Limit Theorems of Probability Theory

Limit Theorems of Probability Theory

Editors

Alexander Tikhomirov
Vladimir Ulyanov

Basel • Beijing • Wuhan • Barcelona • Belgrade • Novi Sad • Cluj • Manchester

Editors
Alexander Tikhomirov
Institute of Physics and
Mathematics
Komi Science Center of Ural
Division of the Russian
Academy of Sciences
Syktyvkar, Russia

Vladimir Ulyanov
Faculty of Computational
Mathematics and Cybernetics
Lomonosov Moscow State
University
Moscow, Russia

Editorial Office
MDPI
St. Alban-Anlage 66
4052 Basel, Switzerland

This is a reprint of articles from the Special Issue published online in the open access journal *Mathematics* (ISSN 2227-7390) (available at: https://www.mdpi.com/si/mathematics/Limit_Theo_Probab_Theory).

For citation purposes, cite each article independently as indicated on the article page online and as indicated below:

Lastname, A.A.; Lastname, B.B. Article Title. *Journal Name* **Year**, *Volume Number*, Page Range.

ISBN 978-3-0365-9192-6 (Hbk)
ISBN 978-3-0365-9193-3 (PDF)
doi.org/10.3390/books978-3-0365-9193-3

© 2023 by the authors. Articles in this book are Open Access and distributed under the Creative Commons Attribution (CC BY) license. The book as a whole is distributed by MDPI under the terms and conditions of the Creative Commons Attribution-NonCommercial-NoDerivs (CC BY-NC-ND) license.

Contents

About the Editors vii

Alexander N. Tikhomirov and Vladimir V. Ulyanov
On the Special Issue "Limit Theorems of Probability Theory"
Reprinted from: *Mathematics* **2023**, *11*, 3665, doi:10.3390/math11173665 1

Xia Wang and Miaomiao Zhang
Large Deviations for the Maximum of the Absolute Value of Partial Sums of Random Variable Sequences
Reprinted from: *Mathematics* **2022**, *10*, 758, doi:10.3390/math10050758 5

Rundong Luo, Yiming Chen and Shuai Song
On the M-Estimator under Third Moment Condition
Reprinted from: *Mathematics* **2022**, *10*, 1713, doi:10.3390/math10101713 17

Friedrich Götze and Andrei Yu. Zaitsev
A New Bound in the Littlewood–OffordProblem
Reprinted from: *Mathematics* **2022**, *10*, 1740, doi:10.3390/math10101740 33

Naiqi Liu, Vladimir V. Ulyanov and Hanchao Wang
On De la Peña Type Inequalities for Point Processes
Reprinted from: *Mathematics* **2022**, *10*, 2114, doi:10.3390/math10122114 39

Alexander N. Tikhomirov and Dmitry A. Timushev
Local Laws for Sparse Sample Covariance Matrices
Reprinted from: *Mathematics* **2022**, *10*, 2326, doi:10.3390/math10132326 53

Mihailo Jovanović, Vladica Stojanović, Kristijan Kuk, Brankica Popović and Petar Čisar
Asymptotic Properties and Application of GSB Process: A Case Study of the COVID-19 Dynamics in Serbia
Reprinted from: *Mathematics* **2022**, *10*, 3849, doi:10.3390/math10203849 91

Yuri Yakubovich, Oleg Rusakov and Alexander Gushchin
Functional Limit Theorem for the Sums of PSI-Processes with Random Intensities
Reprinted from: *Mathematics* **2022**, *10*, 3955, doi:10.3390/math10213955 119

Igor Borisov and Maman Jetpisbae
Poissonization Principle for a Class of Additive Statistics
Reprinted from: *Mathematics* **2022**, *10*, 4084, doi:10.3390/math10214084 137

Shuya Kanagawa
Asymptotic Expansions for Symmetric Statistics with Degenerate Kernels
Reprinted from: *Mathematics* **2022**, *10*, 4158, doi:10.3390/math10214158 157

Alexander Bulinski and Nikolay Slepov
Sharp Estimates for Proximity of Geometric and Related Sums Distributions to Limit Laws
Reprinted from: *Mathematics* **2022**, *10*, 4747, doi:10.3390/math10244747 167

Yasunori Fujikoshi and Tetsuro Sakurai
High-Dimensional Consistencies of KOO Methods for the Selection of Variables in Multivariate Linear Regression Models with Covariance Structures
Reprinted from: *Mathematics* **2023**, *11*, 671, doi:10.3390/math11030671 205

Alexander N. Tikhomirov
Limit Theorem for Spectra of Laplace Matrix of Random Graphs
Reprinted from: *Mathematics* **2023**, *11*, 764, doi:10.3390/math11030764 . . . . **221**

Gerd Christoph and Vladimir V. Ulyanov
Second Order Chebyshev–Edgeworth-Type Approximations for Statistics Based on Random Size Samples
Reprinted from: *Mathematics* **2023**, *11*, 1848, doi:10.3390/math11081848 . . . . **247**

Yoon-Tae Kim and Hyun-Suk Park
Bound for an Approximation of Invariant Density of Diffusions via Density Formula in Malliavin Calculus
Reprinted from: *Mathematics* **2023**, *11*, 2302, doi:10.3390/math11102302 . . . . **265**

Manuel L. Esquível and Nadezhda P. Krasii
On Structured Random Matrices Defined by Matrix Substitutions
Reprinted from: *Mathematics* **2023**, *11*, 2505, doi:10.3390/math11112505 . . . . **283**

About the Editors

Alexander Tikhomirov

Alexander Tikhomirov has been a professor at the Institute of Physics and Mathematics, Komi Science Center of Ural Division of the Russian Academy of Sciences, Russia, since 2008. Professor Tikhomirov received his Ph.D. degree in mathematics from St. Petersburg State University, Russia, in 1977 and his Habilitation (Doctor of Sciences) from the Steklov Mathematical Institute of the Russian Academy of Sciences, Russia, in 1996. From 1997 to 2020, he worked at the Faculty of Mathematics at Syktyvkar State University, where he became a full professor in 1998. His research focuses on random matrices, strong mixing conditions, limit theorems, and circular law.

Vladimir Ulyanov

Vladimir Ulyanov is currently a professor at the Faculty of Computational Mathematics and Cybernetics, Lomonosov Moscow State University, Russia, and a professor at the Faculty of Social Sciences, National Research University—Higher School of Economics, Russia. He received his Ph.D. degree from Lomonosov Moscow State University in 1978 and his Habilitation (Doctor of Sciences) from Steklov Mathematical Institute of the Russian Academy of Sciences in 1994. He was awarded the State Prize of the USSR for Young Scientists in 1987. He worked as an Alexander von Humboldt Research Fellow in Germany from 1991 to 1993 and a JSPS Research Fellow in Japan in 1999 and 2004, respectively. He has worked as a visiting professor/researcher at Bielefeld University, Germany; the University of Leiden; the University de Paris V; the University of Hong Kong; the Institute of Statistical Mathematics in Tokyo; the National University of Singapore; the University of Melbourne; Shandong University, China, etc. He is currently a Member of the Bernoulli Society. His research lies in limit theorems of probability theory, vector-valued random variables, weak limit theorems, Gaussian processes, approximation in statistics, and transforms of probability distributions.

Editorial

On the Special Issue "Limit Theorems of Probability Theory"

Alexander N. Tikhomirov [1,2,*] and Vladimir V. Ulyanov [2,3,4,*]

1. Institute of Physics and of Mathematics, Komi Science Center of Ural Branch of RAS, 167982 Syktyvkar, Russia
2. Faculty of Computer Science, HSE University, 109028 Moscow, Russia
3. Faculty of Computational Mathematics and Cybernetics, Lomonosov Moscow State University, 119991 Moscow, Russia
4. Institute for Financial Studies, Shandong University, Jinan 250100, China
* Correspondence: sasha-tikh@yandex.ru (A.N.T.); vulyanov@hse.ru (V.V.U.)

M. Loeve wrote that "the fundamental limit theorems of Probability theory may be classified into two groups. One group deals with the problem of limit laws of sequences of some of random variables, the other deals with the problem of limits of random variables, in the sense of almost sure convergence, of such sequences. These problems will be labeled, respectively, the Central Limit Problem (CLP) and the Strong Central Limit Problem (SCLP). Like all mathematical problems, the CLP and SCLP are not static; as answers to old queries are discovered they experience the usual development and new problems arise".

The papers in this Special Issue present new directions and new advances for limit theorems in probability theory and its applications. The list of topics is extensive, and it includes classical models of sums of both independent and various types of dependent random variables, probabilities of large deviations, functional limit theorems, and limit theorems for random processes, in high-dimensional spaces, for spectra of random matrices and random graphs, and more.

In [1], Xia Wang and Miaomiao Zhang obtain a large deviation principle for the maximum of the absolute value of partial sums of independent, identically distributed, centered, random variables. It is assumed that tail probabilities for "positive" and "negative" tails of the summand have the same exponential decrease.

Estimating the expected value of a random variable via data-driven methods is one of the most fundamental problems in statistics. In [2], Rundong Luo, Yiming Chen, and Shuai Song present an extension of Olivier Catoni's classical M-estimators of the empirical mean, which focus on heavy-tailed data by imposing more precise inequalities on exponential moments of Catoni's estimator. The authors show that their estimators behave better than Catoni's estimators, both in practice and theory. The results obtained are illustrated on modeled and real data.

Paper [3], by Friedrich Götze and Andrei Yu Zaitsev, deals with studying a connection of the Littlewood–Offord problem to estimations of the concentration functions of some symmetric, infinitely divisible distributions. It is shown that the concentration function of a weighted sum of independent, identically distributed, random variables is estimated in terms of the concentration function of a symmetric, infinitely divisible distribution, whose spectral measure is concentrated on the set of plus–minus weights.

There has been a renewed interest in exponential concentration inequalities for stochastic processes in probability and statistics over the last three decades. De la Peña established a good exponential inequality for a discrete time, locally square, integrable martingale. In [4],, Naiqi Liu, Vladimir V. Ulyanov, and Hanchao Wang obtain de la Peña's inequalities for a stochastic integral of multivariate point processes. The proof is primarily based on the Doléans-Dade exponential formula and the optional stopping theorem. As an application, they obtain an exponential inequality for block counting process in the Λ–coalescent.

Citation: Tikhomirov, A.N.; Ulyanov, V.V. On the Special Issue "Limit Theorems of Probability Theory". *Mathematics* **2023**, *11*, 3665. https://doi.org/10.3390/math11173665

Received: 8 August 2023
Accepted: 16 August 2023
Published: 25 August 2023

Copyright: © 2023 by the authors. Licensee MDPI, Basel, Switzerland. This article is an open access article distributed under the terms and conditions of the Creative Commons Attribution (CC BY) license (https://creativecommons.org/licenses/by/4.0/).

In [5], Alexander N. Tikhomirov and Dmitry A. Timushev prove the local Marchenko–Pastur law for sparse sample covariance matrices that corresponded to rectangular observation matrices and sparse probability. The new bounds of the distance between Laplace transforms of the empirical spectral distribution function of the sparse sample covariance matrices and the Marchenko–Pastur law distribution function are obtained in the complex domain. It is assumed that a sparse probability and the moments of the matrix elements satisfy some conditions.

In see [6], Mihailo Jovanović, Vladica Stojanović, Kristijan Kuk, Brankica Popović, and Petar Čisar describe one of the non-linear (and non-stationary) stochastic models, the Gaussian, or Generalized, Split-BREAK (GSB) process, which is used in the analysis of time series with pronounced and accentuated fluctuations. In the beginning, the stochastic structure of the GSB process and its important distributional and asymptotic properties are given. To that end, a method based on characteristic functions (CFs) was used. Various procedures for the estimation of model parameters, asymptotic properties, and numerical simulations of the obtained estimators are also investigated. Finally, as an illustration of the practical application of the GSB process, an analysis of the dynamics and stochastic distribution of the infected and immunized populations in relation to COVID-19 in the Republic of Serbia is presented.

The Poisson Stochastic Index process (PSI-process) represents a special kind of a random process, when the discrete time of a random sequence is replaced by the continuous time of a "counting" process of a Poisson type. In [7], Yuri Yakubovich, Oleg Rusakov, and Alexander Gushchin establish a functional limit theorem for normalized cumulative sums of PSI-processes in the Skorokhod space. This theorem can be used in different ways. The PSI-processes are very simple, and some results can be obtained directly for their sums and imply the corresponding facts of the limiting stationary Gaussian process. On the other hand, the theory of stationary Gaussian processes has been deeply developed in the last few decades, and some results of this theory can have consequences for pre-limiting processes, which model a number of real life phenomena.

In [8], Igor Borisov and Maman Jetpisbaev consider a class of additive functionals of a finite or countable collection of the group frequencies of an empirical point process that corresponds to, at most, a countable partition of the sample space. Under broad conditions, it is shown that the asymptotic behavior of the distributions of such functionals is similar to the behavior of the distributions of the same functionals of the accompanying Poisson point process. However, the Poisson versions of the additive functionals under consideration, unlike the original ones, have the structure of sums (finite or infinite) of independent random variables, which allows them to reduce the asymptotic analysis of the distributions of additive functionals of an empirical point process to classical problems of the theory of summation of independent random variables.

In [9], Shuya Kanagawa investigates asymptotic expansions for U-statistics and V-statistics with degenerate kernels, and finds the order estimates for the remainder terms. It implies the corresponding results for the Cramér–von Mises statistics of a uniform distribution on (0,1). The scheme of the proof is based on three steps. The first one is the almost certain convergence in a Fourier series expansion of the kernel function. The key condition for the convergence is the nuclearity of a linear operator defined by the kernel function. The second one is a representation of U-statistics or V-statistics, by single sums of Hilbert space valued random variables. The third one is the application of asymptotic expansions for single sums of Hilbert space valued random variables.

In [10], Alexander Bulinski and Nikolay Slepov study the convergence rate in the famous Rényi theorem by means of the Stein method refinement. Namely, it is demonstrated that the new estimate of the convergence rate of the normalized geometric sums to exponential laws involving the ideal probability metric of the second order is sharp. Some recent results concerning the convergence rates in Kolmogorov and Kantorovich metrics are extended as well. In contrast to many previous works, there are no assumptions that the summands of geometric sums are positive and have the same distribution. For the first time, an analogue of the Rényi theorem is established for the model of exchangeable random variables. Furthermore, within this model, a sharp estimate of convergence rate to a specified mixture of distributions is provided. The convergence rate of the appropriately normalized random sums of random summands to the generalized gamma distribution is estimated. Here, the number of summands follows the generalized negative binomial law. The sharp estimates of the proximity of random sums of random summand distributions to the limit law are established both for independent summands and for the model of exchangeable ones. The inverse to the equilibrium transformation of the probability measures is introduced and, in this way, a new approximation of the Pareto distributions by exponential laws is proposed. The integral probability metrics, and the techniques of integration with respect to sign measures, are essentially employed.

In [11], Yasunori Fujikoshi and Tetsuro Sakurai consider the high-dimensional consistencies of KOO methods for selecting response variables in multivariate linear regression with some covariance structures. The method, which was named the knock-one-out (KOO) method, determines "selection" or "no selection" for each variable by comparing the model that removes that variable and the full model. It is assumed that the covariance structure is one of three covariance structures: (1) an independent covariance structure with the same variance, (2) an independent covariance structure with different variances, and (3) a uniform covariance structure. A sufficient condition for model selection consistency is obtained using a KOO method under a high-dimensional asymptotic framework, such that sample size, the number of response variables, and the number of explanatory variables are large.

In [12], Alexander N. Tikhomirov considers the limit of the empirical spectral distribution of Laplace matrices of generalized random graphs. Applying the Stieltjes transform method, the author proves under general conditions that the limit spectral distribution of Laplace matrices converges with the free convolution of the semicircular law and the normal law.

In [13], Gerd Christoph and Vladimir V. Ulyanov complete their studies on the formal construction of asymptotic approximations for statistics based on a random number of observations. Second-order Chebyshev–Edgeworth expansions of asymptotically normally or chi-squared distributed statistics from samples with negative binomial or Pareto-like distributed random sample sizes are obtained. The results can have applications for a wide spectrum of asymptotically normally or chi-square distributed statistics. Random, non-random, and mixed scaling factors for each of the studied statistics produce three different limit distributions. In addition to the expected normal or chi-squared distributions, Student's t-, Laplace, Fisher, gamma, and weighted sums of generalized gamma distributions also occur.

The Kolmogorov and total variation distance between the laws of random variables have upper bounds are represented by the L^1-norm of densities when random variables have densities. In [14], Yoon-Tae Kim and Hyun-Suk Park derive an upper bound, in terms of densities such as the Kolmogorov and total variation distance, for several probabilistic distances (e.g., Kolmogorov distance, total variation distance, Wasserstein distance, Forter–Mourier distance, etc.) between the laws of F and G in the case where a random variable F follows the invariant measure that admits a density and a differentiable random variable G, in the sense of Malliavin calculus, and also allows a density function.

In [15], Manuel L. Esquível and Nadezhda P. Krasii describe the structure of the random matrices by deterministic matrices, forming the skeletons of the random matrices. The authors propose to use an algorithm of matrix substitutions with entries in a finite field of integers that modulo some prime number, akin to the algorithm of one dimensional automatic sequences. A random matrix has the structure of a given skeleton if, to the same number of an entry of the skeleton in the finite field, it corresponds a random variable having, at least, as its expected value, the correspondent value of the number in the finite field. Affine matrix substitutions are introduced, and fixed-point theorems that allow for the consideration of steady states of the structure, which are essential for an efficient observation, are proven. For some more restricted classes of structured random matrices, the parameter estimation of the entries is addressed, as well as the convergence in law, and also some aspects of the spectral analysis of the random operators associated with the random matrix. Finally, aiming at possible applications, it is shown that there is a procedure to associate a canonical random surface to every random structured matrix of a certain class.

In summary, this Special Issue proposes and develops new mathematical methods and approaches, new algorithms and research frameworks, and their applications to solve various nontrivial practical problems. We strongly believe that the selected topics and results will be attractive and useful to the international scientific community, and will contribute to further research in the field of limit theorems in probability theory.

Acknowledgments: The research activity of the Guest Editors was conducted within the framework of the HSE University Basic Research Programs and within the program of the Moscow Center for Fundamental and Applied Mathematics, Lomonosov Moscow State University.

Conflicts of Interest: The authors declare no conflict of interest.

References

1. Wang, X.; Zhang, M. Large Deviations for the Maximum of the Absolute Value of Partial Sums of Random Variable Sequences. *Mathematics* **2022**, *10*, 758. [CrossRef]
2. Luo, R.; Chen, Y.; Song, S. On the M-Estimator under Third Moment Condition. *Mathematics* **2022**, *10*, 1713. [CrossRef]
3. Götze, F.; Zaitsev, A.Y. A New Bound in the Littlewood–Offord Problem. *Mathematics* **2022**, *10*, 1740. [CrossRef]
4. Liu, N.; Ulyanov, V.V.; Wang, H. On De la Peña Type Inequalities for Point Processes. *Mathematics* **2022**, *10*, 2114. [CrossRef]
5. Tikhomirov, A.N.; Timushev, D.A. Local Laws for Sparse Sample Covariance Matrices. *Mathematics* **2022**, *10*, 2326. [CrossRef]
6. Jovanović, M.; Stojanović, V.; Kuk, K.; Popović, B.; Čisar, P. Asymptotic Properties and Application of GSB Process: A Case Study of the COVID-19 Dynamics in Serbia. *Mathematics* **2022**, *10*, 3849. [CrossRef]
7. Yakubovich, Y.; Rusakov, O.; Gushchin, A. Functional Limit Theorem for the Sums of PSI-Processes with Random Intensities. *Mathematics* **2022**, *10*, 3955. [CrossRef]
8. Borisov, I.; Jetpisbaev, M. Poissonization Principle for a Class of Additive Statistics. *Mathematics* **2022**, *10*, 4084. [CrossRef]
9. Kanagawa, S. Asymptotic Expansions for Symmetric Statistics with Degenerate Kernels. *Mathematics* **2022**, *10*, 4158. [CrossRef]
10. Bulinski, A.; Slepov, N. Sharp Estimates for Proximity of Geometric and Related Sums Distributions to Limit Laws. *Mathematics* **2022**, *10*, 4747. [CrossRef]
11. Fujikoshi, Y.; Sakurai, T. High-Dimensional Consistencies of KOO Methods for the Selection of Variables in Multivariate Linear Regression Models with Covariance Structures. *Mathematics* **2023**, *11*, 671. [CrossRef]
12. Tikhomirov, A.N. Limit Theorem for Spectra of Laplace Matrix of Random Graphs. *Mathematics* **2023**, *11*, 764. [CrossRef]
13. Christoph, G.; Ulyanov, V.V. Second Order Chebyshev–Edgeworth-Type Approximations for Statistics Based on Random Size Samples. *Mathematics* **2023**, *11*, 1848. [CrossRef]
14. Kim, Y.-T.; Park, H.-S. Bound for an Approximation of Invariant Density of Diffusions via Density Formula in Malliavin Calculus. *Mathematics* **2023**, *11*, 2302. [CrossRef]
15. Esquível, M.L.; Krasii, N.P. On Structured Random Matrices Defined by Matrix Substitutions. *Mathematics* **2023**, *11*, 2505. [CrossRef]

Disclaimer/Publisher's Note: The statements, opinions and data contained in all publications are solely those of the individual author(s) and contributor(s) and not of MDPI and/or the editor(s). MDPI and/or the editor(s) disclaim responsibility for any injury to people or property resulting from any ideas, methods, instructions or products referred to in the content.

Article

Large Deviations for the Maximum of the Absolute Value of Partial Sums of Random Variable Sequences

Xia Wang * and Miaomiao Zhang

Faculty of Science, College of Statistics and Date Science, Beijing University of Technology, Beijing 100124, China; zhangmiaomiaoqd@163.com
* Correspondence: wangxia@bjut.edu.cn

Abstract: Let $\{\xi_i : i \geq 1\}$ be a sequence of independent, identically distributed (i.i.d. for short) centered random variables. Let $S_n = \xi_1 + \cdots + \xi_n$ denote the partial sums of $\{\xi_i\}$. We show that sequence $\{\frac{1}{n} \max_{1 \leq k \leq n} |S_k| : n \geq 1\}$ satisfies the large deviation principle (LDP, for short) with a good rate function under the assumption that $P(\xi_1 \geq x)$ and $P(\xi_1 \leq -x)$ have the same exponential decrease.

Keywords: large deviation principle; principle of the largest term; maximum of the absolute value of partial sums

1. Introduction

Throughout this paper, on a probability space $\{\Omega, \mathcal{F}, P\}$, let $\{\xi_i : i \geq 1\}$ be a sequence of independent, identically distributed (i.i.d.) centered random variables that take real values. Denote the partial sums $S_n := \sum_{i=1}^n \xi_i$ of sequence $\{\xi_i : i \geq 1\}$.

The seminal paper of Cramer [1] motivates our work. Cramer obtained that $\{\frac{1}{n} S_n : n \geq 1\}$ satisfies large deviation principle (LDP) with rate function $\Lambda^*(x)$ (see Theorem 1) under finite moments, which is the famous Cramer condition, i.e., if there exists a $\delta > 0$ such that $Ee^{\lambda |X_1|} < \infty$ for all $|\lambda| < \delta$. Cramer theorem has the following form for any measurable set $B \subset \mathbb{R}$:

$$- \inf_{x \in B^\circ} \Lambda^*(x) \leq \liminf_{n \to \infty} \frac{1}{n} \log P(\frac{S_n}{n} \in B) \quad (1)$$

$$\leq \limsup_{n \to \infty} \frac{1}{n} \log P(\frac{S_n}{n} \in B) \leq -\inf_{x \in \bar{B}} \Lambda^*(x). \quad (2)$$

where B° denotes the interior of B and $\bar{B}$ denotes its closure. We call inequality (1) the large deviations lower bound and inequality (2) the large deviations upper bound. If both hold, then sequence $\{\frac{1}{n} S_n : n \geq 1\}$ satisfies LDP with rate function $\Lambda^*(x)$. In other words, the theory of LDP deals with large fluctuations and the probability of such large fluctuations decays exponentially.

The tail probability $P(S_n \geq nx)$ of independent random variables was researched in detail in many papers. Nagaev [2] obtained that partial sums $\{\frac{1}{n} S_n : n \geq 1\}$ for i.i.d. random variables and found that it satisfies LDP under the assumption that $P(\xi_1 \geq x)$ decreases similarly to a power function. Soon, Nagaev [3] obtained the bounds for probabilities of partial sums of independent random variables, by weakening the requirement, on the hypothesis that generalized and ordinary moments are finite. Under Cramer condition, Kiesel and Stadtmuller [4] extended Cramer theorem to weighted sums of i.i.d. random variables. Moreover, Gantert, Ramanan and Rembart [5] researched the LDP for weighted sums of i.i.d. random variables with stretched exponential tails.

The tail probability $P(\max_{1\leq k\leq n} S_k \geq nx)$ has been researched in depth. Under the Cramer condition, Borovkov and Korshunov [6] conducted work for time-homogeneous Markov chain and Shklyaev [7] conducted work for i.i.d. random variables; both obtained LDP. Soon after, Kozlov [8] obtained LDP results by applying a direct probability approach to $P(\max_{1\leq k\leq n} S_k \geq nx)$ of i.i.d. non-degenerate random variables, which obey the Cramer condition. Lately, Fan, Grama and Liu [9] established the LDP for sequence $\{\frac{1}{n}\max_{1\leq k\leq n} S_k : n \geq 1\}$ of martingale differences random variables under finite subexponential moments condition.

Feller [10] mentioned the importance of the estimation of tail probability $P(\max_{1\leq k\leq n} |S_k| \geq nx)$, which has attracted broad attention in recent decades. Recently, Li [11] established the upper bound estimation for probability $P(\max_{1\leq k\leq n} |S_k| \geq nx)$ of martingale differences random variables bounded in L^p. For strictly stationary and negatively associated random variables, Xing and Yang [12] obtained some exponential inequalities for the maximum of the absolute value of partial sums via classical techniques based on blocking and truncation. Moreover, the upper bound estimation for tail probability $P(\max_{1\leq k\leq n} |S_k| \geq nx)$ for martingale differences random variables was obtained by Fan, Grama and Liu [13] in situations where conditional subexponential moments are bounded.

The above results demonstrate that the research for probability $\{\frac{1}{n}\max_{1\leq k\leq n} |S_k| : n \geq 1\}$ only obtained large deviations upper bound. To fill this gap, we shall primarily obtain the result that sequence $\{\frac{1}{n}\max_{1\leq k\leq n} |S_k| : n \geq 1\}$ of i.i.d. random variables satisfies LDP under the assumption that $P(\xi_1 \geq x)$ and $P(\xi_1 \leq -x)$ have the same exponential decrease (see Corollary 1), i.e., we obtain large deviations lower bound and large deviations upper bound.

This article is organized as follows. We firstly introduce the necessary knowledge about definitions and theorems that we need in Section 2. Then, the main theorems and corollaries are presented in Section 3. Moreover, in Section 4, we provide the lemmas needed to prove the conclusions and proofs of our main results.

2. Preliminaries

Before we present our results and proofs, we introduce some definitions and theorems that can be found in cf. [14,15].

Definition 1. *(1) A function I: $\mathcal{F} \to [0, \infty]$ is called a rate function if it is non-negative and lower semicontinuous, i.e., the level sets $\{x : I(x) \leq \alpha\}$ are closed, for $\alpha \in \mathbb{R}$. (2) A rate function I is said to be good if, in addition, its level sets are compact.*

Definition 2. *We say that a sequence of random variables $\{\xi_i : i \geq 1\}$ satisfies LDP in $\mathbb{R}$ with rate function I if I is a rate function and, for any measurable set $B \in \mathcal{B}(\mathbb{R})$, the following is the case:*

$$-\inf_{x\in B^\circ} I(x) \leq \liminf_{n\to\infty} \frac{1}{n}\log P(\xi_n \in B)$$

$$\leq \limsup_{n\to\infty} \frac{1}{n}\log P(\xi_n \in B) \leq -\inf_{x\in \bar{B}} I(x),$$

where B° denotes the interior of B, and $\bar{B}$ denotes its closure.

Theorem 1. *(Cramer's theorem) Let $\{\xi_i : i \geq 1\}$ be a sequence of i.i.d. real value random variables on $(\Omega, \mathcal{F}, P)$. Let partial sums $S_n = \sum_{i=1}^n \xi_i$, and let $\Lambda(\theta)$ be log moment generating function of ξ_1, i.e., $\Lambda(\theta) = \log E e^{\theta \xi_1}$, and let $\Lambda^*(x)$ be convex conjugate of Λ, i.e., $\Lambda^*(x) =$*

$\sup_{\theta \in R}\{\theta \xi - \Lambda(\theta)\}$. Then, $\{\frac{S_n}{n} : n \geq 1\}$ satisfies LDP with rate function $\Lambda^*(x)$ in $\mathbb{R}$ if Λ is finite in a neighborhood of zero, i.e., for any measurable set $B \subset \mathbb{R}$ of the following:

$$-\inf_{x \in B^\circ} \Lambda^*(x) \leq \liminf_{n \to \infty} \frac{1}{n} \log P(\frac{S_n}{n} \in B)$$

$$\leq \limsup_{n \to \infty} \frac{1}{n} \log P(\frac{S_n}{n} \in B) \leq -\inf_{x \in \bar{B}} \Lambda^*(x).$$

Theorem 2. *(Principle of the largest term)* Let a_n and b_n be sequences in $\mathbb{R}^+$. Then, the following is the case:

$$\limsup_{n \to \infty} \frac{1}{n} \log(a_n + b_n) \leq \limsup_{n \to \infty} \frac{1}{n} \log(a_n) \vee \limsup_{n \to \infty} \frac{1}{n} \log(b_n),$$

and the following is the case.

$$\liminf_{n \to \infty} \frac{1}{n} \log(a_n + b_n) \geq \liminf_{n \to \infty} \frac{1}{n} \log(a_n) \vee \liminf_{n \to \infty} \frac{1}{n} \log(b_n).$$

3. Main Results

Let $\{\xi_i : i \geq 1\}$ be a sequence of i.i.d. centered random variables and denote $S_n := \sum_{i=1}^{n} \xi_i$. Then, we shall investigate the LDP for the sequence of $\{\frac{1}{n} \max_{1 \leq k \leq n} |S_k| : n \geq 1\}$. The main results of this paper are as follows.

Theorem 3. Let $\{\xi_i : i \geq 1\}$ be a sequence of i.i.d. random variables. If $E\xi_1 = 0$, $E\xi_1^2 < \infty$ and for some constants $\alpha \in (0,1)$, $0 < C_1 \leq C_2$, the following is the case:

$$-C_2 \leq \liminf_{x \to \infty} \frac{1}{x^\alpha} \log P(\xi_1 \geq x) \leq \limsup_{x \to \infty} \frac{1}{x^\alpha} \log P(\xi_1 \geq x) \leq -C_1,$$

then for all $x > 0$, we have the following.

$$-C_2 x^\alpha \leq \liminf_{n \to \infty} \frac{1}{n^\alpha} \log P(\max_{1 \leq k \leq n} S_k \geq nx)$$

$$\leq \limsup_{n \to \infty} \frac{1}{n^\alpha} \log P(\max_{1 \leq k \leq n} S_k \geq nx) \leq -C_1 x^\alpha.$$

Theorem 4. Let $\{\xi_i : i \geq 1\}$ be a sequence of i.i.d. random variables. If $E\xi_1 = 0$ and for some constants $\alpha \in (0,1)$, $0 < C_1 \leq C_2$, $0 < C_3 \leq C_4$, the following is the case:

$$-C_2 \leq \liminf_{x \to \infty} \frac{1}{x^\alpha} \log P(\xi_1 \geq x) \leq \limsup_{x \to \infty} \frac{1}{x^\alpha} \log P(\xi_1 \geq x) \leq -C_1,$$

$$-C_4 \leq \liminf_{x \to \infty} \frac{1}{x^\alpha} \log P(\xi_1 \leq -x) \leq \limsup_{x \to \infty} \frac{1}{x^\alpha} \log P(\xi_1 \leq -x) \leq -C_3,$$

then for all $x > 0$, we have the following.

$$-(C_2 \wedge C_4) x^\alpha \leq \liminf_{n \to \infty} \frac{1}{n^\alpha} \log P(\max_{1 \leq k \leq n} |S_k| \geq nx)$$

$$\leq \limsup_{n \to \infty} \frac{1}{n^\alpha} \log P(\max_{1 \leq k \leq n} |S_k| \geq nx) \leq -(C_1 \wedge C_3) x^\alpha.$$

Corollary 1. Let $\{\xi_i : i \geq 1\}$ be a sequence of i.i.d. random variables. If $E\xi_i = 0$, and for some constants $\alpha \in (0,1)$, $C > 0$, we have the following:

$$\lim_{x \to \infty} \frac{1}{x^\alpha} \log P(\xi_1 \geq x) = -C,$$

$$\lim_{x \to \infty} \frac{1}{x^\alpha} \log P(\xi_1 \leq -x) = -C,$$

then for all $x > 0$, the following is obtained.

$$\lim_{n \to \infty} \frac{1}{n^\alpha} \log P(\max_{1 \leq k \leq n} |S_k| \geq nx) = -Cx^\alpha.$$

Then, $\{\frac{1}{n} \max_{1 \leq k \leq n} |S_k| : n \geq 1\}$ satisfies LDP with the good rate function $I(x) = Cx^\alpha$.

4. Proofs of Main Results

To prove our main results, we need the following lemmas, and we also will provide their proofs.

Lemma 1. For a random variable ξ_1 with $E\xi_1 = 0$, we assume $E(\xi_1^2 \exp\{(\xi_1^+)^\alpha\}) < \infty$, for some constant $\alpha \in (0,1)$. Set $\eta_1 = \xi_1 1_{\{\xi_1 \leq y\}}$, for $y > 0$. Then, the following is the case.

$$Ee^{y^{\alpha-1}\eta_1} \leq 1 + \frac{y^{2\alpha-2}}{2} E(\xi_1^2 \exp\{(\xi_1^+)^\alpha\}).$$

Proof of Lemma 1. By Taylor's expansion, we can obtain

$$e^{y^{\alpha-1}\eta_1} \leq 1 + y^{\alpha-1}\eta_1 + \frac{y^{2\alpha-2}\eta_1^2}{2} e^{y^{\alpha-1}\eta_1^+}.$$

The following is the case:

$$\begin{aligned}
\eta_1^+ &= \xi_1 1_{\{0 \leq \xi_1 \leq y\}} \\
&\leq y^{1-\alpha} \xi_1^\alpha 1_{\{0 \leq \xi_1 \leq y\}} \\
&\leq y^{1-\alpha} (\xi_1^+)^\alpha,
\end{aligned}$$

and $\eta_1^2 \leq \xi_1^2$. Then, we obtain the following.

$$\begin{aligned}
Ee^{y^{\alpha-1}\eta_1} &\leq 1 + y^{\alpha-1} E\eta_1 + \frac{y^{2\alpha-2}}{2} E(\eta_1^2 e^{y^{\alpha-1}\eta_1^+}) \\
&\leq 1 + y^{\alpha-1} E\xi_1 + \frac{y^{2\alpha-2}}{2} E(\xi_1^2 \exp\{(\xi_1^+)^\alpha\}) \\
&= 1 + \frac{y^{2\alpha-2}}{2} E(\xi_1^2 \exp\{(\xi_1^+)^\alpha\}).
\end{aligned}$$

Thus, we complete the proof of Lemma 1. □

Lemma 2. Assume $\{\xi_i : i \geq 1\}$ is an i.i.d. random variables sequence. If $E\xi_1 = 0$, and for some constants $\alpha \in (0,1)$, $C > 0$, $E\xi_1^2 \exp\{(\xi_1^+)^\alpha\} < \infty$,

$$\limsup_{x \to \infty} \frac{1}{x^\alpha} \log P(\xi_1 \geq x) \leq -C,$$

then for all $x > 0$, the following is the case.

$$\limsup_{n \to \infty} \frac{1}{n^\alpha} \log P(\max_{1 \leq k \leq n} S_k \geq nx) \leq -Cx^\alpha.$$

Proof of Lemma 2. Set $\eta_i = \xi_i 1_{\{\xi_i \leq y\}}$ for $y > 0$. Then, the following is the case.

$$P(\max_{1 \leq k \leq n} S_k \geq x) \leq P(\max_{1 \leq k \leq n} \sum_{i=1}^{k} \eta_i \geq x) + P(\max_{1 \leq k \leq n} \sum_{i=1}^{k} \xi_i 1_{\{\xi_i > y\}} > 0)$$

$$= P(\sum_{i=1}^{k} \eta_i \geq x, \exists k \in [1, n]) + P(\max_{1 \leq i \leq n} \xi_i > y)$$

$$:= P_1 + P_2. \tag{3}$$

For all $x > 0$, denote stopping time

$$T(x) = \min\{k \in [1, n] : \sum_{i=1}^{k} \eta_i \geq x\} \text{ and } \min \varnothing = 0.$$

We easily obtain

$$1_{\{\sum_{i=1}^{k} \eta_i \geq x,\, \exists k \in [1,n]\}} = \sum_{k=1}^{n} 1_{\{T(x)=k\}}.$$

In order to obtain the upper bound of P_1, we consider martingale $Z(\lambda) = \{(Z_k(\lambda), \mathcal{F}_k) : k \geq 0\}$, where $\mathcal{F}_k = \sigma(\xi_1, \xi_2, \cdots, \xi_k), k \geq 0$, and the following is the case.

$$Z_k(\lambda) = \prod_{i=1}^{k} \frac{exp\{\lambda \eta_i\}}{Eexp\{\lambda \eta_i\}}, \qquad Z_0(\lambda) = 1.$$

Let the following be the case.

$$Z_{T(x) \wedge k}(\lambda) = \prod_{i=1}^{T(x) \wedge k} \frac{exp\{\lambda \eta_i\}}{Eexp\{\lambda \eta_i\}}, \qquad Z_0(\lambda) = 1.$$

By the property of martingale, then $\{(Z_{T(x) \wedge k}(\lambda), \mathcal{F}_k) : k \geq 0\}$ is also a martingale. Because $E(Z_{T(x) \wedge n}(\lambda)) = E(Z_0(\lambda)) = 1$, then we define the probability measure $dP_\lambda := Z_{T(x) \wedge n} dP$ and define the expectation with respect to P_λ by E_λ.

$$P_1 = E_\lambda[Z_{T(x) \wedge n}(\lambda)^{-1} 1_{\{\sum_{i=1}^{k} \eta_i \geq x,\, \exists k \in [1,n]\}}]$$

$$= E_\lambda[(\prod_{i=1}^{T(x) \wedge n} \frac{exp\{\lambda \eta_i\}}{Eexp\{\lambda \eta_i\}})^{-1} \sum_{k=1}^{n} 1_{\{T(x)=k\}}]$$

$$= \sum_{k=1}^{n} E_\lambda[(\prod_{i=1}^{T(x) \wedge n} \frac{exp\{\lambda \eta_i\}}{Eexp\{\lambda \eta_i\}})^{-1} 1_{\{T(x)=k\}}]$$

$$= \sum_{k=1}^{n} E_\lambda[(\prod_{i=1}^{k} \frac{exp\{\lambda \eta_i\}}{Eexp\{\lambda \eta_i\}})^{-1} 1_{\{T(x)=k\}}]$$

$$= \sum_{k=1}^{n} E_\lambda[exp\{-\sum_{i=1}^{k} \log \frac{exp\{\lambda \eta_i\}}{Eexp\{\lambda \eta_i\}}\} 1_{\{T(x)=k\}}]$$

$$= \sum_{k=1}^{n} E_\lambda[exp\{-\lambda \sum_{i=1}^{k} \eta_i + \sum_{i=1}^{k} \log Ee^{\lambda \eta_i}\} 1_{\{T(x)=k\}}]$$

$$= \sum_{k=1}^{n} E_\lambda[exp\{-\lambda \sum_{i=1}^{k} \eta_i + k \log Ee^{\lambda \eta_1}\} 1_{\{T(x)=k\}}]. \tag{4}$$

Under the conditions of Lemma 2, we take $\lambda = y^{\alpha-1}$, and by Lemma 1, and $\log(1 + t) \leq t$, for $\forall t \geq 0$, we obtain the following.

$$\log E e^{y^{\alpha-1}\eta_1} \leq \log(1 + \frac{y^{2\alpha-2}}{2}E(\xi_1^2 \exp\{(\xi_1^+)^\alpha\}))$$
$$\leq \frac{y^{2\alpha-2}}{2}E(\xi_1^2 \exp\{(\xi_1^+)^\alpha\}). \tag{5}$$

On the set $\{T(x) = k\}$, we obtain $\sum_{i=1}^{k}\eta_i \geq x$. Combining this fact with (4) and (5), we obtain that, for all $x > 0$, the following is the case.

$$P_1 \leq \sum_{k=1}^{n} E_\lambda(\exp\{-\lambda x + n\frac{y^{2\alpha-2}}{2}E(\xi_1^2 \exp\{(\xi_1^+)^\alpha\})\}1_{\{T(x)=k\}})$$
$$\leq \exp\{-y^{\alpha-1}x + n\frac{y^{2\alpha-2}}{2}E(\xi_1^2 \exp\{(\xi_1^+)^\alpha\})\}E_\lambda(\sum_{k=1}^{n}1_{\{T(x)=k\}})$$
$$\leq \exp\{-y^{\alpha-1}x + n\frac{y^{2\alpha-2}}{2}E(\xi_1^2 \exp\{(\xi_1^+)^\alpha\})\}. \tag{6}$$

Next, using the Markov inequality, we obtain the following.

$$P_2 = P(\bigcup_{i=1}^{n}\{\xi_i > y\})$$
$$\leq nP(\xi_1 > y)$$
$$\leq nP(\xi_1^2 \exp\{(\xi_1^+)^\alpha\} > y^2 \exp\{y^\alpha\})$$
$$\leq \frac{n}{y^2}\exp\{-y^\alpha\}E(\xi_1^2 \exp\{(\xi_1^+)^\alpha\}). \tag{7}$$

Let $y = x$. Combining (3), (6) and (7) together, we obtain the following.

$$P(\max_{1\leq k \leq n} S_k \geq x)$$
$$\leq \exp\{-x^\alpha + \frac{nE(\xi_1^2 \exp\{(\xi_1^+)^\alpha\})}{2x^{2-2\alpha}}\} + \frac{nE(\xi_1^2 \exp\{(\xi_1^+)^\alpha\})}{x^2}e^{-x^\alpha}$$
$$= e^{-x^\alpha}(\exp\{\frac{nE(\xi_1^2 \exp\{(\xi_1^+)^\alpha\})}{2x^{2-2\alpha}}\} + \frac{nE(\xi_1^2 \exp\{(\xi_1^+)^\alpha\})}{x^2}).$$

Now, we replace x by nx in the above inequality; then, the following is obtained.

$$P(\max_{1\leq k \leq n} S_k \geq nx) \leq e^{-n^\alpha x^\alpha}(\exp\{\frac{E(\xi_1^2 \exp\{(\xi_1^+)^\alpha\})}{2n^{1-2\alpha}x^{2-2\alpha}}\} + \frac{E(\xi_1^2 \exp\{(\xi_1^+)^\alpha\})}{nx^2}).$$

Take log and limsup to both sides and use the principle of the largest term; here, we obtain the LDP upper bound.

$$\limsup_{n\to\infty}\frac{1}{n^\alpha}\log P(\max_{1\leq k \leq n} S_k \geq nx) \leq -x^\alpha.$$

Now we end the proof of Lemma 2. □

In the following, we prove Theorem 3.

Proof of Theorem 3. (i) Firstly, we prove the upper bound. Let $\varepsilon \in (0,1)$ be fixed, $\xi_1' = C_1^{\frac{1}{\alpha}} \xi_1 (\frac{C_1 - \varepsilon}{C_1})^\beta$, $\beta > \frac{1}{\alpha}$. By the condition given in Theorem 3, we have the following:

$$\limsup_{x \to \infty} \frac{1}{x^\alpha} \log P(\xi_1 \geq x) \leq -C_1,$$

we obtain for $\forall \varepsilon > 0$, $\exists x_0$, such that when $x > x_0$,

$$\frac{\log P(\xi_1 \geq x)}{x^\alpha} \leq -C_1 + \varepsilon;$$

that is,

$$P(\xi_1 \geq x) \leq \exp\{-(C_1 - \varepsilon)x^\alpha\}.$$

Thus, for $\forall \varepsilon > 0$, $\exists x_0$, such that when $x > x_0$,

$$P(\xi_1' \geq x) \leq \exp\{-(C_1 - \varepsilon)^{1 - \alpha\beta} C_1^{\alpha\beta - 1} x^\alpha\}.$$

Then, the following is the case:

$$E\{(\xi_1'^+)^2 \exp\{(\xi_1'^+)^\alpha\}\} = \int_0^\infty P(\xi_1' \geq x)(2x + \alpha x^{\alpha - 1}) e^{x^\alpha} dx$$

$$\leq 2 \int_0^\infty x e^{-\theta x^\alpha} dx + \alpha \int_0^\infty x^{\alpha + 1} e^{-\theta x^\alpha} dx$$

$$< \infty,$$

where $\theta = (C_1 - \varepsilon)^{1 - \alpha\beta} C_1^{\alpha\beta - 1} - 1$, $\theta > 0$.
Because $E\xi_1^2 < \infty$, one can easily obtain $E(\xi_1')^2 = C_1^{\frac{2}{\alpha}} (\frac{C_1 - \varepsilon}{C_1})^{2\beta} E\xi_1^2 < \infty$. Then, we obtain the following.

$$E(\xi_1')^2 \exp\{(\xi_1'^+)^\alpha\} = E((\xi_1')^2 \exp\{(\xi_1'^+)^\alpha\} 1_{\{\xi_1' \geq 0\}} + (\xi_1')^2 \exp\{(\xi_1'^+)^\alpha\} 1_{\{\xi_1' < 0\}})$$

$$= E((\xi_1')^2 \exp\{(\xi_1'^+)^\alpha\} 1_{\{\xi_1' \geq 0\}} + (\xi_1')^2 1_{\{\xi_1' < 0\}})$$

$$\leq E(\xi_1'^+)^\alpha \exp\{(\xi_1'^+)^\alpha\} + E(\xi_1')^2$$

$$< \infty.$$

Thus, sequence $\{\xi_i'\}$ satisfies the conditions of Lemma 2, and we denote $S_k' = \sum_{i=1}^k \xi_i'$. Then, we obtain, for all $x > 0$, the following.

$$\limsup_{n \to \infty} \frac{1}{n^\alpha} \log P(\max_{1 \leq k \leq n} S_k' \geq nx)$$

$$= \limsup_{n \to \infty} \frac{1}{n^\alpha} \log P(C_1^{\frac{1}{\alpha}} (1 - \frac{\varepsilon}{C_1})^\beta \max_{1 \leq k \leq n} S_k \geq nx)$$

$$\leq -x^\alpha.$$

Thus, we obtain the following.

$$\limsup_{n \to \infty} \frac{1}{n^\alpha} \log P(\max_{1 \leq k \leq n} S_k \geq nx) \leq -C_1 (1 - \frac{\varepsilon}{C_1})^{\alpha\beta} x^\alpha.$$

Letting $\varepsilon \to 0$, we obtain the following.

$$\limsup_{n \to \infty} \frac{1}{n^\alpha} \log P(\max_{1 \leq k \leq n} S_k \geq nx) \leq -C_1 x^\alpha. \tag{8}$$

(ii) Next, we will prove the lower bound.

Because $\{\xi_i : i \geq 1\}$ is an i.i.d sequence, the following is the case.

$$P(\max_{1 \leq k \leq n} S_k \geq nx) \geq P(S_n \geq nx)$$

$$= P(\xi_1 + \sum_{i=2}^{n} \xi_i \geq n(\varepsilon + x) - n\varepsilon)$$

$$\geq P(\{\sum_{i=2}^{n} \xi_i \geq -n\varepsilon\} \cap \{\xi_1 \geq n(\varepsilon + x)\})$$

$$= P(\sum_{i=2}^{n} \xi_i \geq -n\varepsilon) P(\xi_1 \geq n(\varepsilon + x)). \tag{9}$$

By using the weak law of large numbers and the following fact:

$$\{\sum_{i=2}^{n} \xi_i \geq -(n-1)\varepsilon\} \subseteq \{\sum_{i=2}^{n} \xi_i \geq -n\varepsilon\},$$

we know the following.

$$\lim_{n \to \infty} P(\sum_{i=2}^{n} \xi_i \geq -n\varepsilon) = 1. \tag{10}$$

Then, by the condition in Theorem 3, $\liminf_{x \to \infty} \frac{1}{x^\alpha} \log P(\xi_1 \geq x) \geq -C_2$, we obtain $\forall \varepsilon > 0, \exists x_0$, s.t. $\forall x > x_0$,

$$\frac{\log P(\xi_1 \geq x)}{x^\alpha} \geq -C_2 - \varepsilon.$$

Then, the following is the case.

$$P(\xi_1 \geq x) \geq \exp\{-(C_2 + \varepsilon)x^\alpha\}.$$

Thus, we obtain the following.

$$P(\xi_1 \geq n(x + \varepsilon)) \geq \exp\{-[(x+\varepsilon)n]^\alpha (C_2 + \varepsilon)\}. \tag{11}$$

Combining (9), (10) and (11) together, we easily obtain the following.

$$\liminf_{n \to \infty} \frac{1}{n^\alpha} \log P(\max_{1 \leq k \leq n} S_k \geq nx)$$

$$\geq \liminf_{n \to \infty} \frac{1}{n^\alpha} \log P(\sum_{i=2}^{n} \xi_i \geq -n\varepsilon) + \liminf_{n \to \infty} \frac{1}{n^\alpha} \log P(\xi_1 \geq n(\varepsilon + x))$$

$$\geq -(C_2 + \varepsilon)(x + \varepsilon)^\alpha.$$

Letting $\varepsilon \to 0$, we obtain the following.

$$\liminf_{n \to \infty} \frac{1}{n^\alpha} \log P(\max_{1 \leq k \leq n} S_k \geq nx) \geq -C_2 x^\alpha. \tag{12}$$

At last, by (8) and (12), we obtain, for all $x > 0$, the following.

$$-C_2 x^\alpha \leq \liminf_{n \to \infty} \frac{1}{n^\alpha} \log P(\max_{1 \leq k \leq n} S_k \geq nx)$$

$$\leq \limsup_{n \to \infty} \frac{1}{n^\alpha} \log P(\max_{1 \leq k \leq n} S_k \geq nx) \leq -C_1 x^\alpha.$$

Thus, we complete the proof of Theorem 3. □

In the following, we prove Theorem 4.

Proof of Theorem 4. By the condition $\liminf\limits_{x\to\infty} \frac{1}{x^\alpha} \log P(\xi_1 \geq x) \leq -C_1$, we obtain for $\forall\, \varepsilon > 0$, $\exists\, x_0$, such that when $\forall x > x_0$, the following.

$$P(\xi_1 \geq x) \leq exp\{-(C_1 - \varepsilon)x^\alpha\}.$$

By condition $\liminf\limits_{x\to\infty} \frac{1}{x^\alpha} \log P(\xi_1 \leq -x) \leq -C_3$, we obtain for $\forall\, \varepsilon > 0$, $\exists\, x_0$, such that when $\forall x > x_0$, $P(\xi_1 \leq -x) \leq exp\{-(C_3 - \varepsilon)x^\alpha\}$.

Thus, we obtain the following.

$$\begin{aligned}
E\xi_1^2 &= \int_0^\infty 2xP(|\xi_1| \geq x)dx \\
&= \int_0^{x_0} 2xP(|\xi_1| \geq x)dx + \int_{x_0}^\infty 2xP(|\xi_1| \geq x)dx \\
&\leq x_0^2 + \int_{x_0}^\infty 2xP(\xi_1 \geq x)dx + \int_{x_0}^\infty 2xP(\xi_1 \leq -x)dx \\
&\leq x_0^2 + \int_{x_0}^\infty 2x\,exp\{-(C_1 - \varepsilon)x^\alpha\}dx + \int_{x_0}^\infty 2x\,exp\{-(C_3 - \varepsilon)x^\alpha\}dx \\
&< \infty.
\end{aligned}$$

Thus, by Theorem 3, we obtain the following:

$$\limsup_{n\to\infty} \frac{1}{n^\alpha} \log P(\max_{1\leq k\leq n} S_k \geq nx) \leq -C_1 x^\alpha,$$

$$\limsup_{n\to\infty} \frac{1}{n^\alpha} \log P(\max_{1\leq k\leq n} S_k \leq -nx) \leq -C_3 x^\alpha,$$

and we know the following.

$$P(\max_{1\leq k\leq n} |S_k| \geq nx) \leq P(\max_{1\leq k\leq n} S_k \geq nx) + P(\max_{1\leq k\leq n} (-S_k) \geq nx).$$

Thus we obtain the following inequality by the principle of the largest term.

$$\begin{aligned}
&\limsup_{n\to\infty} \frac{1}{n^\alpha} \log P(\max_{1\leq k\leq n} |S_k| \geq nx) \\
&\leq \limsup_{n\to\infty} \frac{1}{n^\alpha} \log(P(\max_{1\leq k\leq n} S_k \geq nx) + P(\max_{1\leq k\leq n} (-S_k) \geq nx)) \\
&\leq \limsup_{n\to\infty} \frac{1}{n^\alpha} \log P(\max_{1\leq k\leq n} S_k \geq nx) \vee \limsup_{n\to\infty} \frac{1}{n^\alpha} \log P(\max_{1\leq k\leq n} (-S_k) \geq nx)) \\
&\leq (-C_1 x^\alpha) \vee (-C_3 x^\alpha) \\
&\leq -(C_1 \wedge C_3)x^\alpha.
\end{aligned} \qquad (13)$$

By the given conditions in Theorem 4, $\liminf\limits_{x\to\infty} \frac{1}{x^\alpha} \log P(\xi_1 \geq x) \geq -C_2$, $\liminf\limits_{x\to\infty} \frac{1}{x^\alpha} \log P(\xi_1 \leq -x) \geq -C_4$, we obtain the following.

$$\liminf_{n\to\infty} \frac{1}{n^\alpha} \log P(\max_{1\leq k\leq n} S_k \geq nx) \geq -C_2 x^\alpha,$$

$$\limsup_{n\to\infty} \frac{1}{n^\alpha} \log P(\max_{1\leq k\leq n} S_k \leq -nx) \geq -C_4 x^\alpha.$$

Since the following is the case:

$$P(\max_{1\leq k\leq n} |S_k| \geq nx) \leq P(\max_{1\leq k\leq n} S_k \geq nx) \vee P(\max_{1\leq k\leq n} (-S_k) \geq nx),$$

then we obtain the following.

$$\liminf_{n\to\infty} \frac{1}{n^\alpha} \log P(\max_{1\leq k\leq n} |S_k| \geq nx)$$
$$\geq \liminf_{n\to\infty} \frac{1}{n^\alpha} \log (P(\max_{1\leq k\leq n} S_k \geq nx) \vee P(\max_{1\leq k\leq n} (-S_k) \geq nx))$$
$$\geq \liminf_{n\to\infty} \frac{1}{n^\alpha} \log P(\max_{1\leq k\leq n} S_k \geq nx) \vee \liminf_{n\to\infty} \frac{1}{n^\alpha} \log P(\max_{1\leq k\leq n} (-S_k) \geq nx))$$
$$\geq (-C_2 x^\alpha) \vee (-C_4 x^\alpha)$$
$$\geq -(C_2 \wedge C_4) x^\alpha. \tag{14}$$

Combining (13) and (14), we complete the proof of Theorem 4. □

Proof of Corollary 1**.** Take $C_1 = C_2 = C_3 = C_4 = C$ in Theorem 4, we can obtain the following easily for all x > 0.

$$\lim_{n\to\infty} \frac{1}{n^\alpha} \log P(\max_{1\leq k\leq n} |S_k| \geq nx) = -C x^\alpha.$$

Because the upper bound and the lower bound are same, we can obtain the fact that $\{\frac{1}{n} \max_{1\leq k\leq n} |S_k| : n \geq 1\}$ satisfies LDP with good rate function $I(x) = Cx^\alpha$. □

5. Conclusions

We obtained LDP for the maximum of the absolute value of partial sums of i.i.d. centered random variables under the assumption that $P(\xi_1 \geq x)$ and $P(\xi_1 \leq -x)$ have the same exponential decrease. For further research, we will consider LDP for the maximum of the absolute value of partial sums of other types of dependent random variables, such as martingale differences and acceptable random variables.

Author Contributions: X.W. is mainly responsible for providing funding acquisition and scientific research. M.Z. is mainly responsible for writing the original draft and scientific research. All authors have read and agreed to the published version of the manuscript.

Funding: This work is supported by the National Natural Science Foundation of China (No. 62072044) and Beijing Natural Science Foundation (No. 1202001).

Data Availability Statement: Not applicable.

Acknowledgments: The authors would like to thank the referees for their very helpful comments.

Conflicts of Interest: The authors declare no conflict of interest.

References

1. Cramer, H. Sur un nouveau théoreme-limite de la théorie des probabilits. *Actual. Sci. Ind.* **1937**, *736*, 5–23.
2. Nagaev, A.V. Integral Limit Theorems Taking Large Deviations Into Account When Cramér's Condition Does Not Hold. I. *Theory Probab. Appl.* **1969**, *14*, 51–64. [CrossRef]
3. Nagaev, S.V. Large deviations for sums of independent random variables. *Ann. Probability* **1979**, *7*, 745–789. [CrossRef]
4. Kiesel, R.; Stadtmuller, U. A Large Deviation Principle for Weighted Sums of Independent Identically Distributed Random Variables. *J. Math. Anal. Appl.* **2000**, *251*, 929–939. [CrossRef]
5. Gantert, N.; Ramanan, K.; Rembart, F. Large Deviations for Weighted Sums of Stretched Exponential Random Variables. *Electron. Commun. Probab.* **2014**, *19*, 1–14. [CrossRef]
6. Borovkov, A.A.; Korshunov, D.A. Large-deviation probabilities for one-dimensional Markov chains. Part 2: Prestationary distributions in the exponential case. *Theory Probab. Appl.* **2001**, *45*, 379–405. [CrossRef]

7. Shklyaev, A.V. Limit theorems for random walk under the assumption of maxima large deviation. *Theory Probab. Appl.* **2011**, *55*, 517–525. [CrossRef]
8. Kozlov, M.V. On Large Deviations of Maximum of a Cramer Random Walk and the Queueing Process. *Theory Probab. Appl.* **2014**, *58*, 76–106. [CrossRef]
9. Fan, X.; Grama, I.; Liu, Q. Deviation inequalities for martingales with applications. *J. Math. Anal. Appl.* **2017**, *448*, 538–566. [CrossRef]
10. Feller, W. The fundamental limit theorems in probability. *Bull. Am. Math. Soc.* **1945**, *51*, 800–832. [CrossRef]
11. Li, Y. A martingale inequality and large deviations. *Stat. Probab. Lett.* **2003**, *62*, 317–321. [CrossRef]
12. Xing, G.; Yang, S. An exponential inequality for strictly stationary and negatively associated random variables. *Commun. -Stat.-Theory Methods* **2009**, *39*, 340–349. [CrossRef]
13. Fan, X.; Grama, I.; Liu, Q. Large deviation exponential inequalities for supermartingales. *Electron. Commun. Probab.* **2012**, *17*, 1–8. [CrossRef]
14. Ganesh, A.; O'Connell, N.; Wischik, D. *Big Queues*; Springer: Berlin/Heidelberg, Germany, 2004.
15. Dembo, A.; Zeitouni, O. *Large Deviations Techniques and Applications*, 2nd ed.; Springer: Berlin/Heidelberg, Germany, 1998.

Article

On the M-Estimator under Third Moment Condition

Rundong Luo [1], Yiming Chen [2,*] and Shuai Song [3]

[1] School of Business, Shandong University, Weihai 264209, China; luorundong@sdu.edu.cn
[2] Institute for Financial Studies, Shandong University, Jinan 250100, China
[3] School of Economics, Shandong University, Jinan 250100, China; songshuai@sdu.edu.cn
* Correspondence: chenyiming960212@mail.sdu.edu.cn; Tel.: +86-187-5312-0985

Abstract: Estimating the expected value of a random variable by data-driven methods is one of the most fundamental problems in statistics. In this study, we present an extension of Olivier Catoni's classical M-estimators of the empirical mean, which focus on the heavy-tailed data by imposing more precise inequalities on exponential moments of Catoni's estimator. We show that our works behave better than Catoni's both in practice and theory. The performances are illustrated in the simulation and real data.

Keywords: M-estimator; Catoni's estimator; empirical mean

MSC: 60E15; 62F35

Citation: Luo, R.; Chen, Y.; Song, S. On the M-Estimator under Third Moment Condition. *Mathematics* **2022**, *10*, 1713. https://doi.org/10.3390/math10101713

Academic Editors: Alexander Tikhomirov and Vladimir Ulyanov

Received: 7 April 2022
Accepted: 7 May 2022
Published: 17 May 2022

Publisher's Note: MDPI stays neutral with regard to jurisdictional claims in published maps and institutional affiliations.

Copyright: © 2022 by the authors. Licensee MDPI, Basel, Switzerland. This article is an open access article distributed under the terms and conditions of the Creative Commons Attribution (CC BY) license (https://creativecommons.org/licenses/by/4.0/).

1. Introduction

In this study, we focused on estimating the mean $m = \mathbb{E}X$ of a real random variable X, supposing that $X_1, \ldots, X_n$ are independent and identically distributed drawn from X. It is well known that the empirical mean $\widehat{m}_n = n^{-1} \sum_{i=1}^{n} X_i$ is the most popular estimator of m, and theoretical properties have been thoroughly studied [1].

However, recent works have concentrated more on the performance of the estimator when the distribution is heavy-tailed (the second moment or fourth moment of the distribution does not exist), which is becoming more and more common in many research fields (see, e.g., Embrechts, Klüppelberg, and Mikosch [2]). When the data have a heavy tail, the traditional method such as the empirical mean performs poorly, and appropriate robust estimators are required, which drives related research on M-estimator (generalizations of Maximum Likelihood estimator) for correction of the outliers (Huber [3]).

There has been a renewed interest in the area of robust statistics over the last several decades. Nemirovsky and Yudin [4], Hsu and Sabato [5], and Jerrum et al. [6] proposed various forms of Median-of-means (MOM) estimators to handle data in different situations. They called for dividing the data into several groups with equal size and then calculating the empirical mean within each group, finally taking the median of these empirical means as the formal MOM estimator, which reduces the impact of heavy-tailed data. Tukey and McLaughlin [7] and Huber and Ronchetti [8] tried to improve the performance of the empirical mean by using a truncation of X (they name it truncated mean), which removed part of the sample containing γn maximum and minimum values depending on the parameter $\gamma \in (0,1)$ and then averaged the remaining values to improve the robustness. Catoni [9], Audibert, and Catoni [10] studied the properties of M-estimation for regression problems. The relevant works about robust techniques in various fields are summarized in Bartlett and Mendelson [11], Maronna [12], Bubeck, and Lugosi [13].

Recently, Catoni [14] modified the empirical mean to a new robust estimator. It is easy to observe that the empirical mean is the solution of the following estimation equation

$$\sum_{i=1}^{n}(X_i - \mu) = 0. \tag{1}$$

If we change the form of Equation (1) to

$$\sum_{i=1}^{n} \phi[\alpha(X_i - \mu)] = 0. \quad (2)$$

The solution of (2) is called Catoni's mean estimator, where $\phi : \mathbb{R} \to \mathbb{R}$ is a non-decreasing differentiable truncation function such that for any $x \in \mathbb{R}$, $-\log(1 - x + x^2/2) \leq \phi(x) \leq \log(1 + x + x^2/2)$, and α is a parameter to ensure the existence of the estimator. We denote Catoni's mean estimator by $\widetilde{m}_{n,\alpha}$. The main purpose of the truncation function is to make $\phi(x)$ grow slower than x, and then the effect of outliers due to heavy tails in X will be diminished. Although $\phi(x)$ is not the derivative of some explicit error function, it still can be considered as an influence function in robust theory.

By a mild assumption that the variance $v = \mathbb{E}[(X - m)^2]$ of the distribution exists and choosing the parameter α to optimize the bounds, Catoni [14] obtained the following performance of $\widetilde{m}_{n,\alpha}$.

Theorem 1. *Let $X_1, \ldots, X_n$ be independent, identically distributed random variables, which are drawn from X. We assume that the mean m and variance v of X exist. For any $x \in \mathbb{R}_+$, and positive integer n such that $n > 2x$. Catoni's mean estimator $\widetilde{m}_{n,\alpha}$ with parameter $\alpha = \sqrt{\dfrac{2x}{nv\left(1 + \frac{2x}{n-2x}\right)}}$ satisfies,*

$$\mathbb{P}\left\{|\widetilde{m}_{n,\alpha} - m| \geq \sqrt{\frac{2vx}{n-2x}}\right\} \leq 2e^{-x}. \quad (3)$$

Moreover, if we choose α to be independent from x as follows, and assume $n > 2(1+x)$, $\alpha = \sqrt{\dfrac{2}{nv}}$, then

$$\mathbb{P}\left\{|\widetilde{m}_{n,\alpha} - m| \geq \frac{1+x}{1-(1+x)/n}\sqrt{\frac{v}{2n}}\right\} \leq 2e^{-x}. \quad (4)$$

The method of Catoni [14] is widely promoted as a robust estimator by Brownlees, Joly, and Lugosi [15], Minsker [16], and Wang et al. [17]. We need to point out here that the parameter α is the solution of the equation where the derivative of Catoni's estimator's deviation with respect to α equals to 0. When $v = 0$, the Catoni's estimator's deviation is 0, and no specific α is needed. This also holds for Theorem 2.

The main contribution of this article is to improve Catoni's estimator under the assumption of the third moment condition, and we named it the third-moment Catoni estimator. Starting from the adjustment of the truncation function denoted by $\psi(x)$ in our work, as Figure 1 shows, the influence function with the third moment performs closer to the true value than the original one of Catoni's. We obtained a more precise exponential moment upper bound, which leads to a better error bound.

Simultaneously, our work had a better performance for the samples drawn from the t-distribution, which is common in many fields of research(see Jones and Faddy [18]). As a special case of the heavy-tailed distribution, the third moment of the t-distribution exists, which satisfies our assumptions about the distribution. We present the superiority of our estimator in a Monte Carlo simulation. We also show the performance of the proposed estimator under a skewed normal distribution to evaluate the adaptability of the estimator to other distributions.

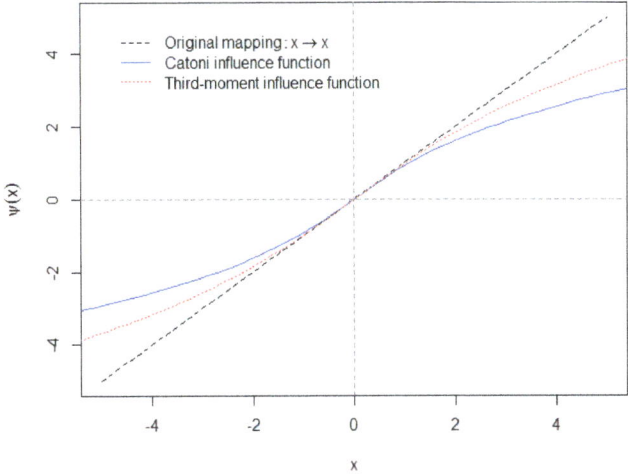

Figure 1. Different chooses of influence function.

The rest of the article is organized as follows. In Section 2, we introduce the main result of the third-moment Catoni's estimator. A Monte Carlo simulation is provided in Section 3 to compare the performance of the proposed estimator with Catoni's estimator for t-distribution. Section 4 examines the performance of the proposed estimator on real data.

2. Main Result

Let $(X_i)_{i=1}^n$ denote an i.i.d. sample drawn from the distribution of X. Let m, v, and s be the mean, variance, and third central moment of X, respectively, which is $\mathbb{E}(X) = m, \mathbb{E}[(X-m)^2] = v,$ and $\mathbb{E}[(X-m)^3] = s$.

The influence function $\psi(x)$ here should be considered wider than the original function as Catoni's to obtain a more accurate exponential moment. In this study, we assumed that

$$\psi(x) = \begin{cases} \log(1 + x + x^2/2 + x^3/6), & x \geq 0 \\ -\log(1 - x + x^2/2 - x^3/6), & x < 0. \end{cases} \quad (5)$$

Our mean estimator $\hat{m}_{n,\alpha}$ is the unique solution of $R_{n,\alpha}(\mu) = 0$, where

$$R_{n,\alpha}(\mu) = \sum_{i=1}^n \psi(\alpha(X_i - \mu)). \quad (6)$$

Next, we present our main result that bounds the $\hat{m}_{n,\alpha} - m$ with the appropriate choice of negative parameter α:

Theorem 2. *Let $X_1, \ldots, X_n$ be independent, identically distributed random variables with finite mean m, variance v, and third central moment s. For any $x > 0$, the error bound between the estimator and the empirical mean satisfies*

$$\mathbb{P}\left\{|\hat{m}_{n,\alpha} - m| \geq 2\left(\sqrt[3]{\frac{q}{2} + \sqrt{\Delta}} + \sqrt[3]{\frac{q}{2} - \sqrt{\Delta}}\right)\right\} \leq 2e^{-x}, \quad (7)$$

where

$$\Delta = \left(\frac{q}{2}\right)^2 + \left(\frac{p}{3}\right)^3, p = \frac{3 + 3v\alpha^2}{\alpha^2}, q = \frac{n\alpha^3 s + 6x - 4n}{n\alpha^3}.$$

Under some technical assumptions that will be mentioned in the following corollary, we have the following upper bound on the probability of the exponential tail:

Corollary 1. Let $X_1, \ldots, X_n$ be independent, identically distributed random variables with finite mean m, variance v and third central moment s. For any $x > 0$ and assume that $n > \frac{3}{2}(1+x)$ and $-\sqrt{\frac{4n^3v^3}{729}} \leqslant s \leqslant \sqrt{\frac{4n^3v^3}{729}}$,

$$\mathbb{P}\left\{|\widehat{m}_{n,\alpha} - m| \geq (1+x)\sqrt{\frac{v}{n}}\right\} \leq 2e^{-x}. \qquad (8)$$

Remark 1. It is obvious that with the assumption that n is a positive integer and satisfies $n > \frac{3}{2}(1+x)$ and $-\sqrt{\frac{4n^3v^3}{729}} \leqslant s \leqslant \sqrt{\frac{4n^3v^3}{729}}$, then

$$\frac{1+x}{1-(1+x)/n}\sqrt{\frac{v}{2n}} \geq (1+x)\sqrt{\frac{v}{n}},$$

By assuming that $\alpha < 0$, we obtained a better estimator bias than (4) in Catoni's result.

Remark 2. When the sample was small, our result was still valid with a small s. We might consider the following example. Let $X_1, \ldots, X_n$ be independent, identically distributed random variables, which are drawn from X. Assuming that the mean $m = 0.01$, variance $v = 1$, $x = 1$, $n = 4$, and whenever $-\sqrt{\frac{4n^3v^3}{729}} \leqslant s \leqslant \sqrt{\frac{4n^3v^3}{729}}$ such as $s = 0.2$, which satisfies the assumption we have

$$\mathbb{P}(|\widehat{m}_{n,\alpha} - 1| \geq 1) \leq \frac{2}{e}.$$

For the convenience of proof, we first present the following lemma (Cardano formula); refer to Høyrup's [19] for more details.

Lemma 1. For any general cubic equation of the form $x^3 + px + q = 0$, one of the roots over the field of real numbers has the form:

$$x = \sqrt[3]{-\frac{q}{2} + \sqrt{\Delta}} + \sqrt[3]{-\frac{q}{2} - \sqrt{\Delta}}, \qquad (9)$$

where the discriminant of the root Δ is as follows, when $\Delta > 0$, the cubic equation has one real root; the cubic equation has three real roots when $\Delta \leq 0$.

$$\Delta = \frac{q^2}{4} + \frac{p^3}{27}.$$

Proof of Theorem 2. Due to the inequality (5) about the $\psi(x)$, we have the following exponential moment inequality of $R_{n,\alpha}(\mu)$, for all $\mu \in \mathbb{R}$:

$$\mathbb{E}\left[e^{R_{n,\alpha}(\mu)}\right] \leq \left(\mathbb{E}\left[1 + \alpha(X - \mu) + \frac{\alpha^2(X-\mu)^2}{2} + \frac{\alpha^3(X-\mu)^3}{6}\right]\right)^n$$
$$= \left(1 + \mathbb{E}[\alpha(X-\mu)] + \mathbb{E}\left[\frac{\alpha^2(X-\mu)^2}{2}\right] + \mathbb{E}\left[\frac{\alpha^3(X-\mu)^3}{6}\right]\right)^n, \qquad (10)$$

with a brief calculation, we have $E[X - \mu]^2 = v + (m - \mu)^2$ and $E[X - \mu]^3 = (m - \mu)^3 + 3v(m - \mu) + s$; so, the inequality (10) can be bounded by the following term:

$$\exp\left(n\alpha(m - \mu) + \frac{n\alpha^2(v + (m - \mu)^2)}{2} + \frac{n\alpha^3}{6}\left((m - \mu)^3 + 3v(m - \mu) + s\right)\right).$$

Similarly,

$$\begin{aligned}
\mathbb{E}\left[e^{-R_{n,\alpha}(\mu)}\right] &\leq \left(\mathbb{E}\left[1 - \alpha(X-\mu) + \frac{\alpha^2(X-\mu)^2}{2} - \frac{\alpha^3(X-\mu)^3}{6}\right]\right)^n \\
&= \left(1 - \mathbb{E}[\alpha(X-\mu)] + \mathbb{E}\left[\frac{\alpha^2(X-\mu)^2}{2}\right] - \mathbb{E}\left[\frac{\alpha^3(X-\mu)^3}{6}\right]\right)^n \\
&= \left(1 - \alpha(m-\mu) + \frac{\alpha^2(v+(m-\mu)^2)}{2} - \frac{\alpha^3}{6}\left((m-\mu)^3 + 3v(m-\mu) + s\right)\right)^n \\
&\leq \exp\left(-n\alpha(m-\mu) + \frac{n\alpha^2(v+(m-\mu)^2)}{2} - \frac{n\alpha^3}{6}\left((m-\mu)^3 + 3v(m-\mu) + s\right)\right).
\end{aligned} \tag{11}$$

Let

$$A_1 = n\alpha(m-\mu) + \frac{n\alpha^2(v+(m-\mu)^2)}{2} + \frac{n\alpha^3}{6}\left((m-\mu)^3 + 3v(m-\mu) + s\right),$$

$$A_2 = -n\alpha(m-\mu) + \frac{n\alpha^2(v+(m-\mu)^2)}{2} - \frac{n\alpha^3}{6}\left((m-\mu)^3 + 3v(m-\mu) + s\right),$$

whenever X_i has a finite third moment s. We can obtain from the Markov inequality that for any $\mu \in \mathbb{R}$ and $x \in \mathbb{R}_+$,

$$\begin{aligned}
\mathbb{P}\{R_{n,\alpha}(\mu) \geq A_1 + x\} &= \mathbb{P}\{\exp(R_{n,\alpha}(\mu)) \geq \exp(A_1 + x)\} \\
&\leq \mathbb{E}\left[e^{R_{n,\alpha}(\mu)}\right] / \exp(A_1 + x) \\
&\leq e^{-x}.
\end{aligned} \tag{12}$$

In the same way, we have

$$\mathbb{P}\{-R_{n,\alpha}(\mu) \geq A_2 + x\} \leq e^{-x}. \tag{13}$$

Then, as shown in Figure 2.

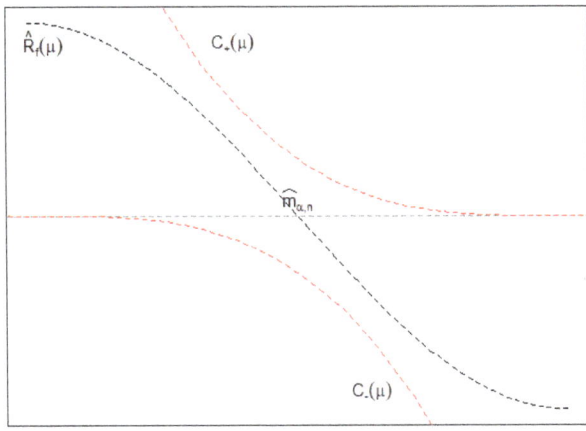

Figure 2. Representation of $\hat{R}_f(\mu)$ and the cubic equation $C_+(\mu)$ and $C_-(\mu)$.

We can control the estimator $\hat{m}_{n,\alpha}$ by the roots of the cubic equation as follows:

$$\begin{aligned}
C_+(\mu) &= A_1 + x = 0, \\
C_-(\mu) &= -A_2 - x = 0.
\end{aligned} \tag{14}$$

Equation (13) above can be regarded as a cubic equation about $m - \mu$. To solve (13), we first convert it into a standard-form one-dimensional cubic equation by letting $y_n = m - \mu - \frac{1}{\alpha}, (n = 1, 2)$, and then we obtain the following equations:

$$y_1^3 + \frac{3 + 3v\alpha^2}{\alpha^2} y_1 + \frac{n\alpha^3 s + 6x - 4n}{n\alpha^3} = 0,$$
$$y_2^3 + \frac{3 + 3v\alpha^2}{\alpha^2} y_2 - \frac{n\alpha^3 s + 6x - 4n}{n\alpha^3} = 0. \tag{15}$$

For any $\alpha \in \mathbb{R}_-$, according to Lemma 1, since $(3 + 3v\alpha^2)/\alpha^2$ is always positive, Δ is always greater than 0. In this case, our equation has one real root and two imaginary roots, which means we can control the $\hat{m}_{n,\alpha}$ by the root of (13) as follows:

$$\mu_+ = m - \frac{1}{\alpha} + \sqrt[3]{\frac{q}{2} - \sqrt{\Delta}} + \sqrt[3]{\frac{q}{2} + \sqrt{\Delta}},$$

$$\mu_- = m - \frac{1}{\alpha} - \sqrt[3]{\frac{q}{2} + \sqrt{\Delta}} - \sqrt[3]{\frac{q}{2} - \sqrt{\Delta}},$$

where the Δ, p, and q are the same as above. We can easily obtain from the formula above that $R_{n,\alpha}(\mu_+) \leq 0$, implying that $\hat{m}_{\alpha,n} < \mu_+$ with probability at least $1 - e^{-x}$, since $R_{n,\alpha}(\mu)$ is a non-increasing function. Similarly, $\hat{m}_{\alpha,n} > \mu_-$ with probability at least $1 - e^{-x}$. Then, by choosing the parameter α, we can derive the performance of the estimator $\hat{m}_{\alpha,n}$ for the bias of the mean m. That is, with probability at least $1 - 2e^{-x}$, we have

$$\mu_- < \hat{m}_{\alpha,n} < \mu_+.$$

The proof of Theorem 2 is completed. □

Proof of Corollary 1. In fact, the right-hand side of (7) can be bounded as follows without limiting the sign of s:

$$|\hat{m}_{n,\alpha} - m| \leq 2\left(\left| \sqrt[3]{\frac{q}{2} + \sqrt{\Delta}} + \sqrt[3]{\frac{q}{2} - \sqrt{\Delta}} \right| \right)$$
$$< 4 \sqrt[3]{\frac{n\alpha^3 s + 6x - 4n}{2n\alpha^3}} \tag{16}$$
$$= 4 \left| \sqrt[3]{-\frac{2}{\alpha^3} + \frac{3x}{n\alpha^3} + \frac{s}{2}} \right|,$$

with the assumption $n > \frac{3}{2}(1 + x)$, which is weaker than Catoni's, (16) can be bounded by

$$4 \left| \sqrt[3]{\frac{2}{\alpha^3} - \frac{2}{\alpha^3} + \frac{s}{2}} \right|$$
$$= 4 \left| \sqrt[3]{\frac{s}{2}} \right|. \tag{17}$$

Moreover, assuming that $-\sqrt{\frac{4n^3v^3}{729}} \leq s \leq \sqrt{\frac{4n^3v^3}{729}}$, we can obtain that (17) is bounded by $(1 + x)\sqrt{\frac{v}{n}}$; then, (8) holds. □

3. Simulation

In this section, we considered the performance of the estimator with respect to the t-distribution on applications by Monte Carlo simulation exercise results. We focused on the performance of the estimator in L_1 regression. Our data were simulated from a linear model generated from a t-distribution regressed by our proposed estimator; we measured the loss of the regression by the minimization of the L_1 norm.

The details of the simulation are as follows: we considered n independent, identically distributed real random variables pairs $(X_1, Y_1), (X_2, Y_2) \ldots, (X_n, Y_n)$ where X_i take their values in $\mathbb{R}^3$ while Y_i in $\mathbb{R}$, and the explanatory variables X_i are drawn from a multivariate normal distribution with 0 mean, and variance is a three-dimensional identity matrix. The response variable Y_i is generated as follows:

$$Y_i = X_i^T \theta + \epsilon_i, \qquad (18)$$

where the parameter vector θ is set to be $(0.25, -0.25, 0.50)$, and ϵ_i is an error term with zero mean and unit variance, which is drawn from a Student t-distribution. Our main goal was to estimate the parameter θ by minimizing the L_1 risk

$$\mathbb{E}\left|Y - X_i^T \theta\right|,$$

and then we defined the the L_1 estimators $\widehat{\theta}_1$, the classical Catoni mean estimator $\widehat{\theta}_2$, and the third-moment Catoni's estimator $\widehat{\theta}_3$ as follows

$$\widehat{\theta}_1 = \arg\min_\theta \widehat{R}_1(\theta) = \arg\min_\theta \frac{1}{n}\sum_{i=1}^n \left|Y_i - X_i^T\theta\right|,$$

$$\widehat{\theta}_2 = \arg\min_\theta \widehat{R}_2(\mu) = \arg\min_\theta \frac{1}{n\alpha}\sum_{i=1}^n \phi\left(\alpha\left(\left|Y_i - X_i^T\theta\right| - \mu\right)\right) = 0, \qquad (19)$$

$$\widehat{\theta}_3 = \arg\min_\theta \widehat{R}_3(\mu) = \arg\min_\theta \frac{1}{n\alpha}\sum_{i=1}^n \psi\left(\alpha\left(\left|Y_i - X_i^T\theta\right| - \mu\right)\right) = 0,$$

where the $\widehat{R}_2(\mu)$, $\widehat{R}_3(\mu)$ is the root of the right side of the equation, respectively; $\phi(x)$ is the widest choice defined in Catoni's result, the parameter $\alpha = 1$, which is the same as Brownless's work; $\psi(x)$ was set as above; and the parameter $\alpha = -1$. The measures for the performance of the estimator are as follows:

$$R\left(\widehat{\theta}_1\right) - R(\theta) = \mathbb{E}\left|Y - X^T\widehat{\theta}_1\right| - \mathbb{E}\left|Y - X^T\theta\right|,$$

$$R\left(\widehat{\theta}_2\right) - R(\theta) = \mathbb{E}\left|Y - X^T\widehat{\theta}_2\right| - \mathbb{E}\left|Y - X^T\theta\right|, \qquad (20)$$

$$R\left(\widehat{\theta}_3\right) - R(\theta) = \mathbb{E}\left|Y - X^T\widehat{\theta}_3\right| - \mathbb{E}\left|Y - X^T\theta\right|.$$

The simulation experiments repeated with different sample sizes, which ranged from 50 to 1000 and with degrees of freedom of the t-distribution ranging from 1 to 7. Each set of the sample size experiments was replicated 1000 times, and for each replication, we evaluated the performance of the regression by the mean of the sample $(X'_1, Y'_1), (X'_2, Y'_2), \ldots, (X'_m, Y'_m)$—that is, i.i.d. with the sample $(X_1, Y_1), (X_2, Y_2) \ldots, (X_n, Y_n)$. We used the following equation to evaluate the performance of the regression, which called excess risk.

$$\widetilde{R}\left(\widehat{\theta}_1\right) = \frac{1}{m}\sum_{i=1}^m \left|Y'_i - Z_i^T\widehat{\theta}_1\right|^2,$$

$$\widetilde{R}\left(\widehat{\theta}_2\right) = \frac{1}{m}\sum_{i=1}^m \left|Y'_i - Z_i^T\widehat{\theta}_2\right|^2, \qquad (21)$$

$$\widetilde{R}\left(\widehat{\theta}_3\right) = \frac{1}{m}\sum_{i=1}^m \left|Y'_i - Z_i^T\widehat{\theta}_3\right|^2.$$

Figure 3 displays the performance of the excess risk for three estimators when $n = 500$ and the degrees of freedom of the t-distribution ranged from 1 to 7; we can obtain that the proposed estimator performs better than the other estimators, which means more stability on the outliers.

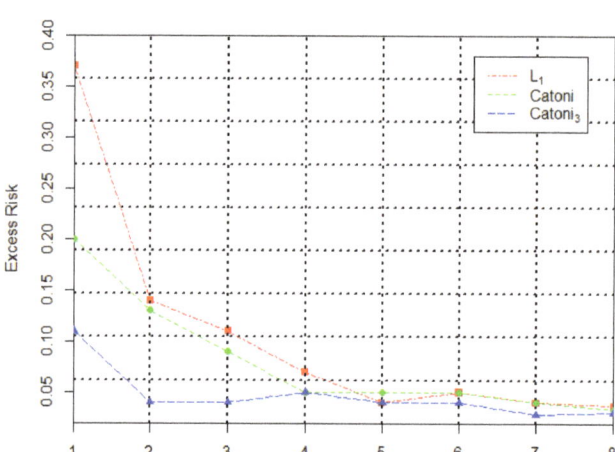

Figure 3. Excess risk varies with degrees of freedom.

The results of the Monte Carlo simulation including the performance of the estimator for different n are presented in Table 1, and we also compared the performance between the proposed estimator and other estimators with various risks in Table 2 where sample size $n = 500$ and degrees of freedom $d = 1$; the L_1 represents the general L_1 regression; the C and C_3 denote the original Catoni estimator and our third-moment Catoni estimator, respectively; and the ER, RB, and SMSE represents the excess risk, relative risk ($\frac{|\|\bar{\hat{\theta}}\|_2 - \|\theta\|_2|}{\|\theta\|_2}$, with $\bar{\hat{\theta}} = \frac{1}{1000}\sum_{j=1}^{1000}\hat{\theta}(j)$), and the square root of the mean square error ($\sqrt{MSE} = \sqrt{\frac{1}{1000}\sum_{j=1}^{1000}[\|\hat{\theta}(j)\|_2 - \|\theta\|_2]^2}$).

We can derive from the table that when the distribution has a heavy tail, our estimator performs better in most cases than the other two estimators, and the excess risk of the estimator decreases as the sample size increases. At the same time, with the degrees of freedom of the t-distribution rising, the tail of the t-distribution becomes thinner, which becomes closer to the normal distribution, and the performance of all procedures on excess risk is significantly improved; additionally, the proposed estimator also performs well for different risks.

Table 1. The excess risk of the L_1, Catoni, and third-moment Catoni regression estimator for different degrees of freedom and sample size n.

		$n = 50$	$n = 100$	$n = 250$	$n = 500$	$n = 1000$
$d=1$	L_1	8.79	5.91	5.75	4.15	3.67
	C	7.53	4.63	4.90	4.07	3.49
	C_3	7.46	4.06	4.84	4.06	3.38
$d=3$	L_1	1.51	1.34	1.22	1.15	1.14
	C	1.38	1.27	1.20	1.15	1.12
	C_3	1.27	1.21	1.14	1.10	1.08
$d=5$	L_1	1.09	1.11	1.08	1.08	1.07
	C	1.08	1.13	1.09	1.10	1.08
	C_3	1.06	1.08	1.03	1.04	1.04
$d=7$	L_1	1.08	1.02	1.05	1.01	1.00
	C	1.05	0.94	1.03	1.00	0.98
	C_3	0.97	0.94	0.90	0.85	0.86

Table 2. Comparisons of the performance between the proposed estimator and other estimators with various risks.

	L_1	C	C_3
ER	4.1561	4.0747	4.0628
RB	0.0398	0.0385	0.0383
SMSE	0.0970	0.0952	0.0947

We also examined the performance of the third-moment Catoni estimator on a skewed normal distribution in Table 3; the model still follows (18) where ϵ follows a skewed normal distribution with shape parameter $\alpha = 1, 3, 5$ and with other settings unchanged. We can draw conclusions from the table that the bias of the improved estimator is still smaller than the original one. However, the deviation in the estimator did not display a significant difference as the shape parameter α changed. We suppose that this results from the tail behavior of the skew normal distribution in that the existence of its fourth moment conflicts with the usual assumption that the fourth moment of heavy tail distribution does not exist. At the same time, neither Catoni's estimator nor our estimator performed better than the estimator obtained by L1 regression.

Table 3. The excess risk of the L_1, Catoni, and third-moment Catoni regression estimator on a skewed normal distribution.

		$n = 50$	$n = 100$	$n = 250$	$n = 500$	$n = 1000$
$s=1$	L_1	0.847	0.829	0.820	0.807	0.784
	C	0.865	0.844	0.825	0.785	0.779
	C_3	0.859	0.837	0.823	0.789	0.781
$s=3$	L_1	0.857	0.833	0.809	0.819	0.798
	C	0.861	0.842	0.829	0.835	0.828
	C_3	0.861	0.843	0.827	0.835	0.824
$s=5$	L_1	0.831	0.825	0.812	0.792	0.782
	C	0.856	0.855	0.850	0.839	0.828
	C_3	0.855	0.855	0.848	0.827	0.822

4. Empirical Analysis

In this section, we used the proposed procedure to research the dataset "tumor cell resistance to death," an artificial dataset consisting of two different types of tumor cells A and B, and the experiment records their resistance to different doses of experimental drugs. The explanatory variable X_i here is the dose of the drug, and the response variable Y_i is the score representing the resistance to death, ranging from 0 to 4. These data are available in the R lqr package; Galarza et al. [20] have studied these data by the quantile regression method.

In Figures 4–7, we display the QQplot and the log-QQplot about the scores for cell A and cell B, and it can be seen that the distribution of both cells lacks normality; however, the normality is satisfied between cells and log-scores; besides, the boxplot and the bee colony diagram in Figures 8 and 9 shows that both cell A and cell B have heavy-tails, which allows us to focus on the following regression model:

$$\log(Y_i) = \beta_0 + \beta_1 X_i,$$

where Y_i and X_i are defined before. Our focus was estimating the parameters β_0 and β_1, the solution of the following equation:

$$\widehat{r}_\beta(u) = \frac{1}{n\alpha} \sum_{i=1}^{n} \psi\left(\alpha\left(\left|\log(Y_i) - \beta_0 - X_i^\top \beta_1\right| - u\right)\right) = 0.$$

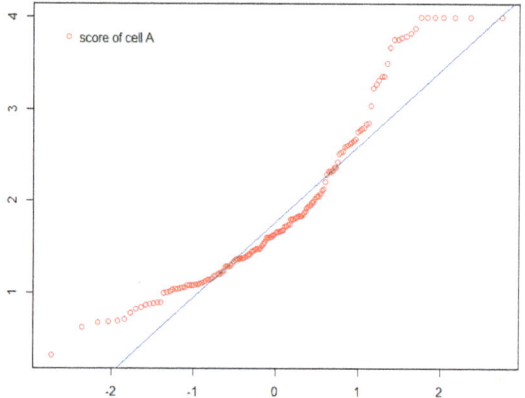

Figure 4. QQplot for cell A.

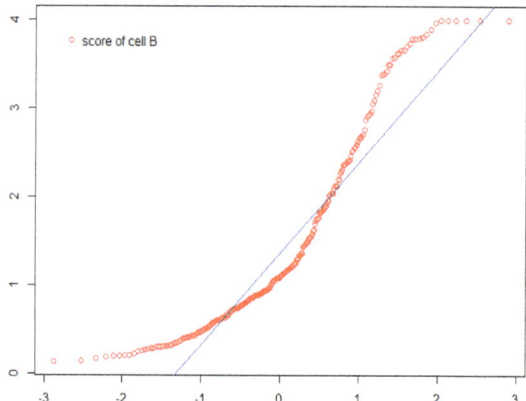

Figure 5. QQplot for cell B.

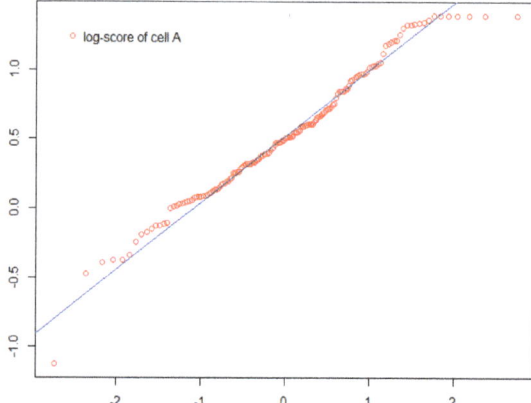

Figure 6. log-QQplot for cell A.

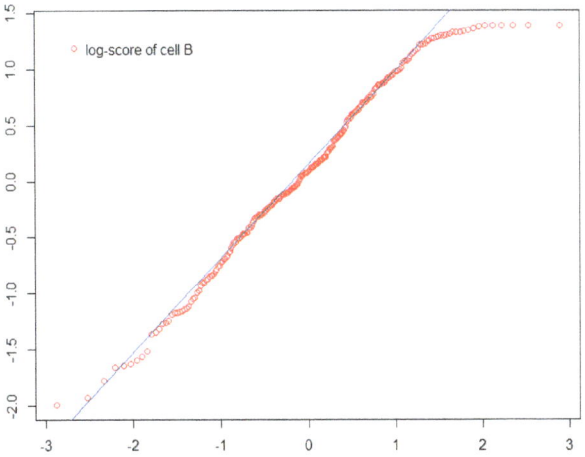

Figure 7. log-QQplot for cell B.

Let $\widehat{R}_C(\beta)$ denote the solution of the $\widehat{r}_\beta(u) = 0$; then, the Catoni regression estimator of β_0 and β_1 is in the form as follows:

$$\arg\min_{\beta_0, \beta_1} \widehat{R}_C(\beta).$$

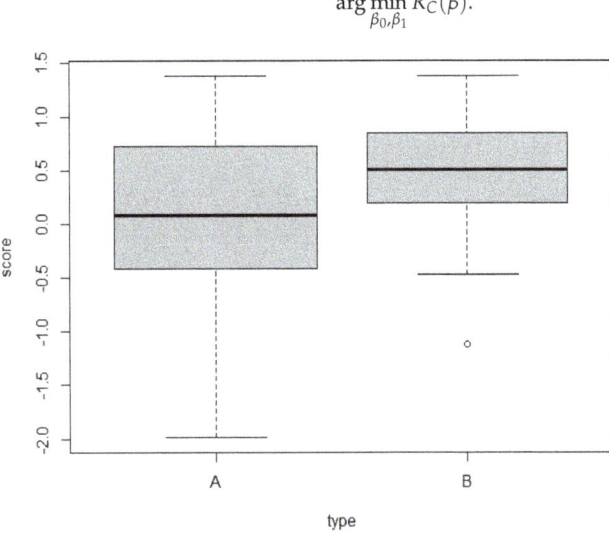

Figure 8. Boxplot about the log-scores for the two types of cells.

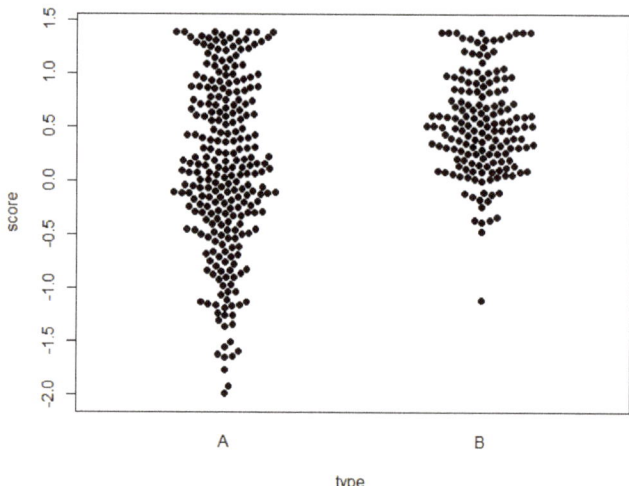

Figure 9. The bee colony diagram about the log-scores for the two types of cells.

Moreover, we compared the proposed estimator with the classical OLS estimator in Figures 10 and 11. The residuals plots are shown in Figures 12–15, from which we can draw the conclusion that the distribution of the residual of the three-order Catoni regression performs more uniformly; furthermore, the Mean Squared Error of the third-moment Catoni regression and OLS regression was 0.1120, 0.1255 for cell A and 0.2268, 0.2335 for cell B, respectively, which indicates that the proposed method is a better regression.

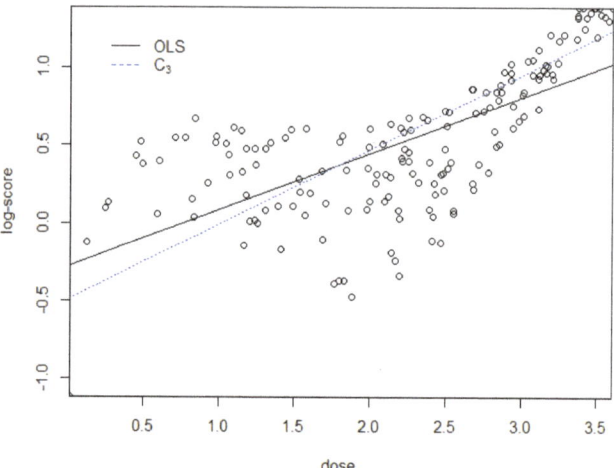

Figure 10. Regression for cell A.

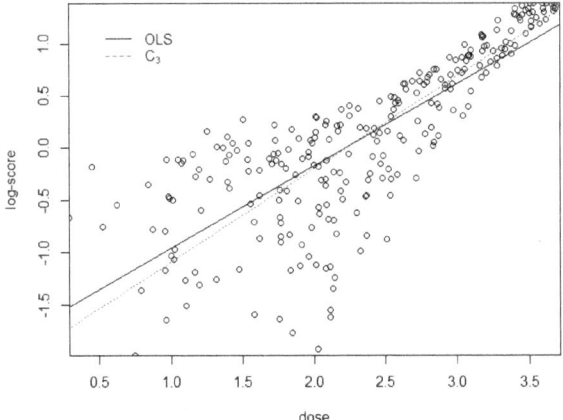

Figure 11. Regression for cell B.

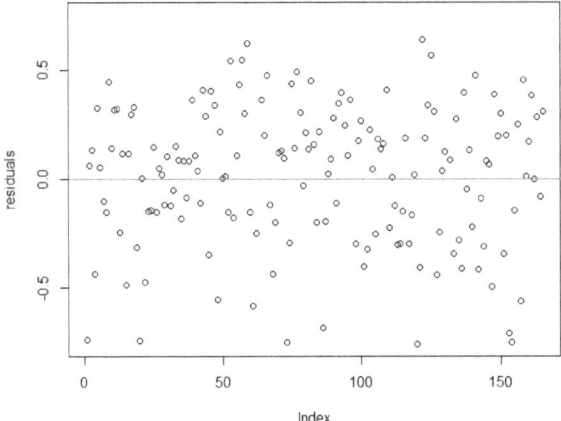

Figure 12. OLS regression residual plot for cell A.

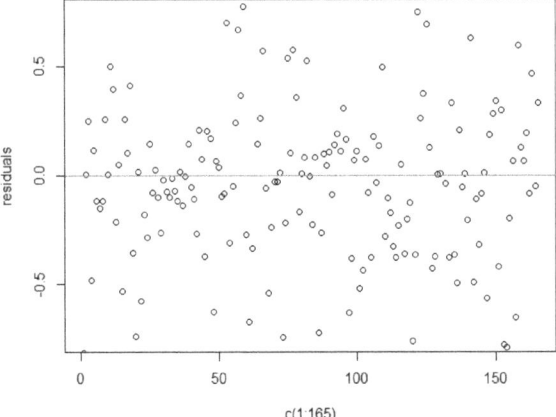

Figure 13. Third-moment Catoni regression residual plot for cell A.

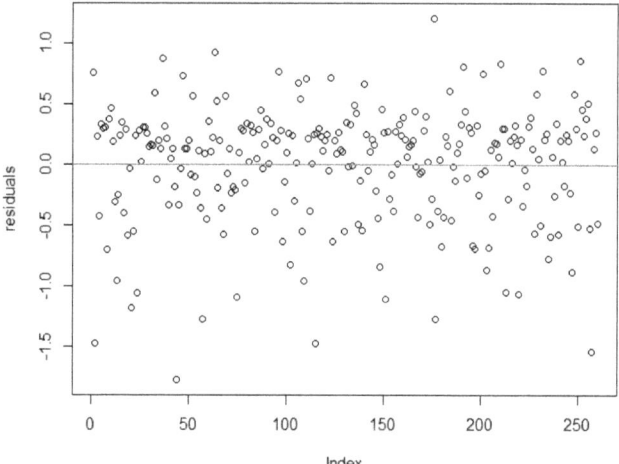

Figure 14. OLS regression residual plot for cell B.

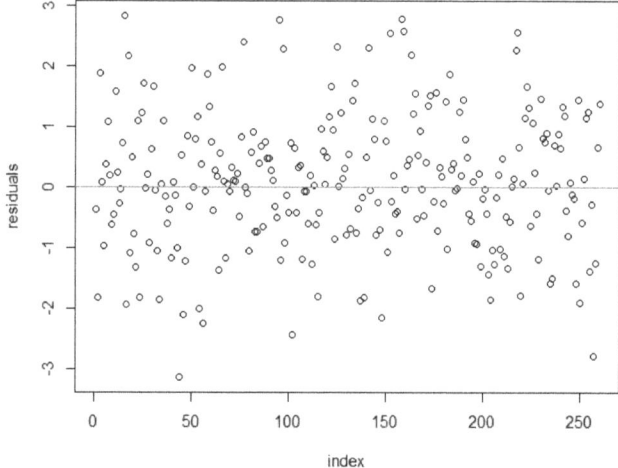

Figure 15. Third-moment Catoni regression residual plot for cell B.

5. Discussion

Estimating the mean of random variables is a classical issue in statistics [1], and it has been well studied in classical statistics; however, with the discovery of heavy-tailed distribution in many research fields, its existence is an important challenge in statistics. When the data have heavy tails, the traditional estimators such as the empirical mean usually perform poorly. Therefore, how to find an appropriate robust procedure is a well-known problem and has aroused great interest. A new estimator based on reconstructing the structure of the empirical mean was proposed by Catoni, which has excellent theoretical properties on the bias.

The Catoni's estimator is based on the existence of the variance v of the random variable. Therefore, with a weaker assumption on the moment conditions, it is an interesting issue whether the estimator has a better performance. In this study, we assumed that the third moment s of the data exists, and a more accurate upper bound of the exponential moment was obtained, which motivates an estimator with a better bias. To a certain extent, the assumption reduces the robustness to outliers, but it has a minimal effect in heavy tails distribution (the fourth moment does not exist). In future work, we have the following goals: first, we believe that our method can be applied as an improved mean estimator to any relevant model as long as the third moment of the distribution has good theoretical properties and wide application; second, it is an interesting idea to discuss and compare the bias bound of the proposed estimator with the minimax bound; finally, the estimation of the variance in regression models is very important in statistical inference. Considering that the deviation of the estimator given in our main theoretical results from the true value can be regarded as the confidence interval based on the known variance; therefore, the proposed estimator is not suitable for the estimation of variance, but it is an interesting issue how a proper variance estimator affects the bias of our estimator; additionally, we will consider variance estimation under heavy-tailed distributions in later work.

Author Contributions: Conceptualization, Y.C.; methodology, Y.C. and R.L.; investigation, Y.C. and R.L.; software, S.S.; writing, Y.C. and R.L.; Y.C. has designed the framework of this study and substantively revised it; R.L. and Y.C. have performed the methodology and simulation; S.S. implements research on empirical analysis research. All authors have read and agreed to the published version of the manuscript.

Funding: This research was supported by the National Natural Science Foundation of China (No. 72073082).

Data Availability Statement: The dataset for the empirical analysis can be derived from the following resource available in CRAN, https://cran.r-project.org/web/packages/lqr/index.html, accessed on 12 February 2022.

Conflicts of Interest: The authors declare no conflict of interest.

References

1. Lugosi, G.; Mendelson, S. Mean estimation and regression under heavy-tailed distributions: A survey. *Found. Comput. Math.* **2019**, *19*, 1145–1190.
2. Embrechts, P.; Kluppelberg, C.; Mikosch, T. *Modelling Extremal Events for Insurance and Finance*; Springer: Berlin/Heidelberg, Germany, 1997.
3. Huber, P. Robust estimation of a location parameter. *Ann. Math. Stat.* **1964**, *35*, 73–101.
4. Nemirovsky, A.; Yudin, D. *Problem Complexity and Method Efficiency in Optimization*; Springer: Berlin/Heidelberg, Germany; Wiley: New York, NY, USA, 1983.
5. Hsu, D.; Sabato, S. Loss minimization and parameter estimation with heavy tails. *J. Mach. Learn. Res.* **2016**, *17*, 1–40.
6. Jerrum, M.; Valiant, L.; Vazirani, V. Random generation of combinatorial structures from a uniform distribution. *Theoret. Comput. Sci.* **1986**, *43*, 169–188.
7. Tukey, J.; McLaughlin, D. Less vulnerable confidence and significance procedures for location based on a single sample: Trimming/Winsorization. I. *Sankhyā Ser. A* **1963**, 331–352.
8. Huber, P.; Ronchetti, E. *Robust Statistics*; Wiley: New York, NY, USA, 2009.
9. Catoni, O. *Statistical Learning Theory and Stochastic Optimization*; Springer: Berlin/Heidelberg, Germany, 2004.
10. Audibert, J.; Catoni, O. Robust linear least squares regression. *Ann. Stat.* **2011**, *39*, 2766–2794.
11. Bartlett, P.; Mendelson, S. Empirical minimization. *Probab. Theory Relat. Fields* **2006**, 311–334.
12. Maronna, R.A.; Martin, D.R.; Yohai, V.J. *Robust Statistics: Theory and Methods*; Springer: New York, NY, USA; Wiley: New York, NY, USA, 2006.
13. Bubeck, S.; Cesa-Bianchi, N.; Lugosi, G. Bandits with heavy tail. *IEEE Trans. Inform. Theory* **2013**, 7711–7717.
14. Catoni, O. Challenging the empirical mean and empirical variance: A deviation study. *Ann. Inst. Henri Poincaré Probab. Stat.* **2012**, *48*, 1148–1185.
15. Brownlees, C.; Joly, E.; Lugosi, G. Empirical risk minimization for heavy-tailed losses. *Ann. Stat.* **2015**, *43*, 2507–2536.
16. Minsker, S. Geometric median and robust estimation in Banach spaces. *Bernoulli* **2015**, *21*, 2308–2335.
17. Wang, Z.; Liu, H.; Zhang, T. Optimal computational and statistical rates of convergence for sparse nonconvex learning problems. *Ann. Stat.* **2014**, *42*, 2164–2201.
18. Jones, M.C.; Faddy, M.J. A skew extension of the t-distribution, with applications. *J. R. Stat. Soc. Ser. B Stat. Methodol.* **2003**, *65*, 159–174. 62E10 (62F10).

19. Høyrup, J. *The Babylonian Cellar Text BM 85200+ VAT 6599*; Springer: Berlin/Heidelberg, Germany; Birkhäuser: Basel, Switzerland, 1992; pp. 315–358.
20. Galarza, C.; Zhang, P.; Lachos, V. Logistic quantile regression for bounded outcomes using a family of heavy-tailed distributions. *Sankhya B* **2021**, *83*, S325–S349.

Article

A New Bound in the Littlewood–Offord Problem

Friedrich Götze [1] and Andrei Yu. Zaitsev [2,3,*]

[1] Fakultät für Mathematik, Universität Bielefeld, Postfach 100131, D-33501 Bielefeld, Germany; goetze@math.uni-bielefeld.de

[2] St. Petersburg Department of Steklov Mathematical Institute, Fontanka 27, St. Petersburg 191023, Russia

[3] Mathematics and Mechanics Faculty, St. Petersburg State University, 7/9 Universitetskaya nab., St. Petersburg 199034, Russia

* Correspondence: zaitsev@pdmi.ras.ru

Abstract: The paper deals with studying a connection of the Littlewood–Offord problem with estimating the concentration functions of some symmetric infinitely divisible distributions. It is shown that the concentration function of a weighted sum of independent identically distributed random variables is estimated in terms of the concentration function of a symmetric infinitely divisible distribution whose spectral measure is concentrated on the set of plus-minus weights.

Keywords: concentration functions; inequalities; the Littlewood–Offord problem; sums of independent random variables

MSC: 60F05; 60E15; 60G50

The aim of the present work is to provide a supplement to the paper of Eliseeva and Zaitsev [1]. We studied a connection of the Littlewood–Offord problem with estimating the concentration functions of some symmetric infinitely divisible distributions. In the study, we repeat the arguments of [1], adding, at the last step, an application of Jensen's inequality.

Let $X, X_1, \ldots, X_n$ be independent identically distributed (i.i.d.) random variables. The concentration function of a $\mathbf{R}^d$-dimensional random vector Y with distribution $F = \mathcal{L}(Y)$ is defined by the equality

$$Q(F, \lambda) = \sup_{x \in \mathbf{R}^d} \mathbf{P}(Y \in x + \lambda B), \quad 0 \leq \lambda \leq \infty,$$

where $B = \{x \in \mathbf{R}^d : \|x\| \leq 1/2\}$. Of course, $Q(F, \infty) = 1$. Let $a = (a_1, \ldots, a_n)$, where $a_k = (a_{k1}, \ldots, a_{kd}) \in \mathbf{R}^d$, $k = 1, \ldots, n$. In this paper, we studied the behavior of the concentration functions of the weighted sums $S_a = \sum_{k=1}^{n} X_k a_k$ with respect to the properties of vectors a_k. Interest in this subject has increased considerably in connection with the study of eigenvalues of random matrices (see, for instance, Friedland and Sodin [2], Rudelson and Vershynin [3,4], Tao and Vu [5,6], Nguyen and Vu [7], Vershynin [8], Tikhomirov [9], Livshyts, Tikhomirov and Vershynin [10], Campos et al. [11]). For a detailed history of the problem, we refer to a review of Nguyen and Vu [12]. The authors of the above articles (see also Halász [13]) called this question the Littlewood–Offord problem, since, for the first time, this problem was considered in 1943 by Littlewood and Offord [14] in connection with the study of random polynomials. They considered a special case, where the coefficients $a_k \in \mathbf{R}$ are one-dimensional, and X takes values ± 1 with probabilities $1/2$.

The recent achievements in estimating the probabilities of singularity of random matrices [9–11] were based on the Rudelson and Vershynin [3,4,8] method of *least common denominator*. Note that the results of [2,4,8] (concerning the Littlewood–Offord problem) were improved and refined in [15–17].

Now, we introduce some notation. In the sequel, let F_a denote the distribution of the sum S_a, let E_y be the probability measure concentrated at a point y, and let G be the distribution of the symmetrized random variable $\widetilde{X} = X_1 - X_2$. For $\delta \geq 0$, we denote

$$p(\delta) = G\{\{z : |z| > \delta\}\}. \tag{1}$$

The symbol c will be used for absolute positive constants which may be different, even in the same formulas.

Writing $A \ll B$ means that $|A| \leq cB$. Furthermore, we will write $A \asymp B$, if $A \ll B$ and $B \ll A$. We will write $A \ll_d B$, if $|A| \leq c(d)B$, where $c(d) > 0$ depends on d only. Similarly, $A \asymp_d B$, if $A \ll_d B$ and $B \ll_d A$. The scalar product in $\mathbf{R}^d$ will be denoted $\langle \cdot, \cdot \rangle$. Later, $\lfloor x \rfloor$ is the largest integer k, such that $k < x$. For $x = (x_1, \ldots, x_n) \in \mathbf{R}^n$, we will use the norms $\|x\|^2 = x_1^2 + \cdots + x_n^2$ and $|x| = \max_j |x_j|$. We denote by $\widehat{F}(t)$, $t \in \mathbf{R}^d$, the characteristic function of d-dimensional distributions F.

Products and powers of measures will be understood in the convolution sense. For infinitely divisible distribution F and $\lambda \geq 0$, we denote by F^λ the infinitely divisible distribution with characteristic function $\widehat{F}^\lambda(t)$.

The elementary properties of concentration functions are well studied (see, for instance, refs [18–20]). It is known that

$$Q(F, \mu) \ll_d (1 + \lfloor \mu/\lambda \rfloor)^d Q(F, \lambda) \tag{2}$$

for any $\mu, \lambda > 0$. Hence,

$$Q(F, c\lambda) \asymp_d Q(F, \lambda). \tag{3}$$

Let us formulate a generalization of the classical Esséen inequality [21] to the multivariate case ([22], see also [19]):

Lemma 1. *Let $\tau > 0$ and let F be a d-dimensional probability distribution. Then,*

$$Q(F, \tau) \ll_d \tau^d \int_{|t| \leq 1/\tau} |\widehat{F}(t)| \, dt. \tag{4}$$

In the general case, $Q(F, \tau)$ cannot be estimated from below by the right hand side of inequality (4). However, if we assume additionally that the distribution F is symmetric and its characteristic function is non-negative for all $t \in \mathbf{R}$, then we have the lower bound:

$$Q(F, \tau) \gg_d \tau^d \int_{|t| \leq 1/\tau} \widehat{F}(t) \, dt, \tag{5}$$

and, therefore,

$$Q(F, \tau) \asymp_d \tau^d \int_{|t| \leq 1/\tau} \widehat{F}(t) \, dt, \tag{6}$$

(see [23] or [18], Lemma 1.5 of Chapter II for $d = 1$). In the multivariate case, relations (5) and (6) may be found in Zaitsev [24]. The use of relation (6) allows us to simplify the arguments of Friedland and Sodin [2], Rudelson and Vershynin [4] and Vershynin [8] which were applied to Littlewood–Offord problem (see [15–17]).

The main result of this paper is a general inequality which reduces the estimation of concentration functions in the Littlewood–Offord problem to the estimation of concentration functions of some infinitely divisible distributions. This result is formulated in Theorem 1.

For $z \in \mathbf{R}$, introduce the distribution H_z with the characteristic function

$$\widehat{H}_z(t) = \exp\left(-\frac{1}{2} \sum_{k=1}^{n} \left(1 - \cos(\langle t, a_k \rangle z)\right)\right). \tag{7}$$

It depends on the vector a. It is clear that H_z is a symmetric infinitely divisible distribution. Therefore, its characteristic function is positive for all $t \in \mathbf{R}^d$.

Recall that $G = \mathcal{L}(X_1 - X_2)$ and $F_a = \mathcal{L}(S_a)$, where $S_a = \sum_{k=1}^{n} X_k a_k$.

Theorem 1. *Let V be an arbitrary one-dimensional Borel measure, such that $\lambda = V\{\mathbf{R}\} > 0$, and $V \leq G$, that is, $V\{B\} \leq G\{B\}$, for any Borel set B. Then, for any $\tau > 0$, we have*

$$Q(F_a, \tau) \ll_d \int_{z \in \mathbf{R}} Q(H_1^\lambda, \tau|z|^{-1}) W\{dz\}, \qquad (8)$$

where $W = \lambda^{-1} V$.

Corollary 1. *For any $\varepsilon, \tau > 0$, we have*

$$Q(F_a, \tau) \ll_d Q(H_1^{p(\tau/\varepsilon)}, \varepsilon), \qquad (9)$$

where $p(\,\cdot\,)$ is defined in (1).

In order to verify Corollary 1, we note that the distribution $G = \mathcal{L}(\widetilde{X})$ may be represented as the mixture

$$G = p_0 G_0 + p_1 G_1, \quad \text{where} \quad p_j = \mathbf{P}\{\widetilde{X} \in A_j\}, \quad j = 0, 1,$$

$A_0 = \{x \colon |x| \leq \tau/\varepsilon\}$, $A_1 = \{x \colon |x| > \tau/\varepsilon\}$, G_j are probability measures defined for $p_j > 0$ by the formula $G_j\{B\} = G\{B \cap A_j\}/p_j$, for any Borel set B. In fact, G_j is the conditional distribution of $\widetilde{X}$, given that $\widetilde{X} \in A_j$. If $p_j = 0$, then we can take G_j as an arbitrary measure.

The conditions of Theorem 1 are satisfied for $V = p_1 G_1$. $\lambda = p_1 = p(\tau/\varepsilon)$, $W = G_1$. Inequalities (2) and (6) imply that

$$\begin{aligned} Q(F_a, \tau) &\ll_d \int_{z \in A_1} Q(H_1^\lambda, \tau|z|^{-1}) W\{dz\} \\ &\leq \sup_{z \geq \tau/\varepsilon} Q(H_1^{p(\tau/\varepsilon)}, \tau/z) = Q(H_1^{p(\tau/\varepsilon)}, \varepsilon), \end{aligned} \qquad (10)$$

proving (9).

Applying Theorem 1 with V of the form

$$V\{dz\} = \left(1 + \lfloor \tau(\varepsilon|z|)^{-1} \rfloor\right)^{-d} G\{dz\}, \qquad (11)$$

and using inequality (2), we obtain.

Corollary 2. *For any $\varepsilon, \tau > 0$, we have*

$$Q(F_a, \tau) \ll_d \lambda^{-1} Q(H_1^\lambda, \varepsilon), \qquad (12)$$

where

$$\lambda = \lambda(G, \tau/\varepsilon) = V\{\mathbf{R}\} = \int_{z \in \mathbf{R}} \left(1 + \lfloor \tau(\varepsilon|z|)^{-1} \rfloor\right)^{-d} G\{dz\}. \qquad (13)$$

It is clear that $\lfloor \tau(\varepsilon|z|)^{-1} \rfloor = 0$ if $|z| > \tau/\varepsilon$. Therefore, $\lambda = \lambda(G, \tau/\varepsilon) \geq p(\tau/\varepsilon)$, hence, $Q(H_1^\lambda, \varepsilon) \leq Q(H_1^{p(\tau/\varepsilon)}, \varepsilon)$. Thus, if $\lambda \gg_d 1$, then inequality (12) of Corollary 2 is stronger than inequality (9) of Corollary 1.

The proof of Theorem 1 is based on elementary properties of concentration functions. We repeat the arguments of [1], adding, at the last step, an application of Jensen's inequality. In [1], inequality (2) was used instead. The main result of [1] does not imply Corollary 2.

Note that H_1^λ is an infinitely divisible distribution with the Lévy spectral measure $M_\lambda = \frac{\lambda}{4} M^*$, where $M^* = \sum_{k=1}^{n} (E_{a_k} + E_{-a_k})$. It is clear that the assertions of Theorem 1 and Corollaries 1 and 2 may be treated as statements about the measure M^*.

Corollary 1 was already proved earlier in [1,25], see also [26] for the case $\tau = 0$. It was used essentially in [25,27] to show that Arak's inequalities for concentration functions may be used for investigations of the Littlewood–Offord problem. Arak has shown that if the concentration function of infinitely divisible distribution is relatively large, then the spectral measure of this distribution is concentrated in a neighborhood of a set with simple arithmetical structure. Together with Corollary 1, this means that a large value of $Q(F_a, \tau)$ implies a simple arithmetical structure of the set $\{\pm a_k\}_{k=1}^{n}$. This statement is similar to the so-called "inverse principle" in the Littlewood–Offord problem (see [5,7,12]).

Note that using the results of Arak [23,28] (see also [18]) one could derive from Corollary 1 inequalities similar to boumds for concentration functions in the Littlewood–Offord problem, which were obtained in a paper of Nguyen and Vu [7] (see also [12]). A detailed discussion of this fact is presented in [25,27]. We noticed that Corollary 2 may be stronger than Corollary 1. Therefore, the results of [25,27] could be improved (in the sense of dependence of constants on the distribution of X_1) replacing an application of Corollary 1 by an application of Corollary 2. The authors are going to devote a separate publication to this topic.

Proof of Theorem 1. Let us show that, for arbitrary probability distribution, W and $\lambda, T > 0$,

$$\log \int_{|t| \leq T} \exp\left(-\frac{1}{2} \sum_{k=1}^{n} \int_{z \in \mathbf{R}} (1 - \cos(\langle t, a_k \rangle z)) \lambda W\{dz\}\right) dt$$

$$\leq \int_{z \in \mathbf{R}} \left(\log \int_{|t| \leq T} \exp\left(-\frac{\lambda}{2} \sum_{k=1}^{n} (1 - \cos(\langle t, a_k \rangle z))\right) dt\right) W\{dz\}$$

$$= \int_{z \in \mathbf{R}} \left(\log \int_{|t| \leq T} \widehat{H}_z^\lambda(t) dt\right) W\{dz\}. \quad (14)$$

It is suffice to prove (14) for discrete distributions $W = \sum_{j=1}^{\infty} p_j E_{z_j}$, where $0 \leq p_j \leq 1$, $z_j \in \mathbf{R}$, $\sum_{j=1}^{\infty} p_j = 1$. Applying in this case the generalized Hölder inequality, we have

$$\int_{|t| \leq T} \exp\left(-\frac{1}{2} \sum_{k=1}^{n} \int_{z \in \mathbf{R}} (1 - \cos(\langle t, a_k \rangle z)) \lambda W\{dz\}\right) dt$$

$$= \int_{|t| \leq T} \exp\left(-\frac{\lambda}{2} \sum_{j=1}^{\infty} p_j \sum_{k=1}^{n} (1 - \cos(\langle t, a_k \rangle z_j))\right) dt$$

$$\leq \prod_{j=1}^{\infty} \left(\int_{|t| \leq T} \exp\left(-\frac{\lambda}{2} \sum_{k=1}^{n} (1 - \cos(\langle t, a_k \rangle z_j))\right) dt\right)^{p_j}. \quad (15)$$

Taking logarithms of the left- and right-hand sides of (15), we get (14). In general cases, we can approximate W by discrete distributions in the sense of weak convergence and pass to the limit. Note also that the integrals $\int_{|t| \leq T} dt$ may be replaced in (14) by the integrals $\int \mu\{dt\}$ with an arbitrary Borel measure μ.

Since for characteristic function $\widehat{U}(t)$ of a random vector Y, we have

$$|\widehat{U}(t)|^2 = \mathbf{E} \exp(i \langle t, \widetilde{Y} \rangle) = \mathbf{E} \cos(\langle t, \widetilde{Y} \rangle),$$

where $\widetilde{Y}$ is the corresponding symmetrized random vector, then

$$|\widehat{U}(t)| \leq \exp\left(-\frac{1}{2}(1 - |\widehat{U}(t)|^2)\right) = \exp\left(-\frac{1}{2}\mathbf{E}(1 - \cos(\langle t, \widetilde{Y} \rangle))\right). \quad (16)$$

According to Theorem 1 and relations $V = \lambda W \leq G$, (14) and (16), applying Jensen's inequality of the form $\exp(\mathbf{E} f(\xi)) \leq \mathbf{E} \exp(f(\xi))$ for any measurable function f and any random variable ξ, we have

$$\begin{aligned}
Q(F_a, \tau) &\ll_d \tau^d \int_{\tau|t| \leq 1} |\widehat{F}_a(t)| \, dt \\
&\ll_d \tau^d \int_{\tau|t| \leq 1} \exp\left(-\frac{1}{2} \sum_{k=1}^n \mathbf{E}\left(1 - \cos(\langle t, a_k \rangle \widetilde{X})\right)\right) dt \\
&= \tau^d \int_{\tau|t| \leq 1} \exp\left(-\frac{1}{2} \sum_{k=1}^n \int_{z \in \mathbf{R}} \left(1 - \cos(\langle t, a_k \rangle z)\right) G\{dz\}\right) dt \\
&\leq \tau^d \int_{\tau|t| \leq 1} \exp\left(-\frac{1}{2} \sum_{k=1}^n \int_{z \in \mathbf{R}} \left(1 - \cos(\langle t, a_k \rangle z)\right) \lambda W\{dz\}\right) dt \\
&\leq \exp\left(\int_{z \in \mathbf{R}} \log\left(\tau^d \int_{\tau|t| \leq 1} \widehat{H}_z^\lambda(t) \, dt\right) W\{dz\}\right) \\
&\leq \int_{z \in \mathbf{R}} \left(\tau^d \int_{\tau|t| \leq 1} \widehat{H}_z^\lambda(t) \, dt\right) W\{dz\}.
\end{aligned} \quad (17)$$

Using (6), we have

$$\tau^d \int_{\tau|t| \leq 1} \widehat{H}_z^\lambda(t) \, dt \asymp_d Q(H_z^\lambda, \tau) = Q(H_1^\lambda, \tau|z|^{-1}). \quad (18)$$

Substituting this formula into (17), we obtain (8). In (18), we have used that $H_z^\lambda = \mathcal{L}(z\eta)$, where η is a random vector with $\mathcal{L}(\eta) = H_1^\lambda$. □

Author Contributions: Investigation, F.G.; Writing—original draft, A.Y.Z. All authors have read and agreed to the published version of the manuscript.

Funding: The authors were supported by SFB 1283/2 2021—317210226 and by the RFBR-DFG grant 20-51-12004. The second author was supported by grant RFBR 19-01-00356.

Institutional Review Board Statement: Not applicable.

Informed Consent Statement: Not applicable.

Data Availability Statement: Not applicable.

Acknowledgments: We are grateful to the anonymous for valuable remarks.

Conflicts of Interest: The authors declare no conflict of interest.

References

1. Eliseeva, Y.S.; Zaitsev, A.Y. On the Littlewood–Offord problem. *J. Math. Sci.* **2016**, *214*, 467–473. [CrossRef]
2. Friedland, O.; Sodin, S. Bounds on the concentration function in terms of Diophantine approximation. *C. R. Math. Acad. Sci. Paris* **2007**, *345*, 513–518. [CrossRef]
3. Rudelson, M.; Vershynin, R. The Littlewood–Offord problem and invertibility of random matrices. *Adv. Math.* **2008**, *218*, 600–633. [CrossRef]
4. Rudelson, M.; Vershynin, R. The smallest singular value of a random rectangular matrix. *Comm. Pure Appl. Math.* **2009**, *62*, 1707–1739. [CrossRef]
5. Tao, T.; Vu, V. Inverse Littlewood–Offord theorems and the condition number of random discrete matrices. *Ann. Math.* **2009**, *169*, 595–632. [CrossRef]
6. Tao, T.; Vu, V. From the Littlewood–Offord problem to the circular law: universality of the spectral distribution of random matrices. *Bull. Amer. Math. Soc.* **2009**, *46*, 377–396. [CrossRef]
7. Nguyen, H.; Vu, V. Optimal inverse Littlewood–Offord theorems. *Adv. Math.* **2011**, *226*, 5298–5319. [CrossRef]
8. Vershynin, R. Invertibility of symmetric random matrices. *Random Struct. Algorithms* **2014**, *44*, 135–182. [CrossRef]
9. Tikhomirov, K. Singularity of random Bernoulli matrices. *Ann. Math.* **2020**, *191*, 593–634. [CrossRef]
10. Livshyts, G.V.; Tikhomirov, K.; Vershynin, R. The smallest singular value of inhomogeneous square random matrices. *Ann. Probab.* **2021**, *49*, 1286–1309. [CrossRef]

11. Campos, M.; Jenssen, M.; Michelen, M.; Sahasrabudhe, J. The singularity probability of a random symmetric matrix is exponentially small. *arXiv* **2021**, arXiv:2105.11384.
12. Nguyen, H.; Vu, V. Small probabilities, inverse theorems and applications. *arXiv* **2013**, arXiv:1301.0019.
13. Halász, G. Estimates for the concentration function of combinatorial number theory and probability. *Period. Math. Hung.* **1977**, *8*, 197–211. [CrossRef]
14. Littlewood, J.E.; Offord, A.C. On the number of real roots of a random algebraic equation. *Rec. Math. [Mat. Sbornik] N.S.* **1943**, *12*, 277–286.
15. Eliseeva, Y.S.; Zaitsev, A.Y. Estimates for the concentration functions of weighted sums of independent random variables. *Theory Probab. Appl.* **2013**, *57*, 670–678. [CrossRef]
16. Eliseeva, Y.S. Multivariate estimates for the concentration functions of weighted sums of independent identically distributed random variables. *Zap. Nauchn. Semin. POMI* **2013**, *412*, 121–137. (In Russian) [CrossRef]
17. Eliseeva, Y.S.; Götze, F.; Zaitsev, A.Y. Estimates for the concentration functions in the Littlewood–Offord problem. *Zap. Nauchn. Semin. POMI* **2013**, *420*, 50–69. (In Russian) [CrossRef]
18. Arak, T.V.; Zaitsev, A.Y. Uniform limit theorems for sums of independent random variables. *Proc. Steklov Inst. Math.* **1988**, *174*, 222.
19. Hengartner, W.; Theodorescu, R. *Concentration Functions*; Academic Press: New York, NY, USA, 1973.
20. Petrov, V.V. *Sums of Independent Random Variables*; De Gruyter: Moscow, Russia, 1972.
21. Esséen, C.-G. On the Kolmogorov–Rogozin inequality for the concentration function. *Z. Wahrscheinlichkeitstheorie Verw. Geb.* **1966**, *5*, 210–216. [CrossRef]
22. Esséen, C.-G. On the concentration function of a sum of independent random variables. *Z. Wahrscheinlichkeitstheorie Verw. Geb.* **1968**, *9*, 290–308. [CrossRef]
23. Arak, T.V. On the approximation by the accompanying laws of n-fold convolutions of distributions with nonnegative characteristic functions. *Theory Probab. Appl.* **1980**, *25*, 221–243. [CrossRef]
24. Zaitsev, A.Y. Multidimensional generalized method of triangular functions. *J. Soviet Math.* **1988**, *43*, 2797–2810. [CrossRef]
25. Eliseeva, Y.S.; Götze, F.; Zaitsev, A.Y. Arak inequalities for concentration functions and the Littlewood–Offord problem. *Theory Probab. Appl.* **2018**, *62*, 196–215.
26. Zaitsev, A.Y. A bound for the maximal probability in the Littlewood–Offord problem. *J. Math. Sci.* **2016**, *219*, 743–746. [CrossRef]
27. Götze, F.; Zaitsev, A.Y. New applications of Arak's inequalities to the Littlewood–Offord problem. *Eur. J. Math.* **2018**, *4*, 639–663. [CrossRef]
28. Arak, T.V. On the convergence rate in Kolmogorov's uniform limit theorem. I. *Theory Probab. Appl.* **1981**, *26*, 219–239. [CrossRef]

Article

On De la Peña Type Inequalities for Point Processes

Naiqi Liu [1], Vladimir V. Ulyanov [2,3] and Hanchao Wang [3,*]

[1] School of Mathematics, Shandong University, Jinan 250100, China; 201711879@mail.sdu.edu.cn
[2] Faculty of Computational Mathematics and Cybernetics, Lomonosov Moscow State University, 119991 Moscow, Russia; vulyanov@cs.msu.ru
[3] Institute for Financial Studies, Shandong University, Jinan 250100, China
* Correspondence: wanghanchao@sdu.edu.cn; Tel.: +86-531-8836-4212

Abstract: There has been a renewed interest in exponential concentration inequalities for stochastic processes in probability and statistics over the last three decades. De la Peña established a nice exponential inequality for a discrete time locally square integrable martingale. In this paper, we obtain de la Peña's inequalities for a stochastic integral of multivariate point processes. The proof is primarily based on Doléans–Dade exponential formula and the optional stopping theorem. As an application, we obtain an exponential inequality for block counting process in $\Lambda-$coalescent.

Keywords: de la Peña's inequalities; purely discontinuous local martingales; stochastic integral of multivariate point processes; Doléans–Dade exponential

MSC: 60E15; 60G55

1. Introduction

Let $S = (S_n)_{n \geq 0}$ be a locally square integrable martingale on $(\Omega, \mathcal{F}, (\mathcal{F}_n)_{n \geq 1}, \mathbb{P})$. The predictable quadratic variation of $S = (S_n)_{n \geq 0}$ is given by

$$<S,S>_n = \sum_{i=1}^{n} \mathbb{E}[((S_i - S_{i-1})^2 | \mathcal{F}_{i-1}].$$

Many authors studied the upper bound of

$$\mathbb{P}(S_n \geq x, <S,S>_n \leq y).$$

The celebrated Freedman inequality is as follows.

Theorem 1 (Freedman [1]). *Let $S = (S_n)_{n \geq 0}$ be a locally square integrable martingale on $(\Omega, \mathcal{F}, (\mathcal{F}_n)_{n \geq 1}, \mathbb{P})$. If $|S_k - S_{k-1}| \leq c$ for each $1 \leq k \leq n$, then*

$$\mathbb{P}(S_n \geq x, <S,S>_n \leq y) \leq \exp\{-\frac{x^2}{2(y + cx)}\}.$$

This result can be regarded as an extension of Hoeffding [2]. Fan, Grama and Liu [3,4], and Rio [5] obtained a series of remarkable extensions of Freedman inequality [1]. See also Bercu et al. [6] for a recent review in this field.

De la Peña [7] establishes a nice exponential inequality for discrete time locally square integrable martingales.

Theorem 2 (De la Peña [7]). *Let $S = (S_n)_{n \geq 0}$ be a locally square integrable and conditionally symmetric martingale on $(\Omega, \mathcal{F}, (\mathcal{F}_n)_{n \geq 1}, \mathbb{P})$. Then,*

$$\mathbb{P}\big(S_n \geq x, \sum_{i=1}^n (S_i - S_{i-1})^2 \leq y\big) \leq \exp\{-\frac{x^2}{2y}\}.$$

This result is quite different from the classical Freedman's inequality. The challenge for obtaining Theorem 1 is to find an approach based on the use of the exponential Markov's inequality. De la Peña constructed a supermartingale to get Theorem 1. Furthermore, Bercu and Touati [8] established the following result for self-normalized martingales, which are similar to Theorem 1.

Theorem 3 (Bercu and Touati [8]). *Let $S = (S_n)_{n \geq 0}$ be a locally square integrable martingale on $(\Omega, \mathcal{F}, (\mathcal{F}_n)_{n \geq 1}, \mathbb{P})$. Then, for all $x, y > 0$, $a \geq 0$ and $b > 0$,*

$$\mathbb{P}\big(\frac{|S_n|}{a + b <S,S>_n} \geq x, <S,S>_n \geq \sum_{i=1}^n (S_i - S_{i-1})^2 + y\big) \leq 2\exp\{-x^2(ab + \frac{b^2 y}{2})\}.$$

It is natural to ask what will happen when we study the continuous-time processes for the above cases? Let $(\Omega, \mathcal{F}, (\mathcal{F}_t)_{t \geq 0}, \mathbb{P})$ be a stochastic basis. $M = (M_t)_{t \geq 0}$ is a continuous locally square integrable martingale. The predictable quadratic variation of M, $<M,M>$, is a continuous increasing process, such that $(M_t^2 - <M,M>_t)_{t \geq 0}$ is a local martingale. However, we cannot define an analogy for M like $\sum_{i=1}^n (S_i - S_{i-1})^2$ in Theorems 1 and 3. Since $M = (M_t)_{t \geq 0}$ has jumps, we can replace $\sum_{i=1}^n (S_i - S_{i-1})^2$ by $\sum_{s \leq t} |\triangle M_s|^2$. It is an interesting problem to consider De la Peña type inequalities for continuous-time local square integrable martingale with jumps. Some authors obtained the concentration inequalities for continuous-time stochastic processes. Bernstein's inequality for local martingales with jumps was given by van der Geer [9]. Khoshnevisan [10] found some concentration inequalities for continuous martingales. Dzhaparidze and van Zanten [11] extended Khoshnevisan's results to martingales with jumps.

This paper focuses on the De la Peña type inequalities for stochastic integrals of multivariate point processes. Stochastic integrals of multivariate point processes are an essential example of purely discontinuous local martingales. Some useful facts and results essential for this paper's proofs will be collected in Section 2. Section 3 will present our main results and give their proofs, while Section 4 will derive an exponential inequality for block counting process in Λ−coalescent as applications. Usually, $c, C, K, \cdots$ denote positive constants, which very often may be different at each occurrence.

2. Preliminaries

Let$(\Omega, \mathcal{F}, (\mathcal{F}_t)_{t \geq 0}, \mathbb{P})$ be a stochastic basis. A stochastic process $M = (M_t)_{t \geq 0}$ is called a purely discontinuous local martingale if $M_0 = 0$ and M is orthogonal to all continuous local martingales. The reader is referred to the classic book [12] due to Jacod and Shiryayev for more information. We shall restrict ourselves to the integer-valued random measure μ on $\mathbb{R}_+ \times \mathbb{R}$ induced by a $\mathbb{R}_+ \times \mathbb{R}$-valued multivariate point process. In particular, let $(T_k, Z_k), k \geq 1$, be a multivariate point process, and define

$$\mu(dt, dx) = \sum_{k \geq 1} \mathbf{1}_{\{T_k < \infty\}} \varepsilon_{(T_k, Z_k)}(dt, dx), \quad (1)$$

where $\varepsilon_{(T_k, Z_k)}$ is the delta measure at point (T_k, Z_k). Then $\mu(\omega; [0, t] \times \mathbb{R}) < \infty$ for all $(\omega, t) \in \Omega \times \mathbb{R}$. Let $\tilde{\Omega} = \Omega \times \mathbb{R}_+ \times \mathbb{R}$, $\tilde{\mathcal{P}} = \mathcal{P} \otimes \mathcal{B}$, where $\mathcal{B}$ is a Borel σ-field on $\mathbb{R}$ and $\mathcal{P}$ a σ-field generated by all left continuous adapted processes on $\Omega \times \mathbb{R}_+$. The predictable function is a $\tilde{\mathcal{P}}$-measurable function on $\tilde{\Omega}$. Let ν be the unique predictable compensator of μ (up to a $\mathbb{P}$-null set). Namely, ν is a predictable random measure such that for any predictable function W, $W * \mu - W * \nu$ is a local martingale, where the $W * \mu$ is defined by

$$W * \mu_t = \begin{cases} \int_0^t \int_{\mathbb{R}} W(s,x)\mu(ds,dx), & \text{if } \int_0^t \int_{\mathbb{R}} |W(s,x)|\mu(ds,dx) < \infty, \\ +\infty, & \text{otherwise.} \end{cases}$$

Note the ν admits the disintegration

$$\nu(dt,dx) = dA_t K(\omega, t; dx), \tag{2}$$

where $K(\cdot, \cdot)$ is a transition kernel from $(\Omega \times \mathbb{R}_+, \mathcal{P})$ into $(\mathbb{R}, \mathcal{B})$, and $A = (A_t)_{t \geq 0}$ is an increasing càdlàg predictable process. For μ in (1), which is defined through multivariate point process, ν admits

$$\nu(dt,dx) = \sum_{n \geq 1} \frac{1}{G_n([t,\infty] \times \mathbb{R})} \mathbf{1}_{\{t \leq T_{n+1}\}} G_n(dt,dx),$$

where $G_n(\omega, ds, dx)$ is a regular version of the conditional distribution of (T_{n+1}, Z_{n+1}) with respect to $\sigma\{T_1, Z_1, \cdots, T_n, Z_n\}$. In particular, if $F_n(dt) = G_n(dt \times \mathbb{R})$, the point process $N = \sum_{n \geq 1} \mathbf{1}_{[T_n, \infty)}$ has the compensator $A_t = \nu([0,t] \times \mathbb{R})$, which satisfies

$$A_t = \sum_{n \geq 1} \int_0^{T_{n+1} \wedge t} \frac{1}{F_n([s,\infty])} F_n(ds).$$

Now, we define the stochastic integrals of multivariate point processes. For a stopping time T, $[T] = \{(\omega, t) : T(\omega) = t\}$ is the graph of T. For μ in (1), define $D = \bigcup_{n=1}^{\infty} [T_n]$. With any measurable function W on $\tilde{\Omega}$, we define $a_t = \nu(\{t\} \times \mathbb{R})$, and

$$\hat{W} * \nu_t = \begin{cases} \int_{\mathbb{R}} W(t,x)\nu(\{t\} \times dx), & \text{if } \int_{\mathbb{R}} |W(t,x)|\nu(\{t\} \times dx) < \infty, \\ +\infty, & \text{otherwise.} \end{cases}$$

We denote by $G_{loc}(\mu)$ the set of all $\tilde{\mathcal{P}}$-measurable real-valued functions W such that $[\sum_{s \leq t}(\widetilde{W}_s)^2]^{1/2}$ is local integrable variation process, where $\widetilde{W}_t = W \mathbf{1}_D(\omega, t) - \hat{W}_t$.

Definition 1. *If $W \in G_{loc}(\mu)$, the stochastic integral of W with respect to $\mu - \nu$ is defined as a purely discontinuous local martingales, the jump process of which is indistinguishable from $\widetilde{W}$.*

We denote the stochastic integral of W with respect to $\mu - \nu$ by $W * (\mu - \nu)$. For a given predictable function W, $W * (\mu - \nu)$ is a purely discontinuous local martingale, which is defined through jump process. It is easy to prove that $W * (\mu - \nu) = W * \mu - W * \nu$. Denote $M = W * (\mu - \nu)$.

Itô's formula for a purely discontinuous local martingale is essential for our proofs. Now, we present Itô's formula for M.

Lemma 1 (Itô's formula, Jacod and Shiryaev [12]). *Let μ be a multivariate point process, ν be the predictable compensator of μ, W be a given predictable function on $\tilde{\Omega}$, and $W \in G_{loc}(\mu)$. Let f be a differentiable function, for $M = W * (\mu - \nu)$ and $t > 0$,*

$$f(M_t) = f(M_0) + \int_0^t f'(M_{s-})dM_s + \sum_{s \leq t}[f(M_s) - f(M_{s-}) - f'(M_{s-})\Delta M_s].$$

Under some conditions, Wang, Lin and Su [13] obtained

$$\mathbb{P}\Big(M_t \geq x, <M,M>_t \leq v^2 \text{ for some } t > 0\Big) \leq \exp\{-\frac{x^2}{2(v^2+cx)}\} \qquad (3)$$

where $<M,M>$ is the predictable quadratic variation process of $M = W * (\mu - \nu)$,

$$<M,M>_t = (W - \hat{W})^2 * \nu_t + \sum_{1 \leq s \leq t}(1-a_s)\hat{W}_s^2.$$

When M is a purely discontinuous local martingale, $\sum_{s \leq \cdot}|\Delta M_s|^2 - <M,M>$ is a local martingale. There will be an interesting problem when the predictable quadratic variation $<M,M>$ in (3) is replaced by the quadratic variation $\sum_{s \leq \cdot}|\Delta M_s|^2$. In this paper, we will estimate the upper bound of two types of tail probabilities:

$$\mathbb{P}\Big(M_t \geq x, \sum_{s \leq t}|\Delta M_s|^2 \leq v^2 \text{ for some } t > 0\Big) \qquad (4)$$

and

$$\mathbb{P}\Big(M_t \geq (\alpha + \beta \sum_{s \leq t}|\Delta M_s|^2)x, \sum_{s \leq t}|\Delta M_s|^2 \geq <M,M>_t + v^2 \text{ for some } t > 0\Big). \qquad (5)$$

It is important to note that the continuity of A implies the quasi-left continuity of M. However, the quasi-left continuity of M can be destroyed easily by changing the filtration in the underlying space. For example, let N be a homogeneous Poisson process with respect to $\mathbb{F}$. Let $(T_n)_{n \geq 0}$ be the sequence of the jump-times of N. The process N is not quasi-left continuous in the filtration $\mathbb{G}$ obtained by enlarging $\mathbb{F}$ initially with the σ-field $\mathcal{R} = \sigma(T_1)$. ($\sigma_n = (1 - \frac{1}{2n})T_1$ is a sequence of $\mathbb{G}$-stopping times announcing T_1). The main purpose of this paper consists in estimating (4) and (5) when M is not quasi-left continuous.

3. The Main Results and Their Proofs

Now, we present our first main result.

Theorem 4. *Let μ be a multivariate point process, ν be the predictable compensator of μ, $a_t = \nu(\{t\} \times \mathbb{R})$, W be a given predictable function on $\tilde{\Omega}$, and $W \in G_{loc}(\mu)$. $M = W * (\mu - \nu)$. Assume $\Delta M \geq -1$. Then, for $x > 0$, $v > 0$,*

$$\mathbb{P}\Big(M_t \geq x, \sum_{s \leq t}|\Delta M_s|^2 \leq v^2 \text{ for some } t > 0\Big) \leq \Big(\frac{v^2+x}{v^2}\Big)^{v^2} e^{-x}.$$

Proof of Theorem 4. For simplicity of notation, put

$$\begin{aligned}S(\lambda)_t &= \int_0^t \int_{\mathbb{R}} (e^{[\lambda(W-\hat{W})-(\lambda+\log(1-\lambda))(W-\hat{W})^2]} - 1 - \lambda(W-\hat{W}))\nu(ds,dx) \\ &\quad + \sum_{s \leq t}(1-a_s)(e^{[-\lambda \hat{W}_s+(\lambda+\log(1-\lambda))(\hat{W}_s)^2]} - 1 + \lambda \hat{W}_s),\end{aligned}$$

where $\lambda \in [0,1)$.

Furthermore,

$$\begin{aligned}
\Delta S(\lambda)_t &= \int_{\mathbb{R}} \left(e^{[\lambda(W-\hat{W})-(\lambda+\log(1-\lambda))(W-\hat{W})^2]} - 1 - \lambda(W-\hat{W}) \right) \nu(\{t\}, dx) \\
&\quad + (1-a_t)(e^{[-\lambda \hat{W}_t + (\lambda+\log(1-\lambda))(\hat{W}_t)^2]} - 1 + \lambda \hat{W}_t) \\
&= e^{[-\lambda \hat{W}_t - (\lambda+\log(1-\lambda))(\hat{W}_t)^2]} \left(\int_{\mathbb{R}} e^{[\lambda W - (\lambda+\log(1-\lambda))(W^2-2W\hat{W})]} \nu(\{t\}, dx) + 1 - a_t \right) \\
&\quad + (1-a_t)(-1 + \lambda \hat{W}_t) - \int_{\mathbb{R}} (1 + \lambda(W-\hat{W})) \nu(\{t\}, dx) \\
&= e^{[-\lambda \hat{W}_t - (\lambda+\log(1-\lambda))(\hat{W}_t)^2]} \left(\int_{\mathbb{R}} e^{[\lambda W - (\lambda+\log(1-\lambda))(W^2-2W\hat{W})]} \nu(\{t\}, dx) + 1 - a_t \right) \\
&\quad + (1-a_t)\lambda \hat{W}_t - 1 - \lambda \int_{\mathbb{R}} (W - \hat{W}) \nu(\{t\}, dx).
\end{aligned}$$

In addition, it is easy to see by noting $a_t \leq 1$,

$$\int_{\mathbb{R}} e^{[\lambda W - (\lambda+\log(1-\lambda))(W^2-2W\hat{W})]} \nu(\{t\}, dx) + 1 - a_t \geq 0,$$

and

$$(1-a_t)\lambda \hat{W}_t = \lambda \int_{\mathbb{R}} (W-\hat{W}) \nu(\{t\}, dx).$$

In combination, we have for all $t > 0$

$$\Delta S(\lambda)_t > -1,$$

where $\lambda \in [0,1)$. For any semimartingale $S(\lambda)_t$, the Doléans–Dade exponential is

$$\mathcal{E}(S(\lambda))_t = e^{S(\lambda)_t - S(\lambda)_0 - \frac{1}{2} <S(\lambda)^c, S(\lambda)^c >_t} \prod_{s \leq t} (1 + \Delta S(\lambda)_t) e^{-\Delta S(\lambda)_t}.$$

We shall first show that the process $\left(e^{[\lambda M_t - (\lambda+\log(1-\lambda)) \sum_{s \leq t} (\Delta M_s)^2]} / \mathcal{E}(S(\lambda))_t \right)_{t \geq 0}$ is a local martingale. Denote $X_t = \lambda M_t - (\lambda + \log(1-\lambda)) \sum_{s \leq t} (\Delta M_s)^2$, $Y_t = \sum_{s \leq t} (\Delta M_s)^2$.

The Itô formula yields

$$\begin{aligned}
e^{X_t} &= 1 + e^{X_{t-}} \cdot X + \sum_{s \leq t} (e^{X_s} - e^{X_{s-}} - e^{X_{s-}} \Delta X_s) \\
&= 1 + \lambda e^{X_{t-}} \cdot M - (\lambda + \log(1-\lambda)) e^{X_{t-}} \cdot Y \\
&\quad + \sum_{s \leq t} (e^{X_s} - e^{X_{s-}} - e^{X_{s-}} \Delta X_s) \\
&= 1 + \lambda e^{X_{t-}} \cdot M + \sum_{s \leq t} (e^{X_s} - e^{X_{s-}} - \lambda e^{X_{s-}} \Delta M_s).
\end{aligned}$$

For X, the jump part of X is

$$\begin{aligned}
\Delta X &= [\lambda(W-\hat{W}) - (\lambda+\log(1-\lambda))(W-\hat{W})^2] 1_D \\
&\quad - \lambda \hat{W} 1_{D^c} + (\lambda+\log(1-\lambda)) \hat{W}^2 1_{D^c}
\end{aligned}$$

where D is the thin set, which is exhausted by $\{T_n\}_{n \geq 1}$. Thus,

$$\sum_{s \leq t} (e^{\Delta X_s} - 1 - \lambda \Delta M_s) - S(\lambda) =: Z_t \quad (6)$$

is a local martingale. Denote $\Xi(\lambda)_t = \sum_{s \leq t} (e^{\Delta X_s} - 1 - \lambda \Delta M_s)$, we have

$$\sum_{s\leq t}(e^{X_s} - e^{X_{s-}} - \lambda e^{X_{s-}}\Delta M_s) - e^{X_-}\cdot S(\lambda)$$
$$= e^{X_-}\cdot \Xi(\lambda) - e^{X_-}\cdot S(\lambda) = e^{X_{t-}}\cdot Z.$$

Thus,

$$e^X - e^{X_-}\cdot S(\lambda)$$
$$= 1 + \lambda e^{X_{t-}}\cdot M + \sum_{s\leq t}(e^{X_s} - e^{X_{s-}} - \lambda e^{X_{s-}}\Delta M_s) - e^{X_-}\cdot S(\lambda)$$
$$= 1 + \lambda e^{X_{t-}}\cdot M + e^{X_{t-}}\cdot Z =: N_1.$$

N_1 is a local martingale. Following the similar arguments in Wang Lin and Su [13], we have $\left(e^{X_t}/\mathcal{E}(S(\lambda))_t\right)_{t\geq 0}$ is a local martingale. In fact, set $H = e^X$, $G = \mathcal{E}(S(\lambda))$, $A = S(\lambda)$ and $f(h,g) = \frac{h}{g}$. The Itô formula yields

$$f(H,G) = 1 + \frac{1}{G_-}\cdot H - \frac{H_-}{G_-^2}\cdot G$$
$$+ \sum_{s\leq \cdot}\left(\Delta f(H,G)_s - \frac{\Delta H_s}{G_{s-}} + \frac{f(H,G)_{s-}}{G_{s-}}\Delta G_s\right).$$

Since $\mathcal{E}(S(\lambda)) = 1 + \mathcal{E}(S(\lambda))_-\cdot S(\lambda)$, we have

$$\frac{1}{G_-}\cdot H - \frac{H_-}{G_-^2}\cdot G$$
$$= \frac{1}{G_-}\cdot H - \frac{H_-}{G_-}\cdot S(\lambda) = \frac{1}{G_-}\cdot (e^X - e^{X_-}\cdot S(\lambda))$$
$$= \frac{1}{G_-}\cdot N_1.$$

Noting that $\Delta G = G_-\Delta A$, $\Delta N_1 = \Delta H - H_-\Delta A$, we have

$$\Delta f(H,G)_s - \frac{\Delta H_s}{G_{s-}} + \frac{f(H,G)_{s-}}{G_{s-}}\Delta G_s = -\frac{\Delta N_{1s}\Delta A_s}{G_{s-}(1+\Delta A_s)},$$

where A is a predictable process, and N is a local martingale. By the property of the Stieltjes integral, we have

$$\sum_{s\leq \cdot}\Delta f(H,G)_s - \frac{\Delta H_s}{G_{s-}} + \frac{f(H,G)_{s-}}{G_{s-}}\Delta G_s = -\frac{\Delta A}{G_-(1+\Delta A)}\cdot N_1. \quad (7)$$

Thus,

$$\left(e^X/\mathcal{E}(S(\lambda))\right) = 1 + \frac{1}{G_-}\cdot N_1 - \frac{\Delta A}{G_-(1+\Delta A)}\cdot N_1$$

is a local martingale.

Let

$$B_1 = \{M_t \geq x, \sum_{s\leq t}|\Delta M_s|^2 \leq v^2 \text{ for some } t > 0\}$$

and

$$\tau_1 = \inf\{t > 0 : M_t \geq x, \sum_{s\leq t}|\Delta M_s|^2 \leq v^2\}.$$

Note by (4.12) in [4], for $\lambda \in [0,1)$ and $x \geq -1$,

$$\exp\{\lambda x + x^2(\lambda + \log(1-\lambda))\} \leq 1 + \lambda x.$$

This implies

$$\int_0^t \int_{-1}^\infty \exp\{\lambda x + (\lambda + \log(1-\lambda))x^2\}\nu^M(ds,dx) \leq \int_0^t \int_{-1}^\infty (1+\lambda x)\nu^M(ds,dx), \quad (8)$$

because $\Delta M_t \geq -1$ for any $t > 0$, where ν^M is the predictable compensate jump measure of M. Inequality (8) implies $S(\lambda) \leq 0$. Since $e^x \geq x+1$ and $e^{S(\lambda)_t} \geq \mathcal{E}(S(\lambda)_t)$,

$$\mathbb{E}[\frac{e^{\lambda X_T}}{e^{S(\lambda)_T}}] \leq \mathbb{E}[\frac{e^{\lambda X_T}}{\mathcal{E}(S(\lambda))_T}] = 1 \quad (9)$$

for any stopping time T. Thus, $U = (U_t)_{t \geq 0}$ is a supermartingale, where

$$U_t = \frac{\exp\{\lambda M_t + (\lambda + \log(1-\lambda))\sum_{s \leq t}(\Delta M_s)^2\}}{\exp\{S(\lambda)_t\}}.$$

Thus, on B_1

$$U_{T_1} \geq \exp\{\lambda x + (\lambda + \log(1-\lambda))v^2\}.$$

We have

$$\mathbb{P}(B_1) \leq \inf_{\lambda \in [0,1)} \exp\{-\lambda x - (\lambda + \log(1-\lambda))v^2\}$$
$$= \left(\frac{v^2+x}{v^2}\right)^{v^2} e^{-x}. \quad (10)$$

$\square$

Put

$$L(\lambda)_t = \int_0^t \int_{\mathbb{R}} (e^{[\lambda(W-\hat{W})+f(\lambda)(W-\hat{W})^2]} - 1 - \lambda(W-\hat{W}))\nu(ds,dx)$$
$$+ \sum_{s \leq t}(1-a_s)(e^{[-\lambda \hat{W}_s + f(\lambda)(\hat{W}_s)^2]} - 1 + \lambda \hat{W}_s),$$

where $f(\lambda) \geq 0$ for $\lambda \geq 0$. We have the following proposition from the proof of Theorem 4.

Proposition 1. *Let μ be a multivariate point process, ν be the predictable compensator of μ, $a_t = \nu(\{t\} \times \mathbb{R})$, W be a given predictable function on $\tilde{\Omega}$. $M = W * (\mu - \nu)$. Denote $\tilde{X}_t = \lambda M_t - f(\lambda)\sum_{s \leq t}(\Delta M_s)^2$, for $\lambda \geq 0$. Then, $e^{\tilde{X}}/\mathcal{E}(L(\lambda))$ is a local martingale.*

In Theorem 4, the condition $\triangle M \geq -1$ plays an important role. In the following theorem, we will present another result, which is the analogy of Theorem 1 in continuous time case.

Theorem 5. *Let μ be a multivariate point process, ν be the predictable compensator of μ, $a_t = \nu(\{t\} \times \mathbb{R})$, W be a given predictable function on $\tilde{\Omega}$, and $W \in G_{loc}(\mu)$. $M = W * (\mu - \nu)$, In addition, define*

$$\tilde{S}(\lambda)_t =: \int_0^t \int_{\mathbb{R}} (e^{[\lambda(W-\hat{W}) - \frac{\lambda^2}{2}(W-\hat{W})^2]} - 1 - \lambda(W-\hat{W}))\nu(ds,dx)$$
$$+ \sum_{s \leq t}(1-a_s)(e^{[-\lambda \hat{W}_s + \frac{\lambda^2}{2}(\hat{W}_s)^2]} - 1 + \lambda \hat{W}_s),$$

and assume that for any $t > 0$ and $\lambda > 0$, $\widetilde{S}(\lambda)_t \leq 0$. Then, for $x > 0$, $v > 0$,

$$\mathbb{P}\left(M_t \geq x, \sum_{s \leq t} |\triangle M_s|^2 \leq v^2 \text{ for some } t > 0\right) \leq \exp\left\{-\frac{x^2}{2v^2}\right\}$$

Proof of Theorem 5. Define

$$V_t = \frac{\exp\{\lambda M_t - \frac{\lambda^2}{2}\sum_{s \leq t} |\triangle M_s|^2\}}{\mathcal{E}(\widetilde{S}(\lambda))_t}.$$

By Proposition 1, V is a local martingale. Note $\widetilde{S}(\lambda)_t \leq 0$ for any $t > 0$ and $\lambda > 0$. We have

$$\mathbb{E}\left[\frac{\exp\{\lambda M_T - \frac{\lambda^2}{2}\sum_{s \leq T}|\triangle M_s|^2\}}{e^{\widetilde{S}(\lambda)_T}}\right] \leq \mathbb{E}[V_T] = 1 \quad (11)$$

for any stopping time T.
    Recall that
$$B_1 = \{M_t \geq x, \sum_{s \leq t} |\triangle M_s|^2 \leq v^2 \text{ for some } t > 0\}$$

and

$$\tau_1 = \inf\{t > 0 : M_t \geq x, \sum_{s \leq t} |\triangle M_s|^2 \leq v^2\}.$$

We have

$$\begin{aligned}
\mathbb{P}(B_1) &\leq \inf_{\lambda \geq 0} \exp\{-\lambda x + \frac{\lambda^2}{2}v^2\} \\
&= \exp\{-\frac{x^2}{2v^2}\}.
\end{aligned} \quad (12)$$

□

Remark 1. *For integrable random variable ξ and a positive number $a > 0$, define*

$$T_a(\xi) = \min(|\xi|, a) sign(\xi).$$

If $\mathbb{E}[\xi] = 0$, and for all $a > 0$, $\mathbb{E}[T_a(\xi)] \leq 0$. Then, ξ is called heavy on left. Bercu and Touati [14] extended Theorem 1 to general case. Let $S = (S_n)_{n \geq 0}$ be a locally square integrable on $(\Omega, \mathcal{F}, (\mathcal{F}_n)_{n \geq 1}, \mathbb{P})$. If

$$\mathbb{E}[T_a(S_n - S_{n-1})|\mathcal{F}_{n-1}] \leq 0 \quad (13)$$

for all $a > 0$ and $n > 0$, Bercu and Touati [14] obtained

$$\mathbb{P}\left(S_n \geq x, \sum_{i=1}^{n}(S_i - S_{i-1})^2 \leq y\right) \leq \exp\{-\frac{x^2}{2y}\}.$$

In fact, our condition, $\widetilde{S}(\lambda)_t \leq 0$, is analogy of (13) in continuous time case. Let $N = (N_t)_{t \geq 0}$ be a homogeneous Poisson point process with parameter κ, and let $(\eta_k)_{k \geq 1}$ be a sequence of i.i.d. r.v.'s with a common distribution function $F(x)$. Assume N is independent of $(\eta_k)_{k \geq 1}$. Define

$$Y_t = \sum_{k=1}^{N_t} \eta_k, \quad t \geq 0. \quad (14)$$

This is a so-called compound Poisson process. The jump measure of Y is given by

$$\mu^Y(dt, dx) = \sum_{k \geq 1} \mathbf{1}_{\{T_k < \infty\}} \varepsilon_{(T_k, \eta_k)}(dt, dx), \quad (15)$$

and the predictable compensator ν^Y is

$$\nu^Y(dt, dx) = \kappa dt F(dx). \tag{16}$$

Thus, $(Y_t - x * \nu_t^Y)_{t \geq 0}$ is a purely discontinuous local martingale. For $(Y_t - x * \nu_t^Y)_{t \geq 0}$,

$$\widetilde{S}(\lambda)_t = \kappa \int_0^t \int_{\mathbb{R}} (e^{[\lambda x - \frac{\lambda^2}{2} x^2]} - 1 - \lambda x) F(dx) ds.$$

If $\mathbb{E}[\eta_k] = 0$ for any $\kappa \geq 1$, $\widetilde{S}(\lambda)_t \leq 0$ implies that

$$\int_{\mathbb{R}} e^{[\lambda x - \frac{\lambda^2}{2} x^2]} F(dx) \leq 1. \tag{17}$$

Bercu and Touati [14] found that if η_k is heavy on the left, then (17) holds. Thus, our condition is an analogy of (13) in continuous time case.

In [7,15], there were obtained a series of exponential inequalities for events involving ratios in the context of continuous martingales, which in turn extended the results in [10]. Su and Wang [16] extended a similar problem for purely discontinuous local martingales in quasi-left continuous case. In this subsection, we obtained the similar inequality for stochastic integrals of a multivariate point process.

Theorem 6. Let μ be a multivariate point process, ν be the predictable compensator of μ, $a_t = \nu(\{t\} \times \mathbb{R})$, W be a given predictable function on $\widetilde{\Omega}$, and $W \in G_{loc}(\mu)$. Denote $M = W * (\mu - \nu)$. Then, for all $x \geq 0, \beta > 0, v > 0 \alpha \in \mathbb{R}$,

$$\mathbb{P}\left(M_t \geq (\alpha + \beta \sum_{s \leq t} |\triangle M_s|^2) x, \sum_{s \leq t} |\triangle M_s|^2 \geq <M, M>_t + v^2 \text{ for some } t > 0\right)$$
$$\leq \exp\{-\frac{x^2}{2}(\alpha\beta + \frac{\beta^2 v^2}{2})\}.$$

Proof of Theorem 6. Recall that $V = (V_t)_{t \geq 0}$ is a local martingale, where

$$V_t = \frac{\exp\{\lambda M_t - \frac{\lambda^2}{2} \sum_{s \leq t} |\triangle M_s|^2\}}{\mathcal{E}(\widetilde{S}(\lambda))_t}.$$

For any stopping time T,

$$\mathbb{E}[\frac{\exp\{\lambda M_T - \frac{\lambda^2}{2} \sum_{s \leq T} |\triangle M_s|^2\}}{\exp\{\widetilde{S}(\lambda)_T\}}] \leq \mathbb{E}[V_T] = 1. \tag{18}$$

By Markov's inequality, we obtain that for all $\lambda > 0$,

$$\mathbb{P}\Big(M_t \geq (\alpha + \beta \sum_{s\leq t}|\triangle M_s|^2)x \text{ and } \sum_{s\leq t}|\triangle M_s|^2 \geq <M,M>_t +v^2 \text{ for some } t>0\Big)$$
$$\leq \mathbb{E}[\exp\{\frac{\lambda}{4}M_{\tau_2} - (\frac{\alpha\lambda x}{4} + \frac{\beta\lambda x}{4}\sum_{s\leq \tau_2}|\triangle M_s|^2)\}1_{B_2}]$$
$$= \exp\{-\frac{\alpha\lambda x}{4}\}\mathbb{E}[\exp\{\frac{\lambda}{4}M_{\tau_2} - \frac{\lambda^2}{8}(\sum_{s\leq \tau_2}|\triangle M_s|^2 + <M,M>_{\tau_2})$$
$$+(\frac{\lambda^2}{8} - \frac{\beta\lambda x}{4})\sum_{s\leq \tau_2}|\triangle M_s|^2 + \frac{\lambda^2}{8}<M,M>_{\tau_2})\}1_{B_2}]$$
$$\leq \exp\{-\frac{\alpha\lambda x}{4}\}\sqrt{\mathbb{E}[\exp\{\frac{\lambda}{2}M_{\tau_2} - \frac{\lambda^2}{4}(\sum_{s\leq \tau_2}|\triangle M_s|^2 + <M,M>_{\tau_2})\}1_{B_2}]}$$
$$\times \sqrt{\mathbb{E}[\exp\{(\frac{\lambda^2}{4} - \frac{\beta\lambda x}{2})\sum_{s\leq \tau_2}|\triangle M_s|^2 + \frac{\lambda^2}{4}<M,M>_{\tau_2}\}1_{B_2}]},$$

where

$$B_2 = \{M_t \geq (\alpha + \beta\sum_{s\leq t}|\triangle M_s|^2)x, \sum_{s\leq t}|\triangle M_s|^2 \geq <M,M>_t +v^2 \text{ for some } t>0\},$$

$$\tau_2 = \inf\{t>0 : M_t \geq (\alpha + \beta\sum_{s\leq t}|\triangle M_s|^2)x, \sum_{s\leq t}|\triangle M_s|^2 \geq <M,M>_t +v^2\}.$$

In fact,

$$\mathbb{E}[\exp\{\frac{\lambda}{2}M_{\tau_2} - \frac{\lambda^2}{4}(\sum_{s\leq \tau_2}|\triangle M_s|^2 + <M,M>_{\tau_2})1_{B_2}\}]$$
$$\leq \sqrt{\mathbb{E}[\frac{\exp\{\lambda M_{\tau_2} - \frac{\lambda^2}{2}\sum_{s\leq \tau_2}|\triangle M_s|^2\}}{\exp\{\widetilde{S}(\lambda)_{\tau_2}\}}1_{B_2}]}\sqrt{\mathbb{E}[\exp\{\widetilde{S}(\lambda)_{\tau_2} - \frac{\lambda^2}{2}<M,M>_{\tau_2}\}]}.$$

By (18)

$$\mathbb{E}[\frac{\exp\{\lambda M_{\tau_2} - \frac{\lambda^2}{2}\sum_{s\leq \tau_2}|\triangle M_s|^2\}}{\exp\{\widetilde{S}(\lambda)_{\tau_2}\}}1_{B_2}] \leq 1.$$

Furthermore,

$$\mathbb{E}[\exp\{\widetilde{S}(\lambda)_{\tau_2} - \frac{\lambda^2}{2}<M,M>_{\tau_2}\}] \leq 1$$

by

$$|\exp\{x - \frac{1}{2}x^2\} - 1 - x| \leq \frac{1}{2}x^2, \quad x \in \mathbb{R}.$$

Taking $\lambda = \beta x$, we get

$$\mathbb{P}(B_2) \leq \exp\{-\frac{x^2}{4}(\alpha\beta + \frac{\beta^2 v^2}{2})\} \times \sqrt{\mathbb{P}(B_2)}.$$

Thus

$$\mathbb{P}\Big(M_t \geq (\alpha + \beta\sum_{s\leq t}|\triangle M_s|^2)x, \sum_{s\leq t}|\triangle M_s|^2 \geq <M,M>_t +v^2 \text{ for some } t>0\Big)$$
$$\leq \exp\{-\frac{x^2}{2}(\alpha\beta + \frac{\beta^2 v^2}{2})\}.$$

☐

From the proof of Theorem 6, we can obtain the following results.

Theorem 7. *Let μ be a multivariate point process, ν be the predictable compensator of μ, $a_t = \nu(\{t\} \times \mathbb{R})$, W be a given predictable function on $\tilde{\Omega}$, and $W \in G_{loc}(\mu)$. Denote $M = W * (\mu - \nu)$. In addition, define*

$$\widetilde{S}(\lambda)_t :=: \int_0^t \int_{\mathbb{R}} (e^{[\lambda(W-\hat{W}) - \frac{\lambda^2}{2}(W-\hat{W})^2]} - 1 - \lambda(W - \hat{W}))\nu(ds, dx)$$
$$+ \sum_{s \leq t}(1 - a_s)(e^{[-\lambda \hat{W}_s + \frac{\lambda^2}{2}(\hat{W}_s)^2]} - 1 + \lambda \hat{W}_s),$$

and assume that for any $t > 0$ and $\lambda > 0$, $\widetilde{S}(\lambda)_t \leq 0$. Then for all $x \geq 0, \beta > 0, v > 0, \alpha \in \mathbb{R}$,

$$\mathbb{P}\left(M_t \geq (\alpha + \beta \sum_{s \leq t} |\triangle M_s|^2)x, \sum_{s \leq t} |\triangle M_s|^2 \geq v^2 \text{ for some } t > 0\right)$$
$$\leq \exp\{-\frac{x^2}{4}(\alpha\beta + \frac{\beta^2 v^2}{2})\}.$$

4. Application

In this section, we will derive exponential inequalities for block counting process in Λ−coalescent. The Λ−coalescent was introduced independently by Pitman [17] and Sagitov [18]. In this paper, the notation and details of Λ−coalescent are from Limic and Talarczyk [19].

Let Λ be an probability measure on $[0,1]$, $\Pi = (\Pi_t)_{t \geq 0}$ is a Markov jump process. Π takes values in the set of partition of $\{1, 2, \cdots\}$. For any $n \geq 1$, the restriction Π^n of Π to $\{1, 2, \cdots, n\}$ is a continuous time Markov chain with the following transitions: when Π^n has b blocks, any given $k-$tuples of blocks coalesces at rate

$$\lambda_{b,k} = \int_0^1 r^{k-2}(1-r)^{b-k}\Lambda(dr)$$

where $2 \leq b \leq n$. Let N_t be the number of blocks of Π_t at t. In fact, $N = (N_t)_{t \geq 0}$ is a point process. Limic and Talarczyk [19] presented integral equation for N. Define

$$\pi(dt, dy, d\mathbf{x}) = \sum_{k \geq 1} \varepsilon_{\{T_k, Y_k, \mathbf{X}^k\}}(dt, dy, d\mathbf{x})$$

where $\{\mathbf{X}^k\}$ is an independent array of i.i.d. random variables $(X_j^k)_{j,k \in \mathbb{N}}$, where X_j^k have uniform distribution on $[0, 1]$. The multivariate point processes π have the compensator $dt\frac{\Lambda(dy)}{y^2}d\mathbf{x}$.

Limic and Talarczyk [19] found that

$$N_t = N_r - \int_r^t \int_0^1 \int_{[0,1]^{\mathbb{N}}} f(N_{s-}, y, \mathbf{x})\pi(ds, dy, d\mathbf{x})$$

for all $0 < r < t$, where

$$f(k, y, \mathbf{x}) = \sum_{j=1}^k 1_{\{x_i \leq y\}} - 1 + 1_{\cap_{j=1}^k \{x_j > y\}}.$$

Define

$$\Psi(k) = \int_0^1 \int_{[0,1]^{\mathbb{N}}} f(k, y, \mathbf{x})]\frac{\Lambda(dy)}{y^2}d\mathbf{x},$$

and
$$t = \int_{v_t}^{\infty} \frac{1}{\Psi(q)} dq,$$

$$M_t = \int_0^t \int_0^1 \int_{[0,1]^{\mathbb{N}}} \frac{f(N_{s-}, y, \mathbf{x})}{v_s} (\pi(dt, dy, d\mathbf{x}) - ds \frac{\Lambda(dy)}{y^2} d\mathbf{x}).$$

$M = (M_t)_{t \geq 0}$ plays important role in the study of Λ−coalescent. Limic and Talarczyk [19] obtained that M is a square integrable martingale. It is not difficult to see that $\triangle M \geq 0$,

$$\sum_{s \leq t} |\triangle M_s|^2 = \int_0^t \int_0^1 \int_{[0,1]^{\mathbb{N}}} \frac{f^2(N_{s-}, y, \mathbf{x})}{v_s^2} \pi(dt, dy, d\mathbf{x})$$

and

$$<M, M>_t = \int_0^t \int_0^1 \int_{[0,1]^{\mathbb{N}}} \frac{f^2(N_{s-}, y, \mathbf{x})}{v_s^2} ds \frac{\Lambda(dy)}{y^2} d\mathbf{x}.$$

We have the following result.

Theorem 8. *Let M be defined as above, we have*

$$\mathbb{P}\left(M_t \geq x, \sum_{s \leq t} |\triangle M_s|^2 \leq v^2 \text{ for some } t > 0\right) \leq \left(\frac{v^2 + x}{v^2}\right)^{v^2} e^{-x}$$

and

$$\mathbb{P}\left(M_t \geq (\alpha + \beta \sum_{s \leq t} |\triangle M_s|^2)x, \sum_{s \leq t} |\triangle M_s|^2 \geq <M, M>_t + v^2 \text{ for some } t > 0\right)$$
$$\leq \exp\{-\frac{x^2}{2}(\alpha\beta + \frac{\beta^2 v^2}{2})\}.$$

where $x \geq 0, \beta > 0, v > 0, \alpha \in \mathbb{R}$.

Author Contributions: Conceptualization, N.L.; methodology, V.V.U. and H.W.; investigation, N.L. and H.W.; writing, V.V.U. and H.W. All authors have read and agreed to the published version of the manuscript.

Funding: This work was supported by National Key R&D Program of China (No.2018YFA0703900), Shandong Provincial Natural Science Foundation (No. ZR2019ZD41).

Institutional Review Board Statement: Not applicable.

Informed Consent Statement: Not applicable.

Conflicts of Interest: The authors declare no conflict of interest.

References

1. Freedman, D. On tail probabilities for martingales. *Ann. Probab.* **1975**, *3*, 100–118. [CrossRef]
2. Hoeffding, W. Probability inequalities for sums of bounded random variables. *J. Amer. Statist. Assoc.* **1963**, *58*, 13–30. [CrossRef]
3. Fan, X.; Grama, I.; Liu, Q. Hoeffding's inequality for supermartingales. *Stoch. Process. Appl.* **2012**, *122*, 3545–3559. [CrossRef]
4. Fan, X.; Grama, I.; Liu, Q. Exponential inequalities for martingales with applications. *Electron. J. Probab.* **2015**, *20*, 1–22. [CrossRef]
5. Rio, E. Extensions of the Hoeffding-Azuma inequalities. *Electron. Commun. Probab.* **2013**, *18*, 1–6. [CrossRef]
6. Bercu, B.; Delyon, B.; Rio, E. *Concentration Inequalities for Sums and Martingales*; Springer: Cham, Switzerland, 2015.
7. De la Peña, V. A general class of exponential inequalities for martingales and ratios. *Ann. Probab.* **1999**, *27*, 537–564. [CrossRef]
8. Bercu, B.; Touati, A. Exponential inequalities for self-normalized martingales with applications. *Ann. Appl. Probab.* **2008**, *18*, 1848–1869. [CrossRef]
9. Van de Geer, S. Exponential inequalities for martingales, with application to maximum likelihood estimation for counting processes. *Ann. Statist.* **1995**, *23*, 1779–1801. [CrossRef]
10. Khoshnevisan, D. Deviation inequalities for continuous martingales. *Stoch. Process. Appl.* **1996**, *65*, 17–30. [CrossRef]
11. Dzhaparidze, K.; van Zanten, J. On Bernstein-type inequalities for martingales. *Stoch. Process. Appl.* **2001**, *93*, 109–117. [CrossRef]

12. Jacod, J.; Shiryaev, A. *Limit Theorems for Stochastic Processes*, 2nd ed.; Grundlehren der Mathematischen Wissenschaften; Springer: Berlin/Heidelberg, Germany, 2003; Volume 288.
13. Wang, H.; Lin, Z.; Su, Z. On Bernstein type inequalities for stochastic integrals of multivariate point processes. *Stoch. Process. Appl.* **2019**, *129*, 1605–1621. [CrossRef]
14. Bercu, B.; Touati, T. New insights on concentration inequalities for self-normalized martingales. *Electron. Commun. Probab.* **2019**, *24*, 1–12. [CrossRef]
15. De la Peña, V.; Klass, M.; Lai, T. Self-normalized processes: Exponential inequalities, moment bounds and iterated logarithm laws. *Ann. Probab.* **2004**, *32*, 1902–1933. [CrossRef]
16. Su, Z.; Wang, H. Exponential concentration inequalities for purely discontinuous martingales. *Sci. Sin. Math.* **2021**. (In Chinese) [CrossRef]
17. Pitman, J. Coalescents with multiple collisions. *Ann. Probab.* **1999**, *27*, 1870–1902. [CrossRef]
18. Sagitov, S. The general coalescent with asynchronous mergers of ancestral lines. *J. Appl. Probab.* **1999**, *36*, 1116–1125. [CrossRef]
19. Limic, V.; Talarczyk, A. Second-order asymptotics for the block counting process in a class of regularly varying $\Lambda-$coalescents. *Ann. Probab.* **2015**, *27*, 1419–1455. [CrossRef]

Article

Local Laws for Sparse Sample Covariance Matrices

Alexander N. Tikhomirov * and Dmitry A. Timushev

Institute of Physics and Mathematics, Komi Science Center of Ural Branch of RAS, 167982 Syktyvkar, Russia; timushev@ipm.komisc.ru
* Correspondence: tikhomirov@ipm.komisc.ru

Abstract: We proved the local Marchenko–Pastur law for sparse sample covariance matrices that corresponded to rectangular observation matrices of order $n \times m$ with $n/m \to y$ (where $y > 0$) and sparse probability $np_n > \log^\beta n$ (where $\beta > 0$). The bounds of the distance between the empirical spectral distribution function of the sparse sample covariance matrices and the Marchenko–Pastur law distribution function that was obtained in the complex domain $z \in \mathcal{D}$ with $\operatorname{Im} z > v_0 > 0$ (where v_0) were of order $\log^4 n/n$ and the domain bounds did not depend on p_n while $np_n > \log^\beta n$.

Keywords: sparse sample covariance matrices; local Marchenko–Pastur law; Stieltjes transformation

MSC: 60F99; 60B20

Citation: Tikhomirov, A.N.; Timushev, D.A. Local Laws for Sparse Sample Covariance Matrices. *Mathematics* **2022**, *10*, 2326. https://doi.org/10.3390/math10132326

Academic Editor: Ninoslav Truhar

Received: 11 May 2022
Accepted: 29 June 2022
Published: 3 July 2022

Publisher's Note: MDPI stays neutral with regard to jurisdictional claims in published maps and institutional affiliations.

Copyright: © 2022 by the authors. Licensee MDPI, Basel, Switzerland. This article is an open access article distributed under the terms and conditions of the Creative Commons Attribution (CC BY) license (https://creativecommons.org/licenses/by/4.0/).

1. Introduction

The random matrix theory (RMT) dates back to the work of Wishart in multivariate statistics [1], which was devoted to the joint distribution of the entries of sample covariance matrices. The next RMT milestone was the work of Wigner [2] in the middle of the last century, in which the modelling of the Hamiltonian of excited heavy nuclei using a large dimensional random matrix was proposed, thereby replacing the study of the energy levels of nuclei with the study of the distribution of the eigenvalues of a random matrix. Wigner studied the eigenvalues of random Hermitian matrices with centred, independent and identically distributed elements (such matrices were later named Wigner matrices) and proved that the density of the empirical spectral distribution function of the eigenvalues of such matrices converges to the semicircle law as the matrix dimensions increase. Later, this convergence was named Wigner's semicircle law and Wigner's results were generalised in various aspects.

The breakthrough work of Marchenko and Pastur [3] gave impetus to new progress in the study of sample covariance matrices. Under quite general conditions, they found an explicit form of the limiting density of the expected empirical spectral distribution function of sample covariance matrices. Later, this convergence was named the Marchenko–Pastur law.

Sample covariance matrices are of great practical importance for the problems of multivariate statistical analysis, particularly for the method of principal component analysis (PCA). In recent years, many studies have appeared that have connected RMT with other rapidly developing areas, such as the theory of wireless communication and deep learning. For example, the spectral density of sample covariance matrices is used in calculations that relate to multiple input multiple output (MIMO) channel capacity [4]. An important object of study for neural networks is the loss surface. The geometry and critical points of this surface can be predicted using the Hessian of the loss function. A number of works that have been devoted to deep networks have suggested the application of various RMT models for Hessian approximation, thereby allowing the use of RMT results to reach specific conclusions about the nature of the critical points of the surface.

Another area of application for sample covariance matrices is graph theory. The adjacency matrix of an undirected graph is asymmetric, so the study of its singular values leads to sample covariance matrices. An example of these graphs is the bipartite random graph, the vertices of which can be divided into two groups in which the vertices are not connected to each other.

If we assume that the probability p_n of having graph edges tends to zero as the number of vertices n increases to infinity, we arrive at the concept of sparse random matrices. The behaviour of the eigenvalues and eigenvectors of a sparse random matrix significantly depends on its sparsity and results that are obtained for non-sparse matrices cannot be applied. Sparse sample covariance matrices have applications in random graph models [5] and deep learning problems [6] as well.

Sparse Wigner matrices have been considered in a number of papers (see [7–10]), in which many results have been obtained. With the symmetrisation of sample covariance matrices, it is possible to apply these results when observation matrices are square. However, when the sample size is greater than the observation dimensions, the spectral limit distribution has a singularity at zero, which requires a different approach. The spectral limit distribution of sparse sample covariance matrices with a sparsity of $np_n \sim n^\epsilon$ (where $\epsilon > 0$ was arbitrary small) was studied in [11,12]. In particular, a local law was proven under the assumption that the matrix elements satisfied the moment conditions $\mathbb{E}|X_{jk}|^q \leq (Cq)^{cq}$. In this paper, we considered a case with a sparsity of $np_n \sim \log^\alpha n$ for $\alpha > 1$ and assumed that the matrix element moments satisfied the conditions $\mathbb{E}|X_{jk}|^{4+\delta} \leq C < \infty$ and $|X_{jk}| \leq c_1(np_n)^{\frac{1}{2}-\varkappa}$ for $\varkappa > 0$.

2. Main Results

We let $m = m(n)$, where $m \geq n$. We considered the independent and identically distributed zero mean random variables X_{jk}, $1 \leq j \leq n$ and $1 \leq k \leq m$ with $\mathbb{E}X_{jk} = 0$ and $\mathbb{E}X_{jk}^2 = 1$ and an independent set of the independent Bernoulli random variables ξ_{jk}, $1 \leq j \leq n$ and $1 \leq k \leq m$ with $\mathbb{E}\xi_{jk} = p_n$. In addition, we supposed that $np_n \to \infty$ as $n \to \infty$. In what follows, we omitted the index n from p_n when this would not cause confusion.

We considered a sequence of random matrices:

$$\mathbf{X} = \frac{1}{\sqrt{mp_n}}(\xi_{jk}X_{jk})_{1 \leq j \leq n, 1 \leq k \leq m}. \tag{1}$$

Denoted by $s_1 \geq \cdots \geq s_n$, the singular values of $\mathbf{X}$ and the symmetrised empirical spectral distribution function (ESD) of the sample covariance matrix $\mathbf{W} = \mathbf{X}\mathbf{X}^*$ were defined as:

$$F_n(x) = \frac{1}{2n} \sum_{j=1}^{n} \left(\mathbb{I}\{s_j \leq x\} + \mathbb{I}\{-s_j \leq x\} \right),$$

where $\mathbb{I}\{A\}$ stands for the event A indicator.

We let $y := y(n,m) = \frac{n}{m}$ and $G_y(x)$ be the symmetrised Marchenko–Pastur distribution function with the density:

$$g_y(x) = \frac{1}{2\pi y|x|}\sqrt{(x^2 - a^2)(b^2 - x^2)}\,\mathbb{I}\{a^2 \leq x^2 \leq b^2\},$$

where $a = 1 - \sqrt{y}$ and $b = 1 + \sqrt{y}$. We assumed that $y \leq y_0 < 1$ for $n, m \geq 1$. When the Stieltjes transformation of the distribution function $G_y(x)$ was denoted by $S_y(z)$ and the Stieltjes transformation of the distribution function $F_n(x)$ was denoted by $s_n(z)$, we obtained:

$$S_y(z) = \frac{-z + \frac{1-y}{z} + \sqrt{(z - \frac{1-y}{z})^2 - 4y}}{2y},$$

$$s_n(z) = \frac{1}{2n}\left[\sum_{j=1}^{n}\frac{1}{s_j - z} + \sum_{j=1}^{n}\frac{1}{-s_j - z}\right] = \frac{1}{n}\sum_{j=1}^{n}\frac{z}{s_j^2 - z^2}.$$

We also put:
$$b(z) = z - \frac{1-y}{z} + 2yS_y(z) = -\frac{1}{S_y(z)} + yS_y(z). \quad (2)$$

In this paper, we proved the so called *local Marchenko–Pastur law* for sparse covariance matrices. We let:
$$\Lambda_n := \Lambda_{n,y}(z) = s_n(z) - S_y(z).$$

For a constant $\delta > 0$, we defined the value $\varkappa = \varkappa(\delta) := \frac{\delta}{2(4+\delta)}$. We assumed that a sparse probability of p_n and that the moments of the matrix elements X_{ij} satisfied the following conditions:

- Condition (C0): for $c_0 > 0$ and $n \geq 1$, we have $np_n \geq c_0 \log^{\frac{2}{\varkappa}} n$;
- Condition (C1): for $\delta > 0$, we have $\mu_{4+\delta} := \mathbb{E}|X_{11}|^{4+\delta} < \infty$;
- Condition (C2): a constant $c_1 > 0$ exists, such that for all $1 \leq j \leq n$ and $1 \leq k \leq m$, we have $|X_{jk}| \leq c_1(np_n)^{\frac{1}{2}-\varkappa}$.

We introduced the quantity $v_0 = v_0(a_0) := a_0 n^{-1} \log^4 n$ with a positive constant a_0. We then introduced the region:
$$\mathcal{D}(a_0) := \{z = u + iv : (1 - \sqrt{y} - v)_+ \leq |u| \leq 1 + \sqrt{y} + v, V \geq v \geq v_0\}.$$

For constants $u_0 > 0$ and V, we defined the region:
$$\widetilde{\mathcal{D}}(a_0, a_1) = \{z = u + iv : |u| \leq u_0, V \geq v \geq v_0, |b(z)| \geq a_1\Gamma_n\}.$$

Next, we introduced some notations. We let:
$$\Gamma_n = 2C_0 \log n \left(\frac{1}{nv} + \min\left\{\frac{1}{np|b(z)|}, \frac{1}{\sqrt{np}}\right\}\right).$$

We introduced the quantity:
$$d(z) = \frac{\operatorname{Im} b(z)}{|b(z)|}$$

and put:
$$d_n(z) := \frac{1}{nv}\left(d(z) + \frac{\log n}{nv|b(z)|}\right) + \frac{1}{np|b(z)|}. \quad (3)$$

We stated the improved bounds for $\Lambda_n(z)$ and put:
$$\mathcal{T}_n := \mathbb{I}\{|b(z)| \geq \Gamma_n\}\left(d_n(z) + d_n^{\frac{3}{4}}(z)\frac{1}{(nv)^{\frac{1}{4}}} + d_n^{\frac{1}{2}}(z)\frac{1}{(nv)^{\frac{1}{2}}}\right)$$
$$+ \mathbb{I}\{|b(z)| \leq \Gamma_n\}\left(\left(\frac{\Gamma_n}{nv}\right)^{\frac{1}{2}} + \Gamma_n^{\frac{1}{2}}\left(\frac{\Gamma_n^{\frac{1}{2}}}{\sqrt{nv}} + \frac{1}{\sqrt{np}}\right)\right).$$

Theorem 1. *Assuming that the conditions (C0)–(C2) are satisfied. Then, for any $Q \geq 1$ the positive constants $C = C(Q, \delta, \mu_{4+\delta}, c_0, c_1)$, $K = K(Q, \delta, \mu_{4+\delta}, c_0, c_1)$ and $a_0 = a_0(Q, \delta, \mu_{4+\delta}, c_0, c_1)$ exist, such that for $z \in \mathcal{D}(a_0)$:*
$$\Pr\left\{|\Lambda_n| \geq K\mathcal{T}_n\right\} \leq Cn^{-Q}.$$

We also proved the following result.

Theorem 2. *Under the conditions of Theorem 1 and for $Q \geq 1$, the positive constants $C = C(Q, \delta, \mu_{4+\delta}, c_0, c_1)$, $K = K(Q, \delta, \mu_{4+\delta}, c_0, c_1)$, $a_0 = a_0(Q, \delta, \mu_{4+\delta}, c_0, c_1)$ and $a_1 = a_1(Q, \delta, \mu_{4+\delta}, c_0, c_1)$ exist, such that for $z \in \widetilde{\mathcal{D}}(a_0, a_1)$:*

$$\Pr\left\{|\operatorname{Im} \Lambda_n| \geq K\mathcal{T}_n\right\} \leq Cn^{-Q}.$$

2.1. Organisation

The paper is organised as follows. In Section 3, we state Theorems 3–5 and several corollaries. In Section 4, the delocalisation is considered. In Section 4, we prove the corollaries that were stated in Section 3. Section 6 is devoted to the proof of Theorems 3–5. In Section 7, we state and prove some auxiliary results.

2.2. Notation

We use C for large universal constants, which may be different from line to line. $S_y(z)$ and $s_n(z)$ denote the Stieltjes transformations of the symmetrised Marchenko–Pastur distribution and the spectral distribution function, respectively. $R(z)$ denotes the resolvent matrix. We let $\mathbb{T} = \{1, \ldots, n\}$, $\mathbb{J} \subset \mathbb{T}$, $\mathbb{T}^{(1)} = \{1, \ldots, m\}$ and $\mathbb{K} \subset \mathbb{T}^{(1)}$. We consider the σ-algebras $\mathfrak{M}^{(\mathbb{J},\mathbb{K})}$, which were generated by the elements of $\mathbf{X}$ (with the exception of the rows from $\mathbb{J}$ and the columns from $\mathbb{K}$). We write $\mathfrak{M}_j^{(\mathbb{J},\mathbb{K})}$ instead of $\mathfrak{M}^{(\mathbb{J}\cup\{j\},\mathbb{K})}$ and $\mathfrak{M}_{l+n}^{(\mathbb{J},\mathbb{K})}$ instead of $\mathfrak{M}^{(\mathbb{J},\mathbb{K}\cup\{l\})}$ for brevity. The symbol $\mathbf{X}^{(\mathbb{J},\mathbb{K})}$ denotes the matrix $\mathbf{X}$, from which the rows with numbers in $\mathbb{J}$ and columns with numbers in $\mathbb{K}$ were deleted. In a similar way, we denote all objects in terms of $\mathbf{X}^{(\mathbb{J},\mathbb{K})}$, such that the resolvent matrix is $\mathbf{R}^{(\mathbb{J},\mathbb{K})}$, the ESD Stieltjes transformation is $s_n^{(\mathbb{J},\mathbb{K})}$, $\Lambda_n^{(\mathbb{J},\mathbb{K})}$, etc. The symbol $\mathbb{E}_j$ denotes the conditional expectation with respect to the σ-algebra $\mathfrak{M}_j$ and $\mathbb{E}_{l+n}$ denotes the conditional expectation with respect to σ-algebra $\mathfrak{M}_{l+n}$. We let $\mathbb{J}^c = \mathbb{T} \setminus \mathbb{J}$ and $\mathbb{K}^c = \mathbb{T}^{(1)} \setminus \mathbb{K}$.

3. Main Equation and Its Error Term Estimation

Note that $F_n(x)$ is the ESD of the block matrix:

$$\mathbf{V} = \begin{bmatrix} \mathbf{O}_n & \mathbf{X} \\ \mathbf{X}^* & \mathbf{O}_m \end{bmatrix},$$

where $\mathbf{O}_k$ is a $k \times k$ matrix with zero elements.

We let $\mathbf{R} = \mathbf{R}(z)$ be the resolvent matrix of $\mathbf{V}$:

$$\mathbf{R} = (\mathbf{V} - z\mathbf{I})^{-1}.$$

By applying the Schur complement, we obtained:

$$\mathbf{R} = \begin{bmatrix} z(\mathbf{XX}^* - z^2\mathbf{I})^{-1} & (\mathbf{XX}^* - z^2\mathbf{I})^{-1}\mathbf{X} \\ \mathbf{X}^*(\mathbf{XX}^* - z^2\mathbf{I})^{-1} & z(\mathbf{X}^*\mathbf{X} - z^2\mathbf{I})^{-1} \end{bmatrix}.$$

This implied:

$$s_n(z) = \frac{1}{n}\sum_{j=1}^n R_{jj} = \frac{1}{n}\sum_{l=1}^m R_{l+n,l+n} + \frac{m-n}{nz}.$$

For the diagonal elements of $\mathbf{R}$, we could write:

$$R_{jj}^{(\mathbb{J},\mathbb{K})} = S_y(z)\left(1 - \varepsilon_j^{(\mathbb{J},\mathbb{K})} R_{jj}^{(\mathbb{J},\mathbb{K})} + y\Lambda_n^{(\mathbb{J},\mathbb{K})} R_{jj}^{(\mathbb{J},\mathbb{K})}\right), \tag{4}$$

for $j \in \mathbb{J}^c$ and:

$$R_{l+n,l+n}^{(\mathbb{J},\mathbb{K})} = -\frac{1}{z + yS_y(z)}\left(1 - \varepsilon_{l+n}^{(\mathbb{J},\mathbb{K})} R_{l+n,l+n}^{(\mathbb{J},\mathbb{K})} + y\Lambda_n^{(\mathbb{J},\mathbb{K})} R_{l+n,l+n}^{(\mathbb{J},\mathbb{K})}\right), \tag{5}$$

for $l \in \mathbb{K}^c$. The correction terms $\varepsilon_j^{(\mathbb{J},\mathbb{K})}$ for $j \in \mathbb{J}^c$ and $\varepsilon_{l+n}^{(\mathbb{J},\mathbb{K})}$ for $l \in \mathbb{K}^c$ were defined as:

$$\varepsilon_j^{(\mathbb{J},\mathbb{K})} = \varepsilon_{j1}^{(\mathbb{J},\mathbb{K})} + \cdots + \varepsilon_{j3}^{(\mathbb{J},\mathbb{K})},$$

$$\varepsilon_{j1}^{(\mathbb{J},\mathbb{K})} = \frac{1}{m}\sum_{l=1}^m R_{l+n,l+n}^{(\mathbb{J},\mathbb{K})} - \frac{1}{m}\sum_{l=1}^m R_{l+n,l+n}^{(\mathbb{J}\cup\{j\},\mathbb{K})},$$

$$\varepsilon_{j2}^{(\mathbb{J},\mathbb{K})} = \frac{1}{mp}\sum_{l=1}^m (X_{jl}^2 \xi_{jl} - p) R_{l+n,l+n}^{(\mathbb{J}\cup\{j\},\mathbb{K})},$$

$$\varepsilon_{j3}^{(\mathbb{J},\mathbb{K})} = \frac{1}{mp}\sum_{1\leq l\neq k\leq m} X_{jl} X_{jk} \xi_{jl} \xi_{jk} R_{l+n,k+n}^{(\mathbb{J}\cup\{j\},\mathbb{K})};$$

and

$$\varepsilon_{l+n}^{(\mathbb{J},\mathbb{K})} = \varepsilon_{l+n,1}^{(\mathbb{J},\mathbb{K})} + \cdots + \varepsilon_{l+n,3}^{(\mathbb{J},\mathbb{K})},$$

$$\varepsilon_{l+n,1}^{(\mathbb{J},\mathbb{K})} = \frac{1}{m}\sum_{j=1}^n R_{jj}^{(\mathbb{J},\mathbb{K})} - \frac{1}{m}\sum_{j=1}^n R_{jj}^{(\mathbb{J},\mathbb{K}\cup\{l+n\})},$$

$$\varepsilon_{l+n,2}^{(\mathbb{J},\mathbb{K})} = \frac{1}{mp}\sum_{j=1}^n (X_{jl}^2 \xi_{jl} - p) R_{jj}^{(\mathbb{J},\mathbb{K}\cup\{l+n\})},$$

$$\varepsilon_{l+n,3}^{(\mathbb{J},\mathbb{K})} = \frac{1}{mp}\sum_{1\leq j\neq k\leq n} X_{jl} X_{kl} \xi_{jl} \xi_{kl} R_{jk}^{(\mathbb{J},\mathbb{K}\cup\{l+n\})}.$$

By summing Equation (4) ($\mathbb{J} = \varnothing$ and $\mathbb{K} = \varnothing$), we obtained the self-consistent equation:

$$s_n(z) = S_y(z)(1 + T_n - y\Lambda_n s_n(z)),$$

with the error term:

$$T_n = \frac{1}{n}\sum_{j=1}^n \varepsilon_j R_{jj}.$$

We let $s_0 > 1$ be positive constant V, depending on δ. The exact values of these constants were defined as below. For $0 < v \leq V$, we defined k_v as:

$$k_v = k_v(V) := \min\{l \geq 0 : s_0^l v \geq V\}.$$

Remembering that:

$$\Lambda_n = \Lambda_n(z) := s_n(z) - S_y(z),$$

and:

$$\Gamma_n = 2C_0 \log n\left(\frac{1}{nv} + \min\left\{\frac{1}{np|b(z)|}, \frac{1}{\sqrt{np}}\right\}\right).$$

We defined:

$$a_n(z) = a_n(u,v) = \begin{cases} \operatorname{Im} b(z) + \Gamma_n, & \text{if } |b(z)| \geq \Gamma_n, \\ \Gamma_n, & \text{if } |b(z)| \leq \Gamma_n. \end{cases}$$

The function $b(z)$ was defined in (2). For a given $\gamma > 0$, we considered the event:

$$\mathcal{Q}_\gamma(v) := \{|\Lambda_n(u+iv)| \leq \gamma a_n(u,v), \text{ for all } u\}$$

and the event:

$$\widehat{\mathcal{Q}}_\gamma(v) = \bigcap_{l=0}^{k_v} \mathcal{Q}_\gamma(s_0^l v).$$

For any γ value, the constant $V = V(\gamma)$ existed, such that:

$$\Pr\{\widehat{\mathcal{Q}}_\gamma(V)\} = 1. \tag{6}$$

It could be $V = \sqrt{2/\gamma}$, for example. In what follows, we assumed that γ and V were chosen so that (6) was satisfied and we wrote:

$$\mathcal{Q} := \widehat{\mathcal{Q}}_\gamma.$$

We defined:

$$\beta_n(z) := \frac{a_n(z)}{nv} + \frac{|A_0(z)|^2}{np},$$

where

$$A_0(z) = yS_y(z) - \frac{1-y}{z}.$$

In this section, we demonstrate the following results.

Theorem 3. *Under the condition (C0), the positive constants $C = C(\delta, \mu_{4+\delta}, c_0)$, $a_0 = a_0(\delta, \mu_{4+\delta}, c_0)$ and $a_1 = a_1(\delta, \mu_{4+\delta}, c_0)$ exist, such that for $z = u + iv \in \widetilde{\mathcal{D}}$:*

$$\mathbb{E}\, |T_n|^q \mathbb{I}\{\mathcal{Q}\} \leq C\Big(F_1 + \cdots + F_6\Big),$$

where

$$F_1 = \frac{a_n^q(z)}{n^q v^q}, \quad F_2 = |S_y(z)|^{2q}\beta_n^q(z)\mathbb{I}\{|b(z)| \geq \Gamma_n\} + |S_y(z)|^{2q}\beta_n^{\frac{q}{2}}(z)\Gamma_n^{\frac{q}{2}},$$

$$F_3 = |S_y(z)|^{2q}\beta_n^{\frac{q}{2}}(z)\Gamma_n^q(\mathbb{I}\{|b(z)| \leq \Gamma_n\}\mathbb{I}\{z \notin \mathcal{D}\})$$
$$+ \left[\frac{|S_y(z)|^{3q}\beta_n^{\frac{q}{2}}(z)a_n^{\frac{q}{2}}(z)}{(nv)^q}\left(|S_y(z)|^q|A_0(z)|^{\frac{q}{2}}\beta_n^{\frac{q}{2}}(z) + \frac{|A_0(z)|^{\frac{q}{2}}}{(np)^{\frac{q}{2}}} + \frac{1}{(nv)^{\frac{q}{2}}}\right)\right],$$

$$F_4 = \frac{|S_y(z)|^{2q}\beta_n^{\frac{q}{2}}(z)}{a_n^{\frac{q}{2}}(z)(nv)^q}\left(|S_y(z)|^q|A_0(z)|^{\frac{q}{2}}\beta_n^{\frac{q}{2}}(z) + \frac{|A_0(z)|^{\frac{q}{2}}}{(np)^{\frac{q}{2}}} + \frac{1}{(nv)^{\frac{q}{2}}}\right),$$

$$F_5 = q^{\frac{q}{2}}|S_y(z)|^{\frac{3q}{2}}\beta_n^{\frac{q}{2}}(z)|A_0(z)|^{\frac{q}{4}}\frac{a_n^{\frac{q}{4}}(z)}{(nv)^{\frac{q}{2}}}(a_n(z) + |b(z)|)^{\frac{q}{2}}$$
$$+ C^q q^{\frac{q}{2}}\left(\frac{a_n(z)|S_y(z)|}{nv}\right)^{\frac{q}{4}}\left(|S_y(z)|^2\beta_n(z)\right)^{\frac{q}{4}}(a_n(z) + |b(z)|)^{\frac{q}{2}}\frac{|S_y(z)|^{\frac{q}{4}}}{(np)^{\frac{q}{4}}}\frac{1}{(nv)^{\frac{q}{4}}}$$
$$+ C^q q^q\left(\frac{|S_y(z)|^2 a_n(z)}{nv}\right)^{\frac{q}{4}}\left(|S_y(z)|^2\beta_n(z)\right)^{\frac{q}{4}}(a_n(z) + |b(z)|)^{\frac{q}{2}}\frac{1}{(nv)^{\frac{q}{2}}},$$

$$F_6 = C^q q^{2(q-1)}(a_n(z) + |b(z)|)^{q-1}|S_y(z)|\beta_n^{\frac{1}{2}}(z)\left[\left(q^{q-1}\frac{|S_y(z)||a_n(z)|}{nv}\right)^{q-1}\frac{1}{(np)^{2\varkappa(q-1)}}\right.$$
$$+ q^q\left(\frac{|S_y(z)||a_n(z)|}{nv}\right)^{q-1}|S_y(z)|^{q-1}\beta_n^{\frac{q-1}{2}}(z)$$
$$+ q^{\frac{3(q-1)}{2}}\left(\frac{|S_y(z)|^2 a_n(z)}{nv}\right)^{\frac{q-1}{2}}\left(\frac{1}{nv}\right)^{q-1} + \frac{q^{2(q-1)}}{(np)^{2(q-1)\varkappa}(nv)^{q-1}}$$
$$+ q^{2(q-1)}\frac{|S_y(z)|^{\frac{q-1}{2}}}{(nv)^{q-1}}\left(\frac{a_n(z)|S_y(z)|}{(nv)}\right)^{\frac{q-1}{2}} + q^{\frac{5(q-1)}{2}}\frac{1}{n^{q-1}v^{q-1}}\left(\frac{|S_y(z)||a_n(z)|}{nv}\right)^{\frac{q-1}{2}}$$
$$+ \left.\frac{q^{3(q-1)}}{(np)^{2(q-1)\varkappa}(nv)^{q-1}}\right].$$

Remark 1. *Theorem 3 was auxiliary. T_n was the perturbation of the main equation in the Stieltjes transformation of the limit distribution. The size of T_n was responsible for the stability of the solution of the perturbed equation. We were interested in the estimates of T_n that were uniform in the domain $\mathcal{D}$ and had an order of $\log n/(nv)$ (such estimates were needed for the proof of the delocalisation of Theorem 6). It was important to know to what extent the estimates depended on both np_n and nv. The estimates behaved differently on the beam and at the ends of the support of the limit distribution (the introduced functions $a_n(z)$ and $b(z)$ were responsible for the behaviour of the estimates, depending on the real part of the argument: on the beam or at the ends of the support of* the limit distribution). For Λ_n estimation, there were two regimes: for $|b(z)| \geq \Gamma_n$, we used the inequality (10) and for $|b(z)| \leq \Gamma_n$, we used the inequality (18).

Corollary 1. *Under conditions of Theorem 3, the following inequalities hold:*

$$\mathbb{I}\{|b(z)| \geq \Gamma_n\} \mathbb{E}\, |T_n|^q \mathbb{I}\{\mathcal{Q}\} \leq C^q |b(z)|^q \Bigg[\Big(\frac{q^2}{(np)^{2\varkappa}}\Big)^{q-1} d_n^{\frac{2q-1}{2}}(z)$$
$$+ d_n^{\frac{3q}{4}}(z)\Big(\frac{q^2}{nv}\Big)^{\frac{q}{4}} + d_n^{\frac{q}{2}}(z)\Big(\frac{q^2}{nv}\Big)^{\frac{q}{2}} + q^{q-1} d_n^{\frac{3q-2}{2}}(z)$$
$$+ q^{2(q-1)} d_n^q(z) \frac{1}{(nv)^{q-1}} + q^{3(q-1)} d_n^{\frac{1}{2}}(z) \frac{1}{(nv)^{q-1}(np)^{2\varkappa(q-1)}} \Bigg] \quad (7)$$

and

$$\mathbb{I}\{\Gamma_n \geq |b(z)|\} \mathbb{E}\, |T_n|^q \mathbb{I}\{\mathcal{Q}\} \leq C^q \Big(\frac{\Gamma_n}{nv} + \frac{1}{np}\Big)^{\frac{q}{2}} \Gamma_n^{\frac{q}{2}}. \quad (8)$$

Corollary 2. *Under the conditions of Theorem 3 and in the domain:*

$$\mathcal{D} = \{z = u + iv : 1 - \sqrt{y} - v \leq |u| \leq 1 + \sqrt{y} + v, V \geq v \geq v_0\},$$

for any $Q > 1$, a constant C exists that depends on Q, such that:

$$\Pr\Big\{|\Lambda_n| > \frac{1}{2}\Gamma_n; \mathcal{Q}\Big\} \leq Cn^{-Q}.$$

Moreover, for $z = u + iv$ to satisfy $v \geq v_0$ and $|z| \geq C \max\{\frac{\sqrt{\log n}}{\sqrt{np}}, \frac{\log^4 n}{(np)^{2\varkappa}}\}$ and for $Q > 1$, a constant C exists that depends on Q, such that:

$$\Pr\Big\{|\operatorname{Im}\Lambda_n| > \frac{1}{2}\Gamma_n; \mathcal{Q}\Big\} \leq Cn^{-Q}.$$

Corollary 3. *Under the conditions of Theorem 3, for $Q \geq 1$, a constant C that depends on Q exists, such that:*

$$\Pr\{\mathcal{Q}\} \geq 1 - Cn^{-Q}.$$

Theorem 4. *Under the conditions of Theorem 1, for $Q \geq 1$, the positive constants $C = C(Q, \delta, \mu_{4+\delta}, c_0, c_1)$ and $a_0 = a_0(Q, \delta, \mu_{4+\delta}, c_0, c_1)$ exists, such that for $z = u + iv \in \mathcal{D}(a_0)$:*

$$\Pr\{|\Lambda_n| \geq \frac{1}{2}\Gamma_n\} \leq Cn^{-Q}.$$

Moreover, for $Q \geq 1$, the positive constants $C = C(Q, \delta, \mu_{4+\delta}, c_0, c_1)$, $C_0 = C_0(Q, \delta, \mu_{4+\delta}, c_0, c_1)$ and $a_0 = a_0(Q, \delta, \mu_{4+\delta}, c_0, c_1)$ exist, such that for $z = u + iv$ satisfying $v \geq v_0$ and $|z| \geq \Gamma_n$:

$$\Pr\Big\{|\operatorname{Im}\Lambda_n| > \frac{1}{2}\Gamma_n\Big\} \leq Cn^{-Q}, \quad (9)$$

where

$$\Gamma_n = C_0 \log n \Big(\frac{1}{nv} + \min\Big\{\frac{1}{np|b(z)|}, \frac{1}{\sqrt{np}}\Big\}\Big).$$

To prove the main result, we needed to estimate the entries of the resolvent matrix.

Theorem 5. *Under the condition (C0) and for $0 < \gamma < \gamma_0$ and $u_0 > 0$, the constants $H = H(\delta, \mu_{4+\delta}, c_0, \gamma, u_0)$, $C = C(\delta, \mu_{4+\delta}, c_0, \gamma, u_0)$, $c = c(\delta, \mu_{4+\delta}, c_0, \gamma, u_0)$, $a_0 = a_0(\delta, \mu_{4+\delta}, c_0, \gamma, u_0)$ and $a_1 = a_1(\delta, \mu_{4+\delta}, c_0, \gamma, u_0)$ exist, such that for $1 \leq j \leq n, 1 \leq k \leq m$ and $z = u + iv \in \widehat{\mathcal{D}}$, we have:*

$$\Pr\{|R_{jk}| > H|S_y(z)|; \widehat{\mathcal{Q}}_\gamma(v)\} \leq Cn^{-c\log n},$$

$$\Pr\{\max\{|R_{j,k+n}|, |R_{j+n,k}|\} > H|S_y(z)|; \widehat{\mathcal{Q}}_\gamma(v)\} \leq Cn^{-c\log n},$$

$$\Pr\{|R_{j+n,k+n}| > H|A_0(z)|; \widehat{\mathcal{Q}}_\gamma(v)\} \leq Cn^{-c\log n},$$

where
$$A_0(z) = yS_y(z) - \frac{1-y}{z}.$$

Corollary 4. *Under the conditions of Theorem 5, for $v \geq v_0$ and $q \leq c\log n$, a constant H exists, such that for $j, k \in \mathbb{T} \cup (\mathbb{T}^{(1)} + n)$:*

$$\mathbb{E}|R_{jk}|^q \mathbb{I}\{\widehat{\mathcal{Q}}_\gamma\} \leq H^q |S_y(z)|^q.$$

4. Delocalisation

In this section, we demonstrate some applications of the main result. We let $\mathbf{L} = (L_{jk})_{j,k=1}^n$ and $\mathbf{K} = (K_{jk})_{j,k=1}^m$ be orthogonal matrices from the SVD of matrix $\mathbf{X}$ s.t.:

$$\mathbf{X} = \mathbf{L}\widetilde{\mathbf{D}}\mathbf{K}^*,$$

where $\widetilde{\mathbf{D}} = \begin{bmatrix} \mathbf{D}_n & \mathbf{O}_{n,m} \end{bmatrix}$ and $\mathbf{D} = \mathrm{diag}\{s_1, \ldots, s_n\}$. Here and in what follows, $\mathbf{O}_{k,n}$ denotes a $k \times n$ matrix with zero entries. The eigenvalues of matrix $\mathbf{V}$ are denoted by λ_j ($\lambda_j = s_j$ for $j = 1, \ldots, n$, $\lambda_j = -s_j$ for $j = n+1, \ldots, 2n$ and $\lambda_j = 0$ for $j = 2n+1, \ldots, n+m$). We let $\mathbf{u}_j = (u_{j,1}, \ldots, u_{j,n+m})$ be the eigenvector of matrix $\mathbf{V}$, corresponding to eigenvalue λ_j, where $j = 1, \ldots, n+m$.

We proved the following result.

Theorem 6. *Under the conditions (C0)–(C2), for $Q \geq 1$, the positive constants $C_1 = C_1(Q, \delta, \mu_{4+\delta}, c_0, c_1)$ and $C_2 = C_2(Q, \delta, \mu_{4+\delta}, c_0, c_1)$ exist, such that:*

$$\Pr\left\{\max_{1 \leq j,k \leq n} |L_{jk}|^2 \leq C_1 \frac{\log^4 n}{n}\right\} \leq C_2 n^{-Q}.$$

Moreover, for $j = 1, \ldots n$, we have:

$$\Pr\left\{\max_{1 \leq j \leq n, 1 \leq k \leq m} |K_{jk}|^2 \leq C_1 \frac{\log^4 n}{n}\right\} \leq C_2 n^{-Q}.$$

Proof. First, we noted that according to [13] based on [14] and Theorem 1, $\tilde{c}_1, \tilde{c}_2, C > 0$ exists, such that:

$$\Pr\{\tilde{c}_1 \leq s_n \leq s_1 \leq \tilde{c}_2\} \geq 1 - Cn^{-Q}.$$

Furthermore, by Lemma 11, we obtained:

$$R_{jj} = \sum_{k=1}^n |L_{jk}|^2 \left(\frac{1}{s_k - z} - \frac{1}{s_k + z}\right) = \int_{-\infty}^\infty \frac{1}{x - z} dF_{nj}(x),$$

where
$$F_{nj}(x) = \frac{1}{2} \sum_{j=1}^n |L_{jk}|^2 (\mathbb{I}\{s_k \leq x\} + \mathbb{I}\{s_k > -x\}).$$

We noted that:

$$\max_{1 \leq j \leq n} |L_{jk}|^2 \leq 2 \sup_{u: |u| \geq \tilde{c}_1/2} (F_{nj}(u + \lambda) - F_{nj}(u)),$$

and

$$F_{nj}(x+\lambda) - F_{nj}(x) = \int_x^{x+\lambda} dF_{nj}(u)$$
$$\leq 2\lambda \int_0^\lambda \frac{\lambda}{(x+\lambda-u)^2 + \lambda^2} dF_{nj}(u) \leq 2\lambda \operatorname{Im} R_{jj}(x+\lambda+i\lambda).$$

These implied that:

$$\sup_{x:|x|\geq \frac{\tilde{c}_1}{2}} |F_{nj}(x+\lambda) - F_{nj}(x)| \leq 2\lambda \sup_{|x|>\frac{\tilde{c}_1}{4}} \operatorname{Im} R_{jj}(x+i\lambda).$$

We chose $\lambda \sim n^{-1}\log^4 n$. Then, by Corollary 4, we obtained:

$$\Pr\left\{\sup_{x:|x|>\frac{\tilde{c}_1}{4}} |F_{nj}(x+\lambda) - F_{nj}(x)| \leq \frac{C\log^4 n}{n}\right\} \geq 1 - Cn^{-Q}.$$

We obtained the bounds for K_{jk} in a similar way. Thus, the theorem was proven. □

5. Proof of the Corollaries

5.1. The Proof of Corollary 4

Proof. We could write:

$$\mathbb{E}|R_{jk}|^q \mathbb{I}\{\mathcal{Q}\} \leq \mathbb{E}|R_{jk}|^q \mathbb{I}\{\mathcal{Q}\} \mathbb{I}\{\mathcal{A}(v)\} + \mathbb{E}|R_{jk}|^q \mathbb{I}\{\mathcal{Q}\} \mathbb{I}\{\mathcal{A}^c(v)\}.$$

Combining this inequality with $|R_{jk}| \leq v^{-1}$, we found that:

$$\mathbb{E}|R_{jk}|^q \mathbb{I}\{\mathcal{Q}\} \leq C^q + v_0^{-q}\mathbb{E}\{\mathbb{I}\{\mathcal{Q}\}\mathbb{I}\{\mathcal{A}^c(v)\}\}.$$

By applying Theorem 5, we obtained what was required.
Thus, the corollary was proven. □

5.2. The Proof of Corollary 2

Proof. We considered the domain $\mathcal{D}$. We noted that for $z \in \mathcal{D}$, we obtained:

$$|z|^2 \geq (1-\sqrt{y}-v)^2 + v^2 \geq \frac{1}{2}(1-\sqrt{y})^2 \text{ and } |A_0(z)| \leq C,$$

and

$$|b(z)| \leq \frac{1-y}{\alpha} + 2\sqrt{y} + B.$$

First, we considered the case $|b(z)| \geq \Gamma_n$. This inequality implied that:

$$|b(z)| \geq \frac{\sqrt{2C_0 \log n}}{\sqrt{np}} \geq \frac{1}{\sqrt{np}}.$$

From there, it followed that:

$$\min\left\{\frac{1}{np|b(z)|}, \frac{1}{\sqrt{np}}\right\} = \frac{1}{np|b(z)|}.$$

Furthermore, for the case $|b(z)| \geq \Gamma_n$, we obtained $|b_n(z)|\mathbb{I}\{\mathcal{Q}\} \geq (1-\gamma)|b(z)|\mathbb{I}\{\mathcal{Q}\}$. We used the inequality:

$$|\Lambda_n|\mathbb{I}\{\mathcal{Q}\} \leq \frac{C|T_n|}{|b(z)|}. \tag{10}$$

By Chebyshev's inequality, we obtained:

$$\Pr\{|\Lambda_n| \geq \frac{1}{2}\Gamma_n; \mathcal{Q}\} \leq \frac{2^q \, \mathbb{E}\, |T_n|^q \mathbb{I}\{\mathcal{Q}\}}{\Gamma_n^q |b(z)|^q}.$$

By applying Corollary 1, we obtained:

$$\Pr\{|\Lambda_n| \geq \frac{1}{2}\Gamma_n; \mathcal{Q}\} \leq \frac{2^q \mathcal{H}_n^q}{\Gamma_n^q},$$

where

$$\mathcal{H}_n^q := C^q \left[\left(\frac{q^{\frac{1}{2}}}{(np)^{2\varkappa}}\right)^{q-1} d_n^{\frac{2q-1}{2}}(z) + d_n^{\frac{3q}{4}}(z)\left(\frac{q^2}{nv}\right)^{\frac{q}{4}} + d_n^{\frac{q}{2}}(z)\left(\frac{q}{nv}\right)^{\frac{q}{2}} \right.$$
$$\left. + q^{q-1} d_n^{\frac{3q-2}{2}}(z) + q^{2(q-1)} d_n^q(z) \frac{1}{(nv)^{q-1}} + q^{3(q-1)} d_n^{\frac{q}{2}}(z) \frac{1}{(nv)^{q-1}(np)^{2\varkappa(q-1)}} \right]. \quad (11)$$

First, we noted that for $q = K \log n$:

$$\frac{d_n(z)}{\Gamma_n} \leq \frac{C}{\log n}. \quad (12)$$

Moreover, for $q = C \log n$:

$$\frac{q^2}{nv\Gamma_n} \leq C \log n. \quad (13)$$

From there, it followed that:

$$C^q d_n^{\frac{3q}{4}}(z) \left(\frac{q^2}{nv}\right)^{\frac{q}{4}} \leq \left(\frac{C}{\log n}\right)^{\frac{q}{2}}. \quad (14)$$

Furthermore:

$$C^q \left(\frac{d_n(z)}{\Gamma_n}\right)^{\frac{q}{2}} \left(\frac{q}{nv\Gamma_n}\right)^{\frac{q}{2}} \leq \left(\frac{C}{\log n}\right)^{\frac{q}{2}}. \quad (15)$$

Using these estimations, we could show that:

$$\frac{2^q \mathcal{H}_n^q}{\Gamma_n^q} \leq \left(\frac{C}{\log n}\right)^{\frac{q}{2}} \quad (16)$$

By choosing $q = K \log n$ and $K > C(Q)$, we obtained:

$$\Pr\{|\Lambda_n| \geq \frac{1}{2}\Gamma_n; \mathcal{Q}\} \leq Cn^{-Q}.$$

Then, we considered the case $|b(z)| \leq \Gamma_n$. In this case:

$$\Gamma_n^{\frac{1}{2}}(\frac{\Gamma_n}{nv} + \frac{1}{np})^{\frac{1}{2}}/\Gamma_n \leq (\frac{1}{nv} + \frac{1}{np\Gamma_n})^{\frac{1}{2}} \leq \frac{C}{\log n}. \quad (17)$$

By applying the inequality $|\Lambda_n(z)| \leq C\sqrt{|T_n|}$ and Corollary 1, we obtained:

$$\Pr\{|\Lambda_n| \geq \frac{1}{2}\Gamma_n; \mathcal{Q}\} \leq \frac{2^q (\frac{\Gamma_n}{nv} + \frac{1}{np})^{\frac{q}{2}}}{\Gamma_n^{\frac{q}{2}}} \leq C^q (\frac{1}{nv} + \frac{1}{np\Gamma_n})^{\frac{q}{2}}.$$

It was then simple to show that:

$$\Pr\{|\Lambda_n| \geq \frac{1}{2}\Gamma_n; \mathcal{Q}\} \leq Cn^{-Q}.$$

Thus, the first inequality was proven. The proof of the second inequality was similar to the proof of the first. We had to use the inequality:

$$|\operatorname{Im} \Lambda_n| \leq C\sqrt{|T_n|}, \qquad (18)$$

which was valid on the real line, instead of $|\Lambda_n| \leq C\sqrt{|T_n|}$, which held in the domain $\widehat{\mathcal{D}}$. Moreover, we noted that for any z value, we obtained:

$$|S_y(z)||A_0(z)| \leq C.$$

Thus, the corollary was proven. □

5.3. Proof of Corollary 3

Proof. According to Theorem 4:

$$\Pr\{|\Lambda_n(z)| \leq \frac{1}{2}\Gamma_n(z); \mathcal{Q}\} \geq 1 - Cn^{-Q}.$$

We noted that for $v = V$:

$$\Pr\{\mathcal{Q}(z)\} = 1.$$

Furthermore:

$$\left|\frac{d\Lambda(z)}{dz}\right| \leq \frac{2}{v^2}.$$

We split the interval $[v_0, V]$ into subintervals by $v_0 < v_1 < \cdots < v_M = V$, such that for $k = 1, \ldots, M$:

$$|\Lambda_n(u + iv_k) - \Lambda_n(u + iv_{k-1})| \leq \frac{1}{2}\Gamma_n(z).$$

We noted that the event $\mathcal{Q}_k = \{|\Lambda_n(u + iv_k)| \leq \frac{1}{2}\Gamma_n(u + iv_k)\}$ implied the event $\widetilde{\mathcal{Q}}_{k+1} = \{|\Lambda_n(u + iv_k)| \leq \Gamma_n\}$. From there, for $v_k \leq v \leq v_{k+1}$, $k = 0, \ldots, M - 1$, we obtained:

$$\Pr\{\mathcal{Q}(u + iv)\} \geq 1 - \Pr\{\mathcal{Q}(u + iv_{k-1})\} - \Pr\{\mathcal{Q}_{k-1}{}^c; \mathcal{Q}(u + iv_{k-1})\} \geq 1 - Cn^{-Q}.$$

□

6. Proof of the Theorems

6.1. Proof of Theorem 1

Proof. We obtained:

$$\Pr\{|\Lambda_n(z)| \geq \mathcal{T}_n\} \leq \Pr\{|\Lambda_n(z)| \geq \mathcal{T}_n; \mathcal{Q}\} + \Pr\{\mathcal{Q}^c\}.$$

The second term in the RHS of the last inequality was bounded by Corollary 3. For z (such that $|b(z)| \geq C\Gamma_n(z)$), we used the inequality:

$$|\Lambda_n(z)| \leq \frac{|T_n|}{|b_n(z)|},$$

the inequality:

$$|b_n(z)| \geq (1 - \gamma)|b(z)|$$

and the Markov inequality. We could write:
$$\Pr\{|\Lambda_n(z)| \geq \mathcal{T}_n\} \leq \frac{\mathbb{E}\{|T_N|^q; \mathcal{Q}\}}{|\mathcal{T}_n|^q |b(z)|^q} + Cn^{-c\log\log n}.$$

We recalled that in the case $|b(z)| \geq \Gamma_n$:
$$\mathcal{T}_n := K\big(\widehat{d}_n(z) + \widehat{d}_n^{\frac{3}{4}}(z)\frac{1}{(nv)^{\frac{1}{4}}} + \widehat{d}_n^{\frac{1}{2}}(z)\frac{1}{(nv)^{\frac{1}{2}}}\big).$$

In the case $|b(z)| \geq \Gamma_n$ and using Corollary 1, we obtained:
$$\Pr\{|\Lambda_n(z)| \geq K\mathcal{T}_n\} \leq \Big(\frac{\mathcal{H}_n}{K\mathcal{T}_n}\Big)^q + Cn^{-c\log\log n}.$$

First, we considered the case $|b(z)| \geq \Gamma_n$. By our definition of $r_n(z)$, we obtained:
$$\Pr\{|\Lambda_n(z)| \geq \mathcal{T}_n\} \leq \Big(C\frac{1}{K\log^{\frac{1}{2}} n}\Big)^q + Cn^{-c\log\log n}. \tag{19}$$

This inequality completed the proof for $|b(z)| \geq \Gamma_n$.

We then considered $|b(z)| \leq \Gamma_n$. We used inequality $|\Lambda_n(z)| \leq \sqrt{|T_n|}$ and Corollary 1 to obtain:
$$\Pr\{|\Lambda_n(z)| \geq \mathcal{T}_n\} \leq \Big(\frac{C}{K}\Big)^q. \tag{20}$$

By choosing a sufficiently large K value, we obtained the proof. Thus, the theorem was proven. □

6.2. Proof of Theorem 2

Proof. The proof of Theorem 2 was similar to the proof of Theorem 1. We only noted that inequality:
$$|\operatorname{Im} \Lambda_n(u + iv)| \leq \sqrt{|T_n|}$$
held for all $u \in \mathbb{R}$. □

6.3. The Proof of Theorem 5

Proof. Using the definition of the Stieltjes transformation, we obtained:
$$s_n(z) = \frac{1}{2n}\Big(\sum_{j=1}^n \frac{1}{s_j - z} + \sum_{j=1}^n \frac{1}{-s_j - z}\Big) = \frac{1}{n}\sum_{j=1}^n \frac{z}{s_j^2 - z^2},$$

and
$$S_y(z) = \frac{-(z^2 - ab) + \sqrt{(z^2 - a^2)(z^2 - b^2)}}{2yz}.$$

It is also well known that for $z = u + iv$:
$$|S_y(z)| \leq \frac{1}{\sqrt{y}}$$

and
$$A_0(z) := -\frac{1}{yS_y(z) + z} = \Big(yS_y(z) - \frac{1-y}{z}\Big).$$

We considered the following event for $1 \leq j \leq n, 1 \leq k \leq m$ and $C > 0$:

$$\mathcal{A}_{jk}(v, \mathbb{J}, \mathbb{K}; C) = \{|R_{jk}^{(\mathbb{J},\mathbb{K})}(u + iv)| \leq C\}.$$

We set:

$$\mathcal{A}^{(1)}(v, \mathbb{J}, \mathbb{K}) = \cap_{j=1}^{n} \cap_{k=1}^{m} \mathcal{A}_{j,k}(v, \mathbb{J}, \mathbb{K}; C|S_y(z)|),$$
$$\mathcal{A}^{(2)}(v, \mathbb{J}, \mathbb{K}) = \cap_{j=1}^{m} \cap_{k=1}^{n} \mathcal{A}_{j+n,k}(v, \mathbb{J}, \mathbb{K}; C|S_y(z)|),$$
$$\mathcal{A}^{(3)}(v, \mathbb{J}, \mathbb{K}) = \cap_{j=1}^{n} \cap_{k=1}^{m} \mathcal{A}_{j,k+n}(v, \mathbb{J}, \mathbb{K}; C|S_y(z)|),$$
$$\mathcal{A}^{(4)}(v, \mathbb{J}, \mathbb{K}) = \cap_{j=1}^{m} \cap_{k=1}^{n} \mathcal{A}_{j+n,k+n}(v, \mathbb{J}, \mathbb{K}; C|A_0(z)|).$$

For $j \in \mathbb{J}^c, k \in \mathbb{K}^c$ and u, we obtained:

$$|R_{jk}^{(\mathbb{J},\mathbb{K})}(z)| \leq \frac{1}{v}.$$

We recalled:

$$a := a_n(u, v) = \begin{cases} \operatorname{Im} b(z) + \Gamma_n, & \text{if } |b(z)| \geq \Gamma_n, \\ \Gamma_n, & \text{if } |b(z)| \leq \Gamma_n. \end{cases}$$

Then:

$$\Gamma_n = \Gamma_n(z) = 2C_0 \log n \left(\frac{1}{nv} + \min\left\{\frac{1}{np|b(z)|}, \frac{1}{\sqrt{np}}\right\}\right).$$

We introduced the events:

$$\hat{\mathcal{Q}}_{\gamma}^{(\mathbb{J},\mathbb{K})}(v) := \bigcap_{l=0}^{k_v} \left\{|\Lambda_n^{(\mathbb{J},\mathbb{K})}(u + is_0^l v)| \leq \gamma a_n(u, s_0^l v) + \frac{|\mathbb{J}| + |\mathbb{K}|}{n s_0^l v}\right\}.$$

It was easy to see that:

$$\hat{\mathcal{Q}}_{\gamma}(v) \subset \hat{\mathcal{Q}}_{\gamma}^{(\mathbb{J},\mathbb{K})}(v).$$

In what follows, we used $\mathcal{Q} := \hat{\mathcal{Q}}_{\gamma}(v)$.

Equations (4) and (5) and Lemma 10 yielded that for $\gamma \leq \gamma_0$ and for $\mathbb{J}, \mathbb{K}$ that satisfied $(|\mathbb{J}| + |\mathbb{K}|)/nv \leq 1/4$, the following inequalities held:

$$|R_{jj}^{(\mathbb{J},\mathbb{K})}| \mathbb{I}\{\mathcal{Q}\} \leq 2|S_y(z)||\varepsilon_j^{(\mathbb{J},\mathbb{K})}||R_{jj}^{(\mathbb{J},\mathbb{K})}| \mathbb{I}\{\mathcal{Q}\} + 2|S_y(z)| \qquad (21)$$

and $|A_0(z)|(|\mathbb{J}| + |\mathbb{K}|)/nv \leq 1/4$,

$$|R_{l+n,l+n}^{(\mathbb{J},\mathbb{K})}| \mathbb{I}\{\mathcal{Q}\} \leq 2|A_0(Z)||\varepsilon_{l+n}^{(\mathbb{J},\mathbb{K})}||R_{l+n,l+n}^{(\mathbb{J},\mathbb{K})}| \mathbb{I}\{\mathcal{Q}\} + 2|A_0(z)|. \qquad (22)$$

We noted that for $|z| \geq \frac{C_1 \log n}{nv}$ and $|\mathbb{J}| \leq C_2 \log n$ under appropriate C_1 and C_2, we obtained $A_0(z)(|\mathbb{J}| + |\mathbb{K}|)/nv \leq 1/4$.

We considered the off-diagonal elements of the resolvent matrix. It could be shown that for $j \neq k \in \mathbb{J}^c$:

$$R_{jk}^{(\mathbb{J},\mathbb{K})} = R_{jj}^{(\mathbb{J},\mathbb{K})}\left(-\frac{1}{\sqrt{mp}} \sum_{l=1}^{m} X_{jl} \xi_{jl} R_{l+n,k}^{(\mathbb{J}\cup\{j\},\mathbb{K})}\right) = R_{jj}^{(\mathbb{J},\mathbb{K})} \zeta_{jk}^{(\mathbb{J},\mathbb{K})}, \qquad (23)$$

for $l \neq k \in \mathbb{K}^c$:

$$R^{(\mathbb{J},\mathbb{K})}_{l+n,k+n} = R^{(\mathbb{J},\mathbb{K})}_{l+n,l+n}\left(-\frac{1}{\sqrt{mp}}\sum_{r=1}^{n}X_{rl}\xi_{rl}R^{(\mathbb{J},\mathbb{K}\cup\{l+n\})}_{k+n,r}\right) = R^{(\mathbb{J},\mathbb{K})}_{l+n,l+n}\zeta^{(\mathbb{J},\mathbb{K})}_{l+n,k+n'} \quad (24)$$

and

$$R^{(\mathbb{J},\mathbb{K})}_{j,k+n} = R^{(\mathbb{J},\mathbb{K})}_{jj}\left(-\frac{1}{\sqrt{mp}}\sum_{r=1}^{m}X_{jr}\xi_{jr}R^{(\mathbb{J}\cup\{j\},\mathbb{K})}_{r+n,l+n}\right) = R^{(\mathbb{J},\mathbb{K})}_{jj}\zeta^{(\mathbb{J},\mathbb{K})}_{j,k+n'}$$

$$R^{(\mathbb{J},\mathbb{K})}_{k+n,j} = R^{(\mathbb{J},\mathbb{K})}_{jj}\left(-\frac{1}{\sqrt{mp}}\sum_{r=1}^{m}X_{jr}\xi_{jr}R^{(\mathbb{J}\cup\{j\},\mathbb{K})}_{r+n,k+n}\right) = R^{(\mathbb{J},\mathbb{K})}_{j,j}\zeta^{(\mathbb{J},\mathbb{K})}_{k+n,j'} \quad (25)$$

where

$$\zeta^{(\mathbb{J},\mathbb{K})}_{jk} = -\frac{1}{\sqrt{mp}}\sum_{l=1}^{m}X_{jl}\xi_{jl}R^{(\mathbb{J}\cup\{j\},\mathbb{K})}_{l+n,k}, \quad \zeta^{(\mathbb{J},\mathbb{K})}_{j+n,k+n} = -\frac{1}{\sqrt{mp}}\sum_{r=1}^{n}X_{rj}\xi_{rj}R^{(\mathbb{J},\mathbb{K}\cup\{j+n\})}_{r,k+n},$$

$$\zeta^{(\mathbb{J},\mathbb{K})}_{j+n,k} = -\frac{1}{\sqrt{mp}}\sum_{l=1}^{m}X_{kl}\xi_{kl}R^{(\mathbb{J}\cup\{k\},\mathbb{K})}_{l+n,j+n}, \quad \zeta^{(\mathbb{J},\mathbb{K})}_{j,k+n} = -\frac{1}{\sqrt{mp}}\sum_{l=1}^{n}X_{lk}\xi_{lk}R^{(\mathbb{J}\cup\{j\},\mathbb{K})}_{l+n,k+n}. \quad (26)$$

Inequalities (21) and (22) implied that:

$$\Pr\{|R_{jj}|\mathbb{I}\{\mathcal{Q}\} > C|S_y(z)|\} \leq \Pr\left\{|\varepsilon_j|\mathbb{I}\{\mathcal{Q}\} > \frac{1}{4}\right\} \quad (27)$$

for $1 \leq j \leq n$ and $C > \frac{4}{\sqrt{y}}$ and that:

$$\Pr\{|R_{l+n,l+n}|\mathbb{I}\{\mathcal{Q}\} > C|A_0(z)|\} \leq \Pr\left\{|\varepsilon_{l+n}|\mathbb{I}\{\mathcal{Q}\} > \frac{1}{4|A_0(z)|}\right\} \quad (28)$$

for $1 \leq l \leq m$ and $C > 2$. Equations (23)–(25) produced:

$$\Pr\{|R_{jk}|\mathbb{I}\{\mathcal{Q}\} > C|S_y(z)|\} \leq \Pr\{|R_{jj}|\mathbb{I}\{\mathcal{Q}\} > C|S_y(z)|\} + \Pr\{|\zeta_{jk}|\mathbb{I}\{\mathcal{Q}\} > 1\}$$

for $1 \leq j \neq k \leq n$ and:

$$\Pr\{|R_{l+n,k+n}|\mathbb{I}\{\mathcal{Q}\} > C|A_0(z)|\} \leq \Pr\{|R_{l+n,l+n}|\mathbb{I}\{\mathcal{Q}\} > C|A_0(z)|\} + \Pr\{|\zeta_{l+n,k+n}|\mathbb{I}\{\mathcal{Q}\} > 1\}$$

for $1 \leq l \neq k \leq m$. Similarly, we obtained:

$$\Pr\{|R_{l,k+n}|\mathbb{I}\{\mathcal{Q}\} > C|S_y(z)|\} \leq \Pr\{|R_{l,l}|\mathbb{I}\{\mathcal{Q}\} > C|S_y(z)|\} + \Pr\{|\zeta_{l,k+n}|\mathbb{I}\{\mathcal{Q}\} > 1\}$$

and

$$\Pr\{|R_{l+n,k}|\mathbb{I}\{\mathcal{Q}\} > C|S_y(z)|\} \leq \Pr\{|R_{k,k}|\mathbb{I}\{\mathcal{Q}\} > C|S_y(z)|\} + \Pr\{|\zeta_{l+n,k}|\mathbb{I}\{\mathcal{Q}\} > 1\}.$$

We noted that for $|z| \leq B$, we obtained:

$$\frac{1}{|A_0(z)|} \leq B + \sqrt{y}.$$

Using Rosenthal's inequality, we found that:

$$\mathbb{E}_j|\zeta_{jk}|^q \leq C^q\left(q^{\frac{q}{2}}(nv)^{-\frac{q}{2}}(\operatorname{Im} R^{(j)}_{kk})^{\frac{q}{2}} + q^q(np)^{-q\varkappa-1}\frac{1}{n}\sum_{l=1}^{m}|R^{(j)}_{k,l+n}|^q\right)$$

for $1 \leq j \neq k \leq n$ and that:

$$\mathbb{E}_{j+n} |\zeta_{j+n,k+n}|^q \leq C^q \Big(q^{\frac{q}{2}}(nv)^{-\frac{q}{2}} (\operatorname{Im} R_{k+n,k+n}^{(j+n)})^{\frac{q}{2}}$$
$$+ q^q(np)^{-q\varkappa-1} \frac{1}{n} \sum_{r=1}^{n} |R_{k+n,r}^{(j+n)}|^q \Big),$$

$$\mathbb{E}_{j} |\zeta_{j,k+n}|^q \leq C^q \Big(q^{\frac{q}{2}}(nv)^{-\frac{q}{2}} (\operatorname{Im} R_{k+n,k+n}^{(j+n)})^{\frac{q}{2}}$$
$$+ q^q(np)^{-q\varkappa-1} \frac{1}{n} \sum_{r=1}^{n} |R_{k+n,r+n}^{(j+n)}|^q \Big),$$

$$\mathbb{E}_{j+n} |\zeta_{j+n,k}|^q \leq C^q \Big(q^{\frac{q}{2}}(nv)^{-\frac{q}{2}} (\operatorname{Im} R_{k+n,k+n}^{(j+n)})^{\frac{q}{2}}$$
$$+ q^q(np)^{-q\varkappa-1} \frac{1}{n} \sum_{r=1}^{n} |R_{k+n,r+n}^{(j+n)}|^q \Big)$$

for $1 \leq j \neq k \leq m$. We noted that:

$$\Pr\{|\varepsilon_j^{(\mathbb{J},\mathbb{K})}| > \frac{1}{4}; \mathcal{Q}\} \leq \Pr\{\mathcal{A}^{(4)}(sv,\mathbb{J},\mathbb{K})^c; \mathcal{Q}\} + \Pr\{|\varepsilon_j^{(\mathbb{J},\mathbb{K})}| > \frac{1}{4}; \mathcal{A}^{(4)}(sv,\mathbb{J},\mathbb{K}); \mathcal{Q}\},$$

$$\Pr\{|\varepsilon_{j+n}^{(\mathbb{J},\mathbb{K})}| > \frac{1}{4|A_0(z)|}; \mathcal{Q}\} \leq \Pr\{\mathcal{A}^{(1)}(sv,\mathbb{J},\mathbb{K})^c; \mathcal{Q}\}$$
$$+ \Pr\{|\varepsilon_{j+n}^{(\mathbb{J},\mathbb{K})}| > 1/(4|A_0(z)|); \mathcal{A}^{(1)}(sv,\mathbb{J},\mathbb{K}); \mathcal{Q};\},$$

$$\Pr\{|\zeta_{jk}^{(\mathbb{J},\mathbb{K})}| > 1; \mathcal{Q}\} \leq \Pr\{\mathcal{A}^{(2)}(sv,\mathbb{J},\mathbb{K})^c; \mathcal{Q}\}$$
$$+ \Pr\{|\zeta_{jk}^{(\mathbb{J},\mathbb{K})}| > 1; \mathcal{A}^{(2)}(sv,\mathbb{J},\mathbb{K}); \mathcal{Q}\},$$

$$\Pr\{|\zeta_{l+n,k+n}^{(\mathbb{J},\mathbb{K})}| > 1; \mathcal{Q}\} \leq \Pr\{\mathcal{A}^{(3)}(sv,\mathbb{J},\mathbb{K})^c; \mathcal{Q}\}$$
$$+ \Pr\{|\zeta_{l+n,k+n}^{(\mathbb{J},\mathbb{K})}| > 1; \mathcal{A}^{(3)}(sv,\mathbb{J},\mathbb{K}); \mathcal{Q};\},$$

$$\Pr\{|\zeta_{j+n,k}^{(\mathbb{J},\mathbb{K})}| > 1; \mathcal{Q}\} \leq \Pr\{\mathcal{A}^{(4)}(sv,\mathbb{J},\mathbb{K})^c; \mathcal{Q}\}$$
$$+ \Pr\{|\zeta_{j+n,k}^{(\mathbb{J},\mathbb{K})}| > 1; \mathcal{Q}; \mathcal{A}^{(4)}(sv,\mathbb{J},\mathbb{K})\},$$

$$\Pr\{|\zeta_{k,j+n}^{(\mathbb{J},\mathbb{K})}| > 1; \mathcal{Q}\} \leq \Pr\{\mathcal{A}^{(4)}(sv,\mathbb{J},\mathbb{K})^c; \mathcal{Q}\}$$
$$+ \Pr\{|\zeta_{k,l+n}^{(\mathbb{J},\mathbb{K})}(v)| > 1; \mathcal{Q}; \mathcal{A}^{(4)}(sv,\mathbb{J},\mathbb{K})\}.$$

Using Chebyshev's inequality, we obtained:

$$\Pr\{|\varepsilon_j^{(\mathbb{J},\mathbb{K})}| > 1/4; \mathcal{Q}; \mathcal{A}^{(4)}\}$$
$$\leq C^q \, \mathbb{E}\left(\mathbb{E}_j |\varepsilon_j|^q \right) \mathbb{I}\{\mathcal{Q}^{(\mathbb{J},\mathbb{K})}\} \mathbb{I}\{\mathcal{A}^{(4)}\}.$$

By applying the triangle inequality to the results of Lemmas (1)–(3) (which were the property of the multiplicative gradient descent of the resolvent matrix), we arrived at the inequality:

$$\mathbb{E}_j \mathbb{I}\{\mathcal{A}^{(4)}(sv,\mathbb{J},\mathbb{K})\}|\varepsilon_j|^q \leq C^q \Bigg[\frac{1}{(nv)^q} + \left(\frac{qs|A_0(z)|^2}{np} \right)^{\frac{q}{2}} + \frac{1}{np}\left(\frac{qs|A_0(z)|}{(np)^{2\varkappa}} \right)^q$$
$$+ \left(\frac{q^2 s(a_n(z) + |A_0(z)|)}{nv} \right)^{\frac{q}{2}} + \frac{1}{np}\left(\frac{qs|A_0(z)|}{(nv)} \right)^{\frac{q}{2}} \left(\frac{q^2}{np} \right)^{\frac{q}{2}}$$
$$+ \left(\frac{q^2 s|A_0(z)|}{(np)^{2\varkappa}} \right)^q \frac{1}{(np)^2} \Bigg].$$

When we set $q \sim \log^2 n$, $nv > C\log^4 n$ and $np > C(\log n)^{\frac{2}{\varkappa}}$ and took into account that $\varkappa < 1/2$ and $|A_0(z)| \le C/|z|$, then we obtained:

$$\mathbb{E}_j |\varepsilon_j|^q \mathbb{I}\{\mathcal{A}^{(4)}(sv, \mathbb{J} \cup \{j\}, \mathbb{K})\} \le Cn^{-c\log n}.$$

Moreover, the constant c could be made arbitrarily large. We could obtain similar estimates for the quantities of $\varepsilon_{l+n}, \zeta_{jk}, \zeta_{j+nk}, \zeta_{jk+n}, \zeta_{j+n,k+n}$. Inequalities (27) and (28) implied:

$$\Pr\{|R_{jj}^{(\mathbb{J},\mathbb{K})}|\mathbb{I}\{\mathcal{Q}\} > C|S_y(z)|\} \le \Pr\{\mathcal{A}^{(4)}(sv, \mathbb{J} \cup \{j\}, \mathbb{K})^c\} + Cn^{-c\log n},$$

$$\Pr\{|R_{l+n,l+n}^{(\mathbb{J},\mathbb{K})}|\mathbb{I}\{\mathcal{Q}\} > C|A_0(z)|\} \le \Pr\{\mathcal{A}^{(1)}(sv, \mathbb{J}, \mathbb{K} \cup \{l\})^c\} + Cn^{-c\log n},$$

$$\Pr\{|R_{jk}^{(\mathbb{J},\mathbb{K})}|\mathbb{I}\{\mathcal{Q}\} > C|S_y(z)|\} \le \Pr\{\mathcal{A}^{(2)}(sv, \mathbb{J}, \mathbb{K} \cup \{l\})^c\} + Cn^{-c\log n},$$

$$\Pr\{|R_{j+n,k}|\mathbb{I}\{\mathcal{Q}\} > C|S_y(z)|\} \le \Pr\{\mathcal{A}^{(4)}(sv, \mathbb{J}, \mathbb{K} \cup \{j\})^c\} + Cn^{-c\log n},$$

$$\Pr\{|R_{k+n,j}|\mathbb{I}\{\mathcal{Q}\} > C|S_y(z)|\} \le \Pr\{\mathcal{A}^{(4)}(sv, \mathbb{J}, \mathbb{K} \cup \{j\})^c\} + Cn^{-c\log n},$$

$$\Pr\{|R_{k+n,j+n}|\mathbb{I}\{\mathcal{Q}\} > C|A_0(z)|\} \le \Pr\{\mathcal{A}^{(3)}(sv, \mathbb{J}, \mathbb{K} \cup \{j\})^c\} + Cn^{-c\log n}.$$

The last inequalities produced:

$$\max_{j,k \in \mathbb{J}^c \cup \mathbb{K}^c} \Pr\{|R_{j,k}^{(\mathbb{J},\mathbb{K})}|\mathbb{I}\{\mathcal{Q}\} > C\} \le Cn^{-c\log n}$$
$$+ \max_{j \in \mathbb{J}^c, k \in \mathbb{K}^c} \max\{\Pr\{\mathcal{A}^c(sv, \mathbb{J} \cup \{j\}, \mathbb{K}; CA_0(z))\}, \Pr\{\mathcal{A}^c(s_0 v, \mathbb{J}, \mathbb{K} \cup \{k\}; CA_0(z))\}.$$

We noted that $k_v \le C\log n$ for $v \ge v_0 = n^{-1}\log^4 n$. So, by choosing c large enough, we obtained:

$$\Pr\{\mathcal{A}^c(v) \cap \mathcal{Q}\} \le Cn^{-c\log n}.$$

This completed the proof of the theorem. $\square$

6.4. The Proof of Theorem 3

Proof. First, we noted that for $z \in \mathcal{D}$, a constant $C = C(y, V)$ exists, such that:

$$|b(z)| \le C.$$

Without a loss of generality, we could assume that $\Gamma_n^{-1} \ge |b(z)|$. We recalled that:

$$a := a_n(z) := a_n(u, v) = \begin{cases} \operatorname{Im} b(z) + \Gamma_n & \text{if } |b(z)| \ge \Gamma_n, \\ \Gamma_n, & \text{if } |b(z)| \le \Gamma_n. \end{cases}$$

Then:

$$\Gamma_n = 2C_0 \log n \left(\frac{1}{nv} + \min\left\{ \frac{1}{np|b(z)|}, \frac{1}{\sqrt{np}} \right\} \right).$$

We considered the smoothing of the indicator $h_\gamma(x)$:

$$h_\gamma(x, v) = \begin{cases} 1, & \text{for } |x| \le \gamma a, \\ 1 - \frac{|x| - \gamma a}{\gamma a}, & \text{for } \gamma a \le |x| \le 2\gamma a, \\ 0, & \text{for } |x| > 2\gamma a. \end{cases}$$

We noted that:

$$\mathbb{I}_{\hat{\mathcal{Q}}_\gamma(v)} \le h_\gamma(|\Lambda_n(u+iv)|, v) \le \mathbb{I}_{\hat{\mathcal{Q}}_{2\gamma}(v)},$$

where, as before:
$$\hat{\mathcal{Q}}_\gamma(v) = \bigcap_{\nu=0}^{k_v} \{|\Lambda_n(u + is_0^\nu v)| \leq \gamma a_n(u, s_0^\nu v)\}.$$

We estimated the value:
$$D_n := \mathbb{E}\,|T_n|^q h_\gamma^q(|\Lambda_n|, v).$$

It was easy to see that:
$$\mathbb{E}\,|T_n|^q \mathbb{I}\{\mathcal{Q}\} \leq D_n.$$

To estimate D_n, we used the approach developed in [15], which refers back to Stein's method. We let:
$$\varphi(z) := \bar{z}|z|^{q-2}.$$

We set:
$$\widehat{T}_n := T_n h_\gamma(|\Lambda_n|, v).$$

Then, we could write:
$$D_n := \mathbb{E}\,\widehat{T}_n \varphi(\widehat{T}_n).$$

The equality:
$$T_n = 1 + \left(z - \frac{1-y}{z}\right)s_n(z) + ys_n^2(z) = b(z)\Lambda_n(z) + y\Lambda_n^2(z)$$

implied that a constant C exists that depends on γ in the definition of $\mathcal{Q}$, such that:
$$|T_n|\,\mathbb{I}\{\mathcal{Q}\} \leq (|b(z)||\Lambda_n(z)| + y|\Lambda_n(z)|^2)\mathbb{I}\{\mathcal{Q}\} \leq C(a_n^2(z) + |b(z)||a_n(z)|)\mathbb{I}\{\mathcal{Q}\} \leq C.$$

We considered:
$$\mathcal{B} := \mathcal{A}^{(1)} \cap \mathcal{A}^{(2)} \cap \mathcal{A}^{(3)} \cap \mathcal{A}^{(4)}.$$

Then:
$$D_n \leq \mathbb{E}\,|T_n|^q \mathbb{I}\{\mathcal{Q}\}\,\mathbb{I}\{\mathcal{B}\} + Cn^{-c\log n}.$$

By the definition of T_n, we could rewrite the last inequality as:
$$D_n := \frac{1}{n}\sum_{j=1}^{n} \mathbb{E}\,\varepsilon_j R_{jj} h_\gamma(|\Lambda_n|, v) \varphi(\widehat{T}_n)\,\mathbb{I}\{\mathcal{B}\} + Cn^{-c\log n}.$$

We set:
$$D_n = D_n^{(1)} + D_n^{(2)} + Cn^{-c\log n}, \qquad (29)$$

where
$$D_n^{(1)} := \frac{1}{n}\sum_{j=1}^{n} \mathbb{E}\,\varepsilon_{j1} R_{jj} h_\gamma(|\Lambda_n|, v) \varphi(\widehat{T}_n)\,\mathbb{I}\{\mathcal{B}\},$$

$$D_n^{(2)} := \frac{1}{n}\sum_{j=1}^{n} \mathbb{E}\,\widehat{\varepsilon}_j R_{jj} h_\gamma(|\Lambda_n|, v) \varphi(\widehat{T}_n)\,\mathbb{I}\{\mathcal{B}\},$$

$$\widehat{\varepsilon}_j := \varepsilon_{j2} + \varepsilon_{j3}.$$

We obtained:
$$\frac{1}{n}\sum_{j=1}^{n} \varepsilon_{j1} R_{jj} = \frac{1}{2n}s_n'(z) + \frac{s_n(z)}{2nz}$$

and this yielded:
$$\left|\frac{1}{n}\sum_{j=1}^{n} \varepsilon_{j1} R_{jj}\right| \leq \frac{C}{nv}\operatorname{Im} s_n(z) + \frac{C}{n} + \frac{C|\Lambda_n|}{n|z|}. \qquad (30)$$

Then, we used:
$$\frac{|S_y(z)|}{|z|} \le \frac{1}{1-y}(y|S_y(z)|^2 + |z||S_y(z)| + 1\}) \le C.$$

Inequality (30) implied that for $z \in \mathcal{D}$:
$$|D_n^{(1)}| \le J_1 D_n^{\frac{q-1}{q}}, \tag{31}$$

where
$$J_1 = C\frac{a_n(z)}{nv}.$$

Further, we considered:
$$\widehat{T}_n^{(j)} = \mathbb{E}_j \widehat{T}_n, \quad T_n^{(j)} = \mathbb{E}_j T_n, \quad \Lambda_n^{(j)} = \mathbb{E}_j \Lambda_n.$$

We noted that by the Jensen inequality, for $q \ge 1$:
$$\mathbb{E}|\widehat{T}_n^{(j)}|^q \le \mathbb{E}|\widehat{T}_n|^q.$$

We represented $D_n^{(2)}$ in the form:
$$D_n^{(2)} = D_n^{(21)} + \cdots + D_n^{(24)}, \tag{32}$$

where
$$D_n^{(21)} := \frac{S_y(z)}{n} \sum_{j=1}^{n} \mathbb{E}\,\widehat{\varepsilon}_j h_\gamma(|\Lambda_n^{(j)}|, v) \varphi(\widehat{T}_n^{(j)}) \,\mathbb{I}\{\mathcal{B}\},$$

$$D_n^{(22)} := \frac{1}{n} \sum_{j=1}^{n} \mathbb{E}\,\widehat{\varepsilon}_j (R_{jj} - S_y(z)) h_\gamma(|\Lambda_n^{(j)}|, v) \varphi(\widehat{T}_n^{(j)}) \,\mathbb{I}\{\mathcal{B}\},$$

$$D_n^{(23)} := \frac{1}{n} \sum_{j=1}^{n} \mathbb{E}\,\widehat{\varepsilon}_j R_{jj}(h_\gamma(|\Lambda_n|, v) - h_\gamma(|\Lambda_n^{(j)}|, v)) \varphi(\widehat{T}_n^{(j)}) \,\mathbb{I}\{\mathcal{B}\},$$

$$D_n^{(24)} := \frac{1}{n} \sum_{j=1}^{n} \mathbb{E}\,\widehat{\varepsilon}_j R_{jj} h_\gamma(|\Lambda_n|, v) (\varphi(\widehat{T}_n) - \varphi(\widehat{T}_n^{(j)})) \,\mathbb{I}\{\mathcal{B}\}.$$

Since $\mathbb{E}_j \widehat{\varepsilon}_j = 0$, we found:
$$D_n^{(21)} = \frac{S_y(z)}{n} \sum_{j=1}^{n} \mathbb{E}\,\widehat{\varepsilon}_j h_\gamma(|\Lambda_n^{(j)}|, v) \varphi(\widehat{T}_n^{(j)}) \,\mathbb{I}\{\mathcal{B}^c\}.$$

From there, it was easy to obtain:
$$|D_n^{(21)}| \le Cn^{-c\log n}. \tag{33}$$

6.4.1. Estimation of $D_n^{(22)}$

Using the representation of R_{jj}, we could write:
$$D_n^{(22)} = \widetilde{D}_n^{(22)} + \widehat{D}_n^{(22)} + \breve{D}_n^{(22)},$$

where

$$\widetilde{D}_n^{(22)} := \frac{S_y(z)}{n} \sum_{j=1}^n \mathbb{E}\,\widehat{\varepsilon}_j^2 R_{jj} h_\gamma(|\Lambda_n^{(j)}|, v)\varphi(\widehat{T}_n^{(j)})\,\mathbb{I}\{\mathcal{B}\},$$

$$\widehat{D}_n^{(22)} := \frac{yS_y(z)}{n} \sum_{j=1}^n \mathbb{E}\,\widehat{\varepsilon}_j \Lambda_n R_{jj} h_\gamma(|\Lambda_n^{(j)}|, v)\varphi(\widehat{T}_n^{(j)})\,\mathbb{I}\{\mathcal{B}\},$$

$$\breve{D}_n^{(22)} := \frac{yS_y(z)}{n} \sum_{j=1}^n \mathbb{E}\,\widehat{\varepsilon}_j \varepsilon_{j1} R_{jj} h_\gamma(|\Lambda_n^{(j)}|, v)\varphi(\widehat{T}_n^{(j)})\,\mathbb{I}\{\mathcal{B}\}$$

By Hölder's inequality:

$$|\widehat{D}_n^{(22)}| \leq \frac{C|S_y(z)|}{n} \sum_{j=1}^n \mathbb{E}^{\frac{1}{q}}\left[\mathbb{E}_j\,|\widehat{\varepsilon}_j||\Lambda_n||R_{jj}|h_\gamma(|\Lambda_n^{(j)}|, v)\,\mathbb{I}\{\mathcal{B}\}\right]^q D_n^{\frac{q-1}{q}}. \tag{34}$$

Further:

$$\mathbb{E}_j\left[|\widehat{\varepsilon}_j||\Lambda_n||R_{jj}|h_\gamma(|\Lambda_n^{(j)}|, v)\,\mathbb{I}\{\mathcal{B}\}\right] \leq C|S_y(z)|\,\mathbb{E}_j\left[|\widehat{\varepsilon}_j||\Lambda_n|h_\gamma(|\Lambda_n^{(j)}|, v)\,\mathbb{I}\{\mathcal{B}\}\right].$$

We obtained:

$$|\Lambda_n|h_\gamma(|\Lambda_n^{(j)}|, v)\,\mathbb{I}\{\mathcal{B}\} \leq |\Lambda_n|h_\gamma(|\Lambda_n|, v)\,\mathbb{I}\{\mathcal{B}\}$$
$$+ |\Lambda_n||h_\gamma(|\Lambda_n|, v) - h_\gamma(|\Lambda_n^{(j)}|, v)|\,\mathbb{I}\{\mathcal{B}\}.$$

In the case $|b_n(z)| \geq \sqrt{|T_n|}$, we obtained:

$$|\Lambda_n| \leq \frac{|T_n|}{|b_n(z)|} \leq \sqrt{|T_n|}.$$

This implied that:

$$|\Lambda_n|h_\gamma(|\Lambda_n|, v)\,\mathbb{I}\{\mathcal{B}\}\mathbb{I}\{\sqrt{|T_n|} \leq |b_n(z)|\} \leq C\sqrt{|T_n|}h(|\Lambda_n|, v).$$

Furthermore, in the case $|b_n(z)| \leq \sqrt{|T_n|}$ and $|b(z)| \geq \Gamma_n$, we obtained:

$$|b_n(z)|\mathbb{I}\{\mathcal{Q}\} \geq (1 - 2\gamma)|b(z)|\mathbb{I}\{\mathcal{Q}\} > c|b(z)|\mathbb{I}\{\mathcal{Q}\}.$$

This implied that:

$$|\Lambda_n|\mathbb{I}\{\mathcal{Q}\} \leq C(\operatorname{Im} b(z) + \Gamma_n)\mathbb{I}\{\mathcal{Q}\} \leq C\sqrt{|T_n|}.$$

For $|b(z)| \leq \Gamma_n$, we could write:

$$\mathbb{E}_j\left[|\widehat{\varepsilon}_j||\Lambda_n||R_{jj}|h_\gamma(|\Lambda_n^{(j)}|, v)\,\mathbb{I}\{\mathcal{B}\}\right] \leq C|S_y(z)|\,\mathbb{E}_j\left[|\widehat{\varepsilon}_j||\Lambda_n|\mathbb{I}\{|\Lambda_n^{(j)}| \leq C\Gamma_n\},\mathbb{I}\{\mathcal{B}\}\right]$$
$$\leq C|S_y(z)|\Gamma_n\,\mathbb{E}_j\left[|\widehat{\varepsilon}_j|\mathbb{I}\{|\Lambda_n^{(j)}| \leq C\Gamma_n\},\mathbb{I}\{\mathcal{B}\}\right].$$

Using this, we concluded that:

$$\mathbb{E}_j\left[|\widehat{\varepsilon}_j||\Lambda_n|h_\gamma(|\Lambda_n^{(j)}|, v)\,\mathbb{I}\{\mathcal{B}\}\right] \leq \mathbb{E}_j^{\frac{1}{2}}|\widehat{\varepsilon}_j|^2\mathbb{I}\{|\Lambda_n^{(j)}| \leq Ca_n(z)\}\mathbb{I}\{\mathcal{B}\}$$
$$\times \left(\mathbb{I}\{|b(z)| \geq \Gamma_n\}\mathbb{E}_j^{\frac{1}{2}}|\widehat{T}_n| + \Gamma_n\mathbb{I}\{|b(z)| \leq \Gamma_n\}\mathbb{I}\{z \notin \mathcal{D}\}\right).$$

By applying Lemmas 2 and 3, we obtained:

$$\mathbb{E}_j\left[|\widehat{\varepsilon}_j||\Lambda_n|h_\gamma(|\Lambda_n^{(j)}|,v)\,\mathbb{I}\{\mathcal{B}\}\right] \leq C\beta_n^{\frac{1}{2}}(z)\Big(\mathbb{E}_j^{\frac{1}{2}}|\widehat{T}_n| + \Gamma_n\mathbb{I}\{|b(z)|\leq \Gamma_n\}\mathbb{I}\{z\notin\mathcal{D}\}\Big). \quad (35)$$

By combining inequalities (34) and (35), $|S_y(z)||A_0(z)|\leq C$ and Young's inequality, we obtained:

$$|\widehat{D}_n^{(22)}| \leq H_1 D_n^{\frac{2q-1}{2q}} + H_2 D_n^{\frac{q-1}{q}}, \quad (36)$$

where

$$H_1 = C|S_y(z)|^2\beta_n^{\frac{1}{2}}(z)\mathbb{I}\{|b(z)|\geq \Gamma_n\},$$
$$H_2 = |S_y(z)|^2\Gamma_n\beta_n^{\frac{1}{2}}(z)\mathbb{I}\{|b(z)|\leq \Gamma_n\}\mathbb{I}\{z\notin\mathcal{D}\}.$$

Hölder's inequality and (35) produced:

$$|\widetilde{D}_n^{(22)}| \leq C|S_y(z)|^2\beta_n(z)D_n^{\frac{q-1}{q}}. \quad (37)$$

6.4.2. Estimation of $D_n^{(23)}$

We noted that:

$$|h_\gamma(|\Lambda_n|,v) - h_\gamma(|\Lambda_n^{(j)}|,v)||R_{jj}|\,\mathbb{I}\{\mathcal{B}\}$$
$$\leq \frac{C}{a_n(z)}|\Lambda_n - \Lambda_n^{(j)}|\,\mathbb{I}\{\max\{|\Lambda_n|,|\Lambda_n^{(j)}|\}\leq 2\gamma a_n(z)\}\,\mathbb{I}\{\mathcal{B}\}.$$

Using Hölder's inequality and Cauchy's inequality, we obtained:

$$D_n^{(23)} \leq \frac{C|S_y(z)|}{a_n(z)}\frac{1}{n}\sum_{j=1}^n \mathbb{E}^{\frac{1}{q}}\Big\{\big[\mathbb{E}_j|\widehat{\varepsilon}_j|^2\mathbb{I}\{\mathcal{Q}\}\mathbb{I}(\mathcal{B})\big]^{\frac{q}{2}}\big[\mathbb{E}_j|\Lambda_n - \Lambda_n^{(j)}|^2\mathbb{I}\{\mathcal{Q}\}\mathbb{I}(\mathcal{B})\big]^{\frac{q}{2}}\Big\} D_n^{\frac{q-1}{q}}.$$

By applying Lemmas 2, 3 and 5, we obtained:

$$D_n^{(23)} \leq C|S_y(z)|a_n^{-1}(z)\beta_n^{\frac{1}{2}}(z)\frac{1}{n}\sum_{j=1}^n \mathbb{E}^{\frac{1}{q}}\big[\mathbb{E}_j|\Lambda_n - \Lambda_n^{(j)}|^2\mathbb{I}\{\mathcal{Q}\}\mathbb{I}(\mathcal{B})\big]^{\frac{q}{2}} D_n^{\frac{q-1}{q}}.$$

6.4.3. Estimation of $D_n^{(24)}$

Using Taylor's formula, we obtained:

$$D_n^{(24)} = \frac{1}{n}\sum_{j=1}^n \mathbb{E}\,\widehat{\varepsilon}_j R_{jj} h_\gamma(|\Lambda_n|,v)(\widehat{T}_n - \widehat{T}_n^{(j)})\varphi'(\widehat{T}_n^{(j)} + \tau(\widehat{T}_n - \widehat{T}_n^{(j)}))\,\mathbb{I}\{\mathcal{B}\},$$

where τ is uniformly distributed across the interval $[0,1]$ and the random variables are independent from each other. Since $\mathbb{I}\{\mathcal{B}\} = 1$ yields $|R_{jj}| \leq C|S_y(z)|$, we found that:

$$|D_n^{(24)}| \leq \frac{C|S_y(z)|}{n}\sum_{j=1}^n \mathbb{E}\,|\widehat{\varepsilon}_j|h_\gamma(|\Lambda_n|,v)|\widehat{T}_n - \widehat{T}_n^{(j)}||\varphi'(\widehat{T}_n^{(j)} + \tau(\widehat{T}_n - \widehat{T}_n^{(j)}))|\,\mathbb{I}\{\mathcal{B}\}.$$

Taking into account the inequality:

$$|\varphi'(\widehat{T}_n^{(j)} + \tau(\widehat{T}_n - \widehat{T}_n^{(j)}))| \leq Cq\Big[|\widehat{T}_n^{(j)}|^{q-2} + q^{q-2}|\widehat{T}_n - \widehat{T}_n^{(j)}|^{q-2}\Big],$$

we obtained:

$$|D_n^{(24)}| \leq \frac{Cq|S_y(z)|}{n} \sum_{j=1}^n \mathbb{E}\,|\hat{\varepsilon}_j| h_\gamma(|\Lambda_n|,v) |\widehat{T}_n - \widehat{T}_n^{(j)}| |\widehat{T}_n^{(j)}|^{q-2} \mathbb{I}\{\mathcal{B}\}$$
$$+ \frac{Cq^{q-1}|S_y(z)|}{n} \sum_{j=1}^n \mathbb{E}\,|\hat{\varepsilon}_j| h_\gamma(|\Lambda_n|,v) |\widehat{T}_n - \widehat{T}_n^{(j)}|^{q-1} \mathbb{I}\{\mathcal{B}\} =: \widehat{D}_n^{(24)} + \widetilde{D}_n^{(24)}.$$

By applying Hölder's inequality, we obtained:

$$\widehat{D}_n^{(24)} \leq \frac{Cq|S_y(z)|}{n} \sum_{j=1}^n \mathbb{E}^{\frac{2}{q}} \left[\mathbb{E}_j\{|\hat{\varepsilon}_j| h_\gamma(|\Lambda_n|,v) |\widehat{T}_n - \widehat{T}_n^{(j)}| \mathbb{I}\{\mathcal{B}\}\}^{\frac{q}{2}} \right] \mathbb{E}^{\frac{q-2}{q}} |\widehat{T}_n^{(j)}|^q.$$

Jensen's inequality produced:

$$\widehat{D}_n^{(24)} \leq \frac{Cq|S_y(z)|}{n} \sum_{j=1}^n \mathbb{E}^{\frac{2}{q}} \left[\mathbb{E}_j\{|\hat{\varepsilon}_j| h_\gamma(|\Lambda_n|,v) |\widehat{T}_n - \widehat{T}_n^{(j)}| \mathbb{I}\{\mathcal{B}\}\}^{\frac{q}{2}} \right] D_n^{\frac{q-2}{q}}.$$

To estimate $\widehat{D}_n^{(24)}$, we had to obtain the bounds for:

$$V_j^{\frac{q}{2}} := \mathbb{E}\left[\mathbb{E}_j\left\{|\hat{\varepsilon}_j| h_\gamma(|\Lambda_n|,v) |\widehat{T}_n - \widehat{T}_n^{(j)}| \mathbb{I}\{\mathcal{B}\}\right\}\right]^{\frac{q}{2}}.$$

Using Cauchy's inequality, we obtained:

$$V_j^{\frac{q}{2}} \leq \mathbb{E}(V_j^{(1)})^{\frac{q}{4}} (V_j^{(2)})^{\frac{q}{4}} \leq \mathbb{E}^{\frac{1}{2}}(V_j^{(1)})^{\frac{q}{2}} \mathbb{E}^{\frac{1}{2}}(V_j^{(2)})^{\frac{q}{2}} \tag{38}$$

where

$$V_j^{(1)} := \mathbb{E}_j |\hat{\varepsilon}_j|^2 \mathbb{I}\{\widehat{\mathcal{Q}}_{2\gamma}(v)\} \mathbb{I}\{\mathcal{B}\},$$
$$V_j^{(2)} := \mathbb{E}_j |\widehat{T}_n - \widehat{T}_n^{(j)}|^2 h_\gamma^2(|\Lambda_n|,v) \mathbb{I}\{\mathcal{B}\}.$$

6.4.4. Estimation of $V_j^{(1)}$

Lemma 2 produced:

$$\mathbb{E}_j |\varepsilon_{j2}|^2 \mathbb{I}\{\widehat{\mathcal{Q}}_{2\gamma}(v)\} \mathbb{I}\{\mathcal{B}\} \leq \frac{C|A_0(z)|^2}{np},$$

and, in turn, Lemma 3 produced:

$$\mathbb{E}_j |\varepsilon_{j3}|^2 \mathbb{I}\{\widehat{\mathcal{Q}}_{2\gamma}(v)\} \mathbb{I}\{\mathcal{B}\} \leq \frac{C}{nv} a_n(z).$$

By summing the obtained estimates, we arrived at the following inequality:

$$V_j^{(1)} \leq \frac{Ca_n(z)}{nv} + \frac{CA_0^2(z)}{np} = \beta_n(z). \tag{39}$$

6.4.5. Estimation of $V_j^{(2)}$

We considered $\widehat{T}_n - \widehat{T}_n^{(j)}$. Since $\widehat{T}_n = T_n h_\gamma(|\Lambda_n|,v)$ and $\widehat{T}_n^{(j)} = \mathbb{E}_j \widehat{T}_n$, we obtained:

$$\widehat{T}_n - \widehat{T}_n^{(j)} = (T_n - T_n^{(j)}) h_\gamma(|\Lambda_n|,v)$$
$$+ T_n^{(j)} \left([h_\gamma(|\Lambda_n|,v) - h_\gamma(|\Lambda_n^{(j)}|,v)] - \mathbb{E}_j T_n \left[h_\gamma(|\Lambda_n|,v) - h_\gamma(|\Lambda_n^{(j)}|,v) \right] \right).$$

Further, we noted that:
$$T_n = \Lambda_n b_n = \Lambda_n b(z) + y\Lambda_n^2,$$

$$T_n^{(j)} z = \Lambda_n^{(j)} b(z) + y\,\mathbb{E}_j\,\Lambda_n^2.$$

Then:
$$\begin{aligned}T_n - T_n^{(j)} &= (\Lambda_n - \Lambda_n^{(j)})(b(z) + 2y\Lambda_n^{(j)})\\ &\quad + y(\Lambda_n - \Lambda_n^{(j)})^2 - y\,\mathbb{E}_j(\Lambda_n - \Lambda_n^{(j)})^2.\end{aligned} \quad (40)$$

We obtained:
$$\begin{aligned}\widehat{T}_n - \widehat{T}_n^{(j)} &= (b(z) + 2y\Lambda_n^{(j)})\Big[(\Lambda_n - \Lambda_n^{(j)})h_\gamma(|\Lambda_n|,v)\Big]\\ &\quad + y\Big[(\Lambda_n - \Lambda_n^{(j)})^2 - \mathbb{E}_j(\Lambda_n - \Lambda_n^{(j)})^2\Big]h_\gamma(|\Lambda_n|,v)\\ &\quad + T_n^{(j)}\Big[(h_\gamma(|\Lambda_n|,v) - h_\gamma(|\Lambda_n^{(j)}|,v) - \mathbb{E}_j(h_\gamma(|\Lambda_n|,v) - h_\gamma(|\Lambda_n^{(j)}|,v))\Big].\end{aligned} \quad (41)$$

Then, we returned to the estimation of $V_j^{(2)}$. Equality (41) implied:

$$\begin{aligned}V_j^{(2)} &\le 4|b(z)|^2\,\mathbb{E}_j\,|\Lambda_n - \Lambda_n^{(j)}|^2 h_\gamma^4(|\Lambda_n|,v)\,\mathbb{I}\{\mathcal{B}\}\\ &\quad + 8y^2\,\mathbb{E}_j\,|\Lambda_n^{(j)}|^2|\Lambda_n - \Lambda_n^{(j)}|^2 h_\gamma^4(|\Lambda_n|,v)\,\mathbb{I}\{\mathcal{B}\}\\ &\quad + 4y^2\Big[\mathbb{E}_j\,|\Lambda_n - \Lambda_n^{(j)}|^4 h_\gamma^4(|\Lambda_n|,v)\Big]\mathbb{I}\{\mathcal{B}\}\\ &\quad + 4y^2\Big[\mathbb{E}_j(\Lambda_n - \Lambda_n^{(j)})^2 h_\gamma(|\Lambda_n|,v)\Big]^2\,\mathbb{E}_j\,h_\gamma^2(|\Lambda_n|,v)\,\mathbb{I}\{\mathcal{B}\}\\ &\quad + 4|T_n^{(j)}|^2\,\mathbb{E}_j\Big[h_\gamma(|\Lambda_n|,v) - h_\gamma(|\Lambda_n^{(j)}|,v)\Big]^2 h_\gamma^2(|\Lambda_n|,v)\,\mathbb{I}\{\mathcal{B}\}\\ &\quad + 4|T_n^{(j)}|^2\Big[\mathbb{E}_j\big(h_\gamma(|\Lambda_n|,v) - h_\gamma(|\Lambda_n^{(j)}|,v)\big)\Big]^2\,\mathbb{E}_j\,h_\gamma^2(|\Lambda_n|,v)\,\mathbb{I}\{\mathcal{B}\}.\end{aligned}$$

We could rewrite this as:
$$V_j^{(2)} \le A_1 + A_2 + A_3 + A_4,$$

$$A_1 = C|b(z)|^2\,\mathbb{E}_j\,|\Lambda_n - \Lambda_n^{(j)}|^2 h_\gamma^4(|\Lambda_n|,v)\mathbb{I}\{\mathcal{B}\},$$
$$A_2 = C\,\mathbb{E}_j\,|\Lambda_n^{(j)}|^2|\Lambda_n - \Lambda_n^{(j)}|^2 h_\gamma^4(|\Lambda_n|,v)\mathbb{I}\{\mathcal{B}\},$$
$$A_3 = C\,\mathbb{E}_j\,|\Lambda_n - \Lambda_n^{(j)}|^4 h_\gamma^2(|\Lambda_n|,v)\big(h_\gamma^2(|\Lambda_n|,v) + \mathbb{E}_j\,h_\gamma^2(|\Lambda_n|,v)\big)\mathbb{I}\{\mathcal{B}\},$$
$$A_4 = C|T_n^{(j)}|^2\,\mathbb{E}_j\Big|h_\gamma(|\Lambda_n|,v) - h_\gamma(|\Lambda_n^{(j)}|,v)\Big|^2\big(h_\gamma^2(|\Lambda_n|,v) + \mathbb{E}_j\,h_\gamma^2(|\Lambda_n|,v)\big)\mathbb{I}\{\mathcal{B}\}.$$

First, we found that:
$$A_1 \le C|b(z)|^2\,\mathbb{E}_j\,|\Lambda_n - \Lambda_n^{(j)}|^2 h_\gamma^4(|\Lambda_n|,v)\mathbb{I}\{\mathcal{B}\}.$$

and

$$A_2 \le Ca_n^2(z)\,\mathbb{E}_j\,|\Lambda_n - \Lambda_n^{(j)}|^2 h_\gamma^4(|\Lambda_n|,v)\mathbb{I}\{\mathcal{B}\}.$$

We noted that:
$$A_3 \le \frac{C}{n^2 v^2}\,\mathbb{E}_j\,|\Lambda_n - \Lambda_n^{(j)}|^2 h_\gamma^2(|\Lambda_n|,v)\mathbb{I}\{\mathcal{B}\}.$$

It was straightforward to see that:

$$|T_n^{(j)}|^2(h_\gamma^2(|\Lambda_n(z)|,v) + \mathbb{E}_j h_\gamma^2(|\Lambda_n(z)|,v)) \leq C(|b(z)|^2 a_n^2(z) + a_n^4(z) + \frac{1}{n^4 v^4}).$$

This bound implied that:

$$A_4 \leq C(|b(z)|^2 a_n^2(z) + a_n^4(z) + \frac{1}{n^4 v^4}) \mathbb{E}_j \left| h_\gamma(|\Lambda_n|,v) - h_\gamma(|\Lambda_n^{(j)}|,v) \right|^2 \mathbb{I}\{\mathcal{B}\}.$$

Further, since:

$$\left| h_\gamma(|\Lambda_n|,v) - h_\gamma(|\Lambda_n^{(j)}|,v) \right| \leq \frac{C}{\gamma a_n(z)} |\Lambda_n - \Lambda_n^{(j)}| \mathbb{I}\{\max\{|\Lambda_n|,|\Lambda_n^{(j)}|\} \leq (1+\gamma)a_n(z)\},$$

we could write:

$$A_4 \leq C(|b(z)|^2 + a_n^2(z)) \mathbb{E}_j |\Lambda_n - \Lambda_n^{(j)}|^2 \mathbb{I}\{\max\{|\Lambda_n|,|\Lambda_n^{(j)}|\} \leq Ca_n(z)\}\mathbb{I}\{\mathcal{B}\}.$$

By combining the estimates that were obtained for $A_1, \ldots, A_4$, we concluded that:

$$V_j^{(2)} \leq C(a_n^2(z) + |b(z)|^2) \mathbb{E}_j |\Lambda_n - \Lambda_n^{(j)}|^2 \mathbb{I}\{\max\{|\Lambda_n|,|\Lambda_n^{(j)}|\} \leq Ca_n(z)\}\mathbb{I}\{\mathcal{B}\}.$$

Inequalities (38) and (39) implied the bounds:

$$V_j^{\frac{q}{2}} \leq C^q \beta_n^{\frac{q}{4}}(z)(a_n^2(z) + |b(z)|^2)^{\frac{q}{4}}$$
$$\times \mathbb{E}\left(\mathbb{E}_j |\Lambda_n - \Lambda_n^{(j)}|^2 \mathbb{I}\{\max\{|\Lambda_n|,|\Lambda_n^{(j)}|\} \leq Ca_n(z)\}\mathbb{I}\{\mathcal{B}\}\right)^{\frac{q}{4}}. \quad (42)$$

We noted that:

$$\widehat{D}_n^{(24)} \leq Cq|S_y(z)|\left(\frac{1}{n}\sum_{j=1}^n V_j\right) D_n^{\frac{q-2}{q}}.$$

Then, Inequality (42) yielded:

$$\widehat{D}_n^{(24)} \leq Cq|S_y(z)|\beta_n^{\frac{1}{2}}(z)(a_n^2(z) + |b(z)|^2)^{\frac{1}{2}}$$
$$\times \frac{1}{n}\sum_{j=1}^n \mathbb{E}^{\frac{2}{q}}\left(\mathbb{E}_j |\Lambda_n - \Lambda_n^{(j)}|^2 \mathbb{I}\{\max\{|\Lambda_n|,|\Lambda_n^{(j)}|\} \leq Ca_n(z)\}\mathbb{I}\{\mathcal{B}\}\right)^{\frac{q}{4}} D_n^{\frac{q-2}{q}}.$$

We rewrote this as:

$$\widehat{D}_n^{(24)} \leq L_1 D_n^{\frac{q-2}{q}}, \quad (43)$$

where

$$L_1 = Cq|S_y(z)|\beta_n^{\frac{1}{2}}(z)(a_n^2(z) + |b(z)|^2)^{\frac{1}{2}}$$
$$\times \frac{1}{n}\sum_{j=1}^n \mathbb{E}^{\frac{2}{q}}\left(\mathbb{E}_j |\Lambda_n - \Lambda_n^{(j)}|^2 \mathbb{I}\{\max\{|\Lambda_n|,|\Lambda_n^{(j)}|\} \leq Ca_n(z)\}\mathbb{I}\{\mathcal{B}\}\right)^{\frac{q}{4}}.$$

6.4.6. Estimation of $\widetilde{D}_n^{(24)}$

We recalled that:

$$\widetilde{D}_n^{(24)} = \frac{C^q q^{q-1}}{n}|S_y(z)|\sum_{j=1}^n \mathbb{E}|\widehat{\varepsilon}_j||\widehat{T}_n - \widehat{T}_n^{(j)}|^{q-1} h_\gamma(|\Lambda_n|,v)\,\mathbb{I}\{\mathcal{B}\}.$$

Using Inequalities (40) and (41) and $a_n(z) \geq \frac{C}{nv}$, we obtained:

$$|\widehat{T}_n - \widehat{T}_n^{(j)}| \leq \left(|b(z)| + |a_n(z)| + \frac{C}{a_n(z)}|T_n^{(j)}|\right)|\Lambda_n - \Lambda_n^{(j)}|\mathbb{I}\{\max\{|\Lambda_n|, |\Lambda_n^{(j)}|\} \leq Ca_n(z)\}.$$

By applying:

$$|T_n^{(j)}|\mathbb{I}\{|\Lambda_n^{(j)}(z)| \leq Ca_n(z)\} \leq C(a_n^2(z) + |b(z)|a_n(z)),$$

we obtained:

$$|\widehat{T}_n - \widehat{T}_n^{(j)}| \leq C(|b(z)| + a_n(z))|\Lambda_n - \Lambda_n^{(j)}|\mathbb{I}\{\max\{|\Lambda_n|, |\Lambda_n^{(j)}|\} \leq Ca_n(z)\}.$$

The last inequality produced:

$$\widetilde{D}_n^{(24)} \leq \frac{C^q q^{q-1}(a_n(z) + |b(z)|)^{q-1}}{n}|S_y(z)|\sum_{j=1}^n \mathbb{E}^{\frac{1}{q}}\left(\mathbb{E}_j|\varepsilon_j|^2 h_\gamma(|\Lambda_n|, v)\mathbb{I}\{\mathcal{B}\}\right)^{\frac{q}{2}}$$

$$\times \mathbb{E}^{\frac{q-1}{q}}\left(\mathbb{E}_j|\Lambda_n - \Lambda_n^{(j)}|^{2q}\mathbb{I}\{\mathcal{B}\}\right)^{\frac{1}{2}}$$

$$\leq C^q q^q |S_y(z)|\beta_n^{\frac{1}{2}}(z)(a_n(z) + |b(z)|)^{q-1}\frac{1}{n}\sum_{j=1}^n \left(\mathbb{E}\left(\mathbb{E}_j|\Lambda_n - \Lambda_n^{(j)}|^{2q}\mathbb{I}\{\mathcal{Q}\}\mathbb{I}\{\mathcal{B}\}\right)\right)^{\frac{q-1}{2q}}.$$

We put:

$$R_n(q) := \frac{1}{n}\sum_{j=1}^n \mathbb{E}\left(\mathbb{E}_j|\Lambda_n - \Lambda_n^{(j)}|^2\mathbb{I}\{\mathcal{B}\}\mathbb{I}\{\mathcal{Q}\}\right)^{\frac{q}{2}}$$

and

$$U_n(q) := \frac{1}{n}\sum_{j=1}^n \mathbb{E}|\Lambda_n - \Lambda_n^{(j)}|^{2q}\mathbb{I}\{\mathcal{B}\}\mathbb{I}\{\mathcal{Q}\}.$$

By applying Lemma 5, we obtained:

$$R_n(q) \leq C^q \frac{|S_y(z)|^q a_n^{\frac{q}{2}}(z)}{(nv)^q}\left(|S_y(z)|^q |A_0(z)|^{\frac{q}{2}}\beta_n^{\frac{q}{2}}(z) + \frac{|A_0(z)|^{\frac{q}{2}}}{(np)^{\frac{q}{2}}} + \frac{1}{(nv)^{\frac{q}{2}}}\right).$$

Finally, using Lemma 6, we obtained:

$$U_n^{\frac{q-1}{2q}}(q) \leq C^q q^{q-1}\left(\frac{a_n(z)}{nv}\right)^{q-1}|S_y(z)|^{2(q-1)}\left(\frac{|A_0(z)|}{(np)^{2\varkappa}}\right)^{q-1}$$

$$+ C^q \left(\frac{a_n(z)}{nv}\right)^{q-1}|S_y(z)|^{2(q-1)}\beta_n^{\frac{q-1}{2}}(z)$$

$$+ C^{q-1}q^{\frac{q-1}{2}}\left(\frac{|S_y(z)|a_n(z)}{nv}\right)^{\frac{q-1}{2}}\left(\frac{|S_y(z)||A_0(z)|}{nvnp}\right)^{\frac{q-1}{2}}$$

$$+ C^{q-1}q^{q-1}\left(\frac{|S_y(z)|}{nv}\right)^{q-1}\left(\frac{|A_0(z)|}{(np)^{2\varkappa}}\right)^{(q-1)} + C^q q^{q-1}\left(\frac{|S_y(z)|}{nv}\right)^{q-1}\left(\frac{a_n(z)}{nv}\right)^{\frac{q-1}{2}}$$

$$+ C^{q-1}q^{\frac{3(q-1)}{2}}\left(\frac{a_n(z)|S_y(z)|}{nv}\right)^{\frac{q-1}{2}}\left(\frac{|A_0(z)||S_y(z)|}{(np)^{2\varkappa}}\right)^{\frac{q-1}{2}}\left(\frac{1}{nv}\right)^{q-1}$$

$$+ C^{q-1}q^{2(q-1)}\frac{|A_0(z)|^{q-1}|S_y(z)|^{q-1}}{(nv)^{q-1}(np)^{2\varkappa(q-1)}}.$$

Using:

$$|S_y(z)||A_0(z)| \leq 1 + 2\sqrt{y},$$

we could write:

$$U_n^{\frac{q-1}{2q}}(q) \leq C^{q-1}q^{q-1}\left(\frac{|S_y(z)|a_n(z)}{nv}\right)^{q-1}\frac{1}{(np)^{2\varkappa(q-1)}}$$

$$+ C^{q-1}\left(\frac{|S_y(z)|a_n(z)}{nv}\right)^{q-1}|S_y(z)|^{q-1}\beta_n^{\frac{q-1}{2}}(z)$$

$$+ C^{q-1}q^{\frac{q-1}{2}}\left(\frac{|S_y(z)|^{\frac{1}{2}}a_n^{\frac{1}{2}}(z)}{nv}\right)^{q-1}\left(\frac{1}{np}\right)^{\frac{q-1}{2}} + C^q q^{q-1}\left(\frac{1}{nv}\right)^{q-1}\left(\frac{1}{np}\right)^{2\varkappa(q-1)}$$

$$+ C^{q-1}q^{q-1}\frac{|S_y(z)|^{\frac{q-1}{2}}}{(nv)^{q-1}}\left(\frac{a_n(z)|S_y(z)|}{(nv)}\right)^{\frac{q-1}{2}}$$

$$+ C^q q^{\frac{3(q-1)}{2}}\frac{1}{n^{q-1}v^{q-1}}\left(\frac{|S_y(z)|a_n(z)}{nv}\right)^{\frac{q-1}{2}}\frac{1}{(np)^{(q-1)\varkappa}}$$

$$+ C^{q-1}q^{2(q-1)}\frac{1}{(nv)^{q-1}(np)^{2\varkappa(q-1)}}.$$

By combining Inequalities (29), (31), (32), (33), (36), (37) and (43) and applying Young's inequality, we obtained the proof. □

6.5. *The Proof of Theorem 4*

Proof. We considered the case $z \in \mathcal{D}$, where

$$\mathcal{D} = \{z = u + iv : (1 - \sqrt{y} - v)_+ \leq |u| \leq 1 + \sqrt{y} + v, V \geq v \geq v_0 = n^{-1}\log^4 n\}.$$

For z, we obtained:

$$2V + (1 + \sqrt{y}) \geq |z| \geq \frac{1}{\sqrt{2}}(1 - \sqrt{y}).$$

This implied that the constant C_1 exists, depending on V, y, such that:

$$|b(z)| \leq C_1.$$

First, we considered the case $|b(z)| \geq \Gamma_n$. Without a loss of generality, we assumed that $C_0 \geq C_1$, where C_0 is the constant in the definition of $a_n(z)$. This meant that $a_n(z) = \operatorname{Im} b(z) + C_0\Gamma_n$. Furthermore:

$$|b_n(z)|\mathbb{I}\{\mathcal{Q}\} \geq (1 - 2\gamma)|b(z)|\mathbb{I}\{\mathcal{Q}\}$$

and

$$|\Lambda_n(z)|\mathbb{I}\{\mathcal{Q}\} \leq C\frac{|T_n|}{|b(z)|}.$$

Using Theorem 3, we obtained:

$$\mathbb{E}|\Lambda_n(z)|^q\mathbb{I}\{\mathcal{Q}\} \leq C^q\frac{q^q(F_1 + \cdots + F_6)}{|b(z)|^q}.$$

We let:

$$d(z) = \frac{\operatorname{Im} b(z) \vee \frac{1}{nv}}{|b(z)|}.$$

The analysis of $F_i/|b(z)|^q$ for $i = 1, \ldots, 6$.

- The bound of $F_1/|b(z)|^q$. By the definition of $a_n(z)$ and F_1, we obtained:

$$F_1/|b(z)|^q \leq C^q \left(\frac{d(z)}{nv} + \frac{1}{np|b(z)|} \right)^q.$$

- The bound of $F_2/|b(z)|^q$. By the definition of F_2, we obtained:

$$F_2/|b(z)|^q \leq C^q |S_y(z)|^{2q} \left(\frac{d(z)}{(nv)} + \frac{1}{(np|b(z)|)} \right)^q.$$

For this, we used $|S_y(z)||A_0(z)| = |1 + zS_y(z)| \leq C$.

- The bound for $F_3/|b(z)|^q$. By the definition of F_3, we obtained:

$$F_3/|b(z)|^q \leq \left(\frac{|S_y(z)|^{\frac{3q}{2}} a_n^{\frac{q}{2}}(z)}{(nv)^q} + \frac{|S_y(z)|^{\frac{q}{2}}}{(nv)^{\frac{q}{2}}(np)^{\frac{q}{2}}} + \frac{|S_y(z)|^q}{(nv)^q} \right) \left(\frac{1}{(np)|b(z)|} + \frac{d(z)}{nv} \right)^q.$$

- The bound of $F_4/|b(z)|^q$. Simple calculations showed that:

$$F_4(z)/|b(z)|^q \leq \left(\frac{|S_y(z)|^{\frac{3q}{2}}}{(nv)^q a_n^{\frac{q}{2}}(z)} + \frac{|S_y(z)|^{\frac{q}{2}}}{a_n^{\frac{q}{2}}(z)(nv)^{\frac{q}{2}}} + \frac{|S_y(z)|^q}{(a_n nv)^{\frac{q}{2}}} \right) \left(\frac{1}{(np)|b(z)|} + \frac{d(z)}{nv} \right)^q.$$

- The bound of $F_5/|b(z)|^q$. We noted that:

$$(a_n(z) + |b(z)|)/|b(z)| \leq C.$$

From there and from the definition of F_5, it followed that:

$$F_5(z)/|b(z)|^q \leq C^q q^{\frac{q}{2}} \left(\left(\frac{d(z)}{nv} + \frac{1}{(np)|b(z)|} \right)^{\frac{3q}{4}} \left(\frac{1}{nv} \right)^{\frac{q}{4}} \right.$$

$$\left. + \left(\frac{d(z)}{nv} + \frac{1}{(np)|b(z)|} \right)^{\frac{q}{2}} \left(\frac{|S_y(z)|}{nv} \right)^{\frac{q}{2}} \right).$$

- The bound of $F_6/|b(z)|^q$. Simple calculations showed that:

$$F_6/|b(z)|^q \le \frac{C^q q^{2(q-1)}}{(np)^{2\varkappa(q-1)}} \frac{\beta_n^{\frac{1}{2}}(z)}{|b(z)|} \left(\frac{d(z)}{nv} + \frac{1}{np|b(z)|}\right)^{q-1}$$
$$+ C^q q^{2(q-1)} \beta_n^{\frac{1}{2}}(z)|b(z)|^{-1} \left(\frac{d(z)}{nv} + \frac{1}{np|b(z)|}\right)^{\frac{3(q-1)}{2}}$$
$$+ \frac{C^q q^{\frac{5(q-1)}{2}}}{(np)^{\frac{q-1}{2}}} \beta_n^{\frac{1}{2}}(z)|b(z)|^{-1} \left(\frac{d(z)}{nv} + \frac{1}{np|b(z)|}\right)^{\frac{(q-1)}{2}} \frac{1}{(nv)^{\frac{q-1}{2}}}$$
$$+ \frac{C^q q^{3q}}{(np)^{2\varkappa(q-1)}} \frac{1}{(nv)^{q-1}}$$
$$+ q^q \frac{|S_y(z)|^{\frac{q-1}{2}}}{(nv)^{q-1}} \frac{\beta_n^{\frac{1}{2}}(z)}{|b(z)|} \left(\frac{d(z)}{nv} + \frac{1}{np|b(z)|}\right)^{\frac{q-1}{2}}$$
$$+ \frac{C^q q^{3q}}{(nv)^{\frac{q-1}{2}}} \frac{\beta_n^{\frac{1}{2}}(z)}{|b(z)|} \left(\frac{d(z)}{nv} + \frac{1}{np|b(z)|}\right)^{\frac{q-1}{2}} \frac{1}{(np)^{\varkappa(q-1)}}$$
$$+ \frac{C^q q^{4(q-1)}}{(np)^{2\varkappa(q-1)}} \frac{1}{(nv)^{q-1}} \frac{\beta_n^{\frac{1}{2}}(z)}{|b(z)|}.$$

We defined:
$$d_n(z) := \frac{d(z)}{nv} + \frac{1}{(np)|b(z)|}.$$

By combining all of these estimations and using:
$$d_n(z)|b(z)| \ge \frac{1}{np},$$

we obtained:
$$\mathbb{I}\{\Gamma_n \le |b(z)|\} \mathbb{E} |\Lambda_n|^q \mathbb{I}\{\mathcal{Q}\} \le C^q q^q (q^{\frac{q}{2}}(nv)^{-\frac{q}{2}} d_n^{\frac{q}{2}}(z) + d_n^q(z)).$$

For $z \in \mathcal{D}$ (such that $\Gamma_n \le |b(z)|$), we could write:
$$\mathbb{E} |\Lambda_n(z)|^q \mathbb{I}\{\mathcal{Q}\} \le C^q q^q (q^{\frac{q}{2}}(nv)^{-\frac{q}{2}} d_n^{\frac{q}{2}}(z) + d_n^q(z)) \le \delta^q \Gamma_n^q.$$

Then, we considered $|b(z)| \le \Gamma_n$. In this case, we used the inequality:
$$|\Lambda_n| \le \sqrt{|T_n|}.$$

In what follows, we assumed that $q \sim \log n$.
The bound of $\mathbb{E}|T_n|^q$ for $|b(z)| \le \Gamma_n$.
- By the definition of $a_n(z)$, we obtained:
$$\frac{a_n(z)}{nv} = \frac{\Gamma_n}{nv}.$$

We could obtain from this that, for sufficiently small $\delta > 0$ values:
$$F_1 \le C^q \Gamma_n^q / (nv)^q \le \delta^q \Gamma_n^{2q}.$$

- We noted that $\Gamma_n \ge \operatorname{Im} b(z) \ge \operatorname{Im} A_0(z)$. This immediately implied that:
$$C^q q^q F_2 \le \delta^q \Gamma_n^{2q}.$$

- We noted that for $\operatorname{Im} b(z) \leq |b(z)| \leq \Gamma_n$, we obtained:
$$\min\{\frac{1}{np|b(z)|}, \frac{1}{\sqrt{np}}\} = \frac{1}{\sqrt{np}}$$
and
$$\frac{1}{np} \leq \delta\Gamma_n^2/\log^2 n.$$

From there, it followed that:
$$C^q q^q \leq \delta^q \Gamma_n^{2q}.$$

- Simple calculations showed that:
$$C^q q^q F_4 \leq \delta^q \Gamma_n^{2q}.$$

- Simple calculation showed that:
$$C^q q^q F_5 \leq C^q \Gamma_n^{4q} \leq \delta^q \Gamma_n^{2q}.$$

- It was straightforward to check that:
$$C^q q^q F_6 \leq C^q \Gamma_n^{3q} \leq \delta^q \Gamma_n^{2q}.$$

By applying the Markov inequality for $\Gamma_n \leq \operatorname{Im} b(z) \leq C$, we obtained:
$$\Pr\{|\Lambda_n| > Kd_n(z)\log n; \mathcal{Q}\} \leq Cn^{-q}.$$

On the other hand, when $\operatorname{Im} b(z) \leq \Gamma_n$, we used the inequality:
$$|\Lambda_n| \leq C|T_n|^{\frac{1}{2}}.$$

By applying the Markov inequality, we obtained:
$$\Pr\{|\Lambda_n(z)| \leq 2\delta\Gamma_n; \mathcal{Q}\} \leq Cn^{-Q}.$$

This implied that:
$$\Pr\{|\Lambda_n(v)| \leq \frac{1}{2}\Gamma_n; \mathcal{Q}\} \leq Cn^{-Q}.$$

We noted that $\mathcal{Q} = \mathcal{Q}(v)$ for $V \geq v \geq v_0$ and that for $V \geq v \geq v_0$:
$$a_n(z) \geq \frac{C\log^2 n}{n}.$$

On the other hand:
$$\sup_u |\Lambda_n(v) - \Lambda_n(v')| \leq \frac{|v-v'|}{v_0^2} \leq n^2|v-v'| = n^2\Delta v.$$

We chose Δv, such that:
$$\sup_u |\Lambda_n(v) - \Lambda_n(v')| \leq \frac{1}{2}\Gamma_n.$$

It was enough to put $\Delta v := n^{-4}$. We let $K := \left[\frac{V-v_0}{\Delta v}\right]$. For $\nu = 0, \ldots, K-1$, we defined:
$$v_\nu = v_0 + \nu\Delta v,$$

and $v_K = V$. We noted that $v_0 < v_1 < \cdots > v_K = V$ and that:

$$\sup_u |\Lambda_n(v_{\nu+1}) - \Lambda_n(v_\nu)| \leq \frac{1}{2}\Gamma_n.$$

We started with $v_K = V$. We noted that:

$$\Pr\{\mathcal{Q}(V)\} = 1.$$

This implied that:

$$\Pr\{|\Lambda_n(v_K)| \leq \frac{1}{2}\Gamma_m\} \leq Cn^{-Q}.$$

From there, it followed that:

$$\Pr\{\mathcal{Q}(v_{K-1})\} \leq Cn^{-Q}.$$

By repeating this procedure and using the union bound, we obtained the proof. Thus, Theorem 4 was proven. □

7. Auxiliary Lemmas

Lemma 1. *Under the conditions of Theorem, for $j \in \mathbb{J}^c$ and $l \in \mathbb{K}^c$, we have:*

$$\max\{|\varepsilon_{j1}^{(\mathbb{J},\mathbb{K})}|, |\varepsilon_{l+n,1}^{(\mathbb{J},\mathbb{K})}|\} \leq \frac{C}{nv}.$$

Proof. For simplicity, we only considered the case $\mathbb{J} = \varnothing$ and $\mathbb{K} = \varnothing$. We noted that:

$$\varepsilon_{j1} = \frac{1}{2m}\left(\left(\operatorname{Tr}\mathbf{R} - \frac{m-n}{z}\right) - \left(\operatorname{Tr}\mathbf{R}^{(j)} - \frac{m-n-1}{z}\right)\right)$$
$$= \frac{1}{2m}\left(\operatorname{Tr}\mathbf{R} - \operatorname{Tr}\mathbf{R}^{(j)}\right) - \frac{1}{2mz}.$$

By applying Schur's formula, we obtained:

$$|\varepsilon_{j1}| \leq \frac{1}{nv}.$$

The second inequality was proven in a similar way. □

Lemma 2. *Under the conditions of Theorem 5, for all $j \in \mathbb{J}^c$, the following inequalities are valid:*

$$\mathbb{E}_j |\varepsilon_{j2}^{(\mathbb{J},\mathbb{K})}|^2 \leq \frac{\mu_4}{np}\frac{1}{n}\sum_{l=1}^m |R_{l+n,l+n}^{(\mathbb{J}\cup\{j\},\mathbb{K})}|^2$$

and

$$\mathbb{E}_{l+n} |\varepsilon_{l+n,2}^{(\mathbb{J},\mathbb{K})}|^2 \leq \frac{\mu_4}{np}\frac{1}{n}\sum_{j=1}^n |R_{jj}^{(\mathbb{J},\mathbb{K}\cup\{l\})}|^2.$$

In addition, for $q > 2$, we have:

$$\mathbb{E}_j |\varepsilon_{j2}^{(\mathbb{J},\mathbb{K})}|^q \leq C^q\left(\frac{q^{\frac{q}{2}}}{(np)^{\frac{q}{2}}}\left(\frac{1}{n}\sum_{l=1}^m |R_{l+n,l+n}^{(\mathbb{J}\cup\{j\},\mathbb{K})}|^2\right)^{\frac{q}{2}} + \frac{q^q}{(np)^{2q\varkappa+1}}\frac{1}{n}\sum_{l=1}^m |R_{l+n,l+n}^{(\mathbb{J}\cup\{j\},\mathbb{K})}|^q\right)$$

and for $l \in \mathbb{K}^c$, we have:

$$\mathbb{E}_{l+n} |\varepsilon_{l+n,2}^{(\mathbb{J},\mathbb{K})}|^q \leq C^q\left(\frac{q^{\frac{q}{2}}}{(np)^{\frac{q}{2}}}\left(\frac{1}{n}\sum_{j=1}^n |R_{jj}^{(\mathbb{J},\mathbb{K}\cup\{l\})}|^2\right)^{\frac{q}{2}} + \frac{q^q}{(np)^{2q\varkappa+1}}\frac{1}{n}\sum_{j=1}^n |R_{jj}^{(\mathbb{J},\mathbb{K}\cup\{l\})}|^q\right).$$

Proof. For simplicity, we only considered the case $\mathbb{J} = \varnothing$ and $\mathbb{K} = \varnothing$. The first two inequalities were obvious. We only considered $q > 2$. By applying Rosenthal's inequality, for $q > 2$, we obtained:

$$\mathbb{E}_j |\varepsilon_{j2}|^q = \frac{1}{(mp)^q} \mathbb{E}_j \left| \sum_{l=1}^m (X_{jl}^2 \tilde{\zeta}_{jl} - p) R_{l+n,l+n}^{(j)} \right|^q$$

$$\leq \frac{C^q}{(mp)^q} \left[q^{\frac{q}{2}} \left(\sum_{l=1}^m \mathbb{E}_j |X_{jl}^2 \tilde{\zeta}_{jl} - p|^2 |R_{l+n,l+n}^{(j)}|^2 \right)^{\frac{q}{2}} \right.$$

$$\left. + q^q \sum_{l=1}^m \mathbb{E}_j |X_{jl}^2 \tilde{\zeta}_{jl} - p|^q |R_{l+n,l+n}^{(j)}|^q \right]$$

$$\leq \frac{C^q}{(mp)^{\frac{q}{2}}} \left[(q\mu_4)^{\frac{q}{2}} \left(\frac{1}{m} \sum_{l=1}^m |R_{l+n,l+n}^{(j)}|^2 \right)^{\frac{q}{2}} \right.$$

$$\left. + \frac{mq^q}{(mp)^{\frac{q}{2}}} \tilde{\mu}_{2q} \frac{1}{m} \sum_{l=1}^m |R_{l+n,l+n}^{(j)}|^q \right]. \tag{44}$$

We recalled that:

$$\tilde{\mu}_r = \mathbb{E} |X_{jk} \tilde{\zeta}_{jk}|^r$$

and under the conditions of the theorem:

$$\tilde{\mu}_{2q} \leq C^q p(np)^{q-2q\varkappa-2} \mu_{4+\delta}.$$

By substituting the last inequality into Inequality (44), we obtained:

$$\mathbb{E}_j |\varepsilon_{j2}|^q \leq C^q \left[\frac{q^{\frac{q}{2}}}{(mp)^{\frac{q}{2}}} \left(\frac{1}{m} \sum_{l=1}^m |R_{l+n,l+n}^{(j)}|^2 \right)^{\frac{q}{2}} + \frac{q^q}{(mp)^{2q\varkappa+1}} \frac{1}{m} \sum_{l=1}^m |R_{l+n,l+n}^{(j)}|^q \right].$$

The second inequality could be proven similarly. □

Lemma 3. *Under the conditions of the theorem, for all $j \in \mathbb{T}_\mathbb{J}$, the following inequalities are valid:*

$$\mathbb{E}_j |\varepsilon_{j3}^{(\mathbb{J},\mathbb{K})}|^2 \leq \frac{C \sum_{l,k=1}^m |R_{l+n,k+n}^{(\mathbb{J} \cup \{j\},\mathbb{K})}(z)|^2}{n^2}$$

and

$$\mathbb{E}_{l+n} |\varepsilon_{l+n,3}^{(\mathbb{J},\mathbb{K})}|^2 \leq \frac{C \sum_{i,k=1}^n |R_{i,k}^{(\mathbb{J},\mathbb{K} \cup \{l\})}(z)|^2}{n^2}.$$

In addition, for $q > 2$, we have:

$$\mathbb{E}_j |\varepsilon_{j3}^{(\mathbb{J},\mathbb{K})}|^q \leq C^q \left(q^q (nv)^{-\frac{q}{2}} \left(\operatorname{Im} s_n^{(j)}(z) - \operatorname{Im} \left\{ \frac{1-y}{z} \right\} \right)^{\frac{q}{2}} \right.$$

$$+ q^{\frac{3q}{2}} (nv)^{-\frac{q}{2}} (np)^{-q\varkappa-1} \frac{1}{n} \sum_{l=1}^m (\operatorname{Im} R_{l+n,l+n}^{(\mathbb{J} \cup \{j\},\mathbb{K})})^{\frac{q}{2}}$$

$$\left. + q^{2q} (np)^{-2q\varkappa} \frac{1}{n^2} \sum_{l=1}^m \sum_{k=1}^m |R_{l+n,k+n}^{(\mathbb{J} \cup \{j\},\mathbb{K})}|^q \right)$$

and for $l \in \mathbb{T}^1_{\mathbb{K}}$, we have:

$$\mathbb{E}_{l+n}|\varepsilon^{(\mathbb{J},\mathbb{K})}_{l+n,3}|^q \leq C^q \Big(q^q(nv)^{-\frac{q}{2}}\big(\operatorname{Im} s_n^{(l)}(z)\big)^{\frac{q}{2}}$$
$$+ q^{\frac{3q}{2}}(nv)^{-\frac{q}{2}}(np)^{-q\varkappa - 1}\frac{1}{n}\sum_{j=1}^m (\operatorname{Im} R_{jj}^{(\mathbb{J},\mathbb{K}\cup\{l+n\})})^q$$
$$+ q^{2q}(np)^{-2q\varkappa} n^{-2}\sum_{j=1}^n\sum_{k=1}^n |R_{kj}^{(\mathbb{J},\mathbb{K}\cup\{l+n\})}|^q\Big).$$

Proof. It sufficed to apply the inequality from Corollary 1 of [16]. □

We recalled the notation:

$$\beta_n(z) = \frac{a_n(z)}{nv} + \frac{|A_0(z)|^2}{np}.$$

Lemma 4. *Under the conditions of the theorem, the following bounds are valid:*

$$\mathbb{E}_j|R_{jj} - \mathbb{E}_j R_{jj}|^2 \mathbb{I}\{\mathcal{Q}\}\mathbb{I}\{\mathcal{B}\} \leq C|S_y(z)|^4 \beta_n(z) \tag{45}$$

and

$$\mathbb{E}_j|R_{jj} - \mathbb{E}_j R_{jj}|^q \mathbb{I}\{\mathcal{Q}\}\mathbb{I}\{\mathcal{B}\} \leq C^q |S_y(z)|^{2q} q^q \Big(q^q \Big(\frac{|A_0(z)|}{(np)^{2\varkappa}}\Big)^q + \beta_n^{\frac{q}{2}}(z)\Big). \tag{46}$$

Proof. We considered the equality:

$$R_{jj} = -\frac{1}{z - \frac{1-y}{z} + y s_n^{(j)}(z)}\Big(1 + \widehat{\varepsilon}_j R_{jj}\Big).$$

It implied that:

$$R_{jj} - \mathbb{E}_j R_{jj} = -\frac{1}{z - \frac{1-y}{z} + y s_n^{(j)}(z)}\Big(\widehat{\varepsilon}_j R_{jj} - \mathbb{E}_j \widehat{\varepsilon}_j R_{jj}\Big). \tag{47}$$

Further, we noted that for a sufficiently small γ value, a constant H existed, such that:

$$\Big|\frac{1}{z - \frac{1-y}{z} + y s_n^{(j)}(z)}\Big|\mathbb{I}\{\mathcal{Q}\} \leq H|S_y(z)|\mathbb{I}\{\mathcal{Q}\}.$$

Hence:

$$\mathbb{E}_j|R_{jj} - \mathbb{E}_j R_{jj}|^2 \mathbb{I}\{\mathcal{Q}\}\mathbb{I}\{\mathcal{B}\} \leq H^2|S_y(z)|^2\Big(\mathbb{E}_j|\widehat{\varepsilon}_j|^2|R_{jj}|^2\mathbb{I}\{\mathcal{Q}\}\mathbb{I}\{\mathcal{B}\}$$
$$+ \mathbb{E}_j \mathbb{I}\{\mathcal{Q}\}\mathbb{I}\{\mathcal{B}\} \mathbb{E}_j|\widehat{\varepsilon}_j|^2|R_{jj}|^2\Big).$$

It was easy to see that:

$$\mathbb{E}_j|\widehat{\varepsilon}_j|^2|R_{jj}|^2\mathbb{I}\{\mathcal{Q}\}\mathbb{I}\{\mathcal{B}\} \leq C|S_y(z)|^2 \mathbb{E}_j|\widehat{\varepsilon}_j|^2\mathbb{I}\{\mathcal{Q}\}\mathbb{I}\{\mathcal{B}\}$$
$$\leq C|S_y(z)|^2\Big(\frac{a_n(z)}{nv} + \frac{|A_0(z)|^2}{np}\Big).$$

We introduced the events:

$$\mathcal{Q}^{(j)} = \Big\{|\Lambda_n^{(j)}| \leq 2\gamma a_n(z) + \frac{1}{nv}\Big\}.$$

It was obvious that:
$$\mathbb{I}\{\mathcal{Q}\} \leq \mathbb{I}\{\mathcal{Q}\}\mathbb{I}\{\mathcal{Q}^{(j)}\}.$$

Consequently:
$$\mathbb{E}_j \mathbb{I}\{\mathcal{Q}\} \mathbb{I}\{\mathcal{B}\} \mathbb{E}_j |\widehat{\varepsilon}_j|^2 |R_{jj}|^2 \leq \mathbb{E}_j \mathbb{I}\{\mathcal{Q}\} \mathbb{I}\{\mathcal{B}\} \mathbb{E}_j |\widehat{\varepsilon}_j|^2 |R_{jj}|^2 \mathbb{I}\{\mathcal{Q}^{(j)}\}.$$

Further, we considered $\widetilde{\mathcal{Q}} = \{|\Lambda_n| \leq 2\gamma a_n(z)\}$. We obtained:
$$\mathbb{I}\{\mathcal{Q}^{(j)}\} \leq \mathbb{I}\{\widetilde{\mathcal{Q}}\}.$$

Then, it followed that:
$$\mathbb{E}_j \mathbb{I}\{\mathcal{Q}\} \mathbb{I}\{\mathcal{B}\} \mathbb{E}_j |\widehat{\varepsilon}_j|^2 |R_{jj}|^2 \leq \mathbb{E}_j \mathbb{I}\{\mathcal{Q}\} \mathbb{I}\{\mathcal{B}\} \mathbb{E}_j |\widehat{\varepsilon}_j|^2 |R_{jj}|^2 \mathbb{I}\{\widetilde{\mathcal{Q}}\}.$$

Next, the following inequality held:
$$\mathbb{E}_j |\widehat{\varepsilon}_j|^2 |R_{jj}|^2 \mathbb{I}\{\widetilde{\mathcal{Q}}\} \leq \mathbb{E}_j |\widehat{\varepsilon}_j|^2 |R_{jj}|^2 \mathbb{I}\{\widetilde{\mathcal{Q}}\}\mathbb{I}\{\widetilde{\mathcal{B}}\} + \mathbb{E}_j |\widehat{\varepsilon}_j|^2 |R_{jj}|^2 \mathbb{I}\{\widetilde{\mathcal{Q}}\}\mathbb{I}\{\widetilde{\mathcal{B}^c}\}. \tag{48}$$

Under the condition C_0 and the inequality $|R_{jj}| \leq v_0^{-1}$, we obtained the bounds:
$$\mathbb{E}_j |\widehat{\varepsilon}_j|^2 |R_{jj}|^2 \mathbb{I}\{\widetilde{\mathcal{Q}}\}\mathbb{I}\{\widetilde{\mathcal{B}^c}\} \leq Cn^{-c\log n}.$$

By applying Lemmas 2 and 3, for the first term on the right side of (48), we obtained:
$$\mathbb{E}_j |\widehat{\varepsilon}_j|^2 |R_{jj}|^2 \mathbb{I}\{\widetilde{\mathcal{Q}}\}\mathbb{I}\{\widetilde{\mathcal{B}}\} \leq C|S_y(z)|^2 \left(\frac{a_n(z)}{nv} + \frac{|A_0(z)|^2}{np}\right).$$

This completed the proof of Inequality (45).
Furthermore, by using representation (47), we obtained:
$$\mathbb{E}_j |R_{jj} - \mathbb{E}_j R_{jj}|^q \mathbb{I}\{\mathcal{Q}\} \mathbb{I}\{\mathcal{B}\} \leq C^q |S_y(z)|^q \mathbb{E} |\widehat{\varepsilon}_j|^q |R_{jj}|^q \mathbb{I}\{\mathcal{Q}\}\mathbb{I}\mathcal{B}\}$$
$$\leq C^q |S_y(z)|^{2q} \mathbb{E}_j |\widehat{\varepsilon}_j|^q \mathbb{I}\{\mathcal{Q}\}\mathbb{I}\mathcal{B}\}.$$

By applying Lemmas 2 and 3, we obtained:
$$\mathbb{E}_j |R_{jj} - \mathbb{E}_j R_{jj}|^q \mathbb{I}\{\mathcal{Q}\} \mathbb{I}\{\mathcal{B}\} \leq C^q |S_y(z)|^{2q} \left(\left(\frac{q|A_0(z)|^2}{np}\right)^{\frac{q}{2}} + \left(\frac{q|A_0(z)|}{(np)^{2\varkappa}}\right)^q \right.$$
$$\left. + \left(\frac{q^2 a_n(z)}{nv}\right)^{\frac{q}{2}} + \left(\frac{q^3 |A_0(z)|}{nv(np)^{2\varkappa}}\right)^{\frac{q}{2}} + \left(\frac{q^2 |A_0(z)|}{(np)^{2\varkappa}}\right)^q \right).$$

By applying Young's inequality, we obtained the required proof. Thus, the lemma was proven. □

Lemma 5. *Under the conditions of the theorem, we have:*
$$\mathbb{E}_j |\Lambda_n - \Lambda_n^{(j)}|^2 \mathbb{I}\{\mathcal{Q}\} \mathbb{I}\{\mathcal{B}\} \leq C \frac{|S_y(z)|^4 |A_0(z)| a_n(z)}{(nv)^2} \beta_n + C \frac{|S_y(z)|^2 |A_0(z)| a_n(z)}{(nv)^2 np}$$
$$+ C \frac{|S_y(z)|^2 a_n(z)}{(nv)^3}.$$

Proof. We set $\widehat{\Lambda}_n^{(j)} = s_n^{(j)}(z) - S_y(z)$. Using Schur's complement formula:
$$\Lambda_n - \widehat{\Lambda}_n^{(j)} = \frac{1}{2n}\left(1 + \frac{1}{np}\sum_{l,k=1}^m X_{jl}X_{jk}\xi_{jl}\xi_{jk}[R^{(j)}]^2_{k+n,l+n}\right)R_{jj}.$$

Since $\widehat{\Lambda}_n^{(j)}$ was measurable with respect to $\mathfrak{M}^{(j)}$, we could write:

$$\Lambda_n - \Lambda_n^{(j)} = (\Lambda_n - \widehat{\Lambda}_n^{(j)}) - \mathbb{E}_j\{\Lambda_n - \widehat{\Lambda}_n^{(j)}\}.$$

We introduced the notation:

$$\eta_{j1} = \frac{1}{np} \sum_{l=1}^{m} (X_{jl}^2 \xi_{jl} - p)[\mathbf{R}^{(j)^2}]_{l+n,l+n},$$

$$\eta_{j2} = \frac{1}{np} \sum_{l=1}^{m} \sum_{k=1, k \neq l}^{m} X_{jl} X_{jk} \xi_{jl} \xi_{jk} [\mathbf{R}^{(j)^2}]_{k+n,l+n}.$$

In this notation:

$$\Lambda_n - \Lambda_n^{(j)} = \frac{1}{n}\left(1 + \frac{1}{n}\sum_{l=1}^{m}[\mathbf{R}^{(j)^2}]_{l+n,l+n}\right)(R_{jj} - \mathbb{E}_j R_{jj})$$
$$+ \frac{1}{n}(\eta_{j1} + \eta_{j2})R_{jj} - \frac{1}{n}\mathbb{E}_j(\eta_{j1} + \eta_{j2})R_{jj}.$$

We noted that:

$$\mathbb{E}_j |\eta_{j1}|^2 \mathbb{I}\{\mathcal{Q}\}\mathbb{I}\{\mathcal{B}\} \leq \frac{C}{n^2 p}\sum_{l=1}^{m}\left|[\mathbf{R}^{(j)^2}]_{l+n,l+n}\right|^2 \mathbb{I}\{\mathcal{Q}^{(j)}\}\mathbb{I}\{\mathcal{B}^{(j)}\}.$$

Since:

$$\left|[\mathbf{R}^{(j)^2}]_{l+n,l+n}\right| \leq \sum_{k=1}^{m}\left|R^{(j)}_{l+n,k+n}\right|^2 \leq \frac{C}{v}\operatorname{Im} R^{(j)}_{l+n,l+n},$$

Theorem 5 produced:

$$\mathbb{E}_j |\eta_{j1}|^2 \mathbb{I}\{\mathcal{Q}\}\mathbb{I}\{\mathcal{B}\} \leq \frac{C}{npv^2}\frac{1}{n}\sum_{l=1}^{m}\left(\operatorname{Im} R^{(j)}_{l+n,l+n}\right)^2 \mathbb{I}\{\mathcal{Q}^{(j)}\}\mathbb{I}\{\mathcal{B}^{(j)}\} \leq \frac{C|A_0(z)|a_n(z)}{npv^2}.$$

Similarly, for the moment of η_{j2}, we obtained the following estimate:

$$\mathbb{E}_j |\eta_{j2}|^2 \mathbb{I}\{\mathcal{Q}\}\mathbb{I}\{\mathcal{B}\} \leq \frac{C}{n^2}\sum_{l,k=1}^{m}\left|[\mathbf{R}^{(j)}]^2_{l+n,k+n}\right|^2 \mathbb{I}\{\mathcal{Q}^{(j)}\}\mathbb{I}\{\mathcal{B}^{(j)}\}$$
$$\leq \frac{C}{n^2}\operatorname{Tr}|\mathbf{R}^{(j)}|^4 \mathbb{I}\{\mathcal{Q}^{(j)}\}\mathbb{I}\{\mathcal{B}^{(j)}\} \leq \frac{C}{nv^3}a_n(z).$$

From the above estimates and Lemma 4, we concluded that:

$$\mathbb{E}_j |\Lambda_n - \Lambda_n^{(j)}|^2 \mathbb{I}\{\mathcal{Q}\}\mathbb{I}\{\mathcal{B}\}$$
$$\leq C\frac{|A_0(z)|a_n(z)}{(nv)^2}\left(\frac{|S_y(z)|^2}{np} + \mathbb{E}_j|R_{jj} - \mathbb{E}_j R_{jj}|^2\right)\mathbb{I}\{\mathcal{Q}\}\mathbb{I}\{\mathcal{B}\} + \frac{C|S_y(z)|^2}{(nv)^2}\frac{a_n(z)}{nv}.$$

Thus, the lemma was proven. □

Lemma 6. *Under the conditions of the theorem, for $2 \leq q \leq c \log n$, we have:*

$$\mathbb{E}_j |\Lambda_n - \Lambda_n^{(j)}|^q \mathbb{I}\{\mathcal{Q}\} \mathbb{I}\{\mathcal{B}\}$$
$$\leq C^q |S_y(z)|^{2q} \frac{a_n^q(z)}{(nv)^q} \left(q^q \left(\frac{|A_0(z)|}{(np)^{2\varkappa}} \right)^q + \beta_n^{\frac{q}{2}}(z) \right) + \frac{Cq^{\frac{q}{2}} |S_y(z)|^q}{(nv)^q (np)^{\frac{q}{2}}} |A_0(z)|^{\frac{q}{2}} a_n^{\frac{q}{2}}(z)$$
$$+ \frac{Cq^q |S_y(z)|^q}{(nv)^q (np)^{2q\varkappa+1}} |A_0(z)|^q + \frac{C^q q^q |S_y(z)|^q}{(nv)^{\frac{3q}{2}}} a_n^{\frac{q}{2}}(z) + \frac{C^q q^{\frac{3q}{2}} |S_y(z)|^q}{(nv)^{\frac{3q}{2}} (np)^{q\varkappa+1}} |A_0(z)|^{\frac{q}{2}} a_n^{\frac{q}{2}}(z)$$
$$+ \frac{C |S_y(z)|^q q^{2q}}{(np)^{2q\varkappa+2} n^q v^q} |A_0(z)|^q.$$

Proof. We used the representation:

$$\Lambda_n - \Lambda_n^{(j)} = \frac{1}{n} \left(1 + \frac{1}{n} \sum_{l=1}^m [\mathbf{R}^{(j)2}]_{l+n,l+n} \right) (R_{jj} - \mathbb{E}_j R_{jj})$$
$$+ \frac{1}{n} (\eta_{j1} + \eta_{j2}) R_{jj} - \frac{1}{n} \mathbb{E}_j (\eta_{j1} + \eta_{j2}) R_{jj}.$$

We noted that by using Rosenthal's inequality:

$$\mathbb{E}_j |\eta_{j1}|^q \mathbb{I}\{\mathcal{Q}\} \mathbb{I}\{\mathcal{B}\} \leq \frac{Cq^{\frac{q}{2}} |A_0(z)|^{\frac{q}{2}} a_n^{\frac{q}{2}}(z)}{v^q n^{\frac{q}{2}} p^{\frac{q}{2}}} + \frac{Cq^q |A_0(z)|^q}{v^q (np)^{2q\varkappa+1}}.$$

Similarly, for the second moment of η_{j2}, we obtained the following estimate:

$$\mathbb{E}_j |\eta_{j2}|^q \mathbb{I}\{\mathcal{Q}\} \mathbb{I}\{\mathcal{B}\} \leq \frac{C^q q^q}{n^{\frac{q}{2}} v^{\frac{3q}{2}}} a_n^{\frac{q}{2}}(z) + \frac{C^q q^{\frac{3q}{2}}}{n^{\frac{q}{2}} v^{\frac{3q}{2}} (np)^{q\varkappa+1}} |A_0(z)|^{\frac{q}{2}} a_n^{\frac{q}{2}}(z) + \frac{C^q q^{2q} |A_0(z)|^q}{(np)^{2q\varkappa+2} v^q}.$$

From the estimates above and Lemma 4, we concluded that:

$$\mathbb{E}_j |\Lambda_n - \Lambda_n^{(j)}|^q \mathbb{I}\{\mathcal{Q}\} \mathbb{I}\{\mathcal{B}\}$$
$$\leq C^q \frac{a_n^q(z)}{(nv)^q} \mathbb{E}_j |R_{jj} - \mathbb{E}_j R_{jj}|^q \mathbb{I}\{\mathcal{Q}\} \mathbb{I}\{\mathcal{B}\} + \frac{C^q q^{\frac{q}{2}} a_n^{\frac{q}{2}}(z) |A_0(z)|^{\frac{q}{2}} |S_y(z)|^q}{(nv)^q (np)^{\frac{q}{2}}}$$
$$+ \frac{C^q q^q |S_y(z)|^q A_0(z)|^q}{(nv)^q (np)^{2q\varkappa+1}}$$
$$+ \frac{C^q q^q a_n^{\frac{q}{2}}(z) |S_y(z)|^q}{(nv)^{\frac{3q}{2}}} + \frac{C^q q^{\frac{3q}{2}} |S_y(z)|^q |A_0(z)|^{\frac{q}{2}} a_n^{\frac{q}{2}}(z)}{(nv)^{\frac{3q}{2}} (np)^{q\varkappa+1}} + \frac{C |S_y(z)|^q q^{2q} |A_0(z)|^q}{(np)^{2q\varkappa+2} n^q v^q}.$$

To finish the proof, we applied Lemma (45) and Inequality (46). Thus, the lemma was proven. □

Lemma 7. *For $1 - \sqrt{y} - v \leq |u| \leq 1 + \sqrt{y} + v$, the following inequality holds:*

$$|b(z)| \leq C a_n(z).$$

Proof. We noted that:

$$b(z) = z - \frac{1-y}{z} + 2y S_y(z) = \sqrt{(z - \frac{1-y}{z})^2 - 4y}$$

and

$$a_n(z) = \mathrm{Im}\{\sqrt{(z - \frac{1-y}{z})^2 - 4y}\} + \frac{1}{nv} + \frac{1}{np}.$$

It was easy to show that for $1 - \sqrt{y} \leq |u| \leq 1 + \sqrt{y}$:

$$\text{Re}\{(z - \frac{1-y}{z})^2 - 4y\} \leq 0.$$

Indeed:

$$\text{Re}\{(z - \frac{1-y}{z})^2 - 4y\} \leq u^2 + \frac{(1-y)^2}{u^2} - 2(1+y).$$

The last expression was not positive for $1 - \sqrt{y} \leq |u| \leq 1 + \sqrt{y}$. From the negativity of the real part, it followed that:

$$\text{Im}\{\sqrt{(z - \frac{1-y}{z})^2 - 4y}\} \geq \frac{1}{\sqrt{2}}\left|\sqrt{(z - \frac{1-y}{z})^2 - 4y}\right|$$

This implied the required proof. Thus, the lemma was proven. □

Lemma 8. *There is an absolute constant $C > 0$, such that for $z = u + iv$:*

$$|\Lambda_n| \leq C \min\{\frac{|T_n|}{|b(z)|}, \sqrt{|T_n|}\}, \tag{49}$$

and that for $z = u + iv$ to satisfy $1 - \sqrt{y} - v \leq |u| \leq 1 + \sqrt{y} + v$ and $v > 0$, the following inequality is valid:

$$|\text{Im}\,\Lambda_n| \leq C \min\{\frac{|T_n|}{|b(z)|}, \sqrt{|T_n|}\}. \tag{50}$$

Proof. We changed the variables by setting:

$$w = \frac{1}{\sqrt{y}}(z - \frac{1-y}{z}), \quad z = \frac{w\sqrt{y} + \sqrt{yw^2 + 4(1-y)}}{2},$$

and

$$\widetilde{S}(w) = \sqrt{y}S_y(z), \widetilde{s}_n(w) = \sqrt{y}s_n(z).$$

In this notation, we could rewrite the main equation in the form:

$$1 + w\widetilde{s}_n(w) + \widetilde{s}_n^2(w) = T_n.$$

It was easy to see that:

$$\Lambda_n = \frac{1}{\sqrt{y}}(\widetilde{s}_n(z) - \widetilde{S}(w)).$$

Then, it sufficed to repeat the proof of Lemma B.1 from [17]. We noted that this lemma implied that Inequality (50) held for all w with $\text{Im}\,w > 0$ (and, therefore, for all z) and that Inequality (49) satisfied $|\text{Re}\,w| \leq 2 + \text{Im}\,w$ for w. From this, we concluded that Inequality (49) held for $z = u + iv$, such that $1 - \sqrt{y} - cv \leq |u| \leq 1 + \sqrt{y} + cv$ for a sufficiently small constant $c > 0$.

Thus, the lemma was proven. □

Lemma 9. *For $z = u + iv$, we have:*

$$|A_0(z)| = \frac{1}{|z + yS_y(z)|} \leq 1 + |b(z)|,$$

and

$$\text{Im}\,A_0(z) \leq \text{Im}\,b(z),$$

where

$$b(z) = z - \frac{1-y}{z} + 2yS_y(z).$$

Proof. First, we noted that:

$$\frac{1}{z+yS_y(z)} = -\left(yS_y(z) - \frac{1-y}{z}\right).$$

Using this, we could write:

$$b(z) = A_0(z) - \frac{1}{A_0(z)}. \tag{51}$$

From there, it followed that:

$$A_0(z) = \frac{b(z) \pm \sqrt{b^2(z)+4}}{2}.$$

This implied that:

$$|A_0(z)| \leq 1 + |b(z)|.$$

Equality (51) yielded:

$$\operatorname{Im} A_0(z) = \frac{|A_0(z)|^2}{1+|A_0(z)|^2} \operatorname{Im} b(z) \leq \operatorname{Im} b(z).$$

Thus, the lemma was proven. □

Lemma 10. *A positive absolute constant B exists, such that:*

$$a_n(z)|A_0(z)| \leq B$$

and

$$|S_y(z)||A_0(z)| \leq C.$$

Proof. First, we considered $|b(z)| \geq \Gamma^{-1}$. Then, for $|z| \geq C\Gamma_n$:

$$a_n(z)|A_0(z)| \leq \Gamma_n(|b(z)|+1) \leq \frac{C\Gamma_n}{|z|} \leq C.$$

In the case $\Gamma_n \leq |b(z)| \leq C$, we obtained:

$$a_n(z)A_0(z) \leq |b(z)|(|b(z)|+1) \leq C(C+1).$$

we then considered the case $|b(z)| \leq \Gamma_n$:

$$a_n(z)A_0(z) \leq (yS_y(z) + \frac{1-y}{|z|})\Gamma_n \leq \sqrt{y}\Gamma_n + 1 - y \leq 1.$$

To prove the second inequality, we considered the equality:

$$|S_y(z)A_0(z)| = |yS_y^2(z) - \frac{1-y}{z}S_y(z)| = |-1 - zS_y(z)| \leq C.$$

Thus, the lemma was proven. □

We let **X** be a rectangular $n \times m$ matrix with $m \geq n$. We let $s_1 \geq \cdots \geq s_n$ be the singular values of matrix **X**. The diagonal matrix with $d_{jj} = s_j$ was denoted by $\mathbf{D}_n = (d_{jk})$ $n \times n$. We let $\mathbf{O}_{n,k}$ be an $n \times k$ matrix with zero entries. We put $\mathbf{O}_n = \mathbf{O}_{n,n}$ and $\widetilde{\mathbf{D}}_n = [\mathbf{D}_n \mathbf{O}_{n,m-n}]$. We let **L** and **K** be orthogonal (Hermitian) matrices, such that the singular value decomposition held:

$$\mathbf{X} = \mathbf{L}\widetilde{\mathbf{D}}_n \mathbf{K}.$$

Furthermore, we let $\mathbf{I}_n$ be the identity of an $n \times n$ matrix and $\mathbf{E}_n = [\mathbf{I}_n \mathbf{O}_{n,m-n}]$. We introduced the matrices $\mathbf{L}_n = \mathbf{L}\mathbf{E}_n$ and $\mathbf{K}_n = \mathbf{K}\mathbf{E}_n^T$. We noted that $\mathbf{L}_n^* = \mathbf{E}_n^T \mathbf{L}^*$ and $\mathbf{K}_n^* = \mathbf{E}_n \mathbf{K}^*$. We introduced the matrix $\mathbf{V} = \begin{bmatrix} \mathbf{O} & \mathbf{X} \\ \mathbf{X}^* & \mathbf{O} \end{bmatrix}$. We considered the matrix $\mathbf{Z} = \frac{1}{\sqrt{2}} \begin{bmatrix} \mathbf{L} & \mathbf{L}_n \\ \mathbf{K}_n & -\mathbf{K} \end{bmatrix}$. We then obtained the following:

Lemma 11.
$$\mathbf{Z}^*\mathbf{V}\mathbf{Z} = \begin{bmatrix} \mathbf{D}_n & \mathbf{O}_n & \mathbf{O}_n \\ \mathbf{O}_n & -\mathbf{D}_n & \mathbf{O}_{m-n,n} \\ \mathbf{O}_{m-n,n} & \mathbf{O}_{m-n,n} & \mathbf{O}_{m-n} \end{bmatrix} =: \widehat{\mathbf{D}}.$$

Proof. The proof followed direct calculations. It was straightforward to see that:
$$\mathbf{Z}^*\mathbf{V} = \frac{1}{\sqrt{2}} \begin{bmatrix} \mathbf{K}_n^*\mathbf{X}^* & \mathbf{L}^*\mathbf{X} \\ -\mathbf{L}_n^*\mathbf{X} & \mathbf{K}^*\mathbf{X} \end{bmatrix} = \frac{1}{\sqrt{2}} \begin{bmatrix} \mathbf{E}_n\widetilde{\mathbf{D}}^T \mathbf{L}^* & \widetilde{\mathbf{D}}\mathbf{K}^* \\ -\mathbf{E}_n\widetilde{\mathbf{D}}\mathbf{K}^* & \widetilde{\mathbf{D}}^T\mathbf{L}^* \end{bmatrix}.$$

Furthermore:
$$\mathbf{Z}^*\mathbf{V}\mathbf{Z} = \frac{1}{2} \begin{bmatrix} \mathbf{E}_n\widetilde{\mathbf{D}}^T + \widetilde{\mathbf{D}}\mathbf{E}_n^T & \mathbf{E}_n\widetilde{\mathbf{D}}^T - \widetilde{\mathbf{D}}_n\mathbf{E}_n^T \\ -\mathbf{E}_n^T\widetilde{\mathbf{D}} + \widetilde{\mathbf{D}}^T\mathbf{E}_n & -\widetilde{\mathbf{D}}^T\mathbf{E}_n - \mathbf{E}_n^T\widetilde{\mathbf{D}} = \widehat{\mathbf{D}} \end{bmatrix}.$$

□

8. Conclusions

In this work, we obtained results by assuming that the conditions (C0)–(C2) were fulfilled. The condition (C2) was of a technical nature. In our investigation on the asymptotic behaviour of the Stieltjes transformation on a beam, this restriction could be eliminated. However, this was a technically cumbersome task that requires separate consideration.

Author Contributions: Writing—original draft, A.N.T. and D.A.T. All authors have read and agreed to the published version of the manuscript.

Funding: This research received no external funding.

Institutional Review Board Statement: Not applicable.

Informed Consent Statement: Not applicable.

Data Availability Statement: Not applicable.

Acknowledgments: The authors wish to thank F. Götze for the several fruitful discussions on this paper.

Conflicts of Interest: The authors declare no conflict of interest.

References

1. Wishart, J. The generalised product moment distribution in samples from a normal multivariate population. *Biometrika* **1928**, *20A*, 32–52. [CrossRef]
2. Wigner, E.P. Characteristic vectors of bordered matrices with infinite dimensions. *Ann. Math.* **1955**, *62*, 548–564. [CrossRef]
3. Marchenko, V.A.; Pastur, L.A. Distribution of eigenvalues for some sets of random matrices. *Mat. Sb.* **1967**, *72*, 507–536.
4. Telatar, E. Capacity of multi-antenna Gaussian channels. *Eur. Trans. Telecomm.* **1999**, *10*, 585–595. [CrossRef]
5. Newman, M. Random graphs as models of networks. In *Handbook of Graphs and Networks*; Bornholdt, S., Schuster, H.G., Eds.; Wiley-VCH: Hoboken, NJ, USA, 2002; pp. 35–68.
6. Granziol, D. Beyond Random Matrix Theory for Deep Networks. *arXiv* **2021**, arXiv:2006.07721v2.
7. Erdős, L.; Knowles, A.; Yau, H.-T.; Yin, J. Spectral statistics of Erdős–Rényi graphs I: Local semicircle law. *Ann. Probab.* **2013**, *41*, 2279–2375. [CrossRef]
8. Erdős, L.; Knowles, A.; Yau, H.-T.; Yin, J. Spectral statistics of Erdős-Rényi graphs II: Eigenvalue spacing and the extreme eigenvalues. *Comm. Math. Phys.* **2012**, *314*, 587–640. [CrossRef]
9. Huang, J.; Landon, B.; Yau, H.-T. Bulk universality of sparse random matrices. *J. Math. Phys.* **2015**, *56*, 123301. [CrossRef]
10. Huang, J.; Yau, H.-T. Edge Universality of Sparse Random Matrices. *arXiv* **2022**, arXiv:2206.06580.

11. Lee, J.O.; Schnelli, K. Tracy–Widom distribution for the largest eigenvalue of real sample covariance matrices with general population. *Ann. Appl. Probab.* **2016**, *26*, 3786–3839. [CrossRef]
12. Hwang, J.Y.; Lee, J.O.; Schnelli, K. Local law and Tracy–Widom limit for sparse sample covariance matrices. *Ann. Appl. Probab.* **2019**, *29*, 3006–3036. [CrossRef]
13. Götze, F.; Tikhomirov, A.N. On the largest and smallest singular values of sparse rectangular random matrices. *Electron. J. Probab.* **2021**, *submitted*.
14. Rudelson, M.; Vershynin, R. Smallest singular value of a random rectangular matrix. *Comm. Pure Appl. Math.* **2009**, *62*, 1707–1739. [CrossRef]
15. Götze, F.; Naumov, A.A.; Tikhomirov, A.N. On the local semicircular law for Wigner ensembles. *Bernoulli* **2018**, *24*, 2358–2400. [CrossRef]
16. Götze, F.; Naumov, A.A.; Tikhomirov, A.N. Moment inequalities for linear and nonlinear statistics. *Theory Probab. Appl.* **2020**, *65*, 1–16. [CrossRef]
17. Götze, F.; Naumov, A.A.; Tikhomirov, A.N. Local Semicircle Law under Moment Conditions. Part I: The Stieltjes Transform. *arXiv* **2016**, arXiv:1510.07350v4.

Article

Asymptotic Properties and Application of GSB Process: A Case Study of the COVID-19 Dynamics in Serbia

Mihailo Jovanović [1,†], Vladica Stojanović [2,*,†], Kristijan Kuk [2,†], Brankica Popović [2,†] and Petar Čisar [2,†]

1 The Office for Information Technologies and eGovernment, 11000 Belgrade, Serbia
2 Department of Informatics & Computer Sciences, University of Criminal Investigation and Police Studies, 11000 Belgrade, Serbia
* Correspondence: vladica.stojanovic@kpu.edu.rs
† These authors contributed equally to this work.

Abstract: This paper describes one of the non-linear (and non-stationary) stochastic models, the GSB (Gaussian, or Generalized, Split-BREAK) process, which is used in the analysis of time series with pronounced and accentuated fluctuations. In the beginning, the stochastic structure of the GSB process and its important distributional and asymptotic properties are given. To that end, a method based on characteristic functions (CFs) was used. Various procedures for the estimation of model parameters, asymptotic properties, and numerical simulations of the obtained estimators are also investigated. Finally, as an illustration of the practical application of the GSB process, an analysis is presented of the dynamics and stochastic distribution of the infected and immunized population in relation to the disease COVID-19 in the territory of the Republic of Serbia.

Keywords: stochastic processes; emphatic fluctuations; non-stationarity; asymptotic normality; Gaussian distribution; estimation; COVID-19

MSC: 60E10; 60F05; 62M10

1. Introduction

Stochastic models which are used in the analysis of time series with pronounced and permanent fluctuations are of particular importance in contemporary research. For this purpose, we start from the basic results of Engle and Smith [1], who first introduced the so-called STOchastic Permanent BREAKing process, popularly called the *STOPBREAK process*. Many authors have since considered the STOPBREAK notion, primarily in the field of econometrics. Some of its modifications were considered, among others, in [2–5], while its application was presented, for instance, in [6–8].

The original modification of the STOPBREAK process, named *the Split-BREAK model*, was introduced in [9]. After that, the general form of this process, named *Gaussian (or Generalized) Split-BREAK (GSB) process*, was proposed in [10–12]. This stochastic model also can be viewed as a generalization of STOPBREAK, as well as a well-known linear Auto-Regressive Moving Average (ARMA) model. In that way, the GSB process has already been applied in analyzing non-linear time series with pronounced and permanent fluctuations. Let us point out that in the mentioned works, of main consideration were the stochastic properties of the stationary components of the GSB process. The main goal of this paper is a more detailed investigation of the non-stationary components (time series) of the GSB model. These series naturally have a more complex stochastic structure, but they are of particular interest in contemporary research [13–18]. To this end, the asymptotic properties of distributions of the GSB series will also be of specific interest.

In addition to the theoretical aspects, the application of the GSB process in describing the dynamics and finding an adequate stochastic distribution of the infected and immunized population with respect to COVID-19 on the territory of the Republic of Serbia was also considered. We point out that many authors who deal with this, still current, issue have contributed various theoretical models that investigate it from several aspects. For instance, rigorous mathematical models, usually based on analyzing and solving systems of partial coupled equations, have been proposed, among others, in [19–21]. On the other hand, works in [22–25] combine deterministic and stochastic approaches, such as multiple and logistic regression, multifactor correlation, and the least squares estimation method, to predict the various effects caused by the COVID-19 pandemic. A particularly interesting approach is given in [26,27] where, to predict the COVID-19 dynamics more accurately, machine learning techniques and the construction of a complete information system are used. Finally, to the best of our knowledge, most stochastic approaches to-date in the analysis of infection, immunization, and other indicators related to the disease of COVID-19 were based on the use of the gamma distribution [21,28], as well as a log-normal distribution [29]. This is precisely one of the reasons why we believe that a different approach is given here, primarily in stochastic modeling and research of this problem. At the same time, let us emphasize that our main goal is to model the temporal dynamics of the COVID-19 disease, based on a formal study of the stochastic structure of the GSB model. In this sense, some other indicators and features of this disease, which can also affect its dynamics (see, for instance [30–32]), can to a certain degree be a limitation of this approach.

In the next section, starting from previous works [9–12], some definitions and basic stochastic properties of the GSB process are discussed. Section 3 contains the main and novel results related to this process's detailed stochastic structure and asymptotic properties, where the method of characteristic functions (CFs) was used as the basic tool. Section 4 presents the procedure for estimating the unknown parameters of the GSB process and an investigation of the asymptotic properties of the obtained estimators. Numerical Monte Carlo simulations of the obtained estimators are considered in Section 5. In addition, the application of the GSB process in describing the dynamics and distribution of the size of infected and immunized populations on the territory of the Republic of Serbia is given here. Finally, concluding remarks are highlighted in Section 6.

2. Definition and Main Properties of the GSB Process

The basic series of GSB processes is defined by the following equality:

$$y_t = m_t + \varepsilon_t. \tag{1}$$

Here, $t = 0, 1, \ldots, T$ are the known time values, (m_t) is the series of the so-called *martingale means*, and (ε_t) are *the innovations*, i.e., series of independent identical distributed (IID) Gaussian $\mathcal{N}(0, \sigma^2)$ random variables (RVs). Moreover, it is considered that (ε_t) is defined on the same probability space $(\Omega, \mathcal{F}, P)$, expanded by some filtration $F = (\mathcal{F}_t)$, i.e., nondecreasing σ-algebras on Ω. In a practical sense, filtration $(\mathcal{F}_t)$ represents a set of "information" at time t. Therefore, it is assumed that, for each $t = 0, 1, \ldots, T$, the RVs ε_t are $\mathcal{F}_t$-adaptive. Accordingly, the conditional expectation, as well as the variance of RVs ε_t, are, respectively,

$$E(\varepsilon_t|\mathcal{F}_{t-1}) = 0, \quad V(\varepsilon_t|\mathcal{F}_{t-1}) = E\left(\varepsilon_t^2 \middle| \mathcal{F}_{t-1}\right) = \sigma^2.$$

On the other hand, for martingale means (m_t), we assume that they are defined by the following recurrence relation:

$$m_t = m_{t-1} + q_{t-1}\varepsilon_{t-1} = m_0 + \sum_{j=0}^{t-1} q_j \varepsilon_j. \tag{2}$$

Here, we can effectively assume that $m_0 \stackrel{as}{=} \mu$ (*const.*) and $\varepsilon_{-1} = \varepsilon_0 \stackrel{as}{=} 0$. Meanwhile, q_t is the so-called *noise indicator*, i.e., the RV that depends on innovations (ε_t) in the following way:

$$q_t = I\left(\varepsilon_{t-1}^2 > c\right) = \begin{cases} 1, & \varepsilon_{t-1}^2 > c \\ 0, & \varepsilon_{t-1}^2 \leq c. \end{cases}$$

The value $c > 0$ represents *the critical value of the reaction*, i.e., the significance of the previous realization of innovations (ε_t) which allow their present values to be included in Equation (2). In other words, value $q_{t-1} = 0$ indicates that there is no change in the martingale mean value m_t, compared to the previous value m_{t-1}. Consequently, the value y_t will be obtained with a "small" fluctuation, which depends only on ε_t. By contrast, in the case of $q_t = 1$ an emphatic (permanent) fluctuation of y_t is registered. Thus, the level of previous realizations of series (ε_t) affects the degree of variations in the series (y_t), that is, it indicates the intensity of fluctuations in the GSB process. Furthermore, according to the previous equalities, it follows that:

$$E(y_t|\mathcal{F}_{t-1}) = m_t + E(\varepsilon_t|\mathcal{F}_{t-1}) = m_t,$$

from which we conclude that the series realizations (y_t) are "close" to the martingale means (m_t). Moreover, it is valid to put:

$$\begin{aligned} E(y_t) &= E[E(y_t|\mathcal{F}_{t-1})] = E(m_t) = E(m_{t-1}) + E(q_{t-1}\varepsilon_{t-1}) \\ &= E(m_{t-1}) = \cdots = E(m_0) = \mu, \end{aligned}$$

i.e., the mean values of the series (y_t) and (m_t) have equal, constant values. We notice that the previous equalities speak a lot about the stochastic nature of the GSB process, that is, the additive decomposition (1). Since the sequence (m_t) is measurable concerning the field $\mathcal{F}_{t-1}$, it represents a component of *predictability and stability* of the GSB process. In contrast, the innovations series (ε_t) is *the deviation factor (white noise)* of the basic GSB series (y_t) in relation to the martingale means (m_t).

Further, we determine the conditional variance of the series (y_t) from the equation:

$$V(y_t|\mathcal{F}_{t-1}) = E(y_t^2|\mathcal{F}_{t-1}) - m_t^2 = 2m_t E(\varepsilon_t) + E(\varepsilon_t^2) = \sigma^2,$$

and from here, one obtains:

$$V(y_t) = E(y_t^2) - \mu^2 = E(m_t^2) + 2E(m_t\varepsilon_t) + E(\varepsilon_t^2) - \mu^2 = V(m_t) + \sigma^2.$$

For each $t = 1, \ldots, T$, it also holds that:

$$\begin{aligned} V(m_t) &= E(m_t^2) - \mu^2 \\ &= E(m_{t-1}^2) + 2E(m_{t-1}q_{t-1}\varepsilon_{t-1}) + E(q_{t-1}^2\varepsilon_{t-1}^2) - \mu^2 \\ &= V(m_{t-1}) + a_c\sigma^2, \end{aligned}$$

where $a_c = E(q_t) = E(q_t^2) = P\{\varepsilon_t^2 > c\}$. It follows that the variance of martingale means (m_t), under the assumption $m_0 \equiv \mu(const.)$, can be expressed as:

$$V(m_t) = ta_c\sigma^2, t \geq 0.$$

From here, the variance of the basic series (y_t) can be obtained as follows:

$$V(y_t) = V(m_t) + \sigma^2 = (ta_c + 1)\sigma^2, \ t \geq 0.$$

According to the previous equalities, the variances of the series (y_t) and (m_t) have non-constant values that depend on the point in time (t) in which they are observed.

Correlation functions of the series (y_t) and (m_t) can be obtained in a similar way. Note that for every $s > t \geq 0$, it holds that:

$$\begin{aligned}Cov(m_t, m_s) &= E(m_t m_s) - \mu^2 = E(m_t m_{s-1}) + E(m_t q_{s-1} \varepsilon_{s-1}) - \mu^2 \\ &= Cov(m_t, m_{s-1}),\end{aligned}$$

and it is easy to see that the covariance of the series (m_t) satisfies:

$$Cov(m_t, m_s) = V(m_t), \quad s > t \geq 0.$$

From here, the correlation function of the martingale means is obtained:

$$\widetilde{K}(s,t) = \frac{Cov(m_t, m_s)}{\sqrt{V(m_t)} \cdot \sqrt{V(m_s)}} = \begin{cases} \frac{\min(s,t)}{\sqrt{s \cdot t}}, & s \neq t \\ 1, & s = t. \end{cases}$$

Similarly, according to equalities:

$$\begin{aligned}Cov(y_t, y_s) &= E(y_t y_s) - \mu^2 = E(y_t m_s) + E(y_t \varepsilon_s) - \mu^2 \\ &= E(m_t m_s) + E(\varepsilon_t m_s) - \mu^2 = Cov(m_t, m_s) + a_c \sigma^2 \\ &= V(m_t) + a_c \sigma^2 = V(y_t), \quad s > t \geq 0,\end{aligned}$$

the correlation function for (y_t), can be obtained as follows:

$$K(s,t) = \begin{cases} \frac{a_c \min(s,t) + 1}{\sqrt{(a_c s + 1) \cdot (a_c t + 1)}}, & s \neq t \\ 1, & s = t. \end{cases}$$

Therefore, both correlation functions depend on the time arguments t, s and indicate the non-stationarity of the series (y_t) and (m_t). This fact requires some more complex techniques to examine their properties. Moreover, note that when $s > t \geq 0$,

$$\lim_{s \to t} \widetilde{K}(s,t) = \lim_{s \to t} \frac{\min(s,t)}{\sqrt{s \cdot t}} = \frac{t}{\sqrt{t^2}} = 1$$
$$\lim_{s \to t} K(s,t) = \lim_{s \to t} \frac{a_c \min(s,t) + 1}{\sqrt{(a_c s + 1) \cdot (a_c t + 1)}} = \frac{a_c t + 1}{\sqrt{(a_c t + 1)^2}} = 1.$$

Thus, the correlation functions of both series (y_t) and (m_t) satisfy the L^2-continuity condition.

At the end of this section, we define *a series of increments of the GSB process* by the following equality:

$$X_t = y_t - y_{t-1}, \quad t = 1, \ldots, T. \tag{3}$$

Almost all authors who have studied STOPBREAK processes highlight the importance of this sequence. This series, as can be easily seen from Equations (1) and (2), can be given in the following form:

$$X_t = \varepsilon_t - \theta_{t-1} \varepsilon_{t-1}, \tag{4}$$

where $\theta_t = 1 - q_t = I(\varepsilon_{t-1}^2 \leq c)$. The series (X_t) is named *a Splitting Moving Average process (of order 1)*, shortened to *Split-MA (1) process*, because it operates in two regimes. Fluctuations of innovations (ε_t) that were emphasized in the previous time moment $(t-1)$ imply $\theta_{t-1} = 0$, so the equality $X_t = \varepsilon_t$ holds. On the other hand, fluctuations that do not exceed the critical value c give a representation of (X_t) in the form of a standard, linear MA (1) process. In this way, (X_t) has similar properties to the MA (1) models, which can be applied in research into it. Thus, taking earlier assumptions, the mean value and variance of this series, obtained by simple computation, are:

$$E(X_t) = 0, \quad V(X_t) = E\left(X_t^2\right) = \sigma^2(b_c + 1),$$

where $b_c = 1 - a_c = P(\varepsilon_{t-1}^2 \leq c)$. Moreover, the covariance of this sequence is:

$$Cov(X_t, X_s) = \begin{cases} (b_c + 1)\sigma^2, & s = t \\ -b_c \sigma^2, & |s - t| = 1 \\ 0, & \text{otherwise,} \end{cases}$$

and obviously has an identical structure to the standard MA (1) series. Based on the obtained covariance, we can easily see that the series (X_t) is stationary and that its correlation function can be written in the form:

$$\rho_X(h) := \frac{Cov(X_t, X_{t+h})}{V(X_t)} = \begin{cases} 1, & h = 0 \\ -b_c/(b_c + 1), & h = \pm 1 \\ 0, & \text{otherwise.} \end{cases}$$

Finally, according to Equations (3) and (4), it follows that:

$$y_t - y_{t-1} = \varepsilon_t - \theta_{t-1}\varepsilon_{t-1}, \; t = 1, \ldots, T,.$$

which can be viewed as a non-linear *Integrated Auto-Regressive Moving Average (ARIMA)* model with "temporary" components ($\theta_{t-1}\varepsilon_{t-1}$). These imply the specific structure of the series (X_t), as well as other components of the GSB process.

In the following section, as we have already pointed out, we also discuss the application of the GSB model in describing the dynamics of infection and immunization of the population on the territory of the Republic of Serbia. As will be seen, this kind of dynamics has pronounced fluctuations that can be described by the non-stationary components of the GSB process, primarily by its main time series (y_t). In that case, due to its stationarity, the Split-MA (1) process plays an important role. As an illustration, Figure 1 shows the realizations of all the above-mentioned series obtained by the Monte Carlo simulation of the GSB model.

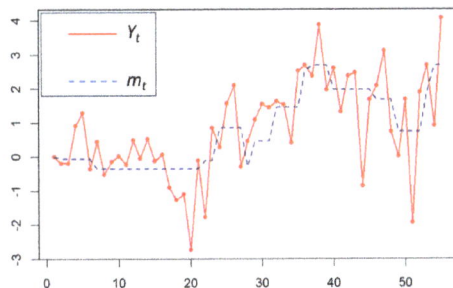
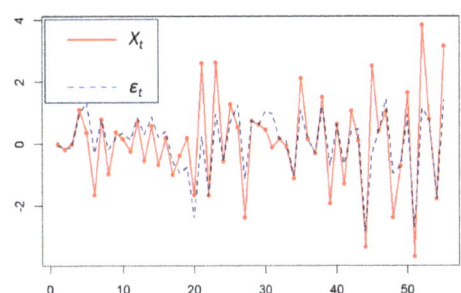

Figure 1. Dynamics of the basic series of the GSB model. (Parameter values are: $\mu = 0$ and $c = \sigma = 1$).

3. Stochastic Distribution and Asymptotic Properties of the GSB Process

In this section, some stochastic properties of the GSB process, regarding the distribution and asymptotic behavior of its basic stochastic components, are discussed in more detail. As explained in the previous section, the GSB model, given by Equations (1)–(4), contains four stochastic components: the basic series (y), innovations (ε_t), the martingale means (m_t), and the series of increments (X_t). At the same time, series (ε_t) and (X_t) represent the stationary components of the GSB process, where (X_t) is "close" to the linear MA model. In general form, the stochastic structure of the series (X_t) is described in [12], where the method of characteristic functions (CFs) was used. Following this approach, the basic stochastic properties of the series (X_t) can be expressed by the following statement.

Theorem 1. Let (X_t) be the Split-MA (1) process defined by Equation (4). For arbitrary $x \in \mathbb{R}$ and $t = 0, \cdot 1, \ldots, T$, the cumulative distribution function (CDF) of this stochastic process is given by:

$$F_X(x) := P\{X_t < x\} = (1 - b_c)F_\varepsilon(x) + b_c F_{\sqrt{2\varepsilon}}(x), \tag{5a}$$

where $F_\varepsilon(x)$ and $F_{2\varepsilon}(x)$ are CDFs of RVs $\varepsilon_t : \mathcal{N}(0, \sigma^2)$ and $\sqrt{2}\varepsilon_t : \mathcal{N}(0, 2\sigma^2)$, respectively.

Proof. For arbitrary $t = 0, 1, \ldots, T$, let us denote the series of RVs $\eta_t = \theta_t \varepsilon_t$. Since θ_t and ε_t are mutually independent RVs, it follows

$$E(\eta_t) = E(\theta_t)E(\varepsilon_t) = 0,$$
$$V(\eta_t) = E(\theta_t^2)E(\varepsilon_t^2) = b_c \sigma^2.$$

Moreover, it is simply shown that $Cov(\eta_t, \eta_{t+h}) = 0$ holds for every $h \neq 0$, i.e., (η_t) is a series of uncorrelated RVs. By applying conditional probabilities, the CDF of these RVs can be obtained as follows:

$$\begin{aligned} F_\eta(x) : &= P\{\eta_t < x\} \\ &= P\{\eta_t < x | \theta_t = 1\} \cdot P\{\theta_t = 1\} + P\{\eta_t < x | \theta_t = 0\} \cdot P\{\theta_t = 0\} \\ &= P\{\varepsilon_t < x\} \cdot P\{\theta_t = 1\} + P\{x > 0\} \cdot P\{\theta_t = 0\} \\ &= b_c F_\varepsilon(x) + (1 - b_c)F_0(x), \end{aligned}$$

where $F_0(x) = I(x > 0)$ is the CDF of the RV $I_0 \stackrel{as}{=} 0$. Based on that, for the CF of the RVs η_t, one obtains:

$$\begin{aligned} \varphi_\eta(u) : &= \int_{-\infty}^{+\infty} e^{iux} F_\eta(dx) = \int_{-\infty}^{+\infty} e^{iux}[b_c F_\varepsilon + (1 - b_c)F_0](dx) \\ &= b_c \varphi_\varepsilon(u) + (1 - b_c)\varphi_0(u). \end{aligned}$$

Here, $\varphi_\varepsilon(u) = e^{-\frac{\sigma^2 u^2}{2}}$ and $\varphi_0(u) \equiv 1$ are CFs of the RVs ε_t и I_0, respectively. By substituting these CFs into the previous equality, we have:

$$\varphi_\eta(u) = 1 + b_c \left(e^{-\frac{\sigma^2 u^2}{2}} - 1 \right),$$

whence, by applying Equation (4), it follows that the CF of RVs X_t is:

$$\begin{aligned} \varphi_X(u) &= \varphi_\varepsilon(u) \cdot \varphi_\eta(u) = e^{-\frac{\sigma^2 u^2}{2}} \left[1 + b_c \left(e^{-\frac{\sigma^2 u^2}{2}} - 1 \right) \right] \\ &= (1 - b_c)e^{-\frac{\sigma^2 u^2}{2}} + b_c e^{-\sigma^2 u^2}. \end{aligned}$$

According to the last equality and Lévy's correspondence theorem (see, e.g., [33] (p. 181)), Equation (5) immediately follows, that is, the statement of the theorem is proved. □

Remark 1. As shown in [12], the CDF of RVs X_t can also be given in the following form:

$$F_X(x) := P\{X_t < x\} = [(1 - b_c)F_0(x) + b_c F_\varepsilon(x)] \otimes F_\varepsilon(x), \tag{5b}$$

where "$\otimes$" denotes the convolution of two (arbitrary) CDFs $F(x)$, $G(x)$:

$$(F \otimes G)(x) := \int_{-\infty}^{+\infty} F(x - y)G(dy).$$

The equivalence of Equations (5a) and (5b) are directly obtained from the fact that CDF $F_0(x)$ is neutral for the convolution operator, i.e.,

$$(F \otimes F_0)(x) = (F_0 \otimes F)(x) = \int_{-\infty}^{+\infty} I(x > y) F(dy) = F(x).$$

Finally, note that by differentiating Equation (5), the probability density function (PDF) of the series (X_t), one obtains:

$$f_X(x) = \frac{1-b_c}{\sigma\sqrt{2\pi}} e^{-\frac{x^2}{2\pi\sigma^2}} + \frac{b_c}{2\sigma\sqrt{\pi}} e^{-\frac{x^2}{4\pi\sigma^2}}.$$

By a similar procedure as in the previous theorem and using the convolutions of CDFs, we describe the stochastic distribution of other components of the GSB process, i.e., the series (m_t) and (y_t). As already shown in the previous section, these series represent non-stationary stochastic processes with a constant mean $\mu = E(m_t) = E(y_t)$. Accordingly, the following statement is valid.

Theorem 2. *Let (y_t) and (m_t) be the time series defined by Equations (1) and (2), respectively, where $m_0 \stackrel{as}{=} \mu$ (const). For arbitrary $x \in \mathbb{R}$ and $t = 0, \cdot 1, \ldots, T$, the CDFs of these series are as follows:*

$$F_m(x,t) := P\{m_t < x\} = \bigotimes_{j=1}^{t} \left[(1-b_c)F_j(x) + b_c F_0(x)\right] \otimes F_\mu(x). \tag{6}$$

$$F_y(x,t) := P\{y_t < x\} = \bigotimes_{j=1}^{t} \left[(1-b_c)F_j(x) + b_c F_0(x)\right] \otimes F_\mu(x) \otimes F_\varepsilon(x). \tag{7}$$

Here, $F_0(x)$ and $F_j(x)$ are the CDFs of previously defined RVs I_0 and ε_t, respectively, and $F_\mu(x) = F_m(x,0)$ is the CDF of the RV $m_0 \stackrel{as}{=} \mu$. In addition, when $T = +\infty$, the following convergences (in distribution) are valid:

$$\frac{1}{\sqrt{t}} m_t \stackrel{d}{\to} \mathcal{N}(0, a_c \sigma^2), \quad \frac{1}{\sqrt{t}} y_t \stackrel{d}{\to} \mathcal{N}(0, a_c \sigma^2), \quad t \to +\infty. \tag{8}$$

Proof. For arbitrary $t = 0, 1, \ldots, T$, let us introduce a series of RVs $\xi_t = q_t \varepsilon_t$. In the same way as in the proof of the previous theorem, it is shown that (ξ_t) is a series of mutually uncorrelated RVs, with $E(\xi_t) = 0$, $D(\xi_t) = a_c \sigma^2$, where $a_c = E(q_t) = P\{\varepsilon_t^2 > c\} = 1 - b_c$. By reapplying the conditional probabilities, the CDF of ξ_t is obtained as follows:

$$\begin{aligned}
F_\xi(x) : &= P\{\xi_t < x\} \\
&= P\{\xi_t < x | q_t = 1\} \cdot P\{q_t = 1\} + P\{\xi_t < x | q_t = 0\} \cdot P\{q_t = 0\} \\
&= P\{\varepsilon_t < x\} \cdot P\{q_t = 1\} + P\{x > 0\} \cdot P\{q_t = 0\} \\
&= a_c F_\varepsilon(x) + (1 - a_c) F_0(x).
\end{aligned}$$

According to this, their corresponding CF is obtained:

$$\begin{aligned}
\varphi_\xi(u) &= \int_{-\infty}^{+\infty} e^{iux} F_\xi(dx) = \int_{-\infty}^{+\infty} e^{iux} [a_c F_\varepsilon + (1-a_c) F_0](dx) \\
&= a_c \varphi_\varepsilon(u) + (1-a_c) \varphi_0(u) = 1 + a_c \left(e^{-\frac{\sigma^2 u^2}{2}} - 1\right) \\
&= (1 - b_c) e^{-\frac{\sigma^2 u^2}{2}} + b_c.
\end{aligned}$$

Applying Equation (2), we find that the CFs of the RVs (m_t) are as follows:

$$\varphi_m(u,t) = \varphi_\mu(u) \prod_{j=0}^{t-1} \varphi_\xi(u) = e^{iu\mu} \left[(1-b_c)e^{-\frac{\sigma^2 u^2}{2}} + b_c \right]^t, \qquad (9)$$

where $\varphi_\mu(u) = e^{iu\mu}$ is CF of the RV $m_0 \stackrel{as}{=} \mu$. Then, Equation (6) immediately follows from Equation (9) and Lévy's correspondence theorem [33] (p. 181).

Similarly, by applying the previous Equations (1) and (9), the CFs of the RVs (y_t) are obtained:

$$\varphi_y(u,t) = \varphi_m(u) \cdot \varphi_\varepsilon(u) = e^{iu\mu - \frac{\sigma^2 u^2}{2}} \left[(1-b_c)e^{-\frac{\sigma^2 u^2}{2}} + b_c \right]^t. \qquad (10)$$

From here, by reapplying the theorem of Lévy, Equation (7) immediately follows.

To prove the second part of the theorem, i.e., Equation (8), note first that the CFs of the RVs $m_t/\sqrt{t}$ and $y_t/\sqrt{t}$, when $t = 1, 2, \ldots$, according to Equations (9) and (10), can be written as follows:

$$\begin{aligned}
\varphi_m\left(\frac{u}{\sqrt{t}}, t\right) &= e^{iu\mu/\sqrt{t}} \left[1 + a_c\left(e^{-\frac{\sigma^2 u^2}{2t}} - 1\right)\right]^t \\
&= e^{iu\mu/\sqrt{t}} \left[1 - \frac{a_c \sigma^2 u^2}{2t} + \sigma\left(\frac{u^2}{t}\right)\right]^t, \\
\varphi_y\left(\frac{u}{\sqrt{t}}, t\right) &= e^{iu\mu/\sqrt{t} - \frac{\sigma^2 u^2}{2t}} \left[1 + a_c\left(e^{-\frac{\sigma^2 u^2}{2t}} - 1\right)\right]^t \\
&= e^{iu\mu/\sqrt{t} - \frac{\sigma^2 u^2}{2t}} \left[1 - \frac{a_c \sigma^2 u^2}{2t} + \sigma\left(\frac{u^2}{t}\right)\right]^t.
\end{aligned}$$

Here, $\sigma(z)$ is an infinitely small value of a higher order than z when $z \to 0$. Hence, for a fixed but arbitrary $u \in \mathbb{R}$, we have:

$$\varphi_m\left(\frac{u}{\sqrt{t}}, t\right) \to e^{-\frac{a_c \sigma^2 u^2}{2}}, \quad \varphi_y\left(\frac{u}{\sqrt{t}}, t\right) \to e^{-\frac{a_c \sigma^2 u^2}{2}}, \quad t \to +\infty,$$

and the convergences thus obtained confirm the asymptotic relations in Equation (8). □

Remark 2. Note again that the proofs of the previous two theorems are based on determining the CFs of the corresponding time series of the GSB process. In this sense, the CFs of the uncorrelated series of RVs (ξ_t) and (η_t) play a fundamental role. The series (ξ_t) and (η_t) can be viewed as "new" innovations with "optional" non-zero values, which essentially describe the stochastic structure of the GSB process. Nevertheless, as the relation $\eta_t + \xi_t \stackrel{as}{=} \varepsilon_t$ holds for each $t = 0, \cdot 1, \ldots, T$, it is sufficient to consider only one of these two series of uncorrelated RVs (which is what was done in the statement of Theorem 2). Moreover, it can be easily shown that CDFs:

$$\begin{aligned}
F_\xi(u) &= (1-b_c)F_\varepsilon(x) + b_c F_0(x), \\
F_\eta(u) &= b_c F_\varepsilon(u) + (1-b_c)F_0(u)
\end{aligned}$$

are continuous almost everywhere, with the only point of discontinuity $x = 0$ where they have "jumps" of the values b_c and $1-b_c$, respectively (see for more detail [34,35]). Therefore, the CDFs of the series (ξ_t) and (η_t) are mixtures of Gaussian and discrete type distribution, usually named *Contaminated Gaussian Distribution* (CGD). This is another important fact that disables an application of some of the standard procedures in the investigation of the properties of non-stationary series (y_t) and (m_t).

On the other hand, Equation (8) shows that even non-stationary time series (m_t) and (y_t) can generate series $\left(m_t/\sqrt{t}\right)$ and $\left(y_t/\sqrt{t}\right)$ that converge toward a normal distribution when $t \to +\infty$. Moreover, based on the properties of the non-stationary components of the GSB process described in Section 2, the time series $(m_t/\sqrt{t})$ has a constant variance $a_c\sigma^2$. These facts will be of importance in the practical application of the GSB process and can be readily observed based on the convergence of the corresponding CFs $\varphi_m(u/\sqrt{t},t)$ and $\varphi_y(u/\sqrt{t},t)$. As an illustration, Figure 2 shows convergences of the modulus of these CFs, for different time indices (t).

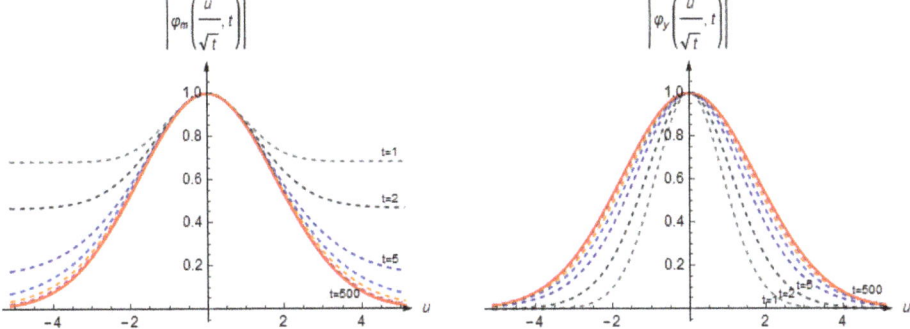

Figure 2. Graphs of the convergence of modulus of the characteristic functions $\varphi_m(u/\sqrt{t},t)$ and $\varphi_y(u/\sqrt{t},t)$, when $t = 1, 2, \ldots, 500$. (Parameter values are: $\mu = c = \sigma = 1$).

At the end of this section, we additionally describe some more asymptotic properties of series obtained by transformations of non-stationary time series (m_t) and (y_t). They also refer to the possibility of finding their asymptotically normal (AN) distributions, which can be shown by the following statement:

Theorem 3. *For arbitrary $\alpha \geq 1$ and time series (y_t) and (m_t), given by Equations (1) and (2), respectively, let us define the so-called α-mean series:*

$$\overline{M}_{t;\alpha} = \frac{1}{t^\alpha}\sum_{j=1}^{t}m_j, \quad \overline{Y}_{t;\alpha} = \frac{1}{t^\alpha}\sum_{j=1}^{t}y_j,$$

Then the following statements hold:

(i). *When $1 \leq \alpha \leq 3/2$, time series $\overline{M}_{t;\alpha}$ and $\overline{Y}_{t;\alpha}$ have an asymptotically normal distribution, i.e., the following relations, when $t \to +\infty$, are valid:*

$$\overline{M}_{t;\alpha} \sim \mathcal{N}\left(\mu t^{1-\alpha}, \frac{a_c\sigma^2 t^{3-2\alpha}}{3}\right), \quad \overline{Y}_{t;\alpha} \sim \mathcal{N}\left(\mu t^{1-\alpha}, \frac{a_c\sigma^2 t^{3-2\alpha}}{3}\right). \tag{11}$$

(ii). *When $\alpha > 3/2$, time series $\overline{M}_{t;\alpha}$ and $\overline{Y}_{t;\alpha}$ asymptotically vanish, i.e.,*

$$\overline{M}_{t;\alpha} \xrightarrow{d} I_0, \quad \overline{Y}_{t;\alpha} \xrightarrow{d} I_0, \quad t \to +\infty. \tag{12}$$

Proof. We show the statement of the theorem first for the time series $\overline{M}_{t;\alpha}$. Based on the definition of time series (m_t), i.e., Equation (2), one obtains:

$$\overline{M}_{t;\alpha} = \frac{1}{t^\alpha}\sum_{j=1}^{t} m_j = \frac{1}{t^\alpha}\sum_{j=1}^{t}\left(m_0 + \sum_{k=0}^{j-1} q_k \varepsilon_k\right)$$

$$= \frac{1}{t^\alpha}\left[tm_0 + \sum_{j=0}^{t-1}(t-j)q_j\varepsilon_j\right] = t^{1-\alpha}m_0 + \sum_{k=1}^{t}\frac{k}{t^\alpha}\xi_{t-k}.$$

Thus, the series $\overline{M}_{t;\alpha}$ is represented as a sum of uncorrelated RVs ξ_{t-k}, $k = 1,\ldots,t$. By applying the well-known properties of the CFs, as well as the expressions for the CF of the series (ξ_t), the CFs of $\overline{M}_{t;\alpha}$ are as follows:

$$\varphi_{\overline{M};\alpha}(u,t) = \varphi_m\left(\frac{u}{t^{\alpha-1}},0\right)\prod_{k=1}^{t}\varphi_\xi\left(\frac{ku}{t^\alpha}\right) = e^{iu\mu t^{1-\alpha}}\prod_{k=1}^{t}\left[1+a_c\left(e^{-\frac{k^2\sigma^2 u^2}{2t^{2\alpha}}}-1\right)\right].$$

Taking the logarithm of the function $\varphi_{\overline{M};\alpha}(u,t)$ gives a function:

$$\psi_M(u,t,\alpha) := \ln\varphi_{\overline{M};\alpha}(u,t) = iu\mu t^{1-\alpha} + \sum_{k=1}^{t} f_k(u,t,\alpha),$$

where $f_k(u,t,\alpha) := \ln\left[1+a_c(\exp(-k^2\sigma^2 u^2 t^{-2\alpha}/2)-1)\right]$. After some computation, we find that, when $0 < a_c < 1$,

$$\frac{\partial f_k(0,t,\alpha)}{\partial u} = \left.\frac{-\frac{a_c k^2 \sigma^2 u}{t^{2\alpha}}e^{-\frac{k^2\sigma^2 u^2}{2t^{2\alpha}}}}{1+a_c\left(e^{-\frac{k^2\sigma^2 u^2}{2t^{2\alpha}}}-1\right)}\right|_{u=0} = 0$$

$$\frac{\partial^2 f_k(0,t,\alpha)}{\partial u^2} = \left.\frac{-\frac{a_c k^2 \sigma^2}{t^{2\alpha}}e^{-\frac{k^2\sigma^2 u^2}{2t^{2\alpha}}}\left((1-a_c)\left(1-\frac{k^2\sigma^2 u^2}{t^{2\alpha}}\right)+a_c e^{-\frac{k^2\sigma^2 u^2}{2t^{2\alpha}}}\right)}{\left(1+a_c\left(e^{-\frac{k^2\sigma^2 u^2}{2t^{2\alpha}}}-1\right)\right)^2}\right|_{u=0} = -\frac{a_c k^2 \sigma^2}{t^{2\alpha}}.$$

Thus, the functions $f_k(u,t,\alpha)$ have local maxima at the point $u = 0$. Using a similar procedure as in [34], that is, by Laplace approximation of functions $f_k(u,t,\alpha)$ at $u = 0$, one obtains:

$$\psi_M(u,t,\alpha) = iu\mu t^{1-\alpha} + \sum_{k=1}^{t}\left[\frac{\partial^2 f_k(0,t,\alpha)}{\partial u^2}\cdot\frac{u^2}{2}+\sigma_k(u^2)\right]$$

$$= iu\mu t^{1-\alpha} + \sum_{k=1}^{t}\left[-\frac{a_c k^2 \sigma^2 u^2}{2t^{2\alpha}}+\sigma_k(t^{-2\alpha}u^2)\right]$$

$$= iu\mu t^{1-\alpha} - \frac{a_c \sigma^2 u^2}{12t^{2\alpha}}t(t+1)(2t+1)+\sigma(t^{3-2\alpha}u^2).$$

Then, by taking the asymptotic value in the last expression, when $t \to +\infty$, it follows:

$$\psi_M(u,t,\alpha) \sim \begin{cases} iu\mu t^{1-\alpha} - a_c\sigma^2 t^{3-2\alpha}/6, & 1 \le \alpha \le 3/2 \\ 0, & \alpha > 3/2. \end{cases}$$

Substituting this expression into the CFs $\varphi_{\overline{M};\alpha}(u,t)$, it is easy to conclude that the first part of the theorem, in the sense of the series $\overline{M}_{t;\alpha}$, is valid.

The proof for the series $\overline{Y}_{t;\alpha}$ is carried out analogously. Using Equation (1), as the previously proven facts, we have that

$$\begin{aligned}\overline{Y}_{t;\alpha} &= \tfrac{1}{t^\alpha}\sum_{j=1}^{t}(m_j+\varepsilon_j) = \overline{M}_{t;\alpha} + \sum_{j=1}^{t}\tfrac{\varepsilon_j}{t^\alpha} = t^{1-\alpha}m_0 + \sum_{k=1}^{t}\tfrac{k}{t^\alpha}\zeta_{t-k} + \sum_{k=0}^{t-1}\tfrac{\varepsilon_{t-k}}{t^\alpha}\\ &= t^{1-\alpha}m_0 + \tfrac{\varepsilon_t}{t^\alpha} + \sum_{k=1}^{t}(1+kq_{t-k})\tfrac{\varepsilon_{t-k}}{t^\alpha}.\end{aligned}$$

Since RVs ε_{t-k}, $k=0,1,\dots,t$, are mutually independent, after some computation, we obtain the CFs of series $\overline{Y}_{t;\alpha}$ as follows:

$$\begin{aligned}\varphi_{\overline{Y};\alpha}(u,t) &= \varphi_m\left(\tfrac{u}{t^{\alpha-1}},0\right)\varphi_\varepsilon\left(\tfrac{u}{t^\alpha}\right)\prod_{k=1}^{t}\left[(1-a_c)\varphi_\varepsilon\left(\tfrac{u}{t^\alpha}\right) + a_c\varphi_\varepsilon\left(\tfrac{(k+1)u}{t^\alpha}\right)\right]\\ &= e^{iu\mu t^{1-\alpha} - \tfrac{\sigma^2 u^2}{2t^{2\alpha}}}\prod_{k=1}^{t}\left[e^{-\tfrac{\sigma^2 u^2}{2t^{2\alpha}}} + a_c\left(e^{-\tfrac{(k+1)^2\sigma^2 u^2}{2t^{2\alpha}}} - e^{-\tfrac{\sigma^2 u^2}{2t^{2\alpha}}}\right)\right]\\ &= e^{iu\mu t^{1-\alpha} - \tfrac{\sigma^2 u^2(t+1)}{2t^{2\alpha}}}\prod_{k=1}^{t}\left[1 + a_c\left(e^{-\tfrac{(k^2+2k)\sigma^2 u^2}{2t^{2\alpha}}} - 1\right)\right].\end{aligned}$$

From here, using the same procedure as in the previous part of the proof, i.e., by taking the logarithm of the function $\varphi_{\overline{Y};\alpha}(u,t)$, and by developing $\psi_Y(u,t,\alpha) := \ln\varphi_{\overline{Y};\alpha}(u,t)$ at the point $u=0$, we have:

$$\begin{aligned}\psi_Y(u,t,\alpha) &= iu\mu t^{1-\alpha} - \tfrac{\sigma^2 u^2(t+1)}{2t^{2\alpha}} + \sum_{k=1}^{t}\ln\left[1 + a_c\left(e^{-\tfrac{(k^2+2k)\sigma^2 u^2}{2t^{2\alpha}}} - 1\right)\right]\\ &= iu\mu t^{1-\alpha} - \tfrac{\sigma^2 u^2(t+1)}{2t^{2\alpha}} - \sum_{k=1}^{t}\left[\tfrac{a_c(k^2+2k)\sigma^2 u^2}{2t^{2\alpha}} + o_k(t^{-2\alpha}u^2)\right]\\ &= iu\mu t^{1-\alpha} - \tfrac{\sigma^2 u^2}{2}\left(t^{1-2\alpha} + t^{-2\alpha}\right) - a_c\tfrac{\sigma^2 u^2}{12t^{2\alpha}}t(t+1)(2t+7)\\ &\quad + o\left(t^{3-2\alpha}u^2\right).\end{aligned}$$

Finally, taking the asymptotic values, when $t\to+\infty$, one obtains:

$$\psi_Y(u,t,\alpha) \sim \begin{cases} iu\mu t^{1-\alpha} - \tfrac{\sigma^2 u^2}{2}\left(t^{1-2\alpha} + t^{-2\alpha} + \tfrac{a_c t^{3-2\alpha}}{3}\right), & 1\le\alpha\le 3/2\\ 0, & \alpha > 3/2.\end{cases}$$

Substituting this expression into CFs $\varphi_{\overline{Y};\alpha}(u,t)$, the entire statement of the theorem is proved. □

Remark 3. In the previous theorem, the case $\alpha = 3/2$ is particularly interesting because Equation (11) then gives the following convergences:

$$\tfrac{1}{t^{3/2}}\sum_{j=1}^{t}m_j \xrightarrow{d} \mathcal{N}\left(0,\tfrac{a_c\sigma^2}{3}\right),\quad \tfrac{1}{t^{3/2}}\sum_{j=1}^{t}y_j \xrightarrow{d} \mathcal{N}\left(0,\tfrac{a_c\sigma^2}{3}\right),\quad t\to+\infty. \tag{13}$$

We will call these convergences, in the usual way, *central limit theorems (CLTs) for the GSB process*. As will be seen below, they will be helpful for estimating the unknown parameters of the GSB process, primarily the conditional variance σ^2.

4. Parameter Estimation Procedures

Now, let us consider the problem of estimation of (unknown) parameters of the GSB process, the critical value (c), mean value (μ), and conditional variance (σ^2). To estimate the first parameter c, a series of increments (X_t) will be used as the (only) observable and stationary component of the GSB model. Recall that we have named this series the Split-MA (1) process because it is close to standard, linear MA models. Although some of the estimation procedures we present here are like standard estimation methods in MA models (see, for instance [36]), the specificity of the Split-MA (1) model requires additional testing and analysis, primarily of the quality of the obtained estimates. To that end, the consistency and asymptotic normality of the estimators were examined. After that, several new approaches were considered, based on the observation of non-stationary time series (y_t). The main goal of these procedures is aimed at obtaining the estimated values of the parameters μ and σ^2.

4.1. Estimates of Critical Value (c)

Let (X_t) be the Split-MA (1) process defined by Equation (4). As we have already shown, the first correlation coefficient of this series is:

$$\rho_X(1) = -\frac{b_c}{1+b_c}, \quad 0 < b_c < 1.$$

From here, by solving on b_c, we get the estimated value of this parameter:

$$\tilde{b}_c = -\frac{\hat{\rho}_X(1)}{1+\hat{\rho}(1)}, \quad 0 < b_c < 1, \tag{14}$$

where:

$$\hat{\rho}_X(1) = \left(\sum_{t=1}^{T} X_t X_{t-1}\right)\left(\sum_{t=1}^{T} X_t^2\right)^{-1}$$

is the estimated value of the first correlation. Based on the estimate $\tilde{b}_c$, the corresponding estimate of the critical value $c = \tilde{c}$ can be determined as a solution to the equation:

$$P\{\varepsilon_t^2 \leq c\} = \tilde{b}_c.$$

According to Equation (14), it is easy to see that $\tilde{b}_c$ and $\tilde{c}$ are appropriate estimates if the following inequalities hold:

$$0 < \tilde{b}_c < 1 \iff -0.5 < \hat{\rho}_X(1) < 0.$$

In [9], it was shown that thus obtained estimators are strictly consistent if the innovations (ε_t) have a continuous distribution. Moreover, the estimates $\tilde{b}_c$ and $\tilde{c}$ will also be asymptotically normal (AN) if the RVs (ε_t) have a symmetric distribution. Note that both conditions are fulfilled in the case of Gaussian innovations $\varepsilon_t : \mathcal{N}(0, \sigma^2)$, when the RVs $(\varepsilon_t/\sigma)^2$ have a χ_1^2 distribution. Thus, the estimate of the critical value $\tilde{c}$ is simply found from the equality:

$$\tilde{c} = \tilde{\sigma}^2 \cdot F_{\chi_1^2}^{-1}(\tilde{b}_c). \tag{15}$$

Here, $\tilde{\sigma}^2$ is the estimated variance of innovations (ε_t) which will be described later.

However, it can be shown that, as for the linear MA series, the estimate $\tilde{b}_c$ is not the most efficient estimate for b_c (asymptotic efficiency of the estimate $\tilde{b}_c$ is analyzed at the end of this subsection). To obtain more efficient estimates of the given parameters, we will modify the well-known Gauss-Newton method of estimating the parameters of nonlinear functions (see, for instance [36]). First, notice that Equation (4) can be written in the form:

$$\varepsilon_t = X_t + \theta_{t-1}\varepsilon_{t-1}, \quad t = 1, \ldots, T$$

or, in functional form,

$$\varepsilon_t(X, \theta) = X_t + \theta_{t-1}\varepsilon_{t-1}(X, \theta). \tag{16}$$

On the other hand, if we define a series of RVs as

$$W_t(X, \theta) = \theta_t W_{t-1}(X, \theta) + \varepsilon_{t-1}(X, \theta), \tag{17}$$

then it is easy to see that the RVs $W_t(X,\theta)$ are $\mathcal{F}_{t-1}$ adapted, for each $t=1,\ldots,T$, and thus independent of ε_t and θ_{t+1}. According to mentioned properties of RVs (θ_t) and (ε_t), it follows that $(W_t(X,\theta))$ is a stationary and ergodic series of RVs (see, for more detail [37]) with $E(W_t(X,\theta))=0$ and correlation function $\rho_W(h)=b_c^{|h|}$, $h=0,\pm 1,\ldots$ To this series, using the procedure described in [38], we add the so-called residual series:

$$R_t(X,\theta) = W_t(X,\theta) - b_c W_{t-1}(X,\theta). \tag{18}$$

The RVs $R_t(X,\theta)$ are also $\mathcal{F}_{t-1}$ adapted and mutually non-correlated, which can easily be shown. Namely, by applying Equations (16)–(18), for any integer $h>0$, one obtains:

$$\begin{aligned}
Cov(R_t(X,\theta), R_{t+h}(X,\theta)) &= E(R_t(X,\theta)R_{t+h}(X,\theta)) \\
&= E[R_t(X,\theta)(W_{t+h}(X,\theta) - b_c W_{t+h-1}(X,\theta))] \\
&= E(R_t(X,\theta)W_{t+h}(X,\theta)) - b_c E(R_t(X,\theta)W_{t+h-1}(X,\theta)) \\
&= E[R_t(X,\theta)\theta_{t+h}W_{t+h-1}(X,\theta)] - b_c E(R_t(X,\theta)W_{t+h-1}(X,\theta)) = 0.
\end{aligned}$$

Thus, Equation (18) defines the series $(W_t(X,\theta))$ as a linear autoregressive (AR) process with innovations $(R_t(X,\theta))$. From here, we obtain another estimate of the unknown parameter $b_c \in (0,1)$ by the following algorithmic procedure:

(1) Applying Equation (14), determine $\widetilde{b}_c$ as (the initial) estimate of b_c, and according to Equation (15), determine estimate $\widetilde{c}$.

(2) Based on Equations (16)–(18) and having obtained an estimate $\widetilde{b}_c$, compute, for each $t=1,\ldots,T$, the values:

$$\widetilde{\theta}_t := I\left(\varepsilon_{t-1}^2\left(X,\widetilde{\theta}\right) \leq \widetilde{c}\right)$$

$$\varepsilon_t\left(X,\widetilde{\theta}\right) := X_t + \widetilde{\theta}_{t-1}\varepsilon_{t-1}\left(X,\widetilde{\theta}\right)$$

$$W_t\left(X,\widetilde{\theta}\right) := \widetilde{\theta}_t W_{t-1}\left(X,\widetilde{\theta}\right) + \varepsilon_{t-1}\left(X,\widetilde{\theta}\right)$$

$$R_t\left(X,\widetilde{\theta}\right) := W_t\left(X,\widetilde{\theta}\right) - \widetilde{b}_c W_{t-1}\left(X,\widetilde{\theta}\right),$$

where $\widetilde{\theta}_0 = 1$, $\varepsilon_0\left(X,\widetilde{\theta}\right) = \varepsilon_{-1}\left(X,\widetilde{\theta}\right) = W_0\left(X,\widetilde{\theta}\right) = 0$.

(3) Using the standard regression procedure, i.e., the correlation function $\rho_W(h)$ when $h=1$, obtain an estimate of b_c in the form:

$$\hat{b}_c = \left(\sum_{t=0}^{T-1} W_t\left(X,\widetilde{\theta}\right)W_{t+1}\left(X,\widetilde{\theta}\right)\right)\left(\sum_{t=1}^{T} W_t^2\left(X,\widetilde{\theta}\right)\right)^{-1}.$$

(4) As in the first step, based on the estimate $\hat{b}_c$, the critical value $\hat{c}$ can be estimated as a solution of the equation (concerning c):

$$P\{\varepsilon_t^2 \leq c\} = \hat{b}_c.$$

We emphasize that in [9], strict consistency and AN of the estimates $\widetilde{b}_c$ and $\widetilde{c}$ as well as $\hat{b}_c$ and $\hat{c}$ was proved. At the same time, the distribution of innovations (ε_t) was not explicitly used there. In the case of GSB process, where innovations are Gaussian distributed, we can express these results as follows:

Theorem 4. *Estimates $\widetilde{b}_c$ and $\hat{b}_c$ are strictly consistent for the parameter b_c, i.e., it is valid that:*

$$\widetilde{b}_c \xrightarrow{as} b_c, \quad \hat{b}_c \xrightarrow{as} b_c, \quad T \to +\infty.$$

Moreover, the estimates $\widetilde{b}_c$ and $\hat{b}_c$ are asymptotically normal for b_c, i.e.,

$$\sqrt{T}\left(\widetilde{b}_c - b_c\right) \xrightarrow{d} \mathcal{N}\left(0, \widetilde{V}\right), \quad \sqrt{T}\left(\hat{b}_c - b_c\right) \xrightarrow{d} \mathcal{N}\left(0, \hat{V}\right), \quad T \to +\infty,$$

where $\widetilde{V}(b_c) = (b_c + 1)^2 \left(2b_c^2 + 4b_c + 1\right)$ and $\hat{V}(b_c) = (1 - b_c)\left(3b_c^2 + 3b_c + 1\right)$.

Remark 4. Based on the previous theorem, the consistency and AN of the estimates $\widetilde{c}$ and $\hat{c}$, as continuous functions of $\widetilde{b}_c$ and $\hat{b}_c$, is also valid (see, for instance [9] or [39] p. 24). Additionally, for any $b_c \in (0,1)$, the inequality $\hat{V}(b_c) \leq \widetilde{V}(b_c)$ holds when the equality is valid only for $b_c = 0$, as can be seen in Figure 3. This means that asymptotic variance $\hat{V}(b_c)$, as a measure of "scattering" $\hat{b}_c$ from the true value b_c, is (significantly) smaller than $\widetilde{V}(b_c)$. So, $\hat{b}_c$ is a more efficient estimate than $\widetilde{b}_c$, which justifies its introduction.

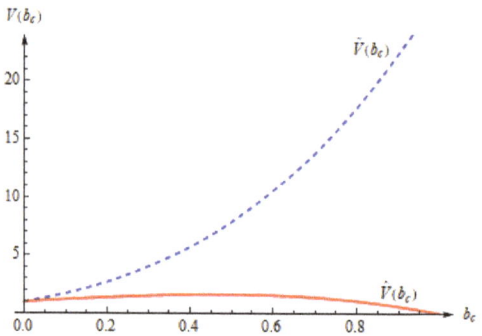

Figure 3. Graphs of the asymptotic variances of the estimates $\widetilde{b}_c$. (dashed line) and $\hat{b}_c$ (solid line), depending on $b_c \in (0, 1)$.

4.2. Estimates of Mean (μ)

As an estimator for the parameter $\mu = E(y_t)$, the sample mean of series (y_t) was usually used:

$$\widetilde{\mu} := \overline{y}_T = \frac{1}{T} \sum_{t=1}^{T} y_t. \tag{19}$$

This estimator is obviously unbiased $E(\widetilde{\mu}) = E(\overline{y}_T) = \mu$, but its variance is not bounded. Namely, using the previously defined α-mean series $\overline{Y}_{T;\alpha}$ when $\alpha = 1$, we can represent the estimator $\widetilde{\mu}$ as a sum of uncorrelated RVs:

$$\widetilde{\mu} = m_0 + \frac{1}{T}\left[\sum_{k=1}^{T}(1 + kq_{T-k})\varepsilon_{T-k} + \varepsilon_T\right].$$

Thus, for the variance of $\widetilde{\mu}$ we get:

$$\begin{aligned}
\widetilde{V} := V(\widetilde{\mu}) &= \tfrac{1}{T^2}\left[\sum_{k=1}^{T} V((1 + kq_{T-k})\varepsilon_{T-k}) + V(\varepsilon_T)\right] \\
&= \tfrac{\sigma^2}{T^2}\left[\sum_{k=1}^{T} E(1 + kq_{T-k})^2 + 1\right] \\
&= \tfrac{\sigma^2}{T^2}\left[\sum_{k=1}^{T}(1 + a_c k(k+2)) + 1\right] \\
&= \tfrac{\sigma^2}{T^2}\left[T + 1 + a_c \tfrac{T(T+1)(2T+7)}{6}\right] \\
&= \tfrac{\sigma^2(T+1)}{T^2}\left(1 + a_c \tfrac{T(2T+7)}{6}\right) \\
&= \tfrac{a_c \sigma^2 T}{3} + \mathcal{O}(T^{-1}) \to +\infty, \quad T \to +\infty.
\end{aligned}$$

Note that, as expected, the variance $\widetilde{V} = V(\widetilde{\mu})$ is asymptotically identical to that in Theorem 3, i.e., as in Equation (11), when $\alpha = 1$. Moreover, $\widetilde{V} = 0$ when $a_c = 0$, that is, in the case of extremely large values of the parameter c. However, in practical applications, this condition is usually not met.

An alternative way to obtain an estimate for μ is to take the sample mean of the mean series $\bar{y}_t$, when $t = 1, \ldots, T$, i.e.,

$$\hat{\mu} := \frac{1}{T}\sum_{t=1}^{T} \bar{y}_t = \frac{1}{T}\sum_{t=1}^{T} \omega_t y_t. \tag{20}$$

Here, $\omega_t := H(T) - H(t-1)$ and $H(t) := \sum_{j=1}^{t} j^{-1}, t = 1, \ldots, T$ are the harmonic numbers, with assumption $H(0) = 0$. Obviously, $\hat{\mu}$ is also an unbiased estimate of the parameter μ, but with weights that are more pronounced at the "older" points of time (t) in which realizations of the series (y_t) are observed. This is consistent with the fact that the covariances of RVs y_t depend on these "older" time indices. Moreover, as shown in Section 2, at these time points, the covariances of RVs y_t are equal to their variances. For these reasons, it is expected that the estimate $\hat{\mu}$ will be more efficient than $\widetilde{\mu}$. Indeed, using a similar procedure as before, we first represent the estimate $\hat{\mu}$ as a sum of uncorrelated RVs:

$$\begin{aligned}\hat{\mu} &= \frac{1}{T}\sum_{t=1}^{T} \omega_t \left(m_0 + \sum_{j=0}^{t-1} q_j \varepsilon_j\right) + \frac{1}{T}\sum_{t=1}^{T} \omega_t \varepsilon_t \\ &= \frac{1}{T}\left[m_0 \sum_{t=1}^{T}\omega_t + \sum_{j=0}^{T-1}\left(q_j \varepsilon_j \sum_{t=j+1}^{T}\omega_t\right) + \sum_{t=1}^{T}\omega_t \varepsilon_t\right].\end{aligned}$$

As for each $j = 1, \ldots, T$, the statement below holds:

$$\sum_{t=j}^{T}\omega_t = \sum_{t=j}^{T}(H(T) - H(t-1)) = \sum_{t=j}^{T}\sum_{k=t}^{T}\frac{1}{k} = T - (j-1)(\omega_j + 1),$$

it follows that it can also be written:

$$\begin{aligned}\hat{\mu} &= \frac{1}{T}\left[T(m_0 + q_0 \varepsilon_0) + \sum_{j=1}^{T-1}(T - j(\omega_{j+1} + 1))q_j \varepsilon_j\right] + \frac{1}{T}\sum_{t=1}^{T}\omega_t \varepsilon_t \\ &= m_0 + q_0 \varepsilon_0 + \frac{1}{T}\sum_{j=1}^{T-1}(c_j q_j + \omega_j)\varepsilon_j + \frac{\varepsilon_T}{T^2},\end{aligned}$$

where $c_j = T - j(\omega_{j+1} + 1)$. Thus, after some computation, the variance of $\hat{\mu}$ one obtains is:

$$\begin{aligned}\hat{V} := V(\hat{\mu}) &= \frac{1}{T^2}\left[\sum_{j=1}^{T-1} E(c_j q_j + \omega_j)^2 E(\varepsilon_j^2) + \frac{E(\varepsilon_T^2)}{T^2}\right] \\ &= \frac{\sigma^2}{T^2}\left[\sum_{j=1}^{T-1}\left(a_c c_j(c_j + 2\omega_j) + \omega_j^2\right) + \frac{1}{T^2}\right] \\ &= \frac{\sigma^2(a_c(T-1)-2)H(T-1)H(T)}{T} + \sigma(H^{-2}(T)) \\ &= a_c \sigma^2 H^2(T) + \sigma(H^{-2}(T)) \to +\infty, \ T \to +\infty.\end{aligned}$$

Notice that the variance of $\hat{V} := V(\hat{\mu})$ is also unbounded, but with a lower asymptotic order than $\widetilde{V} = V(\widetilde{\mu})$, since:

$$\lim_{T\to +\infty}\frac{V(\hat{\mu})}{V(\widetilde{\mu})} = \lim_{T\to +\infty}\frac{H^2(T)}{T} = 0.$$

This means that the estimate $\hat{\mu}$ is (asymptotically) more efficient than $\tilde{\mu}$, which can be seen in Figure 4. Here are shown 3D plots of both variances $\tilde{V}$ and $\hat{V}$, which were observed as functions of two variables $a_c \in (0,1)$ and $T > 0$.

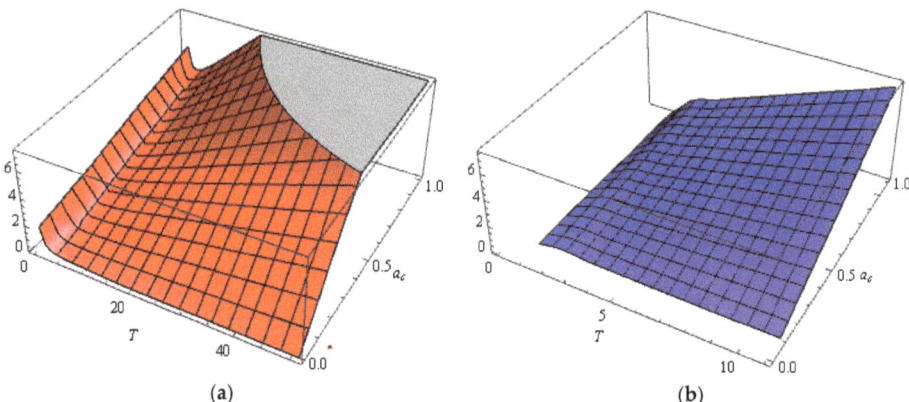

Figure 4. Variances shown as 3D plots of the estimate $\tilde{\mu}$ (a) and estimate $\hat{\mu}$ (b), depending on $a_c \in (0,1)$ and $T > 0$. (The variance of innovations is $\sigma^2 = 1$).

4.3. Estimates of Variance (σ^2)

Let us consider determining the estimates of the third unknown parameter σ^2, which represents the variance of the innovations (ε_t), that is, the conditional variance of the base series (y_t). It is precisely these facts that enable different estimation procedures for the parameter σ^2. First, notice that based on the previously obtained estimates $\tilde{b}_c$ and $\hat{b}_c$, i.e., the modeled innovation values (ε_t) given by Equation (16), the variance σ^2 can be easily estimated. The usual estimation procedure is based on sampling variance:

$$\tilde{\sigma}^2 = \frac{1}{T}\sum_{t=1}^{T} \varepsilon_t^2\left(X,\tilde{\theta}\right) \text{ or } \hat{\sigma}^2 = \frac{1}{T}\sum_{t=1}^{T} \varepsilon_t^2(X,\hat{\theta}). \tag{21}$$

Here, $\varepsilon_t\left(X,\tilde{\theta}\right)$ are $\varepsilon_t(X,\hat{\theta})$ modeled innovation values obtained from the estimates $\tilde{b}_c$ and $\hat{b}_c$, respectively. Notice that in the case of Gaussian innovations (ε_t), the estimates given by Equation (21) are identical to the maximum likelihood estimators. Indeed, the log-likelihood function then reads as follows:

$$L(y_1,\ldots,y_T;\sigma^2) = -\frac{T}{2}\ln(2\pi\sigma^2) - \frac{1}{2\sigma^2}\sum_{t=1}^{T}(y_t - m_t)^2,$$

and by solving the equation $\partial L(y_1,\ldots,y_T;\sigma^2)/\partial\sigma^2 = 0$, the estimate of σ^2 is obtained as in Equation (21), that is, as the sample variance of the series (ε_t). Thus, the consistency and AN of both estimates $\tilde{\sigma}^2$ and $\hat{\sigma}^2$ can be readily shown. We note that due to their equivalence, only the estimate $\hat{\sigma}^2$ will be further considered (see Theorem below).

On the other hand, note that the previous estimation procedure is based on unobservable, modeled values of innovations (ε_t). Another approach to estimating the variance σ^2 is based on the so-called two-stage procedure, using the previously estimated parameter $\hat{b}_c$. By applying the equality $V(X_t) = E(X_t^2) = \sigma^2(b_c + 1)$, as well as the sample variance of the series (X_t), we can obtain an estimate:

$$\hat{\sigma}_X^2 = \frac{1}{T\left(\hat{b}_c + 1\right)}\sum_{t=1}^{T} X_t^2. \tag{22}$$

Then, it follows:

Theorem 5. *Estimates $\hat{\sigma}^2$ and $\hat{\sigma}_X^2$ are strictly consistent for the parameter σ^2, i.e., it is valid to put:*

$$\hat{\sigma}^2 \xrightarrow{as} \sigma^2, \quad \hat{\sigma}_X^2 \xrightarrow{as} \sigma^2, \quad T \to +\infty.$$

Moreover, the estimates $\hat{\sigma}^2$ and $\hat{\sigma}_X^2$ are asymptotically normal for σ^2, i.e.,

$$\sqrt{T}\left(\hat{\sigma}^2 - \sigma^2\right) \xrightarrow{d} \mathcal{N}(0, V_1), \quad \sqrt{T}\left(\hat{\sigma}_X^2 - \sigma^2\right) \xrightarrow{d} \mathcal{N}(0, V_2), \quad T \to +\infty, \tag{23}$$

where $V_1 = 2\sigma^4$ and $V_2 = \sigma^4 \left(2 + 11 b_c - b_c^2\right)\left(1 + 2 b_c - 3 b_c^3\right)^{-1}$.

Proof. Since $\left(\varepsilon_t^2\right)$ is an IID series of RVs, the stationarity and ergodicity of this series are apparent. Applying the strong low of large numbers (SLLS), it follows:

$$\hat{\sigma}^2 = \frac{1}{T}\sum_{t=1}^{T} \varepsilon_t^2(X,\hat{\theta}) \xrightarrow{as} \sigma^2.$$

Furthermore, it can easily be shown that $V\left(\hat{\sigma}^2\right) = 2\sigma^4/T$ is the variance of the estimate $\hat{\sigma}^2$. Thus, applying the central limit theorem (CLT), the first convergence in Equation (23) is obtained.

To prove the properties of the estimate $\hat{\sigma}_X^2$, we note that $\left(X_t^2\right)$ is also a stationary and ergodic series of RVs. If SLLS is now applied to the following statistics:

$$\overline{X}_t^2 := \frac{1}{T}\sum_{t=1}^{T} X_t^2, \tag{24}$$

then one obtains:

$$\frac{1}{T}\sum_{t=1}^{T} X_t^2 \xrightarrow{as} \sigma^2(b_c + 1).$$

At the same time, according to Theorem 4, we have that $\hat{b}_c$ is a strongly consistent estimator of b_c, i.e., $\hat{b}_c + 1 \xrightarrow{as} b_c + 1$, when $T \to +\infty$. Thus, the last two convergences give:

$$\hat{\sigma}_X^2 = \frac{\overline{X}_t^2}{\hat{b}_c + 1} \xrightarrow{as} \sigma^2, \quad T \to +\infty.$$

To prove the AN of the estimate $\hat{\sigma}_X^2$, note first that the sequence $\left(X_t^2\right)$ is 1-dependent, in the sense of Definition 6.3.1 in [36] (p. 245). According to Cauchy-Swarz and Minkowski inequalities, applied to Equation (4), i.e., the sixth moment of the sum $X_t = \varepsilon_t + (-\theta_{t-1}\varepsilon_{t-1})$, it follows that:

$$E|X_t|^6 \leq \left[\left(E|\varepsilon_t|^6\right)^{1/6} + \left(b_c\, E|\varepsilon_{t-1}|^6\right)^{1/6}\right]^6$$

$$\leq 15\sigma^6 \left(1 + b_c^{1/6}\right)^6 < +\infty.$$

Then, the Hoeffding-Robbins theorem [40] can be applied, based on which it follows:

$$\sqrt{T}\overline{X}_t^2 = T^{-1/2}\sum_{t=1}^{T} X_t^2 \xrightarrow{d} \mathcal{N}\left(\sigma^2(b_c + 1), V_0\right), \tag{25}$$

for which:

$$\begin{aligned}V_0 &= V(X_t^2) + 2\text{Cov}(X_t^2, X_{t+1}^2) = E(X_t^4) + 2E(X_t^2 X_{t+1}^2) - 3\sigma^4(1+b_c)^2 \\ &= 3\sigma^4(1+3b_c) + 2\sigma^4(1+4b_c+b_c^2) - 3\sigma^4(1+b_c)^2 \\ &= \sigma^4(2+11b_c - b_c^2).\end{aligned}$$

By applying the almost sure convergence of the estimate $\hat{b}_c$ and the previously obtained convergence in Equation (25), we have

$$\sqrt{T}\hat{\sigma}_X^2 = \frac{\sqrt{T}\overline{X_t^2}}{\hat{b}_c + 1} \xrightarrow{d} \mathcal{N}(\sigma^2, V_2), \quad T \to +\infty,$$

where $V_2 = V_0/\hat{V}(b_c)$. Thus, according to Theorem 4, the second convergence in Equation (23) is obtained. □

Remark 5. As in Theorem 4, by comparing the asymptotic variances V_1 and V_2 for the estimates $\hat{\sigma}^2$ and $\hat{\sigma}_X^2$, respectively, it is easy to see that inequality $V_1 \leq V_2$ holds. At the same time, the equality $V_1 = V_2 = 2\sigma^4$ is valid only when $b_c = 0$ (Figure 5a), so the estimator $\hat{\sigma}^2$ is more efficient than $\hat{\sigma}_X^2$.

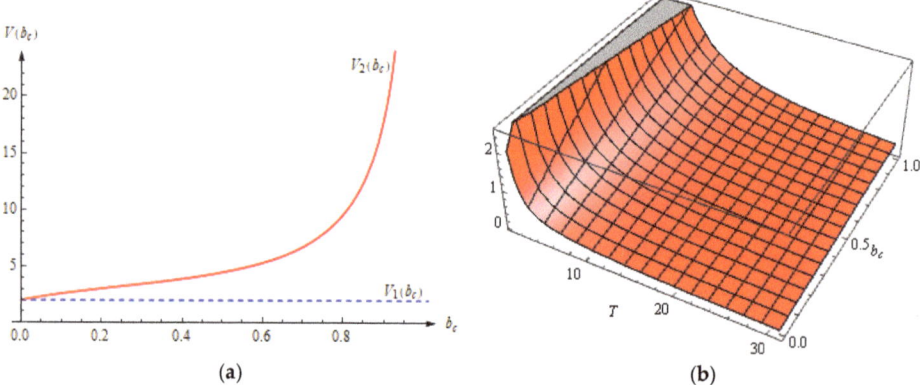

Figure 5. (a) Graphs of the asymptotic variances of the estimates $\hat{\sigma}^2$ (dashed line) and $\hat{\sigma}_X^2$ (solid line), depending on $b_c \in (0,1)$. (b) Plot in 3D of the variance of statistics $\overline{X_t^2}$, depending on $b_c \in (0,1)$ and $T > 0$. (The variance of the innovations is $\sigma^2 = 1$).

However, according to the proof of the previous theorem, it can be easily seen that for the variance of the statistics $\overline{X_t^2}$, given by Equation (24), is valid (Figure 5b):

$$V(\overline{X_t^2}) = \frac{\sigma^4(2+11b_c - b_c^2)}{T} \to 0, \quad T \to +\infty.$$

Thus, $\overline{X_t^2}$ can be used as an estimator of the "hybrid" parameter $\sigma^2(b_c + 1)$, which will be of interest for practical research, that is, the application of the GSB model discussed below.

Finally, another approach to finding estimates of the variance σ^2 is based on the observations of the non-stationary series (y_t). Applying Theorem 3, i.e., the previously proven convergence in Equation (13), we have:

$$\overline{Y}_{T;3/2} := \frac{1}{T^{3/2}} \sum_{t=1}^{T} y_t \xrightarrow{d} \mathcal{N}\left(0, \frac{a_c \sigma^2}{3}\right), \quad T \to +\infty.$$

If we now consider the statistics:

$$S_T^2 := \overline{Y}_{T;3/2}^2 = \frac{1}{T^3}\left(\sum_{t=1}^T y_t\right)^2 = \frac{1}{T^3}\sum_{j=1}^T\sum_{k=1}^T y_j y_k, \qquad (26)$$

after some computation, one obtains:

$$\begin{aligned}
E(S_T^2) &= \frac{1}{T^3}\sum_{j=1}^T\sum_{k=1}^T E(y_j y_k) = \frac{1}{T^3}\sum_{j=1}^T\sum_{k=1}^T \left[Cov(y_j y_k) + \mu^2\right] \\
&= \frac{1}{T^3}\sum_{j=1}^T\sum_{k=1}^T \left[\sigma^2(\min\{j,k\}a_c + 1) + \mu^2\right] \\
&= \frac{\sigma^2}{T^3}\left[a_c \sum_{j=1}^T\left(j + 2\sum_{k=1}^{j-1} k\right) + T^2\right] + \frac{\mu^2}{T} = \frac{\sigma^2}{T^3}\left(a_c\sum_{j=1}^T j^2 + T^2\right) + \frac{\mu^2}{T} \\
&= \frac{\sigma^2 a_c}{6T^2}(T+1)(2T+1) + \frac{\sigma^2+\mu^2}{T} \rightarrow \frac{a_c\sigma^2}{3}, \; T \rightarrow +\infty.
\end{aligned}$$

Thus, S_T^2 is an asymptotically unbiased estimator for $a_c\sigma^2/3$, and using the estimate $\hat{a}_c = 1 - \hat{b}_c$, an estimator of the parameter σ^2 can be taken as:

$$\hat{\sigma}_Y^2 := \frac{3}{\hat{a}_c}S_T^2 = \frac{3}{\hat{a}_c T^3}\sum_{j=1}^T\sum_{k=1}^T y_j y_k. \qquad (27)$$

5. Numerical Simulation and Application of the GSB Process

As already mentioned in the introductory section, two important aspects related to the practical implementation of the GSB process will be explored here. Firstly, numerical Monte Carlo simulations of previously obtained GSB estimators are analyzed. Then, based on actual data, the GSB process was applied to analyze the dynamics and distribution of the infected and immunized population with respect to COVID-19 disease in the territory of the Republic of Serbia.

5.1. Numerical Simulations of GSB Estimators

We first describe a pseudo-algorithm for estimating the parameters of the GSB model based on $N = 1000$ independent Monte Carlo replications of the GSB series. To that end, we assume that all series have size $T = 500$, which is close to the length of the actual series to be considered below. The primary aim is to examine the convergence, i.e., the quality of the previously proposed estimators on a sample of a given length. Therefore, corresponding estimation errors will also be investigated for this purpose. Using the previously presented theoretical facts, the pseudo-algorithm for estimating the parameters of the GSB process can be formulated as follows:

1. In the first estimation step, compute the sample correlation $\hat{\rho}_X(1)$ for a series of increments (X_t). If the condition $-0.5 < \hat{\rho}_X(1) < 0$ is fulfilled, by using Equation (14), the estimator $\tilde{b}_c$ can be obtained.
2. Compute statistics $\overline{X}_t^2$, given by Equation (24), as an estimate of the "hybrid" parameter $\sigma^2(b_c + 1)$. The following variance estimator is then obtained:

$$\hat{\sigma}_X^2 = \frac{\overline{X}_t^2}{\tilde{b}_c + 1}.$$

3. According to Equation (15) and previously obtained estimates $\tilde{b}_c$ and $\hat{\sigma}_X^2$, compute the estimator $\tilde{c} = \hat{\sigma}_X^2 \cdot F_{\chi_1^2}^{-1}(\tilde{b}_c)$.

4. By using the estimate $\tilde{c}$, for each $t = 1, \ldots, T$, generate the (modeled) values of series (ε_t) and (m_t), by applying the iterative procedure:

$$\begin{cases} \varepsilon_t = y_t - m_t, \\ m_t = m_{t-1} + \varepsilon_{t-1} I\{\varepsilon_{t-2}^2 \geq \tilde{c}\}, \end{cases} \quad (28)$$

where $\varepsilon_0 = \varepsilon_{-1} = 0$, and $m_0 = y_0 = \hat{\mu}$ is given by Equation (20).

5. According to previously obtained series (ε_t), and by using Equation (21), compute a (more efficient) variance estimator $\tilde{\sigma}^2$.
6. By applying the Gauss-Newton procedure, i.e., Equations (16)–(18), the estimate $\hat{b}_c$ can be obtained.
7. According to previously obtained estimates $\hat{b}_c$ and $\tilde{\sigma}^2$, compute the estimator $\hat{c} = \tilde{\sigma}^2 \cdot F_{X_1^2}^{-1}(\hat{b}_c)$.

We point out that in the above-mentioned pseudo algorithm, the 2nd stage can be replaced by the following alternative step:

2'. Compute statistics S_T^2, given by Equation (26), and estimate the "hybrid" parameter $a_c \sigma^2 / 3$. Then, according to Equation (27), the variance σ^2 can be estimated as:

$$\hat{\sigma}_Y^2 := \frac{3}{\tilde{a}_c} S_T^2,$$

where $\tilde{a}_c = 1 - \tilde{b}_c$.

By applying this pseudo-algorithm, the obtained values of the estimated parameters can be summarized as shown in Table 1, where their average values (Mean), minimums (Min.), maximums (Max.) can also be seen, along with the appropriate mean squared errors of estimation (MSEE) given in parentheses. Furthermore, testing results concerning the AN of thus obtained estimates are also presented in Table 1. To that end, Anderson-Darling and Cramer-von Mises normality tests were used. Their test statistics (denoted as AD and W, respectively), as well as their corresponding p-values, were calculated using procedures from the R-package "nortest" [41].

According to the obtained values, it is evident that most estimators have a property of the AN. This applies even to the estimates of the mean value $\tilde{\mu}$ and $\hat{\mu}$, which are obtained from realizations of non-stationary GSB-series (y_t). As already explained, this is related to Theorems 2 and 3, which respectively describe the AN properties of the series $(y_t/\sqrt{t})$ and so-called α-means series. Notice that the asymptotic variance of these estimators is not bounded, hence there is a large range of their observed values. On the other hand, the AN property is not particularly emphasized in the case where the critical value (c) is estimated. This is because both estimates $\tilde{c}$ and $\hat{c}$ are obtained by the three-step procedure: estimates for the parameters b_c and σ^2 should first be determined, and only then for c. In the case of variance estimators $\tilde{\sigma}^2$ and $\hat{\sigma}^2$, obtained based on modeled innovations (ε_t), it is easy to see that they have the highest and almost the same efficiency. Furthermore, the values of the estimator $\hat{\sigma}_X^2$ are only slightly "weaker" than $\tilde{\sigma}^2$ and $\hat{\sigma}^2$. This is expected since, according to Theorem 5, the AN property holds for all these variance estimators. However, the estimate $\hat{\sigma}_Y^2$ is by far the weakest variance estimate and can be omitted from further analysis. Moreover, based on previously obtained theoretical results, also confirmed through simulations, the most robust estimates of the unknown parameters c, μ, σ^2 are $\hat{c}$, $\hat{\mu}$, $\hat{\sigma}^2$, respectively. For those reasons, these estimators will be used for GSB modeling of actual data on COVID-19, which will be discussed below.

Table 1. Summary statistics of estimated parameters of the GSB process, obtained by a Monte Carlo study, along with realized statistics of normality tests.

Parameters Estimators	Statistics	Values	AD (p-Value)	W (p-Value)
Mean ($\widetilde{\mu}$)	Min.	−24.9395	0.2886	0.0415
	Mean	−0.0192	(0.6161)	(0.6545)
	(MSEE)	(7.2791)		
	Max.	26.8691		
Mean ($\hat{\mu}$)	Min.	−20.0310	0.3363	0.0453
	Mean	−0.00806	(0.5056)	(0.5845)
	(MSEE)	(4.6055)		
	Max.	19.7987		
Critical value ($\widetilde{c}$)	Min.	0.3849	1.0160 *	0.1449 *
	Mean	1.0904	(0.0112)	(0.0278)
	(MSEE)	(0.5069)		
	Max.	1.6481		
Critical value ($\hat{c}$)	Min.	0.5105	0.5647	0.1074
	Mean	0.9844	(0.1435)	(0.0889)
	(MSEE)	(0.1587)		
	Max.	1.5033		
Variance ($\widetilde{\sigma}_2$)	Min.	0.8271	0.3144	0.0494
	Mean	0.9991	(0.5446)	(0.5182)
	(MSEE)	(0.0630)		
	Max.	1.2182		
Variance ($\hat{\sigma}_2$)	Min.	0.8248	0.3247	0.0546
	Mean	1.0002	(0.5231)	(0.4459)
	(MSEE)	(0.0631)		
	Max.	1.2118		
Variance ($\hat{\sigma}_Y^2$)	Min.	0.7796	0.4018	0.0588
	Mean	1.0034	(0.3584)	(0.3921)
	(MSEE)	(0.0842)		
	Max.	1.3340		
Variance ($\hat{\sigma}_X^2$)	Min.	0.1104	90.626 **	16.522 **
	Mean	1.0937	($<2.2 \times 10^{-16}$)	(7.37×10^{-10})
	(MSEE)	(1.4183)		
	Max.	1.6313		

* $p < 0.05$, ** $p < 0.01$.

5.2. Application of the GSB Process: A Case Study of COVID-19 Dynamics

In this section we give, as an illustration, a practical application of the GSB process in stochastic modeling of actual data. In other words, as mentioned in the introductory section, we will show that it can be an adequate stochastic model for describing the dynamics of the infected and vaccinated population in relation to the SARS-CoV2 virus on the territory of the Republic of Serbia. To that end, we observe realizations of two time series (U_t) and (V_t) which, daily, represents the total number of infected persons, i.e., persons vaccinated with the first dose of the vaccine, starting from 24 December 2020 (the start date of vaccination in Serbia) and ending with 6 June 2022. The dynamics of both time series, length $T = 529$, are shown in Figure 6.

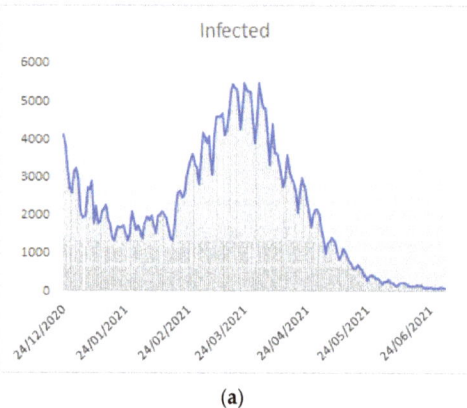
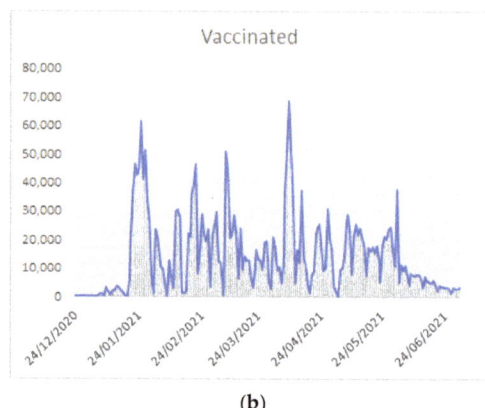

Figure 6. Dynamics of the total infected (**a**) and vaccinated population (**b**) in relation to the virus SARS-CoV2 on the territory of the Republic of Serbia.

The main statistical indicators of these series (also labeled as Series A and Series B, respectively) are shown in the following Table 2. Based on thus obtained values, it can be concluded that these are time series with distinct, pronounced fluctuations. For instance, the average number of infected people is (approximately) 3650 per day, ranging from 60 to 19,901 infected people. Similar to that, the average number of vaccinated persons is 6348 per day, but the range of vaccinated persons varies from only 4 to as many as 68,678 persons per day. Therefore, we further consider the possibility that the GSB process can be used here as an appropriate stochastic model. For this purpose, as basic sequences, we observe the realizations of the so-called *log-volumes*, i.e., logarithmic values of series (U_t) and (V_t):

$$y_t^{(1)} := \ln(U_t), \ y_t^{(2)} := \ln(V_t), \ t = 0, 1, \ldots, T. \tag{29}$$

Notice that the main goal of this transformation is to obtain more evenly distributed values of both series, and although based on increasing of the logarithmic function, the emphasis of fluctuations will remain. Additionally, inequalities $U_t, V_t \geq 1$ implies the non-negativity of both log-volumes series $\left(y_t^{(1)}, y_t^{(2)} \geq 0\right)$.

Table 2. Basic statistical indicators of observed actual series.

Statistics	Infected (A)	Vaccinated (B)
Mean	3650.84	6336
Median	2000	2960
Mode	1366	45
Stand. deviation	3650.84	1026.38
Minimum	60	4
Maximum	19,901	68,678
Kurtosis	8.1189	8.2609
Skewness	2.1418	2.7009

Further, using the log-volumes as a basic series, and using Equation (3), the series of increments $\left(X_t^{(1)}\right), \left(X_t^{(2)}\right)$ are determined entirely. Based on them, the estimates of GSB process parameters can be obtained by applying the pseudo-algorithm presented above. We emphasize that here the estimation procedure is repeated twice, i.e., for both series (A and B). Thus, modeled values of martingale means and innovations series, generated by Equation (29), are as follows:

$$\begin{cases} \varepsilon_t^{(j)} = y_t^{(j)} - m_t^{(j)}, \\ m_t^{(j)} = m_{t-1}^{(j)} + \varepsilon_{t-1}^{(j)} I\left\{ \left(\varepsilon_{t-2}^{(j)}\right)^2 \geq \widetilde{c} \right\}, \end{cases} \quad (30)$$

where $j = 1, 2$. As initial values of the iterative procedure (30), as before, we have taken $\varepsilon_0^{(j)} = \varepsilon_{-1}^{(j)} = 0$, as well as $m_0^{(j)} = y_0^{(j)} = \widehat{\mu}$. Table 3 contains the basic statistical indicators of the actual series, log-volumes $(y_t^{(j)})$ and increments $\left(X_t^{(j)}\right)$, as well as modeled series, martingale means $\left(m_t^{(j)}\right)$ and innovations $\left(\varepsilon_t^{(j)}\right)$.

Table 3. Basic statistical indicators of actual and modeled series.

Statistics	Series A				Series B			
	$y_t^{(1)}$	$X_t^{(1)}$	$m_t^{(1)}$	$\varepsilon_t^{(1)}$	$y_t^{(2)}$	$X_t^{(2)}$	$m_t^{(2)}$	$\varepsilon_t^{(2)}$
Mean	7.4041	−0.0033	7.4111	−0.0054	7.3544	−0.0068	8.9349	−0.1769
Median	7.5976	−0.0336	7.6061	−0.0332	7.9940	−0.0566	9.4269	−0.1106
Stand. deviation	1.3247	0.1948	1.3244	0.1912	2.0546	1.0036	1.7589	1.0238
Minimum	4.0943	−0.5990	4.0943	−0.5990	1.3863	−5.0554	1.0986	−6.6837
Maximum	9.8985	0.9125	9.8985	0.7390	11.1372	5.5147	11.3099	4.5209
Kurtosis	2.3419	4.3332	2.3305	3.7214	2.4071	10.1761	3.6732	10.2208
Skewness	−0.5493	0.6114	−0.5605	0.4518	−0.4958	0.4290	−1.0703	−0.1625

By analyzing thus obtained values, an interesting connection can be observed, which can be explained by the previous theoretical results. Firstly, the average values of the log-volumes are "close" to the averages of the martingale means, which is in accordance with the equality $E(y_t) = E(m_t)$. Moreover, with series A, almost equal values of other statistical indicators (standard deviations, for instance) are noticeable. This can also be seen by comparing the corresponding statistical indicators of increments $\left(X_t^{(1)}\right)$ and innovations $\left(\varepsilon_t^{(1)}\right)$, which will be explained below. Table 4 shows the above-mentioned estimators obtained according to the previously described procedures. In addition, some other estimates are shown, such as the sample linear correlation $\widehat{\rho}_X(1)$ and estimates of the value b_c. Accordingly, note that the condition $-0.5 < \widehat{\rho}_X(1) < 0$ is fulfilled in the cases of both series. Moreover, let us notice, for instance, that the estimated values for σ^2 in the case of Series B are "close" to unity, so it can be assumed that innovations (ε_t) in this case have a standard $\mathcal{N}(0, 1)$ distribution.

Table 4. Estimated values of GSB process parameters.

Parameters	Series A	Series B
$\widetilde{\mu}$	7.4041	7.3544
$\widehat{\mu}$	7.4454	8.1409
$\widehat{\rho}_X(1)$	−0.0126	−0.2577
$\widetilde{b}_c$	0.0127	0.3472
$\widetilde{c}$	0.0003	0.2118
$\widehat{b}_c$	0.0953	0.4436
$\widehat{c}$	0.0006	0.3477
$\widetilde{\sigma}^2$	0.0413	1.0462
$\widehat{\sigma}^2$	0.0403	1.0634
$\widehat{\sigma}_X^2$	0.0375	1.0053

As we have already pointed out, the most robust estimators of the GSB process are $\widehat{c}$, $\widehat{\mu}$, $\widehat{\sigma}^2$ and based on them, modeled values of the series $(m_t^{(j)})$ and $(\varepsilon_t^{(j)})$ were obtained. Let us recall that these series, respectively, represent the stability and the impact of fluctuations in the dynamics of the total number of infected and vaccinated people. The agreement between the modeled series and the actual data can be seen in Figure 7a where, along with the empirical values of the log-volumes ($y_t^{(j)}$), modeled values of martingale means ($m_t^{(j)}$) are given. On the other hand, the agreement of a series of increments, i.e., the Split-MA(1) process ($X_t^{(j)}$) with innovations ($\varepsilon_t^{(j)}$) is shown in Figure 7b.

It should also be noted that the high agreement between the actual and modeled series is particularly noticeable in the case of series A. This can be explained theoretically, in the way it was done in Section 2. If at some points in time, innovations ($\varepsilon_t^{(1)}$) have a pronounced fluctuation, they become equal to increments ($X_t^{(1)}$) at the next moment. The agreement between the realizations of these two series will be all the better if, in addition to large and pronounced fluctuations of ($\varepsilon_t^{(1)}$), the critical value c is relatively small. Note that this is precisely the case with series A, where "small" estimated values of the parameter c indicate the possibility that the true value of this parameter is $c = 0$ (or, equivalently, $b_c = 0$). If the sample size is large enough, this assumption can be formally tested by the null hypothesis $H_0 : c = 0$ or, equivalently, $H_0 : b_c = 0$. According to Theorem 4, testing procedures can be based on the normal distribution, that is, using some standard, well-known statistical tests.

Note that in that case, the series of increments ($X_t^{(1)}$) is equalized with innovations ($\varepsilon_t^{(1)}$). This implies that ($y_t^{(j)}$) is a series with independent increments, i.e.,

$$X_t^{(1)} = y_t^{(1)} - y_{t-1}^{(1)} = \varepsilon_t^{(1)} \iff y_t^{(1)} = y_{t-1}^{(1)} + \varepsilon_t^{(1)}. \tag{31}$$

According to Equation (1), it follows that $y_{t-1}^{(1)} = m_t^{(1)}$, so all "information from the past" is contained in the previous realization of the series ($y_t^{(1)}$). In that way, the entire statistical analysis of this series, i.e., the dynamics of the infected population, gains simplicity; namely, series A then has (only) two stochastic components ($y_t^{(1)}$) and ($\varepsilon_t^{(1)}$), i.e., it represents a random walk series.

Finally, using the inverse transformations of those given in Equation (29), PDFs of actual series (U_t) and (V_t) are readily obtained:

$$f_U(x,t) = \frac{1}{x} f_y^{(1)}(\ln x, t), \quad f_V(x,t) = \frac{1}{x} f_y^{(2)}(\ln x, t). \tag{32}$$

Here, $f_y^{(j)}(\ln x, t), j = 1, 2$ are the PDFs of log-volumes ($y_t^{(j)}$), obtained by differentiating the CDFs given by Equation (9), which can be done simply. Still, due to the non-stationarity of the mentioned series, which also depends on time, it is necessary to apply some numerical procedures to calculate their PDFs. For this purpose, the R-package "distr" [42] has been used, and the results of the applied procedure are shown in Figure 8.

Here are the empirical distributions, i.e., histograms of the number of infected and vaccinated persons per day, with their fitted PDFs, obtained using Equations (32). Due to the non-stationarity of the time series (U_t) and (V_t), as well as the comparison of the theoretical PDFs, fitting was also performed for the PDFs $f_U(x,t)$ and $f_V(x,t)$ of length $t = 50, 10, \ldots, 500 < T = 529$ (shown with dashed lines in Figure 8). In the case of the infected population (Series A), according to Equation (31) and the condition $c \approx 0$, it follows that RVs $y_t^{(1)}$ have (an approximately) normal $\mathcal{N}(\mu, (t+1)\sigma^2)$ distribution. Thus, RVs U_t will have (an approximately) log-normal distribution, shown with the solid line in Figure 8a. Note that this result is close to that obtained in [29]. Nevertheless, the distribution of the number of vaccinated population (Series B), shown with the solid line in Figure 8b, has a more pronounced "peak" close to the origin. It can also be explained by previous theoretical results, primarily given in Theorem 2, i.e., by Equation (8), which concerns the asymptotic behavior of the main GSB series (y_t).

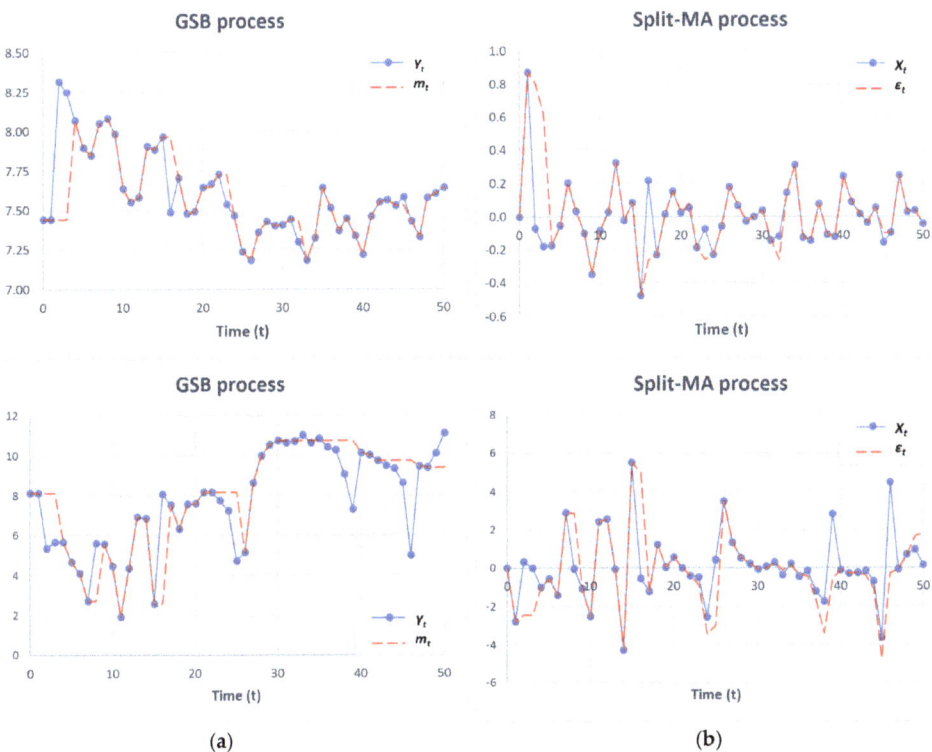

Figure 7. Graphs of empirical and modeled data: (**a**) log-volumes (solid lines) and martingale means (dashed lines); (**b**) Split-MA(1) process (solid lines) and innovations series (dashed lines). The upper panels represent the dynamics of the COVID-19 infection (Series A), and the lower panels represent the dynamics of the vaccinated population (Series B).

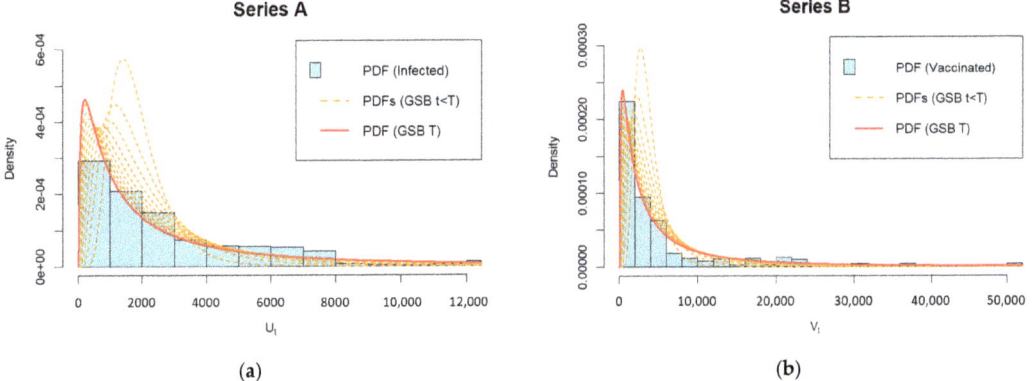

Figure 8. Empirical distributions of actual data (histograms) and their fitted PDFs (lines), obtained by the proposed estimation procedure: (**a**) distribution of the infected population (Series A); (**b**) distribution of the vaccinated population (Series B).

6. Conclusions

The stochastic analysis of the GSB process presented in this paper confirms its possibility in modeling actual time series with pronounced fluctuations. The applied methods of dynamic and statistical analysis, based on this process, aim here to understand the long-term tendency of the SARS-COV2 virus behavior, as well as the immunization process. Along with other contemporary research, we hope this one can help further development of successful methods of overcoming the pandemic. To this end, notice that new strains of the SARS-CoV2 virus, which are very common, can affect the overall symptoms as well as the disease dynamics of COVID-19 (see, c.f. [43–45]). They may therefore change the dynamics of both time series investigated here. This may therefore be a new goal and motivation for some future research.

Finally, let us emphasize that one of the main stochastic advantages of the GSB model is that it allows the simultaneous use of both stationary and non-stationary components. Thereby, the asymptotic behavior of the GSB time series as well as the corresponding estimates thus obtained are of particular importance. It should also be noted that the proposed parameter estimation procedure can be implemented algorithmically in a relatively simple way. Additionally, some other estimation methods, such as the Empirical Characteristic Function (ECF) method described in [12] can be used. As shown in [11,12], it can also be used to model some other types of real data with pronounced and persistent fluctuations.

Author Contributions: Conceptualization, M.J.; data curation, M.J.; formal analysis, V.S.; methodology, K.K.; project administration, B.P.; software, K.K. and B.P.; supervision, V.S.; validation, P.Č.; visualization, P.Č.; writing—original draft, M.J., V.S. and K.K.; writing—review and editing, B.P. All authors have read and agreed to the published version of the manuscript.

Funding: This research was funded by the Ministry of Education, Science and Technological Development of the Republic of Serbia. (Grant number: III 47016.)

Data Availability Statement: Not applicable.

Acknowledgments: The authors would like to thank the Electronic Government of the Republic of Serbia and the Institute for Public Health "Milan Jovanović-Batut" for providing datasets used in this research.

Conflicts of Interest: The authors declare no conflict of interest.

References

1. Engle, R.F.; Smith, A.D. Stochastic Permanent Breaks. *Rev. Econ. Stat.* **1999**, *81*, 553–574. [CrossRef]
2. Diebold, F.X.; Inoue, A. Long Memory and Regime Switching. *J. Econom.* **2001**, *105*, 131–159. [CrossRef]
3. Gonzalo, J.; Martínez, O. Large Shocks vs. Small Shocks. (Or does size matter? May be so.). *J. Econom.* **2006**, *135*, 311–347. [CrossRef]
4. Dendramis, Y.; Kapetanios, G.; Tzavalis, E. Level Shifts in Stock Returns Driven by Large Shocks. *J. Empir. Financ.* **2014**, *29*, 41–51. [CrossRef]
5. Dendramis, Y.; Kapetanios, G.; Tzavalis, E. Shifts in Volatility Driven by Large Stock Market Shocks. *J. Econom. Dynam. Control* **2015**, *55*, 130–147. [CrossRef]
6. Huang, B.-N.; Fok, R.C.W. Stock Market Integration—an Application of the Stochastic Permanent Breaks Model. *Appl. Econ. Lett.* **2001**, *8*, 725–729. [CrossRef]
7. González, A. A Smooth Permanent Surge Process. In *SSE/EFI Working Paper Series in Economics and Finance No. 572*; Stockholm School of Economics, The Economic Research Institute: Stockholm, UK, 2004.
8. Kapetanios, G.; Tzavalis, E. Modeling Structural Breaks in Economic Relationships Using Large Shocks. *J. Econom. Dynam. Control* **2010**, *34*, 417–436. [CrossRef]
9. Stojanović, V.; Popović, B.Č.; Popović, P. The Split-BREAK Model. *Braz. J. Probab. Stat.* **2011**, *25*, 44–63. [CrossRef]
10. Stojanović, V.; Popović, B.Č.; Popović, P. Stochastic Analysis of GSB Process. *Publ. Inst. Math.* **2014**, *95*, 149–159. [CrossRef]
11. Stojanović, V.; Popović, B.Č.; Popović, P. Model of General Split-BREAK Process. *REVSTAT Stat. J.* **2015**, *13*, 145–168.
12. Stojanović, V.; Milovanović, G.V.; Jelić, G. Distributional Properties and Parameters Estimation of GSB Process: An Approach Based on Characteristic Functions. *ALEA—Lat. Am. J. Probab. Math. Stat.* **2016**, *13*, 835–861. [CrossRef]
13. Xu, Z.; Wang, H.; Zhang, H.; Zhao, K.; Gao, H.; Zhu, Q. Non-Stationary Turbulent Wind Field Simulation of Long-Span Bridges Using the Updated Non-Negative Matrix Factorization-Based Spectral Representation Method. *Appl. Sci.* **2019**, *9*, 5506. [CrossRef]

14. Granero-Belinchón, C.; Roux, S.G.; Garnier, N.B. Information Theory for Non-Stationary Processes with Stationary Increments. *Entropy* **2019**, *21*, 1223. [CrossRef]
15. Zhao, D.; Gelman, L.; Chu, F.; Ball, A. Novel Method for Vibration Sensor-Based Instantaneous Defect Frequency Estimation for Rolling Bearings Under Non-Stationary Conditions. *Sensors* **2020**, *20*, 5201. [CrossRef] [PubMed]
16. Qu, C.; Li, J.; Yan, L.; Yan, P.; Cheng, F.; Lu, D. Non-Stationary Flood Frequency Analysis Using Cubic B-Spline-Based GAMLSS Model. *Water* **2020**, *12*, 1867. [CrossRef]
17. Aguejdad, R. The Influence of the Calibration Interval on Simulating Non-Stationary Urban Growth Dynamic Using CA-Markov Model. *Remote Sens.* **2021**, *13*, 468. [CrossRef]
18. Narr, C.F.; Chernyavskiy, P.; Collins, S.M. Partitioning Macroscale and Microscale Ecological Processes Using Covariate-Driven Non-Stationary Spatial Models. *Ecol. Appl.* **2022**, *32*, e02485. [CrossRef]
19. Vaz, S.; Torres, D.F.M. A Discrete-Time Compartmental Epidemiological Model for COVID-19 with a Case Study for Portugal. *Axioms* **2021**, *10*, 314. [CrossRef]
20. Alqahtani, R.T.; Musa, S.S.; Yusuf, A. Unravelling the Dynamics of the COVID-19 Pandemic with the Effect of Vaccination, Vertical Transmission and Hospitalization. *Results Phys.* **2022**, *39*, 105715. [CrossRef]
21. Ghosh, S.; Volpert, V.; Banerjee, M. An Epidemic Model with Time Delay Determined by the Disease Duration. *Mathematics* **2022**, *10*, 2561. [CrossRef]
22. Almeshal, A.M.; Almazrouee, A.I.; Alenizi, M.R.; Alhajeri, S.N. Forecasting the Spread of COVID-19 in Kuwait Using Compartmental and Logistic Regression Models. *Appl. Sci.* **2020**, *10*, 3402. [CrossRef]
23. Rossi, C.; Bonanomi, A.; Oasi, O. Psychological Wellbeing during the COVID-19 Pandemic: The Influence of Personality Traits in the Italian Population. *Int. J. Environ. Res. Public Health* **2021**, *18*, 5862. [CrossRef]
24. Ponkratov, V.; Kuznetsov, N.; Bashkirova, N.; Volkova, M.; Alimova, M.; Ivleva, M.; Vatutina, L.; Elyakova, I. Predictive Scenarios of the Russian Oil Industry; with a Discussion on Macro and Micro Dynamics of Open Innovation in the COVID-19 Pandemic. *J. Open Innov. Technol. Mark. Complex.* **2020**, *6*, 85. [CrossRef]
25. Hassan, S.M.; Riveros Gavilanes, J.M. First to React Is the Last to Forgive: Evidence from the Stock Market Impact of COVID-19. *J. Risk Financ. Manag.* **2021**, *14*, 26. [CrossRef]
26. Flora, J.; Khan, W.; Jin, J.; Jin, D.; Hussain, A.; Dajani, K.; Khan, B. Usefulness of Vaccine Adverse Event Reporting System for Machine-Learning Based Vaccine Research: A Case Study for COVID-19 Vaccines. *Int. J. Mol. Sci.* **2022**, *23*, 8235. [CrossRef] [PubMed]
27. Kouamé, K.-M.; Mcheick, H. An Ontological Approach for Early Detection of Suspected COVID-19 among COPD Patients. *Appl. Syst. Innov.* **2021**, *4*, 21. [CrossRef]
28. Sarría-Santamera, A.; Abdukadyrov, N.; Glushkova, N.; Russell Peck, D.; Colet, P.; Yeskendir, A.; Asúnsolo, A.; Ortega, M.A. Towards an Accurate Estimation of COVID-19 Cases in Kazakhstan: Back-Casting and Capture–Recapture Approaches. *Medicina* **2022**, *58*, 253. [CrossRef] [PubMed]
29. Shim, E.; Choi, W.; Song, Y. Clinical Time Delay Distributions of COVID-19 in 2020–2022 in the Republic of Korea: Inferences from a Nationwide Database Analysis. *J. Clin. Med.* **2022**, *11*, 3269. [CrossRef]
30. Jankhonkhan, J.; Sawangtong, W. Model Predictive Control of COVID-19 Pandemic with Social Isolation and Vaccination Policies in Thailand. *Axioms* **2021**, *10*, 274. [CrossRef]
31. Queirós-Reis, L.; Gomes da Silva, P.; Gonçalves, J.; Brancale, A.; Bassetto, M.; Mesquita, J.R. SARS-CoV-2 Virus−Host Interaction: Currently Available Structures and Implications of Variant Emergence on Infectivity and Immune Response. *Int. J. Mol. Sci.* **2021**, *22*, 10836. [CrossRef] [PubMed]
32. Xu, L.; Xie, L.; Zhang, D.; Xu, X. Elucidation of Binding Features and Dissociation Pathways of Inhibitors and Modulators in SARS-CoV-2 Main Protease by Multiple Molecular Dynamics Simulations. *Molecules* **2022**, *27*, 6823. [CrossRef]
33. Williams, D. *Probability with Martingales*; Cambridge University Press: Cambridge, UK, 1991.
34. Stojanović, V.; Popović, B.Č.; Milovanović, G.V. The Split-SV model. *Comput. Statist. Data Anal.* **2016**, *100*, 560–581. [CrossRef]
35. Stojanović, V.; Kevkić, T.; Jelić, G. Application of the Homotopy Analysis Method in Approximation of Convolutions Stochastic Distributions. *Univ. Politeh. Buchar. Sci. Bull.* **2017**, *79*, 103–112.
36. Fuller, W.A. *Introduction to Statistical Time Series*; John Wiley & Sons: New York, NY, USA, 1996.
37. Popović, B.Č. The First Order Random Coefficient (RC) Autoregressive Time Series. *Sci. Rev.* **1992**, *21–22*, 131–136.
38. Lawrence, A.J.; Lewis, P.A.W. Reversed Residuals in Autoregressive Time Series Analysis. *J. Time Series Anal.* **1992**, *13*, 253–266. [CrossRef]
39. Serfling, R.J. *Approximation Theorems of Mathematical Statistics*, 2nd ed.; John Wiley & Sons: Hoboken, NJ, USA, 2002.
40. Hoeffding, W.; Robbins, H. The central limit theorem for dependent random variables. *Duke Math. J.* **1948**, *15*, 773–780. [CrossRef]
41. Gross, L. Tests for normality. R Package Version 1.0-2. 2013. Available online: http://CRAN.R-project.org/package=nortest (accessed on 21 September 2022).
42. Ruckdeschel, P.; Kohl, M.; Stabla, T.; Camphausen, F. S4 Classes for Distributions. *R News* **2006**, *6*, 2–6. Available online: https://CRAN.R-project.org/doc/Rnews (accessed on 21 September 2022).
43. Sivakumar, B.; Deepthi, B. Complexity of COVID-19 Dynamics. *Entropy* **2022**, *24*, 50. [CrossRef]

44. Beškovnik, B.; Zanne, M.; Golnar, M. Dynamic Changes in Port Logistics Caused by the COVID-19 Pandemic. *J. Mar. Sci. Eng.* **2022**, *10*, 1473. [CrossRef]
45. Zakharov, V.; Balykina, Y.; Ilin, I.; Tick, A. Forecasting a New Type of Virus Spread: A Case Study of COVID-19 with Stochastic Parameters. *Mathematics* **2022**, *10*, 3725. [CrossRef]

Article

Functional Limit Theorem for the Sums of PSI-Processes with Random Intensities

Yuri Yakubovich [1,*], Oleg Rusakov [1] and Alexander Gushchin [2,3]

[1] Mathematics and Mechanics Faculty, St. Petersburg State University, 199034 St. Petersburg, Russia
[2] Steklov Mathematical Institute of Russian Academy of Sciences, 119991 Moscow, Russia
[3] Faculty of Economic Sciences, National Research University Higher School of Economics, 109028 Moscow, Russia
* Correspondence: y.yakubovich@spbu.ru

Abstract: We consider a sequence of i.i.d. random variables, $(\xi) = (\xi_i)_{i=0,1,2,\dots}$, $\mathbb{E}\xi_0 = 0$, $\mathbb{E}\xi_0^2 = 1$, and subordinate it by a doubly stochastic Poisson process $\Pi(\lambda t)$, where $\lambda \geq 0$ is a random variable and Π is a standard Poisson process. The subordinated continuous time process $\psi(t) = \xi_{\Pi(\lambda t)}$ is known as the PSI-process. Elements of the triplet $(\Pi, \lambda, (\xi))$ are supposed to be independent. For sums of n, independent copies of such processes, normalized by $\sqrt{n}$, we establish a functional limit theorem in the Skorokhod space $D[0, T]$, for any $T > 0$, under the assumption $\mathbb{E}|\xi_0|^{2h} < \infty$ for some $h > 1/\gamma^2$. Here, $\gamma \in (0, 1]$ reflects the tail behavior of the distribution of λ, in particular, $\gamma \equiv 1$ when $\mathbb{E}\lambda < \infty$. The limit process is a stationary Gaussian process with the covariance function $\mathbb{E}e^{-\lambda u}$, $u \geq 0$. As a sample application, we construct a martingale from the PSI-process and establish a convergence of normalized cumulative sums of such i.i.d. martingales.

Keywords: functional limit theorem; Poisson stochastic index process; pseudo-Poisson process; random intensity

MSC: 60F17; 60G10; 60G44

1. Introduction

The Poisson Stochastic Index process (PSI-process) represents a special kind of a random process when the discrete time of a random sequence is replaced by the continuous time of a "counting" process of a Poisson type.

Throughout this paper, we consider the triplet $\{\Pi, \lambda, (\xi)\}$ of jointly independent components defined on a probability space $\{\Omega, \mathcal{F}, \mathbb{P}\}$. Here, Π is a standard Poisson process on $\mathbb{R}_+ := \{t \in \mathbb{R} : t \geq 0\}$, λ is an almost surely (a.s.) non-negative random variable, which plays a role of random intensity, and (ξ) denotes a random sequence $\xi_0, \xi_1, \dots$ of independent and identically distributed (i.i.d.) random variables. Let us define a PSI-process in the following way:

$$\psi(t; \lambda) \equiv \psi(t) := \xi_{\Pi(\lambda t)}, \qquad t \in \mathbb{R}_+. \tag{1}$$

The mechanism of PSI-processes is reduced to sequential replacements of terms of the "driven" sequence (ξ) at arrival times of the "driving" doubly stochastic Poisson process $\Pi(\lambda t)$.

Let us introduce a "natural" filtration $\mathbb{F} \equiv (\mathcal{F}_t)_{t \in \mathbb{R}_+}$, generated by the PSI-process

$$\mathcal{F}_t := \sigma\{\Pi(\lambda s), s \leq t; \xi_0, \dots \xi_k, k \leq \Pi(\lambda t)\} \subset \mathcal{F}. \tag{2}$$

Note that if the distribution of ξ_0 has no atoms, then the natural filtration $\mathbb{F}$ coincides with a filtration, which is generated by a compound Poisson type process with the random intensity λ: $Y(t) := \sum_{k=0}^{\Pi(\lambda t)} \xi_k$ starting at the random point ξ_0. (In the case when ξ_0 has an atom at 0, some jumps of $\Pi(\lambda t)$ may be "missed" in Y, the process Y is known as *a stuttering compound Poisson* process. A similar phenomenon happens with a PSI-process when ξ_0 has any atom, not necessarily at 0. For details we refer to [1].)

PSI-processes may have a lot of interpretations. For instance, in insurance models and their applications: while a compound Poisson process $Y(t)$ is monitoring the cumulative value of claims up to a current time t, the corresponding PSI-process $\psi(t)$ is monitoring the last claim.

Another interpretation arises in models of information channels. Here, (ξ) plays a role of random loads on an information channel. The driving doubly stochastic Poisson process $\Pi(\lambda t)$ affects (ξ) in the following manner. At arrival points of the driving process $\Pi(\lambda t)$, the current term of (ξ) is replaced with the next term.

In view of these interpretations, as well as from a point of view of the classical probability theory, it makes sense to consider sums of independent PSI-processes. In this paper, we confine ourselves to the case when all terms in these sums are identically distributed PSI-processes and when the terms of the driven sequences have a finite second moment. Without loss of generality, we assume that $\mathbb{E}\xi_0 = 0$ and $\mathbb{E}\xi_0^2 = 1$. Let $\psi^{(k)}$, $k = 1, 2, \ldots$, denote independent copies of ψ. Note that the Poisson processes in the definition (1) are also independent in different copies, as well as the time change factors $\lambda_k \stackrel{d}{=} \lambda$, for any $k \in \mathbb{N}$. Introduce

$$\zeta_n(t) := \frac{1}{\sqrt{n}} \sum_{k=1}^{n} \psi^{(k)}(t; \lambda_k), \qquad n \in \mathbb{N}, \quad t \geq 0, \tag{3}$$

the normalized cumulative sum. Note that ζ_n is a stationary process for any n.

When one of the processes $\psi^{(1)}, \ldots, \psi^{(n)}$ changes its value, all the values of other processes remain the same a.s. Hence, the change mechanism behind the sums of type (3) can be described as a projection of some information from past to future and replacement of other information with new independent values. This can be opposed to autoregression schemes, which are based on contractions of information. This mechanism of projection survives after a passage to the limit as $n \to \infty$. Hence, if the limit exists in some sense, it has to be described by so-called "trawl" or "upstairs represented" processes introduced by O. E. Barndorf-Nielsen [2,3] and R. Wolpert, M.Taqqu [4], respectively. A relationship of PSI-processes with trawl processes is discussed briefly in [5].

Our main result is a functional limit theorem for normalized cumulative sums (3) (Theorem 1): random processes ζ_n weakly converge, as $n \to \infty$, in the Skorokhod space of càdlàg functions defined on a compact $[0, T]$, $T > 0$. The limit process ζ is Gaussian, centered, stationary, and its covariance function is $L_\lambda(|t - s|)$, $s, t \in \mathbb{R}_+$, where L_λ denotes the Laplace transform of the random intensity λ. In a simpler case of non-random intensity λ, the analogous functional limit theorem has been established by the second author in [6]. In this case, the limit is necessarily an Ornstein–Uhlenbeck process. Introducing a random intensity significantly widens the class of possible limiting processes but makes a proof of the corresponding functional limit theorem more involved. Our method of proof is essentially based on a detailed analysis of a modulus of continuity for the PSI-process.

In our research, we came upon the following interesting phenomena, which occurs if $\mathbb{E}\lambda = +\infty$. Then, the fatter the tail of λ is, the more moments of ξ_0 are needed for the relative compactness of the family $(\zeta_n)_{n \in \mathbb{N}}$. When $\mathbb{E}\lambda < \infty$, our method of proof requires just a condition $\mathbb{E}|\xi_0|^{2+\varepsilon} < \infty$, for some $\varepsilon > 0$.

As an example of a functional of the PSI-process, we construct a martingale adapted to the natural filtration $(\mathcal{F}_t)$ generated by the PSI-process defined in (2). Consider a pathwise integrated PSI-process

$$\Psi(t) := \int_0^t \psi(s) ds \tag{4}$$

and define a so-called M-process associated with the PSI-process as

$$M(t; \lambda) \equiv M(t) := \lambda \Psi(t) + \psi(t) - \xi_0, \quad t \geq 0. \tag{5}$$

Suppose that λ is a positive constant and $\mathbb{E}\xi_0 = 0$. Then, $M(t)$ is an $(\mathcal{F}_t)$-martingale, starting at the origin. The proof presented in Section 3 is reduced to a direct calculation and exploits the fact that the pair (Ψ, ψ) is an $\mathbb{R}^2$-valued Markov process (moreover, a strong Markov process with respect to $(\mathcal{F}_t)$).

This example shows that the PSI-process $\psi(t)$ is the stationary solution of the Langevin equation driven by the martingale $M(t)$:

$$d\psi(t) = -\lambda \psi(t) + dM(t). \tag{6}$$

As one of the consequences of our main result, we obtain as a limit the classical martingale $\sqrt{2\lambda}W(t)$, $t \geq 0$, which replaces $M(t)$ in (6). Here and below, $W(t)$ is a standard Brownian motion.

Remark that if λ is a non-degenerate random variable, then $M(t; \lambda)$ is not measurable with respect to $\mathcal{F}_t$, and hence, it is not an $(\mathcal{F}_t)$-martingale. However, if we supplement $\mathcal{F}_0$ with $\sigma(\lambda)$ to generate an initially enlarged filtration $(\mathcal{F}_t^\lambda)$, then the M-process becomes a local martingale with respect to the new adjusted filtration. If $\mathbb{E}\lambda < \infty$, then it is a martingale (see Proposition 2).

Suppose now as usual that $\mathbb{E}\xi_0^2 = 1$. Direct application of Theorem VIII.3.46 [7] (p. 481) allows us to obtain a functional limit theorem for the martingale $M(t)$, i.e., for

$$\overline{M}_n := \frac{1}{\sqrt{n}} \sum_{i=1}^{n} M^{(i)}(t), \tag{7}$$

where $M^{(i)}(t)$, $i = 1, 2, \ldots$, are independent copies of $M(t)$. Here, the convergence takes place in the Skorokhod space, and the limit process is $\sqrt{2\mathbb{E}\lambda}W(t)$, $t \geq 0$.

The rest of the paper is organized as follows. In Section 2, we introduce some notation and formulate our main result, Theorem 1. In Section 3, the M-process described above is studied in some details, as an example of the application of Theorem 1. Another example of the PSI-process such that the normalized cumulative sums do not converge in the Skorokhod space is constructed in Section 4 in order to show that some conditions are indeed necessary in a functional limit theorem. Section 5 collects some auxiliary facts about PSI-processes and their modulus of continuity. In Section 6, we study sums of PSI-processes and prove our main result. We finish the article with some conclusions in Section 7.

2. Main Results

Let $(\xi) = (\xi_0, \xi_1, \ldots)$ be a sequence of random variables. Consider an independent of (ξ) standard Poisson process $\Pi(t)$, $t \geq 0$. Then, one can subordinate the sequence by the Poisson process to obtain a continuous time process

$$\psi(t) = \xi_{\Pi(t)}, \quad t \geq 0.$$

Consider also a non-negative random variable λ, which is independent of (ξ) and Π. The time-changed Poisson process $\Pi(\lambda t)$ is a Poisson process with random intensity, also known as (a specific case of) a Cox process or a doubly stochastic Poisson process. We consider the PSI-process with the random time-change

$$\psi(t; \lambda) = \xi_{\Pi(\lambda t)}, \quad t \geq 0. \tag{8}$$

We call $\psi(t; \lambda)$ the *Poisson stochastic index process*, or PSI-process for short.

It turns out that if random variables ξ_i, $i = 0, 1, \ldots$, are uncorrelated and have zero expectations and unit variances, then the covariance function for $\psi(t; \lambda)$ is equal to the Laplace transform of λ

$$L_\lambda(u) = \mathbb{E}e^{-\lambda u}, \quad u \geq 0. \tag{9}$$

Lemma 1. *Let $(\xi) = (\xi_0, \xi_1, \dots)$ be a sequence of uncorrelated random variables with $\mathbb{E}\xi_i \equiv 0$ and $\mathbb{E}\xi_i^2 \equiv 1$. Let λ be a non-negative random variable and $\Pi(t)$ be a standard Poisson process. Suppose that (ξ), λ, and Π are mutually independent. Then, for any $s, t \geq 0$*

$$\mathrm{Cov}\big(\psi(s;\lambda), \psi(t;\lambda)\big) = L_\lambda(|t-s|).$$

In particular, ψ is a wide sense stationary process.

Proof. First note that $\mathbb{E}\,\psi(s,\lambda) = 0$ since any $\mathbb{E}\xi_i = 0$. Hence, $\mathrm{Cov}\big(\psi(s;\lambda), \psi(t;\lambda)\big) = \mathbb{E}\,\psi(s;\lambda)\psi(t;\lambda)$. Suppose without loss of generality that $0 \leq s \leq t$. Given λ, one has

$$\begin{aligned}
\mathbb{E}(\psi(s;\lambda)\psi(t;\lambda)|\lambda) &= \mathbb{E}\big(\xi_{\Pi(\lambda s)}\xi_{\Pi(\lambda t)}\big|\lambda\big) \\
&= \mathbb{E}\big(\mathbf{1}\{\Pi(\lambda s) = \Pi(\lambda t)\}\big|\lambda\big) \\
&= \mathbb{E}\big(\mathbf{1}\{\Pi(\lambda(t-s)) = 0\}\big|\lambda\big) \\
&= e^{-\lambda(t-s)}.
\end{aligned}$$

Here and below, $\mathbf{1}\{A\}$ denotes the indicator of an event A. We used the assumption that $\mathbb{E}\,\xi_i\xi_j = \delta_{ij}$, the Kronecker delta, and also the stationarity of the increments of the Poisson process. Taking expectation with respect to λ yields the result. □

Remark 1. *Unlike [8], we allow λ to have an atom at 0, which implies that $\lim_{u\to\infty} L_\lambda(u) = \mathbb{P}(\lambda = 0) > 0$.*

Corollary 1. *Let the triplet $(\Pi, \lambda, (\xi))$ satisfy the assumptions of Lemma 1. Then, the processes (ζ_n) defined in (3) as normalized cumulative sums of independent copies of $\psi(t;\lambda)$ converge in the sense of finite dimensional distributions (f.d.d.), as $n \to \infty$, to a stationary centered Gaussian process $\zeta(t)$ with the covariance function $\mathrm{Cov}(\zeta(s), \zeta(t)) = L_\lambda(|t-s|)$, $s, t \in \mathbb{R}_+$.*

Proof. This is an immediate consequence of the central limit theorem (CLT) for vectors. Indeed, for any fixed time moments $0 \leq t_1 < \dots < t_d$, the finite-dimensional distributions of $\big(\psi^{(k)}(t_1; \lambda_k), \dots, \psi^{(k)}(t_d; \lambda_k)\big)$ are i.i.d. for different k and have zero mean and the covariation matrix

$$B = \big(L_\lambda(|t_i - t_j|)\big)_{i,j=1}^d. \quad \square$$

Lemma 1 emphasizes a special role played by the Laplace transform L_λ in the study of PSI-processes with random intensities. We will need asymptotics of the Laplace transform L_λ in the right neighborhood of 0.

Assumption 1. *For some $\gamma \in (0, 1]$ and any $\varepsilon > 0$, the Laplace transform (9) of λ satisfies*

$$1 - L_\lambda(s) = o(s^{\gamma - \varepsilon}), \qquad s \downarrow 0. \tag{10}$$

It is well known that (10) holds with $\gamma = 1$ if $\mathbb{E}\lambda < \infty$ or with $\gamma \in (0, 1]$ if the tail $\mathbb{P}(\lambda > x)$ of λ varies regularly of index $-\gamma$ at $x \to \infty$, see, e.g., [9] (Theorem 8.1.6).

Below, we shall always suppose that terms of the sequence (ξ) are i.i.d., hence uncorrelated, and satisfy the assumptions of Lemma 1. By Corollary 1, random processes (ζ_n) have a limit ζ as $n \to \infty$ but in the rather weak f.d.d. sense. The aim of this paper is to establish a more strong result, a functional limit theorem for (ζ_n) in an appropriate functional space. If Assumption 1 holds, then the covariance function of the limiting process $\zeta(t)$ behaves in a controllable way at 0, and $\zeta(t)$ has a version with almost surely continuous paths because $\gamma > 0$ in (10), see, e.g., [10] (§9.2). Our main result is that, under additional moment assumptions $\mathbb{E}|\xi_0|^{2h} < \infty$ for some $h > 1/(\gamma^2)$ (where γ is the exponent in (10)), the convergence indeed takes place in the Skorokhod space $D[0, T]$, for any $T > 0$.

Theorem 1. *Consider a triplet $(\Pi, \lambda, (\xi))$ that consists of a standard Poisson process Π, a non-negative random variable λ satisfying Assumption 1, and a sequence $(\xi) = (\xi_0, \xi_1, \dots)$ of i.i.d. random variables such that $\mathbb{E}\xi_0 = 0$ and $\mathbb{E}\xi_0^2 = 1$. Elements of the triplet are supposed to be independent and to satisfy the condition*

$$\mathbb{E}|\xi_0|^{2h} < \infty \quad \text{for some} \quad h > \frac{1}{\gamma^2}. \tag{11}$$

Let $(\Pi_k, \lambda_k, (\xi^{(k)}))$, $k = 1, 2, \dots$, be a sequence of independent copies of the triplet $(\Pi, \lambda, (\xi))$, $\psi^{(k)} \equiv \psi^{(k)}(t; \lambda_k)$ be the PSI-process (1) constructed from the k-th triplet, and ζ_n be defined by (3). Then, for any $T > 0$, the sequence of stochastic processes $(\zeta_n(t))$ converges in the Skorokhod space $D[0, T]$, as $n \to \infty$, to a zero mean stationary Gaussian process $\zeta(t)$ with the covariance function $\mathbb{E}\,\zeta(s)\zeta(t) = L_\lambda(|s - t|)$, $s, t \in [0, T]$.

Remark 2. *Nowadays, it is common to consider a weak convergence in the space $D[0, \infty)$. Due to specific features of our model (stationary of ζ_n for every n, continuity of ζ), this implies a weak convergence in $D[0, T]$ for all $T > 0$. Since we essentially use the results from Billingsley's book [11] that deals with $D[0, T]$, we prefer to formulate our results in $D[0, T]$, $T > 0$, as in Theorem 1.*

We prove Theorem 1 in Section 6 and now proceed with studying some of its consequences.

3. Example: A PSI-Martingale

Recall the definition (2) of the natural filtration $\mathbb{F}$ given in the Introduction. Note that since PSI-processes (with non-random λ) belong to a so-called class of "Pseudo-Poisson processes" [12] (Ch. X), they have the Markov property with the following transition probabilities: for $x \in \mathbb{R}$; $t, u \in \mathbb{R}_+$,

$$\mathbb{P}(\psi(t+u) \leq x \mid \psi(t) = x_0) = \mathbb{P}(\Pi(\lambda u) > 0)\mathbb{P}(\xi_0 \leq x) + \mathbb{P}(\Pi(\lambda u) = 0)\mathbf{1}\{x_0 \leq x\}$$
$$= \left(1 - e^{-\lambda u}\right)\mathbb{P}(\xi_0 \leq x) + e^{-\lambda u}\mathbf{1}\{x_0 \leq x\}.$$

Denote the pathwise integrated PSI-process $\Psi(t) = \int_0^t \psi(s)\,ds$. Note that a pair (Ψ, ψ) is an $\mathbb{R}^2$-valued Markov process, although Ψ itself is not Markovian.

Proposition 1 (The PSI-martingale). *Assume that $\xi_0, \xi_1, \dots$ are i.i.d. and $\mathbb{E}\xi_0 = 0$. Then, for a non-random $\lambda > 0$, the stochastic process $M(t)$ defined in (5) is a starting at the origin $\mathbb{F}$-martingale for $t \in \mathbb{R}_+$.*

Proof. Let us introduce a slightly modified $\mathcal{M}$-process

$$\mathcal{M}(t) := \lambda \Psi(t) + \psi(t) = M(t) + \xi_0.$$

First, we show that it is an $\mathbb{F}$-martingale starting at the random point ξ_0. Since the pair $(\Psi(t), \psi(t))$ is a Markov process adapted to the filtration $(\mathcal{F}_t)$, and $\mathcal{M}(t)$ is determined by $(\Psi(t), \psi(t))$, we have

$$\mathbb{E}(\mathcal{M}(t+u)|\mathcal{F}_t) = \mathbb{E}(\mathcal{M}(t+u)|\Psi(t), \psi(t)), \quad \forall u, t \geq 0. \tag{12}$$

Let $0 < T_1 < T_2 < \cdots$ be jump times of the driving Poisson process $\Pi(\lambda t)$. Denote the random period $\theta(t) = \min\{T_k : T_k > t\} - t$; that is the time for which the Poisson process $\Pi(\lambda s)$ does not change after time t. For each fixed t, the period $\theta(t)$ has the exponential distribution with the intensity λ. Using this notation, we can calculate

$$\mathbb{E}(\psi(t+u)|\Psi(t),\psi(t)) = \psi(t)\,\mathbb{E}\,\mathbf{1}\{\theta(t) > u\} = \psi(t)\,e^{-\lambda u}, \tag{13}$$

$$\mathbb{E}(\Psi(t+u)|\Psi(t),\psi(t)) = \Psi(t) + \psi(t)\,\mathbb{E}\min\{\theta(t),u\} = \Psi(t) + \psi(t)\frac{1-e^{-\lambda u}}{\lambda}. \tag{14}$$

Multiplying (14) by λ and adding (13), we obtain $\mathbb{E}(\mathcal{M}(t+u)|\Psi(t),\psi(t)) = \mathcal{M}(t)$, which proves the assertion about $\mathcal{M}(t)$ due to (12).

Now, the claim of Proposition 1 easily follows from $\sigma(\Psi(t),\psi(t)) \subset \mathcal{F}_t$ and $\mathbb{E}(\xi_0|\mathcal{F}_t) = \xi_0$. □

As it has been mentioned in the Introduction, for a random non-degenerate λ, the process $M(t)$ is not $\mathcal{F}_t$-measurable, and the filtration $\mathbb{F}$ should be augmented by $\sigma(\lambda)$:

$$\mathcal{F}_t^\lambda := \sigma\{\,\Pi(\lambda s), s \le t;\ \xi_0,\ldots \xi_k, k \le \Pi(\lambda t);\ \lambda\,\}; \qquad \mathbb{F}^\lambda := (\mathcal{F}_t^\lambda)_{t \in \mathbb{R}_+}. \tag{15}$$

The following analog of Proposition 1 holds, but the proof is more tricky.

Proposition 2 (The PSI-martingale with random intensity). *Assume that* $(\xi) = (\xi_0, \xi_1, \ldots)$ *is a sequence of i.i.d. random variables with* $\mathbb{E}\xi_0 = 0$, $\Pi = \Pi(t)$ *is a standard Poisson process, a random variable λ is positive a.s.; λ, (ξ), and Π are independent. Then, the stochastic process $M(t; \lambda)$, $t \ge 0$, defined in (5) is a local martingale with respect to $\mathbb{F}^\lambda$. If $\mathbb{E}\lambda < \infty$, then $M(t)$ is a martingale.*

Proof. Let $0 < \tau_1 < \tau_2 < \ldots$ be jump times of the Poisson process $\Pi(t)$ and $T_k := \tau_k/\lambda$ corresponding jump times of the process $\Pi(\lambda t)$. Recall that filtrations $\mathbb{F} = (\mathcal{F}_t)_{t \ge 0}$ and $\mathbb{F}^\lambda = (\mathcal{F}_t^\lambda)_{t \ge 0}$ are defined in (2) and (15), respectively. It is easy to check that a set $A \in \mathcal{F}$ belongs to $\mathcal{F}_t$ (resp. to $\mathcal{F}_t^\lambda$), $t \ge 0$, if and only if $A \cap \{T_k \le t < T_{k+1}\} = A \cap \{\Pi(\lambda t) = k\} \in \mathcal{G}_k$ (resp. $A \cap \{T_k \le t < T_{k+1}\} \in \mathcal{G}_k^\lambda$) for every $k = 0, 1, \ldots$. Here,

$$\mathcal{G}_k := \sigma\{T_1, \ldots, T_k;\ \xi_0, \ldots \xi_k\,\} = \sigma\{\tau_1, \ldots, \tau_k;\ \xi_0, \ldots \xi_k\,\},$$

the latter equality being held if $\lambda = const$, and

$$\mathcal{G}_k^\lambda := \sigma\{T_1, \ldots, T_k;\ \xi_0, \ldots \xi_k;\ \lambda\,\} = \sigma\{\tau_1, \ldots, \tau_k;\ \xi_0, \ldots \xi_k;\ \lambda\,\}.$$

In particular, the filtrations $(\mathcal{F}_t)_{t \ge 0}$ and $(\mathcal{F}_t^\lambda)_{t \ge 0}$ are right-continuous.

First, we calculate the $\mathbb{F}^\lambda$-compensator of the locally integrable process

$$\Pi(\lambda t) = \sum_{n=1}^\infty \mathbf{1}\{t \ge T_n\}.$$

Since, for $\lambda = const$, $\Pi(\lambda t)$ is a Poisson process with intensity λ, its $\mathbb{F}$-compensator is λt. This means that $\Pi(\lambda t) - \lambda t$ is an $\mathbb{F}$-martingale. Denoting $N(t) := \Pi(t) - t$, this can be written as

$$\mathbb{E}\Big\{\big(N(\lambda t) - N(\lambda s)\big)\mathbf{1}\{\Pi(\lambda s) = k\}f(\tau_1, \ldots, \tau_k;\ \xi_0, \ldots \xi_k)\Big\} = 0$$

for every $0 \le s < t$, $k = 0, 1, \ldots$, and any bounded Borel function f from $\mathbb{R}^{2k+1}$ in $\mathbb{R}$. Consider now the case of random λ. Note that $\mathbb{E}\big(\Pi(\lambda t)\mathbf{1}\{\lambda \le k\}\big) \le kt < \infty$ for any t and $k \ge 1$. This allows us to take a conditional expectation given λ in the expression below, where f is as above and g is a bounded measurable function from $\mathbb{R}$ to $\mathbb{R}$:

$$\mathbb{E}\Big\{\big(N(\lambda t) - N(\lambda s)\big)\mathbf{1}\{\Pi(\lambda s) = k\}f(\tau_1, \ldots, \tau_k;\ \xi_0, \ldots \xi_k)g(\lambda)\mathbf{1}\{\lambda \le k\}\Big\}$$

$$= \mathbb{E}\,\mathbb{E}\Big\{\big(N(\lambda t) - N(\lambda s)\big)\mathbf{1}\{\Pi(\lambda s) = k\}f(\tau_1, \ldots, \tau_k;\ \xi_0, \ldots \xi_k)g(\lambda)\mathbf{1}\{\lambda \le k\}\,\Big|\,\lambda\Big\} = 0.$$

This means
$$0 = \mathbb{E}\left\{(N(\lambda t) - N(\lambda s))\mathbf{1}\{\lambda \leq k\}\big|\mathcal{F}_s^\lambda\right\} = \mathbb{E}(N(\lambda t \wedge \sigma_k) - N(\lambda s \wedge \sigma_k)|\mathcal{F}_s^\lambda),$$

where $\sigma_k = 0$ if $\lambda > k$ and $\sigma_k = +\infty$ otherwise. We conclude that $N(\lambda t)$ is an $\mathbb{F}^\lambda$-local martingale, and λt is the $\mathbb{F}^\lambda$-compensator of $\Pi(\lambda t)$.

The same proof shows that
$$K(\lambda t) := \sum_{n=1}^\infty \xi_n \mathbf{1}\{t \geq T_n\}$$

is an $\mathbb{F}^\lambda$-local martingale. Indeed, it is a compound Poisson process with zero mean; hence, it itself is an $\mathbb{F}$-martingale for a deterministic λ. To ensure that the corresponding expectation is finite, we note that $\mathbb{E}(K(\lambda t)\mathbf{1}\{\lambda \leq k\}) \leq \sum_{n=1}^\infty \mathbb{E}|\xi_n|\mathbb{P}(t \geq T_n, \lambda \leq k) \leq \mathbb{E}|\xi_0|\mathbb{E}(\Pi(\lambda t)\mathbf{1}\{\lambda \leq k\}) < \infty$.

The final step of the proof is to determine the $\mathbb{F}^\lambda$-compensator of the process
$$J(\lambda t) := \sum_{n=1}^\infty \xi_{n-1}\mathbf{1}\{t \geq T_n\}$$

We can represent $J(\lambda t)$ as the pathwise Lebesgue–Stieltjes integral of a predictable process
$$H(\lambda t) := \sum_{n=1}^\infty \xi_{n-1}\mathbf{1}\{T_{n-1} < t \leq T_n\}$$

with respect to $\Pi(\lambda t)$. Note that the integral process
$$\int_{(0,t]} H(\lambda t)\mathrm{d}\Pi(\lambda t)$$

is a process with $\mathbb{F}^\lambda$-locally integrable variation because its variation up to σ_k is estimated from above similarly to $K(\lambda t)$. This allows us to conclude that the $\mathbb{F}^\lambda$-compensator of $J(\lambda t)$ is the Lebesgue–Stieltjes integral process of $H(\lambda t)$ with respect to the $\mathbb{F}^\lambda$-compensator of $\Pi(\lambda t)$, see, e.g., Theorem 2.21 (2) in [13], i.e., the $\mathbb{F}^\lambda$-compensator of $J(\lambda t)$ equals
$$\int_{(0,t]} H(\lambda t)\lambda \mathrm{d}t = \lambda\Psi(t).$$

Summarizing, we obtain that the $\mathbb{F}^\lambda$-compensator of
$$\psi(t) - \xi_0 = \sum_{n=1}^\infty (\xi_n - \xi_{n-1})\mathbf{1}\{t \geq T_n\} = K(\lambda t) - J(\lambda t),$$

that is $-\lambda\Psi(t)$.

Finally, the quadratic variation of M is
$$[M,M]_t = \sum_{k=1}^\infty (\xi_k - \xi_{k-1})^2 \mathbf{1}\{T_k \leq t\}. \tag{16}$$

Hence, if $\mathbb{E}\lambda < \infty$,
$$\mathbb{E}([M,M]_t)^{1/2} \leq \mathbb{E}\sum_{k=1}^\infty |\xi_k - \xi_{k-1}|\mathbf{1}\{T_k \leq t\}$$
$$\leq 2\mathbb{E}|\xi_0|\mathbb{E}\sum_{k=1}^\infty \mathbf{1}\{T_k \leq t\} \leq 2\mathbb{E}|\xi_0|\mathbb{E}\Pi(\lambda t) = 2t\mathbb{E}|\xi_0|\mathbb{E}\lambda.$$

Therefore, $M(t)$ is a martingale according to Davis' inequality (see [14] (Ch. 9)). □

If we assume also that $\mathbb{E}\xi_0^2 = 1$, then the $\mathbb{F}^\lambda$-martingale $M(t)$ has $\mathbb{E}M(t)^2 < \infty$ for all $t \in \mathbb{R}_+$. Its quadratic variation is calculated in (16). The variance of $M(t)$ can then be calculated as follows:

$$\operatorname{Var} M(t) = \mathbb{E}\,[M,M]_t = \mathbb{E}\sum_{k=1}^\infty (\xi_k - \xi_{k-1})^2 \mathbf{1}\{T_k \le t\} = \mathbb{E}(\xi_1 - \xi_0)^2\,\mathbb{E}\,\Pi(\lambda t) = 2t\,\mathbb{E}\lambda\,.$$

If $\mathbb{E}\lambda < \infty$ (in particular, if λ is not random), then the variance of $M(t)$ is finite for any $t \in \mathbb{R}_+$. Hence, direct application of Theorem VIII.3.46 [7] (p. 481) allows us to obtain a functional limit theorem for properly normalized sums of independent copies $M^{(i)}(t)$, $i = 1, 2, \ldots$, of the martingale $M(t)$, i.e., for the processes

$$\overline{M}_n(t) := \frac{1}{\sqrt{n}} \sum_{i=1}^n M^{(i)}(t), \quad n = 1, 2, \ldots, \quad t \ge 0.$$

Here, the convergence takes place in the Skorokhod space, and the limit process is $\sqrt{2\mathbb{E}\lambda}\,W(t)$, where $W(t)$, $t \ge 0$, is a standard Brownian motion.

Assume now that $\lambda > 0$ is non-random. It is easy to see that the mapping $(\psi(t))_{t \in [0,T]} \mapsto (M(t))_{t \in [0,T]}$ is continuous in the Skorokhod space $D[0,T]$, for any $T > 0$. Hence, as a corollary of Theorem 1, we reconstruct the above result that the convergence $\overline{M}_n \to \sqrt{2\lambda}\,W$ takes place in the Skorokhod space, under the condition that $\mathbb{E}|\xi_0|^{2+\varepsilon} < \infty$, for some $\varepsilon > 0$.

4. Counterexample: Diverging Sums

For $\beta > 1$, denote $\mu_\beta = \frac{\beta}{\beta-1}$ and consider a function

$$f_\beta(x) = \begin{cases} \beta(x + \mu_\beta)^{-\beta-1}, & x \ge -1/(\beta-1), \\ 0, & x < -1/(\beta-1) \end{cases}$$

of $x \in \mathbb{R}$. This is a probability density. Let ξ be a random variable with this density, then, by the choice of μ_β the mean $\mathbb{E}\xi = 0$ for any $\beta > 1$, and $\operatorname{Var}\xi = \frac{\beta}{(\beta-2)(\beta-1)^2} < \infty$ for any $\beta > 2$. Moreover, all absolute moments of non-negative order less than β exist, while $\mathbb{E}|\xi|^\beta = \infty$. The tail distribution function is $\mathbb{P}(\xi > x) = (x + \mu_\beta)^{-\beta}$ for $x \ge -1/(\beta-1)$. Let $(\xi) = (\xi_0, \xi_1, \ldots)$ be a sequence of i.i.d. random variables distributed as ξ.

For $\alpha > 0$, let λ be independent of (ξ) and have the tail distribution function $\mathbb{P}(\lambda > x) = (x+1)^{-\alpha}$ for $x \ge 0$. The Laplace transform of λ can be expressed in terms of the (upper) incomplete Gamma function function

$$\Gamma(\alpha, x) = \int_x^\infty e^{-y} y^{\alpha-1}\,dy.$$

By a simple change of variables, we obtain

$$L_\lambda(s) = \mathbb{E}\,e^{-s\lambda} = \alpha e^s s^\alpha \Gamma(-\alpha, s), \quad s > 0. \qquad (17)$$

The asymptotics of $L_\lambda(s)$ as $s \downarrow 0$ can be read, say, from Theorem 8.1.6 [9] (p. 333): as $s \downarrow 0$,

$$1 - L_\lambda(s) \sim \begin{cases} \Gamma(1-\alpha)s^\alpha, & \alpha \in (0,1), \\ s \log \frac{1}{s}, & \alpha = 1, \\ \frac{s}{\alpha-1}, & \alpha > 1. \end{cases}$$

Hence, λ satisfies Assumption 1 with $\gamma = \min\{\alpha, 1\}$.

Let $\Pi(t)$ be a standard Poisson process, independent of both (ξ) and λ. Define a PSI-process $\psi(t; \lambda)$ with the random intensity λ as in (1).

Consider independent copies $\psi^{(k)}(t; \lambda_k)$, $k = 1, 2, \ldots$, where λ_k are independent copies of λ, and let $(\zeta_n(t))$ be their normalized cumulative sums, as in (3). The CLT for vectors implies that, for $\beta > 2$ and $\alpha > 0$, in terms of finite-dimensional distributions, the processes (ζ_n) converge, as $n \to \infty$, to a stationary centered Gaussian process with the covariance function $\beta(\beta-2)^{-1}(\beta-1)^{-2}L_\lambda(u)$, $u \geq 0$. We claim that, nevertheless, for certain parameters $\alpha > 0$ and $\beta > 2$, the functional limit theorem cannot hold true for these (ζ_n). The proof is based on the following technical result.

Proposition 3. *One can find n_0 such that for any $n \geq n_0$, with probability not less than $1/16$, one of the PSI-processes $\psi^{(1)}(t;\lambda_1),\ldots,\psi^{(n)}(t,\lambda_n)$ has a jump of size at least $n^{1/(\alpha\beta)}$, for $t \in [0,1]$.*

Proof. Define for $n = 1, 2, \ldots$

$$\mu_n := \max\{\lambda_1, \ldots, \lambda_n\}.$$

The cumulative distribution function of μ_n is

$$F_n(x) := \mathbb{P}(\mu_n \leq x) = \left(1 - (x+1)^{-\alpha}\right)^n, \quad x \geq 0.$$

Notice that $\lim_{n \to \infty} F_n(n^{1/\alpha}) = e^{-1}$. Hence, for large enough n, there exists $\varkappa \in \{1,\ldots,n\}$ such that $\lambda_\varkappa \geq n^{1/\alpha}$ with probability not less than $1/2$. Since $\Pi_\varkappa$ is independent of $\lambda_\varkappa$ and the Poisson distribution is asymptotically symmetric around its mean as the parameter becomes large, we may claim that $\mathbb{P}(\Pi_\varkappa(\lambda_\varkappa) > n^{1/\alpha} | \lambda_\varkappa \geq n^{1/\alpha}) > 1/3$. Hence, with probability not less than $1/6$ among PSI-process $\psi^{(1)}, \ldots, \psi^{(n)}$, at least one process $\psi^{(\varkappa)}$ engages more than $n^{1/\alpha}$ random variables $(\xi_i^{(\varkappa)})$ on the time interval $[0,1]$; that is, $\Pi_\varkappa(\lambda_\varkappa) \geq m := \lfloor n^{1/\alpha} \rfloor + 1$. Here and below for $x \in \mathbb{R}$, we denote $\lfloor x \rfloor = \max\{n \in \mathbb{Z} : n \leq x\}$ the floor function.

Consider now $\eta_{\varkappa,m} := \max\{\xi_1^{(\varkappa)}, \ldots, \xi_m^{(\varkappa)}\}$. For any fixed n, they are i.i.d. and have the cumulative distribution function

$$G_m(x) := \mathbb{P}(\eta_{\varkappa,m} \leq x) = \left(1 - (x + \mu_\beta)^{-\beta}\right)^m, \quad x > -1/(\beta - 1),$$

and $\eta_{\varkappa,m} > m^{1/\beta}$ with probability not less than $1/2$ for all m large enough, because $G_m(m^{1/\beta}) = \left(1 - (m^{1/\beta} + \mu_\beta)^{-\beta}\right)^m \to e^{-1}$ as $m \to \infty$. This maximum is attained on some $\xi_j^{(\varkappa)}$, and with probability $3/4$ at least one of $\xi_{j-1}^{(\varkappa)}$ and $\xi_{j+1}^{(\varkappa)}$ is less than $2^{1/\beta} - \mu_\beta < 0$. (We neglect a situation when the maximum is attained for $j = 1$ or $j = m$, which happens with the probability $2/m$, see, e.g., [15].) It means that, for large m, $\psi^{(\varkappa)}(t, \lambda_\varkappa)$ has at least one jump greater than $m^{1/\beta}$, with probability at least $3/8$.

Combining the above estimates and using the independence between $\Pi(\lambda_\varkappa t)$ and the corresponding driven sequence $(\xi^{(\varkappa)})$, we see that, with probability not less than $1/16$, the process $\psi^{(\varkappa)}(t;\lambda_\varkappa)$, $t \in [0,1]$, has a jump of size at least $m^{1/\beta} \geq n^{1/(\alpha\beta)}$, for all $n \geq n_0 = n_0(\alpha, \beta)$. □

Since all these PSI-processes jump at different moments of time a.s., the jump of any process is not compensated by other PSI-processes and makes a contribution to ζ_n. If $\alpha\beta \leq 2$, then after the scaling by $\sqrt{n}$ in (3), the size of the jump that exists according to Proposition 3 exceeds $n^{1/(\alpha\beta)-1/2} \not\to 0$ as $n \to \infty$. Hence, the limit in the Skorokhod space $D[0,1]$, if it exists, should have jumps with positive probability. However, it is well known that the stationary Gaussian process with the covariance function $const \cdot L_\lambda(u)$, $u \geq 0$, where $L_\lambda(u)$ is given by (17), has a continuous modification a.s. This contradiction shows that the convergence $\zeta_n \to \zeta$ cannot take place in $D[0,1]$ as $n \to \infty$.

Remark 3. *The considered counterexample suggests that the correct condition for the functional limit theorem could be $\mathbb{E}|\xi_0|^{2h} < \infty$ for some $h > 1/\gamma$. Theorem 1 is proved under the more restrictive condition $h > 1/\gamma^2$. In the case $\mathbb{E}\lambda < \infty$, Assumption 1 holds with $\gamma = 1$, so both inequalities become $h > 1$. In the more interesting case $\mathbb{E}\lambda = \infty$, we conjecture that the less restrictive inequality $h > 1/\gamma$ should be enough. The only place in our proof where we need*

$h > 1/\gamma^2$ is Lemma 4, which is proved with a straightforward and rather rough approach. A more sophisticated technique is needed to show that the same or similar result holds if $h > 1/\gamma$.

5. Modulus of Continuity for PSI-Processes with Random Intensity

We need to bound the probability of large changes of the PSI-process with random intensity. The following result builds a base for such bounds.

Proposition 4. *Consider a PSI-process ψ defined by* (1). *Then, for any fixed $\delta > 0$,*

$$\mathbb{P}\Big(\sup_{0 \le t \le \delta} |\psi(t;\lambda) - \psi(0;\lambda)| \ge r\Big) = \int_{-\infty}^{\infty} \big[1 - L_\lambda\big(\delta(1 - F(x+r) + F(x-r))\big)\big] dF(x) \quad (18)$$

at least for all $r > 0$ such that $F(x)$ and $F(x+r)$ have no common discontinuity points.

Proof. Suppose first that λ is fixed. If there are no jumps of $\Pi(\lambda t)$ on $[0,\delta] \ni t$, then $\psi(t;\lambda) = \psi(0,\lambda) = \xi_0$ for all $t \in [0,\delta]$. If $\Pi(\lambda t)$ has $k > 0$ jumps on $[0,\delta]$, then

$$\sup_{0 \le t \le \delta} |\psi(t;\lambda) - \psi(0;\lambda)| = \max\{|\xi_1 - \xi_0|, \ldots, |\xi_k - \xi_0|\}.$$

Since (ξ_i) are i.i.d., conditioning on the value of $\xi_0 = x$, we obtain

$$\mathbb{P}\big(\max\{|\xi_1 - \xi_0|, \ldots, |\xi_k - \xi_0|\} < r\big) = \int_{-\infty}^{\infty} \mathbb{P}(|\xi_1 - x| < r)^k dF(x)$$

and if $F(x)$ and $F(x+r)$ have no common discontinuities as functions of x, it implies

$$\mathbb{P}\big(\max\{|\xi_1 - \xi_0|, \ldots, |\xi_k - \xi_0|\} \ge r\big) = 1 - \int_{-\infty}^{\infty} \big(F(x+r) - F(x-r)\big)^k dF(x).$$

For a fixed λ, the process $\Pi(\lambda t)$ has k jumps on $[0,\delta]$ with probability $\frac{(\lambda\delta)^k}{k!} e^{-\lambda\delta}$, so by the law of total probability,

$$\mathbb{P}\Big(\sup_{0 \le s \le \delta} |\psi(s;\lambda) - \psi(0;\lambda)| \ge r \,\Big|\, \lambda\Big)$$

$$= \sum_{k=1}^{\infty} \Big(1 - \int_{-\infty}^{\infty} \big(F(x+r) - F(x-r)\big)^k dF(x)\Big) \frac{(\lambda\delta)^k}{k!} e^{-\lambda\delta}$$

$$= 1 - e^{-\lambda\delta} - e^{-\lambda\delta} \int_{-\infty}^{\infty} \Big(\exp\big(\lambda\delta(F(x+r) - F(x-r))\big) - 1\Big) dF(x)$$

$$= \int_{-\infty}^{\infty} \Big(1 - \exp\big(-\lambda\delta(1 - F(x+r) + F(x-r))\big)\Big) dF(x),$$

where changing the order of summation and integration is justified by Fubini's theorem, and the last line follows by simple manipulations using $\int_{-\infty}^{\infty} dF(x) = 1$. The claim (18) follows by taking expectation with respect to λ, and again, the order of integration can be changed by Fubini's theorem. □

The equality (18) easily implies a bound for the probability in the left-hand part of (18) in terms of the so-called concentration function of a random variable ξ defined as

$$Q_\xi(r) = \sup_{x \in \mathbb{R}} \mathbb{P}(x \le \xi \le x + r).$$

The straightforward calculation shows that (18) implies that

$$\mathbb{P}\Big(\sup_{0 \le t \le \delta} |\psi(t;\lambda) - \psi(0;\lambda)| \ge r\Big) \le 1 - L_\lambda\big(\delta(1 - Q_{\xi_0}(2r))\big). \quad (19)$$

However, we need a more explicit bound. To obtain such bound, we analyze the behavior of the Laplace transform $L_\lambda(s)$ for small s. It is postulated in Assumption 1, but for applications, it is convenient to obtain an explicit inequality. It can always be done by slightly reducing the power of s.

Lemma 2. *If λ satisfies Assumption 1, then for any $\varepsilon \in (0, \gamma)$, there exists a constant $C > 0$ such that*

$$0 \leq 1 - L_\lambda(s) \leq Cs^{\gamma - \varepsilon}, \quad s \geq 0. \tag{20}$$

Proof. Since $(1 - L_\lambda(s))s^{-\gamma + \varepsilon} \to 0$ as $s \downarrow 0$, according to (10), the inequality (20) holds with $C = 1$ when $s \in [0, s_0)$ for some sufficiently small $s_0 = s_0(\gamma, \varepsilon, L_\lambda)$. The inequality for $s \geq s_0$ can be fulfilled by increasing C if necessary. □

A combination of the above statements gives an estimate for the probability of big changes of the PSI-process with random intensity on a small interval, provided that we can bound the tail probability for an individual random variable ξ_0, say under some moment assumptions.

Proposition 5. *Suppose that the PSI-process $\psi(t; \lambda)$ with the random intensity λ defined by (1) satisfies the assumptions of Proposition 4, that λ satisfies Assumption 1, and that $\mathbb{E}|\xi_0|^{2h} < \infty$ for some $h > 0$. Then, for any $\varepsilon \in (0, \gamma)$, there exists a constant $C > 0$ such that for all $r > 0$ and $\delta \in [0, 1]$*

$$\mathbb{P}\left(\sup_{0 \leq t \leq \delta} |\psi(t; \lambda) - \psi(0; \lambda)| \geq r\right) \leq C\delta^{\gamma - \varepsilon} r^{-2h(\gamma - \varepsilon)}. \tag{21}$$

Proof. Denote for short $m_{2h} := \mathbb{E}|\xi_0|^{2h} < \infty$ by assumption. Take $r > 0$, then for any $|x| < r/2$

$$1 - F(x + r) + F(x - r) = \mathbb{P}(\xi_0 \leq x - r \text{ or } \xi_0 > x + r) \leq \mathbb{P}(|\xi_0| \geq r/2) \leq \frac{2^{2h} m_{2h}}{r^{2h}}$$

by Markov's inequality. Thus, since L_λ does not increase

$$\int_{-r/2}^{r/2} \left[1 - L_\lambda\left(\delta(1 - F(x + r) + F(x - r))\right)\right] dF(x) \leq 1 - L_\lambda\left(4^h m_{2h} \delta r^{-2h}\right). \tag{22}$$

On the other hand, $1 - L_\lambda(\delta(1 - F(x + r) + F(x - r))) \leq 1 - L_\lambda(\delta)$ for any $x \in \mathbb{R}$ and $r \geq 0$. Hence, for any $\varepsilon > 0$, again by the Markov inequality applied to $|\xi_0|^{2h(\gamma - \varepsilon)}$, one has

$$\left(\int_{-\infty}^{-r/2} + \int_{r/2}^{\infty}\right) \left[1 - L_\lambda\left(\delta(1 - F(x + r) + F(x - r))\right)\right] dF(x)$$

$$\leq (1 - L_\lambda(\delta))\mathbb{P}(|\xi_0| \geq r/2) \leq (1 - L_\lambda(\delta)) \frac{2^{2h(\gamma - \varepsilon)} m_{2h(\gamma - \varepsilon)}}{r^{2h(\gamma - \varepsilon)}}. \tag{23}$$

Combining (22) and (23) and using Lemma 2, we obtain the result. □

6. Sums of PSI-Processes

Since the limit of the normalized cumulative sums (ζ_n) is an a.s. continuous stochastic process, we can use Theorem 15.5 from Billingsley's book [11] (p. 127), which gives the conditions for convergence of processes from the Skorokhod space $D[0, 1]$ to a process with realizations lying in $C[0, 1]$ a.s., in terms of the modulus of continuity

$$\omega_\zeta(\delta) = \sup_{\substack{s, t \in [0, 1] \\ |s - t| \leq \delta}} \{|\zeta(s) - \zeta(t)|\}. \tag{24}$$

It claims that if

(i) for any $\varepsilon > 0$ there exists t such that $\mathbb{P}\big(|\zeta_n(0)| > t\big) \leq \varepsilon$ for all $n \geq 1$;
(ii) for any positive ε and w there exist $\delta \in (0,1)$ and n_0 such that

$$\mathbb{P}\big(\omega_{\zeta_n}(\delta) \geq w\big) \leq \varepsilon, \qquad n \geq n_0; \tag{25}$$

(iii) (ζ_n) converges weakly in terms of finite-dimensional distributions to some random function ζ as $n \to \infty$,

then (ζ_n) converges to ζ as $n \to \infty$, in $D[0,1]$ and ζ is continuous a.s.

In order to bound ω_{ζ_n} in probability, Billingsley suggests to use a corollary to Theorem 8.3 in the same book, which can be formulated as follows. Suppose that ζ is some random element in $D[0,1]$, then for any $\delta > 0$ and $w > 0$

$$\mathbb{P}\big(\omega_\zeta(\delta) \geq 3w\big) \leq \sum_{i=0}^{\lfloor 1/\delta \rfloor - 1} \mathbb{P}\Big(\sup_{t \in [i\delta, (i+1)\delta]} |\zeta(t) - \zeta(i\delta)| \geq w\Big). \tag{26}$$

The sum (26) can be estimated efficiently in our settings because ζ_n is stationary by construction for any n. Hence, all the probabilities in the sum (26) are the same and

$$\mathbb{P}\big(\omega_{\zeta_n}(\delta) \geq 3w\big) \leq \frac{1}{\delta} \mathbb{P}\Big(\sup_{t \in [0,\delta]} |\zeta_n(t) - \zeta_n(0)| \geq w\Big). \tag{27}$$

Remark 4. *Actually, the events whose probabilities are added in the right-hand side of (26) are dependent since for a large n and a small δ, an appearance of a big ($\geq \varepsilon$) jump of ζ_n on $[0, \delta]$ suggests that there are many jumps of some $\psi^{(i)}(t; \lambda_i)$, and hence, the correspondent λ_i is large; so it is probable that there would be many jumps on other intervals and a probability of a big jump is not too small. Perhaps this observation can be used to find a better bound than the union bound (27), but we have not used it.*

In order to check assumption (ii) of Billingsley's theorem, we apply the following two-stage procedure. We use (27) to bound the "global" probability of jumps greater than w on some interval of the length δ. We aim to show that for any $w > 0$ and $\varepsilon > 0$, one can find positive C, τ, and δ such that

$$\mathbb{P}\Big(\sup_{t \in [0,\delta]} |\zeta_n(t) - \zeta_n(0)| \geq w\Big) \leq C\delta^{1+\tau} \quad \text{and} \quad C\delta^\tau < \varepsilon \tag{28}$$

for all n greater than some n_0. To this end, we first show that one can find positive C, τ, δ, and n_0 such that (28) holds for $n = n_0$ and then analyze the local structure of ζ_n to show that (28) actually holds for all $n \geq n_0$.

Our analysis of $\sup_{t \in [0,\delta]} |\zeta_n(t) - \zeta_n(0)|$ is based on the results of Section 5. Consider the Poisson processes with random intensity $\Pi_i(\lambda_i t)$, $i = 1, \ldots, n$, used in the construction of $\psi^{(1)}, \ldots, \psi^{(n)}$, and denote $\kappa_n(\delta)$ the (random) number of these processes that have at least one jump on $[0, \delta]$:

$$\kappa_n(\delta) := \sum_{i=1}^n \mathbf{1}\{\Pi_i(\lambda_i \delta) > 0\}. \tag{29}$$

This is a binomial random variable with n trials and the success probability

$$p_1 \equiv p_1(\delta) := 1 - L_\lambda(\delta). \tag{30}$$

Lemma 2 provides an upper bound for $p_1(\delta)$. We are interested just in the case when $p_1(\delta)$ is small compared to $1/n$, that is, when $\mathbb{E}\kappa_n(\delta)$ is small. Then, the probability that $\kappa_n(\delta) \geq b$ decays fast enough even for an appropriately chosen but fixed b.

Lemma 3. *Let λ satisfy Assumption 1. Then, for any $a > 1/\gamma$, $b > a/(a\gamma - 1)$ and $c > 0$, one can find positive τ and δ_0 such that for all n satisfying $n\delta^{1/a} \leq c$, it holds*

$$\mathbb{P}(\kappa_n(\delta) \geq b) \leq \delta^{1+\tau}, \qquad \delta \in (0, \delta_0).$$

Proof. The well-known Chernoff bound [16] (Theorem 2.1) ensures that for any $t \geq 0$,

$$\mathbb{P}(\kappa_n(\delta) \geq np_1(\delta) + t) \leq \exp(-f(t/(np_1(\delta)))np_1(\delta)), \tag{31}$$

where $f(x) = (1+x)\log(1+x) - x$. For $a > 1/\gamma$, Lemma 2 along with the assumption $n\delta^{1/a} \leq c$ guarantee that $np_1(\delta) \leq C\delta^{\gamma - 1/a - \varepsilon}$ for any $\varepsilon \in (0, \gamma)$ and some C (which may depend on ε). Taking $\varepsilon < \gamma - 1/a$ yields $np_1(\delta) \to 0$ as $\delta \downarrow 0$. Plugging $t = b - np_1(\delta)$, which is positive for small δ, into (31) gives

$$\begin{aligned}\log \mathbb{P}(\kappa_n(\delta) \geq b) &\leq -f((b/(np_1(\delta))) - 1)np_1(\delta) \\ &= -b(\log b - 1) + b\log(np_1(\delta)) - np_1(\delta) \\ &\leq -b(\log b - 1 - \log c) + b(\gamma - 1/a - \varepsilon)\log \delta.\end{aligned}$$

Restricting ε further to be less than $\gamma - 1/a - 1/b$, which is positive by the assumptions, implies that the coefficient of $\log \delta$, that is $b(\gamma - 1/a - \varepsilon)$, is bigger than 1, and Lemma 3 is proved. □

Lemma 4. *Suppose that the random λ satisfies Assumption 1 and that $\mathbb{E}|\xi_0|^{2h} < \infty$ for some $h > 1/\gamma^2$. Let $0 < c_1 < c_2 < \infty$. Then for any $a \in (1/\gamma, (h\gamma - 1)/(1 - \gamma))$ (with the right bound understood as ∞ if $\gamma = 1$) and for any fixed $w > 0$, there exist positive δ_0 and τ such that for all $n \in [c_1\delta^{-1/a}, c_2\delta^{-1/a}]$*

$$\mathbb{P}\Big(\sup_{t \in [0,\delta]} |\zeta_n(t) - \zeta_n(0)| \geq w\Big) \leq \delta^{1+\tau}, \qquad \delta \in (0, \delta_0]. \tag{32}$$

Proof. Let $a > 1/\gamma$ and $w > 0$ be fixed. Denote for short $\delta = n^{-a}$. By the law of total probability,

$$\begin{aligned}&\mathbb{P}\Big(\sup_{t \in [0,\delta]} |\zeta_n(t) - \zeta_n(0)| \geq w\Big) \\ &= \sum_{k=0}^{n} \mathbb{P}\Big(\sup_{t \in [0,\delta]} |\zeta_n(t) - \zeta_n(0)| \geq w \mid \kappa_n(\delta) = k\Big)\mathbb{P}(\kappa_n(\delta) = k) \\ &\leq \sum_{k=1}^{b-1} \mathbb{P}\Big(\sup_{t \in [0,\delta]} |\zeta_n(t) - \zeta_n(0)| \geq w \mid \kappa_n(\delta) = k\Big)\mathbb{P}(\kappa_n(\delta) = k) + \mathbb{P}(\kappa_n(\delta) \geq b) \end{aligned} \tag{33}$$

for any integer $b \geq 2$. Consider an event $\kappa_n(\delta) = k \geq 1$, which means that not more than some k of n processes $\psi^{(1)}, \ldots, \psi^{(n)}$ jump on $[0, \delta]$, and other $n - k$ processes are constant. Then, $\sup_{t \in [0,\delta]} |\zeta_n(t) - \zeta_n(0)| \geq w$ implies that at least one of k PSI-processes that jumps on $[0, \delta]$ changes by more than $w\sqrt{n}/k$. So, for $k \geq 1$,

$$\begin{aligned}&\mathbb{P}\Big(\sup_{t \in [0,\delta]} |\zeta_n(t) - \zeta_n(0)| \geq w \mid \kappa_n(\delta) = k\Big) \\ &\leq k\mathbb{P}\Big(\sup_{t \in [0,\delta]} |\psi(t; \lambda) - \psi(0; \lambda)| \geq w\sqrt{n}/k \mid \Pi(\lambda \cdot) \text{ jumps on } [0, \delta]\Big) \\ &= \frac{k}{p_1}\mathbb{P}\Big(\sup_{t \in [0,\delta]} |\psi(t; \lambda) - \psi(0; \lambda)| \geq w\sqrt{n}/k\Big). \end{aligned} \tag{34}$$

Proposition 5 provides a bound for the probability in the right-hand part of (34), and since $\kappa_n(\delta)$ has the binomial distribution with the parameters n and p_1, using the total probability formula, we continue (33) as

$$
\mathbb{P}\Big(\sup_{t\in[0,\delta]}|\zeta_n(t)-\zeta_n(0)|\geq w\Big)
$$
$$
\leq \sum_{k=1}^{b-1} k\,\mathbb{P}\Big(\sup_{t\in[0,\delta]}|\psi(t;\lambda)-\psi(0;\lambda)|\geq w\sqrt{n}/k\Big)\binom{n}{k}p_1^{k-1}(1-p_1)^{n-k}+\mathbb{P}\big(\kappa_n(\delta)\geq b\big)
$$
$$
\leq C\sum_{k=1}^{b-1} k\binom{n}{k}\Big(\frac{k^{2h}\delta^k}{w^{2h}n^h}\Big)^{\gamma-\varepsilon}+\mathbb{P}\big(\kappa_n(\delta)\geq b\big) \tag{35}
$$

for any $\varepsilon\in(0,\gamma)$, $h>0$ such that $\mathbb{E}|\xi_0|^{2h}<\infty$, and some C depending on the choice of ε, where the last inequality follows from Proposition 5.

Suppose now that $h>1/\gamma^2$. Then $1/\gamma<(h\gamma-1)/(1-\gamma)$, where the right part is understood as ∞ if $\gamma=1$. Choose $a\in(1/\gamma,(h\gamma-1)/(1-\gamma))$ and an integer $b>a/(a\gamma-1)$. Then, by Lemma 3, there exists a positive τ such that $\mathbb{P}(\kappa_n(\delta)\geq b)\leq\delta^{1+\tau}$ for small enough δ. Bounds $c_1\delta^{-1/a}\leq n\leq c_2\delta^{-1/a}$ give

$$
k\binom{n}{k}\Big(\frac{k^{2h}\delta^k}{w^{2h}n^h}\Big)^{\gamma-\varepsilon}\leq\frac{k^{2h(\gamma-\varepsilon)}}{(k-1)!w^{2h(\gamma-\varepsilon)}}\frac{n^k\delta^{k(\gamma-\varepsilon)}}{n^{h(\gamma-\varepsilon)}}\leq\frac{c_2^k k^{2h(\gamma-\varepsilon)}}{c_1^{h(\gamma-\varepsilon)} w^{2h(\gamma-\varepsilon)}}\delta^{k(\gamma-\varepsilon-1/a)+h(\gamma-\varepsilon)/a}.
$$

Choosing $\varepsilon<\gamma-1/a$ ensures that the power of δ is minimal for $k=1$, and the inequality $a<(h\gamma-1)/(1-\gamma)$ guarantees that for $k=1$ this power $\gamma+(h\gamma-1)/a-(1+h/a)\varepsilon>1$ for small enough ε; thus, (32) follows from (35). □

The estimates that are used in the proof of Lemma 4 essentially rely on the relation between δ and n. Therefore, this argument cannot be used to provide a bound (28) uniformly for all $n\geq n_0$. In order to obtain such bound, we apply the technique close to the one used in Billingsley's book [11] (Ch. 12). If we impose some moment condition on ξ_0, then the following bound holds:

Lemma 5. *Suppose that* $\mathbb{E}\xi_0=0$, $\mathbb{E}\xi_0^2=1$ *and* $\mathbb{E}|\xi_0|^{2h}<\infty$ *for some* $h>1$. *Then, for some constant* $C>0$ *and for all* $n=1,2,\ldots$ *and* $0\leq s<t\leq 1$

$$
\mathbb{E}\big|\zeta_n(t)-\zeta_n(s)\big|^{2h}\leq C\max\{p_1(t-s)^h,p_1(t-s)n^{1-h}\}, \tag{36}
$$

where $p_1(\cdot)$ *is defined by* (30).

Proof. Due to stationarity of ζ_n for each n, it is enough to consider the case $s=0$. For any $t\geq 0$, we can represent the increment $\zeta_n(t)-\zeta_n(0)$ as a sum of i.i.d. random variables

$$
\zeta_n(t)-\zeta_n(0)\stackrel{d}{=}\frac{1}{\sqrt{n}}\sum_{i=1}^n\eta_i, \tag{37}
$$
$$
\eta_i\stackrel{d}{=}(\xi_1-\xi_0)\mathbf{1}\{\Pi(\lambda t)>0\}. \tag{38}
$$

Each summand η_i has a symmetric distribution, and two factors in the right-hand part of (38) are independent. By Rosenthal's inequality (see, e.g., [17] (Th. 2.9)), we obtain

$$
\mathbb{E}\big|\zeta_n(t)-\zeta_n(0)\big|^{2h}\leq Cn^{-h}\max\Big\{\Big(\operatorname{Var}\sum_{i=1}^n\eta_i\Big)^h,n\,\mathbb{E}|\eta_1|^{2h}\Big\} \tag{39}
$$

for some constant $C>0$. Both moments can be easily evaluated. Since the summands are i.i.d.,

$$
\operatorname{Var}\sum_{i=1}^n\eta_i=n\operatorname{Var}\eta_1=np_1(t)\operatorname{Var}(\xi_1-\xi_0)=2np_1(t),
$$

because $\mathbb{E}\,\mathbf{1}\{\Pi(\lambda t)>0\}=p_1(t)$. Similarly,

$$
\mathbb{E}|\eta_1|^{2h}=p_1(t)\,\mathbb{E}\,|\xi_1-\xi_0|^{2h}.
$$

Plugging these two values into (39), we readily obtain (36), maybe with another constant C than in (39). □

Corollary 2. *Suppose that Assumption 1 holds, and $h > 1/\gamma$ in the settings of Lemma 5. Then, for any fixed $w > 0$, one can find positive δ_1 and τ such that for all $n \geq (t-s)^{-(\gamma+1)/(h+1)}$ it holds*

$$\mathbb{P}(|\zeta_n(t) - \zeta_n(s)| \geq w) \leq (t-s)^{1+\tau}, \qquad t-s \in (0, \delta_1]. \tag{40}$$

Proof. By the Markov inequality, we have

$$\mathbb{P}(|\zeta_n(t) - \zeta_n(s)| \geq w) \leq \mathbb{E}|\zeta_n(t) - \zeta_n(s)|^{2h} w^{-2h}, \qquad 0 \leq s < t \leq 1.$$

Lemma 5 gives a bound for the right-hand side in terms of $p_1(t-s)$ and n. Lemma 2 provides the upper bound for $p_1(t-s)$, and the condition on n imposed in the claim implies $n^{-1} \leq (t-s)^{(\gamma+1)/(h+1)}$. Hence, for any $\varepsilon > 0$, there exists a constant $C' > 0$ such that for all $0 \leq s < t \leq 1$

$$\mathbb{P}(|\zeta_n(t) - \zeta_n(s)| \geq w) \leq C' \max\{(t-s)^{h(\gamma-\varepsilon)}, (t-s)^{\gamma-\varepsilon+(h-1)(\gamma+1)/(h+1)}\}.$$

Taking $\varepsilon = (h\gamma - 1)/(h+1)$, which is positive by the assumptions, makes both exponents above equal: $h(\gamma - \varepsilon) = \gamma - \varepsilon + (h-1)(\gamma+1)/(h+1) = 1 + \varepsilon$. Hence, this choice of ε yields (40) with $\tau = \varepsilon$ for all $0 \leq s < t \leq 1$, but with a constant in the right-hand side of the inequality. Reducing to $t - s$ lying in a proper interval $(0, \delta_1]$ allows us to get rid of the constant. □

Proof of Theorem 1. Without loss of generality, we may assume $T = 1$ (otherwise perform a non-random time change $t \mapsto t/T$). We need to show that the conditions of Theorem 15.5 of [11] (recalled in the beginning of Section 6) hold. Condition (iii) was already verified (see Corollary 1), and it implies condition (i). So it remains to check condition (ii), which follows from (28).

Suppose that we are given positive ε and w and want to find δ and n_0 such that (25) holds. Lemma 4 applied with $c_1 = 1/2$, $c_2 = 2$ implies that for some positive δ_0, τ and any $a \in (1/\gamma, (h\gamma - 1)/(1 - \gamma))$ inequality (32) holds for $\delta \in (0, \delta_0]$. Corollary 2 guarantees that for some positive δ_1, inequality (40) holds for n sufficiently large and $\delta \in (0, \delta_1]$, and in our application below, the lower bound on n will be fulfilled if $a < (h+1)/(\gamma+1)$. Choose some $a \in (1/\gamma, \min\{(h\gamma - 1)/(1 - \gamma), (h+1)/(\gamma+1)\})$ (this interval is not empty if $h > 1/\gamma^2$), fix a positive $\delta \leq \min\{\delta_0, \delta_1\}$ and let $n_0 = \lfloor \delta^{-1/a} \rfloor$.

For this choice of parameters, Lemma 4 (again with $c_1 = 1/2$, $c_2 = 2$) ensures that (28) holds for all $n \in [n_0, 2n_0]$. Suppose now that $n > 2n_0$ and let $m = \lfloor n^a \delta \rfloor$. (Note that $a > 1/\gamma \geq 1$, so $m \geq 2$ if $n > 2n_0$.) Then for $c_1 = 1/2$, $c_2 = 2$ we have $n \in [c_1(\delta/m)^{-1/a}, c_2(\delta/m)^{-1/a}]$, so (32) holds with δ/m instead of δ, implying that for any $i = 1, \ldots, m$

$$\mathbb{P}\left(\sup_{t \in [\delta(i-1)/m, \delta i/m]} |\zeta_n(t) - \zeta_n(\delta(i-1)/m)| \geq w\right) \leq (\delta/m)^{1+\tau}, \tag{41}$$

due to the stationarity of ζ_n. Let

$$Z_m(\delta) := \max_{i=1,\ldots,m} \{|\zeta_n(\delta i/m) - \zeta_n(0)|\}.$$

Take $s = i\delta/m$ and $t = j\delta/m$ for some $0 \leq i < j \leq m$. Now, we aim to apply Corollary 2 for these s and t. Note that $t - s \in (0, \delta_1]$ by the choice of δ, so it remains to check that the assumption $n \geq (t-s)^{-(\gamma+1)/(h+1)}$ holds. Indeed, $t - s \geq \delta/m$ and $m/\delta \leq n^a$; thus, $(t-s)^{-(\gamma+1)/(h+1)} \leq n^{a(\gamma+1)/(h+1)} < n$ by the choice of a. Hence, Corollary 2 implies

$$\mathbb{P}\big(|\zeta_n(j\delta/m) - \zeta_n(i\delta/m)| \geq w\big) \leq \big((j-i)\delta/m\big)^{1+\tau'}$$

for some $\tau' > 0$. Hence, Theorem 12.2 from Billingsley's book [11] implies that

$$\mathbb{P}\big(Z_m(\delta) \geq w\big) \leq K\delta^{1+\tau'} \tag{42}$$

for some $K > 0$, which depends on τ' but not on δ.

Suppose now that $Z_m(\delta) < w$ and $\sup_{t \in [\delta(i-1)/m, \delta i/m]} |\zeta_n(t) - \zeta_n(\delta(i-1)/m)| < w$ for all $i = 1, \ldots, m$. Then, $\sup_{t \in [0,\delta]} |\zeta_n(t) - \zeta_n(0)| < 2w$ by the triangle inequality. Hence,

$$\mathbb{P}\big(\sup_{t \in [0,\delta]} |\zeta_n(t) - \zeta_n(0)| \geq 2w\big) \leq \mathbb{P}\big(Z_m(\delta) \geq w\big) + m\mathbb{P}\big(\sup_{t \in [0,\delta/m]} |\zeta_n(t) - \zeta_n(0)| \geq w\big) \leq (K+1)\delta^{1+\tau_1}$$

with $\tau_1 = \min\{\tau, \tau'\}$, by inequalities (41) and (42). This argument works for any $\delta \leq \min\{\delta_0, \delta_1\}$, with δ_0 and δ_1 given by Lemma 4 and Corollary 2, and choosing $\delta > 0$ small enough, one can guarantee that $(K+1)\delta^{\tau_1} \leq \varepsilon$. This proves (28) (with $2w$ instead of w, but $w > 0$ is arbitrary) for all $n \geq n_0$, and the claim follows by application of Theorem 15.5 from Billingsley's book [11]. □

7. Conclusions

The functional limit theorem for normalized cumulative sums of PSI-processes (Theorem 1) can be used in opposite directions. The PSI-processes are very simple, and some results can be obtained directly for their sums and imply the corresponding facts for the limiting stationary Gaussian process ζ. On the other hand, the theory of stationary Gaussian processes has been deeply developed in the last few decades, and some results of this theory can have consequences for the pre-limiting processes (ζ_n), which model a number of real life phenomena.

When $\gamma < 1$ in Assumption 1, there is some gap between the conditions implied by the counterexample of Section 4, that is $\mathbb{E}|\xi_0|^{2/\gamma+\varepsilon} < \infty$ for some $\varepsilon > 0$, and the actual condition $\mathbb{E}|\xi_0|^{2/\gamma^2+\varepsilon} < \infty$ (see (11)) under which Theorem 1 is proven. Also, if $\mathbb{E}\lambda < \infty$, it is still unclear if just the finiteness of the variance $\mathbb{E}\xi_0^2 < \infty$ would be sufficient for the convergence in the Skorokhod space.

Author Contributions: Writing – original draft, Y.Y., O.R. and A.G.; Writing – review & editing, Y.Y., O.R. and A.G. All authors have read and agreed to the published version of the manuscript.

Funding: The reported study was funded by RFBR, project number 20-01-00646 A.

Data Availability Statement: Not applicable.

Acknowledgments: The authors express their gratitude to A.V. Liulintsev (the last year student at the Math. and Mech. Dept. of St. Petersburg State University, a participant of the project 20-01-00646 A) for active discussion of M-processes studied in Section 3.

Conflicts of Interest: The authors declare no conflict of interest. The funders had no role in the design of the study; in the collection, analyses, or interpretation of data; in the writing of the manuscript; or in the decision to publish the results.

References

1. Rusakov, O.; Yakubovich, Y. Poisson processes directed by subordinators, stuttering Poisson and pseudo-Poisson processes, with applications to actuarial mathematics. *J. Phys. Conf. Ser.* **2021**, *2131*, 022107. [CrossRef]
2. Barndorff-Nielsen, O.E. Stationary infinitely divisible processes, *Braz. J. Probab. Stat.* **2011**, *25*, 294–322.
3. Barndorff-Nielsen, O.E.; Benth, F.E.; Veraart, A.E.D. *Ambit Stochastics*; Springer Nature: Cham, Switzerland, 2018.
4. Wolpert, R.L.; Taqqu, M.S. Fractional Ornstein-Uhlenbeck Lévy processes and the Telecom process: Upstairs and downstairs. *Signal Process.* **2005**, *85*, 1523–1545. [CrossRef]
5. Rusakov, O.; Yakubovich, Y. On PSI, trawl, and ambit stochastics. In Proceedings of the 7th International Conference on Stochastic Methods (ICSM-7), Gelendzhik, Russia, 2–9 June 2022; To appear in *Theory Probab. Appl.*

6. Rusakov, O.V. Tightness of sums of independent identically distributed pseudo-Poisson processes in the Skorokhod space. *Zap. Nauchn. Sem. POMI* **2015**, *442*, 122–132. (In Russian). English transl. in *J. Math. Sci.* **2017**, *225*, 805–811. [CrossRef]
7. Jacod, J.; Shiryaev, A.N. *Limit Theorems for Stochastic Processes*, 2nd ed.; Springer: Berlin, Germany, 2002.
8. Rusakov, O. V. Pseudo-Poissonian processes with stochastic intensity and a class of processes generalizing the Ornstein–Uhlenbeck process. *Vestn. St. Petersb. Univ. Math. Mech. Astron.* **2017**, *4*, 247–257. (In Russian). English transl. in *Vestn. St.Petersb. Univ. Math.* **2017**, *50*, 153–160. [CrossRef]
9. Bingham, N.H.; Goldie, C.M.; Teugels, J.L. *Regular Variation*; Encyclopedia of Mathematics and its Applications, 27; Cambridge University Press: Cambridge, UK, 1987.
10. Cramér H.; Leadbetter, M.R. *Stationary and Related Stochastic Processes*; Reprint of the 1967 original; Dover Publications, Inc.: Mineola, NY, USA, 2004.
11. Billingsley, P. *Convergence of Probability Measures*; John Wiley and Sons: Hoboken, NJ, USA, 1968.
12. Feller, W. *An Introduction to Probability Theory and Its Applications*, 2nd ed.; John Wiley & Sons, Inc.: New York, NY, USA; London, UK; Sydney, Australia, 1971; Volume II.
13. Gushchin, A.A. *Stochastic Calculus for Quantitative Finance*; ISTE Press: London, UK; Elsevier Ltd.: Oxford, UK, 2015.
14. Karandikar, R.L.; Rao, B.V. *Introduction to Stochastic Calculus*; Indian Statistical Institute Series; Springer: Singapore, 2018.
15. Nevzorov, V.B. *Records: Mathematical Theory*; Translations of Mathematical Monographs, Volume 194; AMS: Providence, RI, USA, 2001; Translated from the Russian manuscript by D. M. Chibisov.
16. Janson, S.; Łuczak, T.; Rucinski, A.*Random Graphs*; Wiley-Interscience Series in Discrete Mathematics and Optimization; Wiley-Interscience: New York, NY, USA, 2000.
17. Petrov, V.V. *Limit Theorems of Probability Theory*; Oxford Studies in Probability, Clarendon Press: Oxford, UK, 1995.

Article

Poissonization Principle for a Class of Additive Statistics

Igor Borisov * and Maman Jetpisbaev

Laboratory of Probability Theory and Mathematical Statistics, Sobolev Institute of Mathematics, Novosibirsk State University, 630090 Novosibirsk, Russia
* Correspondence: sibam@math.nsc.ru

Abstract: In this paper, we consider a class of additive functionals of a finite or countable collection of the group frequencies of an empirical point process that corresponds to, at most, a countable partition of the sample space. Under broad conditions, it is shown that the asymptotic behavior of the distributions of such functionals is similar to the behavior of the distributions of the same functionals of the accompanying Poisson point process. However, the Poisson versions of the additive functionals under consideration, unlike the original ones, have the structure of sums (finite or infinite) of independent random variables that allows us to reduce the asymptotic analysis of the distributions of additive functionals of an empirical point process to classical problems of the theory of summation of independent random variables.

Keywords: empirical point process; Poisson point process; Poissonization; group frequency; additive functional

MSC: 60F05

Citation: Borisov, I.; Jetpisbaev, M. Poissonization Principle for a Class of Additive Statistics. *Mathematics* **2022**, *10*, 4084. https://doi.org/10.3390/math10214084

Academic Editors: Alexander Tikhomirov and Vladimir Ulyanov

Received: 5 September 2022
Accepted: 29 October 2022
Published: 2 November 2022

Publisher's Note: MDPI stays neutral with regard to jurisdictional claims in published maps and institutional affiliations.

Copyright: © 2022 by the authors. Licensee MDPI, Basel, Switzerland. This article is an open access article distributed under the terms and conditions of the Creative Commons Attribution (CC BY) license (https://creativecommons.org/licenses/by/4.0/).

1. Introduction

In this paper, we study a class of additive functionals (statistics) of a finite or countable collection of group frequencies constructed by a sample of size n with a finite or countable partition of the sample space. Under broad conditions, it is shown that, as $n \to \infty$, the asymptotic behavior of distributions of the additive functionals under consideration is completely similar to the behavior of distributions of the same functionals of the accompanying Poisson point process. From here it is easy to establish that the above-mentioned weak convergence is equivalent to that for the same additive functionals but with independent group frequencies, which are constructed, respectively, using a finite or countable collection of independent copies of the original sample, when we fix in the i-th partition element only the points from the i-th independent copy of the original sample. In other words, in the case under consideration, we remove the dependence of the initial group frequencies with a multinomial distribution. This phenomenon makes it possible to directly use the diverse tool of the summation theory of independent random variables to study the limiting behavior of the additive statistics being considered.

The structure of this paper is as follows. In Section 2, we introduce the empirical and accompanying Poisson vector point processes and formulate some important results regarding their connection. In Section 3, we introduce a class of additive statistics and give a number of examples. Section 4 contains the main result of the paper, i.e., a duality theorem, which states that an original additive statistic with some normalizing and centering constants weakly converges to a limit if, and only if, their Poisson version with the same normalizing and centering constants weakly converges to the same limit. In Section 5, we discuss some applications of the duality theorem. In Section 6, we present moment inequalities connecting the original additive statistics and their Poisson versions. Section 7 is devoted to asymptotic analysis of first two moments of additive statistics connected with an infinite multinomial urn model. Section 8 contains proofs of all results of the paper. Finally, in Section 9, we summarize the results and discuss some their extensions.

2. Empirical and Poisson Point Processes

Let $\{X_i^{(k)}, i \geq 1\}$, $k = \overline{1,m}$ be a finite set of independent copies of a sequence of independent identically distributed random variables with values in an arbitrary measurable space $(\mathfrak{X}, \mathcal{A})$ and distribution P. For any natural $n_1, \ldots, n_m$, consider m independent empirical point processes based on respective samples $X_1^{(k)}, \ldots, X_{n_k}^{(k)}$, $k = \overline{1,m}$:

$$V_{n_k}^{(k)}(A) := \sum_{i=1}^{n_k} I_A(X_i^{(k)}), \quad k = \overline{1,m}, \quad A \in \mathcal{A}.$$

Define the m independent accompanying Poisson point processes as

$$\Pi_{n_k}^{(k)}(A) := \sum_{i=1}^{\pi_k(n_k)} I_A(X_i^{(k)}), \quad k = \overline{1,m}, \quad A \in \mathcal{A},$$

where $\pi_k(t)$, $k = \overline{1,m}$, are independent standard Poisson processes on the positive half-line, which do not depend on all sequences $\{X_i^{(k)}; i \geq 1\}$, $k = \overline{1,m}$. In other words, $\Pi_{n_k}(A) = V_{\pi_k(n_k)}(A)$ for all $k = \overline{1,m}$. We consider the point processes $V_{n_k}(\cdot)$ and $\Pi_{n_k}(\cdot)$ as stochastic processes with trajectories from the measurable space $(\mathbb{B}^\mathcal{A}, \mathcal{C})$ of all bounded functions indexed by the elements of the set $\mathcal{A}$, with the σ-algebra $\mathcal{C}$ of all cylindrical subsets of the space $\mathbb{B}^\mathcal{A}$. The distributions of stochastic processes $V_{n_k}(\cdot)$ and $\Pi_{n_k}(\cdot)$ on $\mathcal{C}$ are defined in a standard way.

Now, we introduce the vector-valued empirical and accompanying Poisson point processes

$$\overline{V}_{\bar{n}}(A) := (V_{n_1}^{(1)}(A), \ldots, V_{n_m}^{(m)}(A)) \equiv \overline{V}_{\bar{n}},$$

$$\overline{\Pi}_{\bar{n}}(A) := (\Pi_{n_1}^{(1)}(A), \ldots, \Pi_{n_m}^{(m)}(A)) \equiv \overline{\Pi}_{\bar{n}},$$

where $\bar{n} = (n_1, n_2, \ldots, n_m)$. The vector-valued point processes $\overline{V}_{\bar{n}}$ and $\overline{\Pi}_{\bar{n}}$ are considered as random elements with values in the measurable space $((\mathbb{B}^\mathcal{A})^m, \mathcal{C}^m)$.

Let $A_0 \in \mathcal{A}$ with $p := P(A_0) \in (0,1)$. Consider the restrictions of the vector point processes $\overline{V}_{\bar{n}}$ and $\overline{\Pi}_{\bar{n}}$ to the set

$$\mathcal{A}_0 := \{A \in \mathcal{A} : A \subseteq A_0\}. \tag{1}$$

These so-called $\mathcal{A}_0$-restrictions are denoted by $\overline{V}_{\bar{n}}^0$ and $\overline{\Pi}_{\bar{n}}^0$, respectively. For the distributions $\mathcal{L}(\overline{V}_{\bar{n}}^0)$ and $\mathcal{L}(\overline{\Pi}_{\bar{n}}^0)$ in the measurable space $((\mathbb{B}^\mathcal{A})^m, \mathcal{C}^m)$, there are the following three assertions (some particular versions of these assertions have been proved in [1,2]).

Theorem 1. *The following inequality is valid:*

$$\mathcal{L}(\overline{V}_{\bar{n}}^0) \leq \frac{1}{(1-p)^m} \mathcal{L}(\overline{\Pi}_{\bar{n}}^0). \tag{2}$$

Corollary 1. *For any non-negative measurable functional F defined on $((\mathbb{B}^\mathcal{A})^m, \mathcal{C}^m)$,*

$$\mathbf{E}F(\overline{V}_{\bar{n}}^0) \leq \frac{1}{(1-p)^m} \mathbf{E}F(\overline{\Pi}_{\bar{n}}^0); \tag{3}$$

the expectation on the right-hand side of (3) *may be infinite at that.*

The following result plays an essential role in proving the main result of the paper—a duality limit theorem for the distributions $\mathcal{L}(\overline{V}_{\bar{n}})$ and $\mathcal{L}(\overline{\Pi}_{\bar{n}})$ (see Theorem 3 below).

Theorem 2. *For each multi-index $\bar{n}$, one can define some vector point processes $\overline{V}_{\bar{n}}^{0*}$ and $\overline{\Pi}_{\bar{n}}^{0*}$ on a common probability space so that they coincide in distribution with the point processes $\overline{V}_{\bar{n}}^0$ and $\overline{\Pi}_{\bar{n}}^0$, respectively, and*

$$\sup_{\mathcal{A}_c \subseteq \mathcal{A}_0} \mathbf{P}\left(\sup_{A \in \mathcal{A}_c} \left\|\overline{V}_{\bar{n}}^{0*}(A) - \overline{\Pi}_{\bar{n}}^{0*}(A)\right\| \neq 0\right) \leq 1 - (1-p)^m < mp, \tag{4}$$

where $\|(z_1, \ldots, z_m)\| := \max_{k \leq m} |z_k|$, and the outer supremum is taken over all at most countable families $\mathcal{A}_c$ of sets from $\mathcal{A}_0$.

Remark 1. *In Theorem 2, the sup-seminorm $\sup_{A \in \mathcal{A}_c} \|\cdot\|$ is obviously measurable with respect to the cylindrical σ-algebra $\mathcal{C}^m$. If instead of $\mathcal{A}_c$ we substitute the entire class $\mathcal{A}_0$ (possibly uncountable) then this measurability may no longer exist (unless, of course, the point processes under consideration do not have the separability property). Nevertheless, the assertion of Theorem 2 remains valid in this case if the probability $\mathbf{P}$ is replaced by the outer probability $\mathbf{P}^*(N_0) := \inf_{N \in \mathcal{C}^m : N \supseteq N_0} \mathbf{P}(N)$. However, the outer probability has only the property of semiadditivity, which makes it difficult to use.*

Let measurable sets $\Delta_1, \Delta_2, \ldots$ form a finite or countable partition of the sample space under the condition $p_i := P(\Delta_i) > 0$ for all i. Without loss of generality, we can assume that the sequence $\{p_i\}$ is monotonically nonincreasing. Denoted by $v_{n_k 1}^{(k)}, v_{n_k 2}^{(k)}, \ldots$, $k = \overline{1,m}$, the corresponding group frequencies are defined by the sample $X_1^{(k)}, \ldots, X_{n_k}^{(k)}$. Put

$$\bar{v}_{i\bar{n}} := \overline{V}_{\bar{n}}(\Delta_i) = \left(v_{n_1 i}^{(1)}, \ldots, v_{n_m i}^{(m)}\right), \quad i = 1, 2, \ldots.$$

Let us agree that everywhere below the limit relation $\bar{n} \to \infty$ will be understood as $n_k \to \infty$ for all $k = \overline{1,m}$.

3. Additive Statistics: Examples

In the paper, we consider a class of additive statistics of the form

$$\Phi_f(\overline{V}_{\bar{n}}) := \sum_{i \geq 1} f_{i\bar{n}}(\bar{v}_{i\bar{n}}), \tag{5}$$

where $f \equiv \{f_{i\bar{n}}\}$ is an array of arbitrary finite functions defined on $\mathbb{Z}_+^m$ under the condition

$$\sum_{i \geq 1} |f_{i\bar{n}}(0, \ldots, 0)| < \infty \quad \forall n, \tag{6}$$

which ensures the correct definition of the functional $\Phi_f(\overline{V}_{\bar{n}})$ in the case of a countable partition of the sample space, since the sum under consideration contains only a finite set of nonzero random vectors $\bar{v}_{i\bar{n}}$. In the case of a finite partition and $m = 1$, additive functionals of the form (5) were considered in [3–5].

We now give some examples of such statistics.

(1) Consider a finite partition $\{\Delta_i; i = 1, \ldots, N\}$ of the sample space. Put $f_{i\bar{n}}(\bar{x}) := \frac{|\bar{x} - \bar{n} p_i|^2}{|\bar{n} p_i|}$, $i = 1, \ldots, N$, where $|\cdot|$ is the standard Euclidean norm in $\mathbb{R}^m$. Then the functional

$$\Phi_{\chi^2}(\overline{V}_{\bar{n}}) := \sum_{i=1}^{N} \frac{|\bar{v}_{i\bar{n}} - \bar{n} p_i|^2}{|\bar{n} p_i|} \tag{7}$$

is an m-variate version of a well-known χ^2-statistic. Note that, in the present paper, we are primarily interested in the case where $N \equiv N(\bar{n}) \to \infty$ as $\bar{n} \to \infty$.

(2) Let now the sizes of all m samples be equal: $n_j = n$, $j = 1, \ldots, m$. In an equivalent reformulation of the original problem, we consider a sample of m-dimensional observations $\{(X_i^1, \ldots, X_i^m); i \leq n\}$ under the main hypothesis that the sample vector coordinates are independent and have the same N-atomic distribution with unknown masses $p_1, \ldots, p_N$. In this case, the log-likelihood function can be represented as the additive functional

$$\Phi_{\log}(\overline{V}_{\bar{n}}) := \sum_{i=1}^{N} (\bar{v}_{i\bar{n}}, \bar{1}) \log p_i,$$

where $\bar{1}$ is the unit vector in $\mathbb{R}^m$ and $(\cdot,\cdot)$ is the Euclidean inner product.

(3) Consider a finite or countable partition $\{\Delta_i; i \geq 1\}$. Let $f_{i\bar{n}}(\bar{x}) \equiv f(\bar{x}) := I_B(\bar{x})$ be the indicator function of some subset $B \subset \mathbb{Z}_+^m$. Then the functional

$$\Phi_{I_B}(\overline{V}_{\bar{n}}) := \sum_{i \geq 1} I_B(\bar{v}_{i\bar{n}}) \tag{8}$$

counts the number of partition elements (cells) containing any number of vector sample observations from the range B in a multinomial scheme (finite or infinite) of placing particles into cells (see [6–12]). Note that in the case of an infinite multinomial scheme in (8), it is additionally assumed that $0 \notin B$.

In the case $m = 2$ and $B = \{(x,y) \in \mathbb{Z}_+^2 : x = 0, y > 0\}$, the two-sample statistic (8) counts the number of nonempty cells after second ("additional") series of trials ("future" sample), which were empty in the first series ("original" sample). Statistics of such a kind play an important role in the theory of species sampling (for example, see [13,14]). In this case the functional (8) is called the number of unseen species in the original sample.

(4) In the case $m = 1$, consider the joint distribution (see [10]) of the random variables

$$\Phi_{I_B}(V_{n_1}), \Phi_{I_B}(V_{n_1+n_2}), \ldots, \Phi_{I_B}(V_{n_1+\ldots+n_m})$$

defined in (8) by the sample $(X_1, \ldots, X_N)$, with $N = n_1 + \ldots + n_m$. It is clear that studying the asymptotic behavior of the joint distribution of these random variables (for example, proving the multidimensional central limit theorem) can be reduced to the study of the limit distributions of the linear combinations of the form

$$a_1 \Phi_{I_B}(V_{n_1}) + a_2 \Phi_{I_B}(V_{n_1+n_2}) + \ldots + a_m \Phi_{I_B}(V_{n_1+\ldots+n_m})$$

for almost all vectors $(a_1, \ldots, a_m)$ with respect to the Lebesgue measure on $\mathbb{R}^m$. It is easy to see that, for any natural $j \leq m$,

$$V_{n_1+\ldots+n_j} = V_{n_1}^{(1)} + \ldots + V_{n_j}^{(j)},$$

where the empirical point processes $V_{n_1}^{(1)}, \ldots, V_{n_j}^{(j)}$ are defined by the above-mentioned independent subsamples. So, in this case, we deal with a functional of the form (5) defined by m independent empirical point processes corresponding to the m independent subsamples $(X_1, \ldots, X_{n_1}), (X_{n_1+1}, \ldots, X_{n_1+n_2}), \ldots, (X_{N-n_m+1}, \ldots, X_N)$, and with the array of functions

$$f_{i\bar{n}}(\bar{x}) \equiv f(x_1, \ldots, x_m) := a_1 I_B(x_1) + a_2 I_B(x_1 + x_2) + \ldots + a_m I_B(x_1 + \ldots + x_m). \tag{9}$$

(5) Consider the stochastic process $\{\Phi_{I_B}(\overline{V}_{\bar{n}}); B \subset \mathbb{Z}_+^m\}$ indexed by all subsets of $\mathbb{Z}_+^m$. As was noted above, studying the asymptotic behavior of the joint distributions of this process can be reduced to studying the asymptotic behavior of the distributions of any linear combinations of corresponding one-dimensional projections of this process, i.e., to studying the asymptotic behavior of the distributions of functionals of the form (5) for $m = 1$ and the array of functions

$$f_{i\bar{n}}(x) \equiv f(x) := a_1 I_{B_1}(x) + a_2 I_{B_2}(x) + \ldots + a_r I_{B_r}(x) \tag{10}$$

for almost all vectors $(a_1, \ldots, a_r)$. For one-point sets, the asymptotic analysis of the above-mentioned joint distributions can be found, for example, in [7–12].

(6) Consider the case $m = 1$ and the functional

$$\Phi_f(V_n) := \sum_{i \geq 1} n p_i I_B(v_{in}), \tag{11}$$

which counts the sampling ratio of the cells containing any number of particles from the range B. For the one-point set $B = \{0\}$, such functional was considered in [9]. In general, if instead of np_i in (11) we consider arbitrary weights $g(n,i) > 0$ (under condition (6)) with one or another interpretation, the functional $\Phi_f(V_n)$ in this case will be interpreted as the total weight of the corresponding cells.

4. Poissonization: Duality Theorem

In this section, we present the main result of the paper—a duality theorem for additive statistics under consideration. First of all, we explain the term "Poissonization". It means that studying the limit behavior of the original additive statistics, we reduce the problem to studying the following "Poissonian version" of the functional (5) under condition (6):

$$\Phi_f(\Pi_{\bar{n}}) := \sum_{i \geq 1} f_{i\bar{n}}(\bar{\pi}_{i\bar{n}}), \qquad (12)$$

where $\bar{\pi}_{i\bar{n}} = \left(\pi_{n_1 i}^{(1)}, \ldots, \pi_{n_m i}^{(m)}\right)$, $\pi_{n_k i}^{(k)} := \Pi_{n_k}(\Delta_i)$, $i \geq 1$, is a sequence of independent Poisson random variables with respective parameters $n_k p_i$. It is clear that the functional (12) is well defined with probability 1 since only a finite number of the vectors $\{\bar{\pi}_{i\bar{n}}\}$ differ from the zero vector. Independence of the summands is a crucial difference of the Poisson version of an additive functional from the original one. Some elements of Poissonization for additive functionals of the form (8) and (10) are contained, for example, in [9,12]. In [9], the author used the well-known representation of an empirical point process as the conditional Poisson point process under the condition that the number of atoms of the accompanying Poisson point process equals n. Moreover, in [9], the simple known representation $\pi(n) = n + O_p(\sqrt{n})$ was employed, where $O_p(\sqrt{n})$ denotes a random variable such that $O_p(\sqrt{n})/\sqrt{n}$ is bounded in probability as $n \to \infty$. In [12], proving the multivariate central limit theorem for the above-mentioned joint distributions (in fact, for functionals of the form (10) in the case of one-point subsets $\{B_i\}$), the authors applied a reduction to the joint distributions of the Poissonian versions of additive functionals using known upper bounds for a multivariate Poisson approximation to a multinomial distribution (see also [15]). The main goal of the paper is to establish a duality theorem, which demonstrates absolute identity of the asymptotic behavior of the distributions of the additive functionals under consideration and their Poissonian versions.

First, we formulate a crucial auxiliary assertion in proving the main result.

Lemma 1. *Let $\{\Delta_{\bar{n}}\}$ be an arbitrary scalar array satisfying the condition $f_{i\bar{n}}(\pi_{i\bar{n}})\Delta_{\bar{n}} \xrightarrow{p} 0$ as $\bar{n} \to \infty$ for every fixed i. Then, for each multiindex $\bar{n}$, one can define on a common probability space a pair of point processes $\overline{V}^*_{\bar{n},\Delta_{\bar{n}}}$ and $\overline{\Pi}^*_{\bar{n},\Delta_{\bar{n}}}$ such that $\mathcal{L}(\overline{V}^*_{\bar{n},\Delta_{\bar{n}}}) = \mathcal{L}(\overline{V}_{\bar{n}})$, $\mathcal{L}(\overline{\Pi}^*_{\bar{n},\Delta_{\bar{n}}}) = \mathcal{L}(\overline{\Pi}_{\bar{n}})$, and for any $\varepsilon > 0$,*

$$\mathbf{P}\left(|\Delta_{\bar{n}}| \left| \Phi_f(\overline{V}^*_{\bar{n},\Delta_{\bar{n}}}) - \Phi_f(\overline{\Pi}^*_{\bar{n},\Delta_{\bar{n}}}) \right| > \varepsilon \right) \to 0 \text{ as } \bar{n} \to \infty. \qquad (13)$$

Remark 2. *Lemma 1 only asserts that the marginal distributions (that is, for each $\bar{n}$ separately) of the arrays $\{\overline{V}^*_{\bar{n},\Delta_{\bar{n}}}, \bar{n} \in \mathbb{Z}^m_+\}$ and $\{\overline{V}_{\bar{n}}, \bar{n} \in \mathbb{Z}^m_+\}$, and also $\{\overline{\Pi}^*_{\bar{n},\Delta_{\bar{n}}}, \bar{n} \in \mathbb{Z}^m_+\}$ and $\{\overline{\Pi}_{\bar{n}}, \bar{n} \in \mathbb{Z}^m_+\}$. Note that the probability in (13) is precisely determined by the marginal distributions of the mentioned random arrays, i.e., formally, it also depends on $\bar{n}$. Without loss of generality, we can assume that pairs of point processes $(\overline{V}^*_{\bar{n},\Delta_{\bar{n}}}, \overline{\Pi}^*_{\bar{n},\Delta_{barn}})$ are independent in $\bar{n}$, and on this extended probability space, the universal probability measure $\mathbf{P}$ in (13) is given in the standard way, which no longer depends on $\bar{n}$. In this case it is correct to speak about the convergence to zero in probability of the sequence of random variables in (13).*

Lemma 1 gives the key to the proof of the following duality theorem, a criterion for the weak convergence of distributions of functionals of the point processes under consideration. The essence of this result is that the asymptotic behavior of the distributions of additive functionals of the point processes $\overline{V}_{\bar{n}}$ and $\overline{\Pi}_{\bar{n}}$ is exactly the same. In addition, one can also indicate a third class of additive functionals (under condition (6)) that has the same property:

$$\Phi_f^* := \sum_{i \geq 1} f_{i\bar{n}}(\bar{v}_{i\bar{n}}^*),$$

where $\{\bar{v}_{i\bar{n}}^*, i \geq 1\}$ is a sequence of independent random vectors such that $\mathcal{L}(\bar{v}_{i\bar{n}}^*) = \mathcal{L}(\bar{v}_{i\bar{n}})$ for all i. The functional Φ_f^* is well defined due to the Borel–Cantelli lemma and the simple estimate $\mathbf{P}(\bar{v}_{i\bar{n}}^* \neq 0) = \mathbf{P}(\bar{v}_{i\bar{n}} \neq 0) \leq m\|\bar{n}\|p_i$.

Let us agree that the symbol «$\Longrightarrow$» in what follows will denote the weak convergence of distributions. The main result of the paper is as follows.

Theorem 3. *Under the conditions of Lemma 1, the following three limit relations are equivalent as $\bar{n} \to \infty$:*

(1) $\mathcal{L}\left(\Phi_f(\overline{V}_{\bar{n}})\Delta_{\bar{n}} - M_{\bar{n}}\right) \Longrightarrow \mathcal{L}(\gamma)$,

(2) $\mathcal{L}\left(\Phi_f(\overline{\Pi}_{\bar{n}})\Delta_{\bar{n}} - M_{\bar{n}}\right) \Longrightarrow \mathcal{L}(\gamma)$,

(3) $\mathcal{L}\left(\Phi_f^* \Delta_{\bar{n}} - M_{\bar{n}}\right) \Longrightarrow \mathcal{L}(\gamma)$,

where $M_{\bar{n}}$ and $\Delta_{\bar{n}}$ are some scalar arrays and γ is some random variable.

5. Applications

Theorem 3 allows us to reduce the asymptotic analysis of the distributions of the additive functionals under consideration to a similar analysis of their Poissonian versions, i.e., to the asymptotic analysis of distributions of sums (finite or infinite) of independent random variables, or to reduce the problem to studying the limit behavior of the distributions $\mathcal{L}\left(\Phi_f(\overline{V}_{\bar{n}})\right)$, absolutely ignoring the dependence of the random variables $\{\bar{v}_{i\bar{n}}, i \geq 1\}$. Note also that, under some rather broad assumptions, the law $\mathcal{L}(\gamma)$ will be infinitely divisible. A detailed analysis of such conditions and corresponding examples will be considered in a separate paper. Here we present only a few of these corollaries, focusing our attention on the equivalence of the first two relations of Theorem 3.

First of all, we note one useful property of the expectations of the functionals under consideration as functions of $\bar{n}$.

Lemma 2. *Let $\max_{\bar{n}} \sup_{\bar{x}} |f_{i\bar{n}}(\bar{x})| \leq C_i$, $\sum_{i \geq 1} C_i p_i < \infty$, and*

$$\sum_{i \geq 1} \mathbf{E}|f_{i\bar{n}}(\bar{\pi}_{i\bar{n}})| < \infty \quad \forall \bar{n}. \tag{14}$$

Then the relations $\lim_{\bar{n} \to \infty} |\mathbf{E}\Phi_f(\overline{V}_{\bar{n}})| = \infty$ and $\lim_{\bar{n} \to \infty} |\mathbf{E}\Phi_f(\overline{\Pi}_{\bar{n}})| = \infty$ are equivalent. In the case of infinite limits,

$$\mathbf{E}\Phi_f(\overline{V}_{\bar{n}}) \sim \mathbf{E}\Phi_f(\overline{\Pi}_{\bar{n}}) \quad \text{as } \bar{n} \to \infty.$$

Remark 3. *For functionals of the form (8) in an infinite multinomial scheme, the conditions of Lemma 2 are typical. Let $m = 1$ and $B := \{j : j > k\}$ for any $k \geq 0$. Then*

$$\lim_{n \to \infty} \mathbf{E}\Phi_f(V_n) = \lim_{n \to \infty} \sum_{i \geq 1} \mathbf{P}(v_{in} > k) = \infty$$

since, by virtue of the law of large numbers, $\lim_{n \to \infty} \mathbf{P}(v_{in} > k) \to 1$ for every fixed i. Moreover, in the case under consideration, obviously, $\mathbf{E}\Phi_f(V_n) \leq n$. Similarly, without any restrictions on the probabilities $\{p_i\}$, the infinite limits in Lemma 2 for functionals of the form (8) (and even more so for (11)) also hold for the set B consisting of all odd natural numbers. Here the limit relation $\lim_{n \to \infty} \mathbf{E}\Phi_f(\overline{\Pi}_{\bar{n}}) \equiv \lim_{n \to \infty} \sum_{i \text{ ge} 1} \mathbf{P}(\pi_{in} \in B) = \infty$ follows immediately from the equality $\mathbf{P}(\pi_{in} \in B) = \frac{1}{2}(1 - e^{-2np_i})$.

It is also worth noting that for some sets B the main contribution to the limit behavior of the series $\sum_{i\geq 1} \mathbf{P}(\pi_{in} \in B)$ can be made not only by their initial segments but also tails. For example, this will be the case for any one-point sets $B_k := \{k\}$ for $k > 0$ if the group probabilities are given as $p_i = Ci^{-1-b}$ or $p_i = ce^{-C_0 i^\alpha}$ for some constants $c, C, C_0, b > 0$ and $\alpha \in (0,1)$. In this case, for any subset B of natural numbers in the definition of the functionals (8) and (11), the expectation limits indicated in Lemma 2 will be infinite (see Section 7 and [9,12]). On the other hand, if $p_i = ce^{-C_0 i}$, then for any one-point set the expectations mentioned will be bounded uniformly in n (see Section 7 and [9,12]). For more complex functionals with kernels (9) or (10) for the above-mentioned distributions $\{p_i\}$, one can find sufficiently broad conditions that ensure unbounded increase in their expectations and variances as $\bar{n} \to \infty$ for almost all vectors $(a_1, \ldots, a_r) \in \mathbb{R}^r$ (see Section 7).

Now we present one of the corollaries of Theorem 3, namely, the law of large numbers for the additive functionals under consideration, setting in this theorem $\Delta_{\bar{n}} := (\mathbf{E}\Phi_f(\overline{\Pi}_{\bar{n}}))^{-1}$, $M_{\bar{n}} := 0$, and $\gamma := 1$.

Corollary 2. *Let the conditions of Lemma 2 be fulfilled. If $|\mathbf{E}\Phi_f(\overline{\Pi}_{\bar{n}})| \to \infty$ as $\bar{n} \to \infty$ then the following criterion holds:*

$$\frac{\Phi_f(\overline{V}_{\bar{n}})}{\mathbf{E}\Phi_f(\overline{V}_{\bar{n}})} \xrightarrow{p} 1 \quad \text{iff} \quad \frac{\Phi_f(\overline{\Pi}_{\bar{n}})}{\mathbf{E}\Phi_f(\overline{\Pi}_{\bar{n}})} \xrightarrow{p} 1;$$

in this case, the normalizations $\mathbf{E}\Phi_f(\overline{V}_{\bar{n}})$ and $\mathbf{E}\Phi_f(\overline{\Pi}_{\bar{n}})$ can be swapped.

Remark 4. *In consideration of Chebyshev's inequality, a sufficient condition for the limit relations in Corollary 2 is as follows:*

$$\frac{\sum_{i\geq 1} \mathbf{D} f_{i\bar{n}}(\tilde{\pi}_{i\bar{n}})}{\left(\sum_{i\geq 1} \mathbf{E} f_{i\bar{n}}(\tilde{\pi}_{i\bar{n}})\right)^2} \to 0.$$

For example, let $f_{i\bar{n}}(\cdot) \geq 0$ and $\sup_{\tilde{x},i,\bar{n}} f_{i\bar{n}}(\tilde{x}) \leq C_0$. Then $\mathbf{D} f_{i\bar{n}}(\tilde{\pi}_{i\bar{n}}) \leq C_0 \mathbf{E} f_{i\bar{n}}(\tilde{\pi}_{i\bar{n}})$ and

$$\frac{\sum_{i\geq 1} \mathbf{D} f_{i\bar{n}}(\tilde{\pi}_{i\bar{n}})}{\left(\sum_{i\geq 1} \mathbf{E} f_{i\bar{n}}(\tilde{\pi}_{i\bar{n}})\right)^2} \leq C_0 \left|\sum_{i\geq 1} \mathbf{E} f_{i\bar{n}}(\tilde{\pi}_{i\bar{n}})\right|^{-1} \to 0.$$

In particular, this estimate is valid in the case $f_{i\bar{n}}(\tilde{x}) \equiv f(\tilde{x}) := I_B(\tilde{x})$, with $0 \notin B$, if only $\mathbf{E}\Phi_f(\overline{\Pi}_{\bar{n}}) = \sum_{i\geq 1} \mathbf{P}(\tilde{\pi}_{i\bar{n}} \in B) \to \infty$.

We now formulate an analog of Lemma 2 for the variances of the functionals under consideration.

Lemma 3. *Under the conditions $\max_{\bar{n}} \sup_{\tilde{x}} |f_{i\bar{n}}(\tilde{x})| \leq C_i \ \forall i$ and $\sum_{i\geq 1} C_i^2 p_i < \infty$ the limit relation $\lim_{\bar{n}\to\infty} \mathbf{D}\Phi_f(\overline{V}_{\bar{n}}) = \infty$ holds if and only if $\lim_{\bar{n}\to\infty} \mathbf{D}\Phi_f(\overline{\Pi}_{\bar{n}}) = \infty$. In the case of infinite limit the following equivalence is valid: $\mathbf{D}\Phi_f(\overline{V}_{\bar{n}}) \sim \mathbf{D}\Phi_f(\overline{\Pi}_{\bar{n}})$ as $\bar{n} \to \infty$.*

Lemma 3 and Theorem 3 imply the following important criterion, which allows us to reduce proving the central limit theorem for additive functionals $\Phi_f(\overline{V}_{\bar{n}})$ to proving the same assertion for the Poissonian version $\Phi_f(\overline{\Pi}_{\bar{n}})$.

Corollary 3. *Under the conditions of Lemma 3 and $\mathbf{D}\Phi_f(\overline{\Pi}_{\bar{n}}) \to \infty$ as $\bar{n} \to \infty$ the limit relation*

$$\mathcal{L}\left(\frac{\Phi_f(\overline{V}_{\bar{n}}) - \mathbf{E}\Phi_f(\overline{V}_{\bar{n}})}{\mathbf{D}^{1/2}\Phi_f(\overline{V}_{\bar{n}})}\right) \Longrightarrow N(0,1) \quad \text{as } \bar{n} \to \infty,$$

is valid if, and only if,

$$\mathcal{L}\left(\frac{\Phi_f(\overline{\Pi}_{\bar{n}}) - \mathbf{E}\Phi_f(\overline{\Pi}_{\bar{n}})}{\mathbf{D}^{1/2}\Phi_f(\overline{\Pi}_{\bar{n}})}\right) \Longrightarrow \mathcal{N}(0,1) \quad \text{as } \bar{n} \to \infty,$$

where $\mathcal{N}(0,1)$ is the standard normal distribution. In this case, the normalizing and centering sequences in these two limit relations can be, respectively, swapped.

In order to prove this corollary we should put in Theorem 3 $\Delta_{\bar{n}} := \mathbf{D}^{-1/2}\Phi_f(\overline{\Pi}_{\bar{n}})$, $M_{\bar{n}} := \mathbf{E}\Phi_f(\overline{V}_{\bar{n}})\mathbf{D}^{-1/2}\Phi_f(\overline{\Pi}_{\bar{n}})$, and $\mathcal{L}(\gamma) := \mathcal{N}(0,1)$. In this case, Lemma 3 allows us only to replace the normalizing and centering sequences in Theorem 3 with some equivalent sequences.

Remark 5. *The validity of the central limit theorem for the sequence $\Phi_f(\overline{\Pi}_{\bar{n}})$ in Theorem 3 will be justified if, say, the third-order Lyapunov condition is met:*

$$\frac{\sum\limits_{i\geq 1}\mathbf{E}|f_{i\bar{n}}(\bar{\pi}_{i\bar{n}}) - \mathbf{E}f_{i\bar{n}}(\bar{\pi}_{i\bar{n}})|^3}{\left(\sum\limits_{i\geq 1}\mathbf{D}f_{i\bar{n}}(\bar{\pi}_{i\bar{n}})\right)^{3/2}} \to 0 \quad \text{as } \bar{n} \to \infty.$$

For example, let $\sup\limits_{\bar{x},i,\bar{n}}|f_{i\bar{n}}(\bar{x})| \leq C_0$. Then it is easy to see that

$$\sum_{i\geq 1}\mathbf{E}|f_{i\bar{n}}(\bar{\pi}_{i\bar{n}}) - \mathbf{E}f_{i\bar{n}}(\bar{\pi}_{i\bar{n}})|^3 \leq 2C_0\sum_{i\geq 1}\mathbf{D}f_{i\bar{n}}(\bar{\pi}_{i\bar{n}}).$$

Thus, if $\mathbf{D}\Phi_f(\overline{\Pi}_{\bar{n}}) \to \infty$ as $\bar{n} \to \infty$, then the Lyapunov condition will be met and the approval of the above investigation will take place. So an important special case $f_{i\bar{n}}(\bar{x}) := I_B(\bar{x})$ is included in the scheme at issue if

$$\mathbf{D}\Phi_{I_B}(\overline{\Pi}_{\bar{n}}) = \sum_{i\geq 1}\mathbf{P}(\bar{\pi}_{i\bar{n}} \in B)(1 - \mathbf{P}(\bar{\pi}_{i\bar{n}} \in B)) \to \infty \quad \text{as } \bar{n} \to \infty.$$

Note that examples for which the specified variance property takes place or is violated are given, for example, in [9].

Finally, here is another consequence of Theorem 3, relating to the asymptotic behavior of χ^2-statistics in (7) at $m = 1$ and $N \equiv N(n) \to \infty$. First of all, note that

$$\mathbf{E}\Phi_{\chi^2}(\Pi_n) = N,$$

$$D_n := \mathbf{D}\Phi_{\chi^2}(\Pi_n) = 2N + \sum_{i=1}^{N}\frac{1}{np_i}.$$

Corollary 4. *Let $N \equiv N(n) \to \infty$ as $n \to \infty$. Then the following two asymptotic relations are equivalent:*

$$\mathcal{L}\left(\frac{\Phi_{\chi^2}(V_n) - N}{D_n^{1/2}}\right) \Longrightarrow \mathcal{N}(0,1), \qquad (15)$$

$$\mathcal{L}\left(\frac{\Phi_{\chi^2}(\Pi_n) - N}{D_n^{1/2}}\right) \Longrightarrow \mathcal{N}(0,1). \qquad (16)$$

Note that in the present case, the requirement of Lemma 1 is met, since each term $\frac{(v_{in}-np_i)^2}{np_i}$ (as a sequence of n) is bounded in probability due to Markov's inequality, and therefore, with the normalizing sequence $\Delta_n := D_n^{-1}$, this term will tend to zero in probability as $n \to \infty$.

Remark 6. *In the relations (15) and (16) we can say just about the double limit when $N, n \to \infty$ because this assertion is missing restrictions on the rate of increase in the sequence $N(n)$. The proposed formulation in Corollary 4, equivalent to the one just mentioned, is more convenient to refer to Theorem 3. Note that the centering sequence E_n can be replaced with its equivalent sequence $\mathbf{E}\Phi_{\chi^2}(V_n) = N - 1$. Replacement in the normalization in (15) the variance D_n with the variance of the χ^2-statistic itself, i.e., by the term (for example, see [16])*

$$\mathbf{D}\Phi_{\chi^2}(V_n) = 2N + \frac{1}{N}\sum_{i=1}^{N}\frac{1}{np_i} - \frac{3N-2}{n},$$

is possible only if these two variances are equivalent. For example, this would be the case if $\min_{i\leq N} np_i \to \infty$. This means that the growth rate of the sequence $N \equiv N(n)$ is subject to appropriate constraints, which is not the case in the above consequence. So, in this assertion we can talk about a double limit as $n, N \to \infty$.

The formulated criterion allows us to establish a fairly general sufficient condition for the asymptotic normality of χ^2-statistics with an increasing number of groups.

Theorem 4. *Let $N \equiv N(n) \to \infty$ as $n \to \infty$. Then the asymptotic relation (15) is valid if*

$$\frac{\sum_{i=1}^{N}(np_i)^{-2}}{\left(N + \sum_{i=1}^{N}(np_i)^{-1}\right)^{3/2}} \longrightarrow 0 \tag{17}$$

as $n \to \infty$.

The problem of finding more or less broad sufficient conditions for asymptotic normality χ^2-statistics with a growing number of groups were studied by many authors in the second half of the last century (for example, see [3–5,16–18]). Note that all known sufficient conditions for the above weak convergence imply fulfillment of the asymptotic relation (17). For example, the condition $\min_{i\leq N} np_i \to \infty$ along with $N \to \infty$ (see [17,18]), obviously immediately entails relation (17). It is equally obvious that the requirement of the so-called regularity of multinomial models (see [3–5]), i.e.,

$$0 < c_1 \leq \min_{i\leq N} Np_i, \quad \max_{i\leq N} Np_i < c_2 < \infty,$$

where the constants c_1 and c_2 are independent of N, also implies (17). On the other hand, it is easy to construct examples in which the regularity requirement of the multinomial model is violated but relation (17) is valid. For example, let $p_i := C_N i^{-1-b}$, $i = 1, \ldots, N$, where $b > 0$ and $C_N := \left(\sum_{i\leq N} i^{-1-b}\right)^{-1}$. It is easy to see that, as $N \to \infty$, the sums $\sum_{i=1}^{N} p_i^{-2}$ and $\sum_{i=1}^{N} p_i^{-1}$ increase as N^{3+2b} and N^{2+b}, respectively. Therefore, as $n, N \to \infty$, the ratio in (17) is equivalent to

$$\frac{N^{3+2b}}{\sqrt{n}(N^{2+b})^{3/2}} = \frac{N^{b/2}}{\sqrt{n}}$$

up to a constant factor. So, here we already need to measure the growth rate N with n. Obviously, in this case, in order to fulfill condition (17), you need to require that $N = o(n^{1/b})$. If the probabilities p_i decrease exponentially then the growth rate zone for N narrows to $o(\log n)$. It is worth to note that for the above-mentioned power-type probabilities at issue the condition $\min_{i\leq N} np_i \to \infty$ implies the asymptotic relation $N = o(n^{1/(b+1)})$ that is more restrictive than the above constraint.

6. Probability and Moment Inequalities

The next theorem is related to estimation of the distribution tails of additive functionals.

Theorem 5. *Let $f_{i\bar{n}}(\cdot) \geq 0$ for all i. Then, for any $x > 0$,*

$$\mathbf{P}(\Phi_f(\overline{V}_{\bar{n}}) \geq x) \leq 2C^* \mathbf{P}(\Phi_f(\overline{\Pi}_{\bar{n}}) \geq x/2), \tag{18}$$

where $C^* := \min_{j \geq 1} \max\{(\sum_{i \leq j} p_i)^{-1}, (\sum_{i > j} p_i)^{-1}\}$. If additionally $\sup_x f_{1\bar{n}}(x) \leq c_0$ then

$$\mathbf{P}(\Phi_f(\overline{V}_{\bar{n}}) \geq x) \leq p_1^{-1} \mathbf{P}(\Phi_f(\overline{\Pi}_{\bar{n}}) \geq x - c_0). \tag{19}$$

Remark 7. *In (19), the constant c_0 may depend on $\bar{n}$. What is more, we can use the truncation of the random variable $f_{1\bar{n}}(v_{i_{\bar{n}}})$ at the level c_0, while adding to the right-hand side of inequality (19) the probability $\mathbf{P}(f_{1\bar{n}}(v_{i_{\bar{n}}}) > c_0)$.*

Corollary 5. *Under the conditions of Theorem 5, let F be a continuous nondecreasing function defined on $\mathbb{R}_+$, with $F(0) = 0$. If $\mathbf{E}F(2\Phi_f(\overline{\Pi}_{\bar{n}})) < \infty$ then*

$$\mathbf{E}F(\Phi_f(\overline{V}_{\bar{n}})) \leq 2C^* \mathbf{E}F(2\Phi_f(\overline{\Pi}_{\bar{n}})). \tag{20}$$

As an example, consider the functional $\Phi_{I_B}(\overline{V}_{\bar{n}})$ defined in (8). Then, as a consequence of (19) and Chernoff's upper bound [19] for the distribution tail of a sum of independent nonidentically distributed Bernoulli random variables (the transition from finite sums to series in this case is obvious), we obtain the following result.

Corollary 6. *Put $M_n(B) := \mathbf{E}\Phi_{I_B}(\overline{\Pi}_{\bar{n}}) = \sum_{i \geq 1} \mathbf{P}(\pi_{in} \in B)$. Then for any $\varepsilon > (M_n(B))^{-1}$ the following inequality holds:*

$$\mathbf{P}\left(\left|\frac{\Phi_{I_B}(\overline{V}_{\bar{n}})}{M_n(B)} - 1\right| > \varepsilon\right) \leq 2p_1^{-1} e^{-\frac{\delta^2 M_n(B)}{2 + \delta}}, \tag{21}$$

where $\delta := \varepsilon - \frac{1}{M_n(B)} > 0$.

Remark 8. *one can replace the Poissonian mean $M_n(B)$ in (21) with the mean $\mathbf{E}\Phi_{I_B}(\overline{V}_{\bar{n}})$, which differs from $M_n(B)$ by no more than 1 due to Barbour–Hall's estimate of the Poisson approximation to a binomial distribution (see [15,20]). Further, if the condition $M_n(B) \to \infty$ is met as $n \to \infty$ then from (21) we obtain not only the law of large numbers (already formulated in Corollary 2), but at a certain growth rate of the sequence $M_n(B)$, the strong law of large numbers (SLLN) (see Section 7). If in the case $m = 1$ we consider the infinite intervals $B \equiv B_k := \{i : i > k\}$ for any $k \in \mathbb{Z}_+$ then the SLLN occurs at any speed of increasing the sequence $M_n(B)$ to infinity. This follows from estimate (21), the monotonicity of the functions $I_{B_k}(x)$, and the simple technique in proving SLLN in [9,21].*

7. Asymptotic Analysis of the Means and Variances of Additive Statistics

In the previous section, it was noted that when proving certain limit theorems for the introduced additive functionals, it is extremely important to have information about the behavior of their means and variances. In this section, for additive statistics (8)–(11), we demonstrate exactly how the asymptotic behavior of these moments is studied. To simplify the notation, we will consider here the case $m = 1$. The subsequent asymptotic analysis is based on the following elementary assertion, which is presented in one way or another in many papers on this topic.

Lemma 4. *Let $f_n(x)$ be a sequence of non-negative, integrable, and piecewise monotonic functions defined on $\mathbb{R}_+$. Suppose that each $f_n(x)$ has M monotonicity intervals, where M is independent of n. Finally, assume that, as $n \to \infty$,*

$$\int_0^\infty f_n(x)dx \to \infty, \quad \sup_{x \geq 0} f_n(x) = o\left(\int_0^\infty f_n(x)dx\right).$$

Then, as $n \to \infty$,

$$\sum_{j>0} f_n(j) \sim \int_0^\infty f_n(x)dx.$$

We now give a few examples of calculating the asymptotics we need.

(1) Let $B_k := \{i : i > k\}$ for any $k \in \mathbb{Z}_+$. In Remark 3 it was already noted that $M_n(B_k) \to \infty$ due to the strong law of large numbers for binomially distributed random variables. However, for specific classes of distributions $\{p_i\}$, one can estimate the growth rate of the sequence $\{M_n(B_k)\}$. For example, let $p_i := Ci^{-1-b}$, where $b > 0$, $i = 1, 2, \ldots$. Then, using Lemma 4 and the well-known connection between the tail of a Poisson distribution and the corresponding gamma distribution, we obtain after integration by parts and a change of the integration variable:

$$M_n(B_k) \equiv \sum_{i \geq 1} \mathbf{P}(\pi_{in} > k) = \sum_{i \geq 1} \gamma_{k+1,1}(np_i)$$

$$\sim (Cn)^{\frac{1}{1+b}} \int_0^\infty \gamma_{k+1,1}(y^{-1-b})dy = \frac{(Cn)^{\frac{1}{1+b}}}{k!}\Gamma\left(k + \frac{b}{1+b}\right), \quad (22)$$

where $\gamma_{k+1,1}(z) := \int_0^z \frac{t^k}{k!}e^{-t}dt$, $\Gamma(z) := \int_0^\infty t^{z-1}e^{-t}dt$, $z > 0$, are the distribution function of the gamma-distribution with parameters $(k+1, 1)$, and the gamma-function, , respectively. For example, if $k = 0$ then the asymptotics of the expectation of the number of nonempty cells is as follows (see [6,9]):

$$M_n(B_0) \sim (Cn)^{\frac{1}{1+b}} \int_0^\infty (1 - e^{-y^{-1-b}})dy = (Cn)^{\frac{1}{1+b}}\Gamma\left(\frac{b}{1+b}\right). \quad (23)$$

By analogy to the arguments in proving (22), after an appropriate change of the integration variable, we obtain for the one-point sets the following asymptotics:

$$M_n(\{k\}) \sim (Cn)^{\frac{1}{1+b}} \int_0^\infty \frac{y^{-k(1+b)}}{k!}e^{-y^{-1-b}}dy$$

$$= \frac{(Cn)^{\frac{1}{1+b}}}{(1+b)k!} \int_0^\infty x^{k-1-\frac{1}{1+b}}e^{-x}dx = \frac{(Cn)^{\frac{1}{1+b}}}{(1+b)k!}\Gamma\left(k - \frac{1}{1+b}\right). \quad (24)$$

Thus, from (24) it follows that for *any subset B of the natural series* in the case under consideration of a power-law decrease in $\{p_i\}$ the following asymptotic representation is true:

$$M_n(B) \sim \frac{(Cn)^{\frac{1}{1+b}}}{(1+b)} \sum_{k \in B} \frac{1}{k!}\Gamma\left(k - \frac{1}{1+b}\right). \quad (25)$$

Note that, due to the countable additivity of the finite measure $M_n(\cdot)$ and the relations (22)–(24), the sum (possibly infinite) in (25) will always be finite.

Remark 9. *Inequality (21), relation (25), and the Borel–Cantelli lemma guarantee that the strong law of large numbers holds for the sequence $\{M_n(B)\}$ for any subsets B of the natural series in the case of a power-law decrease in the probabilities $\{p_i\}$. Moreover, what has been said and the above asymptotics are also preserved for probabilities of the form $p_i := C(i)i^{-1-b}$, where $C(x)$ is a slowly varying function under certain minimal constraints (see [9,12]). In this case, in the asymptotic relations (22)–(25) instead of C one should substitute $C(n)$.*

Asymptotic behavior of the variances of the functionals $\Phi_{I_B}(\overline{\Pi}_n)$ for some B and broad conditions on the rate of decrease in the sequence $\{p_i\}$ is given in [9]. Here we only demonstrate how this variance is calculated for *arbitrary* subsets B of the natural series under the above conditions on $\{p_i\}$. Analogously with (22) we have for the infinite intervals B_k:

$$D_n(B_k) := \mathbf{D}\Phi_{I_{B_k}}(\overline{\Pi}_n) = \sum_{i\geq 1} \mathbf{P}(\pi_{in} > k) - \sum_{i\geq 1} \mathbf{P}^2(\pi_{in} > k)$$

$$= \sum_{i\geq 1} \gamma_{k+1,1}(np_i) - \sum_{i\geq 1} \gamma^2_{k+1,1}(np_i) \sim (Cn)^{\frac{1}{1+b}} \int_0^\infty \left(\gamma_{k+1,1}(y^{-1-b}) - \gamma^2_{k+1,1}(y^{-1-b}) \right) dy. \quad (26)$$

Similarly to proving (24), we derive the asymptotics of the variance for the one-point sets:

$$D_n(\{k\}) = \sum_{i\geq 1} \mathbf{P}(\pi_{in} = k) - \sum_{i\geq 1} \mathbf{P}^2(\pi_{in} = k)$$

$$= \frac{(Cn)^{\frac{1}{1+b}}}{(1+b)} \left(\int_0^\infty \frac{1}{k!} x^{k-1-\frac{1}{1+b}} e^{-x} dx - \int_0^\infty \frac{1}{(k!)^2} x^{2k-1-\frac{1}{1+b}} e^{-2x} dx \right)$$

$$= \frac{(Cn)^{\frac{1}{1+b}}}{(1+b)k!} \left(\Gamma\left(k - \frac{1}{1+b}\right) - \frac{2^{\frac{1}{1+b}-2k}}{k!} \Gamma\left(2k - \frac{1}{1+b}\right) \right). \quad (27)$$

Although the set function $D_n(\cdot)$ is not additive, the extension to arbitrary subsets B of the natural series of computing the asymptotics of $D_n(B)$ presents no difficulty. Along with formula (25), which gives one term in the resulting asymptotics, we use the following representation for the second sum:

$$\sum_{i\geq 1} \mathbf{P}^2(\pi_{in} \in B) \sim \frac{(Cn)^{\frac{1}{1+b}}}{1+b} \int_0^\infty \left(\sum_{k\in B} \frac{x^k}{k!} \right)^2 x^{-1-\frac{1}{1+b}} e^{-2x} dx$$

$$= \frac{(Cn)^{\frac{1}{1+b}}}{1+b} \sum_{k,l\in B} \frac{2^{\frac{1}{1+b}-k-l}}{k!l!} \Gamma\left(k+l - \frac{1}{1+b}\right). \quad (28)$$

Thus, the difference between the right-hand sides of (25) and (28) determines the asymptotic of $D_n(B)$ for any subset of the natural series.

(2) The asymptotics of the first two moments for the functionals (10) for pairwise disjoint sets $\{B_j\}$ is derived in exactly the same way. In the case of one-point sets $B_j := \{k_j\}$, the asymptotic behavior of the first moment immediately follows from the previous calculations. As for the variance, we should first note that, due to the orthogonality of the indicator random variables under consideration, we have

$$\mathbf{D} \sum_{s=1}^r a_s I_{B_s}(\pi_{in}) = \sum_{s=1}^r a_s^2 \mathbf{P}(\pi_{in} = k_s) - \left(\sum_{s=1}^r a_s \mathbf{P}(\pi_{in} = k_s) \right)^2$$

$$= \sum_{s=1}^r a_s^2 \mathbf{P}(\pi_{in} = k_s) - \sum_{j,s=1}^r a_s a_j \mathbf{P}(\pi_{in} = k_s) \mathbf{P}(\pi_{in} = k_j).$$

Summation over i of the resulting expression and the previous calculations give the desired asymptotics:

$$\mathbf{D}\Phi_f(\Pi_n) \sim \frac{(Cn)^{\frac{1}{1+b}}}{b+1} \sum_{s,j=1}^r \left[\frac{a_s^2}{rk_s!} \Gamma\left(k_s - \frac{1}{b+1}\right) - \frac{2^{\frac{1}{b+1}-k_s-k_j} a_s a_j}{k_s! k_j!} \Gamma\left(k_s + k_j - \frac{1}{b+1}\right) \right].$$

148

We note the resulting representation can vanish on the set of vectors $(a_1, \ldots, a_r)$ of zero Lebesgue measure in $\mathbb{R}^r$, i.e., on the surface defined by the relation $\sum_{s,j=1}^{r} B_{s,j} a_s a_j = 0$ for some coefficients $\{B_{s,j}\}$.

For infinite intervals of the form $B_j := \{i : i > k_j\}$, the variance is studied in a similar way. We assume without loss of generality that $k_1 \leq k_2 \leq \ldots \leq k_r$. To calculate the variance of this functional, it suffices for us to restrict ourselves to the second moment, since the asymptotics of the first one has already been studied. We have

$$\mathbf{E}\left(\sum_{s=1}^{r} a_s I(\pi_{in} > k_s)\right)^2 = \sum_{s=1}^{r} a_s^2 \mathbf{P}(\pi_{in} > k_s) + 2\mathbf{E}\sum_{j=1}^{r-1} a_j I(\pi_{in} > k_j) \sum_{s>j}^{r} a_s I(\pi_{in} > k_s)$$

$$= \sum_{s=1}^{r} a_s^2 \mathbf{P}(\pi_{in} > k_s) + 2\mathbf{E}\sum_{j=1}^{r-1} a_j \sum_{s>j}^{r} a_s I(\pi_{in} > k_s)$$

$$= \sum_{s=1}^{r} a_s^2 \mathbf{P}(\pi_{in} > k_s) + 2\sum_{j=1}^{r-1} a_j \sum_{s>j}^{r} a_s \mathbf{P}(\pi_{in} > k_s).$$

Further calculations in essence have already been made earlier. So, finally we obtain

$$\mathbf{D}\Phi_f(\Pi_n) \sim (Cn)^{\frac{1}{1+b}} \sum_{s,j=1}^{r} \left[\frac{a_s^2}{r} \int_0^{\infty} \Gamma_{k_s+1,1}(v^{-1-b}) dv - a_s a_j \int_0^{\infty} \Gamma_{k_s+1,1}(v^{-1-b}) \Gamma_{k_j+1,1}(v^{-1-b}) dv\right]$$

with comments similar to the above regarding the zeroing of the double sum.

To conclude this section, we give an example where the above-mentioned moments of the functional under consideration do not tend to infinity as n grows. We put $p_j = e^{-Cj}$, with $C := \log 2$. Let us show that

$$\sup_n \sum_{j\geq 1} \mathbf{P}(\pi_{nj} = k) < \infty.$$

This estimate obviously implies that the first two moments of the functional $\Phi_{I_B}(\Pi_n)$ are uniformly bounded in n for $B := \{k\}$. Indeed, one has

$$\sum_{j\geq 1} \mathbf{P}(\pi_{nj} = k) = \frac{n^k}{k!} \sum_{j\geq 1} e^{-ne^{-Cj}} e^{-Ckj} \leq \frac{e^{Ck} n^k}{k!} \int_1^{\infty} e^{-ne^{-Cx}} e^{-Ckx} dx$$

$$= \frac{e^{Ck} n^k}{Ck!} \int_0^{e^{-C}} e^{-nt} t^{k-1} dt = \frac{e^{Ck}}{Ck!} \int_0^{ne^{-C}} e^{-u} u^{k-1} du;$$

here we used the estimate $e^{-ne^{-Cj}} e^{-Ckj} \leq e^{Ck} e^{-ne^{-Cx}} e^{-Ckx}$ for all $x \in [j, j+1]$, also representing the integral over the semiaxis $[0, \infty)$ as a series of integrals over the indicated segments of unit length. If $n \to \infty$ then the integral in the last expression converges monotonically to the quantity $\Gamma(k)$, which proves our assertion. Note also that a similar example is given in [9].

8. Proofs

Proof of Theorem 1. The assertion of the theorem is essentially a consequence of some results from [1,2,22,23]. First we introduce the necessary notation and recall the assertions from [22,23] we need.

Let $\{Y_i\}$ be a sequence of independent identically distributed random elements taking values in a measurable Abelian group $(\mathcal{G}, \mathcal{A})$ with measurable operation «+». Assume that the zero (neutral) element 0, as a one-point set, belongs to σ-algebra $\mathcal{A}$ and $p := \mathbf{P}(Y_1 \neq 0) \in (0,1)$. Denote by $\{Y_i^0\}$ a sequence of independent identically distributed random variables with marginal distribution

$$\mathcal{L}(Y_1^0) = \mathcal{L}(Y_1 | Y_1 \neq 0),$$

and also put $S_n := \sum_{i=1}^n Y_i$ and $S_n^0 := \sum_{i=1}^n Y_i^0$. In [1,2,22], the following assertion was obtained. □

Lemma 5. *For any natural n, the following representations are valid:*

$$\mathcal{L}(S_n) = \mathcal{L}(S_{\nu(n,p)}^0), \quad \mathcal{L}(S_{\pi(n)}) = \mathcal{L}(S_{\pi(np)}^0), \quad (29)$$

where $\mathcal{L}(\nu(n,p)) \equiv B_{n,p}$, is the binomial distribution with parameters n and p, $\pi(t)$ is a standard Poisson process; wherein the pair $(\nu(n,p), \pi(np))$ does not depend on the sequence $\{X_i^0\}$.

The second important assertion gives an estimate for the Radon–Nikodim derivative of the binomial distribution with respect to the accompanying Poisson law (see [23]).

Lemma 6. *For all $p \in (0,1)$ and natural n, the following estimate holds:*

$$\sup_{k \geq 0} \frac{B_{n,p}(k)}{\mathcal{L}(\pi(np))(k)} \leq \frac{1}{1-p}. \quad (30)$$

Remark 10. *There are other estimates for this Radon–Nikodim derivative. For example, in [24], it was established that*

$$\sup_{k \geq 0} \frac{B_{n,p}(k)}{\mathcal{L}(\pi(np))(k)} \leq \frac{2}{\sqrt{1-p}}$$

for any n and $p \in (0,1)$. Note that for $p \geq 3/4$ this estimate is more accurate than (30).

It is clear that it is enough to prove the assertion for $m = 1$. A proof of the general case is carried out by induction on m and immediately follows from the total probability formula and an estimate for the conditional probability when $m-1$ coordinates of the vector $\overline{V}_n$ are fixed. From (29) and (30) and the total probability formula (when the sequence $\{Y_i^0\}$ is fixed) we obtain the inequality

$$\mathcal{L}(S_n) \leq \frac{1}{1-p} \mathcal{L}(S_{\pi(n)}). \quad (31)$$

Now we put $Y_i := I_A(X_i^{(1)})$, $A \in \mathcal{A}_0$, where $\mathcal{A}_0$ is defined in (1). Consider the Abelian group

$$\mathcal{G} := \left\{ \sum_{i=1}^k e_i I_A(z_i), A \in \mathcal{A}_0; \forall k \geq 1, \forall z_i \in \mathfrak{X}, \forall e_i = -1, 1 \right\}$$

and equip this group with the cylindric σ-algebra. It is clear that $Y_i \in \mathcal{G}$ and the following is true: $\mathbf{P}(Y_1 \neq 0) = P(A_0) = p \in (0,1)$. So, inequality (2) follows from (31) and the above-mentioned induction on m.

Proof of Theorem 2. We will carry out our reasoning in the generality and notation of the proof of Theorem 1. Both relations (29) will be the basis of construction where the sequence $\{Y_i^0\}$ is assumed to be the same in constructing the sums S_n^0 and $S_{\pi(n)}^0$ on a common probability space. So, to prove the first two assertion of the theorem, we only need to construct on the common probability space the random variables $\nu(n,p)$ and π_{np} so that they would be as close as possible to each other. The resulting probability space will be the direct product of the two probability spaces where are, respectively, defined the sequence of independent identically distributed random variables $\{Y_i^0\}$ and the above-mentioned pair of scalar indices. For the optimal definition of random indices $\nu(n,p)$ and π_{np} on a common probability space, we use Dobrushin's theorem (see [25]), which guarantees the existence of marginal copies $\nu^*(n,p)$ and π^*_{np} of the mentioned random indices defined on a common probability space so that

$$\mathbf{P}(\nu^*(n,p) \neq \pi^*_{np}) = d_{TV}(\mathcal{L}(\nu(n,p)), \mathcal{L}(\pi_{np})), \tag{32}$$

where $d_{TV}(\cdot, \cdot)$ is the total variation distance between distributions. Now we use the well-known estimate of Poisson approximation to a binomial distribution (see [15,20]):

$$d_{TV}(\mathcal{L}(\nu(n,p)), \mathcal{L}(\pi_{np})) \leq p \wedge (np^2) \leq p. \tag{33}$$

Using the described construction to each of the m independent coordinates of the vector point processes under consideration, we easily obtain from (32) and (33) the assertion of the theorem. □

Proof of Lemma 1. Fix a multi-index $\bar{n}$. Let us assume that the point processes $\overline{V}_{\bar{n}}$ and $\overline{\Pi}_{\bar{n}}$ are defined on the same probability space in one way or another. Then for any natural k we have the estimate

$$|\Phi_f(\overline{V}_{\bar{n}}) - \Phi_f(\overline{\Pi}_{\bar{n}})| \leq \sum_{i \geq k} |f_{i\bar{n}}(\bar{\nu}_{i\bar{n}}) - f_{i\bar{n}}(\bar{\pi}_{i\bar{n}})| + \zeta_{k\bar{n}}, \tag{34}$$

where $\zeta_{k\bar{n}} := \sum_{i<k} |f_{i\bar{n}}(\bar{\nu}_{i\bar{n}})| + \sum_{i<k} |f_{i\bar{n}}(\bar{\pi}_{i\bar{n}})|$. Put $\mathcal{A}_0 := \bigcup_{i \geq k} \Delta_i$, $p(k) := \mathbf{P}(\mathcal{A}_0) = \sum_{i \geq k} p_i$. Note that the tail of the series on the right-hand side of inequality (34) is a functional of the $\mathcal{A}_0$-restrictions of the studied vector point processes defined on common probability space. So we can use Theorem 2, which guarantees the existence of an absolute coupling (depending on k) of the mentioned $\mathcal{A}_0$-restrictions with the following lower bound for the coincidence probability (see (4); here, in order not to clutter up the notation, we omit the upper symbol «*»):

$$\mathbf{P}\begin{pmatrix} (\nu^{(1)}_{n_1 k}, \nu^{(1)}_{n_1 k+1}, \ldots) = (\pi^{(1)}_{n_1 k}, \pi^{(1)}_{n_1 k+1}, \ldots) \\ (\nu^{(2)}_{n_2 k}, \nu^{(2)}_{n_2 k+1}, \ldots) = (\pi^{(2)}_{n_2 k}, \pi^{(2)}_{n_2 k+1}, \ldots) \\ \ldots \quad \ldots \quad \ldots \\ (\nu^{(m)}_{n_m k}, \nu^{(m)}_{n_m k+1}, \ldots) = (\pi^{(m)}_{n_m k}, \pi^{(m)}_{n_m k+1}, \ldots) \end{pmatrix}$$

$$= \mathbf{P}\left(\sup_{\Delta_j, j \geq k} \left\| V^0_{\bar{n}}(\Delta_j, \ldots, \Delta_j) - \Pi^0_{\bar{n}}(\Delta_j, \ldots, \Delta_j) \right\| = 0 \right) \geq (1 - p(k))^m. \tag{35}$$

Hence, the coupling method of Theorem 2 vanishes the first term on the right-hand side of (34) with a probability no less than $(1 - p(k))^m$.

Further, by virtue of estimate (2) we conclude that $\mathcal{L}(\bar{\nu}_{i\bar{n}}) \leq \frac{1}{(1-p_i)^m} \mathcal{L}(\bar{\pi}_{i\bar{n}})$ for any i. Therefore, by virtue of the conditions of the theorem, we have $\Delta_{\bar{n}} f_{i\bar{n}}(\bar{\nu}_{i\bar{n}}) \xrightarrow{p} 0$ for any i for $\bar{n} \to \infty$. So, for any given (obviously, such construction exists) random variable $\zeta_{k\bar{n}}$ on the same probability space with the $\mathcal{A}_0$-restrictions of the point processes mentioned above, there is the relation $\Delta_{\bar{n}} \zeta_{k\bar{n}} \xrightarrow{p} 0$ for $\bar{n} \to \infty$ for any fixed k. Therefore, using the diagonal method, one can choose $k \equiv k(\bar{n}) \to \infty$ for $\bar{n} \to \infty$, for which $\Delta_{\bar{n}} \zeta_{k\bar{n}} \xrightarrow{p} 0$ as $\bar{n} \to \infty$. After constructing the point processes under consideration on a common probability space by the method of Theorem 2 for each $\bar{n}$ and already chosen $k(\bar{n})$ (in this case, obviously, $p(k(n)) \to 0$), the limit relation (13) will hold. Lemma 1 is proved. □

Proof of Theorem 3. The equivalence of items 1 and 2 directly follows from Lemma 1 and the evident two-sided estimate

$$\mathbf{P}(\xi \leq x - \varepsilon) - \mathbf{P}(|\xi - \eta| > \varepsilon) \leq \mathbf{P}(\eta \leq x) \leq \mathbf{P}(\xi \leq x + \varepsilon) + \mathbf{P}(|\xi - \eta| > \varepsilon)$$

for any $x \in \mathbb{R}$, $\varepsilon > 0$, and arbitrary random variables ξ and η defined on a common probability space. It remains to put

$$\xi := \Phi_f(\overline{V}^*_{\bar{n},\Delta_{\bar{n}}})\Delta_{\bar{n}} - M_{\bar{n}}, \quad \eta := \Phi_f(\overline{\Pi}^*_{\bar{n},\Delta_{\bar{n}}})\Delta_{\bar{n}} - M_{\bar{n}},$$

where the point processes $V^*_{\bar{n},\Delta_{\bar{n}}}$ and $\overline{\Pi}^*_{\bar{n},\Delta_{\bar{n}}}$ are defined in Lemma 1.

We now prove the equivalence of items 2 and 3 of the theorem. To this end we need to reformulate the assertion in Lemma 1 where we substitute Φ^*_f for the functional $\Phi_f(\overline{V}_{\bar{n}})$. As the resulting probability space in this assertion, we consider the direct product of the probability spaces where ν_{ni} and π_{ni} are defined by Dobrushin's theorem. We only note that, after such construction,

$$\mathbf{P}(\{\tilde{\nu}^*_{i\bar{n}}, i \geq k\} \equiv \{\tilde{\pi}_{i\bar{n}}, i \geq k\}) \geq 1 - m \sum_{i \geq k} p_i \sim 1$$

if only $k \to \infty$. Further, we repeat the corresponding reasoning in the proof of Lemma 1 (using the corresponding analog of (34)) as well as the above-mentioned arguments in proving the equivalence of items 1 and 2. □

Proof of Lemma 2. We restrict ourselves to the case $m = 2$. For an arbitrary m, the assertion can be easily proved by induction on m using analogues of the estimates that will be given below. So we have

$$\mathbf{E}\Phi_f(\overline{V}_{\bar{n}}) = \sum_{i \geq 1} \sum_{k_1,k_2 \geq 0} f_{i\bar{n}}(k_1,k_2) \mathbf{P}(\nu^{(1)}_{in_1} = k_1) \mathbf{P}(\nu^{(2)}_{in_2} = k_2),$$

$$\mathbf{E}\Phi_f(\overline{\Pi}_{\bar{n}}) = \sum_{i \geq 1} \sum_{k_1,k_2 \geq 0} f_{i\bar{n}}(k_1,k_2) \mathbf{P}(\pi^{(1)}_{in_1} = k_1) \mathbf{P}(\pi^{(2)}_{in_2} = k_2);$$

here the introduction of the operator $\mathbf{E}$ under the summation sign in the second formula is legal due to (14) and Fubini's theorem. Now, estimate the total variation distance between the distributions of the vectors $(\nu^{(1)}_{in_1}, \nu^{(2)}_{in_2})$ and $(\pi^{(1)}_{in_1}, \pi^{(2)}_{in_2})$:

$$\sum_{k_1,k_2 \geq 0} |\mathbf{P}(\nu^{(1)}_{in_1} = k_1)\mathbf{P}(\nu^{(2)}_{in_2} = k_2) - \mathbf{P}(\pi^{(1)}_{in_1} = k_1)\mathbf{P}(\pi^{(2)}_{in_2} = k_2)|$$

$$\leq \sum_{k_1,k_2 \geq 0} |\mathbf{P}(\nu^{(1)}_{in_1} = k_1) - \mathbf{P}(\pi^{(1)}_{in_1} = k_1)|\mathbf{P}(\nu^{(2)}_{in_2} = k_2)$$

$$+ \sum_{k_1,k_2 \geq 0} |\mathbf{P}(\nu^{(2)}_{in_2} = k_2) - \mathbf{P}(\pi^{(2)}_{in_2} = k_2)|\mathbf{P}(\pi^{(1)}_{in_1} = k_1)$$

$$= \sum_{k_1 \geq 0} |\mathbf{P}(\nu^{(1)}_{in_1} = k_1) - \mathbf{P}(\pi^{(1)}_{in_1} = k_1)| + \sum_{k_2 \geq 0} |\mathbf{P}(\nu^{(2)}_{in_2} = k_2) - \mathbf{P}(\pi^{(2)}_{in_2} = k_2)|.$$

We now use once more Barbour–Hall's upper bound (see [15,20]) for the total variation distance between the distributions $\mathcal{L}\left(\nu^{(j)}_{in_j}\right)$ and $\mathcal{L}\left(\pi^{(j)}_{in_j}\right)$:

$$\sum_{k_j \geq 0} |\mathbf{P}(\nu^{(j)}_{in_j} = k_j) - \mathbf{P}(\pi^{(j)}_{in_j} = k_j)| < 2p_i, \quad j = \overline{1,m}.$$

Then the total variation distance between the distributions of the bivariate vectors under consideration is estimated as follows:

$$\sum_{k_1,k_2 \geq 0} |\mathbf{P}(\nu^{(1)}_{in_1} = k_1)\mathbf{P}(\nu^{(2)}_{in_2} = k_2) - \mathbf{P}(\pi^{(1)}_{in_1} = k_1)\mathbf{P}(\pi^{(2)}_{in_2} = k_2)| \leq 4p_i.$$

Therefore,

$$\left| \sum_{i\geq 1} \sum_{k_1,k_2\geq 0} f_{i\bar{n}}(k_1,k_2) \mathbf{P}(v_{in_1}^{(1)} = k_1) \mathbf{P}(v_{in_2}^{(2)} = k_2) \right.$$

$$\left. - \sum_{i\geq 1} \sum_{k_1,k_2\geq 0} f_{i\bar{n}}(k_1,k_2) \mathbf{P}(\pi_{in_1}^{(1)} = k_1) \mathbf{P}(\pi_{in_2}^{(2)} = k_2) \right|$$

$$\leq \sum_{i\geq 1} C_i \sum_{k_1,k_2\geq 0} \left| \mathbf{P}(v_{in_1}^{(1)} = k_1) \mathbf{P}(v_{in_2}^{(2)} = k_2) - \mathbf{P}(\pi_{in_1}^{(1)} = k_1) \mathbf{P}(\pi_{in_2}^{(2)} = k_2) \right| \leq 4 \sum_{i\geq 1} C_i p_i$$

or

$$|\mathbf{E}\Phi_f(\overline{V}_{\bar{n}}) - \mathbf{E}\Phi_f(\overline{\Pi}_{\bar{n}})| \leq 4 \sum_{i\geq 1} C_i p_i.$$

From here we obtain the assertion we need. □

Proof of Lemma 3. As in the proof of Lemma 2, we restrict ourselves to the case $m=2$. It is clear that we need to examine two series

$$S_1(\overline{V}_{\bar{n}}) := \sum_{i\geq 1} \sum_{k_1,k_2\geq 0} f_{i\bar{n}}^2(k_1,k_2) \mathbf{P}(v_{in_1}^{(1)} = k_1) \mathbf{P}(v_{in_2}^{(2)} = k_2),$$

$$S_2(\overline{V}_{\bar{n}}) := \sum_{i\geq 1} \left(\sum_{k_1,k_2\geq 0} f_{i\bar{n}}(k_1,k_2) \mathbf{P}(v_{in_1}^{(1)} = k_1) \mathbf{P}(v_{in_2}^{(2)} = k_2) \right)^2,$$

In the same way as in the proof of Lemma 1, we obtain

$$|S_1(\overline{V}_{\bar{n}}) - S_1(\overline{\Pi}_{\bar{n}})| \leq 4 \sum_{i\geq 1} C_i^2 p_i.$$

Similarly,

$$|S_2(\overline{V}_{\bar{n}}) - S_2(\overline{\Pi}_{\bar{n}})|$$
$$\leq \sum_{i\geq 1} 2C_i \sum_{k_1,k_2\geq 0} |f_{i\bar{n}}(k_1,k_2)| \left| \mathbf{P}(v_{in_1}^{(1)} = k_1) \mathbf{P}(v_{in_2}^{(2)} = k_2) - \mathbf{P}(\pi_{in_1}^{(1)} = k_1) \mathbf{P}(\pi_{in_2}^{(2)} = k_2) \right|$$

$$\leq 4 \sum_{i\geq 1} C_i^2 p_i.$$

From these estimates it follows that

$$|\mathbf{D}\Phi_f(\overline{\Pi}_{\bar{n}}) - \mathbf{D}\Phi_f(\overline{V}_{\bar{n}})| \leq 8 \sum_{i\geq 1} C_i^2 p_i,$$

whence we obtain the assertion of Lemma 2. □

Proof of Theorem 4. By Corollary 4, it suffices to present conditions for the asymptotic normality of the Poisson version of the χ^2-statistic, i.e., conditions for the feasibility of relation (16). As such, we take the Lyapunov condition of third order. Indeed, consider the following scheme of series of independent in each series of centered random variables:

$$\xi_{in} := \frac{(\pi_{in} - np_i)^2}{np_i} - 1, \quad i = 1, \ldots, N(n), \ n \geq 1.$$

The Lyapunov condition of third order, which guarantees the fulfillment of the central limit theorem (16), is as follows:

$$D_n^{-3/2} \sum_{i=1}^{N(n)} \mathbf{E}|\xi_{in}|^3 \to 0 \quad \text{as } n \to \infty. \tag{36}$$

In order to estimate the absolute third moment in (36), we need the well-known recurrence relation for the central moments of the Poisson distribution:

$$\mathbf{E}(\pi_\lambda - \lambda)^n = \lambda \sum_{k=0}^{n-2} C_{n-1}^k \mathbf{E}(\pi_\lambda - \lambda)^k, \quad n \geq 2,$$

where π_λ is a Poisson random variable with parameter λ. From here it follows that

$$\mathbf{E}(\pi_\lambda - \lambda)^6 = 15\lambda^3 + 25\lambda^2 + \lambda,$$

and using the elementary estimate $|a^2 - 1|^3 \leq 4(a^6 + 1)$, we obtain

$$\mathbf{E}|\zeta_{in}|^3 \leq \frac{4}{(np_i)^3}\left(15(np_i)^3 + 25(np_i)^2 + np_i\right) + 4 = 64 + \frac{100}{np_i} + \frac{4}{(np_i)^2}.$$

It is clear that, to prove relation (36) it suffices to verify that, under the conditions of the theorem,

$$\frac{64N + 100\sum_{i=1}^N \frac{1}{np_i} + 4\sum_{i=1}^N \frac{1}{(np_i)^2}}{\left(2N + \sum_{i=1}^N \frac{1}{np_i}\right)^{3/2}}$$

$$\leq 100\left(2N + \sum_{i=1}^N \frac{1}{np_i}\right)^{-1/2} + \frac{4\sum_{i=1}^N \frac{1}{(np_i)^2}}{\left(N + \sum_{i=1}^N \frac{1}{np_i}\right)^{3/2}} \to 0,$$

that is true in virtue of (17). □

Proof of Theorem 5. For any natural k, denote

$$\Phi_f^{(k)}(\overline{V}_\hbar) := \sum_{i \leq k} f_{i\hbar}(\bar{v}_{i\hbar}).$$

$$\mathbf{P}\left(\Phi_f(\overline{V}_\hbar) \geq x\right) \leq \mathbf{P}\left(\Phi_f^{(k)}(\overline{V}_\hbar) \geq \frac{x}{2}\right) + \mathbf{P}\left(\Phi_f(\overline{V}_\hbar) - \Phi_f^{(k)}(\overline{V}_\hbar) \geq \frac{x}{2}\right). \quad (37)$$

In the notation of Theorem 1, let $V_\hbar^0$ be the restriction of the point process $\overline{V}_\hbar$ to the set $A_0 := \bigcup_{i \leq k} \Delta_i$ with hit probability $p := \sum_{i \leq k} p_i$. Under the sign of the first probability of the right-hand side of inequality (37), instead of the point process $\overline{V}_\hbar$, we can substitute $V_\hbar^0$ and use inequality (2) for the distributions of the restrictions of the corresponding point processes.

The difference

$$\Phi_f(\overline{V}_\hbar) - \Phi_f^{(k)}(\overline{V}_\hbar) = \sum_{i > k} f_{i\hbar}(\bar{v}_{i\hbar})$$

is also an additive functional of the restriction of the point process $\overline{V}_\hbar$ to the additional set $A_0 := \bigcup_{i > k} \Delta_i$ with hit probability $p := \sum_{i > k} p_i$. For this functional, we also use estimate (2). As a result, from (37) and Theorem 1, taking into account the non-negativity of the terms $f_{i\hbar}(\cdot)$, we obtain

$$\mathbf{P}\left(\Phi_f(\overline{V}_\hbar) \geq x\right) \leq \left(\sum_{i > k} p_i\right)^{-m} \mathbf{P}\left(\Phi_f^{(k)}(\overline{\Pi}_\hbar) \geq \frac{x}{2}\right)$$

$$+ \left(\sum_{i \leq k} p_i\right)^{-m} \mathbf{P}\left(\Phi_f(\overline{\Pi}_\hbar) - \Phi_f^{(k)}(\overline{\Pi}_\hbar) \geq \frac{x}{2}\right) \leq 2C^* \mathbf{P}\left(\Phi_f(\overline{\Pi}_\hbar) \geq \frac{x}{2}\right).$$

The theorem is proved. □

Proof of Corollary 5. is based on the following well-known equality. If ζ is a non-negative random variable with finite mean then

$$\mathbf{E}\zeta = \int_0^\infty \mathbf{P}(\zeta \geq x)dx.$$

Using successively this equality for ζ equal to $\Phi_f(\overline{V}_{\bar{n}})$ or $2\Phi_f(\overline{\Pi}_{\bar{n}})$, we easily obtain from (18) the moment inequality (20). □

9. Conclusions

In this paper, we discuss a remarkable asymptotic property of a wide class of additive statistics that allows us to ignore the dependence of the summands in the additive structure of the statistics under consideration and to reduce asymptotic analysis of their distributions to the classical theory of the central limit problem. As consequences, we obtain refinements of certain results concerning the limit behavior of some known classes of additive statistics. Although we limited ourselves only to the law of large numbers and the central limit theorem for the statistics at issue, in the model under consideration it is possible to study sufficient conditions for the weak convergence of their distributions to other infinitely divisible laws as well. In fact, we deal here with a variant of Poisson approximation of empirical point processes, or in other words, with a compound Poisson approximation of an n-th partial sum of independent random variables taking values in some function space. So, in the present paper we deal with the classical subject of Probability Theory and the Poisson approximation of sums of independent multivariate random variables (for example, see [1,12,22,23]).

Moreover, one can reformulate the above-mentioned Poissonization duality theorem for more general U-statistic-type functionals

$$U_f(\overline{V}_n) := \sum_{i_1 \leq \ldots \leq i_m} f_{\bar{n},i_1,\ldots,i_m}(\bar{v}_{\bar{n},i_1}, \ldots, \bar{v}_{\bar{n},i_m}),$$

where $f \equiv \{f_{\bar{n},i_1,\ldots,i_m}(\cdot)\}$ is an array of finite functions defined on $\mathbb{Z}_+^d$, with $d := \sum_{k \leq m} n_k$, satisfying only the restriction

$$\sum_{i_1 \leq \ldots \leq i_m} |f_{\bar{n},i_1,\ldots,i_m}(0,\ldots,0)| < \infty \quad \forall \bar{n}.$$

For example, in this more general setting, one can study the limit behavior of the functionals

$$U_I(V_n) := \sum_{i \geq 1} I_{\bar{A}}(v_{i-1,n}) I_A(v_{i,n}) \cdots I_A(v_{i+m-1,n}) I_{\bar{A}}(v_{i+m,n}),$$

where $\bar{A}$ is the complement of an arbitrary subset $A \subset \mathbb{Z}_+$, with $0 \notin A$, and $v_{0n} := 0$. These functionals count the number of success chains of length m in the dependent (finite or infinite) Bernoulli trials $\{I_A(v_{i,n}); i \geq 1\}$.

Author Contributions: Conceptualization, I.B.; formal analysis, I.B. and M.J.; methodology, I.B.; writing—original draft, I.B. and M.J.; writing—review and editing, I.B. All authors have read and agreed to the published version of the manuscript.

Funding: The study of I. Borisov was supported by the Russian Science Foundation, project no. 22-21-00414.

Acknowledgments: The authors thank the anonymous reviewers for careful reading of the paper and insightful comments and suggestions.

Conflicts of Interest: The authors declare no conflict of interest.

References

1. Borisov, I.S. Poisson approximation of the partial sum process in Banach spaces. *Sib. Math. J.* **1996**, *37*, 627–634. [CrossRef]
2. Borisov, I.S. Moment inequalities connected with accompanying Poisson laws in Abelian groups. *Int. J. Math. Math. Sci.* **2003**, *44*, 2771–2786. [CrossRef]
3. Medvedev, J.I. Some theorems on the asymptotic distribution of the χ^2 statistic. *Dokl. Akad. Nauk SSSR* **1970**, *192*, 987–989. (In Russian)
4. Medvedev, Y.I. Decomposable statistics in a polynomial scheme. I. *Theory Probab. Appl.* **1977**, *22*, 1–15. [CrossRef]
5. Medvedev, Y.I. Decomposable statistics in a polynomial scheme. II. *Theory Probab. Appl.* **1978**, *22*, 607–615. [CrossRef]

6. Bahadur, R.R. On the number of distinct values in a large sample from an infinite discrete distribution. *Proc. Nat. Inst. Sci. India* **1960**, *26A*, 67–75.
7. Kolchin, V.F.; Sevastyanov, B.A.; Chistyakov, V.P. *Random Assignments*; Nauka: Moscow, Russia, 1976.
8. Darling, D.A. Some limit theorems associated with multinomial trials. In *Fifth Berkeley Symposium on Mathematical Statistics and Probability*; Part 1. Berkley–Los Angelos; University of California Press: Berkeley, CA, USA , 1967; Volume 2, pp. 345–350.
9. Karlin, S. Central limit theorems for certain infinite urn schemes. *J. Math. Mech.* **1967**, *17*, 373–401. [CrossRef]
10. Chebunin, M.; Kovalevskii, A.P. Functional central limit theorems for certain statistics in an infinite urn scheme. *Stat. Probab. Lett.* **2016**, *119*, 344–348. [CrossRef]
11. Sevastyanov, B.A.; Chistyakov, V.P. Asymptotic Normality in a Classical Problem with Balls. *Theory Probab. Appl.* **1964**, *9*, 198–211. [CrossRef]
12. Barbour, A.D.; Gnedin, A.V. Small counts in the infinite occupancy scheme. *Electr. J. Probab.* **2009**, *14*, 365–384. [CrossRef]
13. Fisher, R.A.; Corbet, A.S.; Williams, C.B. The relation between the number of species and the number of individuals in a random sample of an animal population. *J. Anim. Ecol.* **1943**, *12*, 42–58 . [CrossRef]
14. Orlitsky, A.; Suresh, A.T.; Wu, Y. Supplementary Information for: Estimating the number of unseen species: A bird in the hand is worth log *n* in the bush. *Proc. Natl. Acad. Sci. USA* **2016**, *1511*, 07428.
15. Barbour, A.D.; Holst, L.; Janson, S. *Poisson Approximation*; Oxford University Press: Oxford, UK, 1992.
16. Kruglov, V.M. The asymptotic behavior of the Pearson statistic. *Theory Probab. Appl.* **2001**, *45*, 69–92. [CrossRef]
17. Steck, G.P. *Limit Theorems for Conditional Distributions*; University of California Press: Berkeley, CA, USA, 1957; Volume 2, pp. 237–284.
18. Tumanyan, S.K. Asymptotic distribution of χ^2-criterion when the size of observations and the number of groups simultaneously increase. *Theory Probab. Appl.* **1956**, *1*, 117–131. [CrossRef]
19. Hagerup, T.; Rüb, C. A guided tour of Chernoff bounds. *Inf. Process. Lett.* **1990**, *33*, 305–308. [CrossRef]
20. Barbour, A.D.; Hall, P. On the rate of Poisson convergence. *Math. Proc. Camb. Philos. Soc.* **1984**, *95*, 473–480. [CrossRef]
21. Loéve, M. *Probability Theory*; Nauchnaya Literatura: Moscow, Russia, 1962. (In Russian)
22. Borisov, I.S. Strong Poisson and mixed approximations of sums of independent random variables in Banach spaces. *Sib. Adv. Math.* **1993**, *3*, 1–13.
23. Borisov, I.S.; Ruzankin, P.S. Poisson approximation for expectations of unbounded functions of independent random variables. *Ann. Probab.* **2002**, *30*, 1657–1680. [CrossRef]
24. Borisov, I.S. Approximation of distributions of von Mises statistics with multidimensional kernels. *Sib. Math. J.* **1991**, *32*, 554–566. [CrossRef]
25. Dobrushin, R.L. Definition of random variables by conditional distributions. *Theory Probab. Appl.* **1970**, *15*, 458–486. [CrossRef]

Article

Asymptotic Expansions for Symmetric Statistics with Degenerate Kernels

Shuya Kanagawa [1,2]

[1] Department of Mathematics, Tokyo Gakugei University, 4-1-1 Nukuikita-machi, Tokyo 184-8501, Japan; skanagaw@tcu.ac.jp
[2] Department of Mathematics, Tokyo City University, 1-28-1 Tamazutsumi, Tokyo 158-8557, Japan

Abstract: Asymptotic expansions for U-statistics and V-statistics with degenerate kernels are investigated, respectively, and the remainder term $O(n^{1-p/2})$, for some $p \geq 4$, is shown in both cases. From the results, it is obtained that asymptotic expansions for the Cramér–von Mises statistics of the uniform distribution $U(0,1)$ hold with the remainder term $O\left(n^{1-p/2}\right)$ for any $p \geq 4$. The scheme of the proof is based on three steps. The first one is the almost sure convergence in a Fourier series expansion of the kernel function $u(x,y)$. The key condition for the convergence is the nuclearity of a linear operator T_u defined by the kernel function. The second one is a representation of U-statistics or V-statistics by single sums of Hilbert space valued random variables. The third one is to apply asymptotic expansions for single sums of Hilbert space valued random variables.

Keywords: U-statistics; V-statistics; asymptotic expansion; integral kernel; nuclearity

MSC: 60B12; 60F05; 62G20

1. Introduction

Asymptotic expansions for symmetric statistics are studied by many people. See, e.g., Callaert–Janssen–Veraverbeke (1980) [1], Withers (1988) [2], Maesono (2004) [3], and so on. They treat U-statistics with non-degenerate kernels. On the other hand, Bentkus—Götze (1999) [4] and Zubayraev (2011) [5] obtained optimal bounds in asymptotic expansions for U-statistics with degenerate kernels. They treat the following modified U-statistics,

$$W_n = \frac{1}{n^2}\sum_{1\leq i<j\leq n}\phi(\xi_i,\xi_j)+\frac{1}{n}\sum_{1\leq i\leq n}\phi_1(\xi_i), \qquad (1)$$

where $\phi(\cdot,\cdot)$ is a symmetric function, $\phi_1(\cdot)$ is a measurable function and $\{\xi_i\}$ are i.i.d. random variables. W_n coincides with V-statistics when

$$\phi_1(x) = \frac{1}{2}\phi(x,x). \qquad (2)$$

If $\phi_1(x) = 0$ for any x, then W_n coincides with U-statistics. They obtained asymptotic expansions with remainder $O(n^{-1})$ for the distribution function of W_n. In this paper, we investigate asymptotic expansions for the simple U-statistics and the V-statistics with degree two defined by

$$U_n = \frac{2}{n^2}\sum_{1\leq i<j\leq n}u(\xi_i,\xi_j), \quad V_n = \frac{1}{n^2}\sum_{1\leq i,j\leq n}u(\xi_i,\xi_j), \qquad (3)$$

respectively. We obtain asymptotic expansions with remainder $O(n^{1-p/2})$ for some $p \geq 4$ for the distribution function of U_n or V_n under some assumptions for $\{\xi_i\}$ and $u(x,y)$. Our scheme of the proof is based on three steps. The first one is the almost sure convergence in a Fourier series expansion of $u(\xi_i, \xi_j)$. The key condition for the convergence is the nuclearity of a linear operator T_u defined by the kernel function $u(x, y)$. The second one is a representation of U-statistics or V-statistics by single sums of Hilbert space valued random variables. The third one is to apply asymptotic expansions for single sums of Hilbert space valued random variables due to Sazonov—Uyanov (1995) [6].

2. Symmetric Statistics

Let $\{\xi_j, j \geq 1\}$ be i.i.d. random variables with a probability distribution μ on an arbitrary measurable space $(X, \mathcal{B})$. Suppose that $u(x_1, x_2, \cdots, x_n)$ is a real valued symmetric function for some $k \geq 1$, i.e.,

$$u(x_1, x_2, \cdots, x_k) = u(x_{i_1}, x_{i_2}, \cdots, x_{i_k}), \tag{4}$$

for any permutation $(i_1, i_2, \cdots, i_k)$ of $(1, 2, \cdots, k)$. A statistics defined by the kernel function $u(x_1, x_2, \cdots, x_k)$ is called a symmetric statistics. The followings are the typical examples of the symmetric statistics.

Example 1. *U-statistics with degree $k \geq 1$:*

$$U_n = \binom{n}{k}^{-1} \sum_{1 \leq i_1 < i_2 < \cdots < i_k \leq n} u(\xi_{i_1}, \xi_{i_2}, \cdots, \xi_{i_k}). \tag{5}$$

Example 2. *V-statistics with degree $k \geq 1$:*

$$V_n = n^{-k} \sum_{1 \leq i_1, i_2, \cdots, i_k \leq n} u(\xi_{i_1}, \xi_{i_2}, \cdots, \xi_{i_k}). \tag{6}$$

In this paper, we treat V-statistics V_n and U-statistics U_n with degree two defined by (3) when the kernel function $u(x, y)$ is degenerate, i.e.,

$$E[u(\xi_1, x)] = 0, \tag{7}$$

for any real number x.

3. Non-Central Limit Theorems for U-Statistics with Degenerate Kernels

Assume that $\{\xi_i\}$ are i.i.d. random variables with a distribution μ. Let $u(x, y)$ be a real valued symmetric function on $\mathbf{R} \times \mathbf{R}$ and square integrable such that

$$E\left[u(\xi_1, \xi_2)^2\right] < \infty. \tag{8}$$

Suppose that $u(x, y)$ is a degenerate kernel satisfying the condition (7). Let $L^2(\mathbf{R}, \mu)$ be the space of all square integrable functions with respect to μ. Then, according to Serfling (1980) [7], we see that the kernel $u(x, y)$ induces a bounded linear operator $L^2(\mathbf{R}, \mu) \to L^2(\mathbf{R}, \mu)$ (trace class) defined by

$$T_u(f) = E[u(\xi_1, x)f(\xi_1)] = \int_{-\infty}^{\infty} u(y, x) f(y) \mu(dy), \quad f \in L^2, \tag{9}$$

which has eigenvalues $\{\lambda_i\}$ and eigenfunctions $\{g_i\}$ satisfying for each $i \geq 1$

$$\begin{cases} E[g_i(\xi_1)] = 0, \quad E\left[g_i^2(\xi_1)\right] = 1 \\ E[g_i(\xi_1)g_j(\xi_1)] = 0 \ (i \neq j), \quad E[u(\xi_1, x)g_i(\xi_1)] = \lambda_i g_i(x) \end{cases}. \tag{10}$$

With respect to (10), see Serfling (1980) [7], pp. 196 and Dunford and Schwartz (1963), pp. 905, 1009, 1083, 1087 for more details. Then we have

$$\lim_{n\to\infty} E\left[\left(u(\xi_i,\xi_j) - \sum_{k=1}^{n} \lambda_k g_k(\xi_i)g_k(\xi_j)\right)^2\right] = 0, \quad (11)$$

for each $i,j \geq 1$. Serfling (1980) [7] showed the non-central limit theorem for U-statistics with degree 2.

Theorem 1. *(Serfling (1980) [7])*
Put $\theta = E[u(\xi_1,\xi_2)]$. Let U_n be a U-statistics with the degenerate kernel $u(x,y)$ defined by

$$U_n = \frac{2}{n^2} \sum_{1 \leq i < j \leq n} u(\xi_i,\xi_j), \quad (12)$$

Let $\{Z_i\}$ be i.i.d. random variables with the standard Normal distribution $N(0,1)$. Then, as $n \to \infty$

$$nU_n \Rightarrow \sum_{j=1}^{\infty} \lambda_j\left(Z_j^2 - 1\right), \quad (13)$$

where "$\Rightarrow$" means the weak convergence in $\mathbf{R}$.

It is well known that the rate of convergence in (13) is $O(n^{-1/2})$ (See, e.g., Serfling (1980) [7] for more details). We obtain asymptotic expansions for U_n and V_n using asymptotic expansions due to Sazonov—Uyanov (1995) [6] for sums of Hilbert space valued i.i.d. random variables in the next section.

4. Asymptotic Expansions for Single Sums which Hit a Ball in a Hilbert Space

In this section we consider an asymptotic expansions for sums of Hilbert space valued random vectors $\{X_i\}$ according to Sazonov—Uyanov (1995) [6]. Let $\{X_i\}$ be a sequence of i.i.d. random vectors in a separable Hilbert space H with $E[X_1] = 0$ and $E\left[\|X_1\|^2\right] = 1$, where $\|x\|^2 = \langle x,x \rangle$ for $x \in H$ and $\langle \cdot,\cdot \rangle$ is the inner product in H. Define the covariance operator V of X_1 by

$$\langle Vx,y \rangle = E[\langle X_1 - E[X_1], x\rangle\langle X_1 - E[X_1], y\rangle], \quad (14)$$

for $x,y \in H$. Denote by $\sigma_1^2 \geq \sigma_2^2 \geq \cdots$ the eigenvalues of V and by $e_1, e_2, \cdots$ be the orthonormal eigenvectors corresponding to the eigenvalues. Put

$$S_n = \frac{1}{\sigma\sqrt{n}} \sum_{i=1}^{n} (X_i - E[X_i]), \quad v_k = \left(\prod_{i=1}^{k} \sigma_i\right)^{-1/k}, \quad c_k(V) = v_k^{k-1}, \quad (15)$$

where $\sigma^2 = E\left[\|X_1 - E(X_1)\|^2\right]$. Define the projection $K : H \to H$ by

$$Ky = \sum_{i=1}^{6k-5} \langle y, e_i \rangle e_i, \quad y \in H. \quad (16)$$

Put

$$\theta_k(L) = \sup\left\{\left|E\left[\exp\left(\sqrt{-1}\langle y, X_1\rangle\right)\right]\right| \,\middle|\, \|Ky\| \geq \frac{1}{L}\right\}. \quad (17)$$

for any $L > 0$. Let Y be the H-valued Gaussian random variables with mean 0 and the covariance operator V. For $a, h \in H$, $r > 0$, $i = 0, 1, \cdots$ we put

$$\Phi_i(a,r) = P\left\{\left\|\left(1 - \frac{i}{n}\right)^{1/2} Y - a\right\| < r\right\}, \tag{18}$$

$$d_h \Phi_i(a,r) = \lim_{t \to \infty} \frac{\Phi_i(a - th, r) - \Phi_i(a,r)}{t}. \tag{19}$$

Define the differential operators d_h^k by

$$d_h^1 \Phi_i(a,r) = d_h \Phi_i(a,r), \quad d_h^k \Phi_i(a,r) = d_h\left(d_h^{k-1} \Phi_i(a,r)\right), \quad k \geq 2. \tag{20}$$

Put

$$\chi_{j,L}' = I\{\|X_j\| < L\} \tag{21}$$

for the indicator $I\{\cdot\}$

$$\chi_{j,t} = \chi_{j,\sqrt{n}(1+t)}' \tag{22}$$

and $\chi_j = \chi_{j,0}$. For positive integers $l_1, l_2, \cdots, l_s$ we put

$$Q_s = \left(d_{X_1 \chi_1}^{l_1} - d_{Y_1}^{l_1}\right) \cdots \left(d_{X_1 \chi_s}^{l_s} - d_{Y_s}^{l_s}\right) \tag{23}$$

and for integers $k \geq 2$, $1 \leq i \leq k - 2$, we put

$$A_i(a,r) = n^{-i/2} \sum_{j=1}^{n} {}'n^{-j} \binom{n}{j} \left(l^{(j)}!\right)^{-1} E(Q_j) \Phi_j(a,r), \tag{24}$$

where $l^{(j)} = l_1! \cdots l_j!$ and $\sum'$ denotes the summation over all, such that

$$l_1 \geq 3, \, l_2 \geq 3, \, \cdots, \, l_j \geq 3, \, l_1 + l_2 + \cdots, + l_j = 2j + i. \tag{25}$$

The following theorem is the key result for the proofs of our theorems.

Theorem 2. *Sazonov—Uyanov (1995) [6]*
Suppose that $E\left[\|X_1\|^p\right] < \infty$ for some $p \geq 4$. For any $t \geq 0$ and integer $k \geq 2$, let L be a positive number, such that

$$E\left[\|X_1\|^2 (1 - \chi_{j,L}')\right] \leq \frac{\sigma_{6k-5}^2}{3}. \tag{26}$$

Then, for $L \leq n^{1/2}$

$$\Delta_n(a,r) := \left| P\{\|S_n - a\| < r\} - P\{\|Y - a\| < r\} - \sum_{i=1}^{k-2} A_i(a,r) \right| \tag{27}$$

$$\leq A(p,s,t)$$

$$+ c(k) \exp\{-s^\alpha\} \left\{ c_{6k-5}(V) E[B_2(a,r)(1 - \chi_1)] + \left(1 + M(a,r)^{k-2}\right) E[B_{k+1}(a,r)(1 - \chi_1)] \right.$$

$$\left. + c_{6k-5}(V) \left(1 + m^3(a,r)|a|\langle Va,a\rangle\right)^{k-2} \left(\frac{L^2}{n}\right)^{(k-1)/2} + \theta_k^{n/(k \log(n/L^2))}(L) \log\left(n/L^2\right) \right\},$$

where for $s = |\|a\| - r|$ and $\alpha \geq \frac{1}{5}$,

$$A(p,s,t) := nE[(1 - \chi_{1,t})] + c_p (1-s)^p n^{1 - p/2} E\left[\|X_1\|^p (\chi_{1,t} - \chi_1)\right], \tag{28}$$

$$B(j,r) = n^{-(j-2)}\left(\|X_1\|^j + m^j(a,r)|\langle X_1,a\rangle|^j\right), \tag{29}$$

$$M(a,r) = m^2(a,r)\langle Va,a\rangle \tag{30}$$

and

$$m(a,r) := \begin{cases} \min\left\{1, \frac{r}{\|a\|}\right\}, & \|a\| > 0 \\ 0, & a = 0 \end{cases}. \tag{31}$$

In addition, the terms in the asymptotic expansion for $\varepsilon > 0$ satisfies the estimates

$$|A_i(a,r)| \leq c(\varepsilon,i)\exp\left\{-\frac{s^2}{2+\varepsilon}\right\}n^{-i/s}c_{6i+3}(V) \tag{32}$$

$$\times E\left[\chi_i\|X_1\|^{i+2} + |\langle X_1,a\rangle|^{i+2}\chi_i m^{i+2}(a,r)\times\right.$$

$$\left.\left\{1 + m^{2(i+2)}(a,r)\left(1 + m^{2(i+2)}(a,r)\langle Va,a\rangle^{i-1}\right)\right\} + M(a,r)^{3i+2}\right]$$

for even i, and if i is odd, then we have

$$|A_i(a,r)| \leq c(\varepsilon,i)\exp\left\{-\frac{s^2}{2+\varepsilon}\right\}n^{-i/s}\left\{c_{6i+3}(V)\left(1 + \left(m^2(a,r)\langle Va,a\rangle^{i-1}\right)\right)\right. \tag{33}$$

$$\times E\left[|\langle X_1,a\rangle|\chi_i m(a,r)\left\{\|X_1\|^2 + \|X_1\|^{i+1} + \langle X_1,a\rangle^{i+1}(a,r)m^{i+1}(a,r)\right\}\right]$$

$$+ c_{6i+3}(V)m(a,r)\langle Va,a\rangle^{1/2}E\left[\chi_i\|X_1\|^{i+1}\right]$$

5. The Sato–Mercer Theorem

In the proofs of our theorems we use the Fourier series expansion for the kernel function $u(\xi_i,\xi_j)$ by eigenvalues and eigenfunction of the linear operator T_u defined by (9). Since (11) holds in the sense of the L^2-convergence, (11) can not be applied to show the asymptotic expansions for U-statistics or V-statistics as it is. We show that $u(\xi_i,\xi_j)$ can be represented by the Fourier series expansion in (11) almost surely using the following Sato–Mercer theorem. (See Sato (1992) [8] for more details.)

Theorem 3. (The Sato–Mercer theorem)
Let X be a separable metric space with a Borel measure ν on X, and $K(x,y)$ be a function on $X \times X$ such that there exists a Borel-measurable subset X_0, such that

$$\nu(X\setminus X_0) = 0. \tag{34}$$

Suppose that $K(x,y)$ is continuous on X_0 and satisfies

$$\int_X\int_X |K(x,y)|^2\nu(dx)\nu(dy) < \infty \tag{35}$$

and

$$\int_X\int_X K(x,y)f(x)\overline{f(y)}\nu(dx)\nu(dy) \geq 0, \tag{36}$$

for any $f \in L^2(X,\nu)$. Then, the linear operator T_K on $L^2(X,\nu)$ defined by

$$T_Kf(x) = \int_X K(x,y)f(y)\nu(dy), \quad f \in L^2(X,\nu) \tag{37}$$

is nuclear if, and only if,

$$\int_X K(x,x)\nu(dx) < \infty \tag{38}$$

holds.

From Theorem 3, we have the next result.

Theorem 4. *Let $\{\xi_j, j \geq 1\}$ be i.i.d. random variables with the distribution μ. Let $u(x,y)$ be a real valued symmetric function on $\mathbf{R} \times \mathbf{R}$ and T_u be a linear operator defined by*

$$T_u f(x) = E[u(\xi_1, x) f(\xi_1)] = \int_{-\infty}^{\infty} u(y,x) f(y) \mu(dy), \quad f \in L^2(\mathbf{R}, \mu). \tag{39}$$

Suppose that $u(x,y)$ is the square integrable degenerate kernel of the linear operator T_u, such that

$$\int_{-\infty}^{\infty} \int_{-\infty}^{\infty} u^2(x,y) \mu(dx) \mu(dy) < \infty, \tag{40}$$

$$\int_{-\infty}^{\infty} \int_{-\infty}^{\infty} u(x,y) f(x) \overline{f(y)} \mu(dx) \mu(dy) \geq 0, \tag{41}$$

for any $f \in L^2(\mathbf{R}, \mu)$ and

$$E[u(\xi_1, x)] = \int_{-\infty}^{\infty} u(y,x) \mu(dy) = 0 \tag{42}$$

for any $x \in \mathbf{R}$. Let $\{\lambda_k\}$ and $\{g_k\}$ be eigenvalues and eingenfunctions of the linear operator T_u, respectively. Suppose

$$\lambda_k \geq 0, \quad k \geq 1. \tag{43}$$

Furthermore assume that there exists a Lebesgue measurable subset $X_0 \subset \mathbf{R}$, such that

$$\mu(X_0) = 1 \tag{44}$$

and $u(x,y)$ is continuous on X_0. Then, we have

$$u(\xi_i, \xi_j) = \sum_{k=1}^{\infty} \lambda_k g_k(\xi_i) g_k(\xi_j) \quad a.s., \tag{45}$$

for each $i, j \geq 1$.

Proof. It is easy to see that from (10)

$$E\left[\sum_{k=1}^{n} |\lambda_k g_k(\xi_i) g_k(\xi_j)|\right] = \sum_{k=1}^{n} E[|\lambda_k g_k(\xi_i) g_k(\xi_j)|] \tag{46}$$

$$= \sum_{k=1}^{n} |\lambda_k| E[|g_k(\xi_i) g_k(\xi_j)|]$$

$$\leq \sum_{k=1}^{n} |\lambda_k| \left\{ E\left[g_k(\xi_i)^2\right] \right\}^{1/2} \left\{ E\left[g_k(\xi_j)^2\right] \right\}^{1/2}$$

$$= \sum_{k=1}^{n} |\lambda_k|,$$

for each $n \geq 1$. Tending $n \to \infty$, (46) implies that

$$E\left[\sum_{k=1}^{\infty} |\lambda_k g_k(\xi_i) g_k(\xi_j)|\right] \leq \sum_{k=1}^{\infty} |\lambda_k|. \tag{47}$$

On the other hand, from (40) and (41), $u(x,y)$ satisfies (35) and (36). Therefore, T_u is nuclear by Theorem 3. Hence, from (43) and the nuclearity of T_u, we have

$$\sum_{k=1}^{\infty} |\lambda_k| = \sum_{k=1}^{\infty} \lambda_k < \infty. \tag{48}$$

From (47) and (48), we have

$$E\left[\sum_{k=1}^{\infty} |\lambda_k g_k(\xi_i) g_k(\xi_j)|\right] < \infty, \tag{49}$$

which implies

$$\sum_{k=1}^{\infty} |\lambda_k g_k(\xi_i) g_k(\xi_j)| < \infty, \quad a.s. \tag{50}$$

Therefore, (45) is proved from (11) and (50). □

Remark 1. *If the symmetric function $u(x,y)$ is piecewise continuous on $\mathbf{R}$, then there exists $X_0 \subset \mathbf{R}$ satisfying (44) such that $u(x,y)$ is continuous on X_0. In the next section, we show a typical example of U- or V-statistics defined by such piecewise continuous function $u(x,y)$ as its kernel function.*

6. Asymptotic Expansions for Degenerate V-Statistics and U-Statistics with Degree 2

For applying Theorem 2 for Hilbert space valued random variables to the proof of asymptotic expansions for V_n, we represent V_n by sums of Hilbert space valued random variables $\{G_i\}$ by the following method.

According to K.—Yoshihara (1994) [9], we introduce a separable Hilbert space H-equipped with the inner product $\langle \cdot, \cdot \rangle$ and the norm $\|\cdot\|$ as follows,

$$H = \left\{ \mathbf{x} = (x_1, x_2, \cdots) \in \mathbf{R}^{\infty} \,\middle|\, \sum_{k=1}^{\infty} |\lambda_k| x_k^2 < \infty \right\}, \tag{51}$$

$$\langle \mathbf{x}, \mathbf{y} \rangle = \sum_{k=1}^{\infty} |\lambda_k| x_k y_k \tag{52}$$

and

$$\|\mathbf{x}\| = \left(\sum_{k=1}^{\infty} |\lambda_k| x_k^2\right)^{1/2}. \tag{53}$$

Using the assumptions of Theorem 4, we have from (10) and (48) that

$$E\left[\sum_{k=1}^{\infty} |\lambda_k| g_k^2(\xi_i)\right] = \sum_{k=1}^{\infty} |\lambda_k| E\left[g_k^2(\xi_i)\right] = \sum_{k=1}^{\infty} |\lambda_k| < \infty, \tag{54}$$

which implies that we can define H-valued random variables by

$$G_i = (g_1(\xi_i), g_2(\xi_i), g_3(\xi_i), \cdots) \tag{55}$$

for each $i \geq 1$. Let $\{U_n, n \geq 1\}$ and $\{V_n, n \geq 1\}$ be U-statistics and V-statistics with degree 2 defined by (3), respectively.

Theorem 5. *Without loss of generality we assume that $\theta = 0$. Suppose that $\{\xi_j, j \geq 1\}$ is a sequence of i.i.d. random variables with the distribution μ. Assume that $u(x,y)$ is a square integrable symmetric function with respect to $\mu \times \mu$ satisfying (40) $\sim$ (42). Suppose that for some $p \geq 4$*

$$E\big[\|G_1\|^p\big] < \infty. \tag{56}$$

Furthermore, without loss of generality, assume that

$$\sum_{k=1}^{\infty} \lambda_k = 1. \tag{57}$$

Let Y be the H-valued Gaussian random variables with mean 0 and the covariance operator V satisfying (14) with the eigenvalues $\sigma_1^2 \geq \sigma_2^2 \geq \cdots$ and the orthogonal eigenvectors $e_1, e_2, \cdots$. For any $t \geq 0$, integer $k \geq 2$, let L be a positive number, such that

$$E\left[\|G_1\|^2 (1 - \chi_{j,L'})\right] \leq \frac{\sigma_{6k-5}^2}{3}. \tag{58}$$

Then, for $L \leq n^{1/2}$ and $\alpha \geq \frac{1}{5}$,

$$\left| P\{|nV_n| \leq r\} - P\{\|Y\| \leq r\} - \sum_{i=1}^{k-2} A_i(0, r) \right| \tag{59}$$

$$\leq A(p, s, t) + c(k) \exp\{-r^\alpha\} [c_{6k-5}(V) E[B_2(0, r)(1 - \chi_1)]$$

$$+ E[B_{k+1}(0, r) \chi_1] + c_{6k-5}(V) \left(\frac{L^2}{n}\right)^{(k-1)/2} + \theta_k^{n/(k \log(n/L^2))} (L) \log(n/L^2),$$

where

$$\|Y\| = \left| \sum_{j=1}^{\infty} \lambda_j (Z_j^2 - 1) \right|, \tag{60}$$

$$A(p, s, t) = nE[(1 - \chi_{1,t})] + c(p)(1 + r)^{-p} n^{1-p/2} E[\|G_1\|^p (\chi_{1,t} - \chi_1)] \tag{61}$$

and

$$B_j(0, r) = n^{-(j-2)/2} \|G_1\|^j. \tag{62}$$

Proof. Put

$$h(\mathbf{x}) = \sum_{k=1}^{\infty} \lambda_k x_k \tag{63}$$

for

$$\mathbf{x} \in H = \left\{ \mathbf{x} = (x_1, x_2, \cdots) \,\bigg|\, \sum_{k=1}^{\infty} |\lambda_k| x_k^2 < \infty \right\} \tag{64}$$

Recall that for each i,

$$\frac{1}{\sqrt{n}} \sum_{i=1}^{n} G_i = \left(\frac{1}{\sqrt{n}} \sum_{i=1}^{n} g_1(\xi_i), \frac{1}{\sqrt{n}} \sum_{i=1}^{n} g_2(\xi_i), \cdots \right) \in H. \tag{65}$$

Then we have

$$nV_n = \frac{1}{n} \sum_{1 \leq i,j \leq n} u(\xi_i, \xi_j) = \frac{1}{n} \sum_{1 \leq i,j \leq n} \sum_{k=1}^{\infty} \lambda_k g_k(\xi_i) g_k(\xi_j) \tag{66}$$

$$= \frac{1}{n} \sum_{k=1}^{\infty} \lambda_k \left\{ \sum_{1 \leq i,j \leq n} g_k(\xi_i) g_k(\xi_j) \right\} = \frac{1}{n} \sum_{k=1}^{\infty} \lambda_k \left\{ \sum_{i=1}^{n} g_k(\xi_i) \right\}^2$$

$$= \left\| \frac{1}{\sqrt{n}} \sum_{i=1}^{n} G_i \right\|.$$

Thus, we can apply Theorem 2 to show Theorem 5. □

Theorem 6. *Suppose that the i.i.d. random variables $\{\xi_i, i \geq 1\}$ obey a continuous distribution. Let $v(x,y)$ be a symmetric function defined by*

$$v(x,y) = \begin{cases} u(x,y), & x \neq y \\ 0, & x = y \end{cases}. \tag{67}$$

Under the same assumptions in Theorem 5, the equation (59) holds for U_n with the degenerate kernel $v(x,y)$.

Proof. Since the i.i.d. random variables $\{\xi_i, i \geq 1\}$ obey a continuous distribution, we have

$$P\{\xi_i \neq \xi_j\} = 1 \quad (i \neq j). \tag{68}$$

Therefore, from (67) and (68)

$$nU_n = \frac{2}{n} \sum_{1 \leq i < j \leq n} u(\xi_i, \xi_j) = \frac{1}{n} \sum_{1 \leq i,j \leq n} v(\xi_i, \xi_j) \quad a.s. \tag{69}$$

Since the right hand side of (69) is the V-statistics with the degenerate kernel $v(x,y)$ satisfying all assumptions of Theorem 5, Theorem 6 holds from Theorem 5. □

Remark 2. *From (10), $E[G_1] = 0$ and $\sigma^2 = E\left[\|G_1\|^2\right] = 1$ in Theorem 5.*

7. Cramer–Von Mises Statistics

There are some examples of U-statistics or V-statistics for which the above theorems are applicable under the assumption of nuclearity of the kernel functions where the above theorems are applicable.

Example 3. *(Cramér-von Mises Statistics, Sato (1992) [8])*
Assume that i.i.d. random variables $\{\xi_j, j \geq 1\}$ obey the uniform distribution $U(0,1)$, i.e., μ is the Lebesgue on $[0,1]$. Define a kernel function $u(x,y)$ by

$$u(x,y) = \int_0^1 \frac{\left(I_{[x,1]}(t) - t\right)\left(I_{[y,1]}(t) - t\right)}{t(1-t)} dt, \quad x,y \in [0,1] \tag{70}$$

satisfies the hypothesis of Theorem 5 or Theorem 6. On the other hand, we have

$$\int_0^1 u(x,x)dx = \int_0^1 dx \int_0^1 \frac{\left(I_{[x,1]}(t) - t\right)^2}{t(1-t)} dt \tag{71}$$

$$= \int_0^1 \frac{dt}{t(1-t)} \int_0^1 \left(I_{[x,1]}(t) - t\right)^2 dx = 1 < \infty.$$

Therefore, the integral operator T_u defined by

$$T_u f(y) = \int_0^1 u(x,y) f(y) dx \tag{72}$$

is nuclear from Theorem 3. Therefore, since the degenerate kernel $u(x,y)$ defined by (70) satisfies all assumptions of Theorem 5, Theorem 5 holds for the Cramér-von Mises Statistics. Furthermore, Theorem 6 also holds for U-statistics with the degenerate kernel $v(x,y)$ defined by (67) and (70).

8. Conclusions

Bentkus—Götze (1999) [4] and Zubayraev (2011) [5] obtained the remainder $O(n^{-1})$ in asymptotic expansions for U-statistics or V-statistics with degenerate kernels. From Theorems 5 and 6, if we assume $E[\|G_1\|^p] \leq \infty$, $p \geq 4$ and some conditions, then we obtain the remainder $O\left(n^{1-p/2}\right)$. Applying Theorem 5, we obtain asymptotic expansions for the Cramér–von Mises statistics of the uniform distribution $U(0,1)$ with the remainder $O\left(n^{1-p/2}\right)$ for any $p \geq 4$.

Funding: Grant-in-Aid Scientific Research (C), No.18K03431, Ministry of Education, Science and Culture, Japan.

Institutional Review Board Statement: Not applicable.

Informed Consent Statement: Not applicable.

Data Availability Statement: The author uses no data.

Acknowledgments: The author would like to express his gratitude to the anonymous referees for their useful comments. He also would like to express his gratitude to V.V. Ulyanov for giving the opportunity to present this work.

Conflicts of Interest: The author declares no conflict of interest.

References

1. Callaert, H.; Janssen, P.; Veraverbeke, N. An edgeworth expansion for U-statistics. *Ann. Stat.* **1980**, *8*, 299–312. [CrossRef]
2. Withers, C.S. Some asymptotics for U-statistics. *Commun. Stat. Theory Methods* **1988**, *17*, 3269–3276. [CrossRef]
3. Maesono, Y. Asymptotic representations of skewness estimators of studentized U-statistics. *Bull. Inform. Cybern.* **2004**, *36*, 91–104. [CrossRef]
4. Bentkus, V.; Götze, F. Optimal bounds in non-Gaussian limit theorems for U-statistics. *Ann. Probab.* **1999**, *27*, 454–521. [CrossRef]
5. Zubayraev, T. Asymptotic analysis for U-statistics and its application to Von Mises statistics. *Open J. Stat.* **2011**, *1*, 139–144. [CrossRef]
6. Sazonov, V.V.; Ul'yanov, V.V. Asymptotic expansions for the probability that the sum of independent random variables hits a ball in a Hilbert space. *Russ. Math. Surv.* **1995**, *50*, 1045–1063. [CrossRef]
7. Serfling, R.J. *Approximation Theorems of Mathematical Statistics*; John Wiley & Sons: Hoboken, NJ, USA, 1980. [CrossRef]
8. Sato, H. Nuclearity of a nonnegative definite integral kernel on a separable metric space. *J. Theor. Probab.* **1992**, *5*, 349–353. [CrossRef]
9. Kanagawa, S.; Yoshihara, K. The almost sure invariance principles of degenerate U-statistics of degree two for stationary random variables. *Stoch. Process. Their Appl.* **1994**, *49*, 347–356. [CrossRef]

Article

Sharp Estimates for Proximity of Geometric and Related Sums Distributions to Limit Laws

Alexander Bulinski [1,*] and Nikolay Slepov [2]

[1] Faculty of Mathematics and Mechanics, Lomonosov Moscow State University, Leninskie Gory 1, 119991 Moscow, Russia
[2] Department of Higher Mathematics, Moscow Institute of Physics and Technology, National Research University, 9 Instituskiy per., Dolgoprudny, 141701 Moscow, Russia
* Correspondence: alexander.bulinski@math.msu.ru

Citation: Bulinski, A.; Slepov, N. Sharp Estimates for Proximity of Geometric and Related Sums Distributions to Limit Laws. *Mathematics* **2022**, *10*, 4747. https://doi.org/10.3390/math10244747

Academic Editors: Alexander Tikhomirov and Vladimir Ulyanov

Received: 29 October 2022
Accepted: 7 December 2022
Published: 14 December 2022

Publisher's Note: MDPI stays neutral with regard to jurisdictional claims in published maps and institutional affiliations.

Copyright: © 2022 by the authors. Licensee MDPI, Basel, Switzerland. This article is an open access article distributed under the terms and conditions of the Creative Commons Attribution (CC BY) license (https://creativecommons.org/licenses/by/4.0/).

Abstract: The convergence rate in the famous Rényi theorem is studied by means of the Stein method refinement. Namely, it is demonstrated that the new estimate of the convergence rate of the normalized geometric sums to exponential law involving the ideal probability metric of the second order is sharp. Some recent results concerning the convergence rates in Kolmogorov and Kantorovich metrics are extended as well. In contrast to many previous works, there are no assumptions that the summands of geometric sums are positive and have the same distribution. For the first time, an analogue of the Rényi theorem is established for the model of exchangeable random variables. Also within this model, a sharp estimate of convergence rate to a specified mixture of distributions is provided. The convergence rate of the appropriately normalized random sums of random summands to the generalized gamma distribution is estimated. Here, the number of summands follows the generalized negative binomial law. The sharp estimates of the proximity of random sums of random summands distributions to the limit law are established for independent summands and for the model of exchangeable ones. The inverse to the equilibrium transformation of the probability measures is introduced, and in this way a new approximation of the Pareto distributions by exponential laws is proposed. The integral probability metrics and the techniques of integration with respect to sign measures are essentially employed.

Keywords: probability metrics; Stein method; geometric sums; generalization of the Rényi theorem; generalized transformation of equilibrium for probability measures and its inverse; generalized gamma distribution

MSC: 60F99; 60E10; 60G50; 60G09

1. Introduction

The theory of sums of random variables belongs to the core of modern probability theory. The fundamental contribution to the formation of the classical core was made by A. de Moivre, J. Bernoulli, P.-S. Laplace, D. Poisson, P.L. Chebyshev, A.A. Markov, A.M. Lyapunov, E. Borel, S.N. Bernstein, P. Lévy, J. Lindeberg, H. Cramér, A.N. Kolmogorov, A.Ya. Khinchin, B.V. Gnedenko, J.L. Doob, W. Feller, Yu.V. Prokhorov, A.A. Borovkov, Yu.V. Linnik, I.A. Ibragimov, A. Rényi, P. Erdös, M. Csörgö, P. Révész, C. Stein, P. Hall, V.V. Petrov, V.M. Zolotarev, J. Jacod and A.N. Shiryaev among others. The first steps led to limit theorems for appropriately normalized partial sums of sequences of independent random variables. Besides the laws of large numbers, special attention was paid to emergence of Gaussian and Poisson limit laws. Note that despite many efforts to find necessary and sufficient conditions for the validity of the central limit theorem (the term was proposed by G. Pólya for a class of limit theorems describing weak convergence of distributions of normalized sums of random variables to the Gaussian law), this problem was completely resolved for independent summands only in the second part of the 20th century in the works by V.M. Zolotarev and V.I. Rotar. Also in the last century, the beautiful theory of infinitely divisible and stable laws was constructed. New developments of infinite divisibility along with classical theory can be found in [1]. For exposition of the theory of stable distributions and their applications, we refer to [2], see also references therein.

Parallel to partial sums of a sequence of random variables (and vectors), other significant schemes have appeared, for instance, the arrays of random variables. Moreover, in physics, biology and other domains, researchers found that it was essential to study the sums of random variables when the number of summands was random. Thus, the random sums with random summands became an important object of investigation. One can mention the branching processes which stem from the 19th century population models by I.J. Bienaymé, F. Galton and H.W. Watson that are still intensively being developed, see, e.g., [3]. In the theory of risk, it is worth recalling the celebrated Cramér–Lundberg model for dynamics of the capital of an insurance company, see, e.g., Ch. 6 in [4]. Various examples of models described by random sums are considered in Ch. 1 of [5], including (see Example 1.2.1) the relationship between certain random sums analysis and the famous Pollaczek–Khinchin formula in queuing theory. A vast literature deals with the so-called geometric sums. There, one studies the sum of independent identically distributed random variables, and the summation index follows the geometric distribution, being independent with summands. Such random sums can model many real world phenomena, e.g., in queuing, insurance and reliability, see the Section "Origin of Geometric Sums" in the Introduction of [6]. Furthermore, a multitude of important stochastic models described by systems of dependent random variables occurred to meet diverse applications, see, e.g., [7]. In particular, the general theory of stochastic processes and random fields arose in the last century (for introduction to random fields, see, e.g., [8]).

An intriguing problem of estimating the convergence rate to a limit law was addressed by A.C. Berry and C.-G. Esseen. Their papers initiated the study of proximity for distribution functions of the normalized partial sums of independent random variables to the distribution function of a standard Gaussian law in the framework of the classical theory of random sums.

To assess the proximity of distributions, we will employ various integral probability metrics. Usually, for random variables Y, Z and a specified class $\mathcal{H}$ of functions $h : \mathbb{R} \to \mathbb{R}$, one sets

$$d_{\mathcal{H}}(Y,Z) := \sup_{h \in \mathcal{H}} |\mathbb{E}[h(Y)] - \mathbb{E}[h(Z)]| \in [0, \infty]. \tag{1}$$

Clearly, $d_{\mathcal{H}}(Y,Z)$ is a functional depending on $law(Y)$ and $law(Z)$, i.e., distributions of Y and Z. A class $\mathcal{H}$ should be rich enough to guarantee that $d_{\mathcal{H}}$ possesses the properties of a metric (or semi-metric). The general theory of probability metrics is presented, e.g., in [9,10]. In terms of such metrics, one often compares the distribution of a random variable Y under consideration with that of a target random variable Z. In Section 2, we recall the definitions of the Kolmogorov and Kantorovich (alternatively called Wasserstein) distances and Zolotarev ideal metrics corresponding to the adequate choice of $\mathcal{H}$, denoted below as $\mathcal{K}$, $\mathcal{H}_1$ and $\mathcal{H}_2$, respectively.

It should be emphasized that for sums of random variables, deep results were established along with creation and development of different methods of analysis. One can mention the method of characteristic functions due to the works of J.Fourier, P.-S.Laplace and A.M.Lyapunov, the method of moments proposed by P.L.Chebyshev and developed by A.A.Markov, the Lindeberg method of employing auxiliary Gaussian random variables and the Bernstein techniques of large and small boxes. In 1972, C.Stein in [11] (see also [12]) introduced the new method to estimate the proximity of the distribution under consideration to a normal law. Furthermore, this powerful method was developed in the framework of classical limit theorems of the probability theory. We describe this method in Section 2. Applying the Stein method along with other tools, one can establish in certain cases the sharp estimates of closeness between a target distribution and other ones in specified metrics (see, e.g., [13,14]). We recommend the books [15,16] and the paper [17] for basic ideas of the ingenious Stein method. The development of this techniques under mild moment restrictions for summands is treated in [18,19]. We mention in passing that there are deep generalizations of Stein techniques involving generators of certain Markov processes; a compact exposition is provided, e.g., on p. 2 of [20].

In the theory of random sums of random summands, the limit theorems with exponential law as a target distribution play a role similar to the central limit theorem for (nonrandom) sums of random variables. Here, one has to underline the principal role of the Rényi classical theorem for geometric sums published in [21]. Recall this famous result. Let $X_1, X_2, \ldots$ be a sequence of independent identically distributed (i.i.d.) random variables such that $\mu := \mathbb{E}[X_1] \neq 0$. Take a geometric random variable N_p with parameter $p \in (0,1)$, defined as follows:

$$\mathbb{P}(N_p = k) = p(1-p)^k, \quad k \in \mathbb{N} \cup \{0\}. \tag{2}$$

Assume that N_p and $(X_n)_{n \in \mathbb{N}}$ are independent. Set $S_0 := 0$, $S_n := X_1 + \ldots + X_n$, $n \in \mathbb{N}$. Then,

$$W_p := \frac{S_{N_p}}{\mathbb{E}[S_{N_p}]} \xrightarrow{\mathcal{D}} Z \sim Exp(1) \text{ as } p \to 0+, \tag{3}$$

where $\xrightarrow{\mathcal{D}}$ stands for convergence in distribution, and Z follows the exponential law $Exp(\lambda)$ with parameter $\lambda = 1$, $\mathbb{E}[S_{N_p}] = \mu(1-p)/p$. In fact, instead of N_p, A.Rényi considered the shifted geometric random variable $N(p)$ such that $\mathbb{P}(N(p) = k) = p(1-p)^{k-1}, k \in \mathbb{N}$. Clearly, N_p has the same law as $N(p) - 1$. He supposed that i.i.d. random variables $X_1, X_2, \ldots$ are non-negative, and $N(p)$ and $(X_n)_{n \in \mathbb{N}}$ are independent. Then, $S_{N(p)}/\mathbb{E}[S_{N(p)}]$ converges in distribution to $Z \sim Exp(1)$ as $p \to 0+$, where $\mathbb{E}[S_{N(p)}] = \mu/p$. It was explained in [22] that both statements are equivalent and the assumption of nonnegativity of summands can be omitted.

Building on the previous investigations discussed below in this section, we study different instances of quantifying the approximation of random sums by limit laws and also extend the Stein method employment. The main goals of our paper are the following: (1) to find sharp estimates (i.e., optimal ones which cannot be diminished) of proximity of geometric sums of independent (in general non-identically distributed) random variables to exponential law using the probability metric $d_{\mathcal{H}_2}$; (2) to prove the new version of the Rényi theorem when the summands are described by a model of exchangeable random variables, establishing the due non-exponential limit law together with an optimal bound of the convergence rate applying $d_{\mathcal{H}_2}$; (3) to obtain the exact convergence rate of appropriately normalized random sums of random summands to the generalized gamma distribution when the number of summands follows the generalized negative binomial distribution employing $d_{\mathcal{H}_2}$; (4) to introduce the inverse transformation to an "equilibrium distribution transformation", give full description of its existence and demonstrate the advantage of applying the Stein method combined with that inverse transform; and (5) to use such approach in deriving the new approximation in the Kolmogorov metric $d_{\mathcal{K}}$ of the Pareto distribution by an exponential one, which is important in signal processing.

The main idea is to apply the Stein method and deduce (Lemma 2) new estimates of the solution of Stein's equation (corresponding to an exponential law $Exp(\lambda)$ as a target distribution) when a function h appearing in its right-hand side belongs to a class $\mathcal{H}_2$. This entails the established sharp estimates. The integral probability metrics and the techniques of integration with respect to sign measures are essentially employed. It should be stressed that we consider random summands which take, in general, positive and negative values and in certain cases need not have the same law.

Now, we briefly comment on the relevance of the five groups of the paper results mentioned above. Some upper bounds for convergence rates in Equation (3) were obtained previously by different tools (the renewal techniques and the memoryless property of the geometric distribution), and the estimates were not sharp. We refer to the results by A.D. Soloviev, V.V. Kalashnikov and S.Y. Vsekhsvyatskii, M. Brown, V.M. Kruglov and V.Yu. Korolev, where the authors either used the Kolmogorov distance or proved specified nonuniform estimates for differences of the corresponding distribution functions. For instance, in [23] the following estimate was proved

$$\sup_{x \in \mathbb{R}} |\mathbb{P}(W_p \leq x) - \mathbb{P}(Z \leq x)| \leq p \frac{\mathbb{E}[X_1^2]}{\mu^2} \max\left\{1, \frac{1}{2(1-p)}\right\},$$

where $Z \sim Exp(1)$. Moreover, this estimate is asymptotically exact when $p \to 0+$. Some improvements are in [24] under certain (hazard rate) assumptions. E.V. Sugakova obtained a version of the Rényi theorem for independent, in general, not identically distributed random variables. We also mention contributions by V.V. Kalashnikov, E.F. Peköz, A. Röllin, N. Ross and T.L. Hung which gave the estimates in terms of the Zolotarev ideal metrics. We do not reproduce all these results here since they can be viewed on pages 3 and 4 of [22] with references where they were published.

In Corollary 3.6 of [25] for nondegenerate i.i.d. positive random variables $X_1, X_2, \ldots$ with mean μ and finite second moment, it was proved that

$$\zeta_2(pS(p), Z(1/\mu)) \leq p(\mathbb{E}[X_1^2] + 2\mu^2),$$

where $S(p) := \sum_{j=1}^{N(p)} X_j$, ζ_2 is the Zolotarev ideal metric of order two, $Z(\lambda) \sim Exp(\lambda)$, $\lambda > 0$. In [22], the estimates for proximity of geometric sums distributions to $Z \sim Exp(1)$ were provided in the Kantorovich and ζ_2 metrics. A substantial contribution of the authors of [22] is the study of random summands $X_1, X_2, \ldots$ that need not be positive (see also [26]). The general estimate for deviation of W_p from $Z \sim Exp(1)$ in the ideal metric of order s was proved in [27]. We do not assume that W_p is constructed by means of i.i.d. random variables and, moreover, demonstrate that our estimate (for summands taking real values) involving the metric $d_{\mathcal{H}_2}$ is sharp.

The exchangeable random variables form an important class having various applications in statistics and combinatorics, see, e.g., [28]. As far as we know, the model of exchangeable random variables is studied in the context of random sums for the first time here. It is interesting that instead of the exponential limit law we indicate explicit expression of the new limit law. In addition, we establish the sharp estimate of proximity of random sums distributions to this law using $d_{\mathcal{H}_2}$.

A natural generalization of the Rényi theorem is to study the summation index following non-geometrical distribution. In this way, the upper bound of the convergence rate of random sums of random summands to generalized gamma distribution was proved in [29]. Theorem 3.1 in [30] contains the estimates in the Kolmogorov and Kantorovich distances for approximations of non-negative random variable law by specified (nongeneralized) gamma distribution. The proof relies on Stein's identity for gamma distribution established in H.M.Luk's PhD thesis (see the reference in [30]). New estimates of the solutions of the gamma Stein equation are given in [31]. We derive the sharp estimate for approximation of random sums by generalized gamma law using the Zolotarev metric of order two. In a quite recent paper [32] the author established deep results concerning further generalizations of the Rényi theorem. Namely, Theorem 1 of [32] demonstrates how one can provide the upper bounds of the convergence rate of specified random sums to a more general law than an exponential one using the estimates in the Rényi theorem. This approach is appealing since the author employs the ideal metric of order $s > 0$. However, the sharpness of these estimates was not examined.

Note that in [33] the important "equilibrium transformation of distributions" was proposed and employed along with the Stein techniques. We will consider this transformation X^e for a random variable X in Section 7 and also tackle other useful transformations. In the present paper, the inverse to the "equilibrium distribution transformation" is introduced. We completely describe the possibility to construct such transformation and provide an explicit formula for the corresponding density. The idea to apply such inverse transformation whenever it exists is based on the result [33] demonstrating that one can obtain a more precise estimate for proximity in the Kantorovich metric between X^e and Z than between X and Z, where $Z \sim Exp(1)$ and $\mathbb{E}[X] = 1$, $\mathbb{E}[X^2] < \infty$. We extend this result. Moreover, we prove that in this way one can obtain a new estimate of approximation of the Pareto distribution by an exponential one. It is shown that our new estimate is advantageous for a wide range of parameters of the Pareto distribution. Let $X^e \sim Pareto(\alpha, \beta)$, i.e., the distribution function of X^e is

$$F^e(x) = 1 - \left(\frac{\beta}{x+\beta}\right)^\alpha, \quad x \geq 0, \ \alpha > 0, \ \beta > 0.$$

We show that the preimage $X \sim Pareto(\alpha + 1, \beta)$. Thus, for any $\alpha > 2, \beta > 0$, one has $d_\mathcal{K}(X^e, Z) \leq 1/(\alpha - 1)$, where $Z \sim Exp(\alpha/\beta)$ and $d_\mathcal{K}$ stands for the Kolmogorov distance. This bound is more precise than the previous ones applied in signal processing, see, e.g., [34].

This paper is organized as follows. After the Introduction, the auxiliary results are provided in Section 2. Here we include the material important for understanding the main results. We recall the concept of probability metrics, consider the Kolmogorov and the Kantorovich distances and examine the Zolotarev ideal metrics. We describe the basic ideas of Stein's method, especially for the exponential target distribution. In this section, we formulate a simple but useful Lemma 1 concerning the essential supremum of the Lipschitz function, an important Lemma 2 giving the solution of the Stein equation for different functional classes. We explain the essential role of the generalized equilibrium transformation proposed in [22] which permits study of the summands taking both positive and negative values. We formulate Lemma 3 to be able to solve an integral equation involving the generalized equilibrium transformation when $\mathbb{E}[X] \neq 0$ and $\mathbb{E}[X^2] < \infty$. The proofs of auxiliary lemmas are placed in Appendix A. Section 3 is devoted to an approximation of the normalized geometric sums W_p by an exponential law. Here, the sharp convergence rate is found (see Theorem 1) by means of the probability metric $d_{\mathcal{H}_2}$. The proof is based on the Lebesgue–Stieltjes integration techniques, the formula of integration by parts for functions of bounded variations, Lemma 2, various limit theorems for integrals and the important result of [22] concerning the estimates involving the Kantorovich distance. In Section 4, for the first time an analog of the Rényi theorem is proved for a model of exchangeable random variables proposed in [35]. We demonstrate (Theorem 2) that, in contrast to Rényi's theorem, the limit distribution for random sums under consideration is a specified mixture of two explicitly indicated laws. Moreover, the sharp convergence rate to this limit law is obtained (Theorem 3) by means of $d_{\mathcal{H}_2}$. In Section 5, the distance between the generalized gamma law and the suitably normalized sum of independent random variables is estimated when the number of summands has the generalized negative binomial distribution. Theorem 4 demonstrates that this estimate is sharp. For the proof, we employ various truncation techniques, the transformations of parameters of initial random variables, the monotone convergence theorem and explicit formula for the generalized gamma distribution moments of order $\delta > 0$, obtained in [27]. Section 6 provides the pioneering study of the same problem in the framework of exchangeable random variables and also gives the sharp estimate for the $d_{\mathcal{H}_2}$ metric (Theorem 5). In Section 7, we introduce the inverse to the equilibrium transformation of the probability measures. Lemma 6 contains a full description of situations when a unique preimage X of a random variable X^e exists and gives an explicit formula for distribution of X. This approach permits us to obtain the new estimates of closeness of probability measures in the Kolmogorov and Kantorovich metrics (Theorem 6). In particular, due to Theorem 6 and Lemmas 2, 6, it becomes possible to find a useful estimate of proximity of the Pareto law to the exponential one (Example 2). Section 8 containing the conclusions and indications for further research work is followed by Appendix A and the list of references.

2. Auxiliary Results

Let $\mathcal{K} := \{h : h_z(x) = \mathbb{I}\{x \leq z\}, \ x, z \in \mathbb{R}\}$, where $\mathbb{I}\{A\} := 1$ if A holds and zero otherwise. The choice $\mathcal{H} = \mathcal{K}$ in Equation (1) corresponds to the Kolmogorov distance. Note that h above is a function in x, whereas z is the index parameterizing the class.

A function $h : \mathbb{R} \to \mathbb{R}$ is called the Lipschitz one if

$$Lip(h) := \sup_{x,u \in \mathbb{R}; x \neq u} \frac{|h(x) - h(u)|}{|x - u|} < \infty. \tag{4}$$

Then,

$$|h(x) - h(u)| \leq C|x - u|, \ x, u \in \mathbb{R}, \tag{5}$$

and in light of Equation (4), $Lip(h)$ is the smallest possible constant C appearing in Equation (5). We write $Lip(C)$, where $C \in [0, \infty)$ for a collection of the Lipschitz functions having $Lip(h) \leq C$. For $s > 0$ set $m = m(s) := \lceil s - 1 \rceil \in \mathbb{N} \cup \{0\}$ (where, for $a \in \mathbb{R}$, $\lceil a \rceil$ stands for the minimal integer number which is equal or greater than a). Introduce a class of functions

$$\mathcal{H}_s := \{h : \mathbb{R} \to \mathbb{R}, \ |h^{(m)}(x) - h^{(m)}(u)| \leq |x - u|^{s-m}, \ x, u \in \mathbb{R}\}, \ s > 0.$$

As usual, $h^{(0)}(x) = h(x)$, $x \in \mathbb{R}$. We write $d_{\mathcal{H}_s}$ for a metric defined according to Equation (1) with $\mathcal{H} = \mathcal{H}_s$. V.M. Zolotarev and many other researchers defined an ideal metric ζ_s of order $s > 0$ involving only bounded functions from $\mathcal{H}_s$. We will use collections $\mathcal{H}_1$ and $\mathcal{H}_2$ without assumption that functions h are bounded on $\mathbb{R}$. This is the reason why we write $d_{\mathcal{H}_s}$ instead of ζ_s. Thus, we employ

$$\mathcal{H}_1 := \{Lip(1)\}, \quad \mathcal{H}_2 := \{h : h' \in Lip(1)\}.$$

Note that in definitions of $\mathcal{H}_2$ we deal with $h \in C^{(1)}$, where the space $C^{(1)}(\mathbb{R})$ consists of functions $h : \mathbb{R} \to \mathbb{R}$ such that $h'(x)$ exists for all $x \in \mathbb{R}$, and h' is continuous on $\mathbb{R}$ (evidently the Lipschitz function is continuous). One calls $d_{\mathcal{H}_1}$ the Kantorovich metric (the term Wasserstein metric appears in the literature as well). One also uses the bounded Kantorovich metric when the class $\mathcal{H}_1$ contains all the bounded functions from $Lip(1)$. The metric ζ_s was introduced in [36] and called an ideal metric in light of its important properties. The properties of ζ_s metrics, where $s > 0$, are collected in Sec. 2 of [32]. We mention in passing that various functionals are ubiquitous in assessing the proximity of distributions. In this regard, we refer, e.g., to [37,38].

To apply the Stein method, we begin with fixing the target random variable Z (or its distribution) and describe a class $\mathcal{H}$ to estimate $d_{\mathcal{H}}(Y, Z)$ for a random variable Y under consideration. Then, the problem is to indicate an operator T (with specified domain of definition) so that the Stein equation

$$Tf(x) = h(x) - \mathbb{E}[h(Z)] \tag{6}$$

has a solution $f_h(x)$, $x \in \mathbb{R}$, for each function $h \in \mathcal{H}$. After that, one can substitute Y instead of x in Equation (6) and take the expectation of both sides, assuming that all these expectations are finite. As a result, one comes to the relation

$$\mathbb{E}[Tf_h(Y)] = \mathbb{E}[h(Y)] - \mathbb{E}[h(Z)]. \tag{7}$$

It is not a priori clear why the estimation of the left-hand side of Equation (7) is more adequate than the estimation of $|\mathbb{E}[h(Y)] - \mathbb{E}[h(Z)]|$ for $h \in \mathcal{H}$. However, in many situations, justifying the method this occurs. The choice of T depends on the distribution of Z. Note that in certain cases (e.g., when Z follows the Poisson law) one considers functions f defined on a subset of $\mathbb{R}$. We emphasize that the construction of operator T is a nontrivial problem, see, e.g., [33,39–41].

The basic idea in this way is the following. For many probability distributions (Gaussian, Laplace, Exponential, etc.), one can find an operator T characterizing the law of a target variable Z. In other words, for a rather large class of functions f, $\mathbb{E}[Tf(Y)] = 0$ if and only if $law(Y) = law(Z)$ (i.e., the laws of Y and Z coincide). Thus, if $|\mathbb{E}[Tf_h(Y)]|$ is small enough for a suitable class of functions h, this leads to the assertion that the law of Y is close (in a sense) to the law of Z. One has to verify that this kind of "continuity" takes place. Clearly, if for any $h \in \mathcal{H}$, where $\mathcal{H}$ defines the integral probability metric in Equation (1), one can find a solution f_h of Equation (6), then the relation $\mathbb{E}[Tf_h(Y)] = 0$ for all $f_h, h \in \mathcal{H}$, yields $d_\mathcal{H}(Y, Z) = 0$ and, consequently, $law(Y) = law(Z)$.

Further, we assume that $Z \sim Exp(\lambda)$, i.e., Z has exponential distribution with parameter $\lambda > 0$. In this case (see, e.g., Sec. 5 in [17]), one uses the operator

$$Tf(x) := f'(x) - \lambda f(x) + \lambda f(0), \quad x \in \mathbb{R}, \quad \lambda > 0, \tag{8}$$

and writes the Stein Equation (6) as follows

$$f'(x) - \lambda f(x) + \lambda f(0) = h(x) - \mathbb{E}[h(Z)], \quad x \in \mathbb{R}. \tag{9}$$

It should be stipulated that $\mathbb{E}[h(Z)] \in \mathbb{R}$ for a test function $h \in \mathcal{H}$, and there exists a differentiable solution f of Equation (9). Therefore, if one can find such solution f, then

$$\mathbb{E}[f'(Y)] - \lambda \mathbb{E}[f(Y)] + \lambda f(0) = \mathbb{E}[h(Y)] - \mathbb{E}[h(Z)] \tag{10}$$

under the hypothesis that all these expectations are finite. If $f : \mathbb{R} \to \mathbb{R}$ is absolutely continuous, then (see, e.g., Theorem 13.18 of [42]) for almost all $x \in \mathbb{R}$ with respect to the Lebesgue measure, there exists $f'(x)$. Moreover, one can find an integrable (on each interval) function $g : \mathbb{R} \to \mathbb{R}$, $x \in \mathbb{R}$, to guarantee, for each $x, u \in \mathbb{R}$, that

$$f(x) = f(u) + \int_u^x g(v) dv, \tag{11}$$

where $g(v) = f'(v)$ for almost all $v \in \mathbb{R}$. Thus, $(Tf)(x)$ is defined for such f according to Equation (8) for almost all $x \in \mathbb{R}$. In general, for an arbitrary random variable Y, one cannot write $\mathbb{E}[(Tf)(Y)]$ since the value of expectation depends on the choice of a version of $(Tf)(x)$, $x \in \mathbb{R}$. Really, let $B \in \mathcal{B}(\mathbb{R})$ be such that $m(B) = 0$, where m stands for the Lebesgue measure. Assume that Y takes values in B. Then, it is clear that $\mathbb{E}[(Tf)(Y)]$ depends on the choice of a function $(Tf)(x)$ version defined on $\mathbb{R}$. However, if the distribution $\mathbb{P}_Y$ of a random variable Y has a density with respect to m, then $\mathbb{E}[(Tf)(Y)]$ will be the same for any version of Tf (with respect to the Lebesgue measure). In certain cases, the Stein operator is applied to smoothed functions (see, e.g., [33,43]). Otherwise, Equation (6) does not hold at each point of $\mathbb{R}$ (see, e.g., Lemma 2.2 in [16]), and complementary efforts are needed. For our study, it is convenient to employ in Equation (8) for T in the capacity of $f'(x)$, $x \in \mathbb{R}$, the right derivative. In many cases, for a real-valued function f defined on a fixed set $D \subset \mathbb{R}$ one considers $\sup_{x \in D} |f(x)|$ as "essential supremum". Recall that a function $\tilde{f}$ is a version of f (and vice versa) if the measure (here the Lebesgue measure) of points x such that $\tilde{f}(x) \neq f(x)$ is zero. The notation $\|f\|_\infty$ means that one takes $\inf_{\tilde{f}} \sup_{x \in D} |\tilde{f}(x)|$, where $\tilde{f}$ belongs to the class of all versions of f. Clearly, $\|f\|_\infty$ will be the same if we change f on a subset of D having a measure which is equal to zero. Thus, we write $\|f'\|_\infty$ instead of $\|g\|_\infty$ appearing in Equation (11). The following simple observation is useful. Its proof is provided in Appendix A.

Lemma 1. *A function h is the Lipschitz function on $\mathbb{R}$ with $Lip(h) = C < \infty$ if and only if h is absolutely continuous and (its essential supremum) $\|h'\|_\infty = C < \infty$.*

Remark 1. Note that $0 \leq h(x) \leq 1$, $x \in \mathbb{R}$, for any $h \in \mathcal{K}$. If, for some positive constant C, $h \in \text{Lip}(C)$, then Equation (5) yields that $|h(x)| \leq C|x| + |h(0)|$. If h' is a Lipschitz function (with $\text{Lip}(h') = C$), then $h''(x)$ exists for almost all $x \in \mathbb{R}$ and an application of Lemma 1 gives

$$|h'(x) - h'(0)| = \left| \int_0^x h''(u) du \right| \leq C|x|, \quad x \in \mathbb{R}.$$

Consequently, $|h'(x)| \leq A|x| + B$ for some positive A, B (one can take $A = C$, $B = |h'(0)|$) and any $x \in \mathbb{R}$. As $h'(x)$ is continuous on each interval, it follows that $|h(x)| \leq ax^2 + b|x| + c$ for some positive a, b, c and all $x \in \mathbb{R}$ ($a = C/2$, $b = |h'(0)|$, $c = |h(0)|$). Therefore, $|h(x)| \leq A_0 x^2 + B_0$ for some positive A_0, B_0 and each $x \in \mathbb{R}$.

Lemma 2. For any $\lambda > 0$ and each $h \in \mathcal{K} \cup \mathcal{H}_1 \cup \mathcal{H}_2$, the equation

$$f'(x) - \lambda f(x) = h(x), \quad x \in \mathbb{R}, \tag{12}$$

has a solution

$$f_h(x) = -e^{\lambda x} \int_x^\infty h(u) e^{-\lambda u} du, \quad x \in \mathbb{R}, \tag{13}$$

where $f_h(0) = -\mathbb{E}[h(Z)]/\lambda$. If $h \in \mathcal{K}$, then for all $x \in \mathbb{R}$ there exists $f_h'(x)$ and $\|f_h'\|_\infty \leq 1$. If $h \in \mathcal{H}_1 \cup \mathcal{H}_2$, then f_h' is defined on $\mathbb{R}$ and $\|f_h'\|_\infty \leq \|h'\|_\infty / \lambda$. For $h \in \mathcal{H}_2$, a function f_h'' is defined on $\mathbb{R}$ and $\|f_h''\|_\infty \leq \min\{2\|h'\|_\infty, \|h''\|_\infty / \lambda\}$.

The right-hand side of Equation (13) is well defined for each $x \in \mathbb{R}$ in light of Remark 1. Lemma 4.1 of [33] contains for $\lambda = 1$ some statements of Lemma 1. We will use the above estimates for any $\lambda > 0$. Estimates for $h \in \mathcal{H}_2$ were not considered in [33]. The proof of Lemma 2 is given in Appendix A.

The following concept was introduced in [33].

Definition 1 ([33]). Let X be a non-negative random variable with finite $\mathbb{E}[X] > 0$. One says that a random variable X^e has distribution of equilibrium with respect to X if for any Lipschitz function $f : \mathbb{R} \to \mathbb{R}$,

$$\mathbb{E}[f(X)] - f(0) = \mathbb{E}[X] \mathbb{E}[f'(X^e)]. \tag{14}$$

Note that Definition 1 deals separately with distributions of X and X^e. One says that X^e is the result of the equilibrium transformation applied to X. The same terminology is used for transition from $law(X)$ to $law(X^e)$. For the sake of completeness, we explain in Appendix A (Comments to Definition 1) why one can take the law of X^e having a density with respect to the Lebesgue measure

$$p^e(x) = \begin{cases} \frac{1}{\mathbb{E}[X]} \mathbb{P}(X > x), & x \geq 0, \\ 0, & x < 0, \end{cases} \tag{15}$$

to guarantee the validity of Equation (14).

Remark 2. For a non-negative random variable X with finite $\mathbb{E}[X] > 0$, one can construct a random variable X^e having a density (15). Accordingly, we then have a random vector (X, X^e) with specified marginal distributions. However, the joint law of X and X^e is not fixed and can be chosen in appropriate way. If $X_1, X_2, \ldots$ is a sequence of independent random variables, we will assume that a sequence $(X_n, X_n^e)_{n \in \mathbb{N}}$ consists of independent vectors, and these vectors are independent with all considered random variables which are independent with $(X_n)_{n \in \mathbb{N}}$.

In the recent paper [22], a generalization of the equilibrium transformation of distributions was proposed without assuming that random variable X is non-negative.

Definition 2 ([22]). *Let X be a random variable having a distribution function $F(x) := \mathbb{P}(X \leq x)$, $x \in \mathbb{R}$. Assume the existence of finite $\mathbb{E}[X] \neq 0$. An equilibrium distribution function corresponding to X (or $F(x)$) is introduced by way of*

$$F^e(x) := \begin{cases} -\frac{1}{\mathbb{E}[X]} \int_{-\infty}^{x} F(u) du, & x \leq 0, \\ -\frac{\mathbb{E}[X^-]}{\mathbb{E}[X]} + \frac{1}{\mathbb{E}[X]} \int_0^x (1 - F(u)) du, & x > 0, \end{cases} \qquad (16)$$

where $X^- := X\mathbb{I}\{X < 0\}$. This function can be written as $F^e(x) = \int_{-\infty}^{x} p^e(u) du$, where

$$p^e(x) = \begin{cases} -\frac{1}{\mathbb{E}[X]} F(x), & x \leq 0, \\ \frac{1}{\mathbb{E}[X]}(1 - F(x)), & x > 0, \end{cases} \qquad (17)$$

thus, p^e is a density (with respect to the Lebesgue measure) of a signed measure Q^e corresponding to F^e. In other words, Equation (17) demonstrates the Jordan decomposition (see, e.g., Sec. 29 of [44]) of Q^e.

Clearly, for a non-negative random variable, the functions defined in Equation (15) and Equation (16) coincide. For a nonpositive random variable, the function F^e appearing in Equation (16) is a distribution function of a probability measure. In general, when X can take positive and negative values, the function introduced in Equation (16) is not a distribution function. We will call F^e the generalized equilibrium distribution function. Note that $|p^e(x)| \leq \frac{1}{|\mathbb{E}[X]|}$. Thus, F^e is the Lipschitz function and consequently continuous ($F^e(x)$ is well defined for each $x \in \mathbb{R}$ since $\mathbb{E}[X]$ is finite and nonzero). Moreover, F^e is absolutely continuous being the Lipschitz function. Each absolutely continuous function has bounded variation. If G is a function of bounded variation, then $G = G_1 - G_2$, where G_1 and G_2 are nondecreasing functions (see, e.g., [42], Theorem 12.18). One can employ the canonical choice $G_1(x) := Var_0^x(G)$, where $Var_a^b(G)$ means the variation of G on $[a, b]$, $-\infty < a \leq b < \infty$ (if $a > b$ then $Var_a^b(G) := -Var_b^a(G)$). If G is right-continuous (on $\mathbb{R}$), then evidently G_1 and G_2 are also right-continuous. Thus, for a right-continuous G having bounded variation, a nondecreasing function G_i in its representation corresponds to a σ-finite measure Q_i on $\mathcal{B}(\mathbb{R})$, $i = 1, 2$. More precisely, there exists a unique σ-finite measure Q_i on $\mathcal{B}(\mathbb{R})$ such that, for each finite interval $(a, b]$, $Q_i((a, b]) = G_i(b) - G_i(a)$, $i = 1, 2$. Recall that one writes for the Lebesgue–Stieltjes integral with respect to a function G

$$\int_{\mathbb{R}} f(u) dG(u) := \int_{\mathbb{R}} f(u) dG_1(u) - \int_{\mathbb{R}} f(u) dG_2(u), \qquad (18)$$

whenever the integrals in the right-hand side exist (with values in $[-\infty, \infty]$), and the cases $\infty - \infty$ or $-\infty + \infty$ are excluded. The integral $\int_{\mathbb{R}} f(u) dG_i(u)$ means the integration with respect to measure Q_i, $i = 1, 2$. The signed measure Q corresponding to G is $Q_1 - Q_2$. Thus, $\int_{\mathbb{R}} f(u) dG(u)$ means the integration with respect to signed measure Q. Note that if $G = U_1 - U_2$ where U_i is right-continuous and nondecreasing ($i = 1, 2$), then

$$\int_{\mathbb{R}} f(u) dG_1(u) - \int_{\mathbb{R}} f(u) dG_2(u) = \int_{\mathbb{R}} f(u) dU_1(u) - \int_{\mathbb{R}} f(u) dU_2(u). \qquad (19)$$

The left-hand side and the right-hand side of Equation (19) make sense simultaneously, and if so, are equal to each other. Indeed, for any finite interval $(a, b]$ ($a \leq b$), one has $G_1(b) - G_1(a) - (G_2(b) - G_2(a)) = U_1(b) - U_1(a) - (U_2(b) - U_2(a))$. Thus, the signed measures corresponding to $G_1 - G_2$ and $U_1 - U_2$ coincide on $\mathcal{B}(\mathbb{R})$. We mention in passing that one can also employ the Jordan decomposition of a signed measure.

For F^e introduced in Equation (16), the analog of Equation (15) has the form

$$\mathbb{E}[f(X)] - f(0) = \mathbb{E}[X] \int_{\mathbb{R}} f'(x) dF^e(x). \qquad (20)$$

Taking into account Equation (17), one can rewrite Equation (20) equivalently as follows

$$\mathbb{E}[f(X)] - f(0) = \int_{(-\infty,0]} f'(x)(-F(x))dx + \int_{(0,\infty)} f'(x)(1-F(x))dx. \quad (21)$$

The right-hand side of the latter relation does not depend on the choice of a version of f'. Due to Theorem 1(d) of [22], Equation (20) is valid for any Lipschitz function f. Evidently, an arbitrary function $f \in \mathcal{H}_2$ need not be the Lipschitz one and vice versa.

Lemma 3. *Let X be a random variable such that $\mathbb{E}[X^2] < \infty$ and $\mathbb{E}[X] \neq 0$. Then, Equation (20) is satisfied for all $f \in \mathcal{H}_2$.*

The proof is provided in Appendix A.

3. Limit Theorem for Geometric Sums of Independent Random Variables

Consider $N_p \sim Geom(p)$, see Equation (2). In other words, N_p has a geometric distribution with parameter p. Let $X_1, X_2, \ldots$ be a sequence of independent random variables such that $\mathbb{E}[X_k] = \mu$, where $\mu \in \mathbb{R}$, $\mu \neq 0$, $k \in \mathbb{N}$. Assume that N_p and $(X_n)_{n \in \mathbb{N}}$ are independent. Consider a normalized geometric sum

$$W_p := \frac{p}{\mu(1-p)} \sum_{k=1}^{N_p} X_k, \quad (22)$$

introduced in Equation (3). Since N_p can take zero value, set, as usual, $\sum_{k=1}^{0} X_k := 0$. One can see that W_p can be viewed as a random sum $S_p := \sum_{k=1}^{N_p} X_k$ normalized by $\mathbb{E}[X]\mathbb{E}[N_p]$.

Lemma 4. *Let $X_1, X_2, \ldots$ and N_p, where $p \in (0,1)$, be random variables described above in this Section. Then, the following relations hold:*

$$\mathbb{E}[W_p] = 1, \quad \mathbb{E}|W_p| \leq \frac{\sup_{k \in \mathbb{N}} \mathbb{E}|X_k|}{|\mu|},$$

$$\mathbb{E}[W_p^2] = \frac{p}{\mu^2(1-p)} \mathbb{E}[X_{N_p+1}^2] + 2. \quad (23)$$

Proof. Recall that

$$\mathbb{E}[N_p] = \sum_{k=1}^{\infty} kp(1-p)^{k-1} = \frac{1-p}{p}, \quad (24)$$

$$\mathbb{E}[N_p^2] = \sum_{k=1}^{\infty} k^2 p(1-p)^{k-1} = \frac{(1-p)(2-p)}{p^2}. \quad (25)$$

Thus, one has

$$\mathbb{E}[W_p] = \frac{p}{\mu(1-p)} \sum_{k=1}^{\infty} k\mu \mathbb{P}(N_p = k) = \frac{p}{1-p} \mathbb{E}[N_p] = 1.$$

Clearly, $\mathbb{E}|X_k| < \infty$ since $\mathbb{E}[X_k]$ is finite ($k \in \mathbb{N}$). Therefore

$$\mathbb{E}|W_p| \leq \frac{p}{|\mu|(1-p)} \sum_{k=1}^{\infty} k\mathbb{E}|X_k|\mathbb{P}(N_p = k) \leq \frac{\sup_{k \in \mathbb{N}} \mathbb{E}|X_k|}{|\mu|}.$$

Set $v_k := \mathbb{E}[X_k^2]$, $k \in \mathbb{N}$. One has

$$\mathbb{E}[S_p^2] = \sum_{k=1}^{\infty} \mathbb{P}(N_p = k) \mathbb{E}\left(\sum_{i=1}^{k} X_i\right)^2 = \sum_{k=1}^{\infty} p(1-p)^k \left(\sum_{i=1}^{k} v_i + k(k-1)\mu^2\right). \quad (26)$$

According to Equations (24) and (25) one derives the formula

$$\sum_{k=1}^{\infty} p(1-p)^k \left(k(k-1)\mu^2\right) = \mu^2 \left(\frac{(1-p)(2-p)}{p^2} - \frac{1-p}{p}\right) = 2\left(\frac{\mu(1-p)}{p}\right)^2. \quad (27)$$

Convergence of the series $\sum_{k=1}^{\infty} p(1-p)^k \sum_{i=1}^{k} v_i$ having non-negative terms holds simultaneously with the validity of inequality $\mathbb{E}[W_p^2] < \infty$. Changing the order of summation, we obtain

$$\sum_{k=1}^{\infty} p(1-p)^k \sum_{i=1}^{k} v_i = \sum_{i=1}^{\infty} (1-p)^i v_i = \left(\frac{1-p}{p}\right) \mathbb{E}[X_{N_p+1}^2].$$

The latter formula and Equations (26), (27) yield

$$\mathbb{E}[W_p^2] = \left(\frac{p}{\mu(1-p)}\right)^2 \mathbb{E}[S_p^2] = \left(\frac{p}{\mu(1-p)}\right)^2 \left(\left(\frac{1-p}{p}\right) \mathbb{E}[X_{N_p+1}^2] + 2\left(\frac{\mu(1-p)}{p}\right)^2\right)$$

$$= \frac{p}{\mu^2(1-p)} \mathbb{E}[X_{N_p+1}^2] + 2.$$

Equation (23) is established. □

The proof of Theorem 3.1 in [45] shows for non-negative i.i.d. random variables $X_1, X_2, \ldots$ (when $\mu = 1$, see Formula (3.15) in [45]) that the equilibrium transformation of W_p distribution has the following form:

$$W_p^e = \frac{p}{\mu(1-p)} \left(\sum_{k=1}^{N_p} X_k + X_{N_p+1}^e\right) = W_p + \frac{p}{\mu(1-p)} X_{N_p+1}^e, \quad (28)$$

where $X_{N_p+1}^e$ means that we construct $X_1^e, X_2^e, \ldots$ and then take a random index $N_p + 1$. In other words,

$$X_{N_p+1}^e = \sum_{n=0}^{\infty} X_{n+1}^e \mathbb{I}\{N_p = n\}.$$

It was explained in Section 2 that a generalized equilibrium distribution function $F_{W_p}^e(x)$ (see Definition 2) need not be a distribution function when the summands $X_1, X_2, \ldots$ can take values of different signs. However, employing this function, one can establish the following result.

Theorem 1. *Let $X_1, X_2, \ldots$ be a sequence of independent random variables having finite $\mathbb{E}[X_k] = \mu$, where $\mu \neq 0$, $k \in \mathbb{N}$. Assume that N_p and $(X_n)_{n \in \mathbb{N}}$ are independent, where $N_p \sim Geom(p)$, $0 < p < 1$. If $Z \sim Exp(1)$, then*

$$d_{\mathcal{H}_2}(W_p, Z) = \frac{\mathbb{E}[X_{N_p+1}^2]}{2\mu^2} \left(\frac{p}{1-p}\right) \quad (29)$$

where W_p was introduced in Equation (22).

Proof. If $\mathbb{E}[W_p^2] = \infty$, then $d_{\mathcal{H}_2}(W_p, Z) = \infty$ since, for a function $h(x) = x^2/2$, $x \in \mathbb{R}$, belonging to $\mathcal{H}_2$, one has $\mathbb{E}[h(W_p)] = \infty$, whereas $\mathbb{E}[h(Z)] < \infty$. According to Equation (23), $\mathbb{E}[W_p^2]$ and $\mathbb{E}[X_{N_p+1}^2]$ are both finite or infinite simultaneously. Consequently, Equation (29) is true when $\mathbb{E}[W_p^2] = \infty$.

Let us turn to the case $\mathbb{E}[W_p^2] < \infty$. At first, we obtain an upper bound for $d_{\mathcal{H}_2}(W_p, Z)$. Take $h \in \mathcal{H}_2$. Applying Lemmas 1 and 2 and Remark 1, one can write due to Stein's Equation (10) that

$$|\mathbb{E}[h(W_p)] - \mathbb{E}[h(Z)]| = |\mathbb{E}[f_h'(W_p)] - \mathbb{E}[f_h(W_p)] + f(0)|. \quad (30)$$

Using the generalized equilibrium distribution transformation (20) one obtains:

$$|\mathbb{E}[f'_h(W_p)] - \mathbb{E}[f_h(W_p)] + f(0)| = \left| \int_\mathbb{R} f'_h(x) \, dF_{W_p}(x) - \int_\mathbb{R} f'_h(x) \, dF^e_{W_p}(x) \right|. \quad (31)$$

Due to Lemma 3 this is true, for $h \in \mathcal{H}_2$, because $f_h \in \mathcal{H}_2$ according to Lemma 2 (with $\lambda = 1$). Next, we employ the relation

$$\int_\mathbb{R} f'_h(x) \, dF_{W_p}(x) - \int_\mathbb{R} f'_h(x) \, dF^e_{W_p}(x) = \int_\mathbb{R} f'_h(x) \, d(F_{W_p} - F^e_{W_p})(x). \quad (32)$$

Evidently, one can write $\int_\mathbb{R} |f'_h(x)| \, dF_{W_p}(x) < \infty$. The notation $dF^e_{W_p}(x)$ in the integral refers to the Lebesgue–Stieltjes integral with respect to a function $F^e_{W_p}(x)$ of bounded variation. In fact, the integral with integrator $dF^e_{W_p}(x)$ means that integration employs a signed measure $Q^+_p - Q^-_p$, where Q^+_p and Q^-_p have the following densities with respect to the Lebesgue measure:

$$q^+_p(x) := (1 - F_{W_p}(x))\mathbb{I}\{(0, \infty)\}, \quad q^-_p(x) := F_{W_p}(x)\mathbb{I}\{(-\infty, 0]\}, \quad x \in \mathbb{R},$$

we took into account that $\mathbb{E}[W_p] = 1$ according to Lemma 4. Then, for any $-\infty < a < b < \infty$, one ascertains that variation of $F^e_{W_p}$ on $[a, b]$ is given by formula $\mathrm{Var}^b_a(F^e_{W_p}) = \int^b_a |p^e_{W_p}(u)| \, du$ (see, e.g., Theorem 4.4.7 [46]). Note that for any $-\infty < a < b < \infty$,

$$\int^b_a |p^e_{W_p}(u)| \, du \leq \mathbb{E}|W_p| < \infty$$

according to Lemma 4. Thus, $F^e_{W_p}$ is a function of bounded variation. In the right-hand side of Equation (32), we take the Lebesgue–Stieltjes integral with respect to the function of bounded variation $(F_{W_p} - F^e_{W_p})(x), x \in \mathbb{R}$. Let $F^e_{W_p}(x) = F^e_{p,1}(x) - F^e_{p,2}(x), x \in \mathbb{R}$, where $F^e_{p,i}$ are nondecreasing right-continuous functions (even continuous since $F^e_{W_p}$ is continuous), $i = 1, 2$. Thus,

$$F_{W_p}(x) - F^e_{W_p}(x) = (F_{W_p}(x) + F^e_{p,2}(x)) - F^e_{p,1}(x), \quad x \in \mathbb{R}.$$

With the help of Equations (18) and (19) one makes sure that, for each $n \in \mathbb{N}$,

$$\int_{(-n,n]} f'_h(x) \, d(F_{W_p} - F^e_{W_p})(x) = \int_{(-n,n]} f'_h(x) \, d(F_{W_p}(x) + F^e_{p,2}(x)) - \int_{(-n,n]} f'_h(x) \, d(F^e_{p,1}(x))$$

$$= \int_{(-n,n]} f'_h(x) \, dF_{W_p}(x) + \int_{(-n,n]} f'_h(x) \, dF^e_{p,2}(x) - \int_{(-n,n]} f'_h(x) \, dF^e_{p,1}(x)$$

$$= \int_{(-n,n]} f'_h(x) \, dF_{W_p}(x) - \int_{(-n,n]} f'_h(x) \, d(F^e_{p,1}(x) - F^e_{p,2}(x))$$

$$= \int_{(-n,n]} f'_h(x) \, dF_{W_p}(x) - \int_{(-n,n]} f'_h(x) \, dF^e_{W_p}(x).$$

All the integrals in the latter formulas are finite. According to Lemma 2 and Remark 1, one can write $|f'_h(x)| \leq A_0|x| + B_0$, where A_0, B_0 are positive constants. Thus, the Lebesgue theorem on dominated convergence ensures that

$$\lim_{n \to \infty} \int_{(-n,n]} f'_h(x) \, dF_{W_p}(x) = \int_\mathbb{R} f'_h(x) \, dF_{W_p}(x),$$

where the latter integral is finite. Indeed,

$$\int_\mathbb{R} (A_0|x| + B_0) \, dF_{W_p}(x) = A_0 \mathbb{E}|W_p| + B_0 < \infty \quad (33)$$

according to Lemma 4. By the same Lemma, one has $\mathbb{E}[W_p] = 1$. Therefore, on account of Equation (17), the following relation holds:

$$\int_{(-n,n]} f_h'(x)\, dF_{W_p^e}(x) = \int_{(-n,0]} f_h'(x)(-F_{W_p}(x))dx + \int_{(0,n]} f_h'(x)(1 - F_{W_p}(x))dx,$$

whereas Corollary 2, Sec. 6, Ch. II of [47] and Lemma 4 entail that

$$\int_{(-\infty,0]} (A_0|x| + B_0) F_{W_p}(x) dx + \int_{(0,\infty)} (A_0|x| + B_0)(1 - F_{W_p}(x)) dx$$
$$\leq A_0 \mathbb{E}[W_p^2] + B_0 \mathbb{E}|W_p| < \infty. \quad (34)$$

The Lebesgue theorem on dominated convergence for σ-finite measures and Equation (34) yield

$$\lim_{n \to \infty} \int_{(-n,n]} f_h'(x) dF_{W_p}^e(x) = \int_{\mathbb{R}} f_h'(x) dF_{W_p}^e(x),$$

where the latter integral is finite. Now, we show that

$$\lim_{n \to \infty} \int_{(-n,n]} f_h'(x)\, d(F_{W_p} - F_{W_p}^e)(x) = \int_{\mathbb{R}} f_h'(x)\, d(F_{W_p} - F_{W_p}^e)(x). \quad (35)$$

Note that $f_h'(x)\mathbb{I}_{(-n,n]}(x) \to f_h'(x)$ at each $x \in \mathbb{R}$ as $n \to \infty$. To apply the version of the Lebesgue theorem to integrals over a signed measure, it suffices (see, e.g., [48], p. 74) to verify that

$$\int_{\mathbb{R}} |f_h'(x)| |d(F_{W_p} - F_{W_p}^e)(x)| < \infty,$$

where $|dG|$ means that one evaluates an integral with respect to the measure corresponding to the total variation of a measure determined by a right-continuous function G of bounded variation. The extension of the Lebesgue theorem on dominated convergence for signed measures is an immediate corollary of the Jordan decomposition mentioned above. Using this decomposition, one obtains the inequality

$$\int_{\mathbb{R}} |f_h'(x)| |d(F_{W_p} - F_{W_p}^e)(x)| \leq \int_{\mathbb{R}} |f_h'(x)| |dF_{W_p}(x)| + \int_{\mathbb{R}} |f_h'(x)| |dF_{W_p}^e(x)|.$$

Due to Remark 1 one has $|f_h'(x)| \leq A_0|x| + B_0$ for all $x \in \mathbb{R}$ and some positive constants A_0, B_0. Then, Equations (33) and (34) yield (as F_{W_p} generates probability measure)

$$\int_{\mathbb{R}} (A_0|x| + B_0) dF_{W_p}(x) + \int_{\mathbb{R}} (A_0|x| + B_0) |dF_{W_p}^e(x)| < \infty.$$

The functions f_h' and $F_{W_p} - F_{W_p}^e$ are right-continuous and have bounded variation. Then each of them can be represented as the difference of right-continuous nondecreasing functions, and using for any $n \in \mathbb{N}$ the integration by parts formula (see, e.g., Theorem 11, Sec. 6, Ch. 2, [47]), one has

$$\int_{(-n,n]} f_h'(x)\, d(F_{W_p} - F_{W_p}^e)(x)$$
$$= f_h'(x)(F_{W_p}(x) - F_{W_p}^e(x))\big|_{-n}^{n} - \int_{(-n,n]} (F_{W_p}(x) - F_{W_p}^e(x)) df_h'(x).$$

Since the integral in the right-hand side of Equation (35) is finite, it holds

$$f_h'(x)(F_{W_p}(x) - F_{W_p}^e(x)) \to 0, \quad x \to -\infty \text{ or } x \to \infty \quad (36)$$

(the proof is similar to the proof of Corollary 2, Sec. 6, Ch. 2 in [47]). Then,

$$\int_{\mathbb{R}} f'_h(x) \, d(F_{W_p} - F^e_{W_p})(x) = -\lim_{n\to\infty} \int_{(-n,n]} (F_{W_p}(x) - F^e_{W_p}(x)) d f'_h(x).$$

The function f'_h is absolutely continuous according to Lemma 2. Hence (see also Equations (36) and (A12) in Appendix A) we get

$$\left| \int_{\mathbb{R}} f'_h(x) \, d(F_{W_p}(x) - F^e_{W_p}(x)) \right| = \lim_{n\to\infty} \left| \int_{(-n,n]} (F_{W_p}(x) - F^e_{W_p}(x)) f''_h(x) \, dx \right|$$
$$\leq \|f''_h\|_\infty \int_{\mathbb{R}} |F_{W_p}(x) - F^e_{W_p}(x)| \, dx \leq \int_{\mathbb{R}} |F_{W_p}(x) - F^e_{W_p}(x)| \, dx, \quad (37)$$

because $\|f''_h\|_\infty \leq \|h'\|_\infty \leq 1$ due to Lemmas 1 and 2. Using the homogeneity of the Kantorovich metric for signed measures which is derived from formula (20) of [22] (see Lemma 1 (a) there) and applying Lemma 3 of that paper, we can write

$$\int_{\mathbb{R}} |F_{W_p}(x) - F^e_{W_p}(x)| \, dx = \frac{p}{|\mu|(1-p)} \int_{\mathbb{R}} |F_{S_{N_p}}(x) - F^e_{S_{N_p}}(x)| \, dx$$
$$\leq \frac{\mathbb{E}[X^2_{N_p+1}]}{2\mu^2} \left(\frac{p}{1-p} \right). \quad (38)$$

Relations (30), (31), (32), (37), (38) and Lemmas 1 and 2 guarantee that $d_{\mathcal{H}_2}(W_p, Z)$ does not exceed the right-hand side of Equation (29).

Now, we turn to the lower bounds for $d_{\mathcal{H}_2}(W_p, Z)$. Choose $h(x) = x^2/2$ as the test function. Since $h \in \mathcal{H}_2$, we can write

$$d_{\mathcal{H}_2}(W_p, Z) \geq |\mathbb{E}[h(W_p)] - \mathbb{E}[h(Z)]| = \frac{1}{2} |\mathbb{E}[W_p^2] - \mathbb{E}[Z^2]|. \quad (39)$$

For a random variable Z following the exponential law $Exp(1)$, one has $\mathbb{E}[Z^2] = 2$. Formula (23) of Lemma 4 yields

$$d_{\mathcal{H}_2}(W_p, Z) \geq \frac{\mathbb{E}[X^2_{N_p+1}]}{2\mu^2} \left(\frac{p}{1-p} \right).$$

Taking into account formula (38), we come to the desired statement. The proof is complete. □

Remark 3. *Evidently,*

$$\mathbb{E}[X^2_{N_p+1}] = \sum_{n=0}^{\infty} \mathbb{E}[X^2_{n+1}] p(1-p)^n.$$

Thus, one obtains

$$\mathbb{E}[X^2_{N_p+1}] \leq \sup_{n \in \mathbb{N}} \mathbb{E}[X^2_n],$$

and the latter inequality becomes an equality when $\mathbb{E}[X^2_n] = \mathbb{E}[X^2_1]$ for all $n \in \mathbb{N}$. Therefore, the statement of Theorem 1 can be written as follows

$$d_{\mathcal{H}_2}(W_p, Z) \leq \frac{\sup_{n\in\mathbb{N}} \mathbb{E}[X^2_n]}{2\mu^2} \left(\frac{p}{1-p} \right),$$

and this becomes an equality when $\mathbb{E}[X^2_n] = \mathbb{E}[X^2_1]$ for all $n \in \mathbb{N}$.

Remark 4. *In [22], the authors proved the following inequality*

$$d_{\mathcal{H}_2}(W_p, Z) \leq \frac{3\mathbb{E}[X^2_{N_p+1}]}{2\mu^2} \left(\frac{p}{1-p} \right).$$

We established the sharp estimate with a factor $1/2$ instead of $3/2$ having employed Equation (20) for a class of functions comprising solutions of the Stein equation for $h \in \mathcal{H}_2$. The estimate with factor $1/2$ was also obtained in the recent paper [49] but for i.i.d. summands. The lower bounds were not provided there. In our Theorem 1, the summands have the same expectations but need not have the same distribution.

Remark 5. *If the summands of W_p are non-negative, we consider W_p^e appearing in Equation (28). Applying Theorem 1(i) [22] to relation (29), one obtains*

$$d_{\mathcal{H}_1}(W_p^e, Z) = \frac{\mathbb{E}[X_{N_p+1}^2]}{2\mu^2} \frac{p}{1-p}.$$

For $i \in \mathbb{N}$, consider a random variable X_i having distribution $Exp(1/\mu)$. Then $X_i^e \sim Exp(1/\mu)$, and, consequently, $X_{N_p+1}^e \sim Exp(1/\mu)$. We can choose X_i^e, $i \in \mathbb{N}$, according to Remark 2. Then, the distribution of W_p^e will be the same if we change $X_{N_p+1}^e$ to X_{N_p+1} in Equation (28). In such a way, W_p^e is a normalized sum of a random number of independent random variables. Using the homogeneity of the Kantorovich metric, one has

$$d_{\mathcal{H}_1}\left(\frac{p}{\mu}\sum_{k=1}^{N_p+1} X_k, (1-p)Z\right) = (1-p)d_{\mathcal{H}_1}\left(\frac{p}{\mu(1-p)}\sum_{k=1}^{N_p+1} X_k, Z\right) = \frac{\mathbb{E}[X_{N_p+1}^2]}{2\mu^2}p. \quad (40)$$

Therefore, for an arbitrary sequence $(X_k)_{k \in \mathbb{N}}$ satisfying conditions of Theorem 1, the upper bound for the left-hand side of Equation (40) is not less than the right-hand side of Equation (40).

4. Limit Theorem for Geometric Sums of Exchangeable Random Variables

Now, we consider exchangeable random variables $X_1, X_2, \ldots$ satisfying the dependence condition proposed in [35]. Namely, assume that for all $n \in \mathbb{N}$, $t_j \in \mathbb{R}$ ($j = 1, \ldots, n$) and some $\rho \in [0, 1]$

$$\mathbb{E}\left[e^{i(t_1 X_1 + \ldots + t_n X_n)}\right] = \rho \mathbb{E}\left[e^{i X_1(t_1 + \ldots + t_n)}\right] + (1-\rho)\prod_{j=1}^{n} \mathbb{E}\left[e^{i t_j X_j}\right], \quad (41)$$

where $i^2 = -1$. The cases of $\rho = 0$ and $\rho = 1$ correspond, respectively, to independent random variables and those possessing the property of comonotonicity. The latter means that for $\rho = 1$ the joint behavior of $X_1, \ldots, X_n$ is strongly correlated and coincides with one of a vector $(X_1, \ldots, X_1)$.

Theorem 2. *Let $X_1, X_2 \ldots$ be exchangeable random variables with $\mathbb{E}[X_1] = \mu$, $\mu \neq 0$ satisfying condition (41) for some $\rho \in (0, 1)$. Suppose that $(X_n)_{n \in \mathbb{N}}$ and N_p are independent, where $N_p \sim Geom(p)$, $p \in (0, 1)$. In contrast to the Rényi theorem, one has*

$$W_p \xrightarrow{\mathcal{D}} Y, \quad p \to 0+,$$

where the law of Y is the following mixture

$$\mathbb{P}_Y = \rho \mathbb{P}_{VX_1/\mu} + (1-\rho)\mathbb{P}_Z, \quad (42)$$

random variables X_1, V are independent and $V \sim Exp(1)$, $Z \sim Exp(1)$.

Proof. Let $\widetilde{X}_1, \widetilde{X}_2, \ldots$ be independent copies of $X_1, X_2, \ldots$, respectively. Suppose that $\widetilde{X}_1, \widetilde{X}_2, \ldots$ are independent with N_p. Set $S_0 := 0$, $\widetilde{S}_0 := 0$, $\widetilde{S}_n := \widetilde{X}_1 + \ldots + \widetilde{X}_n$, $n \in \mathbb{N}$. Denote the characteristic function of a random variable ξ by $f_\xi(t)$, $t \in \mathbb{R}$. For each $t \in \mathbb{R}$, using Equation (41), one has

$$f_{S_{N_p}}(t) = \sum_{n=0}^{\infty} \mathbb{E}\left[e^{itS_n}\right]\mathbb{P}(N_p = n)$$

$$= \mathbb{P}(N_p = 0) + \sum_{n=1}^{\infty} \left(\rho\mathbb{E}\left[e^{iX_1 tn}\right] + (1-\rho)\prod_{j=1}^{n}\mathbb{E}\left[e^{it\tilde{X}_j}\right]\right)\mathbb{P}(N_p = n)$$

$$= p + \sum_{n=0}^{\infty} \left(\rho\mathbb{E}\left[e^{iX_1 tn}\right] + (1-\rho)\prod_{j=1}^{n}\mathbb{E}\left[e^{it\tilde{X}_j}\right]\right)\mathbb{P}(N_p = n) - \rho p - (1-\rho)p$$

$$= \rho f_{X_1 N_p}(t) + (1-\rho)\sum_{n=0}^{\infty} f_{\tilde{S}_n}(t)\mathbb{P}(N_p = n) = \rho f_{X_1 N_p}(t) + (1-\rho)f_{\tilde{S}_{N_p}}(t).$$

For each $t \in \mathbb{R}$, one has

$$f_{W_p}(t) = \rho f_{\frac{p}{\mu(1-p)}X_1 N_p}(t) + (1-\rho)f_{\widetilde{W}_p}(t), \tag{43}$$

where $\widetilde{W}_p = \frac{p}{\mu(1-p)}\sum_{j=1}^{N_p}\tilde{X}_j$.

According to the classical Rényi theorem, $\widetilde{W}_p \xrightarrow{D} Z$ as $p \to 0+$, where $Z \sim Exp(1)$. Note that $T_p := \frac{p}{1-p}N_p \xrightarrow{D} V$ as $p \to 0+$, where $V \sim Exp(1)$. In fact, one can apply Theorem 1 with $X_j \equiv 1, j \in \mathbb{N}$ to check this. For each $t \in \mathbb{R}$, taking into account that T_p and X_1 are independent and applying the Lebesgue theorem on dominated convergence, we see that

$$\mathbb{E}\left[e^{itT_p X_1}\right] = \mathbb{E}\left[\mathbb{E}e^{itT_p X_1}|X_1\right] = \int_{\mathbb{R}}e^{itT_p x}dF_{X_1}(x) \to \int_{\mathbb{R}}e^{itVx}dF_{X_1}(x) = \mathbb{E}\left[e^{itVX_1}\right], \ p \to 0+,$$

since X_1 and V are independent. Hence,

$$\frac{p}{\mu(1-p)}X_1 N_p \xrightarrow{D} \frac{VX_1}{\mu}, \ p \to 0+$$

is true. In light of Equation (43),

$$W_p \xrightarrow{D} Y, \ p \to 0+,$$

here the law of Y is the mixture of distributions VX_1/μ and Z provided by Equation (42). The proof is complete. □

Theorem 3. *Assume that N_p and $(X_n)_{n\in\mathbb{N}}$ satisfy conditions of Theorem 2. Let $\mu_2 = \mathbb{E}[X_1^2]$. Then,*

$$d_{\mathcal{H}_2}(W_p, Y) = \frac{\mu_2}{2\mu^2}\left(\frac{p}{1-p}\right). \tag{44}$$

Proof. Relation (43) for characteristic functions implies that the following equality of distributions holds

$$W_p \stackrel{D}{=} \frac{p}{\mu(1-p)}\left((1-\mathbb{I}_\rho)N_p X_1 + \mathbb{I}_\rho \tilde{S}_{N_p}\right), \tag{45}$$

where indicator $\mathbb{I}_\rho$ equals 1 and 0 with probabilities $1-\rho$ and ρ, respectively, and is independent of all the variables under consideration. Assume at first that $\mu_2 < \infty$. Then, for $h \in \mathcal{H}_2$,

$$\mathbb{E}[h(W_p)] = \rho\mathbb{E}\left[h\left(\frac{p}{\mu(1-p)}N_p X_1\right)\right] + (1-\rho)\mathbb{E}[h(\widetilde{W}_p)].$$

In view of Equation (42) one has

$$\mathbb{E}[h(Y)] = \rho \mathbb{E}\left[h\left(\frac{VX_1}{\mu}\right)\right] + (1-\rho)\mathbb{E}[h(Z)].$$

The latter two formulas and the triangle inequality yield

$$|\mathbb{E}[h(W_p)] - \mathbb{E}[h(Y)]|$$
$$\leq \rho \left| \mathbb{E}\left[h\left(\frac{p}{\mu(1-p)}N_p X_1\right)\right] - \mathbb{E}\left[h\left(\frac{VX_1}{\mu}\right)\right] \right| + (1-\rho)\left|\mathbb{E}[h(\widetilde{W}_p)] - \mathbb{E}[h(Z)]\right|. \quad (46)$$

By means of Theorem 1 we have

$$\sup_{h \in \mathcal{H}_2} |\mathbb{E}[h(\widetilde{W}_p)] - \mathbb{E}[h(Z)]| = \frac{\mu_2}{2\mu^2}\left(\frac{p}{1-p}\right). \quad (47)$$

For each $h \in \mathcal{H}_2$, taking into account the independence of X_1, N_p, V, one can write

$$\left|\mathbb{E}\left[h\left(\frac{p}{\mu(1-p)}N_p X_1\right)\right] - \mathbb{E}\left[h\left(\frac{VX_1}{\mu}\right)\right]\right|$$
$$= \left|\int_\mathbb{R} \left(\mathbb{E}\left[h\left(\frac{p}{\mu(1-p)}N_p X_1\right)\right] - \mathbb{E}\left[h\left(\frac{xV}{\mu}\right)\right]\right) dF_{X_1}(x)\right|.$$

Due to homogeneity of $d_{\mathcal{H}_2}$ we infer from Theorem 1 that

$$\sup_{h \in \mathcal{H}_2}\left|\mathbb{E}\left[h\left(\frac{p}{\mu(1-p)}N_p X_1\right)\right] - \mathbb{E}\left[h\left(\frac{xV}{\mu}\right)\right]\right| = d_{\mathcal{H}_2}\left(\frac{px}{\mu(1-p)}N_p, \frac{xV}{\mu}\right)$$
$$= \left(\frac{x}{\mu}\right)^2 d_{\mathcal{H}_2}\left(\frac{p}{(1-p)}\sum_{k=1}^{N_p}1, V\right) = \frac{1}{2}\left(\frac{x}{\mu}\right)^2 \frac{p}{1-p}.$$

Consequently, it holds

$$\left|\mathbb{E}\left[h\left(\frac{p}{\mu(1-p)}N_p X_1\right)\right] - \mathbb{E}\left[h\left(\frac{VX_1}{\mu}\right)\right]\right|$$
$$\leq \frac{p}{2(1-p)}\int_\mathbb{R}\left(\frac{x}{\mu}\right)^2 dF_{X_1}(x) = \frac{\mu_2}{2\mu^2}\left(\frac{p}{1-p}\right). \quad (48)$$

Equations (46), (47) and (48) lead to the upper bound for $d_{\mathcal{H}_2}(W_p, Y)$.

Note that a function $h(x) = x^2/2$, $x \in \mathbb{R}$, belongs to $\in \mathcal{H}_2$ and therefore

$$\sup_{\mathcal{H}_2}|\mathbb{E}[h(W_p)] - \mathbb{E}[h(Y)]| \geq \frac{1}{2}\left(\mathbb{E}[W_p^2] - \mathbb{E}[Y^2]\right). \quad (49)$$

Note that $\mathbb{E}[Z^2] = \mathbb{E}[V^2] = 2$ because $Z \sim Exp(1)$ and $V \sim Exp(1)$. The random variables X_1, V, Z are independent. Thus, in light of Equation (42), one has

$$\mathbb{E}[Y^2] = 2\rho\frac{\mu_2}{\mu^2} + 2(1-\rho). \quad (50)$$

By means of Equations (45), (23) and (25) we obtain

$$\mathbb{E}[W_p^2] = \left(\frac{p}{\mu(1-p)}\right)^2 \rho \mathbb{E}[N_p^2]\mathbb{E}[X_1^2] + (1-\rho)\mathbb{E}[\widetilde{W}_p^2]$$
$$= \left(\frac{p}{\mu(1-p)}\right)^2 \rho \frac{(1-p)(2-p)}{p^2}\mu_2 + (1-\rho)\left(\frac{p}{\mu^2(1-p)}\mu_2 + 2\right) =$$
$$= \frac{\mu_2}{\mu^2}\left(\rho\frac{2-p}{1-p} + (1-\rho)\frac{p}{1-p}\right) + 2(1-\rho). \quad (51)$$

Equations (50) and (51) permit to find $\mathbb{E}[W_p^2] - \mathbb{E}[Y^2]$. Hence Equation (49) leads to the inequality

$$\sup_{\mathcal{H}_2}|\mathbb{E}[h(W_p)] - \mathbb{E}[h(Y)]|$$

$$\geq \left(\frac{1}{2}\right)\frac{\mu_2}{\mu^2}\left(\rho\left(\frac{2-p}{1-p}-2\right) + (1-\rho)\frac{p}{1-p}\right) = \left(\frac{1}{2}\right)\frac{\mu_2}{\mu^2}\frac{p}{1-p}. \quad (52)$$

Now, let $\mu_2 = \infty$. Then, $d_{\mathcal{H}_2}(W_p, Y) = \infty$ according to Equation (52). The proof is complete. □

5. Convergence of Random Sums of Independent Summands to Generalized Gamma Distribution

Statements concerning weak convergence of geometric sums distributions to exponential law are often just particular cases of more general results concerning the convergence of random sums of random summands to generalized gamma law when the number of summands follows the generalized negative binomial distribution, see, e.g., [27,29,49]). The recent work [29] demonstrated how it is possible to study the mentioned general case employing the estimates of proximity of geometric sums distributions to exponential law. We introduce some notation to apply Theorem 1 for analysis of the distance between the distributions of random sums and the generalized gamma law.

Introduce a random variable $G_{r,\lambda}$ such that $G_{r,\lambda} \sim G(r,\lambda)$, where $G(r,\lambda)$ is the gamma law with positive parameters r and λ, i.e., its density with respect to the Lebesgue measure has the form

$$g(z;r,\lambda) = \frac{\lambda^r z^{r-1}}{\Gamma(r)} e^{-\lambda z}\mathbb{I}_{(0,\infty)}(z), \quad z \in \mathbb{R},$$

$\Gamma(r)$ being the gamma function. For $r = 1$, one has $G(1,\lambda) = Exp(\lambda)$. Clearly, for $a > 0$, $aG_{r,\lambda} \sim G(r,\lambda/a)$. Set $G_{r,\alpha,\lambda}^* := G_{r,\lambda}^{1/\alpha}$, where $\alpha > 0$. One says that random variable $G_{r,\alpha,\lambda}^*$ has the generalized gamma distribution $G^*(r,\alpha,\lambda)$. According to Equation (5) of [29], the density of $G_{r,\alpha,\lambda}^*$ is given by formula

$$g^*(z;r,\alpha,\lambda) = \frac{|\alpha|\lambda^r z^{\alpha r-1}}{\Gamma(r)} e^{-\lambda z^\alpha}\mathbb{I}_{(0,\infty)}(z), \quad z \in \mathbb{R}.$$

Also it is known (see Equation (6) in [29]) that, for $r \in (0,1)$, $\alpha \in (0,1]$ and $\lambda > 0$, the following relation holds

$$g^*(z;r,\alpha,\lambda) = \int_0^1 \frac{u}{1-u} e^{-\frac{u}{1-u}z} q(u;r,\alpha,\lambda)\,du, \quad z > 0, \quad (53)$$

where q is a density of a specified random variable $Y_{r,\alpha,\lambda}$ such that support of its distribution belongs to $(0,1)$ (see Remark 3 [49]). We only note that for $\alpha = 1$ the density q admits a representation

$$q\left(u;r,1,\frac{b}{1-b}\right) = b^r\left(\frac{\sin \pi r}{\pi}\right)\frac{(1-u)^{r-1}}{u(u-b)^r}\mathbb{I}_{(b,1)}(u), \quad b \in (0,1).$$

Consider a random variable $N_{r,\alpha,p}^*$ having the generalized negative binomial distribution $GNB(r,\alpha,p)$, where $r > 0$, $\alpha \neq 0$ and $p \in (0,1)$, i.e.,

$$\mathbb{P}(N_{r,\alpha,p}^* = k) = \int_0^\infty \frac{z^k}{k!} e^{-z} g^*\left(z;r,\alpha,\frac{p}{1-p}\right) dz, \quad k = 0, 1, \ldots \quad (54)$$

Thus $GNB(r,\alpha,p)$ has a mixed Poisson distribution. One can verify that $GNB(r,1,p)$ coincides with $NB(r,p)$, where $NB(r,p)$ is the negative binomial law. Recall that $N_{r,p} \sim NB(r,p)$ if

$$\mathbb{P}(N_{r,p} = k) = \frac{\Gamma(k+r)}{k!\Gamma(r)} p^r (1-p)^k, \ k = 0, 1, \ldots$$

Note also that $N_{1,p} \sim Geom(p)$.

Introduce the random variables

$$W^*_{r,\alpha,p} := \frac{1}{\mu}\left(\frac{p}{1-p}\right)^{1/\alpha} \sum_{k=1}^{N^*_{r,\alpha,p}} X_k, \quad S^*_{r,\alpha,p} := \sum_{k=1}^{N^*_{r,\alpha,p}} X_k, \tag{55}$$

where $N^*_{r,\alpha,p} \sim GNB(r,\alpha,p)$, $r > 0$, $\alpha \neq 0$, $p \in (0,1)$, and $\mathbb{E}[X_k] = \mu$, $\mu \neq 0$, $k \in \mathbb{N}$. We assume that $(X_n)_{n\in\mathbb{N}}$ and $N^*_{r,\alpha,p}$ are independent, where $r > 0$, $\alpha \neq 0$, $p \in (0,1)$.

Theorem 4. *Let $(X_n)_{n\in\mathbb{N}}$ be a sequence of independent random variables having $\mathbb{E}[X_n] = \mu$, $\mu \neq 0$, $n \in \mathbb{N}$. Then, for $W^*_{r,\alpha,p}$ introduced in Equation (55) with parameters $r \in (0,1)$, $\alpha \in (0,1]$, $p \in (0,1)$ and $G_{r,1}$ having the gamma distribution $G(r,1)$, the following relation holds*

$$d_{\mathcal{H}_2}(W^*_{r,\alpha,p}, G^{1/\alpha}_{r,1}) = \frac{1}{2\mu^2}\left(\frac{p}{1-p}\right)^{2/\alpha} \int_0^1 \mathbb{E}[X^2_{N_u+1}]\left(\frac{1-u}{u}\right) q\left(u; r, \alpha, \frac{p}{1-p}\right) du, \tag{56}$$

whenever the right-hand side of Equation (56) is finite. Here, $N_u := N^*_{1,1,u}$, $N_u \sim Geom(u)$, $u \in (0,1)$ and q appeared in Equation (53).

Proof. Without loss of generality, we can assume that $\mu = 1$; otherwise, we consider $\widetilde{X}_n := \frac{X_n}{\mu}$, $n \in \mathbb{N}$. For such sequence, $\mathbb{E}[\widetilde{X}^2_{N_u+1}] = \frac{1}{\mu^2}\mathbb{E}[X^2_{N_u+1}]$. Note that $\frac{1-p}{p}G_{r,1}$ has the same distribution as $G_{r,p/(1-p)}$. Applying the homogeneity property of the ideal probability metric of order two, one has

$$d_{\mathcal{H}_2}(W^*_{r,\alpha,p}, G^{1/\alpha}_{r,1}) = \left(\frac{p}{1-p}\right)^{2/\alpha} d_{\mathcal{H}_2}\left(S^*_{r,\alpha,p}, G^{1/\alpha}_{r,p/(1-p)}\right).$$

The proof of Theorem 1 [29] starts with establishing for any bounded Borel function h, $r \in (0,1)$, $\alpha \in (0,1]$ and $p \in (0,1)$, that

$$\mathbb{E}\left[h(G^{1/\alpha}_{r,p/(1-p)})\right] = \int_0^1 \mathbb{E}\left[h\left(\frac{1-u}{u}Z\right)\right] q\left(u; r, \alpha, \frac{p}{1-p}\right) du, \tag{57}$$

where $Z \sim Exp(1)$, and

$$\mathbb{E}\left[h(S^*_{r,\alpha,p})\right] = \int_0^1 \mathbb{E}\left[h(S^*_{1,1,u})\right] q\left(u; r, \alpha, \frac{p}{1-p}\right) du. \tag{58}$$

Let us examine these relations for each $h \in \mathcal{H}_2$. Recall that in light of Remark 1 $|h(x)| \leq A_0 x^2 + B_0$ for some positive constants A_0 and B_0 (which depend on h), we write $h = h^+ - h^-$, where $h^+(x) := h(x)\mathbb{I}\{h(x) \geq 0\}$, $h^-(x) := -h(x)\mathbb{I}\{h(x) \leq 0\}$. Set $h_n(x) := h^+(x)\mathbb{I}_{(-n,n]}(x)$, $n \in \mathbb{N}$. Then, h_n and $n \in \mathbb{N}$ are bounded Borel functions such that for each $x \in \mathbb{R}$, $0 \leq h_n(x) \nearrow h^+(x)$ as $n \to \infty$. Hence, the monotone convergence theorem yields

$$\mathbb{E}\left[h^+(G^{1/\alpha}_{r,p/(1-p)})\right] = \lim_{n\to\infty} \mathbb{E}\left[h_n(G^{1/\alpha}_{r,p/(1-p)})\right].$$

Note that, for each $u \in (0,1)$, $\mathbb{E}\left[h_n\left(\frac{1-u}{u}Z\right)\right] \nearrow \mathbb{E}\left[h^+\left(\frac{1-u}{u}Z\right)\right]$. Applying the monotone convergence theorem once again, we obtain

$$\int_0^1 \mathbb{E}\left[h^+\left(\frac{1-u}{u}Z\right)\right] q\left(u; r, \alpha, \frac{p}{1-p}\right) du = \lim_{n\to\infty} \int_0^1 \mathbb{E}\left[h_n\left(\frac{1-u}{u}Z\right)\right] q\left(u; r, \alpha, \frac{p}{1-p}\right) du.$$

So, Equation (57) is valid if instead of h belonging to $\mathcal{H}_2$ we write h^+. Obviously, $0 \leq h^+(x) \leq |h(x)| \leq A_0 x^2 + B_0$, $x \in \mathbb{R}$, $n \in \mathbb{R}$. Thus,

$$\mathbb{E}\left[h^+\left(G^{1/\alpha}_{r,p/(1-p)}\right)^2\right] \leq A_0 \mathbb{E}(G^{2/\alpha}_{r,p/(1-p)}) + B_0 < \infty.$$

According to [27] (page 8), for $\delta > 0$, one has

$$\mathbb{E}[(G^*_{r,\alpha,\lambda})^\delta] = \frac{\Gamma(r + \frac{\delta}{\alpha})}{\lambda^{\delta/\alpha} \Gamma(r)}. \tag{59}$$

This permits us to write $\mathbb{E}(G^{2/\alpha}_{r,p/(1-p)}) = \mathbb{E}\left[(G^*_{r,1,p/(1-p)})^{2/\alpha}\right] < \infty$.

In the same manner, we demonstrate that Equation (57) is valid if instead of $h \in \mathcal{H}_2$ we take h^-. Moreover, $\mathbb{E}[h^-(G^{1/\alpha}_{r,p/(1-p)})]$ is finite. Therefore, Equation (57) holds for any $h \in \mathcal{H}_2$, and for such h, $\mathbb{E}[h(G^{1/\alpha}_{r,p/(1-p)})]$ is finite.

By the monotone convergence theorem $\mathbb{E}[h^+(S^*_{r,\alpha,p})] = \lim_{n \to \infty} \mathbb{E}[h_n(S^*_{r,\alpha,p})]$. In a similar way, $\mathbb{E}[h_n(S^*_{1,1,u})] \nearrow \mathbb{E}[h^+(S^*_{1,1,u})]$ as $n \to \infty$, and applying this theorem once again, we obtain

$$\int_0^1 \mathbb{E}[h^+(S^*_{1,1,u})] q\left(u; r, \alpha, \frac{p}{1-p}\right) du = \lim_{n \to \infty} \int_0^1 \mathbb{E}[h_n(S^*_{1,1,u})] q\left(u; r, \alpha, \frac{p}{1-p}\right) du.$$

Taking into account that Equation (58) is valid for bounded Borel functions h_n, one ascertains that Equation (58) holds if we replace h by h^+. To show the latter integral is finite, we note that $0 \leq h^+(x) \leq |h(x)| \leq A_0 x^2 + B_0$, for some positive A_0, B_0 and all $x \in \mathbb{R}$. Formula (23) of Lemma 4 yields, for each $u \in (0, 1)$,

$$\mathbb{E}[(S^*_{1,1,u})^2] \leq \frac{1-u}{u} \mathbb{E}[X^2_{N_u+1}] + 2\frac{(1-u)^2}{u^2}.$$

It was assumed above that the right-hand side of Equation (56) is finite. So,

$$\int_0^1 \mathbb{E}\left(A_0\left(\frac{1-u}{u} \mathbb{E}[X^2_{N_u+1}] + 2\frac{(1-u)^2}{u^2}\right) + B_0\right) q\left(u; r, \alpha, \frac{p}{1-p}\right) du < \infty,$$

since in light of Equation (57), taking $h(x) = 1$ and $h(x) = \frac{x^2}{2}$ (these functions belong to $\mathcal{H}_2$), $x \in \mathbb{R}$, we obtain, respectively,

$$\int_0^1 q\left(u; r, \alpha, \frac{p}{1-p}\right) du = 1,$$

$$\mathbb{E}[Z^2] \int_0^1 \frac{(1-u)^2}{u^2} q\left(u; r, \alpha, \frac{p}{1-p}\right) du = \mathbb{E}(G^{2/\alpha}_{r,p/(1-p)}) < \infty. \tag{60}$$

We demonstrate analogously that Equation (58) holds upon replacing $h \in \mathcal{H}_2$ with h^- and if the right-hand side of Equation (56) is finite, it follows that

$$\int_0^1 \mathbb{E}[h^-(S^*_{1,1,u})] q\left(u; r, \alpha, \frac{p}{1-p}\right) du$$

is finite as well. Consequently, Equation (58) is established for each $h \in \mathcal{H}_2$ (whenever the right-hand side of Equation (56) is finite) and $\mathbb{E}[h(S^*_{r,\alpha,p})]$ is finite for such h. Therefore, for $h \in \mathcal{H}_2$ and fixed α, r, p, one has

$$\mathbb{E}[h(S^*_{r,\alpha,p})] - \mathbb{E}[h(G^{1/\alpha}_{r,p/(1-p)})]$$
$$= \int_0^1 \left(\mathbb{E}[h(S^*_{1,1,u})] - \mathbb{E}\left[h\left(\frac{1-u}{u}Z\right)\right] \right) q\left(u;r,\alpha,\frac{p}{1-p}\right) du =: J(h).$$

By Theorem 1, for $h \in \mathcal{H}_2$, it holds

$$\left| \mathbb{E}[h(S^*_{1,1,u})] - \mathbb{E}\left[h\left(\frac{1-u}{u}Z\right)\right] \right| \le d_{\mathcal{H}_2}\left(S^*_{1,1,u}, \frac{1-u}{u}Z\right) = \left(\frac{1-u}{u}\right)^2 d_{\mathcal{H}_2}\left(\frac{u}{1-u}S^*_{1,1,u}, Z\right)$$

$$\le \left(\frac{1-u}{u}\right)^2 \frac{u}{1-u}\left(\frac{1}{2}\right)\mathbb{E}[X^2_{N_u+1}] = \left(\frac{1}{2}\right)\frac{1-u}{u}\mathbb{E}[X^2_{N_u+1}],$$

where we take into account that $N^*_{1,1,u} \sim NB(1,u)$, and $NB(1,u)$ coincides with $Geom(u)$. Thus, $\frac{u}{1-u}S^*_{1,1,u}$ can be written as

$$\frac{u}{1-u}\sum_{k=1}^{N_u} X_k,$$

where $N_u \sim Geom(u)$, N_u and $(X_k)_{k \in \mathbb{N}}$ are independent.

Therefore, for each $h \in \mathcal{H}_2$, $\left(\frac{p}{1-p}\right)^{2/\alpha}|J(h)|$ is bounded by the right-hand side of Equation (56), and so the desired upper bound is obtained (recall that $\mu = 1$).

Now, we turn to the lower bound of $d_{\mathcal{H}_2}(W^*_{r,\alpha,p}, G^{1/\alpha}_{r,1})$. Take $h(x) = x^2/2$ belonging to $\mathcal{H}_2$. Then, applying Equation (23) to evaluate $\mathbb{E}\left[(S^*_{1,1,u})^2\right]$, one has

$$d_{\mathcal{H}_2}(W^*_{r,\alpha,p}, G^{1/\alpha}_{r,1})$$
$$\ge \frac{1}{2}\left(\frac{p}{1-p}\right)^{2/\alpha} \left| \int_0^1 \left(\mathbb{E}[(S^*_{1,1,u})^2] - \left(\frac{1-u}{u}\right)^2 \mathbb{E}[G^2_{1,1}] \right) q\left(u;r,\frac{p}{1-p}\right) du \right|$$
$$= \frac{1}{2}\left(\frac{p}{1-p}\right)^{2/\alpha} \int_0^1 \left(\frac{1-u}{u}\right) \mathbb{E}[X^2_{N_u+1}] q\left(u;r,\frac{p}{1-p}\right) du, \quad (61)$$

where $G_{1,1} = Z \sim Exp(1)$. Thus, Equation (61) completes the proof. □

Corollary 1. *Let conditions of Theorem 4 be satisfied and also $\mu_2 = \sup_{n \in \mathbb{N}} \mathbb{E}[X^2_n] < \infty$. Then, the right-hand side of Equation (56) is finite and*

$$d_{\mathcal{H}_2}(W^*_{r,\alpha,p}, G^{1/\alpha}_{r,1}) \le \frac{\mu_2}{2\mu^2}\left(\frac{p}{1-p}\right)^{1/\alpha} \frac{\Gamma(r+\frac{1}{\alpha})}{\Gamma(r)}.$$

The inequality becomes an equality if $\mu_2 = \mathbb{E}[X^2_n]$ for all $n \in \mathbb{N}$. In particular, if $\alpha = 1$ then $\frac{\Gamma(r+1)}{\Gamma(r)} = r$.

Proof. According to Equation (57), for $h(x) = x$, $x \in \mathbb{R}$,

$$\mathbb{E}[G^{1/\alpha}_{r,p/(1-p)}] = \mathbb{E}[Z] \int_0^1 \left(\frac{1-u}{u}\right) q\left(u;r,\alpha,\frac{p}{1-p}\right) du.$$

Thus, the following relation is valid.

$$\int_0^1 \left(\frac{1-u}{u}\right) q\left(u;r,\alpha,\frac{p}{1-p}\right) du = \mathbb{E}[G^{1/\alpha}_{r,p/(1-p)}]. \quad (62)$$

Due to [27] (see page 8 there), for $\delta > 0$, one has $\mathbb{E}[G^*_{r,\alpha,\lambda}] = \frac{\Gamma(r+1/\alpha)}{\lambda^{1/\alpha}\Gamma(r)}$. Therefore,

$$\mathbb{E}[G_{r,p/(1-p)}^{1/\alpha}] = \mathbb{E}[G_{r,\alpha,p/(1-p)}^{*}] = \left(\frac{1-p}{p}\right)^{\frac{1}{\alpha}} \frac{\Gamma(r+\frac{1}{\alpha})}{\Gamma(r)}.$$

For $\alpha = 1$, we obtain $\mathbb{E}[G_{r,p/(1-p)}] = \frac{1-p}{p}\frac{\Gamma(r+1)}{\Gamma(r)} = r\frac{(1-p)}{p}$. □

6. Convergence of Random Sums of Exchangeable Summands to Generalized Gamma Distribution

Consider the model of exchangeable random variables $X_1, X_2, \ldots$ described in Section 4. Introduce the distribution of a random variable $U_{r,\alpha,\lambda}^{*}$ as the following mixture

$$\mathbb{P}_{U_{r,\alpha,\lambda}^{*}} = \rho \mathbb{P}_{\left(\frac{V_{r,\alpha,\lambda}^{*} X_1}{\mu}\right)} + (1-\rho) \mathbb{P}_{Z_{r,\alpha,\lambda}^{*}}, \tag{63}$$

where $\rho \in [0,1]$, $\alpha > 0$, $r > 0$, $\mu := \mathbb{E}[X_1]$, $\mu \neq 0$, random variables $X_1, V_{r,\alpha,\lambda}^{*}$ are independent, $V_{r,\alpha,\lambda}^{*} \sim G^{*}(r,\alpha,\lambda)$, $Z_{r,\alpha,\lambda}^{*} \sim G^{*}(r,\alpha,\lambda)$. Since $\mathbb{E}[G_{r,\lambda}^{2/\alpha}] = \frac{\Gamma(r+2/\alpha)}{\lambda^{2/\alpha}\Gamma(r)}$ (see, e.g., page 8 [27]), one has

$$\mathbb{E}[(U_{r,\alpha,\lambda}^{*})^2] = \left(\rho\frac{\mathbb{E}[X_1^2]}{\mu^2} + (1-\rho)\right)\frac{\Gamma(r+2/\alpha)}{\lambda^{2/\alpha}\Gamma(r)}. \tag{64}$$

Due to the properties of generalized gamma distributions, for any positive number c,

$$\frac{1}{c^\alpha}U_{r,\alpha,\lambda}^{*} = \frac{1}{c^\alpha}\left((1-\mathbb{I}_\rho)\frac{V_{r,\alpha,\lambda}^{*} X_1}{\mu} + \mathbb{I}_\rho Z_{r,\alpha,\lambda}^{*}\right)$$

$$= \left((1-\mathbb{I}_\rho)\frac{V_{r,\alpha,\lambda}^{*} X_1}{\mu} + \mathbb{I}_\rho Z_{r,\alpha,c\lambda}^{*}\right) = U_{r,\alpha,c\lambda}^{*}, \tag{65}$$

where indicator $\mathbb{I}_\rho$ equals 1 and 0 with probabilities $1-\rho$ and ρ, respectively, and is independent with all the variables under consideration. Note that $U_{1,1,1}^{*}$ has the same distribution as a random variable Y, having the law defined in Equation (42). Recall that the generalized negative binomial distribution $GNB(r,\alpha,p)$ is the law of a random variable $N_{r,\alpha,p}^{*}$, see Equation (54). We will use the following result.

Lemma 5. If $r > 0$, $\alpha \neq 0$, $p \in (0,1)$, then for $N_{r,\alpha,p}^{*} \sim GNB(r,\alpha,p)$ one has

$$\mathbb{E}[N_{r,\alpha,p}^{*}] = \mathbb{E}[G_{r,\alpha,p/(1-p)}^{*}], \quad \mathbb{E}[N_{r,\alpha,p}^{*}(N_{r,\alpha,p}^{*}-1)] = \mathbb{E}[(G_{r,\alpha,p/(1-p)}^{*})^2]. \tag{66}$$

Proof. According to Equation (54), for each $n \in \mathbb{N}$,

$$\sum_{k=1}^{n} k\mathbb{P}(N_{r,\alpha,p}^{*}=k) = \int_0^\infty z \sum_{k=1}^{n} \frac{z^{k-1}}{(k-1)!} e^{-z} g^{*}(z;r,\alpha,\frac{p}{1-p}) \, dz,$$

$$\sum_{k=2}^{n} k(k-1)\mathbb{P}(N_{r,\alpha,p}^{*}=k) = \int_0^\infty z^2 \sum_{k=2}^{n} \frac{z^{k-2}}{(k-2)!} e^{-z} g^{*}(z;r,\alpha,\frac{p}{1-p}) \, dz.$$

The desired statement follows from the monotone convergence theorem for the Lebesgue integral by letting $n \to \infty$. □

Theorem 5. Let $X_1, X_2 \ldots$ be exchangeable random variables, introduced in Section 4, such that $\mathbb{E}[X_1] = \mu$, $\mathbb{E}[X_1^2] = \mu_2 < \infty$. Assume that for some $\rho \in (0,1)$ Equation (41) holds. Suppose that $(X_n)_{n \in \mathbb{N}}$ and $N_{r,\alpha,p}^{*}$ are independent, where $N_{r,\alpha,p}^{*} \sim GNB(r,\alpha,p)$. Then, for $W_{r,\alpha,p}^{*}$ defined in Equation (55) with parameters $r \in (0,1)$, $\alpha \in (0,1]$, $p \in (0,1)$ and $U_{r,\alpha,1}^{*}$ given in Equation (63), one has

$$d_{\mathcal{H}_2}(W^*_{r,\alpha,p}, U^*_{r,\alpha,1}) = \frac{\mu_2}{2\mu^2}\left(\frac{p}{1-p}\right)^{1/\alpha}\frac{\Gamma(1+\frac{1}{\alpha})}{\Gamma(r)}. \tag{67}$$

Proof. Without loss of generality, we can assume that $\mu = 1$; otherwise, we consider $\widetilde{X}_n := X_n/\mu$, $n \in \mathbb{N}$. For such sequence, $\widetilde{\mu}_2 = \mathbb{E}\widetilde{X}_1^2 = \mu_2/\mu^2$. Note that Equation (58) is true for dependent summands (see Theorem 1 [29]). Furthermore, for bounded $h(t)$, $t \in \mathbb{R}$, function $h_x(t) = h(xt)$ is also bounded for any $x \in \mathbb{R}$. Thus, an employment of Equation (63) gives

$$\mathbb{E}[h(U^*_{r,\alpha,\lambda})] = \rho \int_{\mathbb{R}} \mathbb{E}[h_x(G^{1/\alpha}_{r,\lambda})]\,dF_{X_1}(x) + (1-\rho)\mathbb{E}[h(G^{1/\alpha}_{r,\lambda})]. \tag{68}$$

Now we apply Equation (57) with bounded h_x and by Fubini's theorem obtain:

$$\int_{\mathbb{R}} \mathbb{E}[h_x(G^{1/\alpha}_{r,\lambda})]\,dF_{X_1}(x) = \int_{\mathbb{R}} \int_0^1 \mathbb{E}\left[h_x\left(\frac{1-u}{u}V^*\right)\right]q(u;r,\alpha,\lambda)\,du\,dF_{X_1}(x)$$
$$= \int_0^1 \mathbb{E}\left[h\left(\frac{1-u}{u}X_1 V^*\right)\right]q(u;r,\alpha,\lambda)\,du, \tag{69}$$

where X_1 and V^* are independent and $V^* \sim Exp(1)$. Apply Equation (57) for the second summand of Equation (68). Then, Equation (69) yields

$$\mathbb{E}[h(U^*_{r,\alpha,\lambda})]$$
$$= \rho \int_0^1 \mathbb{E}\left[h\left(\frac{1-u}{u}X_1 V^*\right)\right]q(u;r,\alpha,\lambda)\,du + (1-\rho)\int_0^1 \mathbb{E}\left[h\left(\frac{1-u}{u}Z^*\right)\right]q(u;r,\alpha,\lambda)\,du$$
$$= \int_0^1 \mathbb{E}\left[h\left(\frac{1-u}{u}U^*_{1,1,1}\right)\right]q(u;r,\alpha,\lambda)\,du, \tag{70}$$

where $Z^* \sim Exp(1)$ and $U^*_{1,1,1}$ have the same distribution as Y, see Equation (42).

Recall that, for $h \in \mathcal{H}_2$, an inequality $|h(x)| \leq A_0 x^2 + B_0$ holds for all $x \in \mathbb{R}$ and some positive constants A_0, B_0 (see Remark 1). Moreover, $\mathbb{E}\big[(U^*_{r,\alpha,\lambda})^2\big] < \infty$ according to Equation (64). So, employing bounded $h_n(x) = h(x)\mathbb{I}_{(-n,n]}(x)$ tending to $h(x) \in \mathcal{H}_2$ as $n \to \infty$, one can invoke the Lebesgue dominated convergence theorem to claim that $\lim_{n\to\infty} \mathbb{E}[h_n(U^*_{r,\alpha,\lambda})] = \mathbb{E}[h(U^*_{r,\alpha,\lambda})]$. We take into account that

$$\int_0^1 \mathbb{E}\left|h_n\left(\frac{1-u}{u}U^*_{1,1,1}\right)\right|q(u;r,\alpha,\lambda)\,du \leq A_0\mathbb{E}\big[(U^*_{1,1,1})^2\big]\int_0^1 \left(\frac{1-u}{u}\right)^2 q(u;r,\alpha,\lambda)\,du + B_0.$$

The integral in the right-hand side of the latter formula is finite by Equation (60) and $\mathbb{E}\big[(U^*_{1,1,1})^2\big] < \infty$ in accord with Equation (64). Thus, it is possible to apply the Lebesgue dominated convergence theorem to obtain

$$\lim_{n\to\infty}\int_0^1 \mathbb{E}\left[h_n\left(\frac{1-u}{u}U^*_{1,1,1}\right)\right]q(u;r,\alpha,\lambda)\,du = \int_0^1 \mathbb{E}\left[h\left(\frac{1-u}{u}U^*_{1,1,1}\right)\right]q(u;r,\alpha,\lambda)\,du$$

for any $h \in \mathcal{H}_2$. So, Equation (70) holds for all $h \in \mathcal{H}_2$.

In a similar way, $\lim_{n\to\infty} \mathbb{E}[h_n(S^*_{r,\alpha,p})] = \mathbb{E}[h(S^*_{r,\alpha,p})]$ for $h \in \mathcal{H}_2$. According to the Cauchy–Bunyakovsky–Schwarz inequality for identically distributed variables $X_1, X_2, \ldots$ we have $|\mathbb{E}[X_i X_j]| \leq \mu_2$ for $i, j \in \mathbb{N}$ and consequently

$$\mathbb{E}\big[(S^*_{r,\alpha,p})^2\big] = \sum_{k=0}^{\infty} \mathbb{P}(N^*_{r,\alpha,p} = k)\mathbb{E}\bigg[\Big(\sum_{j=1}^{k} X_j\Big)^2\bigg]$$
$$\leq \mu_2 \sum_{k=0}^{\infty} \mathbb{P}(N^*_{r,\alpha,p} = k)k^2 = \mu_2 \mathbb{E}\big[(N^*_{r,\alpha,p})^2\big]. \tag{71}$$

Equations (59) and (66) entail that $\mathbb{E}\big[(N_{r,\alpha,p}^*)^2\big] < \infty$. Thus, the dominated convergence theorem guarantees that $\lim_{n\to\infty} \mathbb{E}[h_n(S_{r,\alpha,p}^*)] = \mathbb{E}[h(S_{r,\alpha,p}^*)]$. Furthermore, one can demonstrate that, for each $h \in \mathcal{H}_2$,

$$\lim_{n\to\infty} \int_0^1 \mathbb{E}[h_n(S_{1,1,u}^*)] q(u;r,\alpha,\lambda)\, du = \int_0^1 \mathbb{E}[h(S_{1,1,u}^*)] q(u;r,\alpha,\lambda)\, du. \tag{72}$$

For this purpose we note that Equation (71) implies

$$\int_0^1 \mathbb{E}|h_n(S_{1,1,u}^*)| q(u;r,\alpha,\lambda)\, du \leq C + A\mu_2 \int_0^1 \mathbb{E}\big[(N_{1,1,u}^*)^2\big] q(u;r,\alpha,\lambda)\, du.$$

According to Equation (66) one has

$$\int_0^1 \mathbb{E}\big[(N_{1,1,u}^*)^2\big] q(u;r,\alpha,\lambda)\, du = \int_0^1 \Big(\mathbb{E}\big[(G_{1,1,u/(1-u)}^*)^2\big] + \mathbb{E}\big[G_{1,1,u/(1-u)}^*\big]\Big) q(u;r,\alpha,\lambda)\, du.$$

The latter integral is finite because one can take $h(x) = x$ and $h(x) = x^2/2$ in Equation (57) and invoke Equation (59). Then, it is possible to use the dominated convergence theorem once again to establish Equation (72).

Now, combining Equation (58) and Equation (70) leads for any $h \in \mathcal{H}_2$ to the relation

$$\mathbb{E}[h(S_{r,\alpha,p}^*)] - \mathbb{E}[h(U_{r,\alpha,p/(1-p)}^*)]$$

$$= \int_0^1 \left(\mathbb{E}[h(S_{1,1,u}^*)] - \mathbb{E}\left[h\left(\frac{1-u}{u}U_{1,1,1}^*\right)\right]\right) q\left(u;r,\alpha,\frac{p}{1-p}\right) du. \tag{73}$$

Note that a random variable $N_{1,1,u}^*$ follows the geometric distribution $Geom(u)$ with parameter $u \in (0,1)$. For each $h \in \mathcal{H}_2$ and any $u \in (0,1)$, by Theorem 3 and in view of $d_{\mathcal{H}_2}$ homogeneity, we obtain

$$\left|\mathbb{E}[h(S_{1,1,u}^*)] - \mathbb{E}\left[h\left(\frac{1-u}{u}U_{1,1,1}^*\right)\right]\right| \leq d_{\mathcal{H}_2}\left(S_{1,1,u}^*, \frac{1-u}{u}U_{1,1,1}^*\right)$$

$$= \left(\frac{1-u}{u}\right)^2 d_{\mathcal{H}_2}(W_u, Y) \leq \left(\frac{1-u}{u}\right)^2 \left(\frac{u}{1-u}\right) \frac{\mu_2}{2} = \left(\frac{1-u}{u}\right) \frac{\mu_2}{2}. \tag{74}$$

Employing Equations (73), (74) and (62) one deduces

$$d_{\mathcal{H}_2}(S_{r,\alpha,p}^*, U_{r,\alpha,p/(1-p)}^*) \leq \frac{\mu_2}{2} \int_0^1 \left(\frac{1-u}{u}\right) q\left(u;r,\alpha,\frac{p}{1-p}\right) du = \frac{\mu_2}{2} \mathbb{E}\big[G_{r,p/(1-p)}^{1/\alpha}\big]. \tag{75}$$

Equation (65) implies by virtue of $d_{\mathcal{H}_2}$ homogeneity that

$$d_{\mathcal{H}_2}(W_{r,\alpha,p}^*, U_{r,\alpha,1}^*) = \left(\frac{p}{1-p}\right)^{2/\alpha} d_{\mathcal{H}_2}(S_{r,\alpha,p}^*, U_{r,\alpha,p/(1-p)}^*). \tag{76}$$

Combining Equations (59), (75) and (76) we conclude that the right-hand side of Equation (67) is an upper bound for $d_{\mathcal{H}_2}(W_{r,\alpha,p}^*, U_{r,\alpha,1}^*)$.

Choosing $h(x) = x^2/2$ in Equation (73), upon employing Equation (52) and Equation (62) one infers:

$$d_{\mathcal{H}_2}(W_{r,\alpha,p}^*, G_{r,1}^{1/\alpha}) \geq$$

$$\geq \frac{1}{2}\left(\frac{p}{1-p}\right)^{2/\alpha} \left|\int_0^1 \left(\mathbb{E}[(S_{1,1,u}^*)^2] - \left(\frac{1-u}{u}\right)^2 \mathbb{E}[(U_{1,1,1}^*)^2]\right) q\left(u;r,\alpha,\frac{p}{1-p}\right) du\right| =$$

$$= \frac{\mu_2}{2}\left(\frac{p}{1-p}\right)^{2/\alpha} \int_0^1 \left(\frac{1-u}{u}\right) q\left(u;r,\alpha,\frac{p}{1-p}\right) du = \frac{\mu_2}{2}\left(\frac{p}{1-p}\right)^{2/\alpha} \mathbb{E}[G_{r,\alpha,p/(1-p)}^*].$$

Using Equation (59) once again, we see that the right-hand side of Equation (67) is a lower bound for $d_{\mathcal{H}_2}(W^*_{r,\alpha,p}, U^*_{r,\alpha,1})$. □

7. Inverse to Equilibrium Transformation

The development of Stein's method is closely connected with various transformations of distributions. Let a random variable $W \geq 0$ and $0 < \mu = \mathbb{E}[W] < \infty$. Then, one says that a random variable W^s has the W-size biased distribution if for all f such that $\mathbb{E}[Wf(W)]$ exists
$$\mathbb{E}[Wf(W)] = \mu \mathbb{E}[f(W^s)].$$

The connection of this transformation with Stein's equation was considered in [50,51]. It was pointed out in [51] that this transformation works well for combinatorial problems, such as counting the number of vertices in a random graph having prespecified degrees, see also [52]. In [53], another transformation was introduced. Namely, if a random variable W has mean zero and variance $\sigma^2 \in (0, \infty)$, then the authors of [53] write (Definition 1.1) that a variable W^* has W-zero biased distribution whenever, for all differentiable f such that $\mathbb{E}Wf(W)$ exists, the following relation holds
$$\mathbb{E}[Wf(W)] = \sigma^2 \mathbb{E}[f'(W^*)].$$

This definition is inspired by an equation $\mathbb{E}[Wf(W)] = \sigma^2 \mathbb{E}[f'(W)]$ characterizing the normal law $N(0, \sigma^2)$. The authors of [53] explain that W^* always exists if $\mathbb{E}[W] = 0$ and $\mathrm{var} W \in (0, \infty)$. Zero-based coupling for products of normal random variables is treated in [54]. In Sec. 2 of [30], it is demonstrated that the gamma distribution is uniquely characterised by the property that its size-biased distribution is the same as its zero-biased distribution. Two generalizations of zero biasing were proposed in [55], see p. 104 of that paper for discussion of these transformations. We refer also to survey [56].

Now, we turn to the equilibrium distribution transformation introduced in [33] and concentrate on approximation of the law under consideration by means of an exponential law, see the corresponding Definition 1 in Section 2.

According to the second part of Theorem 2.1 of [33] (in our notation), for $Z \sim Exp(1)$ and non-negative random variable X with $\mathbb{E}[X] = 1$ and $\mathbb{E}[X^2] < \infty$ the following estimate holds
$$d_{\mathcal{H}_1}(X, Z) \leq 2\mathbb{E}|X^e - X|,$$

and at the same time
$$d_{\mathcal{H}_1}(X^e, Z) \leq \mathbb{E}|X^e - X|. \tag{77}$$

The authors of [33] also proved that $d_K(X^e, Z) \leq \mathbb{E}|X^e - X|$. Notice that the estimate for $d_{\mathcal{H}_1}(X^e, Z)$ is more precise than that for $d_{\mathcal{H}_1}(X, Z)$.

Now we turn to Equation (77) and demonstrate how to find the distribution of X when we know the distribution of X^e. In other words, we concentrate on the inverse of an equilibrium distribution transformation.

Assume that $\mathbb{E}[X] > 0$. Recall that a random variable X^e exists if $F^e(x)$ appearing in Equation (16) is a distribution function. The latter statement for $\mathbb{E}[X] > 0$ is equivalent to nonnegativity of X. Indeed, for non-negative X, $F^e(x)$ coincides with a distribution function having a density (15). If $F^e(x)$ is a distribution function and $\mathbb{E}[X] > 0$ in Equation (16), then $F^e(x) \geq 0$ for $x < 0$ only if $F(x) = 0$ for $x < 0$.

Thus a random variable X^e has a (version of) density $p^e(x)$ introduced in Equation (15). Obviously, the function $p^e(x)$ has the following properties. It is nonincreasing on $[0, \infty)$ and $p^e(x) = 0$ for $x < 0$. This density is right-continuous on $[0, \infty)$ and consequently $p^e(0) < \infty$. Now, we are able to provide a full description of the class of densities for random variables X^e relevant to all non-negative X with positive mean.

Lemma 6. *Let a non-negative random variable X^e have a version of density (with respect to the Lebesgue measure) $p^e(x)$, $x \in \mathbb{R}$, such that this function is nonincreasing on $[0, \infty)$, $p^e(x) = 0$ for*

$x < 0$, and there is finite $\lim_{x \to 0+} p^e(x)$. Then, there exists a unique preimage of X^e distribution having the distribution function F continuous at $x = 0$. Namely,

$$F(x) = \begin{cases} 1 - \frac{p^e(x)}{p^e(0)}, & x \geq 0, \\ 0, & x < 0. \end{cases} \tag{78}$$

Proof. First of all, note that $p^e(0) > 0$ as otherwise $p^e(x) = 0$ for all $x \in \mathbb{R}$ (p^e is a nonincreasing function on $[0, \infty)$). We also know that there exist a left-sided limit and a right-sided limit of p^e at each point $x \in (0, \infty)$ as well as the right-sided limit of p^e at $x = 0$. The set of discontinuity points of p^e is at most countable, and we can take a version which is right continuous at each point of $[0, \infty)$. Then, Equation (78) introduces a distribution function. Consider a random variable X with distribution function F and check the validity of Equation (14).

The integration by a parts formula yields, for any $b > 0$,

$$1 \geq \int_0^b p^e(x)\,dx = bp^e(b) + p^e(0) \int_0^b x\,dF(x). \tag{79}$$

Summands in the right-hand side of Equation (79) are non-negative. Therefore, for any $b > 0$, $\mathbb{E}[X\mathbb{I}(X \leq b)] \leq 1/p^e(0)$. Hence, the monotone convergence theorem implies that $\mathbb{E}[X]$ is finite. According to Equation (78)

$$bp^e(b)/p^e(0) = b(1 - F(b)) = b\mathbb{P}(X > b) \to 0, \quad b \to \infty, \tag{80}$$

since $\mathbb{E}[X] < \infty$. Taking in the Equation (79) limit as $b \to \infty$, one obtains $1 = p^e(0)\mathbb{E}[X]$. Now, we are ready to verify Equation (14). For any Lipschitz function f, $\mathbb{E}[f(X)]$ is finite and

$$\mathbb{E}[f(X)] = \int_0^\infty f(x)dF(x) = -\frac{1}{p^e(0)} \int_0^\infty f(x)dp^e(x).$$

Taking into account Equation (80), we infer that $f(b)p^e(b) \to 0$ as $b \to \infty$. Consequently, applying integration by parts once again (f has bounded variation), we obtain

$$\mathbb{E}[X]\mathbb{E}[f'(X^e)] = \frac{1}{p^e(0)} \int_0^\infty f'(x)p^e(x)\,dx = \frac{1}{p^e(0)} \int_0^\infty p^e(x)df(x)$$
$$= \frac{1}{p^e(0)} \left[-f(0)p^e(0) - \int_0^\infty f(x)dp^e(x) \right] = \mathbb{E}[f(X)] - f(0).$$

Uniqueness of X distribution corresponding to X^e is a consequence of Equation (15) and continuity of $F(x)$ at $x = 0$. Indeed, assume that for X_1 and X_2 one has $X_1^e = X_2^e$. Then, Equation (15) yields that for almost all $x \geq 0$,

$$\frac{1}{\mathbb{E}[X_1]}\mathbb{P}(X_1 > x) = \frac{1}{\mathbb{E}[X_2]}\mathbb{P}(X_2 > x), \tag{81}$$

and therefore $\mathbb{P}(X_1 > x) = c\mathbb{P}(X_2 > x)$, where c is a positive constant (the equilibrium distribution in Definition 1 is introduced for random variables with positive expectation only). Since $\mathbb{P}(X_1 = 0) = \mathbb{P}(X_2 = 0) = 0$, one has $\mathbb{P}(X_1 > 0) = \mathbb{P}(X_2 > 0) = 0$. Let $x_n \to 0+$, $n \to \infty$, where the points x_n belong to the set considered in Equation (81) to ensure that $c = 1$. Thus, distributions of X_1 and X_2 coincide. □

Remark 6. *Let X_p be the Bernoulli random variable taking values 1 and 0 with probabilities p and $1 - p$, respectively. Then, it is easily seen that the distribution of X_p^e is uniform on $[0, 1]$. Thus, in contrast to Lemma 6, without assumption of continuity of F at a point $x = 0$ one can not guarantee, in general, the preimage uniqueness for the inverse transformation to the equilibrium one.*

In the proof of Lemma 6, we find out that $\mathbb{E}[X] = 1/p^e(0)$. Set $\lambda = p^e(0)$, $Z \sim Exp(\lambda)$. Then, $\mathbb{E}[X] = \mathbb{E}[Z]$. Further, we suppose that this choice of λ is made.

Recall that random variables U and V are stochastically ordered if either $\mathbb{P}(U \leq x) \leq \mathbb{P}(V \leq x)$, for every $x \in \mathbb{R}$, or the opposite inequality holds (for all $x \in \mathbb{R}$). Now, we clarify one of the Theorem 2.1 of [33] statements (see also Theorem 3 [22], where the result similar to Theorem 2.1 of [33] is formulated employing the generalized distributions).

Theorem 6. *Let a random variable X^e satisfy conditions of Lemma 6, and $\mathbb{E}[X^e] < \infty$ and X be a preimage of the equilibrium transformation. Then, Equation (77) holds. Moreover, the inequality becomes an equality when X and X^e are stochastically ordered.*

Proof. Apply the Stein Equation (10) along with equilibrium transformation (14). Then, in light of $\mathbb{E}[X] = \frac{1}{\lambda}$ and $\mathbb{E}f_h(X) - f_h(0) = \frac{1}{\lambda}\mathbb{E}f'_h(X^e)$, we can write

$$\left|\mathbb{E}[h(X^e)] - \mathbb{E}[h(Z)]\right| = \left|\mathbb{E}\big(f'_h(X^e) - \lambda f_h(X^e)\big) + \lambda f(0)\right|$$
$$= \lambda\left|\mathbb{E}\big(f_h(X^e) - f_h(X)\big)\right| \leq \lambda\|f'_h\|_\infty \mathbb{E}|X^e - X| \leq \|h'\|_\infty \mathbb{E}|X^e - X|. \quad (82)$$

The last inequality in (82) is true due to Lemma 2. Now, we demonstrate that equality in (82) can be attained. Taking $h(x) = x - \frac{1}{\lambda}$, we have a solution $f_h(x) = -\frac{1}{\lambda}x$ of Equation (12). Then,

$$\left|\mathbb{E}[h(X^e)] - \mathbb{E}[h(Z)]\right| = \lambda\left|\mathbb{E}\big(f_h(X^e) - f_h(X)\big)\right| = \left|\mathbb{E}(X^e - X)\right|.$$

Employing the integration by parts formula, one can show that the expression in the right-hand side of the last equality is equal to the Kantorovich distance between X and X^e when these variables are stochastically ordered. Note that $x(1 - F(x)) \to 0$, $x(1 - F^e(x)) \to 0$ as $x \to \infty$ and $xF(x) \to 0$, $xF^e(x) \to 0$ as $x \to -\infty$ because $\mathbb{E}[X]$ and $\mathbb{E}[X^e]$ are finite. Thus,

$$\left|\mathbb{E}[X^e] - \mathbb{E}[X]\right| = \left|\int_\mathbb{R} x\big(dF_{X^e}(x) - dF_X(x)\big)\right|$$
$$= \left|-\int_\mathbb{R} \big(F_{X^e}(x) - F_X(x)\big)dx\right| = \int_\mathbb{R}|F_{X^e}(x) - F_X(x)|\,dx,$$

since $F_{X^e}(x) \geq F_X(x)$ (or $\leq$) for all $x \in \mathbb{R}$. It is well-known that the Kantorovich distance is the minimal one for the metric $\tau(U, V) = \mathbb{E}|U - V|$ (see, e.g., [9], Ch. 1, §1.3). Therefore,

$$\int_\mathbb{R}|F_{X^e}(x) - F_X(x)|\,dx = \inf \mathbb{E}|U - V|,$$

where the infimum has taken over all joint laws (U, V) such that $\mathbb{P}_U = \mathbb{P}_{X^e}$ and $\mathbb{P}_V = \mathbb{P}_X$ (see also Remark 2 and [10], Corollary 5.3.2). Consequently, in the framework of Theorem 6, $\left|\mathbb{E}[X^e] - \mathbb{E}[X]\right| = \mathbb{E}|X^e - X|$. □

Remark 7. *One can show that by means of Lemma 2 and Equation (82) it is possible to provide an estimate*

$$d_\mathcal{K}(X^e, Z) \leq \lambda \mathbb{E}|X^e - X|. \quad (83)$$

For each function h belonging to $\mathcal{K}$, in a similar way to Equation (82), one can apply Equation (10) together with equilibrium transformation. Now, it is sufficient to study the Stein equation with right derivative. Formula (13) gives a solution of the Stein equation according to Lemma 2. Note that for f_h, the right derivative coincides almost everywhere with the derivative, and the law of X^e is absolutely continuous according to Equation (15). Thus, for the Lipschitz function f_h (see Lemma 2), one can use an equilibrium transformation.

Example 1. Consider the distribution functions $F_\varepsilon(x)$ of random variables X_ε, taking values ε and $2-\varepsilon$ with probabilities $1/2$, $0 < \varepsilon < 1$. Formula (15) yields that X_ε^e has the following piece-line structure

$$F_\varepsilon^e(x) = \begin{cases} 0, & \text{if } x < 0, \\ x, & \text{if } 0 \leq x < \varepsilon, \\ x/2 + \varepsilon/2, & \text{if } \varepsilon \leq x < 2-\varepsilon, \\ 1, & \text{if } 2-\varepsilon \leq x. \end{cases}$$

If $\varepsilon \geq 1/2$ then, for all $x \in \mathbb{R}$, the following inequality holds: $F_\varepsilon^e(x) \geq F_\varepsilon(x)$, i.e., X_ε and X_ε^e are stochastically ordered. We see that for $\varepsilon < 1/2$, the inequality is violated in the right neighborhood of a point ε. Thus, there are beside the stochastically ordered pairs (X, X^e) also those of a different kind.

Now, we turn to another example of stochastically ordered X and X^e.

Example 2. Take X^e having the Pareto distribution. The notation $X^e \sim Pareto(\alpha, \beta)$ means that X^e has a density $f^e(x) = \frac{\alpha \beta^\alpha}{(x+\beta)^{\alpha+1}}$ ($x \geq 0$) and the corresponding distribution function $F^e(x) = 1 - \left(\frac{\beta}{x+\beta}\right)^\alpha$, where $x \geq 0$, $\alpha > 0$, $\beta > 0$.

Further, we consider only $\alpha > 1$, since in this case there exists finite $\mathbb{E}[X^e] = \frac{\beta}{\alpha-1}$. By means of Lemma 6, we obtain the distribution of the preimage of the equilibrium transformation

$$F(x) = 1 - \frac{f^e(x)}{f^e(0)} = 1 - \frac{\alpha \beta^\alpha}{(x+\beta)^{\alpha+1}} \frac{\beta^{\alpha+1}}{\alpha \beta^\alpha} = 1 - \left(\frac{\beta}{x+\beta}\right)^{\alpha+1}, \quad x \geq 0.$$

Thus one can state that $X \sim Pareto(\alpha+1, \beta)$. It is not difficult to see that $F^e(x) \leq F(x)$ for $x \in \mathbb{R}$, i.e., the random variables X^e and X are stochastically ordered. Due to Theorem 6, one has

$$d_{\mathcal{H}_1}(X^e, Z) = \mathbb{E}|X^e - X| = \mathbb{E}[X^e] - \mathbb{E}[X] = \frac{\beta}{\alpha-1} - \frac{\beta}{\alpha} = \frac{\beta}{\alpha(\alpha-1)}, \tag{84}$$

$$d_{\mathcal{K}}(X^e, Z) \leq \frac{\alpha}{\beta} \mathbb{E}|X^e - X| = \frac{1}{\alpha-1}.$$

In such a way we find the bound for the Kolmogorov distance between the distributions $Pareto(\alpha, \beta)$ and $Exp(\alpha/\beta)$. This relation demonstrates the convergence rate of $d_1(X^e, Z)$ to zero as $\alpha \to \infty$. The estimate is nontrivial for $\alpha > 2$.

Remark 8. It is interesting that estimation of the proximity of the Pareto law to the Exponential one became important in signal processing, see [34] and references therein. Let $X \sim Pareto(\alpha, \beta)$, where $\alpha > 0$, $\beta > 0$, and $Z \sim Exp(\lambda)$. In [34], the author indicates that the Pinsker–Csiszár inequality was employed to derive

$$d_{\mathcal{K}}(X, Z) \leq \sqrt{2 D_{KL}(X||Z)}, \tag{85}$$

where $D_{KL}(X||Z)$ is the Kullback–Leibler divergence between laws of X and Z. More precisely, in the left-hand side of Equation (85) one can write the total variation distance $d_{TV}(X, Z)$ between distributions of X and Z. Clearly, $d_{\mathcal{K}}(X, Z) \leq d_{TV}(X, Z)$. By evaluating $D_{KL}(X||Z)$ and performing an optimal choice of parameter λ, it was demonstrated (formula (19) in [34]) that, for $\alpha > 1$ and any $\beta > 0$,

$$d_{\mathcal{K}}(X, Z) \leq \sqrt{\frac{2}{\alpha(\alpha-1)}}. \tag{86}$$

if $\lambda = \frac{\alpha-1}{\beta}$. The author of [34] on page 8 writes that in his previous work [57] the inequality

$$d_\mathcal{K}(X, Z) \leq \frac{3}{\alpha} \tag{87}$$

was established with the same choice of λ. Next, he also writes that "in the most cases $\alpha > 2$" and notes that the estimate in Equation (86) involving the Kullback–Leibler divergence is more precise for $\alpha > \frac{9}{7}$ than the estimate in Equation (87) obtained by the Stein method. Moreover, on page 4 of [34] we read: "The problem with the Stein approach is that the bounds do not suggest a suitable way in which, for a given Pareto model, an appropriate approximating Exponential distribution can be specified". However, we have demonstrated that application of the inverse equilibrium transformation together with the Stein method permits indicating, whenever $\alpha > 2$, the corresponding Exponential distribution with proximity closer than the right-hand sides of Equation (86) and Equation (87) can provide.

8. Conclusions

Our principle goal was to find the sharp estimates of the proximity of random sums distributions to exponential and more general laws. This goal is achieved when we employ the probability metric $d_{\mathcal{H}_2}$. Thus, it would be valuable to find the best possible approximations of random sums distributions by means of specified laws using the metrics ζ_s of order $s > 0$. The results of [32] provide the basis for this approach.

There are various complementary refinements of the Rényi theorem. One approach is related to the employment of Brownian motion. It is interesting that in [58] (p. 1071) the authors proposed an explanation of the Rényi theorem involving the embedding theorem. We provide a little bit different complete proof. Let $X_1, X_2, \ldots$ be i.i.d. random variables with mean $\mu := \mathbb{E}X_1$ and $\sigma^2 := \text{var}X_1 < \infty$, whereas $S_n, n \in \mathbb{N}$, denote the corresponding partial sums. According to Theorem 12.6 of [59], which is due to A.V. Skorokhod and V. Strassen, there exists a standard Brownian motion $B(t), t \geq 0$, (perhaps it is defined on an extension of initial probability space) such that

$$\frac{1}{\sqrt{t}} \sup_{0 \leq u \leq t} |S_{[u]} - \mu u - \sigma B(u)| \xrightarrow{\mathbb{P}} 0, \quad t \to \infty, \tag{88}$$

and

$$\lim_{t \to \infty} \frac{S_{[t]} - \mu t - \sigma B(t)}{\sqrt{2t \log \log t}} = 0 \quad \text{a.s.}, \tag{89}$$

where $\xrightarrow{\mathbb{P}}$ stands for convergence in probability, and a.s. means almost surely. Thus, in light of Equation (89), we can write, for $t \geq 0$,

$$S_{[t]} = \mu t + \sigma B(t) + R(t), \tag{90}$$

where $\sup_{0 \leq u \leq t} R(u)/\sqrt{t} \xrightarrow{\mathbb{P}} 0$ and $R(t)/\sqrt{2t \log \log t} \to 0$ a.s. when $t \to \infty$. Substitute N_p (see Equation (2)) in Equation (90) instead of t. It is easily seen that $N_p \xrightarrow{\mathbb{P}} \infty$ (i.e., for each $t > 0$, one has $\mathbb{P}(N_p \leq t) \to 0$ as $p \to 0+$) and by means of characteristic functions one can verify that $pN_p \xrightarrow{D} Z$ as $p \to 0+$, where $Z \sim Exp(1)$. Therefore, $\mu p N_p \xrightarrow{D} \mu Z, p \to 0+$. In the proof of Lemma 4, we showed (Equation (24)) that $\mathbb{E}[N_p] = (1-p)/p$. Consequently,

$$\text{var}[pB(N_p)] = p^2 \mathbb{E}[B(N_p)^2] = p^2 \sum_{k=0}^{\infty} \mathbb{E}[B(k)^2] p(1-p)^k$$

$$= p^2 \sum_{k=0}^{\infty} kp(1-p)^k = p^2 \mathbb{E}[N_p] = p^2 \frac{1-p}{p} = p(1-p) \to 0, \quad p \to 0+.$$

Hence, $p\sigma B(N_p) \xrightarrow{\mathbb{P}} 0$ as $p \to 0+$. Now, we demonstrate that $pR(N_p) \xrightarrow{\mathbb{P}} 0$, $p \to 0+$. For any $\varepsilon > 0$ and any $t > 0$,

$$\mathbb{P}(p|R(N_p)| > \varepsilon) \leq \mathbb{P}(p|R(N_p)| > \varepsilon, N_p \leq t) + \mathbb{P}(N_p > t)$$
$$\leq \mathbb{P}(p \sup_{0 \leq u \leq t} |R(u)| > \varepsilon) + \mathbb{P}(N_p > t).$$

In light of Equation (88), for arbitrary $\gamma > 0$ and $\varepsilon > 0$, one can take $t_0 = t_0(\gamma)$ such that $\mathbb{P}(\sup_{0 \leq u \leq t_0} |R(u)| > \varepsilon \sqrt{t_0}) < \gamma/2$. Then, for any $0 < p \leq 1/\sqrt{t_0}$, we obtain

$$\mathbb{P}(p \sup_{0 \leq u \leq t_0} |R(u)| > \varepsilon) < \gamma/2.$$

Since $N_p \xrightarrow{\mathbb{P}} \infty$, we can find $p_0 > 0$ such that $\mathbb{P}(N_p > t_0) < \gamma/2$ if $0 < p \leq p_0$. Therefore, $R(N_p) \xrightarrow{\mathbb{P}} 0$ as $p \to 0+$. The Slutsky lemma yields the desired relation

$$pS_{N_p} \xrightarrow{\mathcal{D}} \mu Z, \quad p \to 0+,$$

which implies Equation (3). However, it seems that there is no clear intuitive reason why the law of the random sum converges to an exponential in the Rényi theorem. Moreover, in Ch. 3, Sec. 2 "The Rényi Limit Theorem" of [20] (see Sec. 2.1 "Motivation"), one can find examples demonstrating that intuition behind the Rényi theorem is poor.

Actually, relation (90) leads to refinements of Equation (3). In [58], it is proved that if X_1 has finite exponential moments and other specified conditions are satisfied then there exists a more sophisticated approximation for distribution of W_p, and its accuracy is estimated. The results are applied to the study of $M/G/1$ queue for both light-tailed and heavy-tailed service time distributions. Note that in [58], Section 5, the authors study the model where the distribution of X_1 can depend on p. For future research, it would be desirable to establish analogues of our theorems for such a model.

The results concerning the accuracy of approximating a distribution under consideration by an exponential law are applicable to some queuing models. Let, for a queue $M/G/1$, the inter-arrival times follow $Exp(\lambda)$ distribution and S stand for the general service time. Introduce the stationary waiting time W and define $\rho := \lambda \mathbb{E}[S]$ to be its load. Due to [60], if $\mathbb{E}[S^3] < \infty$ then $(1-\rho)W \xrightarrow{\mathcal{D}} Z$ as $\rho \to 1$, where $Z \sim Exp(1)$. Theorem 3.1 of [45] contains an upper bound of $d_{\mathcal{H}_1}(W_p, Z)$, where $Z \sim Exp(1)$. This estimate is used by the authors for analysis of queueing systems with a single server. It would be interesting to obtain the sharp approximations in the framework of queueing systems.

For the model of exchangeable random variables, Theorem 2 in Section 2 ensures the weak convergence of distributions under consideration to specified mixture of explicitly indicated laws. Theorem 3 proves the sharp convergence rate estimate to this limit law by means of the ideal probability metric of the second order. It would be worthwhile to establish such an estimate of the distributions proximity applying the Lévy–Prokhorov distance because convergence in this metric is equivalent to the weak convergence of distributions of random variables. All the more, at present there is no unified theory of probability metrics. In this regard, one can mention Proposition 1.2 of [17] stating that if a random variable Z has the Lebesgue density bounded by C then, for any random variable Y,

$$d_{\mathcal{K}}(Y, Z) \leq \sqrt{C d_{\mathcal{H}_1}(Y, Z)}.$$

However, this estimate only gives the sub-optimal convergence rates. We also highlight the important total variation distance d_{TV}. The authors of [61] study the sum $W := \sum_{j \in J} X_j$, where $\{X_j, j \in J\}$ is a family of locally dependent non-negative integer-valued random variables. Using the perturbations of Stein's operator, they establish the upper bounds for $d_{TV}(W, M)$ where the law of M is a mixture of Poisson distribution and either binomial or negative binomial distribution. It would be desirable to obtain the sharp estimates and, moreover, consider a more general model where the set of summation is random. In this connection, it seems helpful to employ the paper [62], where the authors proved results concerning the weak convergence of distributions of statistics constructed from samples of random size. In addition, it would be interesting to extend these results to stratified samples by invoking Lemma 1 of [63].

Special attention is paid to various generalizations of the geometric sums. In Theorem 3.3 of [64], the authors consider random sums with summation index $T_n := Y_1 + \ldots + Y_n$, where $Y_1, Y_2, \ldots$ are i.i.d. random variables following the geometric law $Geom(p)$, see Equation (2). Then, they show that $S_{T_n}/\mathbb{E}[S_{T_n}]$ converge in distribution to the gamma law with certain parameters as $p \to 0+$. In [62], it is demonstrated that the Linnik and the Mittag–Leffler laws arise naturally in the framework of limit theorems for random sums. Hopefully, in future the complete picture of limit laws involving general theory of distributions mixtures will appear. In addition, it is desirable to study various models of random sums of dependent random variables. On this track, it could be useful to consider the decompositions of exchangeable random sequences extending the fundamental de Finetti theorem, see, e.g., [65].

One can try to generalize the results of Section 7 for accumulative laws proposed in [66]. These laws are akin to both the Pareto distribution and the lognormal distribution. In addition, we refer to [43] where the "variance-gamma distributions" were studied. These distributions form a four-parameter family and comprise as special and limiting cases the normal, gamma and Laplace distributions. Employment of these distributions permits enlarging a range of applications in modeling and fitting real data.

To complete the indication of further research directions, we note that the next essential and nontrivial step is to establish the limit theorem in functional spaces for processes generated by a sequence of random sums of random variables. For such stochastic processes, one can obtain the analogues of the classical invariance principles.

Author Contributions: Conceptualization, A.B. and N.S.; methodology, A.B and N.S.; formal analysis, A.B. and N.S.; investigation, A.B. and N.S.; writing—original draft preparation, A.B. and N.S.; writing—review and editing, A.B. and N.S.; supervision, A.B.; project administration, A.B.; funding acquisition, A.B. All authors have read and agreed to the published version of the manuscript.

Funding: The work was supported by the Lomonosov Moscow State University project "Fundamental Mathematics and Mechanics".

Institutional Review Board Statement: Not applicable.

Informed Consent Statement: Not applicable.

Data Availability Statement: Not applicable.

Acknowledgments: The authors are grateful to Alexander Tikhomirov for invitation to present manuscript for this issue. In addition, they would like to thank three anonymous Reviewers for the careful reading of the manuscript and valuable remarks.

Conflicts of Interest: The authors declare no conflict of interest.

Appendix A

Proof of Lemma 1. If $Lip(h) = C < \infty$, then h is absolutely continuous (see, e.g., §13 in [42]), and consequently there exists $h'(x)$ for almost all $x \in \mathbb{R}$. Thus, $|h'(x)| \leq C$ for almost all $x \in \mathbb{R}$ in light of Equation (4). Assume that essential supremum $\|h'\|_\infty = C_0 < C$. Then, for any $\varepsilon > 0$, one can find a version of h', defined on $\mathbb{R}$, such that $\sup_{x \in \mathbb{R}} |h'(x)| \leq C_0 + \varepsilon$. (It was explained in Section 2 that one can consider a measurable extension of h' to $\mathbb{R}$). Then, due to Equation (11) with h instead of f we obtain Equation (5) with $C_0 + \varepsilon$ instead of C. Consequently, $Lip(h) \leq C_0 < C$. We come to the contradiction.

On the other hand, let h be absolutely continuous. Then, for almost all $x \in \mathbb{R}$, there exists $h'(x)$ and Equation (11) is valid for h instead of f. Assume that essential supremum

$\|h'\|_\infty = C < \infty$. Then, for any $\varepsilon > 0$ there is a version of h' such that $\sup_{x \in \mathbb{R}} |h'(x)| \leq C + \varepsilon$. According to Equation (11), the relation (5) holds with $C + \varepsilon$ instead of C. Since $\varepsilon > 0$ can be taken as an arbitrary small, one can claim that $Lip(h) \leq C$. Suppose that $Lip(h) \leq C_0 < C$. Then, for almost all $x \in \mathbb{R}$, there exists h' and $|h'| \leq C_0$. Thus, we found a version with $\|h'\|_\infty \leq C_0$. The contradiction shows that $Lip(h) = C$. Hence, the desired statement is proved. □

Proof of Lemma 2. Let x_0 be a continuity point of a function $h \in \mathcal{K} \cup \mathcal{H}_1 \cup \mathcal{H}_2$. Then, the same is true for a function $h(u)e^{-\lambda u}$, $u \in \mathbb{R}$. Hence, the function $\int_x^\infty h(u)e^{-\lambda u} du$ has a derivative $-h(x_0)e^{-\lambda x_0}$ at point x_0 (in light of Remark 1 an integral $\int_x^\infty h(u)e^{-\lambda u} du$ is well defined for any $x \in \mathbb{R}$). Thus, for each point x of continuity h there exists

$$f'_h(x) = -\lambda e^{\lambda x} \int_x^\infty h(u)e^{-\lambda u} du - e^{\lambda x}(-h(x)e^{-\lambda x}) = \lambda f_h(x) + h(x). \tag{A1}$$

For each fixed $z \in \mathbb{R}$ and a function $h(x) = \mathbb{I}\{x \leq z\}$, where $x \in \mathbb{R}$, Equation (12) is verified in a similar way for the right derivative f_h at point $z \in \mathbb{R}$. Taking $x = 0$ in Equation (12), we obtain $-\mathbb{E}[h(Z)]/\lambda$. Evidently, $-e^{\lambda x} \int_x^\infty e^{-\lambda u} du = -1/\lambda$. Therefore, Equation (A1) yields

$$f'_h(x) = -\lambda e^{\lambda x} \int_x^\infty (h(u) - h(x))e^{-\lambda u} du. \tag{A2}$$

If a function h belongs to $\mathcal{K}$, then, for any $u, x \in \mathbb{R}$, the following inequality holds $|h(u) - h(x)| \leq 1$. Consequently, for $h \in \mathcal{K}$, one has $\|f'_h\|_\infty \leq 1$ (where f'_h means a right derivative of a version of f'_h, and we operate with essential supremum).

Taking into account Lemma 1, for a function $h \in \mathcal{H}_1$ and any $x \leq u$, one can write $|h(u) - h(x)| \leq Lip(h)(u-x) = \|h'\|_\infty (u-x)$. For $h \in \mathcal{H}_2$ and $x \leq u$, by the Lagrange finite-increments formula, $|h(u) - h(x)| \leq |h'(v)|(u-x) \leq \|h'\|_\infty (u-x)$, where $x < v < u$. Hence, for any $x \in \mathbb{R}$ and $h \in \mathcal{H}_1 \cup \mathcal{H}_2$,

$$|f'_h(x)| = \lambda e^{\lambda x} \int_x^\infty (h(u) - h(x))e^{-\lambda u} du \leq \lambda e^{\lambda x} \|h'\|_\infty \int_x^\infty (u-x)e^{-\lambda u} du = \frac{\|h'\|_\infty}{\lambda}$$

since

$$\lambda e^{\lambda x} \int_x^\infty (u-x)e^{-\lambda u} du = \int_0^\infty \lambda v e^{-\lambda v} dv = \frac{1}{\lambda}. \tag{A3}$$

Taking into account Equation (12), one can see that, for any $h \in \mathcal{H}_2$, $f'_h = \lambda f_h + h$, where f_h and h have derivatives at each point $x \in \mathbb{R}$. Using Equation (A2) and Equation (A3), we obtain, for $x \in \mathbb{R}$,

$$f''_h(x) = \lambda f'_h(x) + h'(x) = -\lambda^2 e^{\lambda x} \int_x^\infty (h(u) - h(x))e^{-\lambda u} du + h'(x)$$

$$= -\lambda^2 e^{\lambda x} \int_x^\infty (h(u) - h(x) - h'(x)(u-x))e^{-\lambda u} du. \tag{A4}$$

By means of Equation (A3) and the Lagrange finite-increments formula we can write

$$|f''_h(x)| \leq 2\|h'\|_\infty \lambda^2 e^{\lambda x} \int_x^\infty (u-x)e^{-\lambda u} du = 2\|h'\|_\infty. \tag{A5}$$

Let us apply the Taylor formula with integral representation of the residual term:

$$h(u) = h(x) + h'(x)(u-x) + R(u,x), \quad R(u,x) = \int_x^u (u-t)h''(t)dt, \quad u, x \in \mathbb{R}. \tag{A6}$$

This representation known for the Riemann integral (see, e.g., [67], §9.17) holds in the framework of the Lebesgue integral if it is possible to use the recurrent integration by parts for $R(u,x)$, i.e.,

$$\int_x^u (u-t)h''(t)dt = -h'(x)(u-x) + \int_x^u h'(t)dt = -h'(x)(u-x) + h(u) - h(x). \quad (A7)$$

Integral in the left-hand side of Equation (A7) exists by virtue of Lemma 1 since $h' \in \text{Lip}(1)$. Therefore, $h''(x)$ is defined for almost all $x \in \mathbb{R}$ and (essential supremum) $\|h''\| \leq 1$. The latter equality in Equation (A7) is obvious since h' is continuous function on $\mathbb{R}$. The first equality in Equation (A7) is valid due to the integration by parts formula for the Lebesgue integral. Indeed, functions $h'(t)$ and $(u-t)$ are absolutely continuous for t belonging to $[x, u]$. Thus, we can apply, e.g., Theorem 13.29 of [42] to justify the first equality in Equation (A7). Consequently, due to Equation (A4) and Equation (A6) one can write

$$|f_h''(x)| \leq \left| -\lambda^2 e^{\lambda x} \int_x^\infty \left(\int_x^u (u-t)h''(t)dt \right) e^{-\lambda u} du \right|$$

$$\leq \frac{\|h''\|_\infty}{2} \left| \int_x^\infty \lambda^2 (u-x)^2 e^{-\lambda(u-x)} du \right| = \frac{\|h''\|_\infty \Gamma(3)}{2\lambda} = \frac{\|h''\|_\infty}{\lambda}, \quad (A8)$$

where $\Gamma(\alpha) := \int_0^\infty u^{\alpha-1} e^{-u} du$, $\alpha > 0$. Relations Equation (A5) and Equation (A8) lead to the last statement of Lemma 2. The proof is complete. □

Comments to Definition 1. For each Lipschitz function f, one can claim that $\mathbb{E}[f(X)]$ is finite since $\mathbb{E}|X| < \infty$ and, in light of Remark 1, one has $|f(x)| \leq C|x| + |f(0)|$, where $C = \text{Lip}(f)$, $x \in \mathbb{R}$. Clearly, it is sufficient to verify Equation (14) for any Lipschitz function f such that $f(0) = 0$ (otherwise we take the Lipschitz function $f(x) - f(0)$, $x \in \mathbb{R}$). Evidently, $p^e(x)$, $x \in \mathbb{R}$, introduced by Equation (15), is a probability density because for non-negative random variable X according to [47], Ch.2, formula (69)

$$\mathbb{E}[X] = \int_{[0,\infty)} \mathbb{P}(X > u) du. \quad (A9)$$

We will show that, for such f and a density p^e of X^e, one has

$$\int_{[0,\infty)} f(u) dF(u) = \int_{[0,\infty)} f'(u) \mathbb{P}(X > u) du, \quad (A10)$$

where F is a distribution function of X and $\mathbb{E}[X] \neq 0$. We take integrals over $[0, \infty)$ as $X \geq 0$ and $p^e(x) = 0$ for $x < 0$.

We know that a function f has a derivative at almost all points $x \in \mathbb{R}$. Therefore, the right-hand side of Equation (A10) does not depend on the choice of a version f' ($\mathbb{P}(X > u)$ is a measurable bounded function). The integral in the right-hand side of Equation (A10) is finite because $\|f'\| \leq C$ in light of Lemma 1 and since the right-hand side of Equation (A9) is finite. One can take the integrals over $(0, \infty)$ in Equation (A10) as $f(0) = 0$ and $m(\{0\}) = 0$, where m stands for the Lebesgue measure.

Function f is a function of finite variation (as f is the Lipschitz function). Therefore, $f = f_1 - f_2$ where f_1 and f_2 are nondecreasing functions. We can take the canonical representation with $f_1(x) = \text{Var}_0^x(f)$ and $f_2(x) = f(x) - f_1(x)$, $x \in \mathbb{R}$, where $\text{Var}_a^b(f)$ is the variation of f on $[a, b]$, $a < b$ (see, e.g., [42], Theorem 12.18). If $f \in \text{Lip}(C)$, then $\text{Var}_a^b(f) \leq C(b-a)$. For $a < c < b$, one has (see, e.g., [42], Lemma 12.15)

$$\text{Var}_a^c(f) + \text{Var}_c^b(f) = \text{Var}_a^b(f).$$

We see that such f_1 and f_2 are the Lipschitz functions when f is the Lipschitz one. Hence, for almost all $x \in \mathbb{R}$, there exist $f_1'(x)$, $f_2'(x)$ and $f'(x) = f_1'(x) - f_2'(x)$. Thus, it is enough to demonstrate that

$$\int_{(0,\infty)} f_i(u) dF(u) = \int_{(0,\infty)} f_i'(u) \mathbb{P}(X > u) du, \quad i = 1, 2.$$

These integrals are finite since f_1 and f_2 are the Lipschitz functions. Note that

$$\int_{(0,\infty)} f_i(u)dF(u) = -\int_{(0,\infty)} f_i(u)d(1-F(u)) = -\int_{(0,\infty)} f_i(u)d\mathbb{P}(X > u).$$

By applying Theorem 11 of Sec. 6, Ch. 2 [47], one obtains, for each $b > 0$, nondecreasing continuous function f_i and a nondecreasing right-continuous function $(-\mathbb{P}(X > u))$, the following formula:

$$\int_{(0,b]} f_i(u)d\mathbb{P}(X > u) = f_i(b)\mathbb{P}(X > b) - f_i(0)\mathbb{P}(X > 0) - \int_{(0,b]} \mathbb{P}(X > u)df_i(u) \quad (A11)$$

$$= f_i(b)\mathbb{P}(X > b) - \int_{(0,b]} \mathbb{P}(X > u)f_i'(u)du.$$

We take into account that $f_i(0) = 0$ and the σ-finite measure Q_i corresponding to f_i is absolutely continuous w.r.t. m, and the Radon–Nikodým derivative $\frac{dQ_i}{dm}(x) = f_i'(x)$, $x \in \mathbb{R}$, $i = 1,2$. In addition, we can write $\mathbb{P}(X > u)$ in Equation (A11) since for at almost all $u \in \mathbb{R}$ the left-limit of this function coincides with $\mathbb{P}(X > u)$ (there exist at most a countable set of jumps of $\mathbb{P}(X > u)$, $u \in \mathbb{R}$). Obviously, $f_i(b)\mathbb{P}(X > b) \to 0$ as $b \to \infty$ because $|f_i(u)| \leq A_i u + B_i$ for some positive A_i, B_i and all $u \in \mathbb{R}$. Indeed, according to formula (73) of Sec. 6, Ch. 2 of [47] the condition $\mathbb{E}|X| < \infty$ yields

$$b\mathbb{P}(|X| > b) \to 0, \quad b \to \infty.$$

By the Lebesgue dominated convergence theorem one infers that

$$\int_{(0,b]} f_i(u)d\mathbb{P}(X > u) \to \int_{(0,\infty)} f_i(u)d\mathbb{P}(X > u), \quad b \to \infty.$$

and

$$\lim_{b\to\infty} \int_{(0,b]} \mathbb{P}(X > u)f_i'(u)du = \int_{(0,\infty)} \mathbb{P}(X > u)f_i'(u)du.$$

This permits to claim the validity of Equation (A10) which entails the desired Equation (15).

Proof of Lemma 3. For $f \in \mathcal{H}_2$, in light of Remark 1 one can state that $|f(x)| \leq A_0 x^2 + B_0$ for some positive numbers A_0 and B_0. Let F be a distribution function of X. Since $\mathbb{E}[X^2] < \infty$, due to Corollary 2, Sec. 6, Ch. 2, v.1, [47] one has

$$x^2 F(x) \to 0, \quad x \to -\infty; \quad x^2(1 - F(x)) \to 0, \quad x \to \infty.$$

Hence, we obtain that $f(x)F(x) \to 0$ as $x \to -\infty$ and $f(x)(1 - F(x)) \to 0$ as $x \to \infty$. Continuous function f has a bounded variation. Thus $f = f_1 - f_2$ where f_1 and f_2 are nondecreasing continuous functions. Thus, for any $a < 0$ and $i = 1,2$, the integration by parts formula (see, e.g., Theorem 11, Sec. 6, Ch. 2, [47]) and Equation (18) give

$$\int_{(a,0]} (f_1(x) - f_2(x))dF(x) = f(0)F(0) - f(a)F(a) - \left(\int_{(a,0]} F(x)df_1(x) - \int_{(a,0]} F(x)df_2(x)\right)$$

$$= f(0)F(0) - f(a)F(a) - \int_{(a,0]} F(x)df(x).$$

We take into account that the integrands are bounded measurable functions and the measures corresponding to F, f_1 and f_2 are finite on any interval $(a,0]$. Therefore such integrals are finite. According to the Lebesgue theorem on dominated convergence (recall that $\mathbb{E}[X^2] < \infty$) one has

$$\lim_{a\to-\infty} \int_{(a,0]} f(x)dF(x) = \int_{(-\infty,0]} f(x)dF(x),$$

and the limit is finite. The monotone convergence theorem for σ-finite measure yields

$$\lim_{a \to -\infty} \left(\int_{(a,0]} F(x) df_1(x) - \int_{(a,0]} F(x) df_2(x) \right) = \int_{(-\infty,0]} F(x) df_1(x) - \int_{(-\infty,0]} F(x) df_2(x).$$

We have seen that $f(a)F(a) \to 0$ as $a \to -\infty$. Hence, in light of Equation (18)

$$\int_{(-\infty,0]} F(x) df_1(x) - \int_{(-\infty,0]} F(x) df_2(x) = \int_{(-\infty,0]} F(x) df(x).$$

Therefore, for $i = 1, 2$, each integral $\int_{(-\infty,0]} F(x) df_i(x)$ is finite as $\int_{(-\infty,0]} F(x) df(x)$ is finite. Thus,

$$\int_{(-\infty,0]} f(x) dF(x) = f(0)F(0) - \int_{(-\infty,0]} F(x) df(x) = f(0)F(0) + \int_{(-\infty,0]} (-F(x)) f'(x) dx,$$

as f is absolutely continuous. Indeed, for any $x \in \mathbb{R}$,

$$f(x) = f(0) + \int_{(0,x]} f'(u) du,$$

where (continuous) $f' \in L^1[a,b]$ for any finite interval $[a,b]$. Thus, $(f')^+ \in L^1[a,b]$ and $(f')^- \in L^1[a,b]$. Set

$$f_1(x) := f(0) + \int_{(0,x]} (f'(u))^+ du, \quad f_2(x) := \int_{(0,x]} (f'(u))^- du.$$

Then f_1 and f_2 are nondecreasing continuous functions on $\mathbb{R}$, $f = f_1 - f_2$ and

$$\int_{(a,0]} F(x) df(x) = \int_{(a,0]} F(x) df_1(x) - \int_{(a,0]} F(x) df_2(x),$$

where these three integrals are finite. For (non-negative) σ-finite measures corresponding to f_1 and f_2, one can write

$$\int_{(a,0]} F(x) df_1(x) = \int_{(a,0]} F(x) (f'(x))^+ dx, \quad \int_{(a,0]} F(x) df_2(x) = \int_{(a,0]} F(x) (f'(x))^- dx.$$

Thus, one has

$$\int_{(a,0]} F(x) df(x) = \int_{(a,0]} F(x) (f'(x))^+ dx - \int_{(a,0]} F(x) (f'(x))^- dx$$

$$= \int_{(a,0]} F(x) ((f'(x))^+ - (f'(x))^-) dx = \int_{(a,0]} F(x) f'(x) dx. \quad (A12)$$

The bound $\|f'\| \le 1$ follows from Lemma 1. Therefore, the Lebesgue theorem on dominated convergence yields (as $\mathbb{E}|X| < \infty$)

$$\lim_{a \to -\infty} \int_{(a,0]} F(x) f'(x) dx = \int_{(-\infty,0]} F(x) f'(x) dx.$$

We have demonstrated that

$$\int_{(-\infty,0]} F(x) df(x) = \int_{(-\infty,0]} F(x) f'(x) dx.$$

In a similar way, we consider $\int_{(0,b]} (1 - F(x)) dx$ and letting $b \to \infty$ come to relation

$$- \int_{(0,\infty)} f(x) d(1 - F(x)) = f(0)(1 - F(0)) + \int_{(0,\infty)} (1 - F(x)) df(x)$$

$$= f(0)(1 - F(0)) + \int_{(0,\infty)} (1 - F(x))f'(x)dx.$$

This establishes Equation (21). □

References

1. Steutel, F.W.; Van Harn, K. *Infinite Divisibility of Probability Distributions on the Real Line*; Marcel Dekker: New York, NY, USA, 2004.
2. Nolan, J.P. *Univariate Stable Distributions. Models for Heavy Tailed Data*; Springer: Cham, Switzerland, 2020.
3. Jagers, P. Branching processes: Personal historical perspective. In *Statistical Modeling for Biological Systems*; Almudevar, A., Oakes, D., Hall, J., Eds.; Springer: Cham, Switzerland, 2020; pp. 1–12. [CrossRef]
4. Schmidli, H. *Risk Theory*; Springer: Cham, Switzerland, 2017.
5. Gnedenko, B.V.; Korolev V.Y. *Random Summation. Limit Theorems and Applications*; CRC Press: Boca Raton, FL, USA, 1996.
6. Kalashnikov V.V. *Geometric Sums: Bounds for Rare Events with Applications*; Kluwer Academic: Dordrecht, The Netherlands, 1997.
7. Pinski, M.A.; Karlin, S. *An Introduction to Stochastic Modeling*, 4th ed.; Academic Press: Amsterdam, The Netherlands, 2011.
8. Bulinski, A.; Spodarev, E. Introduction to random fields. In *Stochastic Geometry, Spacial Statistics and Random Fields. Asymptotic Methods*; Spodarev, E., Ed.; Springer: Berlin, Germany, 2013; pp. 277–336. [CrossRef]
9. Zolotarev, V.M. *Modern Theory of Summation of Random Variables*; De Gruyter: Berlin, Germany, 1997.
10. Rachev, S.T.; Klebanov, L.B.; Stoyanov, S.V.; Fabozzi, F.J. *The Methods of Distances in the Theory of Probability and Statistics*; Springer: New York, NY, USA, 2013.
11. Stein, C. A bound for the error in the normal approximation to the distribution of a sum of dependent random variables. In *Proceedings of the Sixth Berkeley Symposium on Mathematical Statistics and Probability, Volume 2: Probability Theory*; Statistical Laboratory of the University of California: Berkeley, CA, USA, 1972; pp. 583–602.
12. Stein, C. *Approximate Computation of Expectations, Institute of Mathematical Statistics Lecture Notes—Monograph Series, 7*; Institute of Mathematical Statistics: Hayward, CA, USA, 1986.
13. Slepov, N.A. Convergence rate of random geometric sum distributions to the Laplace law. *Theory Probab. Appl.* **2021**, *66*, 121–141. [CrossRef]
14. Tyurin, I.S. On the convergence rate in Lyapunov's theorem. *Theory Probab. Appl.* **2011**, *55*, 253–270. [CrossRef]
15. Barbour, A.D.; Chen, L.H.Y. (Eds.) *An Introduction to Stein's Method*; World Scientific: Singapore, 2005.
16. Chen, L.H.Y.; Goldstein, L.; Shao, Q.-M. *Normal Approximation by Stein's Method*; Springer: Heidelberg, Germany, 2011.
17. Ross, N. Fundamentals of Stein's method. *Probab. Surv.* **2011**, *8*, 210–293. [CrossRef]
18. Arras, B.; Breton, J.-C.; Deshayes, A.; Durieu, O.; Lachièze-Rey, R. Some recent advances for limit theorems. *ESAIM Proc. Surv.* **2020**, *68*, 73–96. [CrossRef]
19. Arras, B.; Houdré, C. *On Stein's Method for Infinitely Divisible Laws with Finite First Moment*, 1st ed.; Springer: Cham, Switzerland, 2019.
20. Chen, P.; Nourdin, I.; Xu, L.; Yang, X.; Zhang, R. Non-integrable Stable Approximation by Stein's Method. *J. Theor. Probab.* **2022**, *35*, 1137–1186. [CrossRef]
21. Rényi, A. (Hungarian) A characterization of Poisson processes. *Magyar Tud. Akad. Mat. Kutató. Int. Közl.* **1957**, *1*, 519–527.
22. Shevtsova, I.; Tselishchev, M. A generalized equilibrium transform with application to error bounds in the Rényi theorem with no support constraints. *Mathematics* **2020**, *8*, 577. [CrossRef]
23. Brown, M. Error bounds for exponential approximations of geometric convolutions. *Ann. Probab.* **1990**, *18*, 1388–1402. [CrossRef]
24. Brown, M. Sharp bounds for exponential approximations under a hazard rate upper bound. *J. Appl. Probab.* **2015**, *52*, 841–850. [CrossRef]
25. Hung, T.L.; Kein, P.T. On the rates of convergence in weak limit theorems for normalized geometric sums. *Bull. Korean Math. Soc.* **2020**, *57*, 1115–1126. [CrossRef]
26. Shevtsova, I.; Tselishchev, M. On the accuracy of the exponential approximation to random sums of alternating random variables. *Mathematics* **2020**, *8*, 1917. [CrossRef]
27. Korolev, V.; Zeifman, A. Bounds for convergence rate in laws of large numbers for mixed Poisson random sums. *Stat. Probab.* **2021**, *168*, 108918. [CrossRef]
28. Aldous, D.J. More Uses of Exchangeability: Representations of Complex Random Structures. In *Probability and Mathematical Genetics: Papers in Honour of Sir John Kingman*; Bingham, N.H., Goldie, C.M., Eds.; Cambridge Univesity Press: Cambridge, UK, 2010.
29. Shevtsova, I.; Tselishchev, M. On the accuracy of the generalized gamma approximation to generalized negative binomial random sums. *Mathematics* **2021**, *9*, 1571. [CrossRef]
30. Liu, Q.; Xia, A. Geometric sums, size biasing and zero biasing. *Electron. Commun. Probab.* **2022**, *27*, 1–13. [CrossRef]
31. Döbler, C.; Peccati, G. The Gamma Stein equation and noncentral de Jong theorems. *Bernoulli* **2018**, *24*, 3384–3421. [CrossRef]
32. Korolev, V. Bounds for the rate of convergence in the generalized Rényi theorem. *Mathematics* **2022**, *10*, 4252. [CrossRef]
33. Peköz, E.A.; Röllin, A. New rates for exponential approximation and the theorems of Rényi and Yaglom. *Ann. Probab.* **2011**, *39*, 587–608. [CrossRef]
34. Weinberg, G.V. Kulback-Leibler divergence and the Pareto-Exponential approximation. *SpringerPlus* **2016**, *5*, 604. [CrossRef]

35. Daly, F. Gamma, Gaussian and Poisson approximations for random sums using size-biased and generalized zero-biased couplings. *Scand. Actuar. J.* **2022**, *24*, 471–487. [CrossRef]
36. Zolotarev, V.M. Ideal metrics in the problem of approximating the distributions of sums of independent random variables. *Theory Probab. Appl.* **1977**, *22*, 433–449. [CrossRef]
37. Gibbs, A.L.; Su, F.E. On choosing and bounding probability metrics. *Int. Stat. Rev.* **2002**, *70*, 419–435. [CrossRef]
38. Janson, S. Probability Distances. 2020. Available online: www2.math.uu.se/~svante (accessed on 1 September 2022).
39. Peköz, E.A.; Röllin, A.; Ross, N. Total variation error bounds for geometric approximation. *Bernoulli* **2013**, *19*, 610–632. [CrossRef]
40. Slepov, N.A. Generalized Stein equation on extended class of functions. In Proceedings of the International Conference on Analytical and Computational Methods in Probability Theory and Its Applications, Moscow, Russia, 23–27 October 2017; pp. 75–79.
41. Ley, C.; Reinert, G.; Swan, Y. Stein's method for comparison of inivariate distributions. *Probab. Surv.* **2017**, *14*, 1–52. [CrossRef]
42. Yeh, J. *Real Analysis. Theory of Measure and Integration*, 2nd ed.; World Scientific: Singapore, 2006.
43. Gaunt, R.E. Wasserstein and Kolmogorov error bounds for variance gamma approximation via Stein's method I. *J. Theor. Probab.* **2020**, *33*, 465–505. [CrossRef]
44. Halmos, P.R. *Measure Theory*; Springer: New York, NY, USA, 1974.
45. Gaunt, R.E.; Walton, N. Stein's method for the single server queue in heavy traffic. *Stat. Probab. Lett.* **2020**, *156*, 108566. [CrossRef]
46. Muthukumar, T. Measure Theory and Lebesgue Integration. 2018. Available online: home.iitk.ac.in/~tmk (accessed on 1 September 2022).
47. Shiryaev, A.N. *Probability-1*; Springer: New York, NY, USA, 2016.
48. Burkill, L.C. *The Lebesgue Integral*; Cambridge University Press: Cambridge, UK, 1963.
49. Korolev, V.; Zeifman, A. Generalized negative binomial distributions as mixed geometric laws and related limit theorems. *Lith. Math. J.* **2019**, *59*, 366–388. [CrossRef]
50. Baldi, P.; Rinott, Y.; Stein, C. A normal approximations for the number of local maxima of a random function on a graph. In *Probability, Statistics and Mathematics, Papers in Honor of Samuel Karlin*; Anderson, T.W., Athreya, K.B., Iglehart, D.L., Eds.; Academic Press: San-Diego, CA, USA, 1989; pp. 59–81. [CrossRef]
51. Goldstein, L.; Rinott, Y. Multivariate normal approximations by Stein's method and size bias couplings. *J. Appl. Prob.* **1996**, *33*, 1–17. [CrossRef]
52. Goldstein, L. Berry-Esseen bounds for combinatorial central limit theorems and pattern occurrences, using zero and size biasing. *J. Appl. Probab.* **2005**, *42*, 661–683. [CrossRef]
53. Goldstein, L.; Reinert, G. Stein's method and the zero bias transformation with application to simple random sampling. *Ann. Appl. Probab.* **1997**, *7*, 935–952. [CrossRef]
54. Gaunt, R.E. On Stein's method for products of normal random variables and zero bias couplings. *Bernoulli* **2017**, *23*, 3311–3345. [CrossRef]
55. Döbler, C. Distributional transformations without orthogonality relations. *J. Theor. Probab.* **2017**, *30*, 85–116. [CrossRef]
56. Arratia, R.; Goldstein, L.; Kochman, F. Size bias for one and all. *Probab. Surv.* **2019**, *16*, 1–61. [CrossRef]
57. Weinberg, G.V. Validity of whitening-matched filter approximation to the Pareto coherent detector. *IET Signal Process* **2012**, *6*, 546–550. [CrossRef]
58. Blanchet, J.; Glinn, P. Uniform renewal theory with applications to expansions of random geometric sums. *Adv. Appl. Prob.* **2007**, *39*, 1070–1097. [CrossRef]
59. Kallenberg, O. *Foundations of Modern Probability*; Springer: New York, NY, USA, 1997.
60. Kingman, J.F.C. On queues in heavy traffic. *J. R. Stat. Soc. Ser. B Stat. Methodol.* **1962**, *24*, 383–392. [CrossRef]
61. Su, Z.; Wang, X. Approximation of sums of locally dependent random variables via perturbation of Stein operator. *arXiv* **2022**, arXiv:2209.09770.v2.
62. Korolev, V.Y.; Zeifman, A.I. Convergence of statistics constructed from samples with random sizes to the Linnik and Mittag-Leffler distributions and their generalizations. *J. Korean Stat. Soc.* **2017**, *46*, 161–181. [CrossRef]
63. Bulinski, A.; Kozhevin, A. New version of the MDR method for stratified samples. *Stat. Optim. Inf. Comput.* **2017**, *5*, 1–18. [CrossRef]
64. Ginag, L.T.; Hung, T.L. An extension of random summations of independent and identically distributed random variables. *Commun. Korean Math. Soc.* **2018**, *33*, 605–618. [CrossRef]
65. Farago, A. Decomposition of Random Sequences into Mixtures of Simpler Ones and Its Application in Network Analysis. *Algorithms* **2021**, *14*, 336. [CrossRef]
66. Feng, M.; Deng, L.-J.; Chen, F.; Perc, M.; Kurths, J. The accumulative law and its probability model: An extension of the Pareto distribution and the log-normal distribution. *Proc. R. Soc. A* **2020**, *476*, 20200019. [CrossRef] [PubMed]
67. Nikolsky, S.M. *A Course of Mathematical Analysis, v. 1*; Mir Publishers: Moscow, Russia, 1987.

Article

High-Dimensional Consistencies of KOO Methods for the Selection of Variables in Multivariate Linear Regression Models with Covariance Structures

Yasunori Fujikoshi [1,*] and Tetsuro Sakurai [2]

[1] Department of Mathematics, Graduate School of Science, Hiroshima University, 1-3-2 Kagamiyama, Hiroshima 739-8626, Japan
[2] School of General and Management Studies, Suwa University of Science, 5000-1 Toyohira, Chino 391-0292, Japan
* Correspondence: fujikoshi_y@yahoo.co.jp

Abstract: In this paper, we consider the high-dimensional consistencies of KOO methods for selecting response variables in multivariate linear regression with covariance structures. Here, the covariance structures are considered as (1) independent covariance structure with the same variance, (2) independent covariance structure with different variances, and (3) uniform covariance structure. A sufficient condition for model selection consistency is obtained using a KOO method under a high-dimensional asymptotic framework, such that sample size n, the number p of response variables, and the number k of explanatory variables are large, as in $p/n \to c_1 \in (0,1)$ and $k/n \to c_2 \in [0,1)$, where $c_1 + c_2 < 1$.

Keywords: consistency property; covariance structures; high-dimensional asymptotic framework; KOO methods; multivariate linear regression

MSC: 62H12; 62H10

Citation: Fujikoshi, Y.; Sakurai, T. High-Dimensional Consistencies of KOO Methods for the Selection of Variables in Multivariate Linear Regression Models with Covariance Structures. *Mathematics* **2023**, *11*, 671. https://doi.org/10.3390/math11030671

Academic Editors: Alexander Tikhomirov and Liangxiao Jiang

Received: 18 November 2022
Revised: 28 December 2022
Accepted: 17 January 2023
Published: 28 January 2023

Copyright: © 2023 by the authors. Licensee MDPI, Basel, Switzerland. This article is an open access article distributed under the terms and conditions of the Creative Commons Attribution (CC BY) license (https:// creativecommons.org/licenses/by/ 4.0/).

1. Introduction

We focus on a multivariate linear regression model of p response variables $y_1, \ldots, y_p$ on a subset of k explanatory variables $x_1, \ldots, x_k$. Suppose that there are n observations on a p-dimensional response vector $\boldsymbol{y} = (y_1, \ldots, y_p)'$ and a k-dimensional explanatory vector $\boldsymbol{x} = (x_1, \ldots, x_k)'$, and let $\mathbf{Y} : n \times p$ and $\mathbf{X} : n \times k$ be the observation matrices of $\boldsymbol{y}$ and $\boldsymbol{x}$ with sample size n, respectively. The multivariate linear regression model including all the explanatory variables under normality is written as follows:

$$\mathbf{Y} \sim \mathrm{N}_{n \times p}(\mathbf{X}\Theta, \Sigma \otimes \mathbf{I}_n), \tag{1}$$

where Θ is a $k \times p$ unknown matrix of regression coefficients, and Σ is a $p \times p$ unknown covariance matrix that is positive definite. $\mathrm{N}_{n \times p}(\cdot, \cdot)$ is the normal matrix distribution, such that the mean of $\mathbf{Y}$ is $\mathbf{X}\Theta$, and the covariance matrix of $\mathrm{vec}(\mathbf{Y})$ is $\Sigma \otimes \mathbf{I}_n$; equivalently, the rows of $\mathbf{Y}$ are independently normal with the same covariance matrix Σ. Here, $\mathrm{vec}(\mathbf{Y})$ is the $np \times 1$ column vector that is obtained by stacking the columns of $\mathbf{Y}$ on top of one another. We assumed that $\mathrm{rank}(\mathbf{X}) = k$.

In multivariate linear regression, the selection of variables for the model is an important concern. One of the approaches is to first consider variable selection models and then apply model selection criteria such as AIC and BIC. Such a criterion for Full Model (1) is expressed as follows:

$$\mathrm{GIC} = -2 \log L(\hat{\Xi}) + dg, \tag{2}$$

where $L(\hat{\Xi})$ is the maximal likelihood, $\Xi = \{\Theta, \Sigma\}$, $d > 0$ is the penalty term, and g is the number of unknown parameters given by $\{kp + \frac{1}{2}p(p+1)\}$. For AIC and BIC, d is defined as 2 and $\log n$, respectively. In the selection of k variables $x_1, \ldots, x_k$, we identified $\{x_1, \ldots, x_k\}$ with the index set $\{1, \ldots, k\} \equiv \omega$, and denote GIC for subset $j \subset \omega$ by GIC_j. Then, the model selection based on GIC chooses the following model:

$$\tilde{j} = \arg\min_j \text{GIC}_j. \tag{3}$$

Here the minimum is usually taken for all combinations of response variables. There are computational problems for the methods based on GIC, including AIC and BIC methods, since we need to compute $2^k - 1$ statistics for the selection of k explanatory variables. To avoid this computational problem, [1] proposed a method that was essentially thanks to [2]. The method, which was named the knock-one-out (KOO) method by [3], determines "selection" or "no selection" for each variable by comparing the model removing that variable and the full model. More precisely, the KOO method chooses the model or the set of variables given by

$$\hat{j} = \{j \in \omega \mid \text{GIC}_{\omega \backslash j} > \text{GIC}_\omega\}, \tag{4}$$

where $\omega \backslash j$ is a short expression for $\omega \backslash \{j\}$, which is the set obtained by removing element j from the set ω. In general, the KOO method can be applied to a method or criterion, not only AIC, a general variable selection criterion or method.

In the literature on multivariate linear regression, numerous papers have dealt with the variable selection problem, as it relates to selecting explanatory variables. When Σ is unknown positive definite, [4–6], for example, indicated that, in a high-dimensional case, AIC and C_p have consistency properties, but BIC is not necessarily consistent. KOO methods in the multivariate regression model were studied by [3] and [7,8]. The KOO method in discriminant analysis; see [9], and [10]. For a review, see [11].

In this paper, we assume that the covariance structure was one of three covariance structures: (1) an independent covariance structure with the same variance, (2) an independent covariance structure with different variances, and (3) a uniform covariance structure. The numbers of unknown parameters in covariance structures (1)–(3) were 1, p, and 2, respectively. Sufficient conditions for the KOO method given by (4) to be consistent were derived under a high-dimensional asymptotic framework, such that sample size n, the number p of response variables, and the number k of explanatory variables were large, as in $p/n \to c_1 \in (0,1)$ and $k/n \to c_2 \in [0,1)$, where $c_1 + c_2 < 1$. Ref. [12] considered similar problems under covariance structures (1), (3), and (4), an autoregressive covariance structure, but did not consider them under (2). Moreover, in the study of asymptotic consistencies, they assumed that k was fixed, but in this paper, k may tend to infinity, such that $k/n \to c_2 \in [0,1)$. From the numerical experiments in [12], we know that the probability of choosing the true model in Cases (1) and (3) results from the following table (Table 1). In variable selection for multivariate linear regression using the KOO method, the probability of selecting the true model is shown in the following table. Here, we examine Cases (1), an independent covariance structure with the same variance, and (3), a uniform covariance structure.

Table 1. KOO Based on AIC.

$k = 3$	KOO Based on AIC		KOO Based on AIC	
(n, p)	(20, 10)	(200, 100)	(20, 10)	(200, 100)
(1)	0.74	1.00	0.77	1.00
(3)	0.47	1.00	0.22	1.00

In this table (Table 1), k is the number of nonzero true explanatory variables, and the true parameter values were omitted. In [12], k was treated as finite. In this paper, k may tend to infinity, such that $k/n \to c_2 \in [0,1)$.

The present paper is organized as follows. In Section 2, we present notations and preliminaries. In Section 3, we state KOO methods with Covariance Structures (1)–(3) in terms of key statistics. Further, an approach for their consistencies is stated in Section 3. In Sections 4–6, we discuss consistency properties of KOO methods under Covariance Structures (1)–(3). In Section 7, our conclusions are discussed.

2. Notations and Preliminaries

Suppose that j denotes a subset of $\omega = \{1,\ldots,k\}$ containing k_j elements, and $\mathbf{X}_j$ denotes the $n \times k_j$ matrix comprising the columns of $\mathbf{X}$ indexed by the elements of j. Then, $\mathbf{X}_\omega = \mathbf{X}$. Further, we assumed that covariance matrix Σ had a covariance structure Σ_c. Then, we have a generic candidate model:

$$M_{c,j} : \mathbf{Y} \sim N_{n \times p}(\mathbf{X}_j \Theta_j, \Sigma_{c,j} \otimes \mathbf{I}_n), \tag{5}$$

where Θ_j is a $k_j \times p$ unknown matrix of regression coefficients. We assumed that $\text{rank}(\mathbf{X}) = k$.

When $\Sigma_{c,j}$ is a $p \times p$ unknown covariance matrix, we could write the GIC in (2) as follows:

$$\text{GIC}_{c,j} = n \log |\hat{\Sigma}_j| + np(\log 2\pi + 1) + d\left\{k_j p + \frac{1}{2}p(p+1)\right\}, \tag{6}$$

where $n\hat{\Sigma}_j = \mathbf{Y}'(\mathbf{I}_n - \mathbf{P}_j)\mathbf{Y}$ and $\mathbf{P}_j = \mathbf{X}_j(\mathbf{X}_j'\mathbf{X}_j)^{-1}\mathbf{X}_j'$. When $j = \omega$, model $M_{c,\omega}$ is called the full model. $\hat{\Sigma}_{c,\omega}$ and $\mathbf{P}_\omega$ are defined from $\hat{\Sigma}_{c,j}$ and $\mathbf{P}_j$ as $j = \omega$, $k_\omega = k$ and $\mathbf{X}_\omega = \mathbf{X}$.

In this paper, we considered the cases in which the covariance matrix Σ_c belonged to each of the following three structures:

(1) Independent covariance structure with the same variance (ICSS).

$$\Sigma_v = \sigma_v^2 \mathbf{I}_p,$$

(2) Independent covariance structure with different variances (ICSD).

$$\Sigma_b = \text{diag}(\sigma_1^2, \ldots, \sigma_p^2),$$

(3) Uniform covariance structure (UCS).

$$\Sigma_u = \sigma_u^2 (\rho_u^{1-\delta_{ij}})_{1 \leq i,j \leq p}.$$

The models considered in this paper can be expressed as in (5) with $\Sigma_{v,j}$, $\Sigma_{b,j}$, and $\Sigma_{u,j}$ for $\Sigma_{c,j}$. Let $f(\mathbf{Y}; \Theta_j, \Sigma_{c,j})$ be the density of $\mathbf{Y}$ in (5) with $\Sigma = \Sigma_{c,j}$. In the derivation of the GIC, under the covariance structure $\Sigma = \Sigma_{c,j}$, we use the following equality:

$$-2 \log \max_{\Theta_j, \Sigma_{c,j}} f(\mathbf{Y}; \Theta_j, \Sigma_{c,j}) = np \log(2\pi)$$
$$+ \min_{\Sigma_{c,j}} \left\{ np \log |\Sigma_{c,j}| + \text{tr} \Sigma_{c,j}^{-1} \mathbf{Y}'(\mathbf{I}_n - \mathbf{P}_j)\mathbf{Y} \right\}. \tag{7}$$

Let $\hat{\Sigma}_{c,j}$ be the quantity minimizing the right-hand side of (7). Then, in our model, it satisfies $\text{tr}\hat{\Sigma}_{c,j}^{-1}\mathbf{Y}'(\mathbf{I}_n - \mathbf{P}_j)\mathbf{Y} = np$, and we obtain

$$\begin{aligned}\text{GIC}_{c,j} &= -2 \log f(\mathbf{Y}; \hat{\Theta}_j, \hat{\Sigma}_c) + dm_{c,j} \\ &= np \log |\hat{\Sigma}_{c,j}| + np(\log 2\pi + 1) + dm_{c,j},\end{aligned} \tag{8}$$

where $m_{c,j}$ is the number of independent unknown parameters under $M_{c,j}$, and d is a positive constant that may depend on n. For AIC and BIC, d is defined by 2 ([13]) and $\log n$ ([14]), respectively.

3. Approach to Consistencies of KOO Methods

Our KOO method is based on

$$T_{c,j;d} = \mathrm{GIC}_{c,\omega\setminus j} - \mathrm{GIC}_{c,\omega}. \tag{9}$$

In fact, the KOO method chooses the following model:

$$\widehat{j}_{c;d} = \left\{ j \mid T_{c,j;d} > 0 \right\}. \tag{10}$$

Its consistency can be proven by showing the following two properties:

$$\mathrm{Q1}: \quad [\mathrm{F1}] \equiv \sum_{j \in j_*} \Pr(T_{c,j;d} \le 0) \to 0, \tag{11}$$

$$\mathrm{Q2}: \quad [\mathrm{F2}] \equiv \sum_{j \notin j_*} \Pr(T_{c,j;d} \ge 0) \to 0, \tag{12}$$

as in [11]. The result can be shown by using the following inequality:

$$\Pr(\widehat{j}_{c;d} = j_*) = \Pr\left(\bigcap_{j \in j_*} {}^{\prime\prime}T_{c,j;d} > 0{}^{\prime\prime} \bigcap_{j \notin j_*} {}^{\prime\prime}T_{c,j;d} < 0{}^{\prime\prime} \right)$$

$$= 1 - \Pr\left(\bigcup_{j \in j_*} {}^{\prime\prime}T_{c,j;d} \le 0{}^{\prime\prime} \bigcup_{j \notin j_*} {}^{\prime\prime}T_{c,j;d} \ge 0{}^{\prime\prime} \right)$$

$$\ge 1 - \sum_{j \in j_*} \Pr(T_{c,j;d} \le 0) - \sum_{j \notin j_*} \Pr(T_{c,j;d} \ge 0).$$

Here, [F1] denotes the probability that true variables are not selected, and [F2] denotes the probability that nontrue variables are selected. Such notations are used for other variable selection methods. x_j is included in the true set of variables if $\theta_j \ne 0$.

Here, we list some of our main assumptions:

A1: The set j_* of the true explanatory variables is included in the full subset, i.e., $j_* \subset \omega$. and the set j_* is finite.

A2: The high-dimensional asymptotic framework:
$p \to \infty$, $n \to \infty$, $k \to \infty$, $p/n \to c_1 \in (0,1)$, $k/n \to c_2 \in [0,1)$, where $0 < c_1 + c_2 < 1$.

A general model selection criterion $\widehat{j}_{c;d}$ is high-dimensionally consistent if

$$\lim \Pr(\widehat{j}_{c;d} = j_*) = 1,$$

under a high-dimensional asymptotic framework. Here, "lim" means the limit under A2.

4. Asymptotic Consistency under an Independent Covariance Structure

In this section, we show an asymptotic consistency of the KOO method on the basis of a general information criterion under an independent covariance structure. A generic candidate model when the set of explanatory variables is j can be expressed as follows:

$$M_{v,j}: \mathbf{Y} \sim \mathrm{N}_{n \times p}(\mathbf{X}_j \Theta_j, \Sigma_{v,j} \otimes \mathbf{I}_n), \tag{13}$$

where $\Sigma_{v,j} = \sigma_{v,j}^2 \mathbf{I}_p$ and $\sigma_{v,j}^2 > 0$. Let us denote the density of $\mathbf{Y}$ under (13) with $f(\mathbf{Y}; \Theta_j, \sigma_{v,j})$. Then, we have

$$-2 \log f(\mathbf{Y}; \Theta_j, \sigma_{v,j}^2) = np \log(2\pi) + np \log \sigma_{v,j}^2$$
$$+ \frac{1}{\sigma_{v,j}^2} \mathrm{tr}(\mathbf{Y} - \mathbf{X}_j \Theta_j)'(\mathbf{Y} - \mathbf{X}_j \Theta_j).$$

Therefore, the maximal estimators of Θ_j and $\sigma_{v,j}^2$ under $M_{v,j}$ are given as follows:

$$\hat{\Theta}_j = (\mathbf{X}_j'\mathbf{X}_j)^{-1}\mathbf{X}_j'\mathbf{Y}, \quad \hat{\sigma}_{v,j}^2 = \frac{1}{np}\mathrm{tr}\mathbf{Y}'(\mathbf{I}_n - \mathbf{P}_j)\mathbf{Y}. \tag{14}$$

General Information Criterion (8) is given by

$$\mathrm{GIC}_{v,j} = np\log\hat{\sigma}_{v,j}^2 + np(\log 2\pi + 1) + dm_{v,j}, \tag{15}$$

where d is a positive constant, and $m_{v,j} = k_j p + 1$.

Using (9) and (15), we have

$$T_{v,j;d} \equiv \mathrm{GIC}_{v,\omega\setminus j} - \mathrm{GIC}_{v,\omega}$$
$$= np\log\left(1 + U_{2j}U_1^{-1}\right) - dp, \tag{16}$$

where

$$U_1 = \mathrm{tr}\mathbf{Y}'(\mathbf{I}_n - \mathbf{P}_\omega)\mathbf{Y} = \sum_{\ell=1}^{p} y_\ell'(\mathbf{I}_n - \mathbf{P}_\omega)y_\ell,$$

$$U_{2j} = \mathrm{tr}\mathbf{Y}'(\mathbf{P}_\omega - \mathbf{P}_{\omega\setminus j})\mathbf{Y} = \sum_{\ell=1}^{p} y_\ell'(\mathbf{P}_\omega - \mathbf{P}_{\omega\setminus j})y_\ell.$$

$U_1/\sigma_{v,j_*}^2$ and $U_{2j}/\sigma_{v,j_*}^2$ are independently distributed as a central and a noncentral chi-squared distribution, respectively. More precisely, assume that

$$\mathrm{E}(\mathbf{Y}) = \mathbf{X}_{j_*}\Theta_{j_*}, \tag{17}$$

and let $\sigma_{v,*}^2 = \sigma_{v,j_*}^2$. Then, using basic distributional properties (see, [15]) on quadratic forms of normal variates and Wishart matrices, we have the following results:

$$\begin{aligned}&(1)\ U_1/\sigma_{v,*}^2 \sim \chi_{(n-k)p}^2,\\ &(2)\ U_{2j}/\sigma_{v,*}^2 \sim \chi_p^2(\delta_{v,j}^2),\\ &(3)\ U_1 \perp U_{2j},\end{aligned} \tag{18}$$

where noncentrality parameter $\tau_{v,j}^2$ is defined by

$$\delta_{v,j}^2 = \frac{1}{\sigma_{v,*}^2}\mathrm{tr}(\mathbf{X}_{j_*}\Theta_{j_*})'(\mathbf{P}_\omega - \mathbf{P}_{\omega\setminus j})\mathbf{X}_{j_*}\Theta_{j_*}.$$

If $j \notin j_*$, $\delta_{v,j}^2 = 0$, and if $j \in j_*$, in general, $\tau_{v,j}^2 \neq 0$. For a sufficient condition for the consistency of the KOO method based on $\mathrm{GIC}_{v,j}$, we assumed

$$\mathrm{A3v}: \text{For any } j \in j_*,\ \delta_{v,j}^2 = \mathrm{O}(np), \text{ and } \lim_{p/n\to c_1}\frac{1}{np}\delta_{v,j}^2 = \eta_{v,j}^2 > 0. \tag{19}$$

Now, we consider thew high-dimensional asymptotic consistency of the KOO method based on $\mathrm{GIC}_{v,j}$ in (15), whose selection method is given by $\hat{j}_{v,j;d} = \{j \mid T_{v,j;d} > 0\}$. When $j \notin j_*$, from (16), we can write

$$T_{v,j;d} = np\log\left\{1 + \chi_p^2/\chi_m^2\right\} - dp, \quad m = (n-k)p.$$

Therefore, we have

$$[F2] = \sum_{j \notin j_*} \Pr(np \log\{1 + \chi_p^2/\chi_m^2\} \geq dp)$$
$$= (k - k_{j_*}) \Pr(U \geq h) \qquad (20)$$
$$\leq (k - k_{j_*}) \Pr(U \geq h_0),$$

where

$$U = \frac{\chi_p^2}{\chi_m^2} - \frac{p}{m-2},$$
$$h = e^{d/n} - 1 - \frac{p}{m-2}, \quad h_0 = \frac{d}{n} - \frac{p}{m-2}. \qquad (21)$$

Note that $h_0 < h$. Then, under the assumption $h_0 > 0$, we have

$$[F2] \leq (k - k_{j_*}) h^{-2\ell} E[U^{2\ell}] \leq (k - k_{j_*}) h_0^{-2\ell} E[U^{2\ell}]. \qquad (22)$$

Related to the assumption $h_0 > 0$, we assumed

$$A4v: d > \frac{np}{m-2} \to \frac{1}{1-c_2}, \text{ and } d = O(n^a), \quad 0 < a < 1. \qquad (23)$$

The first part in A4v implies $h_0 > 0$. It is easy to see that

$$E[U^2] = \frac{2p(m+p-2)}{(m-2)^2(m-4)} = O((n^2p)^{-1}).$$

Here, for the first equality, assumption $m > 4$ is required. Further, $h_0^{-2} = O(n^{2(1-a)})$. Therefore, from (22), we have that $[F2] \to 0$.

When $j \in j_*$, we can write $T_{v,j;d} = np \log\{1 + \chi_p^2(\delta_{v,j}^2)/\chi_m^2\} - dp$. Therefore, we can express [F1] as

$$[F1] = \sum_{j \in j_*} \Pr(\widetilde{T}_{v,j;d} \leq 0),$$

where

$$\widetilde{T}_{v,j;d} = \frac{p}{n} \log\left\{1 + \frac{\chi_p^2(\delta_{v,j}^2)}{\chi_m^2}\right\} - \frac{d}{n}.$$

Assumptions A3v and A4v easily show that

$$\widetilde{T}_{v,j;d} \to c_1 \log(1 + \eta_{v,j}^2) > 0.$$

This implies that $\Pr(\widetilde{T}_{v,j;d} \leq 0) \to 0$.

These imply the following theorem.

Theorem 1. *Suppose that Assumptions A1, A2 A3v, and A4v are satisfied. Then, the KOO method based on general information criteria* $GIC_{v,j}$ *defined by* (15) *is asymptotically consistent.*

An alternative approach for "[F1] $\to 0$". When $j \in j_*$, we can write

$$T_{v,j;d} = np \log\{1 + \chi_p^2(\delta_{v,j}^2)/\chi_m^2\} - dp.$$

Therefore, we have

$$[\text{F1}] = \sum_{j \in j_*} \Pr(np \log\{1 + \chi_p^2(\delta_{v,j}^2)/\chi_m^2\} \leq dp)$$
$$= \sum_{j \in j_*} \Pr(\widetilde{U}_j \leq \widetilde{h}_j),$$

where, for $j \in j_*$,

$$\widetilde{U}_j = \frac{\chi_p^2(\delta_{v,j}^2)}{\chi_m^2} - \frac{p + \delta_{v,j}^2}{m-2}, \quad \widetilde{h}_j = e^{d/n} - 1 - \frac{p + \delta_{v,j}^2}{m-2} = h - \frac{\delta_{v,j}^2}{m-2}.$$

Then, under $d = O(n^a)(0 < a < 1)$, A3v in (19) and the assumption $\widetilde{h}_j < 0$ (or equivalently $h < \delta_j^2/(m-2)$), we have

$$[\text{F1}] \leq k_{j_*} \max_j |\widetilde{h}_j|^{-2\ell} \mathrm{E}[\widetilde{U}^{2\ell}].$$

It is easily seen that

$$\mathrm{E}[\widetilde{U}_j^2] = \frac{2(p + 2\delta_{v,j}^2)(m + p - 2 + \delta_{v,j}^2)}{(m-2)^2(m-4)} = O((n^2 p)^{-1}),$$

where $m > 4$ and under $d = n^a (0 < a < 1)$ and A3v,

$$|\widetilde{h}_j|^2 \to \frac{\eta_{v,j}^2}{c_1(1 - c_2)}.$$

These imply that $[\text{F1}] \to 0$. In this approach, it was assumed that $\widetilde{h}_j < 0$ (or equivalently $h < \delta_j^2/(m-2)$).

5. Asymptotic Consistency under an Independent Covariance Structure with Different Variances

In this section, we assumed that covariance matrix Σ had an independent covariance matrix with different variances, i.e., $\Sigma = \Sigma_b = \mathrm{diag}(\sigma_{b1}^2, \ldots, \sigma_{bp}^2)$. First, let us consider deriving a key statistic $T_{b,j;d} = \mathrm{GIC}_{b,\omega \setminus j} - \mathrm{GIC}_{b,\omega}$. Consider a candidate model with $\mathrm{E}(\mathbf{Y}) = \mathbf{X}\Theta$,

$$M_{b,\omega} : \mathbf{Y} \sim \mathrm{N}_{n \times p}(\mathbf{X}\Theta, \Sigma_b \otimes \mathbf{I}_n). \tag{24}$$

Let the density in the full model be expressed as $f(\mathbf{Y}; \Theta, \Sigma_b)$. Then, we have

$$-2 \log f(\mathbf{Y}; \Theta, \Sigma_b) = np \log(2\pi)$$
$$+ \sum_{\ell=1}^{p} \left\{ n \log \sigma_{b\ell}^2 + \frac{1}{\sigma_{b\ell}^2}(\mathbf{y}_\ell - \mathbf{X}\theta_\ell)'(\mathbf{y}_\ell - \mathbf{X}\theta_\ell) \right\}.$$

It holds that

$$-2 \log \max_{\Theta, \Sigma_b} f(\mathbf{Y}; \Theta, \Sigma_b) = np(\log 2\pi + 1)$$
$$+ \sum_{\ell=1}^{p} n \log \frac{1}{n} \mathbf{y}_\ell'(\mathbf{I}_n - \mathbf{P}_\omega)\mathbf{y}_\ell. \tag{25}$$

Next, consider the model removing the jth explanatory variable from the full model $M_{b,\omega}$, which is denoted by $M_{b,\omega\setminus j}$ or $M;b,\omega\setminus j$. Similarly,

$$-2\log \max_{M;b,\omega\setminus j} f(\mathbf{Y};\Theta,\Sigma_b) = np(\log 2\pi + 1)$$
$$+ \sum_{\ell=1}^{p} n\log \frac{1}{n} \mathbf{y}'_\ell(\mathbf{I}_n - \mathbf{P}_{\omega\setminus j})\mathbf{y}_\ell. \tag{26}$$

Using (25) and (26), we can obtain a general information criterion (8) for two models, $M_{b,\omega}$ and $M_{b,\omega\setminus j}$, and we have

$$T_{b,j;d} \equiv \text{GIC}_{b,\omega\setminus j} - \text{GIC}_{b,\omega}$$
$$= \sum_{\ell=1}^{p} n\log\left(1 + U_{2\ell}U_{1\ell}^{-1}\right) - dp, \tag{27}$$

where

$$U_{1\ell} = \mathbf{y}'_\ell(\mathbf{I}_n - \mathbf{P}_\omega)\mathbf{y}_\ell, \quad \ell = 1,\ldots,p,$$
$$U_{2\ell} = \mathbf{y}'_\ell(\mathbf{P}_\omega - \mathbf{P}_{\omega\setminus j})\mathbf{y}_\ell, \quad \ell = 1,\ldots,p.$$

Let us assume that

$$\mathrm{E}(\mathbf{Y}) = \mathbf{X}_{j_*}\Theta_{j_*} \text{ and } \sigma^2_{b,*} = \sigma^2_{b,j_*}. \tag{28}$$

Then, as in (18), we have the following results:

$$\begin{aligned}&(1)\ U_{1\ell}/\sigma^2_{b,*} \sim \chi^2_{n-k}, \quad \ell = 1,\ldots,p,\\&(2)\ U_{2\ell}/\sigma^2_{b,*} \sim \chi^2_1(\delta^2_{b,j;\ell}), \quad \ell = 1,\ldots,p,\\&(3)\ U_{1\ell}, U_{2\ell}, (\ell = 1,\ldots,p) \text{ are independent,}\end{aligned} \tag{29}$$

where noncentral parameters $\delta^2_{b,j;\ell}$ are defined by

$$\delta^2_{b,j;\ell} = \frac{1}{\sigma^2_{b,*}}(\mathbf{X}_{j_*}\boldsymbol{\theta}^{(\ell)}_*)'(\mathbf{P}_\omega - \mathbf{P}_{\omega\setminus j})(\mathbf{X}_{j_*}\boldsymbol{\theta}^{(\ell)}_*),$$

with $\Theta_* = (\boldsymbol{\theta}^{(1)}_*,\ldots,\boldsymbol{\theta}^{(p)}_*)$. If $j \notin j_*$, $\delta^2_{b,j;\ell} = 0$, and if $j \in j_*$, $\delta^2_{b,j;\ell} \neq 0$. For a sufficient condition for consistency of the KOO method based on $\text{GIC}_{b,j}$, we assumed

A3b : For any $j \in j_*$, $\lim(n-k)^{-1}\delta^2_{b,j;\ell} = \eta^2_{b,j;\ell} > 0$, and

$$\lim \frac{1}{p}\sum_{\ell=1}^{p}\log\left\{1 + \frac{1}{n-k}\delta^2_{b,j;\ell}\right\} \to \eta^2_{b,j} > 0. \tag{30}$$

Now, we consider the high-dimensional asymptotic consistency of the KOO method based on $T_{b,j;d}$ in (9), whose selection method is given by $\hat{j}_{v,j;d} = \{j \mid T_{b,j;d} > 0\}$. When $j \notin j_*$, we have

$$[\text{F2}] = \sum_{j\notin j_*}\Pr(\sum_{\ell=1}^{p} n\log\{1 + U_{2\ell}U_{1\ell}^{-1}\} \geq d)$$
$$\leq \sum_{j\notin j_*}\sum_{\ell=1}^{p}\Pr(n\log\{1 + U_{2\ell}U_{1\ell}^{-1}\} \geq d).$$

This implies that

$$[F2] \leq p(k - k_{j_*}) \Pr(n \log\{1 + \chi_1^2/\chi_{n-k}^2\} \geq d)$$
$$= p(k - k_{j_*}) \Pr(V \geq r), \quad (31)$$

where

$$V = \frac{\chi_1^2}{\chi_{n-k}^2} - \frac{1}{n-k-2},$$
$$r = e^{d/n} - 1 - \frac{1}{n-k-2}, \quad r_0 = \frac{d}{n} - \frac{1}{n-k-2}. \quad (32)$$

Note that $r_0 < r$. Then, under the assumption $r_0 > 0$, we have

$$[F2] \leq p(k - k_{j_*}) r^{-2\ell} E[V^{2\ell}] \leq p(k - k_{j_*}) r_0^{-2\ell} E[V^{2\ell}]. \quad (33)$$

Related to the assumption $r_0 > 0$, we assumed

$$\text{A4b}: d > \frac{n}{n-k-2} \to \frac{1}{1-c_2}, \text{ and } d = O(n^a), \quad 0 < a < 1. \quad (34)$$

The first part in A4b implies $r_0 > 0$. It is easy to see that

$$E[V^2] = \frac{2(n-k-1)}{(n-k-2)^2(n-k-4)} = O((n^2)^{-1}).$$

Further, $r_0^{-2} = O(n^{2(1-a)})$. Therefore, from (33), we have that $[F2] \to 0$.

When $j \in j_*$, we can write $T_{b,j;d} = n \sum_{\ell=1}^{p} \log\{1 + U_{2\ell} U_{1\ell}^{-1}\} - dp$. Therefore, we can express [F1] as follows:

$$[F1] = \sum_{j \in j_*} \Pr(\widetilde{T}_{b,j;d} \leq 0),$$

where

$$\widetilde{T}_{b,j;d} = \frac{1}{p} \sum_{\ell=1}^{p} \log\left\{1 + \frac{\chi_{1;\ell}^2(\delta_{b,j;\ell}^2)}{\chi_{n-k;\ell}^2}\right\} - \frac{d}{n}.$$

Assumptions A3b and A4b easily show that

$$\widetilde{T}_{b,j;d} \to \eta_{b,j}^2 > 0.$$

This implies that $\Pr(\widetilde{T}_{b,j;d} \leq 0) \to 0$.
These imply the following theorem.

Theorem 2. *Suppose that Assumptions A1, A2, A3b and A4b are satisfied. Then, the KOO method based on $T_{b,j;d}$ in (27) is asymptotically consistent.*

Let us consider an alternative approach for "[F1] $\to 0$" as in the case of independent covariance structure. When $j \in j_*$, we can write

$$[F1] = \sum_{j \in j_*} \Pr\left(\sum_{\ell=1}^{p}\left\{n\log\left(1 + \frac{\chi^2_{1;\ell}(\delta^2_{b,j;\ell})}{\chi^2_{n-k;\ell}}\right) - d\right\} \le 0\right)$$

$$\le \sum_{j \in j_*}\sum_{\ell=1}^{p} \Pr\left(n\log\left(1 + \frac{\chi^2_{1;\ell}(\delta^2_{b,j;\ell})}{\chi^2_{n-k;\ell}}\right) - d \le 0\right)$$

$$= \sum_{j \in j_*}\sum_{\ell=1}^{p} \Pr\left(\widetilde{V}_{j,\ell} \le \widetilde{r}_{j,\ell}\right).$$

Here, for $j \in j_*$,

$$\widetilde{V}_{j,\ell} = \frac{\chi^2_{1;\ell}(\delta^2_{b,j;\ell})}{\chi^2_{n-k;\ell}} - \frac{1 + \delta^2_{b,j;\ell}}{n-k-2}, \quad \ell = 1, \ldots, p,$$

$$\widetilde{r}_{j,\ell} = e^{d/n} - 1 - \frac{1 + \delta^2_{b,j;\ell}}{n-k-2} = r - \frac{\delta^2_{b,j}}{n-k-2}, \quad \ell = 1, \ldots, p,$$

where r is the same one as in (32). Note that $\chi^2_{1;\ell}(\delta^2_{b,j;\ell}), \ell = 1, \ldots, p$ are distributed as a noncentral distribution $\chi^2_1(\delta^2_{b,j;\ell})$, and they are independent. Then, under the assumption $\widetilde{r}_j < 0$ (or equivalently $r < \delta^2_{bj;\ell}/(n-k-2)$), we have

$$[F1] \le k_{j_*} \sum_{\ell=1}^{p} |\widetilde{r}_{j,\ell}|^{-2s} E[\widetilde{V}^{2s}_{j,\ell}], \quad s = 1, 2, \ldots. \tag{35}$$

In the above upper bound, it holds that

$$|\widetilde{r}_{j,\ell}| \sim \delta^2_{b,j;\ell}/(n-k) \to \eta^2_{b,j;\ell}. \tag{36}$$

Useful bounds are obtained by giving the first few moments of $\widetilde{V}_{j;\ell}$. For example,

$$E[\widetilde{V}^2_{j,\ell}] = \frac{2(1 + 2\delta^2_{v,j;\ell})(n-k-1+\delta^2_{v,j;\ell})}{(n-k-2)^2(n-k-4)} = O(n^{-1}),$$

$$E[\widetilde{V}^4_{j,\ell}] = O(n^{-2}).$$

Then, Bound (35) with $s = 2$ can be asymptotically expressed as follows:

$$k_{j_*} \sum_{\ell=1}^{p} \eta^{-4}_{b,j;\ell} E[\widetilde{V}^4_{j,\ell}] = k_{j_*} p\left(\frac{1}{p}\sum_{\ell=1}^{p} \eta^{-4}_{b,j;\ell}\right) \times O(n^{-2}).$$

The above expression is $O(n^{-1})$ under the assumption that $\frac{1}{p}\sum_{\ell=1}^{p} \eta^{-4}_{b,j;\ell}$ tends to a quantity.

6. Asymptotic Consistency under a Uniform Covariance Structure

In this section, we show an asymptotic consistency of KOO method based on a general information criterion under a uniform covariance structure. First, following [12], we derive a $GIC_{u,j}$ as in (6), and a key statistic $T_{u,j;d}$ as in (9). A uniform covariance structure is given by

$$\Sigma_u = \sigma^2_u(\rho^{1-\delta_{ij}}_u) = \sigma^2_u\{(1-\rho_u)\mathbf{I}_p + \rho_u\mathbf{1}_p\mathbf{1}'_p\}, \tag{37}$$

with Kronecker delta δ_{ij}. The covariance structure is expressed as follows:

$$\Sigma_u = \alpha\left(\mathbf{I}_p - \frac{1}{p}\mathbf{G}_p\right) + \beta\frac{1}{p}\mathbf{G}_p,$$

where

$$\alpha = \sigma_u^2(1-\rho_u), \quad \beta = \sigma_u^2\{1+(p-1)\rho_u\}, \quad \mathbf{G}_p = \mathbf{1}_p\mathbf{1}_p',$$

and $\mathbf{1}_p = (1,\ldots,1)'$. Matrices $\mathbf{I}_p - \frac{1}{p}\mathbf{G}_p$ and $\frac{1}{p}\mathbf{G}_p$ are orthogonal idempotent matrices, so we have

$$|\Sigma_u| = \beta\alpha^{p-1}, \quad \Sigma_u^{-1} = \frac{1}{\alpha}\left(\mathbf{I}_p - \frac{1}{p}\mathbf{G}_p\right) + \frac{1}{\beta}\cdot\frac{1}{p}\mathbf{G}_p.$$

Now, we consider the multivariate regression model $M_{u,j}$ given by

$$M_{u,j}: \mathbf{Y} \sim N_{n\times p}(\mathbf{X}_j\Theta_j, \Sigma_{u,j}\otimes \mathbf{I}_n), \tag{38}$$

where $\Sigma_{u,j} = \alpha_j(\mathbf{I}_p - p^{-1}\mathbf{G}_p) + \beta_j p^{-1}\mathbf{G}_p$. Let $\mathbf{H} = (\mathbf{h}_1, \mathbf{H}_2)$ be an orthogonal matrix where $\mathbf{h}_1 = p^{-1/2}\mathbf{1}_p$, and let

$$\mathbf{W}_j = \mathbf{Y}'(\mathbf{I}_n - \mathbf{P}_j)\mathbf{Y} \text{ and } \mathbf{U}_j = \mathbf{H}'\mathbf{W}_j\mathbf{H}.$$

Here, $\mathbf{h}_1$ is a characteristic vector of $\Sigma_{u,j}$, and each column vector of $\mathbf{H}_2$ is a characteristic vector of $\Sigma_{u,j}$. Let the density function of $\mathbf{Y}$ under $M_{u,j}$ be denoted by $f(\mathbf{Y};\Theta_j,\alpha_j,\beta_j)$. Then, we have

$$g(\alpha_j,\beta_j) = -2\log\max_{\Theta_j} f(\mathbf{Y};\Theta_j,\alpha_j,\beta_j)$$
$$= np\log(2\pi) + n(p-1)\log\alpha_j + n\log\beta_j + \text{tr}\Psi_j^{-1}\mathbf{U}_j,$$

where $\Psi_j = \text{diag}(\beta_j,\alpha_j,\ldots,\alpha_j)$. Therefore, the maximum likelihood estimators of α_j and β_j under $M_{u,j}$ are given by

$$\hat{\alpha}_j = \frac{1}{n(p-1)}\text{tr}\mathbf{H}_2'\mathbf{Y}'(\mathbf{I}_n - \mathbf{P}_j)\mathbf{Y}\mathbf{H}_2,$$
$$\hat{\beta}_j = \frac{1}{n}\mathbf{h}_1'\mathbf{Y}'(\mathbf{I}_n - \mathbf{P}_j)\mathbf{Y}\mathbf{h}_1.$$

The number of independent parameters under $M_{u,j}$ is $m_j = k_j p + 2$. Noting that Ψ_j is diagonal, we can obtain the general information criterion (GIC) in (8) for $\mathbf{Y}$ in (38) as follows:

$$\text{GIC}_{u,j} = n(p-1)\log\hat{\alpha}_j + n\log\hat{\beta}_j + np(\log 2\pi + 1) + d(k_j p + 2). \tag{39}$$

Therefore, we have

$$T_{u,j;d} \equiv \text{GIC}_{u,\omega\setminus j} - \text{GIC}_{u,\omega}$$
$$= n(p-1)\log\left\{\hat{\alpha}_{\omega\setminus j}(\hat{\alpha}_\omega)^{-1}\right\} + n\log\left\{\hat{\beta}_{\omega\setminus j}\left(\hat{\beta}_\omega\right)^{-1}\right\} - dp \tag{40}$$
$$= Z_{1j} + Z_{2j}.$$

Here, Z_{1j} and Z_{2j} are defined as follows:

$$Z_{1j} = n(p-1)\log\left\{1 + V_{2j}^{(1)}\left(V_1^{(1)}\right)^{-1}\right\} - d(p-1),$$
$$Z_{2j} = n\log\left\{1 + V_{2j}^{(2)}\left(V_1^{(2)}\right)^{-1}\right\} - d, \tag{41}$$

using the following $V_1^{(i)}, V_{2j}^{(i)}, i = 1, 2$:

$$V_1^{(1)} = \text{tr}\mathbf{H}_2'\mathbf{Y}(\mathbf{I}_n - \mathbf{P}_\omega)\mathbf{Y}\mathbf{H}_2, \quad V_{2j}^{(1)} = \text{tr}\mathbf{H}_2'\mathbf{Y}'(\mathbf{P}_\omega - \mathbf{P}_{\omega\setminus j})\mathbf{Y}\mathbf{H}_2,$$
$$V_1^{(2)} = h_1'\mathbf{Y}'(\mathbf{I}_n - \mathbf{P}_\omega)\mathbf{Y}h_1, \quad V_{2j}^{(2)} = h_1'\mathbf{Y}'(\mathbf{P}_\omega - \mathbf{P}_{\omega\setminus j})\mathbf{Y}h_1.$$

Related to the distributional reductions of $Z_{1j}, Z_{2j}, j = 1, \ldots, k$, we use the following Lemma frequently.

Lemma 1. *Let $\mathbf{W}$ have a noncentral Whishart distribution $W_p(m, \Sigma; \Omega)$. Let the covariance matrix Σ be decomposed into characteristic roots and vectors as follows:*

$$\Sigma = \mathbf{H}\Lambda\mathbf{H}'$$
$$= (\mathbf{H}_1, \ldots, \mathbf{H}_h)\text{diag}(\lambda_1\mathbf{I}_{q_1}, \ldots, \lambda_h\mathbf{I}_{q_h})(\mathbf{H}_1, \ldots, \mathbf{H}_h)',$$

where $\lambda_1 > \ldots > \lambda_h > 0$ and $\mathbf{H}$ is an orthogonal matrix. Then, $\text{tr}\mathbf{H}_j'\mathbf{W}_j\mathbf{H}_j, i = 1, \ldots, h$ are independently distributed to noncentral chi-squared distributions with mk_j degrees of freedom and noncentrality parameters $\delta_j^2 = \text{tr}\mathbf{H}_j'\Omega\mathbf{H}_j$.

Proof. The result may be proven by considering the characteristic function of $(\text{tr}\mathbf{H}_1'\mathbf{W}\mathbf{H}_1, \ldots, \text{tr}\mathbf{H}_q'\mathbf{W}\mathbf{H}_q)$ which is expressed as follows (see Theorem 2.1.2 in [15]):

$$E\left[e^{it_1\text{tr}\mathbf{H}_1'\mathbf{W}\mathbf{H}_1 + \cdots + it_h\text{tr}\mathbf{H}_h'\mathbf{W}\mathbf{H}_h}\right]$$
$$= E[\text{etr}(\mathbf{K})]$$
$$= |\mathbf{I}_p - 2\Sigma\mathbf{K}|^{-m/2}\text{etr}\left\{\Omega\mathbf{K}(\mathbf{I}_p - 2\Sigma\mathbf{K})^{-1}\right\},$$

where $\mathbf{K} = it_1\mathbf{H}_1\mathbf{H}_1' + \cdots + it_1\mathbf{H}_q\mathbf{H}_q'$. The result can be easily obtained by checking that the above last expression equals

$$\prod_{j=1}^q (1 - 2it_j)^{-nk_j/2}\exp\left\{\frac{it_j}{1 - 2it_j}\text{tr}\mathbf{H}_j'\Omega\mathbf{H}_j\right\}.$$

□

Assume that the true model is expressed as

$$M_{u,j_*}: \mathbf{Y} \sim N_{n\times p}(\mathbf{X}_{j_*}\Theta_{j_*}, \Sigma_{u,*} \otimes \mathbf{I}_n), \quad (42)$$

where $\Sigma_{u,*} = \alpha_*(\mathbf{I}_p - p^{-1}\mathbf{G}_p) + \beta_*p^{-1}\mathbf{G}_p$. Using Lemma 1, we have the following lemma.

Lemma 2. *Under True Model (42), it holds that*

(1) $V_1^{(1)}/\alpha_*$ *and* $V_{2j}^{(1)}/\alpha_*$ *are independently distributed to a central chi-squared distribution $\chi^2_{(p-1)(n-k)}$ and a noncentral chi-squared distribution $\chi^2_{p-1}(\delta_{1j}^2)$, respectively.*

(2) $V_1^{(2)}/\beta_*$ *and* $V_{2j}^{(2)}/\beta_*$ *are independently distributed to a central chi-squared distribution χ^2_{n-k} and a noncentral chi-squared distribution $\chi^2_1(\delta_{2j}^2)$, respectively.*

(3) *Noncentrality parameters δ_{1j}^2 and δ_{2j}^2 are defined as follows:*

$$\delta_{1j}^2 = \frac{1}{\alpha_*}\text{tr}\mathbf{H}_2'(\mathbf{X}_{j_*}\Theta_{j_*})'(\mathbf{P}_\omega - \mathbf{P}_{\omega\setminus j})(\mathbf{X}_{j_*}\Theta_{j_*})\mathbf{H}_2$$
$$\delta_{2j}^2 = \frac{1}{\beta_*}h_1'(\mathbf{X}_{j_*}\Theta_{j_*})'(\mathbf{P}_\omega - \mathbf{P}_{\omega\setminus j})(\mathbf{X}_{j_*}\Theta_{j_*})h_1.$$

Here, if $j \notin j_*$, then $\delta_{1j}^2 = 0$ and $\delta_{2j}^2 = 0$.

Now, we consider the high-dimensional asymptotic consistency of the KOO method based on $T_{b,j;d}$ in (27), whose selection method is given by $\hat{j}_{v,j;d} = \{j \mid T_{b,j;d} > 0\}$. For a sufficient condition for the consistency of $\hat{j}_{v,j;d}$, we assumed

A3u: For any $j \in j_*$, $\delta_{1j}^2 = O(np)$, $\delta_{2j}^2 = O(n)$ and

$$\lim \frac{1}{np}\delta_{1j}^2 = \eta_{1j}^2 > 0, \quad \lim \frac{1}{n}\delta_{2j}^2 = \eta_{2j}^2 > 0, \tag{43}$$

When $j \notin j_*$, we have

$$[F2] = \sum_{j \notin j_*} \{\Pr(Z_{1j} + Z_{2j} \geq 0)\}$$

$$\leq \sum_{j \notin j_*} \{\Pr(Z_{1j} \geq 0) + \Pr(Z_{2j} \geq 0)\}$$

$$= (k - k_{j_*})\left\{\Pr(Z^{(1)} \geq s_0^{(1)}) + \Pr(Z^{(2)} \geq s_0^{(2)})\right\}.$$

Here,

$$Z^{(1)} = \frac{\chi_{p-1}^2}{\chi_{(p-1)(n-k)}^2} - \frac{p-1}{(p-1)(n-k) - 2},$$

$$s^{(1)} = e^{d/n} - 1 - \frac{p-1}{(p-1)(n-k) - 2}, \quad s_0^{(1)} = \frac{d}{n} - \frac{p-1}{(p-1)(n-k) - 2},$$

$$Z^{(2)} = \frac{\chi_1^2}{\chi_{n-k}^2} - \frac{1}{n-k-2},$$

$$s^{(2)} = e^{d/n} - 1 - \frac{1}{n-k-2}, \quad s_0^{(2)} = \frac{d}{n} - \frac{1}{n-k-2}.$$

Note that $s_0^{(1)} < s^{(1)}$ and $s_0^{(2)} < s^{(2)}$. Then, under the assumption that $s_0^{(1)} > 0$ and $s_0^{(2)} > 0$, we have

$$[F2] \leq (k - k_{j_*})\left[\left(s_0^{(1)}\right)^{-2\ell} E\left[(Z^{(1)})^{2\ell}\right] + \left(s_0^{(2)}\right)^{-2\ell} E\left[(Z^{(2)})^{2\ell}\right]\right]. \tag{44}$$

Related to assumptions $s_0^{(1)} > 0$ and $s_0^{(2)} > 0$, we assumed

$$\text{A4u}: d > \frac{n(p-1)}{(p-1)(n-k) - 2} \to \frac{1}{1 - c_2}, \quad d > \frac{n}{n-k-2} \to \frac{1}{1-c_2},$$

$$\text{and } d = O(n^a), \quad 0 < a < 1. \tag{45}$$

The first part in A4u implies $s_0^{(1)} > 0$ and $s_0^{(2)} > 0$. It is easy to see that

$$E[(Z^{(1)})^2] = \frac{2(p-1)^2(n-k+1)}{\{(p-1)(n-k) - 2\}^2\{(p-1)(n-k) - 4\}} = O((n^3)^{-1}),$$

$$E[(Z^{(2)})^2] = \frac{2(n-k-1)}{(n-k-2)^2(n-k-4)} = O((n^2)^{-1}).$$

Further, $(s_0^{(1)})^{-2} = O(n^{2(1-a)})$ and $(s_0^{(2)})^{-2} = O(n^{2(1-a)})$. Therefore, from (44), we have that $[F2] \to 0$.

When $j \in j_*$, we can write $T_{b,j;d} = n\sum_{\ell=1}^{p} \log\{1 + U_{2\ell}U_{1\ell}^{-1}\} - dp$. Therefore, we can express [F1] as follows:

$$[F1] = \sum_{j \in j_*} \Pr(\widetilde{T}_{b,j;d} \leq 0),$$

where

$$\widetilde{T}_{b,j;d} = \frac{1}{p}\sum_{\ell=1}^{p}\log\left\{1+\frac{\chi^2_{1;\ell}(\delta^2_{b,j;\ell})}{\chi^2_{n-k;\ell}}\right\} - \frac{d}{n}.$$

Assumptions A3b and A4b easily show that

$$\widetilde{T}_{v,j;d} \to \log(1+\gamma^2_{v,j}) > 0.$$

This implies that $\Pr(\widetilde{T}_{v,j;d} \leq 0) \to 0$, and $[F1] \to 0$.
These imply the following theorem.

Theorem 3. *Suppose that Assumptions A1, A2, A3u and A4u are satisfied. Then, the KOO method based on $T_{u,j;d}$ in (40) is asymptotically consistent.*

7. Concluding Remarks

In this paper, we considered selecting regression variables in a p variate regression model with one of three covariance structures: (1) ICSS (an independent covariance structure with the same variance), (2) ICSD (an independent covariance structure with different variances), and (3) UCS (a uniform covariance structure). It was proposed to use a KOO method on the basis of a general information criterion with a penalty term d. We indicated high-dimensional consistencies of the KOO methods with $d = O(n^a), 0 < a < 1$. Ref. [12] studied the asymptotic consistencies of KOO methods in (1) and (3). However, in their approach, the number of explanatory variables was fixed; in this paper, the number of explanatory variables may have tended to infinity. KOO methods may be feasible in computation. The idea goes back to [1], and [2]. However, high-dimensional properties were recently studied in [7–9,11].

A high-dimensional study of the KOO method under an autoregressive covariance structure (AUTO), and extending our results to the case of non-normality remain as future work.

Author Contributions: Conceptualization, Y.F.; Methodology, Y.F. and T.S.; Software, T.S.; Writing—original draft, Y.F. and T.S.; Writing—review & editing, Y.F. All authors have read and agreed to the published version of the manuscript.

Funding: This research received no external funding.

Data Availability Statement: Not applicable.

Acknowledgments: The authors would like to express their gratitude to Vladimir V. Ulyanov and the three referees for their valuable comments and suggestions.

Conflicts of Interest: The authors declare no conflict of interest.

References

1. Nishii, R.; Bai, Z.D.; Krishnaia, P.R. Strong consistency of the information criterion for model selection in multivariate analysis. *Hiroshima Math. J.* **1988**, *18*, 451–462. [CrossRef]
2. Zhao, L.C.; Krishnaia, P.R.; Bai, Z.D. On detection of the number of signals in presence of white noise. *J. Multivar. Anal.* **1986**, *20*, 1–25. [CrossRef]
3. Bai, Z.; Fujikoshi, Y.; Hu, J. *Strong Consistency of the AIC, BIC, Cp and KOO Methods in High-Dimensional Multivariate Linear Regression*; Hiroshima Statistical Research Group: Hiroshima, Japan, 2018; TR; 18-09.
4. Yanagihara, H.; Wakaki, H.; Fujikoshi, Y. A consistency property of the AIC for multivariate linear models when the dimension and the sample size are large. *Electron. J. Stat.* **2015**, *9*, 869–897. [CrossRef]
5. Fujikoshi, Y.; Sakurai, T.; Yanagihara, H. Consistency of high-dimensional AIC-type and C_p-type criteria in multivariate linear regression. *J. Multivar. Anal.* **2014**, *123*, 184–200. [CrossRef]
6. Fujikoshi, Y.; Sakurai, T. High-dimensional consistency of rank estimation criteria in multivariate linear Model. *J. Multivar. Anal.* **2016**, *149*, 199–212. [CrossRef]

7. Oda, R.; Yanagihara, H. A fast and consistent variable selection method for high-dimensional multivariate linear regression with a large number of explanatory variables. *Electron. J. Stat.* **2020**, *14*, 1386–1412. [CrossRef]
8. Oda, R.; Yanagihara, H. A consistent likelihood-based variable selection method in normal multivariate linear regression. In *Intelligent Decision Technologies*; Czarnowski, I., Ed.; Springer: Singapore, 2021; Volume 238, pp. 391–401.
9. Fujikoshi, Y.; Sakurai, T. Consistency of test-based method for selection of variables in high-dimensional two group-discriminant analysis. *Jpn. J. Stat. Data Sci.* **2019**, *2*, 155–171. [CrossRef]
10. Oda, R.; Suzuki, Y.; Yanagihara, H.; Fujikoshi, Y. A consistent variable selection method in high-dimensional canonical discriminant analysis. *J. Multivar. Anal.* **2020**, *175*, 1–13. [CrossRef]
11. Fujikoshi, Y. High-dimensional consistencies of KOO methods in multivariate regression model and discriminant analysis. *J. Multivar. Anal.* **2022**, *188*, 104860. [CrossRef]
12. Sakurai, T.; Fujikoshi, Y. Exploring consistencies of information criterion and test-based criterion for high-dimensional multivariate regression models under three covariance structures. In *Festschrift in Honor of Professor Dietrich von Rosen's 65th Birthday*; Holgerson, T., Singnull, M., Eds.; Springer: Berlin, Germany, 2020; pp. 313–334.
13. Akaike, H. Information theory and an extension of the maximum likelihood principle. In *2nd International Symposium on Information Theory*; Petrov, B.N., Csáki, F., Eds.; Akadémiai Kiadó: Budapest, Hungary, 1973; pp. 267–281.
14. Schwarz, G. Estimating the dimension of a model. *Ann. Stat.* **1978**, *6*, 461–464. [CrossRef]
15. Fujikoshi, Y.; Ulyanov, V.V.; Shimizu, R. *Multivariate Statistics: High-Dimensional and Large-Sample Approximations*; Wiley: Hobeken, NJ, USA, 2010.

Disclaimer/Publisher's Note: The statements, opinions and data contained in all publications are solely those of the individual author(s) and contributor(s) and not of MDPI and/or the editor(s). MDPI and/or the editor(s) disclaim responsibility for any injury to people or property resulting from any ideas, methods, instructions or products referred to in the content.

Article

Limit Theorem for Spectra of Laplace Matrix of Random Graphs

Alexander N. Tikhomirov

Institute of Physics and of Mathematics, Komi Science Center of Ural Branch of RAS, 167982 Syktyvkar, Russia; tikhomirov@ipm.komisc.ru

Abstract: We consider the limit of the empirical spectral distribution of Laplace matrices of generalized random graphs. Applying the Stieltjes transform method, we prove under general conditions that the limit spectral distribution of Laplace matrices converges to the free convolution of the semicircular law and the normal law.

Keywords: semicircular law; random graph; normal law; Stieltjes transform; Laplace matrix

MSC: 60B20; 60C05

1. Introduction and Summary

The spectral theory of random graphs is a branch of mathematics that has been studied intensively in the literature in recent decades. The asymptotic behavior of eigenvalues and eigenvectors of matrices associated with graphs, adjacency matrices and Laplace matrices, in particular (see definition below), as the number of vertices of the graph tends to infinity is investigated. See for instance [1–8]. The adjacency matrix of the generalized Erdős–Rènyi random graph is a special case of the generalized Wigner matrix (matrices with elements that are independent up to symmetry, with zero means and different variances). Many deep results have been obtained recently for such matrices. Methods of studying of the spectrum asymptotics of the adjacency matrices are the same as for the spectrum asymptotics of Wigner matrices—these are the method of moments and the Stieltjes transform method. It should be noted that the most profound results for the spectrum of Wigner random matrices were obtained by the methods related to the Stieltjes transform; see [3,9,10].

Laplace matrices have one significant difference—the dependence of the diagonal elements on the remaining elements of the matrix. This significantly complicates the study. For instance, the limit distribution of the empirical spectral function of the Laplace matrix of a complete graph (non-random) was found firstly in 2006; see [11]. In most of the works devoted to the study of the spectrum asymptotics of Laplace matrices of random graphs, the method of moments is used; see [2,4,12]. In this paper, we consider the empirical spectral distribution function of the Laplace matrices of both weighted and unweighted generalized Erdős-Rényi random graphs. We have obtained simple sufficient conditions for the convergence of the empirical spectral distribution function of the Laplace matrices of random graphs to a distribution function that is a free convolution of the semicircular law and the standard normal law. The conditions are expressed in terms of the properties of the graph edge probability matrix and the weight variance matrix (for weighted graphs). To prove the convergence, we exclusively use the Stieltjes transform method.

We consider a non-oriented simple graph (without loops and with simple edges) $\{V, E\}$ with vertices $|V| = n$ and set of edges E such that edges $e \in E$ are independent and have probability p_e. Consider the adjacency $n \times n$ matrix

$$\mathbf{A} = [A_{jk}], \tag{1}$$

where
$$A_{jk} = \begin{cases} 0, & \text{if } (j,k) \notin E, \\ 1, & \text{if } (j,k) \in E. \end{cases}$$

Define a degree of vertex $j \in V$ as
$$d_j := \sum_{k:(j,k) \in E} A_{jk}.$$

We shall assume that A_{jk} for $1 \leq j \leq k \leq n$ are independent and $\mathbb{E} A_{jk} = p_{jk}^{(n)}$. Note that $\mathbb{E} d_j = \sum_{k:k \neq j} p_{jk}^{(n)}$. We have that matrix $\mathbf{A}$ is symmetric, i.e., $A_{jk} = A_{kj}$, and that r.v.'s A_{jk} for $1 \leq j \leq k \leq n$ are independent. We introduce the quantity

$$\widehat{a}_n = \frac{1}{n} \sum_{j,k=1}^{n} p_{jk}^{(n)} (1 - p_{jk}^{(n)}). \tag{2}$$

We introduce the diagonal matrix
$$\mathbf{D} = \text{diag}(d_1, \ldots, d_n),$$

normalized and centered Laplace matrix of not weighted graph G defined as

$$\widehat{\mathbf{L}} = \frac{1}{\sqrt{\widehat{a}_n}} \Big[(\mathbf{D} - \mathbf{A}) - \mathbb{E}(\mathbf{D} - \mathbf{A}) \Big].$$

We shall consider the weighted graphs $\widetilde{G} = (V, E, w)$ as well with weight function $w_{jk} = w_{kj} = X_{jk}$, where, for $1 \leq j \leq k \leq n$, there are independent random variables s.t.

$$\mathbb{E} X_{jk} = 0, \quad \mathbb{E} X_{jk}^2 = \sigma_{jk}^2.$$

The distribution of X_{jk} may depend on n, but for brevity, we shall omit the index n in the notations. We introduce the quantity

$$a_n = \frac{1}{n} \sum_{i,j=1}^{n} p_{ij}^{(n)} \sigma_{ij}^2. \tag{3}$$

The quantity a_n may be interpreted as the expected mean degree of graph $\widetilde{G}$. With graph $\widetilde{G}$, we consider the adjacency matrix

$$\widetilde{\mathbf{A}} = [A_{ij} X_{ij}]$$

and normalized Laplace or Markov matrix

$$\widetilde{\mathbf{L}} = \frac{1}{\sqrt{a_n}} (\widetilde{\mathbf{D}} - \widetilde{\mathbf{A}}),$$

where
$$\widetilde{\mathbf{D}} = \text{diag}(\widetilde{d}_1, \ldots, \widetilde{d}_n) \text{ with } \widetilde{d}_i = \sum_{j:j \neq i} A_{ij} X_{ij}.$$

We shall denote by $\lambda_1(\mathbf{B}) \geq \lambda_2(\mathbf{B}) \geq \cdots \geq \lambda_n(\mathbf{B})$ ordered eigenvalues of a symmetric $n \times n$ matrix $\mathbf{B}$. We shall consider the spectrum of matrices $\widetilde{\mathbf{L}}$, and $\widehat{\mathbf{L}}$. For brevity of notation, we shall write $\widetilde{\mu}_j = \lambda_j(\widetilde{\mathbf{L}})$, and $\widehat{\mu}_j = \lambda_j(\widehat{\mathbf{L}})$. We introduce the corresponding empirical spectral distributions (ESDs)

$$\widehat{G}_n(x) := \frac{1}{n} \sum_{j=1}^{n} \mathbb{I}\{\widehat{\mu}_j \leq x\}, \quad \widetilde{G}_n(x) := \frac{1}{n} \sum_{j=1}^{n} \mathbb{I}\{\widetilde{\mu}_j \leq x\}. \tag{4}$$

In the paper [11], in 2006, it was shown under conditions $p_{ij}^{(n)} \equiv 1$ and $\sigma_{ij}^2 \equiv 1$, for any $1 \leq i,j \leq n$, that ESD $\widetilde{G}_n(x)$ weakly converges in probability to the non-random distribution function $G(x)$, which is defined as a free convolution of the Gaussian distribution function and the semicircular distribution function (the definition of free convolution see, for instance, in [13]).

In [4], in 2010, the authors considered the limit of $\widetilde{G}_n(x)$ for weighted Erdös–Renyi graphs ($p_{ij}^{(n)} \equiv p_n$) with equivariance weights ($\sigma_{ij}^2 \equiv \sigma^2$). Assuming that p_n bounded away from zero and one, and that random variables X_{ij} have the fourth moment, they proved that $\widetilde{G}_n(x)$ weakly converges to the same function $G(x)$.

In [14], in 2020, Yizhe Zhu considered the so-called graphon approach to the limiting spectral distribution of Wigner-type matrices. The author described the moments of the limit spectral measure in terms 2279–2375, of graphon of the variance profile matrix $\Sigma = (\sigma_{ij}^2)$ and number of trees with a fixed number of vertices. Recently, Chatterjee and Hazra published the paper [12] in which the approach of Zhu was developed.

In [15], in 2021, the author stated simple conditions on probabilities p_{ij} for the convergence of ESD of adjacency matrices to the semicircular law. In the present paper, we consider the convergence of ESD $\widehat{G}_n(x)$ and $\widetilde{G}_n(x)$ under similar conditions to the function $G(x)$.

First, we formulate some conditions which we shall use in the present paper.

- Condition $CP(0)$:
$$a_n \to \infty, \text{ as } n \to \infty. \tag{5}$$

- Condition $CP(0a)$: There exists a constant C_0 s.t.
$$\sup_{n \geq 1} \max_{1 \leq j,k \leq n} \frac{1}{a_n} p_{jk}^{(n)} \sigma_{jk}^2 \leq C_0 < \infty.$$

- Condition $CP(1)$:
$$\lim_{n \to \infty} \frac{1}{na_n} \sum_{j=1}^n \sum_{k=1}^n |p_{jk}^{(n)} \sigma_{jk}^2 - \frac{a_n}{n}| = 0.$$

- Condition $CX(1)$: For any $\tau > 0$
$$L_n(\tau) := \frac{1}{na_n} \sum_{i,j=1}^n p_{ij}^{(n)} \mathbb{E} X_{ij}^2 \mathbb{I}\{|X_{ij}| > \tau \sqrt{a_n}\} \to 0 \text{ as } n \to \infty. \tag{6}$$

Remark 1. *Condition $CP(1)$ is equivalent to the following two conditions together*
- Condition $CP(1a)$:
$$\lim_{n \to \infty} \frac{1}{n} \sum_{j=1}^n |\frac{1}{a_n} \sum_{k=1}^n p_{jk}^{(n)} \sigma_{jk}^2 - 1| = 0. \tag{7}$$

- Condition $CP(1b)$:
$$\lim_{n \to \infty} \frac{1}{na_n} \sum_{j=1}^n \sum_{k=1}^n |p_{jk}^{(n)} \sigma_{jk}^2 - \frac{1}{n} \sum_{l=1}^n p_{jl}^{(n)} \sigma_{jl}^2| = 0.$$

The main result of the present paper is the following theorem.

Theorem 1. *Let conditions $CP(0)$, $CP(0a)$, $CP(1)$, $CX(1)$ hold. Then, ESDs $\widetilde{G}_n(x)$ converge in probability to the distribution function $G(x)$, which is the additive free convolution of the standard normal distribution function and the semi-circular distribution function:*

$$\lim_{n\to\infty} \widetilde{G}_n(x) = G(x).$$

Corollary 1. *Assume that $\sigma_{jk}^2 \equiv \sigma^2$ and $p_{jk}^{(n)} \equiv p_n$ for any $1 \leq j,k \leq n$ and any $n \geq 1$. Assume that $np_n \to \infty$ as $n \to \infty$ and assume that condition $CX(1)$ holds. Then, ESDs $\widetilde{G}_n(x)$ converge in probability to the distribution function $G(x)$, which is the additive free convolution of the standard normal distribution function and the semi-circular distribution function:*

$$\lim_{n\to\infty} \widetilde{G}_n(x) = G(x).$$

Proof of Corollary. Note that in the case $p_{jk}^{(n)} \equiv p_n$ and $\sigma_{jk}^2 = \sigma^2$, we have

$$a_n = np_n\sigma^2.$$

Condition $CP(0)$ is fulfilled. Moreover, it is simple to see that all conditions of Theorem 1 are fulfilled. □

Theorem 2. *Let conditions*

$$\widehat{a}_n \to \infty \text{ as } n \to \infty, \tag{8}$$

and

$$\lim_{n\to\infty} \frac{1}{n\widehat{a}_n} \sum_{j=1}^{n}\sum_{k=1}^{n} |p_{jk}^{(n)}(1 - p_{jk}^{(n)}) - \frac{\widehat{a}_n}{n}| = 0 \tag{9}$$

hold. Then, ESDs $\widehat{G}_n(x)$ converge in probability to the distribution function $G(x)$, which is the additive free convolution of the standard normal distribution function and the semicircular distribution function,

$$\lim_{n\to\infty} \widehat{G}_n(x) = G(x).$$

In what follows, we shall omit the superscript (n) in the notations of $p_{ij}^{(n)}$, writing p_{ij} instead.

2. Toy Example

Consider graph $\{V, E\}$ with clique number $d = d(n)$ where $|V| = n$. The clique number of graph G is the size of the largest clique or a maximal clique of the graph. Let $\mathcal{M}$ denote the clique of the graph. Define the weights of vertices as follows

$$W_i = \begin{cases} d, & \text{if } i \in \mathcal{M} \\ 1, & \text{otherwise.} \end{cases}$$

We introduce edge probabilities as follows

$$p_{ij} = W_iW_j/d^2 = \begin{cases} \frac{1}{d^2}, & \text{if } i \notin \mathcal{M}, j \notin \mathcal{M}, \\ \frac{1}{d}, & \text{if } i \in \mathcal{M}, j \notin \mathcal{M}, \text{ or } i \notin \mathcal{M}, j \in \mathcal{M}, \\ 1, & \text{if } i, j \in \mathcal{M}. \end{cases} \tag{10}$$

We assume that $\sigma_{jk}^2 \equiv \sigma^2 = 1$, for $1 \leq j, k \leq n$. In this case, we have

$$\sum_{j,k=1}^{n} p_{jk} = (\frac{n-d}{d} + d)^2, \tag{11}$$

and
$$a_n = \frac{n}{d^2}(1+\alpha_n)^2, \text{ where } \alpha_n = \frac{d(d-1)}{n}. \tag{12}$$

Proposition 1. *Under condition*
$$\lim_{n\to\infty}\frac{d^2(n)}{n} = 0 \tag{13}$$
conditions $CP(0)$, $CP(0a)$ and $CP(1)$ hold.

Proof. We have
$$\frac{1}{na_n}\sum_{j,k=1}^{n}|p_{jk}-\frac{a_n}{n}| = \frac{1}{na_n}(\frac{1}{d^2}(2\alpha_n+\alpha_n^2)(n-d)^2 + 2|\frac{1}{d}-\frac{1}{d^2}(1+\alpha_n)^2|d(n-d) +$$
$$d^2(1-\frac{1}{d^2}(1+\alpha_n)^2)$$
$$= \frac{\alpha_n(1+2\alpha_n)(n-d)^2}{n^2(1+\alpha_n)^2} + 2|1-\frac{1}{d}(1+\alpha_n)^2|\frac{d^2(n-d)}{n^2(1+\alpha_n)^2}$$
$$+ \frac{d^4}{n^2(1+\alpha_n)^2}(1-\frac{1}{d^2}(1+\alpha_n)^2). \tag{14}$$

It is straightforward to check that for $d = d(n)$ satisfying the condition (13), we have $\alpha_n = o(1)$, $a_n \to \infty$ as $n \to \infty$ and
$$\lim_{n\to\infty}\frac{1}{na_n}\sum_{j,k=1}^{n}|p_{jk}-\frac{a_n}{n}| = 0. \tag{15}$$

That means that the conditions $CP(0a)$ and $CP(1)$ hold. Furthermore,
$$\max_{1\leq k\leq n}\sum_{l=1}^{n}p_{kl} \leq \frac{n}{d}+d. \tag{16}$$

It is straightforward to check as well that
$$\sup_{n\geq 1}\frac{\max_{1\leq k,l\leq n}p_{kl}}{a_n} \leq C_0. \tag{17}$$

Thus, Proposition 1 is proved. □

3. Proof of Theorem 1

We shall use the method of the Stieltjes transform for the proof of Theorem 1. Introduce the resolvent matrix of matrix $\widetilde{L}$,
$$\mathbf{R} := \mathbf{R}_{\widetilde{L}}(z) = (\widetilde{L} - z\mathbf{I})^{-1},$$
where $\mathbf{I} := \mathbf{I}_n$ denotes a $n \times n$ unit matrix. Let $m_n(z)$ denote the Stieltjes transform of the empirical spectral distribution function of matrix $\widetilde{L}$,
$$m_n(z) = \int_{-\infty}^{\infty}\frac{1}{x-z}d\widetilde{G}_n(x) = \frac{1}{n}\text{Tr}\mathbf{R}.$$

For the proof of Theorem 1, it is enough to prove the convergence of the Stieltjes transforms for any fixed $z = u + iv$ with $v > 0$; moreover, it is enough to prove that $m_n(z)$ converges to some function, say $s(z)$, in some set with a non-empty interior. According to Lemma A2, it is enough to prove the convergence of the expected Stieltjes transform $s_n(z) = \mathbb{E} m_n(z) = \mathbb{E} \frac{1}{n} \text{Tr} \mathbf{R}$ only. Using Lemma A1, the result of Theorem 1 follows from the relation

$$s_n(z) - s_g(z + s_n(z)) \to 0 \text{ as } n \to \infty,$$

where $s_g(z)$ denotes the Stieltjes transform of the standard Gaussian distribution,

$$s_g(z) = \frac{1}{\sqrt{2\pi}} \int_{-\infty}^{\infty} \frac{1}{x-z} \exp\{-\frac{x^2}{2}\} dx.$$

First, we need some additional notations. By $\widetilde{\mathbf{L}}^{(j)}$, we denote the matrix obtained from $\widetilde{\mathbf{L}}$ by replacing diagonal entries $\widetilde{L}_{ll}, l = 1, \ldots, n$ with $\widetilde{L}_{ll}^{(j)} = \frac{1}{\sqrt{a_n}} \sum_{r \neq j} A_{lr} X_{lr}$. Note that the diagonal entries of matrix $\widetilde{\mathbf{L}}^{(j)}$ (except $\widetilde{L}_{jj}^{(j)}$) do not depend on the r.v. values X_{jk}, A_{jk} for $k = 1, \ldots, n$. We denote by $\widetilde{\mathbf{D}}^{(j)}$ the diagonal matrix with diagonal entries $\widetilde{D}_{ll}^{(j)} = \frac{1}{\sqrt{a_n}} A_{jl} X_{jl}$. Denote by $\widetilde{\mathbf{R}}^{(j)}$ the resolvent matrix corresponding to the matrix $\widetilde{\mathbf{L}}^{(j)}$,

$$\widetilde{\mathbf{R}}^{(j)} = (\widetilde{\mathbf{L}}^{(j)} - z\mathbf{I})^{-1}.$$

We have

$$\mathbf{R} = \widetilde{\mathbf{R}}^{(j)} - \mathbf{R} \widetilde{\mathbf{D}}^{(j)} \widetilde{\mathbf{R}}^{(j)}. \tag{18}$$

Using this formula, we may write

$$R_{jj} = \widetilde{R}_{jj}^{(j)} - \frac{1}{\sqrt{a_n}} \sum_{r=1}^{n} A_{jr} X_{jr} R_{jr} \widetilde{R}_{rj}^{(j)}. \tag{19}$$

According to Lemma A5, we obtain

$$\lim_{n \to \infty} \left| \frac{1}{n} \text{Tr} \mathbf{R} - \frac{1}{n} \sum_{j=1}^{n} \widetilde{R}_{jj}^{(j)} \right| = 0. \tag{20}$$

Furthermore, let us denote by $\widetilde{\mathbf{L}}^{(j,0)}$ the matrix obtained from $\widetilde{\mathbf{L}}^{(j)}$ by deleting both the j-th column and j-th row. $\widetilde{\mathbf{R}}^{(j,0)}$ denotes the resolvent matrix corresponding to the matrix $\widetilde{\mathbf{L}}^{(j,0)}$. Using the Schur complement formula, we may write

$$\widetilde{R}_{jj}^{(j)} = \frac{1}{\widetilde{L}_{jj}^{(j)} - z - \sum_{l,k: l \neq j, k \neq j} [\widetilde{R}^{(j,0)}(z)]_{kl} \widetilde{L}_{jl} \widetilde{L}_{jk}}. \tag{21}$$

Introduce the following notations

$$\varepsilon_{j1} := \sum_{l \neq k: l \neq j, k \neq j} [\widetilde{R}^{(j,0)}]_{kl} \widetilde{L}_{jl} \widetilde{L}_{jk}, \quad \varepsilon_{j2} = \frac{1}{a_n} \sum_{k: k \neq j} [\widetilde{R}^{(j,0)}]_{kk} (A_{jk} - p_{jk}) X_{jk}^2,$$

$$\varepsilon_{j3} = \frac{1}{a_n} \sum_{k: k \neq j} [\widetilde{R}^{(j,0)}]_{kk} p_{jk} (X_{jk}^2 - \sigma_{jk}^2),$$

$$\varepsilon_{j4} = \frac{1}{a_n} \sum_{k: k \neq j} [\widetilde{R}^{(j,0)}]_{kk} (p_{jk} \sigma_{jk}^2 - \frac{1}{n} \sum_{l=1}^{n} p_{jl} \sigma_{jl}^2),$$

$$\varepsilon_{j5} = \frac{1}{n} \sum_{k: k \neq j} \widetilde{R}_{kk}^{(j,0)} (\frac{1}{a_n} \sum_{l=1}^{n} p_{jl} \sigma_{jl}^2 - 1),$$

$$\varepsilon_{j6} = \frac{1}{n} \sum_{k: k \neq j} \widetilde{R}_{kk}^{(j,0)} - \frac{1}{n} \sum_{k=1}^{n} R_{kk},$$

$$\varepsilon_{j7} = \frac{1}{n} \sum_{k=1}^{n} [R]_{kk} - \mathbb{E} \frac{1}{n} \sum_{k=1}^{n} [R(z)]_{kk}.$$

Put $\varepsilon_j = \sum_{\nu=1}^{7} \varepsilon_{j\nu}$. Let

$$\zeta_j := \widetilde{L}_{jj}^{(j)} = \frac{1}{\sqrt{a_n}} \sum_{k \neq j} A_{jk} X_{jk}.$$

In these notations, we may write

$$\mathbb{E}[\widetilde{R}^{(j)}]_{jj} = \mathbb{E} \frac{1}{\zeta_j - z - s_n(z) - \varepsilon_j}.$$

We continue as follows

$$\mathbb{E}\widetilde{R}_{jj}^{(j)} = \mathbb{E} \frac{1}{\zeta_j - z - s_n(z)} + \mathbb{E} \frac{\varepsilon_j}{\zeta_j - z - s_n(z)} \widetilde{R}_{jj}^{(j)}. \tag{22}$$

Summing the last equality in $j = 1, \ldots, n$, we obtain

$$s_n(z) = \mathbb{E} \frac{1}{\zeta_\mathbb{J} - z - s_n(z)} + \mathbb{E} \frac{\varepsilon_\mathbb{J}}{\zeta_\mathbb{J} - z - s_n(z)} R_{\mathbb{J}\mathbb{J}}^{(\mathbb{J})} + \mathbb{E}(R_{\mathbb{J},\mathbb{J}} - \widetilde{R}_{\mathbb{J},\mathbb{J}}^{(\mathbb{J})}), \tag{23}$$

where $\mathbb{J}$ denotes a random variable which is uniform distributed on the set $\{1, \ldots, n\}$ and independent on all other random variables. Denote by $F_n(x)$ the distribution function of $\zeta_\mathbb{J}$ and let

$$\Delta_n = \sup_x |F_n(x) - \Phi(x)|,$$

where $\Phi(x)$ denotes the distribution function of the standard normal law. Denote the Stieltjes transform of the standard normal law by $s_g(z)$,

$$s_g(z) = \int_{-\infty}^{\infty} \frac{1}{x - z} d\Phi(x).$$

Note that

$$\mathbb{E} \frac{1}{\zeta_\mathbb{J} - z - \widehat{s}_n(z)} - s_g(z + \widehat{s}_n(z)) = \int_{-\infty}^{\infty} \frac{1}{x - z - \widehat{s}_n(z)} d(F_n(x) - \Phi(x)). \tag{24}$$

Integrating by part, we obtain

$$|\mathbb{E} \frac{1}{\zeta_\mathbb{J} - z - \widehat{s}_n(z)} - s_g(z + \widehat{s}_n(z))| \leq 2v^{-2} \Delta_n. \tag{25}$$

According to Lemma A3,

$$|\mathbb{E} \frac{1}{\zeta_\mathbb{J} - z - s_n(z)} - s_g(z + s_n(z))| \to 0 \text{ as } n \to \infty. \tag{26}$$

Note that

$$|\mathbb{E} \frac{\varepsilon_\mathbb{J}}{\zeta_\mathbb{J} - z - s_n(z)} R_{\mathbb{J}\mathbb{J}}| \leq v^{-2} \mathbb{E}|\varepsilon_\mathbb{J}|. \tag{27}$$

It remains to prove that $\mathbb{E}|\varepsilon_\mathbb{J}| \to 0$ and $\mathbb{E}(R_{\mathbb{J},\mathbb{J}} - \widetilde{R}_{\mathbb{J},\mathbb{J}}^{(\mathbb{J})}) \to 0$ as $n \to \infty$. The last claim follows from Lemmas A6–A11, Lemma A2 and equality (20).

Thus, Theorem 1 is proved.

4. The Proof of Theorem 2

Similar to the previous section, we may write that diagonal entries of matrix $\widehat{L}$

$$\widehat{\zeta}_j = \frac{1}{\sqrt{\widehat{a}_n}} \sum_{k \neq j} (A_{jk} - p_{jk}). \tag{28}$$

Let $\widehat{R} = (\widehat{L} - z\mathbf{I})^{-1}$ denote the resolvent matrix of the matrix $\widehat{L}$. Let $j \in \{1, \ldots, n\}$ be fixed. We denote by $\widehat{L}^{(j)}$ the matrix obtained from $\widehat{L}$ by replacing diagonal entries $\widehat{L}_{ll}$, $l = 1, \ldots, n$ with $\widehat{L}_{ll}^{(j)} = \frac{1}{\sqrt{\widehat{a}_n}} \sum_{r \neq j} (A_{lr} - p_{lr})$. Let $\widehat{D}^{(j)} = \widehat{L} - \widehat{L}^{(j)}$. By definition, $\widehat{D}^{(j)} = \text{diag}(\widehat{d}_1^{(j)}, \ldots, \widehat{d}_n^{(j)})$ is a diagonal matrix with $\widehat{d}_{ll}^{(j)} = \frac{1}{\sqrt{\widehat{a}_n}} (A_{jl} - p_{jl})$, for $l = 1, \ldots, n$. Note that diagonal entries of matrix $\widehat{L}^{(j)}$ (except $\widehat{L}_{jj}^{(j)}$) do not depend on the r.v. values A_{jk} for $k = 1, \ldots, n$. By $\widehat{L}^{(j,0)}$, we denote the matrix obtained from $\widehat{L}^{(j)}$ by deleting both the j-th column and j-th row. $\widehat{R}^{(j,0)}$ denotes the resolvent matrix corresponding to the matrix $\widehat{\mathbf{L}}^{(j,0)}$. Analogously to (21), we represent the diagonal entries of resolvent matrix $\widehat{\mathbf{R}}^{(j)} = (\widehat{\mathbf{L}}^{(j)} - z\mathbf{I})^{-1}$ in the form

$$\widehat{R}_{jj}^{(j)} = \frac{1}{\widehat{L}_{jj}^{(j)} - z - \sum_{l,k: l \neq j, k \neq j} \widehat{R}_{kl}^{(j,0)} \widehat{L}_{jl} \widehat{L}_{jk}}. \tag{29}$$

Introduce the following notations

$$\widehat{\varepsilon}_{j1} := \sum_{l \neq k: l \neq j, k \neq j} [\widehat{R}^{(j,0)}]_{kl} \widehat{L}_{jl} \widehat{L}_{jk}, \quad \widehat{\varepsilon}_{j2} = \frac{1}{\widehat{a}_n} \sum_{k: k \neq j} [\widehat{R}^{(j,0)}]_{kk} ((A_{jk} - p_{jk})^2 - p_{jk}(1 - p_{jk}))$$

$$\widehat{\varepsilon}_{j3} = \frac{1}{\widehat{a}_n} \sum_{k: k \neq j} \widehat{R}_{kk}^{(j,0)} \left(p_{jk}(1 - p_{jk}) - \frac{\widehat{a}_n}{n} \right),$$

$$\widehat{\varepsilon}_{j4} = \frac{1}{n} \sum_{k: k \neq j} \widehat{R}_{kk}^{(j,0)} - \frac{1}{n} \sum_{k=1}^n \widehat{R}_{kk},$$

$$\widehat{\varepsilon}_{j5} = \frac{1}{n} \sum_{k=1}^n \widehat{R}_{kk} - \mathbb{E} \frac{1}{n} \sum_{k=1}^n \widehat{R}_{kk}.$$

Put $\widehat{\varepsilon}_j = \sum_{\nu=1}^5 \widehat{\varepsilon}_{j\nu}$. Let

$$\widehat{\zeta}_j := \widehat{L}_{jj}^{(j)} = \frac{1}{\sqrt{\widehat{a}_n}} \sum_{k \neq j} (A_{jk} - p_{jk}).$$

In these notations, we may write

$$\mathbb{E}[\widehat{R}^{(j)}]_{jj} = \mathbb{E} \frac{1}{\widehat{\zeta}_j - z - \widehat{s}_n(z) - \widehat{\varepsilon}_j},$$

where $\widehat{s}_n(z) = \mathbb{E} \frac{1}{n} \text{Tr} \widehat{\mathbf{R}}$. We continue as follows

$$\mathbb{E}[\widehat{R}^{(j)}]_{jj} = \mathbb{E} \frac{1}{\widehat{\zeta}_j - z - \widehat{s}_n(z)} + \mathbb{E} \frac{\widehat{\varepsilon}_j}{\widehat{\zeta}_j - z - \widehat{s}_n(z)} \widehat{R}_{jj}^{(j)}(z). \tag{30}$$

Summing the last equality in $j = 1, \ldots, n$, we obtain

$$\widehat{s}_n(z) = \mathbb{E} \frac{1}{\widehat{\zeta}_\mathbb{J} - z - \widehat{s}_n(z)} + \mathbb{E} \frac{\widehat{\varepsilon}_\mathbb{J}}{\widehat{\zeta}_\mathbb{J} - z - \widehat{s}_n(z)} \widehat{R}_{\mathbb{J}\mathbb{J}}^{(\mathbb{J})} + \mathbb{E}(\widehat{R}_{\mathbb{J}\mathbb{J}} - \widehat{R}_{\mathbb{J}\mathbb{J}}^{\mathbb{J}}), \tag{31}$$

where $\mathbb{J}$ denotes a random variable which is uniform distributed on the set $\{1, \ldots, n\}$ and independent on all other random variables. Similar to inequality (25), we have

$$\left| \mathbb{E} \frac{1}{\widehat{\zeta}_j - z - \widehat{s}_n(z)} - s_g(z + \widehat{s}_n(z)) \right| \leq \frac{1}{v^2} \widehat{\Delta}_n. \tag{32}$$

According to Lemma A12

$$\left| \mathbb{E} \frac{1}{\widehat{\zeta}_j - z - \widehat{s}_n(z)} - s_g(z + \widehat{s}_n(z)) \right| \to 0 \text{ as } n \to \infty. \tag{33}$$

Furthermore, since $\text{Im } z + \text{Im } s_n(z) \geq v$ and $|\widehat{R}_{\mathbb{J}\mathbb{J}}^{(\mathbb{J})}| \leq v^{-1}$, we have

$$\left| \mathbb{E} \frac{\widehat{\varepsilon}_\mathbb{J}}{\widehat{\zeta}_\mathbb{J} - z - \widehat{s}_n(z)} \widehat{R}_{\mathbb{J}\mathbb{J}}^{(\mathbb{J})} \right| \leq v^{-2} \mathbb{E}|\widehat{\varepsilon}_\mathbb{J}|. \tag{34}$$

By Lemmas A13–A17,

$$\lim_{n \to \infty} \mathbb{E}|\widehat{\varepsilon}_\mathbb{J}| = 0. \tag{35}$$

Furthermore, we note that

$$\widehat{\mathbf{R}} = \widehat{\mathbf{R}}^{(\mathbb{J})} - \widehat{\mathbf{R}}^{(\mathbb{J})} \widehat{\mathbf{D}}^{(\mathbb{J})} \widehat{\mathbf{R}}. \tag{36}$$

This relation implies that

$$|\mathbb{E}(\widehat{R}_{JJ} - \widehat{R}_{JJ}^{(J)})| \leq \max_{1 \leq j \leq n} \mathbb{E}\|\widehat{\mathbf{R}} - \widehat{\mathbf{R}}^{(j)}\| \leq v^{-2} \max_{1 \leq j \leq n} \mathbb{E}\|\widehat{\mathbf{D}}^{(j)}\|. \tag{37}$$

It is straightforward to check that

$$\mathbb{E}\|\widehat{\mathbf{D}}^{(j)}\| \leq \frac{1}{\sqrt{a_n}} \mathbb{E} \max_{1 \leq l \leq n} |A_{jl} - p_{jl}| \leq \frac{1}{\sqrt{a_n}} \to 0 \text{ as } n \to \infty. \tag{38}$$

Combining relations (33), (35), (38), we obtain

$$\varkappa_n(z) := s_n(z) - s_g(z + s_n(z)) \to 0 \text{ as } n \to \infty. \tag{39}$$

The last relation and Lemma A1 completed the proof of Theorem 2. Thus, Theorem 2 is proved.

Funding: This research received no external funding.

Institutional Review Board Statement: Not applicable.

Informed Consent Statement: Not applicable.

Data Availability Statement: Not applicable.

Conflicts of Interest: The author declares no conflict of interest.

Appendix A

Definition of Additive Free Convolution

We give the definition of the additive free convolution of distribution functions following the paper [16] (Section 5).

Definition A1. *A pair $(\mathcal{A}, \varphi)$ consisting of a unital algebra $\mathcal{A}$ and a linear functional $\varphi : \mathcal{A} \to \mathbb{C}$ with $\varphi(1) = 1$ is called the free probability space. Elements of $\mathcal{A}$ are called random variables, the numbers $\varphi(a_{i(1)} \cdots a_{i(n)})$ for such random variables $a_1, \ldots, a_k \in \mathcal{A}$ are called moments, and the collection of all moments is called the joint distribution of $a_1, \ldots, a_k$. Equivalently, we may say that the joint distribution of $a_1, \ldots, a_k$ is given by the linear functional $\mu_{a_1, \ldots, a_k} : \mathbb{C}\langle X_1, \ldots, X_k \rangle \to \mathbb{C}$ with $\mu_{a_1, \ldots, a_k}(P(X_1, \ldots, X_k)) = \varphi(P(a_1, \ldots, a_k))$, where $\mathbb{C}\langle X_1, \ldots, X_k \rangle$ denotes the algebra of all polynomials in k non-commutative indeterminantes $X_1, \ldots, X_k$.*

If for a given element $a \in \mathcal{A}$ there exists a unique probability measure μ_a on $\mathbb{R}$ such that $\int t^k d\mu_a(t) = \varphi(a^k)$ for all $k \in \mathbb{N}$, we identify the distribution of a with the probability measure μ_a.

Definition A2. *Let $(\mathcal{A}, \varphi)$ be a non-commutative probability space.*

(1) *Let $(\mathcal{A}_i)_{i \in I}$ be a family of unital sub-algebras of $\mathcal{A}$. The sub-algebras $\mathcal{A}_i$ are called free independent if, for any positive integer k, $\varphi(a_1 \cdots a_k) = 0$ whenever the following set of conditions holds: $a_j \in \mathcal{A}_{i(j)}$ (with $i(j) \in I$) for $j = 1, \ldots, k$, $\varphi(a_j) = 0$ for all $j = 1, \ldots, k$ and neighboring elements are from taken different sub-algebras, i.e., $i(1) \neq i(2), i(2) \neq i(3), \ldots, i(k-1) \neq i(k)$.*

(2) *Let $(\mathcal{A}'_i)_{i \in I}$ be a family of subset of $\mathcal{A}$. The subsets $\mathcal{A}'_i$ are called free or freely independent if their generated initial sub-algebras are free, i.e., if $(\mathcal{A}_i)_{i \in I}$ are free, where for each $i \in I$, $\mathcal{A}_i$ is the smallest initial sub-algebra of $\mathcal{A}$ which contains $\mathcal{A}'_i$.*

(3) *Let $(a_i)_{i \in I}$ be a family of elements from $\mathcal{A}$. The elements a_i are called free independent if the subsets $(\{a_i\})_{i \in I}$ are free.*

Consider two random variables a and b which are free. Then, distributions of $a + b$ (in the sense of linear functionals) depend only on the distribution of a and b.

Definition A3. *For free random variables a and b, the distribution of $a + b$ is called the free additive convolution of μ_a and μ_b and is denoted by*

$$\mu_{a \boxplus b} = \mu_a \boxplus \mu_b.$$

To compute the free convolution of concrete distributions, we may use the so-called R-transform introduced by Voiculescu [17]. Let $s(z)$ be the Stieltjes transform of some distribution function $F(x)$. Denote by $s^{-1}(z)$ the inverse function of $s(z)$ in the science of composition. Define R-transform as follows

$$R(z) = -s^{-1}(z) - \frac{1}{z}.$$

Let $F(x)$ be the semicircle distribution function. Its Stieltjes transform satisfies the equation

$$s^2(z) + zs(z) + 1 = 0$$

Denote by $R_{sc}(z)$ the R-transform of the semicicular law. Simple calulations show that

$$R_{sc}(z) = z.$$

We denote dy $R_{fc}(z)$ the R-transform of the free convolution semicircular law and Gaussian law. Let R_g denote the R-transform of the standard normal law. Then

$$R_{fc}(z) = R_{sc}(z) + R_g(z).$$

See for instance, refs. [18,19]. Using the definition of the R-transform via the Stieltjes transform, we obtain

$$-s_{fc}^{-1}(z) = z - s_g^{-1}(z).$$

It is straightforward to show that this equality implies

$$s_{fc}(z) = s_g(z + s_{fc}(z)). \tag{A1}$$

We prove the following simple but important lemma.

Lemma A1. *Let a sequence of Stieltjes transforms of the distribution functions $F_n(x)$ satisfy the equations*

$$s_n(z) = s_g(z + s_n(z)) + \varkappa_n(z), \tag{A2}$$

where

$$\varkappa_n(z) \to 0 \text{ as } n \to \infty.$$

Then, the distribution functions $F_n(x)$ weakly converge to the distribution function $F_{fc}(x)$, which is free convolution of the semicircular law and the standard normal law.

Proof. It is enough to prove that the Stieltjes transform $s_n(z)$ converges in some region with non-empty interior to the Stieltjes transform $s_{fc}(z)$, which satisfies equation (A1). We shall consider the region of $z = u + iv$ with $v > \sqrt{2}$. Since the derivative of $s_g(z)$ does not exceed the level $1/v^2$, we may write

$$|s_n(z) - s_m(z)| \leq \frac{1}{2}|s_n(z) - s_m(z)| + |\varkappa_n(z)| + |\varkappa_m(z)|.$$

or

$$|s_n(z) - s_m(z)| \leq 2|\varkappa_n(z)| + 2|\varkappa_m(z)| \to 0 \text{ as } n, m \to \infty. \tag{A3}$$

The sequence of the Stieltjes transforms $s_n(z)$ is Cauchy; consequently, there exists a limit say $s_{fc}(z)$ of this sequence,

$$\lim_{n \to \infty} s_n(z) = s_{fc}(z).$$

Taking the limit in the equation (A2), we obtain

$$s_{fc}(z) = s_g(z + s_{fc}(z)).$$

The last equality implies that $s_{fc}(z)$ is the Stieltjes transform of the semicircular law and the standard Gaussian law. Thus, Lemma is proved. □

Appendix B. Weighted Graphs

Appendix B.1. Variance of Stieltjes Transform of Empirical Measure

In this section, we estimate the variance of $m_n(z) = \frac{1}{n}\text{Tr}\mathbf{R}$, where $\mathbf{R} := \mathbf{R_L}(z) = (\widetilde{\mathbf{L}} - z\mathbf{I})^{-1}$. We prove the following Lemma.

Lemma A2. *For any $z = u + iv$ with $v > 0$, the following inequality holds*

$$\lim_{n \to \infty} \mathbb{E}\left|\frac{1}{n}\text{Tr}\mathbf{R} - \frac{1}{n}\mathbb{E}\text{Tr}\mathbf{R}\right| = 0. \tag{A4}$$

Proof. The proof of this lemma is using the martingale representation of $\zeta - \mathbb{E}\zeta$. This method in Random Matrix Theory was firstly used by Girko, see for instance [20]. We introduce the sequence of σ-algebras $\mathfrak{M}_k$ generated by random variables $X_{j,l}$ for $1 \leq j, l \leq k$. It is easy to see that $\mathfrak{M}_k \subset \mathfrak{M}_{k+1}$. Denote by $\mathbb{E}_k$ the conditional expectation with respect to σ-algebra $\mathfrak{M}_k$. For $k = 0$, $\mathbb{E}_0 = \mathbb{E}$. Introduce random variables

$$\gamma_k := \mathbb{E}_k \frac{1}{n}\text{Tr}\mathbf{R} - \mathbb{E}_{k-1}\frac{1}{n}\text{Tr}\mathbf{R}. \tag{A5}$$

The sequence of γ_k, for $k = 1, \ldots, n$ is martingale difference and

$$\frac{1}{n}\text{Tr}\mathbf{R} - \mathbb{E}\frac{1}{n}\text{Tr}\mathbf{R} = \sum_{k=1}^{n} \gamma_k.$$

Introduce the sub-matrices $\widetilde{\mathbf{L}}^{(k)}$ obtained from $\widetilde{\mathbf{L}}$ by deleting both the k-th row and k-th column. Denote by $\mathbf{R}^{(k)} = \mathbf{R}^{(k)}(z)$ the corresponding resolvent matrix, $\mathbf{R}^{(k)}(z) = (\widetilde{\mathbf{L}}^{(k)} - z\mathbf{I})^{-1}$. Note that the matrix $\widetilde{\mathbf{L}}^{(k)}$ depends on the random variables X_{kl}, $l = 1, \ldots, n$ via diagonal entries. To overcome this difficulty, we introduce the matrix $\widetilde{\mathbf{L}}^{(k,0)}$ obtained from $\widetilde{\mathbf{L}}^{(k)}$ by replacing diagonal entries with $\widehat{L}_{jj}^{(k)} := \frac{1}{\sqrt{a_n}} \sum_{l:l \neq k, l \neq j} A_{jl} X_{jl}$. The corresponding resolvent matrix is denoted via $\mathbf{R}^{(k,0)}$. We have now

$$\mathbb{E}_k \text{Tr} \mathbf{R}^{(k,0)} = \mathbb{E}_{k-1} \mathbf{R}^{(k,0)}.$$

This allows us to write

$$\gamma_k = \mathbb{E}_k\left(\frac{1}{n}(\text{Tr}\mathbf{R} - \text{Tr}\mathbf{R}^{(k)}) - \mathbb{E}_{k-1}\left(\frac{1}{n}(\text{Tr}\mathbf{R} - \text{Tr}\mathbf{R}^{(k)})\right)\right)$$
$$+ \mathbb{E}_k\left(\frac{1}{n}(\text{Tr}\mathbf{R}^{(k)} - \text{Tr}\mathbf{R}^{(k,0)})\right) - \mathbb{E}_{k-1}\left(\frac{1}{n}(\text{Tr}\mathbf{R}^{(k)} - \text{Tr}\mathbf{R}^{(k,0)})\right) =: \gamma_k^{(1)} + \gamma_k^{(2)}.$$

By the overlapping theorem, for $z = u + iv$,

$$\left|\frac{1}{n}\text{Tr}\mathbf{R}_L(z) - \frac{1}{n}\text{Tr}\mathbf{R}^{(k)}(z)\right| \leq \frac{1}{nv}. \tag{A6}$$

From here, we immediately obtain

$$|\gamma_k^{(1)}| \leq \frac{2}{nv},$$

and

$$\sum_{k=1}^{n} \mathbb{E}|\gamma_k|^2 \leq \frac{4}{nv^2}. \tag{A7}$$

To complete the proof, it remains to show that

$$\lim_{n \to \infty} \sum_{k=1}^{n} \mathbb{E}|\gamma_k^{(2)}|^2 = 0. \tag{A8}$$

Note that

$$\mathbb{E}|\gamma_k^{(2)}|^2 \leq 2\mathbb{E}\left|\frac{1}{n}\text{Tr}\mathbf{R}^{(k)} - \frac{1}{n}\text{Tr}\mathbf{R}^{(k,0)}\right|^2. \tag{A9}$$

Introduce the diagonal matrix $\mathbf{D}^{(k)}$ with diagonal entries

$$D_{ll}^{(k)} = \frac{1}{\sqrt{a_n}} A_{kl} X_{kl}, \quad l \neq k.$$

In these notations, we have

$$\frac{1}{n}\text{Tr}\mathbf{R}^{(k)} - \frac{1}{n}\text{Tr}\mathbf{R}^{(k,0)} = \frac{1}{n}\text{Tr}\mathbf{R}^{(k)}\mathbf{D}^{(k,0)}\mathbf{R}^{(k,0)} = \frac{1}{n\sqrt{a_n}} \sum_{l \neq k, j \neq k} R_{ij}^{(k)} A_{kj} X_{kj} R_{jl}^{(k,0)}. \tag{A10}$$

This implies that

$$\sum_{k=1}^{n} \mathbb{E}|\gamma_k^{(2)}|^2 \leq \frac{4}{n^2 a_n} \sum_{k=1}^{n} \mathbb{E}|\sum_{j\neq k} A_{kj} X_{kj} (\sum_{l\neq k} R_{lj}^{(k)} R_{jl}^{(k,0)})|^2. \quad (A11)$$

We continue this inequality as follows

$$\sum_{k=1}^{n} \mathbb{E}|\gamma_k^{(2)}|^2 \leq \frac{8}{n^2 a_n} \sum_{k=1}^{n} \mathbb{E}|\sum_{j\neq k} A_{kj} X_{kj} (\sum_{l\neq k} R_{lj}^{(k)} R_{jl}^{(k,0)}) \mathbb{I}\{A_{kj}|X_{kj}| \leq \tau\sqrt{a_n}\})|^2$$
$$+ \frac{8}{n^2 a_n} \sum_{k=1}^{n} \mathbb{E}|\sum_{j\neq k} A_{kj} X_{kj} (\sum_{l\neq k} R_{lj}^{(k)} R_{jl}^{(k,0)}) \mathbb{I}\{A_{kj}|X_{kj}| > \tau\sqrt{a_n}\}|^2. \quad (A12)$$

Applying Cauchy's inequality to the second term in the right-hand side of the last inequality, we obtain

$$\frac{8}{n^2 a_n} \sum_{k=1}^{n} \mathbb{E}|\sum_{j\neq k} A_{kj} X_{kj} (\sum_{l\neq k} R_{lj}^{(k,0)} R_{jl}^{(k)}) \mathbb{I}\{A_{kj}|X_{kj}| > \tau\sqrt{a_n}\}|^2$$
$$\leq \frac{8}{n a_n} \sum_{k=1}^{n} \sum_{j\neq k} \mathbb{E} A_{jk} X_{kj}^2 |\sum_{l\neq k} R_{lj}^{(k)} R_{jl}^{(k,0)}|^2 \mathbb{I}\{A_{kj}|X_{kj}| > \tau\sqrt{a_n}\}. \quad (A13)$$

It is straightforward to check that

$$|\sum_{l\neq k} R_{lj}^{(k)} R_{jl}^{(k,0)}|^2 \leq v^{-4}. \quad (A14)$$

Using this bound, we obtain

$$\frac{8}{n^2 a_n} \sum_{k=1}^{n} \mathbb{E}|\sum_{j\neq k} A_{kj} X_{kj} (\sum_{l\neq k} R_{lj}^{(k)} R_{jl}^{(k,0)}) \mathbb{I}\{A_{kj}|X_{kj}| > \tau\sqrt{a_n}\}|^2 \leq 8v^{-4} L_n(\tau). \quad (A15)$$

We estimate now the first term in the r.h.s. of (A12). Using that

$$\mathbf{R}^{(k)} = \mathbf{R}^{(k,0)} + \mathbf{R}^{(k,0)} \mathbf{D}^{(k)} \mathbf{R}^{(k)}, \quad (A16)$$

we may write

$$\frac{8}{n^2 a_n} \sum_{k=1}^{n} \mathbb{E}|\sum_{j\neq k} A_{kj} X_{kj} (\sum_{l\neq k} R_{lj}^{(k)} R_{jl}^{(k,0)}) \mathbb{I}\{A_{kj}|X_{kj}| \leq \tau\sqrt{a_n}\}|^2$$
$$\leq \frac{8}{n^2 a_n} \sum_{k=1}^{n} \mathbb{E}|\sum_{j\neq k} A_{kj} X_{kj} (\sum_{l\neq k} R_{lj}^{(k,0)} R_{jl}^{(k,0)}) \mathbb{I}\{A_{kj}|X_{kj}| \leq \tau\sqrt{a_n}\}|^2$$
$$+ \frac{8}{n^2 a_n^2} \sum_{k=1}^{n} \mathbb{E}|\sum_{j\neq k} A_{kj} X_{kj} (\sum_{l\neq k} \sum_{s=1}^{n} X_{ks} A_{ks} R_{ls}^{(k,0)} R_{sj}^{(k)} R_{jl}^{(k,0)}) \mathbb{I}\{A_{kj}|X_{kj}| \leq \tau\sqrt{a_n}\}|^2. \quad (A17)$$

By the independence of random variables $A_{jk} X_{jk}$ for $j=1,\ldots,n$ and matrix $\widehat{\mathbf{R}}^{(k,0)}$, we have

$$\frac{8}{n^2 a_n} \sum_{k=1}^{n} \mathbb{E}|\sum_{j\neq k} A_{kj} X_{kj} (\sum_{l\neq k} R_{lj}^{(k,0)} R_{jl}^{(k,0)}) \mathbb{I}\{A_{kj}|X_{kj}| \leq \tau\sqrt{a_n}\}|^2$$
$$\leq \frac{8}{n^2 a_n v^4} \sum_{k=1}^{n} \sum_{j\neq k} p_{jk} \sigma_{jk}^2 + \frac{1}{n^2 a_n^2 \tau^2 v^4} \sum_{k=1}^{n} (\sum_{j=1}^{n} p_{jk} \mathbb{E} X_{jk}^2 \mathbb{I}\{|X_{jk}| > \tau\sqrt{a_n}\})^2$$
$$\leq \frac{8}{nv^4} + \left(\frac{L_n(\tau)}{\tau v^2}\right)^2. \quad (A18)$$

For the second term in the r.h.s. of (A17), we have

$$\frac{8}{n^2 a_n^2} \sum_{k=1}^{n} \mathbb{E} \Big| \sum_{j\neq k} A_{kj} X_{kj} \Big(\sum_{l\neq k} \sum_{s=1}^{n} X_{ks} A_{ks} R_{ls}^{(k,0)} R_{sj}^{(k)} R_{jl}^{(k,0)} \Big) \mathbb{I}\{A_{kj}|X_{kj}| \leq \tau\sqrt{a_n}\} \Big|^2$$

$$= \frac{8}{n^2 a_n^2} \sum_{k=1}^{n} \mathbb{E} \Big| \sum_{s\neq k} A_{ks} X_{ks} \Big(\sum_{j=1}^{n} X_{kj} A_{kj} \sum_{l\neq k} R_{ls}^{(k,0)} R_{sj}^{(k)} R_{jl}^{(k,0)} \mathbb{I}\{A_{kj}|X_{kj}| \leq \tau\sqrt{a_n}\} \Big) \Big|^2$$

$$\leq \frac{8}{n a_n^2} \sum_{k=1}^{n} \mathbb{E} \sum_{s\neq k} A_{ks}|X_{ks}|^2 \Big| \sum_{j=1}^{n} X_{kj} A_{kj} \sum_{l\neq k} R_{ls}^{(k,0)} R_{sj}^{(k)} R_{jl}^{(k,0)} \mathbb{I}\{A_{kj}|X_{kj}| \leq \tau\sqrt{a_n}\} \Big|^2. \tag{A19}$$

Note that

$$\sum_{r=1}^{n} |R_{rj}^{(k)}| \Big| \sum_{l\neq k} \widehat{R}_{lr}^{(k)} \widehat{R}_{jl}^{(k)} \Big| \leq \Big(\sum_{r=1}^{n} |R_{jr}^{(k)}|^2 \Big)^{\frac{1}{2}} \Big(\sum_{r=1}^{n} |[R^{(k,0)}]_{jr}^2|^2 \Big)^{\frac{1}{2}} \leq v^{-3}. \tag{A20}$$

Using this inequality, we obtain

$$\frac{8}{n^2 a_n^2} \sum_{k=1}^{n} \mathbb{E} \Big| \sum_{j\neq k} A_{kj} X_{kj} \Big(\sum_{l\neq k} \sum_{r=1}^{n} X_{kr} A_{kr} R_{lr}^{(k,0)} R_{rj}^{(k)} R_{jl}^{(k,0)} \Big) \Big|^2 \prod_{r=1}^{n} \mathbb{I}\{A_{kr}|X_{kr}| \leq \tau\sqrt{a_n}\}$$

$$\leq \frac{8\tau^2}{n a_n v^6} \sum_{k=1}^{n} \sum_{j\neq k} p_{jk} \sigma_{jk}^2 = \frac{8\tau^2}{v^6}. \tag{A21}$$

Combining inequalities (A7), (A12), (A20), we obtain

$$\mathbb{E}|\text{Tr}\mathbf{R} - \mathbb{E}\text{Tr}\mathbf{R}|^2 \leq \frac{C}{nv^2} + \frac{C\tau^2}{v^6} + \frac{CL_n(\tau)}{v^4}. \tag{A22}$$

Passing to the limit first in $n \to \infty$ and then in $\tau \to 0$, we obtain

$$\lim_{n\to\infty} \mathbb{E} \Big| \frac{1}{n}(\text{Tr}\mathbf{R} - \mathbb{E}\text{Tr}\mathbf{R}) \Big|^2 = 0. \tag{A23}$$

Thus, lemma is proved. □

In what follows, we shall assume that $z = u + iv$ is fixed.

Appendix B.2. Convergence of Diagonal Entries Distribution Functions of Laplace Matrices to the Normal Law

Lemma A3. *Under conditions $CP(0)$ and $CX(0)$, we have*

$$\lim \frac{1}{n} \sum_{j=1}^{n} \frac{\max_{1\leq k\leq n} p_{jk} \sigma_{jk}^2}{a_n} = 0. \tag{A24}$$

Proof. We fix arbitrary $\tau > 0$. We may write

$$\frac{1}{n} \sum_{j=1}^{n} \frac{\max_{1\leq k\leq n} p_{jk} \sigma_{jk}^2}{a_n} \leq \tau^2 + \frac{1}{na_n} \sum_{j=1}^{n} \sum_{k=1}^{n} p_{jk} \mathbb{E}|X_{jk}|^2 \mathbb{I}\{|X_{jk}| < \tau\sqrt{a_n}\}. \tag{A25}$$

By condition $CX(0)$, we obtain

$$\limsup_{n\to\infty} \frac{1}{n} \sum_{j=1}^{n} \frac{\max_{1\leq k\leq n} p_{jk} \sigma_{jk}^2}{a_n} \leq \tau^2.$$

Because τ is arbitrary, we obtain the claim. □

Lemma A4. *Under conditions $CP(0)$, $CP(2)$ and $CX(0)$, $CX(1)$, we have*

$$\lim_{n\to\infty} \sup_x |F_n(x) - \Phi(x)| = 0 \tag{A26}$$

Proof. Let $\mathbb{J}$ be an independent on A_{jk} and X_{jk} random variable uniform distributed on the set $\{1,\ldots,n\}$. We consider the characterictic function of $\zeta_\mathbb{J} = \frac{1}{\sqrt{a_n}} \sum_{k=1}^n A_{\mathbb{J},k} X_{\mathbb{J},k}$, $f_n(t) = \mathbb{E}\exp\{it\zeta_\mathbb{J}\} = \frac{1}{n}\sum_{j=1}^n \mathbb{E}\exp\{it\zeta_j\}$. Introduce the following set of indices

$$\mathcal{M} = \mathcal{M}_1 \cap \mathcal{M}_2 \cap \mathcal{M}_3, \tag{A27}$$

where

$$\mathcal{M}_1 := \left\{ j \in \{1,\ldots,n\} : \frac{1}{a_n} |\sum_{k=1}^n p_{jk}\sigma_{jk}^2 - 1| \le \frac{1}{16} \right\},$$

$$\mathcal{M}_2 := \left\{ j \in \{1,\ldots,n\} : \frac{1}{a_n} \sum_{k=1}^n p_{jk}\mathbb{E}X_{jk}^2 \mathbb{I}\{|X_{jk}| > \tau\sqrt{a_n}\} \le \frac{1}{16} \right\},$$

$$\mathcal{M}_3 := \left\{ j \in \{1,\ldots,n\} : \frac{1}{a_n} \max_{1 \le k \le n} p_{jk}\sigma_{jk}^2 \le \frac{1}{16t^2} \right\}. \tag{A28}$$

We denote by $\mathcal{A}^c$ the complement set of $\mathcal{A}$ and by $|\mathcal{A}|$, we denote the cardinality of set $\mathcal{A}$. Note that by condition $CP(1)$

$$\frac{|\mathcal{M}_1^c|}{n} \le 16 \frac{1}{na_n} \sum_{j=1}^n \sum_{k=1}^n |p_{jk}\sigma_{jk}^2 - \frac{a_n}{n}| \to 0, \text{ as } n \to \infty. \tag{A29}$$

Analogously, by $CX(1)$,

$$\frac{|\mathcal{M}_2^c|}{n} \le 16 L_n(\tau) \to 0, \text{ as } n \to \infty. \tag{A30}$$

Finally, by Lemma A3

$$\frac{|\mathcal{M}_3^c|}{n} \le 16t^2 \frac{1}{na_n} \sum_{j=1}^n \max_{1 \le k \le n} p_{jk}\sigma_{jk}^2 \to 0 \text{ as } n \to \infty. \tag{A31}$$

Combining the last three relations, we obtain

$$\lim_{n \to \infty} \frac{|\mathcal{M}^c|}{n} = 0. \tag{A32}$$

Note that by the independence of A_{jk} and X_{jk},

$$f_{nj}(t) := \mathbb{E}\exp\{\frac{it}{\sqrt{a_n}}\zeta_j\} = \prod_{k=1}^n \mathbb{E}\exp\{\frac{it}{\sqrt{a_n}} A_{jk} X_{jk}\} =: \prod_{k=1}^n f_{njk}(t).$$

Furthermore,

$$f_{njk}(t) = 1 + p_{jk}(\mathbb{E}\exp\{\frac{it}{\sqrt{a_n}} X_{jk}\} - 1), \tag{A33}$$

and by condition $CP(0)$

$$|f_{njk}(t) - 1| \le \frac{t^2}{2a_n} p_{jk}\sigma_{jk}^2 \le \frac{t^2}{2a_n} \max_{1 \le j,k \le n} p_{jk}\sigma_{jk}^2 \to 0 \text{ as } n \to \infty. \tag{A34}$$

Without loss of generality, we may assume that

$$\max_{1 \le j m k \le n} |f_{njk}(t) - 1| \le \frac{1}{4}, \tag{A35}$$

and applying Taylor's formula, we write that

$$\ln f_{njk}(t) = p_{jk}\left(\mathbb{E}\exp\{\frac{it}{\sqrt{a_n}} X_{jk}\} - 1\right) + 2\theta(t) p_{jk}^2 \left|\mathbb{E}\exp\{\frac{it}{\sqrt{a_n}} X_{jk}\} - 1\right|^2, \tag{A36}$$

where $\theta(t)$ denotes some function such that $|\theta(t)| \leq 1$. Futhermore, by Taylor's formula

$$\mathbb{E}\exp\{\frac{it}{\sqrt{a_n}}X_{jk}\} - 1 = -\frac{t^2}{2a_n}\sigma_{jk}^2 + \theta_1(t)\frac{|t|^3}{6a_n^{\frac{3}{2}}}\mathbb{E}|X_{jk}|^3\mathbb{I}\{|X_{jk}|\leq \tau\sqrt{a_n}\}$$
$$+ \theta_2(t)|\mathbb{E}\left|\exp\{\frac{it}{\sqrt{a_n}}X_{jk}\} - 1 - \frac{it}{\sqrt{a_n}}X_{jk} + \frac{t^2}{2a_n}X_{jk}^2\right|\mathbb{I}\{|X_{jk}| > \tau\sqrt{a_n}\}, \quad \text{(A37)}$$

where $\theta_i(t)$, $i = 1, 2$ denotes some functions such that $|\theta_i(t)| \leq 1$. Using this equality, we may write

$$\ln f_{njk}(t) = -\frac{t^2}{2a_n}p_{jk}\sigma_{jk}^2 + \theta_1(t)\frac{\tau|t|^3}{6a_n}p_{jk}\sigma_{jk}^2$$
$$+ \theta_2(t)\frac{t^2}{a_n}p_{jk}\mathbb{E}|X_{jk}|^2\mathbb{I}\{|X_{jk}| \geq \tau\sqrt{a_n}\} + \theta_3(t)\frac{t^4}{4a_n^2}p_{jk}^2\sigma_{jk}^4. \quad \text{(A38)}$$

Summing this equality by $k = 1\ldots, n$, we obtain

$$\ln f_{nj}(t) = -\frac{t^2}{2}\frac{1}{a_n}\sum_{k=1}^{n}p_{jk}\sigma_{jk}^2 + \theta_i(t)\tau\frac{|t|^3}{6a_n}\sum_{k=1}^{n}p_{jk}\sigma_{jk}^2$$
$$+ \theta_2(t)\frac{t^2}{a_n}\sum_{k=1}^{n}p_{jk}\mathbb{E}|X_{jk}|^2\mathbb{I}\{|X_{jk}| \geq \tau\sqrt{a_n}\}$$
$$+ \theta_3(t)\frac{t^4}{4}\frac{\max_{1\leq j,k\leq n}p_{jk}\sigma_{jk}^2}{a_n}\frac{1}{a_n}\sum_{k=1}^{n}p_{jk}\sigma_{jk}^2. \quad \text{(A39)}$$

For $\frac{8}{17|t|} > \tau > 0$, we have

$$|\ln f_{nj}(t) + \frac{t^2}{2}| \leq \frac{t^2}{3}. \quad \text{(A40)}$$

This implies that for $j \in \mathcal{M}$

$$|f_{nj}(t) - \exp\{-\frac{t^2}{2}\}| \leq C\Big(t^2(|\frac{1}{a_n}\sum_{k=1}^{n}p_{jk}\sigma_{jk}^2 - 1| + \frac{1}{a_n}\sum_{k=1}^{n}p_{jk}\mathbb{E}|X_{jk}|^2\mathbb{I}\{|X_{jk}| > \tau\sqrt{a_n}\})$$
$$+ \tau|t|^3 + \frac{t^4\max_{1\leq j,k\leq n}p_{jk}\sigma_{jk}^2}{a_n}\Big). \quad \text{(A41)}$$

From this inequality, it follows that

$$|f_n(t) - \exp\{-\frac{t^2}{2}\}| \leq \frac{2|\mathcal{M}^c|}{n}$$
$$+ \frac{1}{n}\sum_{j=1}^{n}\Big(t^2(|\frac{1}{a_n}\sum_{k=1}^{n}p_{jk}\sigma_{jk}^2 - 1| + \frac{1}{a_n}\sum_{k=1}^{n}p_{jk}\mathbb{E}|X_{jk}|^2\mathbb{I}\{|X_{jk}| > \tau\sqrt{a_n}\})$$
$$+ \tau|t|^3 + \frac{t^4\max_{1\leq j,k\leq n}p_{jk}\sigma_{jk}^2}{a_n}\Big). \quad \text{(A42)}$$

By conditions $CP(0)$ and $CX(0)$, relation (A32) and Lemma A3, we obtain

$$\lim_{n\to\infty}f_n(t) = \exp\{-\frac{t^2}{2}\}. \quad \text{(A43)}$$

Thus, the lemma is proved. □

Lemma A5. *Under the conditions of Theorem 1, we have*

$$\lim_{n\to\infty}\frac{1}{n}\sum_{j=1}^{n}\mathbb{E}|R_{jj} - \widetilde{R}_{jj}^{(j)}| = 0. \quad \text{(A44)}$$

Proof. By $\|\mathbf{V}\|$, we shall denote the operator norm of matrix $\mathbf{V}$. Matrices $\widetilde{\mathbf{R}}^{(j)}$ and $\widetilde{\mathbf{D}}^{(j)}$ are defined in the beginning of Section 3 before the relation (18). Note that

$$\|\mathbf{R}\widetilde{\mathbf{D}}^{(j)}\widetilde{\mathbf{R}}^{(j)}\| \leq v^{-2}\|\widetilde{\mathbf{D}}^{(j)}\|. \tag{A45}$$

It is easy to check that

$$\frac{1}{n}\sum_{j=1}^{n}\mathbb{E}|R_{jj} - \widetilde{R}_{jj}^{(j)}| \leq \frac{1}{n}\sum_{j=1}^{n}\mathbb{E}\|\mathbf{R} - \widetilde{\mathbf{R}}^{(j)}\|. \tag{A46}$$

Using that

$$\mathbf{R} = \widetilde{\mathbf{R}}^{(j)} - \mathbf{R}\widetilde{\mathbf{D}}^{(j)}\widetilde{\mathbf{R}}^{(j)}, \tag{A47}$$

we obtain

$$\|\mathbf{R} - \widetilde{\mathbf{R}}^{(j)}\| \leq v^{-2}\|\widetilde{\mathbf{D}}^{(j)}\|. \tag{A48}$$

Futhermore, for any $\tau > 0$, we have

$$\mathbb{E}\|\widetilde{\mathbf{D}}^{(j)}\| \leq \frac{1}{\sqrt{a_n}}\mathbb{E}\max_{1\leq l\leq n, l\neq j}\{|X_{jl}|A_{jl}\} \leq \tau + \frac{1}{\tau a_n}\sum_{l=1}^{n}p_{jl}\mathbb{E}X_{jl}^2\mathbb{I}\{|X_{jl}| > \tau\sqrt{a_n}\}. \tag{A49}$$

Summing this inequality in $j = 1, \ldots, n$, we obtain

$$\frac{1}{n}\sum_{j=1}^{n}\mathbb{E}|R_{jj} - \widetilde{R}_{jj}^{(j)}| \leq v^{-2}(\tau + \frac{1}{\tau}L_n(\tau)). \tag{A50}$$

Since τ is arbitrary, this inequality and condition $CX(0)$ together imply (A44). Thus, Lemma A5 is proved. □

Appendix B.3. *The Bounds of* $\frac{1}{n}\sum_{j=1}^{n}\mathbb{E}|\varepsilon_{j\nu}|$, *for* $\nu = 1, \ldots, 7$

Lemma A6. *Under the conditions of Theorem 1, we have*

$$\frac{1}{n}\sum_{j=1}^{n}\mathbb{E}|\varepsilon_{j1}| \leq \frac{\tau}{v} + \frac{1}{v}\left(\frac{\max_{1\leq j,k\leq n}p_{jk}\sigma_{jk}^2}{a_n}\right)^{\frac{1}{2}}L_n(\tau)^{\frac{1}{2}}. \tag{A51}$$

Proof. By definition of ε_{j1}, we may write

$$\varepsilon_{j1} := \frac{1}{a_n}\sum_{l\neq k: l\neq j, k\neq j}[\widetilde{R}^{(j,0)}]_{kl}A_{jk}A_{jl}X_{jk}X_{jl}. \tag{A52}$$

Applying the Cauchy inequality, we obtain

$$\frac{1}{n}\sum_{j=1}^{n}\mathbb{E}|\varepsilon_{j1}| \leq \left(\frac{1}{n}\sum_{j=1}^{n}\mathbb{E}|\varepsilon_{j1}|^2\right)^{\frac{1}{2}}. \tag{A53}$$

Simple calculations show that

$$\frac{1}{n}\sum_{j=1}^{n}\mathbb{E}|\varepsilon_{j1}| \leq \left(\frac{1}{na_n^2}\sum_{j=1}^{n}\sum_{k\neq j}\sum_{l\neq j}\mathbb{E}|\widetilde{R}_{kl}^{(j,0)}|^2 p_{jk}p_{jl}\sigma_{jk}^2\sigma_{jl}^2\right)^{\frac{1}{2}}, \tag{A54}$$

We introduce the following notations

$$\mathbf{W}_j = (|\widetilde{R}_{kl}^{(j,0)}|^2)_{k,l=1}^n, \quad \mathbf{H}_j = (p_{j1}\sigma_{j1}^2, \ldots, p_{jn}\sigma_{jn}^2)^T. \tag{A55}$$

In these notations, we write

$$\frac{1}{n}\sum_{j=1}^{n}\mathbb{E}|\varepsilon_{j1}| \leq \left(\frac{1}{na_n^2}\sum_{j=1}^{n}\mathbf{H}^{(j)T}\mathbf{W}^{(j)}\mathbf{H}^{(j)}\right)^{\frac{1}{2}}.$$

Using that
$$\sum_{l=1}^{n}|\widetilde{R}_{kl}^{(j,0)}|^2 \leq \frac{1}{v^2}, \quad (A56)$$

we obtain that the spectral norm of matrix $\mathbf{W}^{(j)}$ satiesfies the inequality

$$\|\mathbf{W}^{(j)}\| \leq \frac{1}{v^2}, \quad (A57)$$

and

$$\|\mathbf{H}^{(j)T}\mathbf{W}^{(j)}\mathbf{H}^{(j)}\| \leq \|\mathbf{W}^{(j)}\|\|\mathbf{H}^{(j)}\|^2 \leq \frac{1}{v^2}\sum_{k=1}^{n}p_{jk}^2\sigma_{jkj}^4. \quad (A58)$$

Using the last bound, we obtain

$$\frac{1}{n}\sum_{j=1}^{n}\mathbb{E}|\varepsilon_{j1}| \leq \frac{1}{v}\left(\frac{1}{na_n^2}\sum_{j=1}^{n}\sum_{k=1}^{n}p_{jk}^2\sigma_{jk}^4\right)^{\frac{1}{2}}. \quad (A59)$$

Furthermore, we apply the bound

$$\sigma_{jk}^2 \leq \tau^2 a_n + \mathbb{E}X_{jk}^2\mathbb{I}\{|X_{jk}| > \tau\sqrt{a_n}\}. \quad (A60)$$

We obtain

$$\frac{1}{n}\sum_{j=1}^{n}\mathbb{E}|\varepsilon_{j1}| \leq \frac{1}{v}\left(\tau^2 + \frac{1}{na_n^2}\sum_{j=1}^{n}\sum_{k=1}^{n}p_{jk}^2\sigma_{jk}^2\mathbb{E}|X_{jk}|^2\mathbb{I}\{|X_{jk}| > \tau\sqrt{a_n}\}\right)^{\frac{1}{2}}. \quad (A61)$$

We continue as follows

$$\frac{1}{n}\sum_{j=1}^{n}\mathbb{E}|\varepsilon_{j1}| \leq \frac{\tau}{v} + \frac{1}{v}\left(\frac{\max_{1\leq j,k\leq n}p_{jk}\sigma_{jk}^2}{a_n}\right)^{\frac{1}{2}}L_n(\tau)^{\frac{1}{2}}.$$

Thus, Lemma is proved. □

Lemma A7. *Under the conditions of Theorem 1, we have*

$$\frac{1}{n}\sum_{j=1}^{n}\mathbb{E}|\varepsilon_{j2}| \leq \frac{1}{v}L_n(\tau) + \frac{\tau}{v}. \quad (A62)$$

Proof. We recall the definition of ε_{j2},

$$\varepsilon_{j2} = \frac{1}{a_n}\sum_{k:k\neq j}[\widetilde{R}^{(j,0)}]_{kk}(A_{jk} - p_{jk})X_{jk}^2. \quad (A63)$$

Using triangle inequality and Cauchy's inequality, we may write

$$\frac{1}{n}\sum_{j=1}^{n}\mathbb{E}|\varepsilon_{j2}| \leq \frac{1}{na_nv}\sum_{j=1}^{n}\sum_{k=1}^{n}p_{jk}\mathbb{E}X_{jk}^2\mathbb{I}\{|X_{jk}| \geq \tau\sqrt{a_n}\}$$

$$+ \left(\frac{1}{na_n^2}\sum_{j=1}^{n}\mathbb{E}\left|\sum_{k:k\neq j}[\widetilde{R}^{(j,0)}]_{kk}(A_{jk} - p_{jk})X_{jk}^2\mathbb{I}\{|X_{jk}| \geq \tau\sqrt{a_n}\}\right|^2\right)^{\frac{1}{2}}. \quad (A64)$$

Since $\mathbb{E}[\widetilde{R}^{(j,0)}]_{kk}(A_{jk} - p_{jk})X_{jk}^2\mathbb{I}\{|X_{jk}| \geq \tau\sqrt{a_n}\} = 0$ and random variables A_{jk}, X_{jk} are independent for $k = 1,\ldots n$ and independent on $[\widetilde{R}^{(j,0)}]_{kk}$, we obtain

$$\frac{1}{n}\sum_{j=1}^{n}\mathbb{E}|\varepsilon_{j2}| \leq \frac{1}{v}L_n(\tau) + \frac{\tau}{v}\left(\frac{1}{na_n}\sum_{j=1}^{n}\sum_{k:k\neq j}p_{jk}\sigma_{jk}^2\right)^{\frac{1}{2}}$$

$$= \frac{1}{v}L_n(\tau) + \frac{\tau}{v} \quad (A65)$$

Thus, the lemma is proved. □

Lemma A8. *Under the conditions of Theorem 1, we have*

$$\frac{1}{n}\sum_{j=1}^{n}\mathbb{E}|\varepsilon_{j3}| \leq \frac{3}{v}L_n(\tau) + \frac{\tau}{v}. \tag{A66}$$

Proof. By definition of ε_{j3}, we have

$$\varepsilon_{j3} = \frac{1}{a_n}\sum_{k:k\neq j}[\widetilde{R}^{(j,0)}(z)]_{kk}p_{jk}(X_{jk}^2 - \sigma_{jk}^2), \tag{A67}$$

We may write

$$\frac{1}{n}\sum_{j=1}^{n}\mathbb{E}|\varepsilon_{j3}| \leq \frac{1}{v}\frac{1}{na_n}\sum_{j=1}^{n}\sum_{k=1}^{n}p_{jk}\mathbb{E}|X_{jk}^2 - \sigma_{jk}^2|\mathbb{I}\{|X_{jk}| > \tau\sqrt{a_n}\}$$

$$+ \frac{1}{n}\sum_{j=1}^{n}\mathbb{E}\left|\frac{1}{a_n}\sum_{k=1}^{n}p_{jk}\widetilde{R}_{kk}^{(j,0)}(X_{jk}^2 - \sigma_{jk}^2)\mathbb{I}\{|X_{jk}| \leq \tau\sqrt{a_n}\}\right| \tag{A68}$$

Furthermore,

$$\frac{1}{na_n}\sum_{j=1}^{n}\sum_{k=1}^{n}p_{jk}\mathbb{E}|X_{jk}^2 - \sigma_{jk}^2|\mathbb{I}\{|X_{jk}| > \tau\sqrt{a_n}\} \leq L_n(\tau)$$

$$+ \frac{1}{na_n}\sum_{j=1}^{n}\sum_{k=1}^{n}p_{jk}\sigma_{jk}^2\mathbb{E}\mathbb{I}\{|X_{jk}| > \tau\sqrt{a_n}\}. \tag{A69}$$

Using inequality (A60), we obtain

$$\frac{1}{na_n}\sum_{j=1}^{n}\sum_{k=1}^{n}p_{jk}\sigma_{jk}^2\mathbb{E}\mathbb{I}\{|X_{jk}| > \tau\sqrt{a_n}\} \leq L_n(\tau)$$

$$+ \frac{1}{na_n}\sum_{j=1}^{n}\sum_{k=1}^{n}p_{jk}\mathbb{E}|X_{jk}|^2\mathbb{I}\{|X_{jk}| > \tau\sqrt{a_n}\}\mathbb{E}\mathbb{I}\{|X_{jk}| > \tau\sqrt{a_n}\} \leq 2L_n(\tau).$$

We estimate now the second term in the right-hand side of (A68). Applying triangle inequality, we obtain

$$\frac{1}{n}\sum_{j=1}^{n}\mathbb{E}\left|\frac{1}{a_n}\sum_{k=1}^{n}p_{jk}\widetilde{R}_{kk}^{(j,0)}(X_{jk}^2 - \sigma_{jk}^2)\mathbb{I}\{|X_{jk}| \leq \tau\sqrt{a_n}\}\right|$$

$$\leq \frac{1}{n}\sum_{j=1}^{n}\left|\frac{1}{a_n}\sum_{k=1}^{n}p_{jk}\mathbb{E}\widetilde{R}_{kk}^{(j,0)}\mathbb{E}(X_{jk}^2 - \sigma_{jk}^2)\mathbb{I}\{|X_{jk}| \leq \tau\sqrt{a_n}\}\right|$$

$$+ \left(\frac{1}{n}\sum_{j=1}^{n}\mathbb{E}\left|\frac{1}{a_n}\sum_{k=1}^{n}\widetilde{R}_{kk}^{(j,0)}(X_{jk}^2\mathbb{I}\{|X_{jk}| \leq \tau\sqrt{a_n}\} - \mathbb{E}X_{jk}^2\mathbb{I}\{|X_{jk}| \leq \tau\sqrt{a_n}\})\right|^2\right)^{\frac{1}{2}}. \tag{A70}$$

Simple calculations show that

$$\frac{1}{n}\sum_{j=1}^{n}\mathbb{E}\left|\frac{1}{a_n}\sum_{k=1}^{n}\widetilde{R}_{kk}^{(j,0)}(X_{jk}^2\mathbb{I}\{|X_{jk}| \leq \tau\sqrt{a_n}\} - \mathbb{E}X_{jk}^2\mathbb{I}\{|X_{jk}| \leq \tau\sqrt{a_n}\})\right|^2$$

$$\leq \frac{1}{v^2 n a_n^2}\sum_{j=1}^{n}\sum_{k=1}^{n}p_{jk}^2\mathbb{E}|X_{jk}|^4\mathbb{I}\{|X_{jk}| \leq \tau\sqrt{a_n}\}$$

$$\leq \frac{\tau^2}{v^2}\frac{1}{na_n}\sum_{j=1}^{n}\sum_{k=1}^{n}p_{jk}\sigma_{jk}^2 = \frac{\tau^2}{v^2}. \tag{A71}$$

Finally, we note that

$$\mathbb{E}(X_{jk}^2 - \sigma_{jk}^2)\mathbb{I}\{|X_{jk}| \leq \tau\sqrt{a_n}\} = \mathbb{E}(X_{jk}^2 - \sigma_{jk}^2)\mathbb{I}\{|X_{jk}| > \tau\sqrt{a_n}\}. \tag{A72}$$

Combining inequalities (A68), (A70), (A71), we obtain the result of the lemma. Thus, the lemma is proved. □

Lemma A9. *Under the conditions of Theorem 1, we have*

$$\frac{1}{n}\sum_{j=1}^{n}\mathbb{E}|\varepsilon_{j4}| \leq \frac{1}{vna_n}\sum_{j=1}^{n}\sum_{k=1}^{n}|p_{jk}\sigma_{jk}^2 - \frac{1}{n}\sum_{l=1}^{n}p_{jl}\sigma_{jl}^2|. \qquad (A73)$$

Proof. By definition of ε_{j4}, we have

$$\varepsilon_{j4} = \frac{1}{a_n}\sum_{k:k\neq j}\widetilde{R}_{kk}^{(j,0)}\left(p_{jk}\sigma_{jk}^2 - \frac{1}{n}\sum_{l=1}^{n}p_{jl}\sigma_{jl}^2\right). \qquad (A74)$$

Using that $|\widetilde{R}_{kk}^{(j,0)}| \leq \frac{1}{v}$, we obtain

$$\frac{1}{n}\sum_{j=1}^{n}\mathbb{E}|\varepsilon_{j4}| \leq \frac{1}{vna_n}\sum_{j=1}^{n}\sum_{k=1}^{n}|p_{jk}\sigma_{jk}^2 - \frac{1}{n}\sum_{l=1}^{n}p_{jl}\sigma_{jl}^2|. \qquad (A75)$$

□

Lemma A10. *Under the conditions of Theorem 1, we have*

$$\frac{1}{n}\sum_{j=1}^{n}\mathbb{E}|\varepsilon_{j5}| \leq \frac{1}{vn}\sum_{j=1}^{n}\left|\frac{1}{a_n}\sum_{l=1}^{n}p_{jl}\sigma_{jl}^2 - 1\right|. \qquad (A76)$$

Proof. Recall that

$$\varepsilon_{j5} = \frac{1}{n}\sum_{k:k\neq j}\widetilde{R}_{kk}^{(j,0)}\left(\frac{1}{a_n}\sum_{l=1}^{n}p_{jl}\sigma_{jl}^2 - 1\right). \qquad (A77)$$

Using that $|\widetilde{R}_{kk}^{(j,0)}| \leq v^{-1}$, we obtain

$$\frac{1}{n}\sum_{j=1}^{n}\mathbb{E}|\varepsilon_{j5}| \leq \frac{1}{vn}\sum_{j=1}^{n}\left|\frac{1}{a_n}\sum_{l=1}^{n}p_{jl}\sigma_{jl}^2 - 1\right|. \qquad (A78)$$

Thus, the lemma is proved. □

Lemma A11. *Under the conditions of Theorem 1, we have*

$$\frac{1}{n}\sum_{j=1}^{n}\mathbb{E}|\varepsilon_{j6}| \leq \frac{\tau}{v^2} + \frac{1}{nv^2\tau}L_n(\tau). \qquad (A79)$$

Proof. By definition of ε_{j6}, we have

$$\varepsilon_{j6} = \frac{1}{n}\sum_{k:k\neq j}[\widetilde{R}^{(j,0)}]_{kk} - \frac{1}{n}\sum_{k=1}^{n}[R]_{kk}. \qquad (A80)$$

By the triangle inequality, we obtain

$$\frac{1}{n}\sum_{j=1}^{n}\mathbb{E}|\varepsilon_{j6}| \leq \frac{1}{n}\sum_{j=1}^{n}\mathbb{E}\left|\frac{1}{n}\mathrm{Tr}\widetilde{\mathbf{R}}^{(j,0)} - \frac{1}{n}\mathrm{Tr}\widetilde{\mathbf{R}}^{(j)}\right| + \frac{1}{n}\sum_{j=1}^{n}\mathbb{E}\left|\frac{1}{n}\mathrm{Tr}\widetilde{\mathbf{R}}^{(j)} - \mathrm{Tr}\mathbf{R}\right|. \qquad (A81)$$

By the overlapping theorem, we have

$$\left|\frac{1}{n}\mathrm{Tr}\widetilde{\mathbf{R}}^{(j,0)} - \frac{1}{n}\mathrm{Tr}\widetilde{\mathbf{R}}^{(j)}\right| \leq \frac{1}{nv}. \qquad (A82)$$

It remains to estimate the second term in the r.h.s. of (A81). Note that

$$\widetilde{\mathbf{R}}^{(j)} - \mathbf{R} = \widetilde{\mathbf{R}}^{(j)}\mathbf{D}^{(j)}\mathbf{R}. \qquad (A83)$$

This equality implies that

$$\operatorname{Tr}\widetilde{\mathbf{R}}^{(j)} - \operatorname{Tr}\mathbf{R} = \frac{1}{\sqrt{a_n}} \sum_{l=1}^{n} \sum_{k=1}^{n} R_{kl} A_{jk} X_{jk} \widetilde{R}_{lk}^{(j)}. \quad \text{(A84)}$$

Summing this equality in j, we obtain

$$\frac{1}{n} \sum_{j=1}^{n} \mathbb{E}|\frac{1}{n}\operatorname{Tr}\widetilde{\mathbf{R}}^{(j)} - \frac{1}{n}\operatorname{Tr}\mathbf{R}| \leq \frac{1}{n^2 \sqrt{a_n}} \sum_{j=1}^{n} \mathbb{E}|\sum_{l=1}^{n} \sum_{k=1}^{n} R_{kl} A_{jk} X_{jk} \widetilde{R}_{lk}^{(j)}|. \quad \text{(A85)}$$

Using that

$$\sum_{l=1}^{n} |R_{kl} \widetilde{R}_{kl}^{(j)}| \leq \frac{1}{v^2}, \quad \text{(A86)}$$

we obtain

$$\frac{1}{n} \sum_{j=1}^{n} \mathbb{E}|\frac{1}{n}\operatorname{Tr}\widetilde{\mathbf{R}}^{(j)} - \frac{1}{n}\operatorname{Tr}\mathbf{R}| \leq \frac{1}{v^2 n^2 \sqrt{a_n}} \sum_{j=1}^{n} \sum_{k=1}^{n} p_{jk} \mathbb{E}|X_{jk}| \mathbb{I}\{|X_{jk}| \leq \tau\sqrt{a_n}\}$$

$$+ \frac{1}{n^2 v^2 a_n \tau} \sum_{j=1}^{n} \sum_{k=1}^{n} p_{jk} \mathbb{E} X_{jk}^2 \mathbb{I}\{|X_{jk}| > \tau\sqrt{a_n}\} \leq \frac{\tau}{v^2} + \frac{1}{n v^2 \tau} L_n(\tau). \quad \text{(A87)}$$

Thus, the lemma is proved. □

Appendix C. Unweigthed Graphs

Appendix C.1. Convergence of Diagonal Entries Distribution Functions of Laplace Matrices to the Normal Law

We denote by $\widehat{F}_n(x)$ the distribution function of random variable $\widehat{\zeta}_J$ and

$$\widehat{\Delta}_n := \sup_x |\widehat{F}_n(x) - \Phi(x)|. \quad \text{(A88)}$$

Lemma A12. *Under the conditions of Theorem 2, we have*

$$\lim_{n \to \infty} \sup_x |\widehat{F}_n(x) - \Phi(x)| = 0. \quad \text{(A89)}$$

Proof. We consider the characteristic function of $\widehat{\zeta}_J$, $\widehat{f}_n(t) = \frac{1}{n} \sum_{j=1}^{n} \mathbb{E} \exp\{it\widehat{\zeta}_j\}$. Introduce the following set of indices

$$\widehat{\mathcal{M}} =:= \left\{ j \in \{1, \ldots, n\} : \frac{1}{\widehat{a}_n} \sum_{k=1}^{n} |p_{jk}(1 - p_{jk}) - \frac{\widehat{a}_n}{n}| \leq \frac{1}{16} \right\}. \quad \text{(A90)}$$

We denote by $\mathcal{A}^c$ a complement set of $\mathcal{A}$ and by $|\mathcal{A}|$, we denote the cardinality of set $\mathcal{A}$. Note that, by condition $CP(1)$,

$$\frac{|\widehat{\mathcal{M}}^c|}{n} \leq 16 \frac{1}{n \widehat{a}_n} \sum_{j=1}^{n} \sum_{k=1}^{n} |p_{jk} \sigma_{jk}^2 - \frac{\widehat{a}_n}{n}| \to 0, \text{ as } n \to \infty. \quad \text{(A91)}$$

Note that, by independence of A_{jk},

$$\widehat{f}_{nj}(t) := \mathbb{E} \exp\{\frac{it}{\sqrt{\widehat{a}_n}} \widehat{\zeta}_j\} = \prod_{k=1}^{n} \mathbb{E} \exp\{\frac{it}{\sqrt{\widehat{a}_n}}(A_{jk} - p_{jk})\} =: \prod_{k=1}^{n} \widehat{f}_{njk}(t)$$

Applying the Taylor formula, we may write

$$\widehat{f}_{njk}(t) = 1 - \frac{t^2 p_{jk}(1 - p_{jk})}{2\widehat{a}_n} + \theta(t) \frac{|t|^3}{6\widehat{a}_n^{\frac{3}{2}}} p_{jk}(1 - p_{jk}), \quad \text{(A92)}$$

where $\theta(t)$ denotes some function such that $|\theta(t)| \leq 1$.

Using this equality, we may write

$$\ln \widehat{f}_{njk}(t) = -\frac{t^2}{2\widehat{a}_n}p_{jk}(1-p_{jk}) + \theta_1(t)\frac{\tau|t|^3}{6\widehat{a}_n^{\frac{3}{2}}}p_{jk}(1-p_{jk})$$
$$+ \theta_2(t)\frac{t^4 p_{jk}^2(1-p_{jk})^2}{\widehat{a}_n^2} + \theta_3(t)\frac{t^6 p_{jk}^2(1-p_{jk})^2}{\widehat{a}_n^3}. \quad \text{(A93)}$$

Summing this equality by $k = 1\ldots, n$, we obtain

$$\ln \widehat{f}_{nj}(t) = -\frac{t^2}{2} - \frac{t^2}{2}\frac{1}{\widehat{a}_n}\sum_{k=1}^{n}(p_{jk}(1-p_{jk}) - \frac{\widehat{a}_n}{n}) + \theta_1(t)\frac{|t|^3}{6\widehat{a}_n^{\frac{3}{2}}}\sum_{k=1}^{n}p_{jk}(1-p_{jk})$$
$$+ \theta_2(t)\frac{t^4}{\widehat{a}_n^2}\sum_{k=1}^{n}p_{jk}^2(1-p_{jk})^2 + \theta_3(t)\frac{t^6}{\widehat{a}_n^3}\sum_{k=1}^{n}p_{jk}^2(1-p_{jk})^2. \quad \text{(A94)}$$

Note that for $j \in \widehat{\mathcal{M}}$,

$$\frac{1}{a_n}\sum_{k=1}^{n}p_{jk}(1-p_{jk}) \leq \frac{17}{16}, \text{ for } j \in \widehat{\mathcal{M}}, \quad \text{(A95)}$$

and

$$\lim_{n\to\infty}\frac{|\widehat{\mathcal{M}}^c|}{n} = 0. \quad \text{(A96)}$$

Similar to (A42), we may write

$$|\widehat{f}_n(t) - \exp\{-\frac{t^2}{2}\}| \leq \frac{2|\widehat{\mathcal{M}}^c|}{n} + \frac{t^2}{2}\frac{1}{n\widehat{a}_n}\sum_{j=1}^{n}\sum_{k=1}^{n}|p_{jk}(1-p_{jk}) - \frac{\widehat{a}_n}{n}|$$
$$+ \frac{C|t|^3}{\sqrt{\widehat{a}_n}} + \frac{Ct^4}{\widehat{a}_n} + \frac{C|t|^6}{\widehat{a}_n^2} \quad \text{(A97)}$$

This inequality implies that

$$\lim_{n\to\infty}\widehat{f}_n(t) = \exp\{-\frac{t^2}{2}\}. \quad \text{(A98)}$$

Thus, Lemma A12 is proved. □

In what follows, we shall assume that $z = u + iv$ is fixed.

Appendix C.2. The Bounds of $\frac{1}{n}\sum_{j=1}^{n}\mathbb{E}|\widehat{\varepsilon}_{jv}|$, for $v = 1,\ldots,5$

Lemma A13. *Under conditions of Theorem 1, we have*

$$\frac{1}{n}\sum_{j=1}^{n}\mathbb{E}|\widehat{\varepsilon}_{j1}| \leq \left(\frac{1}{4a_n v^2}\right)^{\frac{1}{2}}. \quad \text{(A99)}$$

Proof. By definition of ε_{j1} we may write

$$\widehat{\varepsilon}_{j1} := \frac{1}{\widehat{a}_n}\sum_{l\neq k: l\neq j, k\neq j}[\widehat{R}^{(j,0)}]_{kl}(A_{jk} - p_{jk})(A_{jl} - p_{jl}). \quad \text{(A100)}$$

Applying the Cauchy inequality, we obtain

$$\frac{1}{n}\sum_{j=1}^{n}\mathbb{E}|\varepsilon_{j1}| \leq \left(\frac{1}{n}\sum_{j=1}^{n}\mathbb{E}|\varepsilon_{j1}|^2\right)^{\frac{1}{2}}. \quad \text{(A101)}$$

Simple calculations show that

$$\frac{1}{n}\sum_{j=1}^{n}\mathbb{E}|\widehat{\varepsilon}_{j1}| \leq \left(\frac{1}{na_n^2}\sum_{j=1}^{n}\sum_{k\neq j}\sum_{l\neq j}\mathbb{E}|\widehat{R}_{kl}^{(j,0)}|^2 p_{jk}p_{jl}(1-p_{jk})(1-p_{jl})\right)^{\frac{1}{2}}$$

$$\leq \left(\frac{1}{4na_n^2}\sum_{j=1}^{n}\sum_{k\neq j}\sum_{l\neq j}\mathbb{E}|\widehat{R}_{kl}^{(j,0)}|^2 p_{jk}(1-p_{jk})\right)^{\frac{1}{2}}$$

$$\leq \left(\frac{1}{4na_n^2 v^2}\sum_{j=1}^{n}\sum_{k\neq j}p_{jk}(1-p_{jk})\right)^{\frac{1}{2}} \leq \left(\frac{1}{4a_n v^2}\right)^{\frac{1}{2}}. \quad \text{(A102)}$$

Thus, Lemma A13 is proved. □

Lemma A14. *Under the conditions of Theorem 1, we have*

$$\frac{1}{n}\sum_{j=1}^{n}\mathbb{E}|\widehat{\varepsilon}_{j2}| \leq \frac{1}{\sqrt{\widehat{a}_n}v}. \quad \text{(A103)}$$

Proof. We recall the definition of $\widehat{\varepsilon}_{j2}$,

$$\widehat{\varepsilon}_{j2} = \frac{1}{\widehat{a}_n}\sum_{k:k\neq j}[\widehat{R}^{(j,0)}]_{kk}((A_{jk}-p_{jk})^2 - p_{jk}(1-p_{jk})). \quad \text{(A104)}$$

Using the triangle inequality and the Cauchy inequality, we may write

$$\frac{1}{n}\sum_{j=1}^{n}\mathbb{E}|\widehat{\varepsilon}_{j2}| \leq \left(\frac{1}{n\widehat{a}_n^2}\sum_{j=1}^{n}\sum_{k=1}^{n}\mathbb{E}|\widehat{R}_{kk}^{(j,0)}|^2 p_{jk}(1-p_{jk})(1-2p_{jk})^2\right)^{\frac{1}{2}}$$

$$\leq \left(\frac{1}{\widehat{a}_n v^2}\frac{1}{n\widehat{a}_n}\sum_{j=1}^{n}\sum_{k=1}^{n}p_{jk}(1-p_{jk})\right)^{\frac{1}{2}} = \left(\frac{1}{\widehat{a}_n v^2}\right)^{\frac{1}{2}}. \quad \text{(A105)}$$

Thus, Lemma A14 is proved. □

Lemma A15. *Under conditions of Theorem 1, we have*

$$\frac{1}{n}\sum_{j=1}^{n}\mathbb{E}|\widehat{\varepsilon}_{j3}| \leq \frac{1}{v}\frac{1}{na_n}\sum_{j=1}^{n}\sum_{k=1}^{n}|p_{jk}(1-p_{jk}) - \frac{\widehat{a}_n}{n}|. \quad \text{(A106)}$$

Proof. By definition of $\widehat{\varepsilon}_{j3}$, we have

$$\widehat{\varepsilon}_{j3} = \frac{1}{a_n}\sum_{k:k\neq j}[\widehat{R}^{(j,0)}]_{kk}(p_{jk}(1-p_{jk}) - \frac{\widehat{a}_n}{n}). \quad \text{(A107)}$$

We may write

$$\frac{1}{n}\sum_{j=1}^{n}\mathbb{E}|\widehat{\varepsilon}_{j3}| \leq \frac{1}{v}\frac{1}{n\widehat{a}_n}\sum_{j=1}^{n}\sum_{k=1}^{n}|p_{jk}(1-p_{jk}) - \frac{\widehat{a}_n}{n}|. \quad \text{(A108)}$$

Thus, Lemma A15 is proved. □

Lemma A16. *Under the conditions of Theorem 1, we have*

$$\frac{1}{n}\sum_{j=1}^{n}\mathbb{E}|\widehat{\varepsilon}_{j4}| \leq \frac{1}{v^2\sqrt{\widehat{a}_n}}. \quad \text{(A109)}$$

Proof. Recall that
$$\widehat{\varepsilon}_{j4} = \frac{1}{n}\sum_{k:k\neq j}\widehat{R}_{kk}^{(j,0)} - \frac{1}{n}\sum_{k=1}^{n}\widehat{R}_{kk}. \tag{A110}$$

Note that
$$\left|\frac{1}{n}\operatorname{Tr}\widehat{\mathbf{R}}^{(j)} - \frac{1}{n}\operatorname{Tr}\widehat{\mathbf{R}}^{(j,0)}\right| \leq \frac{1}{nv}. \tag{A111}$$

Furthermore,
$$\widehat{\mathbf{R}} - \widehat{\mathbf{R}}^{(j)} = \widehat{\mathbf{R}}\widehat{\mathbf{D}}^{(j)}\widehat{\mathbf{R}}^{(j)}. \tag{A112}$$

Recall that $\|\mathbf{A}\|$ denotes the operator norm of matrix $\mathbf{A}$. The last equality and inequality $\max\{\|\widehat{\mathbf{R}}\|, \|\widehat{\mathbf{R}}^{(j)}\|\} \leq v^{-1}$ implies that
$$\left|\frac{1}{n}\operatorname{Tr}(\widehat{\mathbf{R}} - \widehat{\mathbf{R}}^{(j)})\right| \leq \|\widehat{\mathbf{R}} - \widehat{\mathbf{R}}^{(j)}\| \leq \|\widehat{\mathbf{R}}\|\|\widehat{\mathbf{D}}^{(j)}\|\|\widehat{\mathbf{R}}^{(j)}\| \leq v^{-2}\|\widehat{\mathbf{D}}^{(j)}\|. \tag{A113}$$

Note that
$$\mathbb{E}\|\widehat{\mathbf{D}}^{(j)}\| \leq \frac{1}{\sqrt{\widehat{a}_n}}\mathbb{E}\max_{1\leq k\leq n}|A_{jk} - p_{jk}| \leq \frac{1}{\sqrt{\widehat{a}_n}}. \tag{A114}$$

Combining the last two inequalities, we obtain the claim. Thus, Lemma A16 is proved. □

Appendix C.3. Variance of $\frac{1}{n}\operatorname{Tr}\widehat{\mathbf{R}}$

In this section, we estimate the variance of $m_n(z) = \frac{1}{n}\operatorname{Tr}\widehat{\mathbf{R}}$, where $\widehat{\mathbf{R}} = \widehat{\mathbf{R}}(z) = (\widehat{\mathbf{L}} - z\mathbf{I})^{-1}$. We prove the following lemma.

Lemma A17. *For any $v > 0$ and $z = u + iv$, the following inequality holds*
$$\lim_{n\to\infty}\mathbb{E}\left|\frac{1}{n}\operatorname{Tr}\widehat{\mathbf{R}} - \mathbb{E}\frac{1}{n}\operatorname{Tr}\widehat{\mathbf{R}}\right| = 0. \tag{A115}$$

Proof. The proof of this lemma is similar to the proof of Lemma A2. We introduce the sequence of σ-algebras $\mathfrak{M}_k$ generated by random variables $A_{j,l}$ for $1 \leq j, l \leq k$. It is easy to see that $\mathfrak{M}_k \subset \mathfrak{M}_{k+1}$. Denote by $\mathbb{E}_k$ the conditional expectation with respect to σ-algebra $\mathfrak{M}_k$. For $k = 0$, $\mathbb{E}_0 = \mathbb{E}$. Introduce random variables
$$\widehat{\gamma}_k := \mathbb{E}_k\left(\frac{1}{n}\operatorname{Tr}\widehat{\mathbf{R}}\right) - \mathbb{E}_{k-1}\left(\frac{1}{n}\operatorname{Tr}\widehat{\mathbf{R}}\right). \tag{A116}$$

The sequence of $\widehat{\gamma}_k$, for $k = 1, \ldots, n$ is a martingale difference and
$$\frac{1}{n}\operatorname{Tr}\widehat{\mathbf{R}} - \mathbb{E}\frac{1}{n}\operatorname{Tr}\widehat{\mathbf{R}} = \sum_{k=1}^{n}\widehat{\gamma}_k.$$

Furthermore, introduce the sub-matrices $\widehat{\mathbf{L}}^{(k)}$ obtained from $\widehat{\mathbf{L}}$ by replacing the diagonal entries with $\widehat{L}_{ll}^{(k)} := \frac{1}{\sqrt{\widehat{a}_n}}\sum_{l:l\neq k,l\neq j}(A_{jl} - p_{jl})$. Denote by $\widehat{\mathbf{R}}^{(k)}(z)$ the corresponding resolvent matrix, $\widehat{\mathbf{R}}^{(k)}(z) = (\widehat{\mathbf{L}}^{(k)} - z\mathbf{I}_{n-1})^{-1}$. We introduce the matrix $\widehat{\mathbf{L}}^{(k,0)}$ obtained from $\widehat{\mathbf{L}}^{(k)}$ by deleting both the k-th row and k-th column. The corresponding resolvent matrix we denote via $\widehat{\mathbf{R}}^{(k,0)}$. We have now
$$\mathbb{E}_k\operatorname{Tr}\widehat{\mathbf{R}}^{(k,0)} = \mathbb{E}_{k-1}\widehat{\mathbf{R}}^{(k,0)}.$$

This allows us to write
$$\widehat{\gamma}_k = \mathbb{E}_k\left(\frac{1}{n}(\operatorname{Tr}\widehat{\mathbf{R}} - \operatorname{Tr}\widehat{\mathbf{R}}^{(k)})\right) - \mathbb{E}_{k-1}\left(\frac{1}{n}(\operatorname{Tr}\widehat{\mathbf{R}} - \operatorname{Tr}\widehat{\mathbf{R}}^{(k)})\right)$$
$$+ \mathbb{E}_k\left(\frac{1}{n}(\operatorname{Tr}\widehat{\mathbf{R}}^{(k)} - \operatorname{Tr}\widehat{\mathbf{R}}^{(k,0)})\right) - \mathbb{E}_{k-1}\left(\frac{1}{n}(\operatorname{Tr}\widehat{\mathbf{R}}^{(k)} - \operatorname{Tr}\widehat{\mathbf{R}}^{(k,0)})\right) =: \widehat{\gamma}_k^{(1)} + \widehat{\gamma}_k^{(2)}.$$

By the overlapping theorem
$$\left|\frac{1}{n}\operatorname{Tr}\widehat{\mathbf{R}}^{(k)} - \frac{1}{n}\operatorname{Tr}\widehat{\mathbf{R}}^{(k,0)}\right| \leq \frac{1}{nv}. \tag{A117}$$

From here, we immediately obtain
$$|\widehat{\gamma}_k^{(2)}| \leq \frac{2}{nv},$$

and
$$\sum_{k=1}^{n} \mathbb{E}|\widehat{\gamma}_k^{(2)}|^2 \leq \frac{4}{nv^2}. \tag{A118}$$

To complete the proof, it remains to show that

$$\lim_{n\to\infty} \sum_{k=1}^{n} \mathbb{E}|\widehat{\gamma}_k^{(1)}|^2 = 0. \tag{A119}$$

Note that

$$\mathbb{E}|\widehat{\gamma}_k^{(1)}|^2 \leq 2\mathbb{E}|\frac{1}{n}\text{Tr}\widehat{\mathbf{R}} - \frac{1}{n}\text{Tr}\widehat{\mathbf{R}}^{(k)}|^2. \tag{A120}$$

Introduce the diagonal matrix $\widehat{\mathbf{D}}^{(k)}$ with diagonal entries

$$\widehat{D}_{ll}^{(k)} = \frac{1}{\sqrt{\widehat{a}_n}}(A_{kl} - p_{kl}), \quad l \neq k.$$

In these notations, we have

$$\frac{1}{n}\text{Tr}\widehat{\mathbf{R}} - \frac{1}{n}\text{Tr}\widehat{\mathbf{R}}^{(k)} = -\frac{1}{n}\text{Tr}\widehat{\mathbf{R}}\widehat{\mathbf{D}}^{(k)}\widehat{\mathbf{R}}^{(k)} = -\frac{1}{n\sqrt{\widehat{a}_n}} \sum_{l \neq k, j \neq k} \widehat{R}_{lj}^{(k)}(A_{kl} - p_{kl})\widehat{R}_{jl}^{(k)}. \tag{A121}$$

This implies that

$$\sum_{k=1}^{n} \mathbb{E}|\widehat{\gamma}_k^{(1)}|^2 \leq \frac{4}{n^2 \widehat{a}_n} \sum_{k=1}^{n} \mathbb{E}|\sum_{j \neq k}(A_{kj} - p_{kj})(\sum_{l \neq k} \widehat{R}_{lj}\widehat{R}_{jl}^{(k)})|^2. \tag{A122}$$

We continue this inequality as follows

$$\sum_{k=1}^{n} \mathbb{E}|\widehat{\gamma}_k^{(1)}|^2 \leq \frac{8}{n^2 \widehat{a}_n} \sum_{k=1}^{n} \mathbb{E}\left|\sum_{j \neq k}(A_{kj} - p_{kj})(\sum_{l \neq k} R_{lj}^{(k)}\widehat{R}_{jl}^{(k)})\right|^2$$
$$\leq \frac{8}{n^2 v^4 \widehat{a}_n} \sum_{k=1}^{n} \sum_{j \neq k} p_{jk}(1 - p_{jk}) \leq \frac{8}{nv^2}. \tag{A123}$$

Inequalities (A118) and (A123) completed the proof. Thus, Lemma A17 is proved. □

References

1. Bordenave, C.; Caputo, P.; Chafai, D. Spectrum of Markov Generatoron Sparse Random Graphs. *Pure Appl. Math.* **2015**, *67*, 621–669. [CrossRef]
2. Bordenave, C.; Lelarge, M.; Massoulice, L. Nonbacktracking spectrum of random graphs. *Ann. Probab.* **2018**, *46*, 1–71. [CrossRef]
3. Dimitriu, I.; Soumik, P. Sparse regular random graphs: Spectral densitry and eigenvectors. *Ann. Probab.* **2012**, *40*, 2197–2235. [CrossRef]
4. Ding, X.; Jiang, T. Spectral Distribution of Adjacency Matrix and Laplace Matrices of Random Graphs. *Ann. Appl. Probab.* **2010**, *20*, 2086–2117. [CrossRef]
5. Tran, L.V.; Vu, V.H.; Wang, K. Sparse random graphs: Eigenvalues and egenvectors. *Random Struct. Algorithms* **2013**, *42*, 110–134. [CrossRef]
6. Brito, G.; Dimitriu, I.; Harris, K.D. Spectral gap in random bipartite biregular graphs and applications. *Comb. Probab. Comput.* **2022**, *31*, 229–267. [CrossRef]
7. Fernando, L.M.; Jeferson, D.S. Spectral density of dense networks and the breakdown of the Wigner semicircle law. *Phys. Rev. Res.* **2020**, *2*, 043116.
8. Liang, S.; Obata, N.; Takanashi, S. Asymptotic spectral analysis of general Erdös–Renyi random graphs. Nonvommutative harmonic analysis with applications to probability. *Banach Cent. Publ. Inst. Math. Acad. Sci.* **2007**, *78*, 211–229.
9. Erdös, L.; Knowles, A.; Yau, H.-T.; Yin, J. Spectral statistics of Erdős–Rényi graphs I: Local semicircle law. *Ann. Probab.* **2013**, *41*, 2279–2375. [CrossRef]
10. Erdös, L.; Knowles, A.; Yau, H.-T.; Yin, J. Spectral statistics of Erdős-Rényi Graphs II: Eigenvalue spacing and the extreme eigenvalues. *Commun. Math. Phys.* **2012**, *314*, 587–640. [CrossRef]
11. Wloodzimer, B.; Amir, D.; Jiang, T. Spectral Measure of Large Random Hankel, Markov and Toeplitz Matrices. *Ann. Probab.* **2006**, *34*, 1–38.
12. Anirban, C.; Rajat, S.H. Spectral Properties for the Laplace of a Generalized Wigner Matrices. *arXiv* **2021**, arXiv:2011.07912v2.
13. Philippe, B. On the Free Convolution with a Semi-circular Distribution. *Indiana Univ. Math. J.* **1997**, *46*, 705–718.
14. Zhu, Y. A Graphon Approach to Limiting Spectral Distribution of Wigner-Type Matrices. *Random Struct. Algorithms* **2020**, *56*, 251–279. [CrossRef]

15. Tikhomirov, A.N. On the Wigner law for Generalized Erdös–Renyi Random Graphs. *Sib. Adv. Math.* **2021**, *31*, 229–236. [CrossRef]
16. Götze, F.; Koesters, H.; Tikhomirov, A. Asymptotic Spectra of Matrix–Valued Functions of Independent Random Matrices and Free Probability. *Random Matrices Theory Appl.* **2014**, *4*, 1–85. [CrossRef]
17. Voiculescu, D. Symmetries of some reduced free product C*-algebras. In *Operator Algebras and Their Connections with Topology and Ergodic Theory. Lecture Notes in Mathematics*; Springer: Berlin, Germany, 1985; Volume 1132, pp. 556–588.
18. Bercovici, H.; Voiculescu, D. $\mathbb{R}$ee convolution of measures with unbounded support. *Indiana Univ. Math. J.* **1993**, *42*, 733–773. [CrossRef]
19. Voiculescu, D. Lectures on free probability theory. In *Lectures on Probability Theory and Statistics. Lecture Notes in Mathematics*; Springer: Berlin, Germany, 2000; Volume 1738, pp. 279–349.
20. Girko, V.L. Spectral theory of random matrices. *Russ. Math. Surv.* **1985**, *40*, 77–120. [CrossRef]

Disclaimer/Publisher's Note: The statements, opinions and data contained in all publications are solely those of the individual author(s) and contributor(s) and not of MDPI and/or the editor(s). MDPI and/or the editor(s) disclaim responsibility for any injury to people or property resulting from any ideas, methods, instructions or products referred to in the content.

Article

Second Order Chebyshev–Edgeworth-Type Approximations for Statistics Based on Random Size Samples

Gerd Christoph [1,*,†] **and Vladimir V. Ulyanov** [2,3,†]

[1] Department of Mathematics, Otto-von-Guericke University Magdeburg, 39016 Magdeburg, Germany
[2] Faculty of Computer Science, HSE University, 101000 Moscow, Russia
[3] Faculty of Computational Mathematics and Cybernetics, Lomonosov Moscow State University, 119991 Moscow, Russia
* Correspondence: gerd.christoph@ovgu.de
† These authors contributed equally to this work.

Abstract: This article completes our studies on the formal construction of asymptotic approximations for statistics based on a random number of observations. Second order Chebyshev–Edgeworth expansions of asymptotically normally or chi-squared distributed statistics from samples with negative binomial or Pareto-like distributed random sample sizes are obtained. The results can have applications for a wide spectrum of asymptotically normally or chi-square distributed statistics. Random, non-random, and mixed scaling factors for each of the studied statistics produce three different limit distributions. In addition to the expected normal or chi-squared distributions, Student's t-, Laplace, Fisher, gamma, and weighted sums of generalized gamma distributions also occur.

Keywords: second order Chebyshev–Edgeworth expansions; negative binomially distributed sample sizes; Pareto-like distributed sample sizes; asymptotically normally distributed statistics; asymptotically chi-square distributed statistics; scaled Student's t-distribution; normal distribution; discrete Pareto distribution; generalized Laplace distribution; weighted sums of generalized gamma distributions

MSC: 62E17; 62H10; 60E05

1. Introduction

To improve the convergence properties of sums of independent identically distributed random variables in the Central Limit Theorem, asymptotic expansions of distribution functions of normalized sums were considered. The history of asymptotic expansions in nonparametric statistics is presented in detail in Wallace [1], Bickel [2], and Hall [3], among others. Chebyshev–Edgeworth expansions, with which we are concerned here, are presented in great detail in Bhattacharya and Rao [4] for random vectors and in Petrov [5] for one-dimensional random variables. For instance, in Pfanzagl [6] and Bentkus et al. [7], the authors emphasize that asymptotic expansions can provide more effective approximations for asymptotic studies in statistical theory. Second order approximations of distribution functions of sums of random variables are of great importance because they take into account the skewness and kurtosis of the random variable in addition to the expected value and the variance, as in the Central Limit Theorem. In Burnashev [8], second order expansions are proved for the asymptotically normally distributed sample median M_m on a sample of size m and its MSE. Based on this, for a Laplace population with density $e^{-|x|}/2$, the actual MSE with exact data is compared numerically with approximations data. For the normal approximation, the influence of the remaining term is below 10% only for $m > 250$, while for the approximation with the second order expansion, the influence of the remaining term is below 10% already from $m = 8$. For a Cauchy population with smooth and heavy tailed density $1/(\pi(1+x^2))$, for the normal approximation, the influence of the remaining term is below 10% for $m \geq 23$, while for the approximation

with the second order expansion, the influence of the remaining term is below 10% already from $m = 11$. Consequently, as Burnashev [8] pointed out, asymptotic expansions can significantly improve the exactness of statistical conclusions, even in the case of a small number of observations. The results in the abovementioned papers are based on non-random sample sizes or non-random number of observations.

When planning statistical studies, situations often arise where the sample sizes are unknown in advance and they are modeled as realizations of random variables. Many models from medicine, finance, risk theory, physics, and reliability lead to samples with random dimensions. For instance, in the papers by Nunes et al. [9,10,11], different models in medical research random size samples were investigated in order to prevent false conclusions. In Esquível et al. [12], the authors give an informative overview of statistical inference with a random number of observations and some applications. Results for mean and variance for normally distributed samples, calculation of quantiles, and interval estimates with random sample size were also proved. Döbler [13] gives a detailed review of the literature on random sums as well as recent results on approximation in various metrics. In Schluter and Trede [14] (Theorem 1, Proposition 1), the authors show, using the convergence of a negative binomial random sum, that the growth rate of cities is Student t-distributed with 2 degrees of freedom. Their empirical investigations verify the result. The references in the above-cited papers provide further applications for random dimension sampling.

Bening et al. [15,16] proved convergence rates and asymptotic expansions for distributions of statistics T_{N_n} based on samples with random dimension $N_n \geq 1$. Here, T_m is a statistic based on a non-random number $m \geq 1$ of independent observations. The random variables size $N_n \geq 1$ form a sequence of integer random sample sizes that depends on a natural parameter n with $N_n \to \infty$ in probability for $n \to \infty$. Inequalities with a convergence rate are assumed for the approximations of the distribution functions of both the normalized statistics T_m and the normalized random sample sizes N_n. As examples, convergence rates and first order asymptotic expansions are derived for the statistics T_{N_n}, where T_m is an asymptotically normal statistic and the random sample size N_n is either negatively binomial or Pareto-like distributed.

In Christoph et al. [17], inequalities for the second order approximations of the distribution functions of normalized negative binomial and Pareto-like sample sizes were proved. Consequently, second order Chebyshev–Edgeworth approximations and the corresponding Cornish–Fisher expansions could be obtained for the distribution of the normalized arithmetic mean of a sample with normalized negative binomial or Pareto-like sample sizes where the remainders are of order $n^{-3/2}$.

The present work provides a supplement to our paper, Christoph and Ulyanov [18], where we have developed a formal second order design for asymptotic Chebyshev–Edgeworth approximations. We considered asymptotically normal statistics with sample size having negative binomial distribution as well as asymptotically chi-squared statistics with Pareto-like distributed sample sizes. In addition to the distributions of statistic T_m and random sample size N_n, three scaling factors for T_{N_n} are also introduced, leading to different expansions. It is the first paper to consider approximations for asymptotic chi-square statistics based on random sample sizes. Some more applications of random sample size sampling were also mentioned.

In the present paper, we provide similar results for asymptotically normal statistics of samples with Pareto-like distributed sample sizes and for asymptotically chi-squared statistics with sample size having negative binomial distribution.

For better reader convenience, we list in Section 2 some notations, conditions, and statements that were also used in Christoph and Ulyanov [18]. Section 3 states the necessary approximations for the statistics T_m and the sample sizes N_n. The dependence of the limit distributions of the scaled statistic T_{N_n} on the distributions of the statistic T_m and the sample size N_n, as well as the scaling factors, is discussed in Section 4. Section 5 then presents the main results. As examples, we consider the same statistic T_m as in

Christoph and Ulyanov [18] (Corollaries 1 and 2), but with changed sample sizes. Section 6 provides the proofs of the main results, leaving three auxiliary lemmas to Appendix A. Conclusions are presented in Section 7.

2. Notation and Preliminaries

Let $(\Omega, \mathcal{A}, \mathbb{P})$ be a probability space on which all occurring random variables are given.

Set positive numbers, real axis, integer part $[y]$ of real y, and indicator function as follows:

$$\mathbb{N}_+ = \{1, 2, \ldots\}, \quad \mathbb{R} = (-\infty, \infty), \quad y - 1 < [y] \leq y \quad \text{and} \quad \mathbb{I}_A = \mathbb{I}_A(x) = \begin{cases} 1, & x \in A \subset \mathbb{R} \\ 0, & x \notin A \subset \mathbb{R} \end{cases}.$$

Let $X_1, X_2, X_3 \ldots \in \mathbb{R}$ be independent identically distributed random variables. Define the statistic

$$T_m := T_m(X_1, \ldots, X_m) \quad \text{with} \quad m \in \mathbb{N}_+,$$

based on the random sample $\{X_1, X_2, \ldots, X_m\}$ with a non-random sample size $m \in \mathbb{N}_+$.

Consider the sequence of discrete random variables $N_1, N_2, \ldots$, depending on an integer parameter $n \geq 1$. This integer $N_n \geq 1$ indicates the random dimension of the observations $X_1, \ldots, X_{N_n}$. Let us assume that the sample size N_n does not depend on $X_1, X_2, X_3 \ldots$, where $N_n \to \infty$ in probability when $n \to \infty$. Define for each $n \in \mathbb{N}_+$ the statistic T_{N_n} obtained from a random sample $\{X_1, X_2, \ldots, X_{N_n}\}$ by

$$T_{N_n}(\omega) := T_{N_n(\omega)}\left(X_1(\omega), X_2(\omega), \ldots, X_{N_n(\omega)}(\omega)\right) \quad \text{for each} \quad \omega \in \Omega. \tag{1}$$

It follows from Esquível et al. [12] (Theorem 2.1.1) that the statistic T_{N_n} is well-defined in (1).

Since we want to prove second order approximations for the statistic T_{N_n} in form of inequalities, we need the corresponding assumptions for the statistic T_m and for the random sample size N_n as well.

For the statistic T_m with $\mathbb{E}T_m = 0$ and the random sample sizes $N_n \in \mathbb{N}_+$ we suppose conditions on the structure of the approximating functions as well as on the convergence rate:

Assumption 1. *There are a distribution function $F(x)$, bounded functions $f_1(x)$, $f_2(x)$ which are differentiable for all $x \neq 0$, $\gamma \in \{-1, -1/2, 0, 1/2, 1\}$, $a > 1/2$ as well as $0 < C_1 < \infty$ such that*

$$\sup_x \left| \mathbb{P}(m^\gamma T_m \leq x) - F(x) - m^{-1/2} f_1(x) - \mathbb{I}_{a>1}(a) \, m^{-1} f_2(x) \right| \leq C_1 m^{-a}, \quad m \leq 1. \tag{2}$$

Assumption 2. *There exists a distribution function $H(y)$ with $H(0+) = 0$, a bounded variation function $h_2(y)$, a sequence of numbers $0 < g_n \uparrow \infty$, $b > 0$, and $0 < C_2 < \infty$ such that for $n \in \mathbb{N}_+$*

$$\left. \begin{array}{ll} \sup_{y \geq 0} \left| \mathbb{P}(g_n^{-1} N_n \leq y) - H(y) \right| \leq C_2 n^{-b}, & \text{for} \quad 0 < b \leq 1, \\ \sup_{y \geq 0} \left| \mathbb{P}(g_n^{-1} N_n \leq y) - H(y) - n^{-1} h_2(y) \right| \leq C_2 n^{-b}, & \text{for} \quad b > 1. \end{array} \right\} \tag{3}$$

Remark 1. *Assumptions 1 and 2 require inequalities for the approximations of T_m and N_n for all $m, n \in \mathbb{N}_+$, leading to inequalities for the approximations of T_{N_n}. See also Remark 5 below on Poisson and binomial random variables N_n. For these sample sizes, we are so far only aware of estimates of the remaining terms with small-o or large-$\mathcal{O}$ convergence rates. About the differences between inequalities and $\mathcal{O}$ order bounds, see, e.g., Fujikoshi and Ulyanov [19] (Chapter 1).*

Remark 2. *In Bening et al. [16], these conditions are formulated more generally. Assumption 1 requires the existence of $f_1, \ldots, f_l$ with $a > l/2$ and Assumption 2 that of $h_1, \ldots, h_k$ with $b > k/2$.*

We restrict ourselves here, as in Christoph and Ulyanov [18], to the required approximation functions.

Assumptions 1 and 2 lead to the approximations for the distribution functions of statistics T_{N_n}:

Proposition 1. (Christoph and Ulyanov [18], Proposition 1) *Let $\gamma \in \{-1, -1/2, 0, 1/2, 1\}$. The statistic T_m and the sample size N_n are supposed to satisfy Assumptions 1 and 2, respectively. Then,*

$$\sup_{x \in \mathbb{R}} \left| \mathbb{P}\left(g_n^{\gamma} T_{N_n} \leq x\right) - G_n(x, 1/g_n) \right| \leq C_1 \mathbb{E}(N_n^{-a}) + (C_3 D_n + C_4) n^{-b}, \tag{4}$$

where $a > 0, b > 0$ are the convergence rates in (2) and (3),

$$G_n(x, 1/g_n) = \int_{1/g_n}^{\infty} \left(F(xy^{\gamma}) + \frac{f_1(xy^{\gamma})}{\sqrt{g_n y}} + \frac{f_2(xy^{\gamma})}{g_n y} \right) d\left(H(y) + \frac{h_2(y)}{n} \right), \tag{5}$$

$$D_n = \sup_x \int_{1/g_n}^{\infty} \left| \frac{\partial}{\partial y} \left(F(xy^{\gamma}) + \frac{f_1(xy^{\gamma})}{\sqrt{g_n y}} + \frac{f_2(xy^{\gamma})}{y g_n} \right) \right| dy, \tag{6}$$

and $f_1(z), f_2(z), h_2(y)$ are given in (2) and (3). The constants C_1, C_3, C_4 do not depend on n.

Bening et al. [16] proved general transfer theorems under the conditions indicated in Remark 2 only for case $\gamma \geq 0$. Therefore, the proof is repeated in Christoph and Ulyanov [20] (Appendix A.1).

3. Second Order Estimates for Both the Statistics T_m and the Sample Sizes N_n

First we consider the following statistics T_m with non-random sample size m and $\mathbb{E} T_m = 0$ with the corresponding second order approximations. Let the asymptotically normal statistic T_m satisfy the following inequality:

$$\left| \mathbb{P}(\sqrt{m} T_m \leq x) - \Phi(x) - \left(m^{-1/2}(p_0 + p_2 x^2) + m^{-1}(p_1 x + p_3 x^3 + p_5 x^5) \mathbb{I}_{a>1}(a) \right) \varphi(x) \right| \leq C m^{-a} \tag{7}$$

with $a > 0$ and $\Phi(x)$ refers to the standard normal distribution function with density function $\varphi(y)$:

$$\Phi(x) = \int_{-\infty}^{x} \varphi(y) dy, \quad x \in \mathbb{R}, \quad \text{and} \quad \varphi(y) = \frac{1}{\sqrt{2\pi}} e^{-y^2/2}, \quad y \in \mathbb{R}.$$

Asymptotically chi-squared distributed statistics T_m satisfy the following inequality:

$$\left| \mathbb{P}(m T_m \leq x) - G_d(x) - m^{-1}(q_1 x + q_2 x^2) g_d(x) \right| \leq C m^{-2}, \tag{8}$$

where $G_d(x)$, $d \in \mathbb{N}_+$, denotes the chi-squared distribution function with d degrees of freedom and the density function $g_d(y)$:

$$g_d(y) = \frac{1}{2^{d/2} \Gamma(d/2)} y^{(d-2)/2} e^{-y/2}, \ y > 0, \ \text{and} \ G_d(x) = \mathbb{P}(\chi_d^2 \leq x) = \int_0^x g_d(y) dy, \ x > 0.$$

In Christoph and Ulyanov [18] (Sections 3.1 and 3.2), some examples of such statistics T_m are given that satisfy (7) or (8) and consequently, Assumption 1.

As already announced, we consider the following random sample sizes N_n with the corresponding second order approximations.

The Pareto-like random sample sizes $N_n(s)$ are defined as follows:

Let $Y_j(s) \in \mathbb{N}_+, j = 1, 2, \ldots$ be independent discrete Pareto II random variables with parameter $s > 0$, which are discretized from continuous Lomax (Pareto II) random variables on $\mathbb{N}_+$, for a review, see, e.g., Buddana and Kozubowski [21]. For $s > 0$, there are defined

$$\mathbb{P}(Y_j(s) \leq k) = \frac{k}{s+k}, \quad N_n(s) = \max_{1 \leq j \leq n} Y_j(s) \quad \text{and} \quad \mathbb{P}(N_n(s) \leq k) = \left(\frac{k}{s+k}\right)^n, \quad n, k \in \mathbb{N}_+. \tag{9}$$

Proposition 2. *(Christoph and Ulyanov [18], Proposition 4) Let $N_n(s)$ be the discrete Pareto-like random variable whose distribution function is given in (9); then, for all integers $n \geq 1$ and fixed positive $s > 0$, we have*

$$\sup_{y>0} \left| \mathbb{P}\left(\frac{N_n(s)}{n} \leq y\right) - W_s(y) - \frac{h_{2;s}(y)}{n} \right| \leq \frac{C_2(s)}{n^2} \tag{10}$$

$$W_s(y) = e^{-s/y} \ y > 0, \quad h_{2;s}(y) = \frac{s\,e^{-s/y}}{2y^2}(s-1+2Q_1(n\,y)), \ y > 0, \tag{11}$$

with jump correcting function $Q_1(y) = 1/2 - (y - [y])$ and $C_2(s) > 0$ does not depend on n. Furthermore,

$$\mathbb{E}(N_n(s))^{-a} \leq C(a,s)\,n^{-\min\{a,2\}}, \tag{12}$$

with optimal bound in (12) for $0 < a \leq 2$, where a is the convergence rate in (7).

Remark 3. *The inverse exponential random variable $W(s)$ with distribution function $H_s(y) = \mathbb{P}(W(s) \leq y) = e^{-s/y}\mathbb{I}_{(0,\infty)}(y)$ and rate parameter $s > 0$ is "heavy tailed" with shape parameter 1 as is $\mathbb{P}(N_n(s) \leq y)$. Thus, the expected values of these two random variables do not exist.*

Suppose the positive integer $N_n(r)$ has a (shifted by 1) negative binomial distribution with probability of success $1/n$, $n \in \mathbb{N}_+$, parameter $r > 0$, probabilities

$$\mathbb{P}(N_n(r) = j) = \frac{\Gamma(j+r-1)}{\Gamma(j)\,\Gamma(r)} \left(\frac{1}{n}\right)^r \left(1 - \frac{1}{n}\right)^{j-1}, \ j \in \mathbb{N}_+ \text{ and } g_n = \mathbb{E}(N_n(r)) = r\,(n-1)+1. \tag{13}$$

In statistical studies, for counting models, the negative binomial and Poisson distributions are the two most important ones. In Schluter and Trede [14] (Section 2.1), the authors emphasize that the negative binomial distribution with its two parameters can typically observe over-dispersion in count data, while this is not the case with the one-parameter Poisson distribution. They proved in a more general framework

$$\lim_{n \to \infty} \sup_y |\mathbb{P}(N_n(r)/g_n \leq y) - G_{r,r}(y)| = 0, \tag{14}$$

while $G_{r,r}(y)$ denotes the gamma distribution that has identical scale and shape parameters $r > 0$, whose density is

$$g_{r,r}(y) = \frac{r^r}{\Gamma(r)} y^{r-1} e^{-ry} \mathbb{I}_{(0,\infty)}(y), \quad y \in \mathbb{R}.$$

In Bening and Korolev [22] (Lemma 2.2), the result (14) was also obtained.

Proposition 3. *(Christoph and Ulyanov [18], Proposition 3) Let $r > 0$. The discrete random variable $N_n(r)$ has probabilities and expected value g_n given in (13). Then, for all $n \in \mathbb{N}_+$:*

$$\sup_{y \geq 0} \left| \mathbb{P}\left(\frac{N_n(r)}{g_n} \leq y\right) - G_{r,r}(y) - \frac{h_{2;r}(y)}{n} \right| \leq C_2(r)\,n^{-\min\{r,2\}}, \tag{15}$$

where $C_2(r) > 0$ does not depend on n and with the jump correcting function $Q_1(y) = 1/2 - (y - [y])$,

$$h_{2;r}(y) = \begin{cases} 0, & \text{for } r \leq 1, \\ \frac{g_{r,r}(y)}{2r}\big((y-1)(2-r)+2Q_1(g_n\,y)\big), & \text{for } r > 1. \end{cases} \tag{16}$$

Moreover, negative moments $\mathbb{E}(N_n(r))^{-a}$ satisfy the estimation for all $r > 0$, $\alpha > 0$

$$\mathbb{E}(N_n(r))^{-\alpha} \leq C(r) \begin{cases} n^{-\min\{r,\alpha\}}, r \neq \alpha \\ \ln(n)\, n^{-\alpha}, r = \alpha \end{cases} \quad (17)$$

and the convergence rate in case $r = \alpha$ cannot be improved.

Remark 4. *Second order Chebyshev–Edgeworth expansions (10) and (15) with $r > 1$ were first proved in Christoph et al. [17] (Theorems 4 and 1). Approximations in (10) and (15) with remainder estimations C_s/n or $C_r\, n^{-\min\{r,1\}}$ are given, e.g., in Bening et al. [16] and Gavrilenko et al. [23]. In Christoph et al. [24] (Corollaries 5.4 and 6.5), leading terms for the negative moments of $N_n(r)$ and $N_n(s)$ are derived that lead to (17) and (12).*

Remark 5. *The negative binomial distribution belongs to the class of Panjer distributions, which also includes the Poisson and binomial distributions. Samples with binomial or Poisson distributed sample sizes were studied among others in the above-cited papers [9–12]. Convergence rate bounds for statistics based on such samples are given in Döbler [13], Korolev [25], Bulinski and Slepov [26]. Döbler [13], Korolev and Shevtsova [27], Sunklodas [28] obtained Berry–Esseen bounds for sums based on samples with binomial and Poisson sample sizes. To the best of the authors' knowledge, Chebyshev–Edgeworth expansions for these lattice distributed random variables have only been proven so far with bounds of small-o or large-$\mathcal{O}$ rates, see, e.g., Petrov [29] (Chapter 6, Theorem 6) or Kolassa and McCullagh [30]. Therefore, inequality (3) in Assumption 2 is not fulfilled.*

4. Limit Distributions of Statistics with Random Size Samples using Different Scaling Factors

We now consider the statistics T_m and the sample sizes N_n, which are supposed to satisfy the inequalities (2) and (3) in Assumptions 1 and 2, respectively. Let us investigate the scaled statistics $g_n^\gamma N_n^{\gamma^*-\gamma} T_{N_n}$ with the sequence $g_n \uparrow \infty$ as $n \to \infty$. We analyze the two cases Φ and G_u as limiting distributions F in Assumption 1 with respect to the exponents γ^* and γ: If $F = \Phi$, then $\gamma^* = 1/2$ and $\gamma \in \{-1/2, 0, 1/2\}$, while if $F = G_u$, then $\gamma^* = 1$ and $\gamma \in \{-1, 0, 1\}$. Then, conditioning on N_n and using (2) and (3), we have

$$\mathbb{P}\left(g_n^\gamma N_n^{\gamma^*-\gamma} T_{N_n} \leq x\right) = \mathbb{P}\left(N_n^{\gamma^*} T_{N_n} \leq x (N_n/g_n)^\gamma\right) = \sum_{m=1}^\infty \mathbb{P}\left(m^{\gamma^*} T_m \leq x(m/g_n)^\gamma\right) \mathbb{P}(N_n = m)$$

$$\stackrel{(2)}{\approx} \mathbb{E}\left(F(x(N_n/g_n)^\gamma)\right) = \int_{1/g_n}^\infty F(xy^\gamma) d\mathbb{P}(N_n/g_n \leq y) \stackrel{(3)}{\approx} \int_{1/g_n}^\infty F(xy^\gamma) dH(y). \quad (18)$$

Consequently, the limit distribution of the scaled statistic $g_n^\gamma N_n^{\gamma^*-\gamma} T_{N_n}$ is a scale mixture of underlying F with mixing distribution H: $\mathbb{P}\left(g_n^\gamma N_n^{\gamma^*-\gamma} T_{N_n} \leq x\right) \to \int_0^\infty F(xy^\gamma) dH(y)$, as $n \to \infty$. Refer to, e.g., Choy and Chan [31], Fujikoshi et al. [32] (Chapter 13), and Fujikoshi and Ulyanov [19] (Chapter 2) and the references therein.

The limiting distributions $\int_{1/g_n}^\infty F(xy^\gamma) dH(y)$ therefore only arise from the leading distributions $F(x)$ and $H(y)$ in the inequalities (2) and (3) and also depend on the parameter γ.

In Christoph and Ulyanov [18] (Sections 5 and 6), the cases $F(x) = \Phi(x)$ with $H(y) = G_{r,r}(y)$ as well as $F(x) = G_u(x)$ with $H(y) = W_s(y)$ were considered. Now, we interchange the distributions of random sample sizes N_n. We first study the limiting distributions of asymptotically normally distributed statistics with Pareto-like distributed sample sizes $N_n(s)$ and also asymptotically chi-squared distributed statistics with negative binomial distributed sample sizes $N_n(r)$. Since $W_s(1/n) = e^{-sn}$ and $G_{r,r}(1/g_n) \leq \frac{r^{r-1}}{\Gamma(r)} g_n^{-r}$ hold, the integral range in the last integral in (18) can be extended from $(1/g_n, \infty)$ to $(0, \infty)$ for further investigations.

4.1. The Case $F(x) = \Phi(x)$ and $H(y) = W_s(y)$

In Christoph and Ulyanov [20,33], asymptotically normally distributed statistics T_m for samples of m-dimensional normally distributed vectors were considered: correlation coefficient as well as the three geometric features: the length of a vector, the distance, and the angle between two vectors. Inequalities for second order approximations for statistic T_m are derived when the dimension m is replaced by Pareto-like distributed random dimension $N_n(s)$. For the median of a sample with random sample size $N_n(s)$ analogous results are shown in Christoph et al. [24] (Section 6). All these asymptotically normally distributed statistics $T_{N_n(s)}$ with Pareto-like random dimensions or sample sizes have the same limiting distribution.

Let $\gamma \in \{1/2, 0, -1/2\}$. Since $\mathbb{E}N_n(s) = \infty$, we choose as $g_n = n$. Then, the limit laws for

$$\mathbb{P}\left(n^\gamma N_n(s)^{1/2-\gamma} T_{N_n(s)} \leq x\right) \text{ are } V_\gamma(x,s) = \int_0^\infty \Phi(x y^\gamma) dH_s(y) = \int_0^\infty \Phi(x y^\gamma) \frac{s}{y^2} e^{-sy} dy.$$

with corresponding densities

$$v_\gamma(x,s) = \frac{s}{\sqrt{2\pi}} \int_0^\infty y^{\gamma-2} e^{-(x^2 y^{2\gamma}/2 + s/y)} dy = \begin{cases} l_{1/\sqrt{s}}(x) = \frac{\sqrt{2s}}{2} e^{-\sqrt{2s}|x|}, & \gamma = \frac{1}{2}, \\ \varphi(x) = \frac{1}{\sqrt{2\pi}} e^{-x^2/2}, & \gamma = 0, \\ s_2^*(x; \sqrt{s}) = \frac{1}{2\sqrt{2s}} \left(1 + \frac{x^2}{2s}\right)^{-3/2}, & \gamma = -\frac{1}{2}, \end{cases} \quad (19)$$

Therefore, the limit distributions $V_\gamma(x,s)$ are the Laplace law $L_{1/\sqrt{s}}(x)$ with density $l_{1/\sqrt{s}}(x)$ and scale parameter $\lambda = 1/\sqrt{s}$ for $\gamma = 1/2$, the standard normal law $\Phi(x)$ and density $\varphi(x)$ for $\gamma = 0$ and for $\gamma = -1/2$ the scaled Student's t-distribution $S_2^*(x; \sqrt{s})$ with 2 degrees of freedom and density $s_2^*(x; \sqrt{s})$. These mixed scale distributions $V_\gamma(x,s)$ are discussed in more detail in Christoph and Ulyanov [20] (Section 4.2).

4.2. The Case $F(x) = G_d(x)$ and $H(y) = G_{r,r}(y)$

Asymptotically chi-squared distributed statistics of samples with random sample size were considered for the first time in Christoph and Ulyanov [18] in case of $H(y) = W_s(y) = e^{-s/y}$, $y > 0$.

Now, negatively binomial distributed sample sizes $N_n(r)$ are considered. With $\gamma \in \{1, 0, -1\}$ and $g_n = \mathbb{E}N_n(r) = r(n-1) + 1$, the limit distributions for

$$\mathbb{P}\left(g_n^\gamma N_n(r)^{1-\gamma} T_{N_n(r)} \leq x\right) \text{ are } V_\gamma(x; d, r) = \int_0^\infty G_d(x y^\gamma) dG_{r,r}(y) = \int_0^\infty G_d(x y^\gamma) \frac{r^r}{\Gamma(r)} y^{r-1} e^{-ry} dy.$$

The corresponding densities are

$$v_\gamma(x; d, r) = \frac{r^r x^{d/2-1}}{\Gamma(r) 2^{d/2} \Gamma(d/2)} \int_0^\infty y^{r+\gamma d/2 - 1} e^{-(x y^\gamma/2 + ry)} dy$$

$$= \begin{cases} f^*(x; d, 2r) = \frac{\Gamma(d/2 + r) x^{d/2-1}}{\Gamma(d/2) \Gamma(r) 2^{d/2} r^{d/2}} \left(1 + \frac{x}{2r}\right)^{-(d+2r)/2}, & \gamma = 1, \\ g_d(x) = \frac{1}{2^{d/2} \Gamma(d/2)} x^{d/2-1} e^{-x/2}, & \gamma = 0, \\ w_{r-d/2}(x; d, r) = \frac{r}{\Gamma(r) \Gamma(d/2)} \left(\frac{xr}{2}\right)^{r/2 + d/4 - 1} K_{r-d/2}(\sqrt{2rx}). & \gamma = -1. \end{cases} \quad (20)$$

We prove (20) for $\gamma = \pm 1$ in Section 6 in the proof of Theorem 2.

The scale mixtures $V_\gamma(x; d, r)$ are the (scaled by d) F-distribution $F^*(x; d, 2r) = F(x/d; d, 2r)$ with parameters $d \in \mathbb{N}_+$ and $r > 0$ and density $f^*(x; d; 2r) = \frac{1}{d} f(\frac{x}{d}; d; 2r)$ for $\gamma = 1$, the chi-squared distribution $G_d(x)$ with d degrees of freedom and density $g_d(x)$ for $\gamma = 0$ and a gamma distribution of generalized type $W_{r-d/2}(x; d, r)$ occurs with density $w_{r-d/2}(x; d, r)$ for $\gamma = -1$. The modified Bessel function of the third kind or Macdonald functions $K_\lambda(u)$ also occurred in Christoph and Ulyanov [18,20] in generalized gamma and Laplace densities.

Remark 6. *The Macdonald function satisfying order-reflection formula $K_{-\lambda}(u) = K_\lambda(u)$ and $K_\lambda(u)$ may be expressed for $\lambda = m + 1/2$ with integer m in closed forms. In Oldham et al. [34] (Formulas 51:4:1 and 26:13:3), the Macdonald functions $K_{-\lambda}(u) = K_\lambda(u)$ for $\lambda = 1/2, 3/2, 5/2, 7/2, 9/2$ are explicitly given. Using Prudnikov et al. [35] (Formulas 2.3.16.1-3), the densities $w_{r-d/2}(x;d,r) = w_{m+1/2}(x;d,r)$ can be calculated:*

$$w_{m+1/2}(x;d,r) = \frac{r^r \, x^{d/2-1}}{\Gamma(r) \, 2^{d/2} \, \Gamma(d/2)} \begin{cases} (-1)^m \sqrt{\pi} \, \frac{\partial^m}{\partial r^m} \left(r^{-1/2} e^{-\sqrt{2rx}} \right), & m = 0, 1, 2, \ldots, \\ (-2)^{-m} \sqrt{\frac{\pi}{r}} \, \frac{\partial^{-m}}{\partial x^{-m}} e^{-\sqrt{2rx}}, & m = 0, -1, -2, \ldots \end{cases} \tag{21}$$

Example 1. *Some densities $w_{m+1/2}(x;d,r)$ for $m = r - (d+1)/2 = -2, -1, 0, 1, 2$:*

$m = -2$	$d = 7, r = 2$	$w_{-3/2}(x;7,2) = \frac{4x}{15} \left(1 + \sqrt{4x}\right) e^{-\sqrt{4x}}$
$m = -1$	$d = 4, r = 3/2$	$w_{-1/2}(x;4,3/2) = \frac{3}{4} \sqrt{3x} \, e^{-\sqrt{3x}}$
$m = 0$	$d = 4, r = 5/2$	$w_{1/2}(x;4,5/2) = \frac{1}{12} \sqrt{25x} \, e^{-\sqrt{5x}}$
$m = 0$	$d = 3, r = 2$	$w_{1/2}(x;3,2) = \sqrt{4x} \, e^{-\sqrt{4x}}$
$m = 1$	$d = 3, r = 3$	$w_{3/2}(x;3,3) = \frac{3}{8} \left(6x + \sqrt{6x}\right) e^{-\sqrt{6x}}$
$m = 2$	$d = 3, r = 4$	$w_{5/2}(x;3,4) = \frac{1}{12} \left((8x)^{3/2} + 24x + 3\sqrt{8x}\right) e^{-\sqrt{8x}}$.

Remark 7. *If $m = r - (d+1)/2$ is an integer, the distribution functions $W_{m+1/2}(x;d,r)$ of the densities $w_{m+1/2}(x;d,r)$ can also be calculated explicitly by substitution and partial integration.*

Example 2. *Distribution functions $W_\lambda(x;d,r)$ for given densities $w_\lambda(x;d,r)$ with $\lambda = \pm 1/2$:*

$$w_{-1/2}(x;4,\tfrac{3}{2}) = \tfrac{3}{4}\sqrt{3x}\,e^{-\sqrt{3x}} \text{ and } W_{-1/2}(x;4,\tfrac{3}{2}) = 1 - \tfrac{1}{2}\left(2\sqrt{3x} + 3x + 2\right)e^{-\sqrt{3x}} \tag{22}$$

$$w_{1/2}(x;4,\tfrac{5}{2}) = \tfrac{25x}{12}e^{-\sqrt{5x}} \text{ and } W_{1/2}(x;4,\tfrac{5}{2}) = 1 - \left(\tfrac{(5x)^{3/2}}{6} + \tfrac{5x}{2} + \tfrac{\sqrt{5x}}{6} + 1\right)e^{-\sqrt{5x}} \tag{23}$$

$$w_{1/2}(x;3,2) = \sqrt{4x}\,e^{-\sqrt{4x}} \text{ and } W_{1/2}(x;3,2) = 1 - (2x + 2\sqrt{x} + 1)e^{-\sqrt{4x}}. \tag{24}$$

Remark 8. *The generalized gamma distribution $G^*(x;\beta,\alpha,\lambda)$ has two shape parameters α and β, a scale parameter λ, and the density*

$$g^*(x;\beta,\alpha,\lambda) = \frac{|\alpha|\,\lambda^\beta}{\Gamma(\beta)} \, x^{\alpha\beta-1} \, e^{-\lambda x^\alpha}, \quad x \geq 0, \quad |\alpha| > 0, \; \beta > 0, \; \lambda > 0. \tag{25}$$

The density (25) is given in Korolev and Zeifman [36] and Korolev and Gorshenin [37] and summarizes many known densities. Generalized gamma distributions are defined in many different ways, but they do not correspond to the ones that occur above.

Remark 9. *The densities $w_{m+1/2}(x;d,r)$ with integer $m = r - (d+1)/2$ are generalized gamma densities $g^*(x;\beta,\alpha,\lambda)$ given in formula (25) or may be represented as linear combinations of such densities. The parameters $\alpha = 1/2$ and $\lambda = \sqrt{2r}$ apply in all densities $g^*(x;\beta,\alpha,\lambda)$. The parameter β also depends on the number of derivatives $m = r - (d+1)/2$ in the densities (21).*

Example 3. *Some linear combinations of generalized gamma densities:*

$$w_{1/2}(x;3,2) = g^*(x;3,1/2,\sqrt{4})$$
$$w_{3/2}(x;3,3) = \tfrac{3}{4}g^*(x;4,1/2,\sqrt{6}) + \tfrac{1}{4}g^*(x;3,1/2,\sqrt{6})$$
$$w_{5/2}(x;3,4) = \tfrac{1}{2}g^*(x;5,1/2,\sqrt{8}) + \tfrac{3}{8}g^*(x;4,1/2,\sqrt{8}) + \tfrac{1}{8}g^*(x;3,1/2,\sqrt{8}).$$

5. Main Results

Inequalities for approximations to scaled statistics $\mathbb{P}\left(g_n^\gamma N_n^{\gamma^*-\gamma} T_{N_n} \leq x\right)$ for $\gamma \in \{0, \pm 1/2, \pm 1\}$ will be presented. Here, $\gamma^* = 1/2$ and $\gamma \in \{0, \pm 1/2\}$ when the statistic T_m is asymptotically normally distributed, or $\gamma^* = 1$ and $\gamma \in \{0, \pm 1\}$ when normalized T_m has chi-squared limit distribution.

5.1. Asymptotically Normal Statistics T_m and Pareto-like Sample Sizes $N_n(s)$

Let asymptotically normal statistic T_m satisfy inequality (7) with coefficients p_k and the rate of convergence $a > 0$. The Pareto-like sample size $N_n = N_n(s)$, $s > 0$, is given in (9), which fulfills the inequality (10). For the scaling factors, select $\gamma^* = 1/2$ and $\gamma \in \{0, \pm 1/2\}$ in formula (18).

Theorem 1. *Under the conditions given above, the following approximations apply:*

i: *Let $\gamma = 1/2$. The non-random scaling factor $\sqrt{n}$ for the statistic $T_{N_n(s)}$ leads to approximations by the Laplace distribution $L_{1/\sqrt{s}}(x)$ with the density $l_{1/\sqrt{s}}(x)$ stated in (19) for $\gamma = 1/2$:*

$$\sup_x \left| \mathbb{P}\left(\sqrt{n}\, T_{N_n(s)} \leq x\right) - L_{1/\sqrt{s};n}(x) \right| \leq C_s\, n^{-\min\{a,2\}}$$

where $a > 0$ is the rate of convergence in (7) and

$$L_{1/\sqrt{s};n}(x) = L_{1/\sqrt{s}}(x) + l_{1/\sqrt{s}}(x) \left(\frac{\mathbb{I}_{\{a>1/2\}}(a)}{\sqrt{n}} \left[p_2 x^2 + p_0 \left(\frac{|x|}{\sqrt{2s}} + \frac{1}{2s} \right) \right] \right.$$
$$\left. + \frac{\mathbb{I}_{\{a>1\}}(a)}{n} \left[p_5 x^3 |x| \sqrt{2s} + p_3 x^3 + \left(p_1 + \frac{s-1}{4} \right) x \left(\frac{|x|}{\sqrt{2s}} + \frac{1}{2s} \right) \right] \right).$$

ii: *Let $\gamma = 0$. The random scaling factor $\sqrt{N_n(s)}$ with $T_{N_n(s)}$ leads to the normal approximation $\Phi(x)$:*

$$\sup_x \left| \mathbb{P}\left(\sqrt{N_n(s)}\, T_{N_n(s)} \leq x\right) - \Phi(x) - \varphi_{n,2}(x) \right| \leq C_s\, n^{-\min\{a,2\}},$$

where $a > 0$ is the rate of convergence in (7) and

$$\varphi_{n,2}(x) = \varphi(x) \left(\frac{\sqrt{\pi}(p_0 + p_2 x^2)}{2\sqrt{sn}} \mathbb{I}_{\{a>1/2\}}(a) + \frac{p_1 x + p_3 x^3 + p_5 x^5}{sn} \mathbb{I}_{\{a>1\}}(a) \right).$$

iii: *Let $\gamma = -1/2$. The mixed scaling factor $n^{-1/2} N_n(s)$ at $T_{N_n(s)}$ results in Scaled Student's t-distribution $S_2^*(x; \sqrt{s})$ with density $s_2^*(x; \sqrt{s})$ given in (19) for $\gamma = -1/2$:*

$$\sup_x \left| \mathbb{P}\left(n^{-1/2} N_n(s)\, T_{N_n(s)} \leq x\right) - S_{n;2}^*(x) \right| \leq C_s\, n^{-\min\{a,2\}},$$

where $a > 0$ is the rate of convergence in (7) and

$$S_{n;2}^*(x;\sqrt{s}) = S_2^*(x;\sqrt{s}) + s_2^*(x;\sqrt{s})\left(\frac{\mathbb{I}_{\{a>1/2\}}(a)}{\sqrt{n}}\left[p_0 + \frac{3p_2x^2\{\partial > \mathcal{K}\}(a)}{(x^2+2s)}\right]\right.$$
$$\left. + \frac{\mathbb{I}_{\{a>1\}}(a)}{n}\left[\frac{3p_1x}{x^2+2s} + \frac{15p_3x^3}{(x^2+2s)^2} + \frac{105p_5x^5}{(x^2+2s)^3} + \frac{3(s-1)x}{4(x^2+2s)}\right]\right).$$

As applications of the Theorem 1, we now examine the Student t-distribution, the Student t-test statistic, and the sample mean as asymptotically normal statistics T_m considered in Christoph and Ulyanov [18] (Section 3.1 and Corollary 1) for the case of negative binomial sample sizes $N_n = N_n(r)$.

Corollary 1. *Let the conditions of Theorem 1 be satisfied:*

i: *Let $\gamma = 1/2$. In case of the Student's t-statistic $T_m = Z/\sqrt{\chi_m^2}$ with m degrees of freedom estimated in [18] (Formula (18)), inequality (7) is valid with $p_0 = p_2 = p_5 = 0$, $p_1 = p_3 = 1/4$ and $a = 2$. The non-random scaling factor $\sqrt{n}$ and Pareto-like $N_n(s)$ sample sizes lead to:*

$$\sup_x \left|\mathbb{P}\left(\frac{\sqrt{n}\,Z}{\sqrt{\chi_{N_n(s)}^2}} \leq x\right) - L_{1/\sqrt{s}}(x) - \frac{l_{1/\sqrt{s}}(x)}{8n}\left(2x^3 + x(1+|x|\sqrt{2s})\right)\right| \leq C_s\, n^{-2}$$

ii: *Let $\gamma = 0$. Let $T_m = (\overline{X}_m - \mu)/\hat{\sigma}_m$ be the Student's t-statistic with sample mean $\overline{X}_m$ and sample variance $\hat{\sigma}_m$, which was considered in [18] (Formulas (21) and (20)). The first order approximation (7) with $p_0 = \lambda_3/6$, $p_2 = \lambda_3/3$, $a = 1$, the Pareto-like random sample sizes $N_n(s)$ and the random scaling factor $\sqrt{N_n(s)}$ result in:*

$$\sup_x \left|\mathbb{P}\left(\sqrt{N_n(s)}\,T_{N_n(s)} \leq x\right) - \Phi(x) - \varphi(x)\frac{\sqrt{\pi}(\lambda_3 + 2\lambda_3 x^2)}{12\sqrt{sn}}\right| \leq C_s\, n^{-1},$$

iii: *Let $\gamma = -1/2$. Considering sample mean $T_m = \overline{X}_m$ estimated in [18] (Formulas (15) and (16)), one has (7) with $p_0 = -p_2 = \lambda_3/6$, $p_1 = \lambda_4/8 - 5\lambda_3^2/24$, $p_3 = -\lambda_4/24 + 5\lambda_3^2/36$, $p_5 = -\lambda_3^2/72$, $a = 3/2$, Pareto-like random sample sizes $N_n(s)$ and mixed scaling factor $n^{-1/2}N_n(s)$, then*

$$\sup_x \left|\mathbb{P}\left(n^{-1/2}N_n(s)\,T_{N_n(s)} \leq x\right) - S_2^*(x;\sqrt{s}) - s_{n;2}^*(x;\sqrt{s})\right| \leq C_s\, n^{-3/2},$$

with

$$s_{n;2}^*(x;\sqrt{s}) = s_2^*(x;\sqrt{s})\left(\frac{1}{\sqrt{n}}\left(\frac{\lambda_3}{6} - \frac{\lambda_3 x^2}{2(x^2+2s)}\right)\right.$$
$$\left. + \frac{1}{n}\left(\frac{(3\lambda_4 - 5\lambda_3^2)x}{8(x^2+2s)} - \frac{5(3\lambda_4 - 10\lambda_5)x^3}{24(x^2+2s)^2} - \frac{35\lambda_3^2 x^5}{24(x^2+2s)^3} + \frac{3(s-1)x}{4(x^2+2s)}\right)\right).$$

5.2. *Asymptotically Chi-Squared Distributed T_m with Negative Binomially Distributed Sample Sizes $N_n(r)$*

Let the asymptotically chi-squared distributed statistics T_m satisfy inequality (8) with coefficients q_1, q_2 and the rate of convergence $a = 2$. The negative binomially distributed sample sizes $N_n = N_n(r)$ with parameter $r > 0$ and success probability $1/n$ are given in (13) and fulfill the inequality (15). For the scaling factors, choose $\gamma^* = 1$ and $\gamma \in \{0, \pm 1\}$ in formula (18).

Theorem 2. *Under the conditions given above, the following approximations apply.*

i: Let $\gamma = 1$. The non-random scaling factor $g_n = \mathbb{E}N_n(r) = r(n-1) + 1$ at statistics $T_{N_n(r)}$ leads to approximations by the scaled F-distribution $F^*(x;d,2r) = F(x/d;d,2r)$ having parameters $d \in \mathbb{N}_+$ and $r > 0$ and density $f^*(x;d;2r) = \frac{1}{d}f(\frac{x}{d};d;2r)$ given in (20) with $\gamma = 1$:

$$\sup_x \left| \mathbb{P}\left(g_n T_{N_n(r)} \leq x\right) - F^*(x;d,2r) - f_n^*(x;d,2r) \right| \leq C_r \begin{cases} n^{-\min\{r,2\}}, & r \neq 2, \\ n^{-2} \ln n, & r = 2, \end{cases}$$

where

$$f_n^*(x;d,2r) = \frac{f^*(x;d,2r)}{g_n} \mathbb{I}_{\{r>1\}}(r) \left(\left(q_1 - \frac{2-r}{2}\right) \frac{x(2r+x)}{2r+d-2} + q_2 x^2 + \frac{x(2-r)}{2} \right). \quad (26)$$

ii: For $\gamma = 0$ and random scaling factor $N_n(r)$ at $T_{N_n(r)}$, the approximation $G_d(x)$ does not change:

$$\sup_x \left| \mathbb{P}\left(N_n(r) T_{N_n(r)} \leq x\right) - G_d(x;n) \right| \leq C_r \begin{cases} n^{-\min\{r,2\}}, & r \neq 2, \\ n^{-2} \ln n, & r = 2, \end{cases}$$

where

$$G_d(x;n) = G_d(x) + \frac{g_d(x)}{g_n} \mathbb{I}_{\{r>1\}}(r)(q_1 x + q_2 x^2) \frac{r}{r-1}.$$

iii: Let $\gamma = -1$ and $r \geq 2$. The mixed scaling factor $g_n^{-1} N_n^2(r)$ at $T_{N_n(r)}$ results in a gamma distribution of generalized type $W_{r-d/2}(x;d,r)$ with density $w_{r-d/2}(x;d,r)$ given in (20) for $\gamma = -1$:

$$\sup_x \left| \mathbb{P}\left(\frac{N_n^2(r)}{g_n} T_{N_n(r)} \leq x\right) - W_{r-d/2;n}(x;d,r) \right| \leq C_r \begin{cases} n^{-2}, & r > 2, \\ n^{-2} \ln n, & r = 2, \end{cases}$$

where

$$\begin{aligned} W_{r-d/2;n}(x;d,r) &= W_{r-d/2}(x;d,r) + \frac{w_{r-d/2}(x;d,r)}{g_n} \mathbb{I}_{\{r>1\}}(r) \left(2 q_2 r x + \frac{(r-2)x}{2} \right. \\ &\quad + \left. \frac{\sqrt{2rx}}{2} \left(2 q_1 + 2 q_2(d+2-2r) + 2 - r\right) \frac{K_{r-d/2-1}(\sqrt{2rx})}{K_{r-d/2}(\sqrt{2rx})} \right). \end{aligned}$$

The restriction $r \geq 2$ in Theorem 2(iii) has a purely proof-technical character. In Proposition 4, a result is shown with $r = 3/2$.

Remark 10. The function $R(u;d,r) = \frac{K_{\lambda-1}(u)}{K_\lambda(u)}$ can be calculated explicitly for $\lambda = m + 1/2$ with integer $m = r - (d+1)/2$. Then, for example, $R(\sqrt{3x};4,3/2) = 1 + \frac{1}{\sqrt{3x}}$ and $R(\sqrt{4x};3,2) = 1$.

Example 4. Let $\gamma = -1$ in (20), $r = 2$ and $d = 3$. Then, for an asymptotically chi-squared distributed test variable T_m satisfying (8), with scale factor $\frac{N_n^2(2)}{2n-1}$, the estimation holds:

$$\sup_{x>0} \left| \mathbb{P}\left(\frac{N_n^2(2)}{2n-1} T_{N_n(2)} \leq x\right) - W_{1/2}(x;3,2) + \frac{w_{1/2}(x;3,2)}{4(2n-1)} \left(\sqrt{4x}\left(q_2\sqrt{4x} + q_1 + q_2\right)\right) \right| \leq C_2 \frac{\ln n}{n^2},$$

where $W_{1/2}(x;3,2)$ and $w_{1/2}(x;3,2)$ are specified in (24).

As applications to Theorem 2, we now examine Hotelling's T_0^2 distribution and normalized quotients of two independent chi-square distributions as asymptotic chi-square distributions, considered in Christoph and Ulyanov [18] (Section 3.2 and Corollary 2) where the sample sizes $N_n = N_n(s)$ had Pareto-like distribution.

Corollary 2. *The conditions of the Theorem 2 shall be fulfilled:*

i: Let $\gamma = 1$. Consider Hotelling's generalized T_0^2-statistic $T_0^2 = T_m = \text{tr}(\mathbf{S}_q \mathbf{S}_m^{-1})$ with independently distributed random matrices $\mathbf{S}_q$ and $\mathbf{S}_m$ having Wishart distributions $W_p(q, \mathbf{I}_p)$ and $W_p(m, \mathbf{I}_p)$, respectively. Then, inequality (8) holds with limit distribution $G_d(x)$, $d = pq$, $q_1 = (p+1-q)/2$ and $q_2 = (p+1+q)/(2d+4)$. The non-random scaling factor $g_n = \mathbb{E}N_n(r)$ by $T_{N_n(r)}$ leads to

$$\sup_x \left| \mathbb{P}\left(g_n T_{N_n(r)} \leq x\right) - F^*(x; pq, 2r) - f_n^*(x; pq, 2r) \right| \leq C_r \begin{cases} n^{-\min\{r,2\}}, & r \neq 2, \\ n^{-2} \ln n, & r = 2, \end{cases} \quad (27)$$

where the scaled F-distribution $F^*(x; pq, 2r)$ with density $f^*(x; pq, 2r)$ is given in (20) for $\gamma = 1$

$$f_n^*(x; pq, 2r) = \frac{f^*(x; pq, 2r)}{g_n} \mathbb{I}_{\{r>1\}}(r) \left(\left(\frac{p+1-q}{2} - \frac{2-r}{2}\right) \frac{x(2r+x)}{2r+pq-2} \right.$$

$$\left. + \frac{(p+1+q)x^2}{(2pq+4)} + \frac{x(2-r)}{2} \right). \quad (28)$$

ii: Let $\gamma = 0$, χ_d^2 and χ_m^2 be independent and $T_m = \chi_d^2/\chi_m^2$ be scale mixtures satisfying inequality (8) with coefficients $q_1 = (d-2)/2$ and $q_2 = -1/2$. Random degrees of freedom $N_n(r)$ instead of m and random scaling factor $N_n(r)$ lead to

$$\sup_{x>0} \left| \mathbb{P}\left(N_n(r) T_{N_n(r)} \leq x\right) - G_d(x; n) \right| \leq C_r \begin{cases} n^{-\min\{r,2\}}, & r \neq 2, \\ n^{-2} \ln n, & r = 2, \end{cases}$$

where

$$G_d(x; n) = G_d(x) + \frac{g_d(x)}{2 g_n} \mathbb{I}_{\{r>1\}}(r)((d-2)x - x^2) \frac{r}{r-1}.$$

iii: Let $\gamma = -1$. The statistics $T_m = \chi_4^2/\chi_m^2$ satisfy the inequality (8) with the limiting distribution $G_4(x)$ and the coefficients $q_1 = 1$ and $q_2 = -1/2$. The mixed scaling factor $g_n^{-1} N_n^2(r)$ at $T_{N_n(r)}$ results in a limiting gamma distribution of generalized type $W_{r-d/2}(x; d, r)$. Only if $r - (d+1)/2 = m$ is an integer, the involved Macdonald functions $K_{r-d/2}(\sqrt{2r x})$ may be explicitly calculated. Since $d = 4$, we choose $r = 5/2$ and find $r - (d+1)/2 = 0$. Then, uniformly in $x > 0$:

$$\left| \mathbb{P}\left(\frac{N_n^2(5/2)}{(5n-3)/2} \frac{\chi_4^2}{\chi_{N_n(5/2)}^2} \leq x \right) - W_{1/2}(x; 4, 5/2) + \frac{w_{1/2}(x; 4, 5/2)}{2(5n-3)} \left(9x - \sqrt{5x}\right) \right| \leq \frac{C_{3/2}}{n^{3/2}},$$

where $W_{1/2}(x; 4, 5/2)$ and $w_{1/2}(x; 4, 5/2)$ are specified in (23).

Remark 11. *In the paper Monahkov [38], an analogous to (27) estimation is shown, but with 11 approximation terms in corresponding formula (28). Instead of (8) with $q_1 = (p+1-q)/2$, $q_2 = (p+1+q)/(2d+4)$ and $d = pq$, the following equivalent inequality is used; see Fujikoshi et al. [39] (Theorem 4.1(ii)):*

$$\sup_x \left| \mathbb{P}\left(m \, \text{tr}\left(\mathbf{S}_q \mathbf{S}_m^{-1}\right) \leq x \right) - G_d(x) - \frac{d}{4m}\left(a_0 G_d(x) + a_1 G_{d+2}(x) + a_2 G_{d+4}(x)\right) \right| \leq \frac{C}{m^2}$$

where $a_0 = q - p - 1$, $a_1 = -2q$, $a_2 = q + p + 1$ with $a_0 + a_1 + a_2 = 0$ and $d = pq$.

Proposition 4. Let $\gamma = -1$. Consider the statistics $T_m = \chi_4^2/\chi_m^2$, satisfying the inequality (8) with the limiting distribution $G_4(x)$, the coefficients $q_1 = 1$ and $q_2 = -1/2$ and the mixed scaling factor $g_n^{-1} N_n^2(r)$ at $T_{N_n(r)}$. If $r = 3/2$ and $d = 4$, then $r - (d+1)/2 = -1$, $g_n = (3n-1)/2$ and, uniformly in $x > 0$:

$$\left| \mathbb{P}\left(\frac{N_n^2(3/2)}{(3n-1)/2} \frac{\chi_4^2}{\chi_{N_n(3/2)}^2} \le x \right) - W_{-1/2}(x;4,3/2) + \frac{w_{-1/2}(x;4,3/2)}{2(3n-1)}\left(7x + \sqrt{3x} + 1\right) \right| \le \frac{C_{3/2}}{n^{3/2}},$$

where $W_{-1/2}(x;4,3/2)$ and $w_{-1/2}(x;4,3/2)$ are specified in (22).

6. Proofs

For the proofs of Theorems 1 and 2, we use Proposition 1. The statistics T_m and the sample size N_n are either asymptotically normally and discretely Pareto-like distributed (i.e., $F = \Phi$ and $H = W_s$) or asymptotically chi-squared and negatively binomially distributed (i.e., $F = G_d$ and $H = G_{r,r}$). In both cases, the size D_n defined in (6) is uniformly bounded for all $n \in \mathbb{N}_+$, see Christoph and Ulyanov [18] (Lemma A1). Next, the bounds that are required in (4) for the negative moments of sample sizes $\mathbb{E}N_n(s)^{-a}$ and $\mathbb{E}N_n(r)^{-a}$ are provided by (12) and (17). Furthermore, it follows from Christoph and Ulyanov [18] (Proposition 2 and Lemma A2) that in both cases the domain of integration of the integrals in the function $G_n(x, 1/g_n)$ defined in (5) can be extended from $(1/g_n, \infty)$ to $(0, \infty)$:

$$\sup_x |G_n(x, 1/g_n) - G_{n,2}(x)| \le C g_n^{-b},$$

where $b = 2$ if $F = \Phi$ and $H = W_s$ or $b = \min\{r, 2\}$ if $F = G_d$ and $H = G_{r,r}$, respectively, and

$$G_{n,2}(x) = \begin{cases} \int_0^\infty F(xy^\gamma)dH(y), & \text{for } 0 < b \le 1/2, \\ \int_0^\infty \left(F(xy^\gamma) + \frac{f_1(xy^\gamma)}{\sqrt{g_n y}} \right) dH(y) =: G_{n,1}(x), & \text{for } 1/2 < b \le 1, \\ G_{n,1}(x) + \int_0^\infty \frac{f_2(xy^\gamma)}{g_n y} dH(y) + \int_0^\infty \frac{F(xy^\gamma)}{n} dh_2(y), & \text{for } b > 1, \end{cases} \quad (29)$$

We still have to calculate the integrals in (29) that contain f_1, f_2, and h_2, respectively.

Proof of Theorem 1. We now consider $F = \Phi$, $H = H_s$ and $\gamma \in \{0; \pm 1/2\}$. Here, $f_1(xy^\gamma) = (p_0 + p_2x^2y^{2\gamma})\varphi(xy^\gamma)$, $f_2(xy^\gamma) = (p_1xy^\gamma + p_3x^3y^{3\gamma} + p_5x^5y^{5\gamma})\varphi(xy^\gamma)$ and we divide the function $h_2(y) = h_{2;s}(y)$ given in (11) into two parts: $h_{2;s}^*(y) = s(s-1)e^{-s/y}/(2y^2)$ and $h_{2;s}^{**}(y) = s Q_1(ny) y^{-2} e^{-s/y}$. The densities of the limit distributions $V_\gamma(x; d, r) = \int_0^\infty \Phi(xy^\gamma)dW_s(y)$ were given in (20). If $\gamma = 1/2$ to calculate the integrals in (29) involving $f_1(x\sqrt{y})$, $f_2(x\sqrt{y})$ and $h_{2;s}^*(y)$ we use Prudnikov et al. [35] (Formulas 2.3.16.2 and 2.3.16.3):

$$\int_0^\infty y^{-m-1/2} e^{-py-q/y} dy = \begin{cases} (-1)^{-m}\sqrt{\pi} \frac{\partial^{-m}}{\partial p^{-m}} \left(p^{-1/2} e^{-2\sqrt{pq}} \right), & m = 0, -1, -2, \ldots \\ (-1)^m \frac{\sqrt{\pi}}{\sqrt{p}} \frac{\partial^m}{\partial q^m} \left(e^{-2\sqrt{pq}} \right), & m = 0, 1, 2, \ldots \end{cases}, \quad p, q > 0, \quad (30)$$

for $p = x^2/2 > 0$, $q = s > 0$ and $m = 0, 1, 2$, respectively. The corresponding integral with $h_{2;s}^{**}(y)$ was estimated in Christoph et al. [17] (see Proof of Theorem 5) by $c(s) e^{-\sqrt{\pi s n}/2} \le C(s) n^{-2}$.

In case of $\gamma = 0$, we obtain $\int_0^\infty \Phi(x)dh_2(y) = \Phi(x)(h_2(\infty) - \lim_{y \to 0} h_2(y)) = 0$. To calculate the integrals with $f_1(x)$ and $f_2(x)$ we use [35] (Formula 2.3.3.1) with $\alpha = 3/2, 2$ and $q = s$:

$$\int_0^\infty y^{-\alpha-1} e^{-q/y} dy \stackrel{1/y=z}{=} \int_0^\infty z^{\alpha-1} e^{-qz} dz = \Gamma(\alpha) q^{-\alpha}, \quad \alpha > 0, \quad q > 0. \quad (31)$$

If $\gamma = -1/2$, the integrals with $f_1(x/\sqrt{y})$, $f_2(x/\sqrt{y})$ and $h_{2,s}^*(x/\sqrt{y})$ are calculated using (31) with $\alpha = 3/2, 5/2, 7/2, 9/2$ and $q = s + x^2/2$. From Christoph and Ulyanov [20] (see Proof of Theorem 8), it follows that holds: $n^{-1} \sup_x \left| \int_0^\infty \Phi(x/\sqrt{y}) dh_{2;s}^{**}(y) \right| \leq C(s) n^{-2}$ and Theorem 1 is proved. □

Proof of Theorem 2. Now, we consider the case $F(x) = G_d(x)$, $H(y) = G_{r,r}(y)$ and $\gamma \in \{0; \pm 1\}$. This combination has not yet been studied in the literature. Only if $\gamma = 1$, there is a result by Monahkov [38]; see Remark 11 above. Then, $f_1(xy^\gamma) = 0$, $f_2(xy^\gamma) = (q_1 x y^\gamma + q_2 x^2 y^{2\gamma}) g_d(x y^\gamma)$ and we divide the function $h_2(y) = h_{2;r}(y)$ given in (16) into two parts: $h_{2;r}^*(y) = (2r)^{-1} g_{r,r}(y)(y-1)(2-r)$ and $h_{2;r}^{**}(y) = r^{-1} g_{r,r}(y) Q_1(g_n y)$.

For $\gamma = 1$, the density $v_1(x; d, r)$ in (20) and the integrals in (29) with $f_2(xy)$ and $h_{2;r}^*(y)$ are computed with (31) for $\alpha = r + d/2$, $r + d/2 - 1$. The integral with $h_{2;r}^{**}(y)$ is estimated in (A1) in Lemma A1. Together with the inequality $|1/g_n - 1/(rn)| \leq \max\{2, r\}(r-1)(rn)^{-2}$, we get (26).

In case of $\gamma = 0$, we obtain $\int_0^\infty G_d(x) dh_2(y) = G_d(x)(h_{2,r}(\infty) - \lim_{y \to 0} h_{2,r}(y)) = 0$. To calculate the integrals with $f_2(x)$, we use (31) with $\alpha = r - 1$ and $q = r$.

If $\gamma = -1$ the density $v_{-1}(x; d, r)$ in (20) and the integrals with $f_2(x/y)$ and $h_{2,r}^*(y)$ are calculated using Prudnikov et al. [35] (Formula 2.3.16.1):

$$\int_0^\infty y^{\alpha-1} e^{-py-q/y} dy = 2(p/q)^{\alpha/2} K_\alpha(2\sqrt{pq}), \quad p, q > 0,$$

with $\alpha = r - d/2$, $r - d/2 - 1$, $r - d/2 - 2$, $p = r$ and $q = x/2$. We use the order-reflection formula $K_\alpha(u) = K_{-\alpha}(u)$ and the recursion formula; see Oldham et al. [34] (Chapter 51.5):

$$K_{r-d/2-2}(\sqrt{2rx}) = K_{d/2+2-r}(\sqrt{2rx}) = \frac{2(d/2-r+1)}{\sqrt{2rx}} K_{d/2-r+1}(\sqrt{2rx}) + K_{d/2-r}(\sqrt{2rx}).$$

The integral with $h_{2;r}^{**}(y)$ is estimated in (A4) in Lemma A2 and Theorem 2 is proved. □

Proof of Proposition 4. We consider $\gamma = -1$, $r = 3/2$ $d = 4$ and $g_n = (3n-1)/2$. The integrals in (29) with $f_2(x/y)$ and $h_{2,r}^*(y)$ are calculated using (30) with $m = -1, -2, -3$, $p = r$ and $q = x/2$. The integral with $h_{2,r}^{**}$ is estimated in (A5) in Lemma A3 and Proposition 4 is proved. □

7. Conclusions

The common goal of the present work and that of Christoph and Ulyanov [18] is to develop formal second order Chebyshev–Edgeworth expansions for sample statistics with random sample sizes. Corresponding expansions are assumed for the statistics with non-random sample sizes as well as for the random sample sizes. The statistics examined are asymptotically normally distributed and, for the first time in this setting, also asymptotically chi-squared distributed. The random sample sizes have negative binomial or Pareto-like distributions. The formal construction of the approximating functions allows the results to be used for a whole family of asymptotically normal or chi-squared distributed statistics. The Student t-distribution with m degrees of freedom, the one-sample Student t-test statistic, and the sample mean are considered as examples of asymptotic normal statistics. Hotelling's generalized T_0^2 statistic and scale mixture of a normalized quotient of two independent chi-squared random variables were studied as examples of the asymptotic chi-squared distributions. In addition, random, non-random, and mixed scaling factors for the statistics are considered, which have a significant influence on the limit distributions. The limit laws are scale mixtures of the normal with mixing gamma or chi-squared with mixing inverse exponential distributions. In addition to the normal distribution and the chi-square distribution, there are a variety of limit distributions: the Laplace, the scaled Student t-, the scaled Fisher, the generalized gamma, and linear combinations of generalized gamma distributions.

The remaining terms in the approximations of the scaled statistics are estimated by inequalities.

Author Contributions: Conceptualization, G.C. and V.V.U.; methodology, V.V.U. and G.C.; formal analysis, G.C. and V.V.U.; investigation, G.C. and V.V.U.; writing—original draft, G.C. and V.V.U.; writing—review and editing, V.V.U. and G.C. All authors have read and agreed to the published version of the manuscript.

Funding: This research received no external funding. It was carried out within the project "Analysis of the quality of approximations in the statistical analysis of multivariate observations" of the Magdeburg University, the program of the Moscow Center for Fundamental and Applied Mathematics, Lomonosov Moscow State University, and HSE University Basic Research Programs.

Institutional Review Board Statement: Not applicable.

Informed Consent Statement: Not applicable.

Data Availability Statement: Not applicable.

Acknowledgments: The authors thank the Editor for his support and the Reviewers for their appropriate comments which have improved the quality of this paper.

Conflicts of Interest: The authors declare no conflict of interest.

Appendix A. Auxiliary Lemmas

Lemma A1. *Let $r > 1$ then*

$$|J_1(x)| = \left| \int_0^\infty G_d(xy) dh_{2;r}^{**}(y) \right| \leq \frac{c(r,d)}{g_n^{r-1}} \quad \text{with} \quad h_{2;r}^{**}(y) = r^{-1} g_{r,r}(y) Q_1(g_n y). \quad \text{(A1)}$$

Proof of Lemma A1. We use the Fourier series expansion of the jump correcting function $Q_1(y)$ at all non-integer points y; see Prudnikov et al. [35] (Formula 5.4.2.9 for $a = 0$):

$$Q_1(y) = \frac{1}{2} - (y - [y]) = \sum_{k=1}^\infty \frac{\sin(2\pi k y)}{k\pi}, \quad y \neq [y], \quad \text{(A2)}$$

and Prudnikov et al. [35] (Formula 2.5.31.4):

$$\int_0^\infty y^{\alpha-1} e^{-py} \sin(by) dy = \frac{\Gamma(\alpha)}{(b^2+p^2)^{\alpha/2}} \sin(\alpha \arctan(b/p)) \quad \text{with} \quad \alpha > -1, b, p > 0. \quad \text{(A3)}$$

Integration by parts in the integral $J_1(x)$, using (A2), interchanging sum and integral and applying (A3) with $\alpha = r + d/2 - 1$, $p = (r + x/2)$ and $b = 2\pi k g_n$ leads to

$$\begin{aligned}
J_1(x) &= -\frac{r^{r-1} x^{d/2}}{\Gamma(r) 2^{d/2} \Gamma(d/2)} \int_0^\infty y^{r+d/2-2} Q_1(g_n y) e^{-(r+x/2)y} dy \\
&= -\frac{r^{r-1} x^{d/2}}{\pi \Gamma(r) 2^{d/2} \Gamma(d/2)} \sum_{k=1}^\infty \frac{1}{k} \int_0^\infty y^{r+d/2-2} e^{-(r+x/2)y} \sin(2\pi k g_n y) dy \\
&= -\frac{r^{r-1} \Gamma(r+d/2-1)}{\pi \Gamma(r) 2^{d/2} \Gamma(d/2)} \sum_{k=1}^\infty \frac{a_k(x;n)}{k}
\end{aligned}$$

with

$$a_k(x;n) = \frac{x^{d/2} \sin\left((r+d/2-1)\arctan(2\pi k g_n/(r+x/2))\right)}{\left((2\pi k g_n)^2 + (r+x/2)^2\right)^{(r+d/2-1)/2}}.$$

Now, we split the exponent $(r+d/2-1)/2 = (r-1)/2 + d/4$ and obtain

$$|a_k(x;n)| \leq \frac{x^{d/2}}{(2\pi k g_n)^{r-1} (r+x/2)^{d/2}} \leq \frac{2^{d/2}}{(2\pi k g_n)^{r-1}}.$$

Since $r > 1$, we find uniform in $x \geq 0$

$$|J_1(x)| \leq \frac{c_1(r,d)}{g_n^{r-1}} \sum_{k=1}^{\infty} k^{-r} = \frac{c(r,d)}{g_n^{r-1}}$$

and Lemma A1 is proved. □

Lemma A2. *Let $r \geq 2$, then*

$$|J_{-1}(x)| = \left|\int_0^\infty G_d(x/y) dh_{2;r}^{**}(y)\right| \leq \frac{c(r,d)}{g_n} \quad \text{with} \quad h_{2;r}^{**}(y) = r^{-1} g_{r,r}(y) Q_1(g_n y). \tag{A4}$$

Proof of Lemma A2. Integration by parts in the integral $J_{-1}(x)$, using the Fourier series expansion (A2), interchanging sum and integral, we find

$$J_{-1}(x) = \frac{r^{r-1} x^{d/2}}{\Gamma(r) 2^{d/2} \Gamma(d/2)} \int_0^\infty y^{r-d/2-2} Q_1(g_n y) e^{-(ry+x/(2y))} dy = \frac{r^{r-1}}{\pi \Gamma(r) 2^{d/2} \Gamma(d/2)} \sum_{k=1}^{\infty} \frac{J_{k,n}(x)}{k}$$

with $J_{k,n}(x) = \int_0^\infty x^{d/2} y^{r-d/2-2} e^{-(ry+x/(2y))} \sin(2\pi k g_n y) dy$.

In the literature, we have only found integrals $J_{k,n}(x)$ with power functions $y^{-1/2}$ and $y^{-3/2}$. Therefore, we integrate by parts in the integral $J_{k,n}(x)$:

$$J_{k,n}(x) = \frac{-1}{2} \int_0^\infty \left((d-2r+4)f_1(x,y) + 2rf_2(x,y) - f_3(x,y)\right) e^{-(ry+x/(2y))} \frac{\cos(2\pi k g_n y)}{2\pi k g_n} dy,$$

where $f_1(x,y) = x^{d/2} y^{r-d/2-3}$, $f_2(x,y) = x^{d/2} y^{r-d/2-2}$ and $f_3(x,y) = x^{d/2+1} y^{r-d/2-4}$.

Since $r \geq 2$ and $d \geq 1$ we obtain $y^{r-2} e^{-ry/2} \leq c_r$ and $(x/y)^{(d-1)/2} e^{-x/(4y)} \leq c_d$. Using (30) with $m = 0, 1, 2$, $p = r/2$, and $q = x/4$ we find

$$\int_0^\infty f_1(x,y) dy \leq c_r c_d x^{1/2} \int_0^\infty y^{-3/2} e^{-(ry/2+x/(4y))} dy = c_r c_d 2\sqrt{\pi} e^{-\sqrt{rx/2}} \leq C_1(r,d),$$

$$\int_0^\infty f_2(x,y) dy \leq c_r c_d x^{1/2} \int_0^\infty \frac{y^{-1/2}}{e^{(ry/2+x/(4y))}} dy = c_r c_d \sqrt{2\pi x/r} e^{-\sqrt{2rx}/2} \leq C_2(r,d),$$

$$\int_0^\infty f_3(x,y) dy \leq c_r c_d x^{3/2} \int_0^\infty \frac{y^{-5/2}}{e^{(ry/2+x/(4y))}} dy = c_r c_d 2\sqrt{\pi}(\sqrt{2rx}+2) e^{-\sqrt{rx/2}} \leq C_3(r,d)$$

and

$$|J_{k,n}| \leq \frac{1}{4\pi k g_n}\left(|d-2r+4|C_1(r,d) + 2rC_2(r,d) + C_3(r,d)\right) \leq \frac{C^*(r,d)}{k g_n}.$$

Hence,

$$|J_{-1}(x)| \leq \frac{r^{r-1}}{\pi \Gamma(r) 2^{d/2} \Gamma(d/2)} \frac{\pi^2}{6 g_n} C^*(r,d) \leq \frac{c(r,d)}{g_n}.$$

Lemma A2 is proved. □

Lemma A3. *Let $\gamma = -1$, $r = 3/2$, $d = 4$ and $g_n = (3n-1)/2$, then*

$$|J_{-1}^*(x)| = \left|\int_0^\infty G_d(x/y) dh_{2;3/2}^{**}(y)\right| \leq \frac{c(3/2,4)}{\sqrt{g_n}} \quad \text{with} \quad h_{2;3/2}^{**}(y) = (2/3) g_{3/2,3/2}(y) Q_1(g_n y). \tag{A5}$$

Proof of Lemma A3. Integration by parts in the integral $J_{-1}^*(x)$, using the Fourier series expansion (A2), interchanging sum and integral, we find

$$J_{-1}^*(x) = \frac{\sqrt{3/2}\, x^2}{4\Gamma(3/2)} \int_0^\infty y^{-5/2} Q_1(g_n y) e^{-(3y/2+x/(2y))} dy = \frac{\sqrt{3/2}}{\sqrt{\pi}} \sum_{k=1}^{\infty} \frac{J_{k,n}^*(x)}{k}$$

with
$$J^*_{k,n}(x) = x^2 \int_0^\infty y^{-5/2} e^{-(3y/2 + x/(2y))} \sin(2\pi k g_n y) dy.$$

Using Prudnikov et al. [35] (Formula 2.5.37.3), with the real constants $p > 0$, $q > 0$ and $b > 0$, we obtain

$$\int_0^\infty y^{-3/2} e^{-py-q/y} \sin(by) dy = \frac{\sqrt{\pi}}{\sqrt{q}} e^{-2\sqrt{q} z_+} \sin(2\sqrt{q} z_-) \quad \text{and} \quad 2z_\pm^2 = \sqrt{p^2 + b^2} \pm p. \tag{A6}$$

It was shown in Christoph et al. [17] (Proof of Theorem 5) that Leibniz's integral rule allows differentiation to q under the integral sign in (A6). Therefore,

$$\int_0^\infty y^{-5/2} e^{-py-q/y} \sin(by) dy = (\sqrt{\pi}/2) e^{-2\sqrt{q} z_+} \left(q^{-3/2} \sin(2\sqrt{q} z_-) \right.$$
$$\left. + 2q^{-1} z_+ \sin(2\sqrt{q} z_-) - 2q^{-1} z_- \cos(2\sqrt{q} z_-) \right).$$

Since $0 < z_- \le z_+$, $p = 3/2$, $q = x/2$, $b = 2\pi k g_n$, $k \ge 1$ and $g_n \ge 1$ we find $z_+ \ge \sqrt{\pi k g_n}$,

$$|J^*_{k,n}(x)| \le x^2 \frac{\sqrt{\pi}}{2} e^{-\sqrt{2x} z_+} \left(\frac{2\sqrt{2}}{x^{3/2}} + \frac{8}{x} z_+ \right) = \frac{\sqrt{\pi}}{z_+} e^{-\sqrt{2x} z_+} \left(\sqrt{2x} z_+ + 4 x z_+^2 \right) \le \frac{e^{-1} + 8 e^{-2}}{\sqrt{k n}}$$

and

$$|J_{-1}(x)| \le \frac{\sqrt{3/2}}{\sqrt{\pi}} \sum_{k=1}^\infty \frac{e^{-1} + 8 e^{-2}}{k^{3/2} \sqrt{g_n}}.$$

Lemma A3 is proved. □

References

1. Wallace, D.L. Asymptotic approximations to distributions. *Ann. Math. Statist.* **1958**, *29*, 635–654. [CrossRef]
2. Bickel, P.J. Edgeworth expansions in nonparametric statistics. *Ann. Statist.* **1974**, *2*, 1–20. [CrossRef]
3. Hall, P. *The Bootstrap and Edgeworth Expansion*; Springer Series in Statistics; Springer: New York, NY, USA, 1992.
4. Bhattacharya, R.N.; Ranga Rao, R. *Normal Approximation and Asymptotic Expansions*; Wiley: New York, NY, USA, 1976.
5. Petrov, V.V. *Limit Theorems of Probability Theory, Sequences of Independent Random Variables*; Clarendon Press: Oxford, UK, 1995.
6. Pfanzagl, J. Asymptotic expansions related to minimum contrast estimators. *Ann. Statist.* **1973**, *1*, 993–1026. [CrossRef]
7. Bentkus, V.; Götze, F.; van Zwet, W.R. An Edgeworth expansion for symmetric statistics. *Ann. Statist.* **1997**, *25*, 851–896. [CrossRef]
8. Burnashev, M.V. Asymptotic expansions for median estimate of a parameter. *Theory Probab. Appl.* **1997**, *41*, 632–645. [CrossRef]
9. Nunes, C.; Capistrano, G.; Ferreira, D.; Ferreira, S.S.; Mexia, J.T. Exact critical values for one-way fixed effects models with random sample sizes. *J. Comput. Appl. Math.* **2019**, *354*, 112–122. [CrossRef]
10. Nunes, C.; Capistrano, G.; Ferreira, D.; Ferreira, S.S.; Mexia, J.T. Random sample sizes in orthogonal mixed models with stability. *Comp. Math. Methods* **2019**, *1*, e1050. [CrossRef]
11. Nunes, C.; Mário, A.; Ferreira, D.; Moreira, E.M.; Ferreira, S.S.; Mexia, J.T. An algorithm for simulation in mixed models with crossed factors considering the sample sizes as random. *J. Comput. Appl. Math.* **2022**, *404*, 113463. [CrossRef]
12. Esquível, M.L.; Mota P.P.; Mexia J.T. On some statistical models with a random number of observations. *J. Stat. Theory Pract.* **2016**, *10*, 805–823. [CrossRef]
13. Döbler, C. New Berry-Esseen and Wasserstein bounds in the CLT for non-randomly centered random sums by probabilistic methods. *ALEA Lat. Am. J. Probab. Math. Stat.* **2015**, *12*, 863–902.
14. Schluter, C.; Trede, M. Weak convergence to the Student and Laplace distributions. *J. Appl. Probab.* **2016**, *53*, 121–129. [CrossRef]
15. Bening, V.E.; Galieva, N.K.; Korolev, V.Y. On rate of convergence in distribution of asymptotically normal statistics based on samples of random size. *Ann. Math. Inform.* **2012**, *39*, 17–28.
16. Bening, V.E.; Galieva, N.K.; Korolev, V.Y. Asymptotic expansions for the distribution functions of statistics constructed from samples with random sizes. *Inform. Appl.* **2013**, *7*, 75–83. (In Russian)
17. Christoph, G.; Monakhov, M.M.; Ulyanov, V.V. Second-order Chebyshev-Edgeworth and Cornish-Fisher expansions for distributions of statistics constructed with respect to samples of random size. *J. Math. Sci.* **2020**, *244*, 811–839; Translated from *Zap. Nauchnykh Semin. POMI* **2017**, *466*, 167–207. [CrossRef]
18. Christoph, G.; Ulyanov, V.V. Chebyshev–Edgeworth-type approximations for statistics based on samples with random sizes. *Mathematics* **2021**, *9*, 775. [CrossRef]
19. Fujikoshi, Y.; Ulyanov, V.V. *Non-Asymptotic Analysis of Approximations for Multivariate Statistics*; Springer: Singapore, 2020.

20. Christoph, G.; Ulyanov, V.V. Second order expansions for high-dimension low-sample-size data statistics in random setting. *Mathematics* **2020**, *8*, 1151; Reprinted in Special Issue: *Stability Problems for Stochastic Models: Theory and Applications*; Zeifman, A., Korolev, V., Sipin, A., Eds.; MPDI: Basel, Switzerland, 2021; pp. 259–286. [CrossRef]
21. Buddana, A.; Kozubowski, T.J. Discrete Pareto distributions. *Econ. Qual. Control.* **2014**, *29*, 143–156. [CrossRef]
22. Bening, V.E.; Korolev, V.Y. On the use of Student's distribution in problems of probability theory and mathematical statistics. *Theory Probab. Appl.* **2005**, *49*, 377–391. [CrossRef]
23. Gavrilenko, S.V.; Zubov, V.N.; Korolev, V.Y. The rate of convergence of the distributions of regular statistics constructed from samples with negatively binomially distributed random sizes to the Student distribution. *J. Math. Sci.* **2017**, *220*, 701–713. [CrossRef]
24. Christoph, G.; Ulyanov, V.V.; Bening, V.E. Second order expansions for sample median with random sample size. *ALEA Lat. Am. J. Probab. Math. Stat.* **2022**, *19*, 339–365. [CrossRef]
25. Korolev, V. Bounds for the rate of convergence in the generalized Rényi theorem. *Mathematics* **2022**, *10*, 4252. [CrossRef]
26. Bulinski, A.; Slepov, N. Sharp estimates for proximity of geometric and related sums distributions to limit laws. *Mathematics* **2022**, *10*, 4747. [CrossRef]
27. Korolev, V.; Shevtsova, I. An improvement of the Berry-Esseen inequality with applications to Poisson and mixed Poisson random sums. *Scand. Actuar. J.* **2012**, *2012*, 81–105. [CrossRef]
28. Sunklodas, J.K. On the normal approximation of a binomial random sum. *Lith. Math. J.* **2014**, *54*, 356–365. [CrossRef]
29. Petrov, V.V. *Sums of Independent Random Variables*; Akademie-Verlag: Berlin, Germany, 1975.
30. Kolassa, J.E.; McCullagh, P. Edgeworth series for lattice distributions. *Ann. Statist.* **1990**, *18*, 981–985. [CrossRef]
31. Choy, T.B.; Chan, J.E. Scale mixtures distributions in statistical modelling. *Aust. N. Z. J. Stat.* **2008**, *50*, 135–146. [CrossRef]
32. Fujikoshi, Y.; Ulyanov, V.V.; Shimizu, R. *Multivariate Statistics. High-Dimensional and Large-Sample Approximations*; Wiley Series in Probability and Statistics; John Wiley & Sons, Inc.: Hoboken, NJ, USA, 2010.
33. Christoph, G.; Ulyanov, V.V. Random dimension low sample size asymptotics. In *Recent Developments in Stochastic Methods and Applications*; Shiryaev, A.N., Samouylov, K.E., Kozyrev, D.V., Eds.; Springer Proceedings in Mathematics & Statistics; Springer International Publishing: Cham, Switzerland, 2021; Volume 371, pp. 215–228, ISBN 978-3-030-83266-7 and 978-3-030-83266-0._16. [CrossRef]
34. Oldham K.B.; Myland, J.C.; Spanier, J. *An Atlas of Functions*, 2nd ed.; Springer Science + Business Media: New York, NY, USA, 2009.
35. Prudnikov, A.P.; Brychkov, Y.A.; Marichev, O.I. *Integrals and Series, Vol. 1: Elementary Functions*, 3rd ed.; Gordon & Breach Science Publishers: New York, NY, USA, 1992.
36. Korolev, V.Y.; Zeifman, A.I. Generalized negative binomial distributions as mixed geometric laws and related limit theorems. *Lith. Math. J.* **2019**, *59*, 366–388. [CrossRef]
37. Korolev, V.Y.; Gorshenin, A. Probability models and statistical tests for extreme precipitation based on generalized negative binomial distributions. *Mathematics* **2020**, *8*, 604. [CrossRef]
38. Monakhov, M.M. Chebyshev–Edgeworth expansions for distributions of generalized Hotelling-type statistics based on random size samples. *Inform. Primen. [Informatics Its Appl.]* **2021**, *15*, 72–81. (In Russian) [CrossRef]
39. Fujikoshi, Y.; Ulyanov, V.V.; Shimizu, R. L_1-norm error bounds for asymptotic expansions of multivariate scale mixtures and their applications to Hotelling's generalized T_0^2. *J. Multivar. Anal.* **2005**, *96*, 1–19. [CrossRef]

Disclaimer/Publisher's Note: The statements, opinions and data contained in all publications are solely those of the individual author(s) and contributor(s) and not of MDPI and/or the editor(s). MDPI and/or the editor(s) disclaim responsibility for any injury to people or property resulting from any ideas, methods, instructions or products referred to in the content.

Article

Bound for an Approximation of Invariant Density of Diffusions via Density Formula in Malliavin Calculus

Yoon-Tae Kim and Hyun-Suk Park *

Division of Data Science and Data Science Convergence Research Center, Hallym University, Chuncheon 24252, Republic of Korea; ytkim@hallym.ac.kr
* Correspondence: hspark@hallym.ac.kr; Tel.: +82-33-248-2036

Abstract: The *Kolmogorov* and *total variation* distance between the laws of random variables have upper bounds represented by the L^1-norm of densities when random variables have densities. In this paper, we derive an upper bound, in terms of densities such as the Kolmogorov and total variation distance, for several probabilistic distances (e.g., Kolmogorov distance, total variation distance, *Wasserstein* distance, *Forter–Mourier* distance, etc.) between the laws of F and G in the case where a random variable F follows the invariant measure that admits a density and a differentiable random variable G, in the sense of Malliavin calculus, and also allows a density function.

Keywords: Malliavin calculus; invariant measure; density function; Stein's bound; fourth moment theorem; probabilistic distance; Scheffe's theorem

MSC: 60H07; 60F17; 60F25;

Citation: Kim, Y.-T.; Park, H.-S. Bound for an Approximation of Invariant Density of Diffusions via Density Formula in Malliavin Calculus. *Mathematics* **2023**, *11*, 2302. https://doi.org/10.3390/math11102302

Academic Editor: Manuel Alberto M. Ferreira

Received: 17 March 2023
Revised: 29 April 2023
Accepted: 2 May 2023
Published: 15 May 2023

Copyright: © 2023 by the authors. Licensee MDPI, Basel, Switzerland. This article is an open access article distributed under the terms and conditions of the Creative Commons Attribution (CC BY) license (https://creativecommons.org/licenses/by/4.0/).

1. Introduction

Let $B = \{B(h), h \in \mathfrak{H}\}$, where $\mathfrak{H}$ is a real separable Hilbert space, be an isonormal Gaussian process defined on some probability space $(\Omega, \mathfrak{F}, \mathbb{P})$ (see Definition 1). The authors in [1] discovered a celebrated central limit theorem, called the "*fourth moment theorem*", for a sequence of random variables belonging to a fixed Wiener chaos associated with B (see Section 2 for the definition of Wiener chaos).

Theorem 1 (Fourth moment theorem). *Let $\{F_n, n \geq 1\}$ be a sequence of random variables belonging to the $q(\geq 2)$th Wiener chaos with $\mathbb{E}[F_n^2] = 1$ for all $n \geq 1$. Then $F_n \xrightarrow{\mathcal{L}} Z$ if and only if $\mathbb{E}[F_n^4] \to 3 = \mathbb{E}[Z^4]$, where Z is a standard Gaussian random variable and the notation $\xrightarrow{\mathcal{L}}$ denotes the convergence in distribution.*

After that, the authors in [2] obtained a quantitative bound of the distances between the laws of F and Z by developing the techniques based on the combination between Malliavin calculus (see, e.g., [3–7]) and Stein's method for normal approximation (see, e.g., [8–10]). These distances can be defined in several ways. More precisely, the distance between the laws of F and Z is given by

$$d(F, Z) \leq C_d \sqrt{\mathbb{E}[(1 - \langle DF, -DL^{-1}F \rangle_{\mathfrak{H}})^2]}. \qquad (1)$$

where D and L^{-1} denote the Malliavin derivative and the pseudo-inverse of the Ornstein–Uhlenbeck generator, respectively (see Definitions 2 and 5), and the constant C_d in (1) only depends on the distance d considered. In the particular case where F is an element in the qth Wiener chaos of B with $\mathbb{E}[F^2] = 1$, the upper bound (1) for Kolmogorov distance ($C_d = 1$) is given by

$$d_{Kol}(F, Z) \leq \sqrt{\frac{q-1}{3q}(\mathbb{E}[F^4] - 3)}. \qquad (2)$$

where $\mathbb{E}[F^4] - 3$ is the fourth cumulant of F.

The application of the Stein's method related to Malliavin calculus has been extended from the normal distribution to the cases of Gamma and Pearson distributions (see e.g., [11,12]). Furthermore, the authors in [13] extend the upper bound (1) to a more general class of probability distribution. For a differentiable random variable in the sense of the Malliavin calculus, they obtain the upper bound of distance between its law and a law of a random variable with a density that is continuous, bounded, and strictly positive in the interval (l, u) $(-\infty \leq l < u \leq \infty)$ with finite variance. Their approach is based on the construction of an ergodic diffusion that has a density p as an invariant measure. The diffusion with the invariant density p has the form

$$dX_t = b(X_t)dt + \sqrt{a(X_t)}dW_t, \qquad (3)$$

where W is a standard Brownian motion. Then, they consider the generator of the diffusion process X and use the integration by parts (see Definition 3 for the integration by parts formula) to find an upper bound for the distance between the law of a differentiable random variable G and the law of a random variable F with density p_F. This bound contains D and L^{-1} as in the bound (1). Precisely, for a suitable class of functions $\mathcal{F}$,

$$\begin{aligned}
&\sup_{f \in \mathcal{F}} |\mathbb{E}[f(G) - f(F)]| \\
&\leq C \mathbb{E}\left[\left|\frac{1}{2}a(G) + \mathbb{E}\left[\langle -DL^{-1}(b(G) - \mathbb{E}[b(G)]), DG\rangle_{\mathfrak{H}} \big| G\right]\right|\right] \\
&\quad + C|\mathbb{E}[b(G)]|.
\end{aligned} \qquad (4)$$

If a random variable G admits a density with respect to the Lebesgue measure, the Kolmogorov (i.e., $\mathcal{F} = \{\mathbf{1}_{(l,z)}; z \in (l, u)\}$) and *total variation* distance ($\mathcal{F} = \{\mathbf{1}_B; B \in \mathcal{B}(\mathbb{R})\}$) can be bounded by

$$\sup_{f \in \mathcal{F}} |\mathbb{E}[f(G) - f(F)]| \leq \int_{-\infty}^{\infty} |p_G(x) - p_F(x)|dx. \qquad (5)$$

We note that Scheffe's theorem implies that the pointwise convergence of densities is stronger than convergence in distribution. In this paper, we assume that the law of G admits a density with respect to the Lebesgue measure. This assumption on G is satisfied for all distributions considered throughout examples in the paper [13]. Using the bound of (4) and the diffusion coefficient in (3) given by

$$a(x) = \frac{-2 \int_l^x (y - m) p_F(y) dy}{p_F(x)},$$

we derive a bound of general distances in the left-hand side of (4), being expressed in terms of the density functions of two random variables F and G as in the case of Kolmogorov and total variation distances. In addition, we deal with the computation of the conditional expectation in (4). When G is general, it is difficult to find an explicit computation of this expectation. The random variables in all examples covered in [13] are just functions of a Gaussian vector. In this case, it is possible to compute the explicit expectation. If the law of these random variables admits a density with respect to the Lebesgue measure, like all examples considered in [13], we can find the formula from which we can easily compute this expectation.

The rest of the paper is organized as follows. Section 2 reviews some basic notations and the results of Malliavin calculus. In Section 3, we describe the construction of a diffusion process with an invariant density p and derive an upper bound between the laws of F and G in terms of densities. In Section 4, we introduce a method that can directly compute the conditional expectation in (4). Finally, as an application of our main results, in Section 5, we obtain an upper bound of an example considered in [13]. Throughout this paper, c (or C) stands for an absolute constant with possibly different values in different places.

2. Preliminaries

In this section, we briefly review some basic facts about Malliavin calculus for Gaussian processes. For a more detailed explanation, see [6,7]. Fix a real separable Hilbert space $\mathfrak{H}$, with inner product $\langle \cdot, \cdot \rangle_{\mathfrak{H}}$.

Definition 1. *We say that a stochastic process $B = \{B(h), h \in \mathfrak{H}\}$ defined on $(\Omega, \mathfrak{F}, P)$ is an isonormal Gaussian process if B is a centered Gaussian family of random variables such that $\mathbb{E}[B(g)B(h)] = \langle g, h \rangle_{\mathfrak{H}}$ for every $g, h \in \mathfrak{H}$.*

For the rest of this paper, we assume that $\mathfrak{F}$ is the σ-field generated by X. To simplify the notation, we write $L^2(\Omega)$ instead of $L^2(\Omega, \mathfrak{F}, P)$. For each $q \geq 1$, we write $\mathcal{H}_q$ to denote the closed linear subspace of $\mathbb{L}^2(\Omega)$ generated by the random variables $H_q(B(h))$, $h \in \mathfrak{H}$, $\|h\|_{\mathfrak{H}} = 1$, where the space H_q is the qth Hermite polynomial. The space $\mathcal{H}_q$ is called the qth Wiener chaos of B. Let $\mathcal{S}$ denote the class of smooth and cylindrical random variables F of the form

$$F = f(B(\varphi_1), \cdots, B(\varphi_m)), \quad m \geq 1, \tag{6}$$

where $f : \mathbb{R}^m \to \mathbb{R}$ is a $\mathcal{C}^\infty$-function such that its partial derivatives have at most polynomial growth, and $\varphi_i \in \mathfrak{H}$, $i = 1, \cdots, m$. Then, the space $\mathcal{S}$ is dense in $L^q(\Omega)$ for every $q \geq 1$.

Definition 2. *For a given integer $p \geq 1$ and $F \in \mathcal{S}$, the pth Malliavin derivative of F with respect to B is the element of $L^2(\Omega; \mathfrak{H}^{\odot p})$, where the space $\mathfrak{H}^{\odot p}$ denotes the symmetric tensor product of $\mathfrak{H}$, defined by*

$$D^p F = \sum_{i_1,\ldots,i_p = 1}^{m} \frac{\partial^p f}{\partial x_1, \ldots, \partial x_p}(B(\varphi_1), \ldots, B(\varphi_n))\varphi_{i_1} \otimes \cdots \otimes \varphi_{i_p}. \tag{7}$$

For a fixed $p \in [1, \infty)$ and an integer $k \geq 1$, we denote by $\mathbb{D}^{k,p}$ the closure of its associated smooth random variable class of $\mathcal{S}$ with respect to the norm

$$\|F\|_{k,p}^p = \mathbb{E}[|F|^p] + \sum_{\ell=1}^{k} \mathbb{E}[\|D^\ell F\|_{\mathfrak{H}^{\otimes \ell}}^p].$$

For a given integer $p \geq 1$, we denote by $\delta^p : L^2(\Omega; \mathfrak{H}^{\otimes p}) \to L^2(\Omega)$ the adjoint of the operator $D^p : \mathbb{D}^{k,2} \to L^2(\Omega; \mathfrak{H}^{\odot q})$, called the *multiple divergence operator* of order p. The domain of δ^p, denoted by $\text{Dom}(\delta^p)$, is the subset of $\mathbb{L}^2(\Omega; \mathfrak{H}^{\otimes p})$ composed of those elements u such that

$$|\mathbb{E}[\langle D^p F, u \rangle_{\mathfrak{H}^{\otimes p}}]| \leq C(\mathbb{E}[|F|^2])^{1/2} \quad \text{for all } F \in \mathbb{D}^{p,2}.$$

Definition 3. *If $u \in \text{Dom}(\delta^p)$, then $\delta^p(u)$ is the element of $L^2(\Omega)$ defined by the duality relationship*

$$\mathbb{E}[F\delta^p(u)] = \mathbb{E}[\langle D^p F, u \rangle_{\mathfrak{H}^{\otimes p}}] \quad \text{for every } F \in \mathbb{D}^{p,2}. \tag{8}$$

The above formula (8) is called an integration by parts formula. For a given integer $q \geq 1$ and $f \in \mathcal{H}^{\odot q}$, the qth multiple integral of f is defined by $I_q(f) = \delta^q(f)$. Let $h \in \mathfrak{H}$ with $\|h\|_{\mathfrak{H}} = 1$. Then, for any integer $q \geq 1$, we have $I_q(h^{\otimes q}) = q! H_q(B(h))$. From this, the linear mapping $I_q : \mathfrak{H}^{\odot q} \to \mathcal{H}_q$ by $I_q(h^{\otimes q}) = q! H_q(B(h))$ has an isometric property. It is well known that any square integrable random variable $F \in L^2(\Omega)$ can be expanded into a series of multiple integrals:

$$F = \mathbb{E}[F] + \sum_{q=1}^{\infty} I_q(f_q),$$

where the series converges in L^2, and the functions $f_q \in \mathfrak{H}^{\odot q}$, $q \geq 1$, are uniquely determined by F. Moreover, if $F \in \mathbb{D}^{m,2}$, then $f_q = \frac{1}{q!}\mathbb{E}[D^q F]$ for all $q \leq m$.

Definition 4. *For a given $F \in L^2(\Omega)$, we say that F belongs to $\text{Dom}(L)$ if*

$$\sum_{q=1}^{\infty} q^2 \mathbb{E}[J_q(F)^2] < \infty,$$

where J_q is the projection operator from $L^2(\Omega)$ into $\mathcal{H}_q$, that is, $J_q(F) = \text{Proj}(F|\mathcal{H}_q), q = 0,1,2\ldots$. For such an F, the operator L is defined through the projection operator J_q, $q = 0,1,2\ldots$, as $LF = -\sum_{q=1}^{\infty} q J_q F$.

It is not difficult to see that the operator L coincides with the infinitesimal generator of the Ornstein–Uhlhenbeck semigroup $\{P_t, t \geq 0\}$. The following gives a crucial relationship between the operator D, δ, and L: Let $F \in L^2(\Omega)$. Then, we have $F \in \text{Dom}(L)$ if and only if $F \in \mathbb{D}^{1,2}$ and $DF \in \text{Dom}(\delta)$. In this case, $\delta(DF) = -LF$, that is, for $F \in L^2(\Omega)$, the statement $F \in \text{Dom}(L)$ is equivalent to $F \in \text{Dom}(\delta D)$.

Definition 5. *For any $F \in L^2(\Omega)$, we define the operator L^{-1}, called the pseudo-inverse of L, as $L^{-1}F = \sum_{q=1}^{\infty} \frac{1}{q} J_q(F)$.*

Note that L^{-1} is an operator with values in $\mathbb{D}^{2,2}$ and $LL^{-1}F = F - \mathbb{E}[F]$ for all $F \in L^2(\Omega)$.

3. Diffusion Process with Invariant Measures

In this section, we explain how a diffusion process is constructed to have an invariant measure μ that admits a density function, say p, with respect to the Lebesgue measure (see [13,14] for more information). Let μ be a probability measure on $I = (l, u)$ ($-\infty \leq l < u \leq \infty$) with a continuous, bounded, and strictly positive density function p. We take a function $b : I \to \mathbb{R}$ that is continuous such that $e \in (l, u)$ exists for which $b(x) > 0$ for $x \in (l, e)$ and $b(x) < 0$ for $x \in (e, u)$ are satisfied. Moreover, the function bp is bounded on I and

$$\int_l^u b(x)p(x)dx = 0. \tag{9}$$

For $x \in I$, let us set

$$a(x) = \frac{2\int_l^x b(y)p_F(y)dy}{p(x)}. \tag{10}$$

Then, the stochastic differential equation (sde)

$$dX_t = b(X_t)dt + \sqrt{a(X_t)}dB_t \tag{11}$$

has a unique ergodic Markovian weak solution with the invariant measure μ.

The authors prove in [15] that the convergence of the elements of a Markov chaos to a Pearson distribution can be still bounded with just the first four moments by using the new concept of a *chaos grade*. Pearson diffusions are examples of the Markov triple and Itô diffusion given by the sde

$$dX_t = -(X_t - m)dt + \sqrt{a(X_t)}dB_t, \tag{12}$$

where m is the expectation of μ, and

$$a(x) = \frac{-2\int_l^x (y-m)p(y)dy}{p(x)} \quad \text{for } x \in (l, u). \tag{13}$$

Let us define

$$\tilde{h}_f(y) = \frac{2\int_l^y (f(u) - \mathbb{E}[f(F)])p(u)du}{a(y)p_F(y)},$$

where F is a random variable having its law of μ. For $f \in \mathcal{C}_0(I)$, where $\mathcal{C}_0(I) = \{f : I \to \mathbb{R} | f \text{ is continuous on } I \text{ vanishing at the boundary of } I\}$, we define

$$h_f(x) = \int_0^x \tilde{h}_f(y)dy.$$

Then, h_f satisfies that

$$f - \mathbb{E}[f(F)] = b(x)h_f'(x) + \frac{1}{2}a(x)h_f''(x).$$

In [13], the authors derive the Stein's bound between the probability measure μ and the law of an arbitrary random variable G. This bound extends the results in [2,12] in the case where μ is a standard Gaussian and Gamma distribution, respectively.

Theorem 2 (Kusuoka and Tudor (2012) [13])**.** *Let F be a random variable having the target law μ with a probability distribution associated to the diffusion given by sde (11). Let G be an I-valued random variable in $\mathbb{D}^{1,2}$ with $b(G) \in \mathbb{L}^2(\Omega)$. Then, for every $f : I \to \mathbb{R}$ such that $\tilde{h}_f$ and $\tilde{h}_f'$ are bounded, the following holds:*

$$\begin{aligned}
&|\mathbb{E}[f(G) - f(F)]| \\
&\leq \|\tilde{h}_f'\|_\infty \mathbb{E}\left[\left|\frac{1}{2}a(G) + \langle -DL^{-1}(b(G) - \mathbb{E}[b(G)]), DG\rangle_\mathfrak{H}\right|\right] \\
&\quad + \|\tilde{h}_f\|_\infty |\mathbb{E}[b(G)]|,
\end{aligned} \tag{14}$$

and

$$\begin{aligned}
&|\mathbb{E}[f(G) - f(F)]| \\
&\leq \|\tilde{h}_f'\|_\infty \mathbb{E}\left[\left|\mathbb{E}\left[\frac{1}{2}a(G) + \langle -DL^{-1}(b(G) - \mathbb{E}[b(G)]), DG\rangle_\mathfrak{H}\Big|G\right]\right|\right] \\
&\quad + \|\tilde{h}_f\|_\infty |\mathbb{E}[b(G)]|.
\end{aligned} \tag{15}$$

When the laws of F and G admit densities p_F and p_G (with respect to Lebesgue measure), respectively, we derive an upper bound (14) in terms of the densities of F and G by using Theorem 2.

Theorem 3. *Let F be a random variable having the law μ with the density p_F associated to the diffusion given by sde (11). Let G be a random variable in $\mathbb{D}^{1,2}$ with $b(G) \in \mathbb{L}^2(\Omega)$. Suppose that the law of G has the density p_G with respect to the Lebesgue measure. Then, for every $f : I \to \mathbb{R}$ such that $\tilde{h}_f$ and $\tilde{h}_f'$ are bounded, we find that*

$$
\begin{aligned}
&|\mathbb{E}[f(G) - f(F)]| \\
&\leq \|h'_f\|_\infty \mathbb{E}\left[\left|\int_G^\infty b(y)\left(\frac{p_F(y)}{p_F(G)} - \frac{p_G(y)}{p_G(G)}\right)dy\right|\right] \\
&\quad + \left(\|h'_f\|_\infty \mathbb{E}\left[\frac{\int_G^\infty p_G(y)dy}{p_G(G)}\right] + \|h_f\|_\infty\right)|\mathbb{E}[b(G)]|.
\end{aligned} \tag{16}
$$

Proof. Let $\varphi : \mathbb{R} \to \mathbb{R}$ be a C^1-function having a bounded derivative φ' with a compact support. Using the integration by parts yields

$$
\begin{aligned}
&\mathbb{E}\left[\varphi'(G)\mathbb{E}\left[\langle -DL^{-1}(b(G) - \mathbb{E}[b(G)]), DG\rangle_\mathfrak{H} | G\right]\right] \\
&= \mathbb{E}\left[\langle -DL^{-1}(b(G) - \mathbb{E}[b(G)]), D\varphi(G)\rangle_\mathfrak{H}\right] \\
&= \mathbb{E}\left[\varphi(G)(b(G) - \mathbb{E}[b(G)])\right] \\
&= -\int_{-\infty}^\infty \varphi(x)\frac{d}{dx}\left(\int_x^\infty (b(y) - \mathbb{E}[b(G)])p_G(y)dy\right)dx \\
&= \left. -\varphi(x)\int_x^\infty (b(y) - \mathbb{E}[b(G)])p_G(y)dy \right|_{-\infty}^\infty \\
&\quad + \int_{-\infty}^\infty \varphi'(x)\int_x^\infty (b(y) - \mathbb{E}[b(G)])p_G(y)dydx \\
&= \mathbb{E}\left[\varphi'(G)\frac{\int_G^\infty (b(y) - \mathbb{E}[b(G)])p_G(y)dy}{p_G(G)}\right].
\end{aligned} \tag{17}
$$

The above equality (17) obviously shows that

$$
\mathbb{E}\left[\langle -DL^{-1}(b(G) - \mathbb{E}[b(G)]), DG\rangle_\mathfrak{H} | G\right] = \frac{\int_G^\infty (b(y) - \mathbb{E}[b(G)])p_G(y)dy}{p_G(G)}. \tag{18}
$$

Using the relations (10) and (17), the first expectation in the right-hand side of (15) can be written as

$$
\begin{aligned}
&\mathbb{E}\left[\left|\frac{1}{2}a(G) + \mathbb{E}\left[\langle -DL^{-1}(b(G) - \mathbb{E}[b(G)]), DG\rangle_\mathfrak{H} | G\right]\right|\right] \\
&= \mathbb{E}\left[\left|\frac{\int_{-\infty}^G b(y)p_F(y)dy}{p_F(G)} + \frac{\int_G^\infty (b(y) - \mathbb{E}[b(G)])p_G(y)dy}{p_G(G)}\right|\right]
\end{aligned} \tag{19}
$$

Since

$$
\frac{\int_I^u b(y)p_F(y)dy}{p_F(G)} = 0,
$$

we have that

$$
\frac{\int_{-\infty}^G b(y)p_F(y)dy}{p_F(G)} = -\frac{\int_G^\infty b(y)p_F(y)dy}{p_F(G)},
$$

This implies that (19) can be written as

$$\mathbb{E}\left[\left|\mathbb{E}\left[\frac{1}{2}a(G) + \langle -DL^{-1}(b(G) - \mathbb{E}[b(G)]), DG\rangle_{\mathfrak{H}}\Big|G\right]\right|\right]$$
$$\leq \mathbb{E}\left[\left|\frac{\int_G^\infty b(y)p_F(y)dy}{p_F(G)} - \frac{\int_G^\infty b(y)p_G(y)dy}{p_G(G)}\right|\right]$$
$$+ |\mathbb{E}[b(G)]|\mathbb{E}\left[\frac{\int_G^\infty p_G(y)dy}{p_G(G)}\right]. \tag{20}$$

Combining (15) and (20) completes the proof of this theorem. □

Remark 1. *In Theorem 2 of [13], the authors prove that if a random variable $G \in \mathbb{D}^{1,2}$ has the invariant measure μ, then $\mathbb{E}[b(G)] = 0$ and*

$$\mathbb{E}\left[\frac{1}{2}a(G) + \langle -DL^{-1}b(G), DG\rangle_{\mathfrak{H}}\Big|G\right] = 0. \tag{21}$$

Furthermore, if μ admits the density p_F, it is obvious from (19) that (21) holds.

Remark 2. *We think it would be interesting to give numerical examples from the computational validity in Theorem 3. In this respect, although not a numerical example, we give a simple example to deduce an upper bound for between the laws of two centered Gaussain random variables.*

Proposition 1. *Let F and G be two centered Gaussian random variables with variances $\sigma_1^2 > 0$ and $\sigma_2^2 > 0$. Then,*

$$d_{\mathcal{F}}(F,G) \leq \sup_{f \in \mathcal{F}} \|h_f'\|_\infty |\sigma_F^2 - \sigma_G^2|, \tag{22}$$

where $\mathcal{F}$ is the class of functions to be chosen depending on the type of the distance d.

Proof. Obviously, the random variable F has the law μ with the density

$$p_F(x) = \frac{1}{\sqrt{2\pi}\sigma_F} \exp\left(-\frac{x^2}{2\sigma_F^2}\right)$$

associated to the diffusion given by sde with $b(x) = -x$ and $a(x) = 2\sigma_F^2$. Since $\mathbb{E}[b(G)] = 0$, the second sum in (16) is vanished. Hence, from Theorem 3, it follows that

$$|\mathbb{E}[f(G) - f(F)]|$$
$$\leq \|h_f'\|_\infty \mathbb{E}\left[\left|e^{\frac{G^2}{2\sigma_F^2}}\int_G^\infty ye^{-\frac{y^2}{2\sigma_F^2}}dy - e^{\frac{G^2}{2\sigma_G^2}}\int_G^\infty ye^{-\frac{y^2}{2\sigma_G^2}}dy\right|\right]$$
$$= \|h_f'\|_\infty \mathbb{E}\left[\left|\sigma_F^2 e^{\frac{G^2}{2\sigma_F^2}}\int_{-\frac{G^2}{2\sigma_F^2}}^\infty e^{-u}du - \sigma_G^2 e^{\frac{G^2}{2\sigma_G^2}}\int_{-\frac{G^2}{2\sigma_G^2}}^\infty e^{-u}du\right|\right]$$
$$= \|h_f'\|_\infty |\sigma_F^2 - \sigma_G^2|. \tag{23}$$

Since the distance $d_{\mathcal{F}}(F,G)$ between two distributions F and G is given by

$$d_{\mathcal{F}}(F,G) = \sup_{f \in \mathcal{F}} |\mathbb{E}[f(G) - f(F)]|,$$

the proof of this proposition is completed. □

Depending on the choice of $\mathcal{F}$, several types of distances can be defined (see Section 5.2). Comparing the upper bound in Proposition 3.6.1 of [6] obtained from an elementary application of Stein's method with the upper bound in (22) is very interesting. This shows that our study is differentiated from the existing ones.

4. Computation of $\mathbb{E}\big[\langle-\mathbf{DL}^{-1}(\mathbf{b}(\mathbf{G})-\mathbb{E}[\mathbf{b}(\mathbf{G})]),\mathbf{DG}\rangle_\mathfrak{H}|\mathbf{G}\big]$

When G is general, it is difficult to find an explicit computation of the right-hand side of (15). In particular, when $\langle - DL^{-1}(b(G) - \mathbb{E}[b(G)]), DG\rangle_\mathfrak{H}$ is not measurable with respect to the σ-field generated by G, there are cases where it is impossible to compute the expectation. The next proposition in [4] contains an explicit example.

Proposition 2. *Let $DG = \Psi_G(B)$, where B is an isonormal Gaussian process and $\Psi_G : \mathbb{R}^\mathfrak{H} \to \mathfrak{H}$ is a uniquely defined measurable function a.e. Then, we have*

$$\langle -DL^{-1}(G - \mathbb{E}[G]), DG\rangle_\mathfrak{H}$$
$$= \int_0^\infty e^{-t}\langle \Psi_G(B), \mathbb{E}'[\Psi_G(e^{-t}B + \sqrt{1-e^{-2t}}B')]\rangle_\mathfrak{H} dt, \tag{24}$$

so that

$$\mathbb{E}\big[\langle -DL^{-1}(G-\mathbb{E}[G]), DG\rangle_\mathfrak{H}|G\big]$$
$$= \int_0^\infty e^{-t}\mathbb{E}\big[\langle \Psi_G(B), \Psi_G(e^{-t}B + \sqrt{1-e^{-2t}}B')\rangle_\mathfrak{H}|G\big]dt. \tag{25}$$

Here, B and B' are defined on the product space $(\Omega \times \Omega', \mathcal{F} \otimes \mathcal{F}', \mathbb{P} \otimes \mathbb{P}')$ such that B' stands for an independent copy of B. $\mathbb{E}$ and $\mathbb{E}'$ denote the expectation with respect to $\mathbb{P} \otimes \mathbb{P}'$ and $\mathbb{P}'$, respectively.

If $G = h(N) - \mathbb{E}[h(N)]$, where $h : \mathbb{R}^d \to \mathbb{R}$ is a $\mathcal{C}^1$-function with bounded derivative and $N = (N_1, \ldots N_d)$ is a d-dimensional Gaussian random variable with zero mean and covariance $\langle h_i, h_j\rangle_\mathfrak{H} = \mathbb{E}[N_i N_j] = (C_{i,j})$, $i,j = 1, \ldots, d$, where $\{h_i, i = 1, \ldots, n\}$ stands for the canonical basis of $\mathfrak{H}$. By using Proposition 2, the following useful formula can be proved:

$$\langle -DL^{-1}(G - \mathbb{E}[G]), DG\rangle_\mathfrak{H}$$
$$= \int_0^\infty e^{-x}\mathbb{E}'\bigg[\sum_{i,j=1}^d C_{i,j}\frac{\partial h}{\partial x_i}(N)\frac{\partial h}{\partial x_j}\left(e^{-x}N + \sqrt{1-e^{-2x}}N'\right)\bigg]dx. \tag{26}$$

In order to show the significance of the bound (15), the authors in [13] consider the several random variables G. Here, among these random variables, we consider random variables with the uniform and Laplace distribution. The random variable defined by

$$G = e^{-\frac{1}{2}(B(f)+B(g))},$$

where $B(f)$ and $B(g)$ are independent standard Gaussian random variables, has the uniform distribution $\mathcal{U}([0,1])$. The authors in [13] compute the right-hand side of (26) to prove that

$$\mathbb{E}[\langle -DL^{-1}(G-\mathbb{E}[G]), DG\rangle_\mathfrak{H}|G] = G(1-G). \tag{27}$$

Computing in this way is tedious and lengthy. To overcome this situation, we can use Equation (18) to prove that (27) holds. Since G has the uniform distribution $\mathcal{U}([0,1])$, we have

$$\mathbb{E}\big[\langle -DL^{-1}(G-\tfrac{1}{2}), DG\rangle_\mathfrak{H}|G\big] = \frac{\int_G^\infty (y-\tfrac{1}{2})\mathbf{1}_{[0,1]}(y)dy}{\mathbf{1}_{[0,1]}(G)}$$
$$= G(1-G). \tag{28}$$

In the case where G has a Laplace distribution, the authors in [13] consider two random variables:

$$G_1 = \frac{1}{2}(B(h_1)^2 + B(h_2)^2 - B(h_3)^2 - B(h_4)^2), \quad (29)$$
$$G_2 = B(h_1)B(h_2) + B(h_3)B(h_4). \quad (30)$$

where h_i, $i = 1,\ldots,4$, are orthonormal functions in $L^2([0,T])$. It can be easily seen that G_i, $i = 1,2$, has the Laplace distribution with parameter 1. In the paper [13], the authors prove, using Theorem 2 in [13], that for $i = 1, 2$,

$$\mathbb{E}\left[\langle -DL^{-1}G_i, DG_i \rangle_{\mathfrak{H}} | G_i\right] = 1 + |G_i|. \quad (31)$$

The authors argue that these identities are difficult to be proven directly. Here, we introduce a method that can directly prove these identities (31) by using the formula given in (18). Since G_i, $i = 1,2$, has a Laplace distribution with parameter 1, we find that for $i = 1, 2$,

$$\mathbb{E}\left[\langle -DL^{-1}(G_i - \frac{1}{2}), DG_i \rangle_{\mathfrak{H}} | G_i\right] = \frac{\frac{1}{2}\int_{G_i}^{\infty} y e^{-|y|} dy}{\frac{1}{2} e^{-|G_i|}}. \quad (32)$$

An elementary computation yields that for $G_i \geq 0$ a.s,

$$\frac{\frac{1}{2}\int_{G_i}^{\infty} y e^{-|y|} dy}{\frac{1}{2} e^{-|G_i|}} = \frac{e^{-G_i}(1 + G_i)}{e^{-G_i}} = 1 + G_i, \quad (33)$$

and for $G_i < 0$ a.s.

$$\frac{\frac{1}{2}\int_{G_i}^{\infty} y e^{-|y|} dy}{\frac{1}{2} e^{-|G_i|}} = \frac{\frac{1}{2}\int_{G_i}^{0} y e^{y} dy + \frac{1}{2}\int_{0}^{\infty} y e^{-y} dy}{\frac{1}{2} e^{G_i}}$$
$$= \frac{e^{G_i}(1 - G_i)}{e^{G_i}} = 1 - G_i. \quad (34)$$

Combining (33) and (34) proves that the identity (31) holds.

5. Example

In this section, we illustrate the upper bound of probabilistic distances in Theorem 3 through an example considered in [13]. We denote the Wiener integral of $h \in L^2([0,T])$ by $W(h)$. Let $\{h_i, i = 1, 2, \ldots\}$ be a sequence of orthonormal bases of $L^2([0,T])$ and $\{G_N, N = 1, 2 \ldots\}$ a sequence of random variables defined by

$$G_N = e^{-\frac{1}{\sqrt{2N}} \sum_{i=1}^{N}(W(h_i)^2 - 1)}. \quad (35)$$

Let F be a random variable having log normal distribution with mean $m = 0$ and variance $\sigma^2 = 1$. Then, the density of F is given by

$$p_F(x) = \frac{1}{\sqrt{2\pi}x} \exp\left(-\frac{1}{2}(\log x)^2\right) \mathbf{1}_{(0,\infty)}(x). \quad (36)$$

Next, we compute the density of the random variable G_N given by (35). We first compute the cumulative distribution function of G_N. Let us set $X_N = \sum_{i=1}^{N} W(h_i)^2$. Then, the random variable $X_N = N - \sqrt{2N} \log G_N$ has a Gamma distribution with parameters $\alpha = \frac{N}{2}$ and $\beta = \frac{1}{2}$, that is,

$$p_{X_N}(x) = \frac{1}{2^{\frac{N}{2}} \Gamma(\frac{N}{2})} x^{\frac{N}{2}-1} e^{-\frac{x}{2}} \mathbf{1}_{(0,\infty)}(x). \quad (37)$$

Using (37), we find that for $x \geq 0$,

$$\begin{aligned}
\mathbb{P}(G_N \leq x) &= \mathbb{P}\left(-\frac{1}{\sqrt{2N}}\sum_{i=1}^{N}(W(h_i)^2 - 1) \leq \log x\right) \\
&= \mathbb{P}(X_N \geq N - \sqrt{2N}\log x) \\
&= \int_{N-\sqrt{2N}\log x}^{\infty} p_{X_N}(y)dy.
\end{aligned} \qquad (38)$$

Differentiating Equation (38) proves that

$$p_{G_N}(x) = \frac{\sqrt{2N}}{x} p_{X_N}(N - \sqrt{2N}\log x). \qquad (39)$$

From (39), it follows that

$$\begin{aligned}
p_{G_N}(x) &= \frac{\sqrt{2N}}{2^{\frac{N}{2}}\Gamma(\frac{N}{2})x}(N - \sqrt{2N}\log x)^{\frac{N}{2}-1} e^{-\frac{1}{2}(N-\sqrt{2N}\log x)} \mathbf{1}_{(0,\infty)}(x) \\
&= \frac{\sqrt{2N}}{2^{\frac{N}{2}}\Gamma(\frac{N}{2})x} \exp\left\{\left(\frac{N}{2} - 1\right)\log(N - \sqrt{2N}\log x)\right. \\
&\qquad\qquad \left. - \frac{1}{2}(N - \sqrt{2N}\log x)\right\} \mathbf{1}_{(0,\infty)}(x).
\end{aligned} \qquad (40)$$

5.1. Scheffe's Theorem

First, we prove that G_N converges in distribution to F by using Scheffe's theorem and then find a convergence rate of the Kolmogorov and total variation distance. The right-hand side of (40) can be written as

$$\begin{aligned}
p_{G_N}(x) &= \frac{\sqrt{2N}}{2^{\frac{N}{2}}\Gamma(\frac{N}{2})x} \exp\left\{\left(\frac{N}{2} - 1\right)\log N - \frac{N}{2}\right\} \\
&\quad \times \exp\left\{\left(\frac{N}{2} - 1\right)\log\left(1 - \sqrt{\frac{2}{N}}\log x\right)\right. \\
&\qquad\qquad \left. + \sqrt{\frac{N}{2}}\log x\right\} \mathbf{1}_{(0,\infty)}(x).
\end{aligned} \qquad (41)$$

For any fixed $x \in (0, \infty)$, we have, from (36) and (41), that

$$\begin{aligned}
p_{G_N}(x) - p_F(x) &= \left[\frac{\sqrt{2N}}{2^{\frac{N}{2}}\Gamma(\frac{N}{2})}\exp\left\{\left(\frac{N}{2} - 1\right)\log N - \frac{N}{2}\right\}\right. \\
&\qquad \left. - \frac{1}{\sqrt{2\pi}}\right]\frac{1}{x}e^{-\frac{1}{2}(\log x)^2} \\
&\quad + \frac{\sqrt{2N}}{2^{\frac{N}{2}}\Gamma(\frac{N}{2})}\exp\left\{\left(\frac{N}{2} - 1\right)\log N - \frac{N}{2}\right\} \\
&\quad \times \frac{1}{x}\left[\exp\left\{\left(\frac{N}{2} - 1\right)\log\left(1 - \sqrt{\frac{2}{N}}\log x\right)\right.\right. \\
&\qquad\qquad \left.\left. + \sqrt{\frac{N}{2}}\log x\right\} - e^{-\frac{1}{2}(\log x)^2}\right] \\
&= A_{1,N} + A_{2,N}.
\end{aligned} \qquad (42)$$

To estimate the first term $A_{1,N}$ in (42), we can use the following specific version of the Stirling formula of the Γ function, incorporating upper and lower bounds (see [16]):

Lemma 1. *Let $S(x) = x^{x-\frac{1}{2}}e^{-x}$. Then for all $x > 0$,*

$$\sqrt{2\pi}S(x) \leq \Gamma(x) \leq \sqrt{2\pi}S(x)e^{\frac{1}{12x}}. \tag{43}$$

The term $|A_{1,N}|$ in (42) can be written as

$$|A_{1,N}| = \frac{1}{\sqrt{2\pi}}|1 - A_{11,N} \times A_{12,N}|\frac{1}{x}e^{-\frac{1}{2}(\log x)^2}, \tag{44}$$

where

$$A_{11,N} = \frac{\sqrt{2\pi}\sqrt{\frac{2}{N}}(\frac{N}{2})^{\frac{N}{2}}e^{-\frac{N}{2}}}{\Gamma(\frac{N}{2})},$$

$$A_{12,N} = \frac{\sqrt{2N}e^{(\frac{N}{2}-1)\log N - \frac{N}{2}}}{2^{\frac{N}{2}}\sqrt{\frac{2}{N}}(\frac{N}{2})^{\frac{N}{2}}e^{-\frac{N}{2}}}.$$

Obviously,

$$A_{12,N} = \frac{\sqrt{2N}2^{\frac{N}{2}-1}(\frac{N}{2})^{\frac{N}{2}-1}}{2^{\frac{N}{2}}\sqrt{\frac{2}{N}}(\frac{N}{2})^{\frac{N}{2}}} = 1. \tag{45}$$

Hence, form (43) and (44),

$$|A_{1,N}| = \frac{1}{\sqrt{2\pi}}\left|\frac{\Gamma(\frac{N}{2}) - \sqrt{2\pi}(\frac{N}{2})^{\frac{N}{2}-\frac{1}{2}}e^{-\frac{N}{2}}}{\Gamma(\frac{N}{2})}\right|$$

$$\leq \frac{1}{\sqrt{2\pi}}(1 - e^{\frac{1}{12N}})$$

$$= \frac{1}{12\sqrt{2\pi N}} + o\left(\frac{1}{N}\right). \tag{46}$$

Using the Taylor expansion of $\log\left(1 - \sqrt{\frac{2}{N}}\log x\right)$

$$\log\left(1 - \sqrt{\frac{2}{N}}\log x\right) = -\sqrt{\frac{2}{N}}\log x - \frac{2}{2N}(\log x)^2 + o_x(N^{-1}),$$

we write $A_{2,N}$ as

$$A_{2,N} = \frac{\sqrt{2N}}{2^{\frac{N}{2}}\Gamma(\frac{N}{2})}\exp\left\{\left(\frac{N}{2} - 1\right)\log N - \frac{N}{2}\right\}$$

$$\times \frac{1}{x}\left[\exp\left\{-\frac{1}{2}(\log x)^2 + o(1)\right\} - e^{-\frac{1}{2}(\log x)^2}\right]. \tag{47}$$

Since

$$\lim_{N\to\infty}\frac{\sqrt{2N}}{2^{\frac{N}{2}}\Gamma(\frac{N}{2})}\exp\left\{\left(\frac{N}{2} - 1\right)\log N - \frac{N}{2}\right\} = \frac{1}{\sqrt{2\pi}},$$

we will have that $\lim_{N\to\infty} A_{2,N} = 0$, and hence, from (42),

$$\lim_{N\to\infty} p_{G_N}(x) = p_F(x) \text{ for all } x \in (0,1).$$

This convergence implies, from Scheffe's theorem, that as $N \to \infty$,

$$\int_0^\infty |p_{G_N}(x) - p_F(x)| dx \to 0.$$

An upper bound for the Kolmogorov and total variation distance is given in (5). Hence, G_N converges in distribution to F. Next, we find the rate of convergence for an upper bound for these distances by using the bound (5). By using the change of variables $\log x = z$, we find, from (36) and (40), that

$$\begin{aligned}
d(G,F) &\leq \int_0^\infty |p_F(x) - p_G(x)| dx \\
&= \int_{-\infty}^\infty \left| \frac{1}{\sqrt{2\pi}} e^{-\frac{z^2}{2}} - \frac{\sqrt{2N}}{2^{\frac{N}{2}} \Gamma(\frac{N}{2})} e^{(\frac{N}{2}-1) \log N - \frac{N}{2}} \right. \\
&\quad \left. \times e^{(\frac{N}{2}-1) \log(1-\sqrt{\frac{2}{N}}z) + \sqrt{\frac{N}{2}} z} \right| dz.
\end{aligned} \quad (48)$$

Using the Taylor expansion of $\log(1 - \sqrt{\frac{2}{N}}z)$, the right-hand side of (48) can be represented as

$$\begin{aligned}
d(G,F) &\leq \frac{1}{2} \int_{-\infty}^\infty \left| \frac{1}{\sqrt{2\pi}} e^{-\frac{z^2}{2}} - \frac{\sqrt{2N}}{2^{\frac{N}{2}} \Gamma(\frac{N}{2})} e^{(\frac{N}{2}-1) \log N - \frac{N}{2}} \right. \\
&\quad \left. \times e^{-\frac{z^2}{2} + \sqrt{\frac{2}{N}} z + o_z(N^{-\frac{1}{2}})} \right| dz \\
&\leq \frac{1}{2} \left| \frac{1}{\sqrt{2\pi}} - \frac{\sqrt{2N}}{2^{\frac{N}{2}} \Gamma(\frac{N}{2})} e^{(\frac{N}{2}-1) \log N - \frac{N}{2}} \right| \int_{-\infty}^\infty e^{-\frac{z^2}{2}} dz \\
&\quad + \frac{\sqrt{2N}}{2^{\frac{N}{2}+1} \Gamma(\frac{N}{2})} e^{(\frac{N}{2}-1) \log N - \frac{N}{2}} \int_{-\infty}^\infty e^{-\frac{z^2}{2}} \\
&\quad \times \left| 1 - e^{\sqrt{\frac{2}{N}} z + o_z(N^{-\frac{1}{2}})} \right| dz \\
&= B_{1,N} + B_{2,N}.
\end{aligned} \quad (49)$$

From (46), it follows that

$$B_{1,N} \leq \frac{C}{\sqrt{N}}. \quad (50)$$

Obviously,

$$\begin{aligned}
B_{2,N} &\leq C \int_{-\infty}^\infty e^{-\frac{z^2}{2}} \left| 1 - e^{\sqrt{\frac{2}{N}} z + \frac{2}{N} + + o_z(N^{-\frac{1}{2}})} \right| dz \\
&\leq \frac{C}{\sqrt{N}}.
\end{aligned} \quad (51)$$

From (50) and (51), we prove that the rate of convergence of the Kolmogorov and total variation distance between the laws of F and G_N is of order $\frac{1}{\sqrt{N}}$.

5.2. General Distance

In this section, we consider general distances between the laws of F and G_N defined by

$$d_{\mathcal{F}}(G_N, F) = \sup_{f \in \mathcal{F}} \left| \mathbb{E}[f(G_N)] - \mathbb{E}[f(F)] \right|, \quad (52)$$

where $\mathcal{F}$ is a class of functions defined on $\mathbb{R}$. Depending on the choice of $\mathcal{F}$, several types of distances can be defined. In addition to the Kolmogorov distance and total variation distance, the following distances can be obtained: for example, if $\mathcal{F} = \{f : \|f\|_L \leq 1\}$, where $\|\cdot\|_L$ denotes the Lipschitz seminorm defined by

$$\|f\|_L = \sup\left\{\frac{|f(x) - f(y)|}{|x - y|} : x \neq y\right\}.$$

then the distance in (52) is called *Wasserstein*. If $\mathcal{F} = \{f : \|f\|_L + \|f\|_\infty \leq 1\}$, the Fortet-Mourier will be obtained. The rate of convergence of this distance can be found by using the bound given in Theorem 3. The drift coefficient of the associated diffusion is given by

$$a(x) = \frac{2e^{m+\frac{\sigma^2}{2}}}{p_F(x)}\left[\Phi\left(\frac{\log x - m}{\sigma}\right) - \Phi\left(\frac{\log x - m}{\sigma} - \sigma\right)\right], \tag{53}$$

where the function Φ denotes the distribution function of the standard Gaussian distribution. Let us set $\bar{G}_N = G_N - \mathbb{E}[G_N]$. From (18) and (39), it follows that

$$\mathbb{E}\left[\langle -DL^{-1}\bar{G}_N, DG \rangle_{\mathfrak{H}} | \bar{G}_N\right]$$

$$= \frac{\int_{G_N}^{\infty}(y - m)p_{G_N}(y)dy}{p_{G_N}(G_N)}$$

$$= \frac{G_N \int_{G_N}^{\infty}(y - m)\frac{\sqrt{2N}}{y}p_{X_N}(N - \sqrt{2N}\log y)dy}{\sqrt{2N}p_{X_N}(N - \sqrt{2N}\log G_N)}$$

$$= \frac{G_N \int_{-\infty}^{X_N}(e^{-\frac{1}{\sqrt{2N}}(x-N)} - m)p_{X_N}(x)dx}{\sqrt{2N}p_{X_N}(X_N)}, \tag{54}$$

where m is the expectation of G_N given by

$$m = e^{\sqrt{\frac{N}{2}}}\left(1 + \sqrt{\frac{2}{N}}\right)^{-\frac{N}{2}}.$$

The right-hand side of (54) can be written as

$$\mathbb{E}\left[\langle -DL^{-1}\bar{G}_N, DG \rangle_{\mathfrak{H}} | \bar{G}_N\right]$$

$$= \frac{e^{\sqrt{\frac{N}{2}}}G_N \int_{-\infty}^{X_N}[e^{-\frac{x}{\sqrt{2N}}} - (1 + \sqrt{\frac{2}{N}})^{-\frac{N}{2}}]p_{X_N}(x)dx}{\sqrt{2N}p_{X_N}(X_N)}$$

$$= \frac{e^{\sqrt{\frac{N}{2}}}G_N X_N^{1-\frac{N}{2}}e^{-\frac{X_N}{2}}}{\sqrt{2N}}$$

$$\times \int_0^{X_N}[e^{-\frac{x}{\sqrt{2N}}} - (1 + \sqrt{\frac{2}{N}})^{-\frac{N}{2}}]x^{\frac{N}{2}-1}e^{-\frac{x}{2}}dx$$

$$= \frac{e^{\sqrt{\frac{N}{2}}}G_N X_N^{1-\frac{N}{2}}e^{-\frac{X_N}{2}}}{\sqrt{2N}}\left\{\int_0^{X_N} x^{\frac{N}{2}-1}e^{-\frac{1}{2}(\sqrt{\frac{2}{N}}+1)x}dx\right.$$

$$\left. - \int_0^{X_N}\left(1 + \sqrt{\frac{2}{N}}\right)^{-\frac{N}{2}}x^{\frac{N}{2}-1}e^{-\frac{x}{2}}dx\right\}. \tag{55}$$

Using the change of variables $\left(\sqrt{\frac{2}{N}}+1\right)x = y$, we express the right-hand side of (55) as

$$\mathbb{E}\left[\langle -DL^{-1}\tilde{G}_N, DG\rangle_{\mathfrak{H}}|\tilde{G}_N\right] = \frac{e^{\sqrt{\frac{N}{2}}}G_N X_N^{1-\frac{N}{2}}e^{\frac{X_N}{2}}}{\sqrt{2N}}\left(1+\sqrt{\frac{2}{N}}\right)^{-\frac{N}{2}}$$
$$\times \int_{X_N}^{(\sqrt{\frac{2}{N}}+1)X_N} x^{\frac{N}{2}-1}e^{-\frac{x}{2}}dx. \qquad (56)$$

By using the expansion

$$\left(1+\sqrt{\frac{2}{N}}\right)^{-\frac{N}{2}} = e^{-\sqrt{\frac{N}{2}}+\frac{1}{2}-\frac{1}{3\sqrt{2N}}+o(N^{-\frac{1}{2}})},$$

the right-hand side of (56) can be expressed as

$$\mathbb{E}\left[\langle -DL^{-1}\tilde{G}_N, DG\rangle_{\mathfrak{H}}|\tilde{G}_N\right] = \frac{e^{\frac{1}{2}-\frac{1}{3\sqrt{2N}}+o(N^{-\frac{1}{2}})}G_N X_N^{1-\frac{N}{2}}e^{\frac{X_N}{2}}}{\sqrt{2N}}$$
$$\times \int_{X_N}^{(\sqrt{\frac{2}{N}}+1)X_N} x^{\frac{N}{2}-1}e^{-\frac{x}{2}}dx. \qquad (57)$$

The change of variables $\frac{x-X_N}{\sqrt{\frac{2}{N}}X_N} = z$ shows that (57) is

$$\mathbb{E}\left[\langle -DL^{-1}\tilde{G}_N, DG\rangle_{\mathfrak{H}}|\tilde{G}_N\right] = \frac{e^{\frac{1}{2}-\frac{1}{3\sqrt{2N}}+o(N^{-\frac{1}{2}})}G_N X_N}{N}$$
$$\times \int_0^1 \left(1+\sqrt{\frac{2}{N}}z\right)^{\frac{N}{2}-1}e^{-\frac{X_N z}{\sqrt{2N}}}dz. \qquad (58)$$

The Taylor expansion of $\log\left(1+\sqrt{\frac{2}{N}}z\right)$, $0 \leq z \leq 1$, is given by

$$\log\left(1+\sqrt{\frac{2}{N}}z\right) = \sqrt{\frac{2}{N}}z - \frac{1}{N}z^2 + o(N^{-1}). \qquad (59)$$

Applying this expansion (59) to a function $\left(1+\sqrt{\frac{2}{N}}z\right)^{\frac{N}{2}-1}$, we have

$$\left(1+\sqrt{\frac{2}{N}}z\right)^{\frac{N}{2}-1} = e^{(\frac{N}{2}-1)\left(\sqrt{\frac{2}{N}}z-\frac{1}{N}z^2+o(N^{-1})\right)}$$
$$= e^{\sqrt{\frac{N}{2}}z-\frac{z^2}{2}+No(N^{-1})}e^{-\sqrt{\frac{2}{N}}z+o(N^{-\frac{1}{2}})}. \qquad (60)$$

Substituting (60) into the integrand in (58) yields that

$$\mathbb{E}\left[\langle -DL^{-1}\tilde{G}_N, DG\rangle_{\mathfrak{H}}|\tilde{G}_N\right] = \frac{e^{\frac{1}{2}-\frac{1}{3\sqrt{2N}}+o(N^{-\frac{1}{2}})}G_N X_N}{N}$$
$$\times \int_0^1 e^{-\frac{z^2}{2}-\frac{X_N z}{\sqrt{2N}}+\sqrt{\frac{N}{2}}z+o(N^{-\frac{1}{2}})}dz. \qquad (61)$$

From (36) and (53), the drift coefficient of diffusion is given by

$$
\begin{aligned}
\frac{1}{2}a(G_N) &= \frac{e^{\frac{1}{2}}}{p_F(G_N)} \int_{\log G_N - 1}^{\log G_N} \frac{1}{\sqrt{2\pi}} e^{-\frac{z^2}{2}} dz \\
&= \sqrt{2\pi} e^{\frac{1}{2}} G_N e^{\frac{1}{2}\left(\frac{1}{\sqrt{2N}}(X_N - N)\right)^2} \int_{-\frac{1}{\sqrt{2N}}(X_N - N) - 1}^{-\frac{1}{\sqrt{2N}}(X_N - N)} \frac{1}{\sqrt{2\pi}} e^{-\frac{z^2}{2}} dz \\
&= \frac{e^{\frac{1}{2}} G_N e^{\frac{1}{4N}(X_N - N)^2}}{\sqrt{2N}} \int_{X_N}^{X_N + \sqrt{2N}} e^{-\frac{(y-N)^2}{4N}} dz \\
&= \frac{e^{\frac{1}{2}} G_N}{\sqrt{2N}} \int_{X_N}^{X_N + \sqrt{2N}} e^{-\frac{(y-X_N)^2}{4N} - \frac{(X_N - N)(y-X_N)}{2N}} dy.
\end{aligned}
\qquad (62)
$$

The use of the change of variables $\frac{(y-X_N)}{\sqrt{2N}} = z$ makes the right-hand side of (62) equal to

$$
\frac{1}{2}a(G_N) = e^{\frac{1}{2}} G_N \int_0^1 e^{-\frac{z^2}{2} - \frac{X_N z}{\sqrt{2N}} + \sqrt{\frac{N}{2}} z} dz. \qquad (63)
$$

From (61) and (63), we write $\frac{1}{2}a(G_N) - g_{\bar{G}_N}(\bar{G}_N) = D_{1,N} + D_{2,N} + D_{3,N}$, where

$$
\begin{aligned}
D_{1,N} &= e^{\frac{1}{2}}\left(1 - e^{-\frac{1}{3\sqrt{2N}} + o(N^{-\frac{1}{2}})}\right) G_N \\
&\quad \times \int_0^1 e^{-\frac{z^2}{2} - \frac{X_N z}{\sqrt{2N}} + \sqrt{\frac{N}{2}} z} dz, \\
D_{2,N} &= e^{\frac{1}{2} - \frac{1}{3\sqrt{2N}} + o(N^{-\frac{1}{2}})} G_N \left(1 - \frac{X_N}{N}\right) \\
&\quad \times \int_0^1 e^{-\frac{z^2}{2} - \frac{X_N z}{\sqrt{2N}} + \sqrt{\frac{N}{2}} z} dz, \\
D_{3,N} &= e^{\frac{1}{2} - \frac{1}{3\sqrt{2N}} + o(N^{-\frac{1}{2}})} G_N \frac{X_N}{N} \\
&\quad \times \int_0^1 e^{-\frac{z^2}{2} - \frac{X_N z}{\sqrt{2N}} + \sqrt{\frac{N}{2}} z} (1 - e^{o(N^{-\frac{1}{2}})}) dz.
\end{aligned}
$$

Lemma 2. *For every $x > 0$, we have*

$$
\mathbb{E}[G_N^x] = e^{\frac{x^2}{2} + o_x(N^{-\beta})}. \qquad (64)
$$

where $0 < \beta < \frac{1}{2}$.

Proof. We write $G_N = e^{\sqrt{\frac{N}{2}}} \times e^{-\frac{X_N}{\sqrt{2N}}}$, where $X_N \sim \Gamma(\frac{N}{2}, \frac{1}{2})$. Hence,

$$
\begin{aligned}
\mathbb{E}[G_N^x] &= e^{x\sqrt{\frac{N}{2}}} \mathbb{E}\left[e^{-\frac{x}{\sqrt{2N}} X_N}\right] \\
&= e^{x\sqrt{\frac{N}{2}}} \left(1 + \frac{2x}{\sqrt{2N}}\right)^{-\frac{N}{2}}.
\end{aligned}
\qquad (65)
$$

Since

$$
\log\left(1 + \frac{2x}{\sqrt{2N}}\right) = \frac{2x}{\sqrt{2N}} - \frac{2x^2}{2N} + o_x(N^{-\alpha}), \quad \alpha < \frac{3}{2},
$$

we have

$$\left(1 + \frac{2x}{\sqrt{2N}}\right)^{-\frac{N}{2}} = e^{-\frac{N}{2}\log\left(1+\frac{2x}{\sqrt{2N}}\right)}$$

$$= e^{-x\sqrt{\frac{N}{2}}+\frac{x^2}{2}+o_x(N^{-\beta})}, \quad 0 < \beta < \frac{1}{2}. \tag{66}$$

Substituting (66) into (65) proves this lemma. □

Next, we estimate $\mathbb{E}[|D_{k,N}|]$, $k = 1, 2, 3$. The Cauchy–Schwartz inequality and Lemma 2 give the estimate

$$\begin{aligned}
\mathbb{E}[|D_{1,N}|] &\leq e^{\frac{1}{2}}|1 - e^{-\frac{1}{3\sqrt{2N}}+o(N^{-\frac{1}{2}})}|\sqrt{\mathbb{E}[G_N^2]} \\
&\quad \times \left(\int_0^1 e^{-z^2}\mathbb{E}[G_N^{2z}]dz\right)^{\frac{1}{2}} \\
&\leq \frac{e}{3\sqrt{2N}}(1+o(1))e^{o(1)} \leq \frac{c}{\sqrt{N}}.
\end{aligned} \tag{67}$$

By Hölder inequality and Lemma 2, we have

$$\begin{aligned}
\mathbb{E}[|D_{2,N}|] &\leq e^{\frac{1}{2}-\frac{1}{3\sqrt{2N}}+o(N^{-\frac{1}{2}})}(\mathbb{E}[G_N^3])^{\frac{1}{3}}\frac{(\mathbb{E}[|N-X_N|^3])^{\frac{1}{3}}}{N} \\
&\quad \times \left(\int_0^1 e^{-\frac{3z^2}{2}}\mathbb{E}[G_N^{3z}]dz\right)^{\frac{1}{3}} \\
&\leq e^{\frac{1}{2}-\frac{1}{3\sqrt{2N}}+o(N^{-\frac{1}{2}})}e^{\frac{3}{2}+o(N^{-\beta})}\left(\mathbb{E}\left[\left(\frac{N-X_N}{\sqrt{2N}}\right)^4\right]\right)^{\frac{1}{4}}\sqrt{\frac{2}{N}} \\
&\quad \times \left(\int_0^1 e^{3z^2+o_z(N^{-\beta})}dz\right)^{\frac{1}{3}} \\
&\leq e^{\frac{1}{2}-\frac{1}{3\sqrt{2N}}+o(N^{-\frac{1}{2}})}e^{\frac{3}{2}+o(N^{-\beta})}\left(3+\frac{12}{N}\right)^{\frac{1}{4}}\sqrt{\frac{2}{N}}e^{1+o(N^{-\beta})} \\
&\leq \frac{c}{\sqrt{N}}.
\end{aligned} \tag{68}$$

Similarly,

$$\begin{aligned}
\mathbb{E}[|D_{3,N}|] &\leq e^{\frac{1}{2}-\frac{1}{3\sqrt{2N}}+o(N^{-\frac{1}{2}})}(\mathbb{E}[G_N^3])^{\frac{1}{3}}\frac{(\mathbb{E}[|X_N|^3])^{\frac{1}{3}}}{N} \\
&\quad \times \left(\int_0^1 e^{-\frac{3z^2}{2}}\mathbb{E}[G_N^{3z}]dz\right)^{\frac{1}{3}}|1-e^{o(N^{-\frac{1}{2}})}| \\
&\leq e^{\frac{1}{2}-\frac{1}{3\sqrt{2N}}+o(N^{-\frac{1}{2}})}e^{\frac{3}{2}+o(N^{-\beta})}(1+o(1)) \\
&\quad \times e^{1+o(N^{-\beta})}|1-e^{o(N^{-\frac{1}{2}})}| \\
&\leq \frac{c}{\sqrt{N}}.
\end{aligned} \tag{69}$$

Combining the bounds in (67), (68) and (69), we obtain

$$\begin{aligned}|\mathbb{E}[f(G_N) - f(F)]| &\leq \|h'_f\|_\infty \mathbb{E}\left[\left|\frac{1}{2}a(G_N) - g_{\bar{G}_N}(\bar{G}_N)\right|\right] \\ &\leq \frac{c}{\sqrt{N}}.\end{aligned} \quad (70)$$

Therefore, we find that the rate of convergence of the general distance is of order $\frac{1}{\sqrt{N}}$.

6. Conclusions and Future Works

When a random variable F follows the invariant measure that admits a density and a differentiable random variable G in the sense of Malliavin allows a density function, this paper derives an upper bound on several probabilistic distances (e.g., Kolmogorov distance, total variation distance, Wasserstein distance, and Forter–Mourier distance, etc.) between the laws of F and G in terms of two densities. Among these distances, it is well known that the upper bound of the Kolmogorov and total variation distance can be easily expressed in terms of densities. The significant feature of our works is to show that the bounds of distances other than the two distances mentioned above can be expressed in some form of two density functions. An insight into the main result of this study is that it is possible by applying our results to express an upper bound for the distance of two distributions in terms of two density functions even when it is difficult to express the distance as a density function of two distributions.

Future works will be carried out in two directions: (1) Using the results worked in this paper, we plan to conduct a study on the upper bound that is more rigorous than the results obtained in the papers [15,17]. (2) In the case when G is a random variable belonging to a fixed Wiener chaos, we will prove the fourth moment theorem by using the bound obtained in this paper.

Author Contributions: Conceptualization, Y.-T.K. and H.-S.P.; Methodology, H.-S.P.; Writing—original draft, H.-S.P.; Writing—review and editing, H.-S.P.; Funding acquisition, H.-S.P. All authors have read and agreed to the published version of the manuscript.

Funding: This research was supported by Hallym University Research Fund (HRF-202209-001).

Data Availability Statement: Not applicable.

Acknowledgments: We are very grateful to the anonymous referees for their suggestions and valuable advice.

Conflicts of Interest: The authors declare no conflict of interest.

References

1. Nualart, D.; Peccati, G. Central limit theorems for sequences of multiple stochastic integrals. *Annu. Probab.* **2005**, *33*, 177–193. [CrossRef]
2. Nourdin, I.; Peccati, G. Stein's method on Wiener Chaos. *Probab. Theory Relat. Fields* **2009**, *145*, 75–118. [CrossRef]
3. Kim, Y.T.; Park, H.S. An Edgeworth expansion for functionals of Gaussian fields and its applications. *Stoch. Process. Appl.* **2018**, *44*, 312–320. [CrossRef]
4. Nourdin, I.; Viens, F.G. Density formula and concentration inequalities with Malliavin calculus. *Electron. J. Probab.* **2009**, *14*, 2287–2309. [CrossRef]
5. Nourdin, I.; Peccati, G. Stein's method meets Malliavin calculus: A short survey with new estimates. In *Recent Development in Stochastic Dynamics and Stochasdtic Analysis*; Interdisciplinary Mathematical Sciences; World Scientific Publishing: Hackensack, NJ, USA , 2010; Volume 8, pp. 207–236
6. Nourdin, I.; Peccati, G. *Normal Approximations with Malliavin Calculus: From Stein's Method to Universality*; Cambridge Tracts in Mathematica; Cambridge University Press: Cambridge, UK, 2012; Volume 192.
7. Nualart, D. *The Malliavin Calculus and Related Topics*, 2nd ed.; Probability and Its Applications; Springer: Berlin Heidelberg, Germany, 2006.
8. Chen, L.H.Y.; Goldstein, L.; Shao, Q-M. *Normal Approximation by Stein's Method*; Probability and Its Applications; Springer: Berlin/Heidelberg, Germany, 2011.

9. Stein, C. A bound for the error in the normal approximation to the distribution of a sum of dependent random variables. In Proceedings of the Sixth Berkeley Symposium on Mathematical Statistics and Probability, Volume II: Probability Theory, Berkeley, CA, USA, 21 June–18 July 1970; University of California Press: Berkeley, CA, USA, 1972; pp. 583–602.
10. Stein, C. *Approximate Computation of Expectations*; IMS: Hayward, CA, USA, 1986.
11. Eden, R.; Viens, F. General upper and lower tail estimates using Malliavin calculus and Stein's equations. *arXiv* **2010**, arXiv:1007.0514.
12. Nourdin, I.; Peccati, G. Non-central convergence of multiple integrals. *Annu. Probab.* **2009**, *37*, 1412–1426.
13. Kusuoka, S.; Tudor, C.A. Stein's method for invariant measures of diffusions via Malliavin calculus. *Stoch. Process. Appl.* **2012**, *122*, 1627–1651. [CrossRef]
14. Bibby, B.M.; Skovgaard, I.M.; Sorensen, M. Diffusion-type models with given marginals and auto-correlation function. *Bernoulli* **2003**, *11*, 191–220.
15. Bourguin, S.; Campese, S.; Leonenko, N.; Taqqu, M.S. Four moments theorem on Markov chaos. *Annu. Probab.* **2019**, *47*, 1417–1446. [CrossRef]
16. Jameson, G.J.O. A simple proof of Stirling's formula for the gamma function. *Math. Gaz.* **2015**, *99*, 68–74 [CrossRef]
17. Azmoodeh, E.; Campese, S.; Poly, G. Fourth moment theorems for Markov diffusion generators. *J. Funct. Anal.* **2014**, *266*, 2341–2359. [CrossRef]

Disclaimer/Publisher's Note: The statements, opinions and data contained in all publications are solely those of the individual author(s) and contributor(s) and not of MDPI and/or the editor(s). MDPI and/or the editor(s) disclaim responsibility for any injury to people or property resulting from any ideas, methods, instructions or products referred to in the content.

Article

On Structured Random Matrices Defined by Matrix Substitutions

Manuel L. Esquível [1,*] **and Nadezhda P. Krasii** [2]

1. Department of Mathematics, FCT NOVA, and CMA New University of Lisbon, 2829-516 Caparica, Portugal
2. Department of Higher Mathematics, Faculty of Informatics and Computer Engineering, Don State Technical University, 344003 Rostov-on-Don, Russia
* Correspondence: mle@fct.unl.pt

Abstract: The structure of the random matrices introduced in this work is given by deterministic matrices—the skeletons of the random matrices—built with an algorithm of matrix substitutions with entries in a finite field of integers modulo some prime number, akin to the algorithm of one dimensional automatic sequences. A random matrix has the structure of a given skeleton if to the same number of an entry of the skeleton, in the finite field, it corresponds a random variable having, at least, as its expected value the correspondent value of the number in the finite field. Affine matrix substitutions are introduced and fixed point theorems are proven that allow the consideration of steady states of the structure which are essential for an efficient observation. For some more restricted classes of structured random matrices the parameter estimation of the entries is addressed, as well as the convergence in law and also some aspects of the spectral analysis of the random operators associated with the random matrix. Finally, aiming at possible applications, it is shown that there is a procedure to associate a canonical random surface to every random structured matrix of a certain class.

Keywords: random fields; random Matrices; random linear operators; notions of recurrence; symbolic dynamics; automata sequences

MSC: 60G60; 60B20; 47B80; 37B20; 37B10; 11B85

Citation: Esquível, M.L.; Krasii, N.P. On Structured Random Matrices Defined by Matrix Substitutions. *Mathematics* **2023**, *11*, 2505. https://doi.org/10.3390/math11112505

Academic Editor: Luca Gemignani

Received: 30 March 2023
Revised: 16 May 2023
Accepted: 16 May 2023
Published: 29 May 2023

Copyright: © 2023 by the authors. Licensee MDPI, Basel, Switzerland. This article is an open access article distributed under the terms and conditions of the Creative Commons Attribution (CC BY) license (https://creativecommons.org/licenses/by/4.0/).

1. Introduction

Let us start with some motivations. A generic problem in *Big Data* analysis may have as a starting point a large matrix having columns to represent the questions and the lines to represent the subject's answers (see [1], p. 28). The typical observed matrix may appear to be random. The questions can admit answers that can be either categorical—and so can be modelled by random variables taking values in a finite set—or be quantitative and be modelled by random variables taking values in some set of numbers; in this case, we can also have random variables taking values in a finite set by consider a partition in intervals of the range of the real valued random variables. A natural generic question about these matrices is to determine the existence of a possible structure of the matrix. One initial idea, to better understand this line of problems, is to build matrices with random entries but with a prescribed structure and try to recover this structure by means of some statistical tests or by the spectral analysis of the matrix. These ideas give a practical motivation for this study.

Let us situate our work in the context of the subject of *substitutions*. The analysis of *scalar* or *string* substitutions so to say, is a widely studied subject for which [2,3] are comprehensive references. Important results in the subject of *substitutions* are to be found also under the denomination of *automated sequences*, for instance in [4,5]. To the best of our present knowledge, the study of matrix valued substitutions has received no special attention in the literature. In this work, we propose a first approach to this topic. There has been work in multidimensional substitutions but in a different perspective than the adopted here that can be studied in [6–8] and in the chapter by J. Peyriére in [9] and other references therein.

An important starting point of the study of spectral statistics of random matrices is the work [10]. In it, the author focuses on three ensembles of asymmetric Gaussian random matrices derived from the Gaussian Orthogonal, Gaussian Unitary and Gaussian Symplectic random matrix ensembles by relaxing the Hermitian character. The three sets of matrices have a common Gaussian probability measure but they exhibit profound differences in their spectral patterns, differences that are qualitatively described in this work although the quantitative description was further improved by other authors. The difficult study of generic properties of random matrices related to the spectral analysis has received much attention in recent years as perfectly demonstrated in the following works: [11–18]. Readable introductions to the subject are presented in [19–25].

For a remarkable general formulation of the circular law that is most useful for our purposes we will refer the following result that conveys the flavour of an universality result that may be a relevant guide for the statistical analysis of possible existing particular types of structure in large observed matrices.

Theorem 1 (Circular law, Tao and Wu [22]). *If M_n is a $n \times n$ matrix with entries that are independent identically distributed with a complex centred and standardised random variable. Then, given,*

$$\mu_{\frac{M}{\sqrt{n}}}(x,y) := \frac{1}{n} \#\{1 \leq i \leq n : \Re \lambda_i \leq x, \Im \lambda_i \leq y\},$$

the empirical spectral distribution of the eigenvalues λ_i of $(1/\sqrt{n})M_n$, we have that the sequence $(\mu_{\frac{M}{\sqrt{n}}}(x,y))_{n \geq 1}$ converges to the uniform measure on the unit disc given by:

$$d\mu_{circular}(x,y) = \frac{1}{\pi} \mathbb{1}_{\{|x|^2+|y|^2 \leq 1\}}(x,y) dx dy.$$

We stress that until this optimal formulation was reached, several other technically involved formulations were obtained attesting the intrinsic difficulty of the subject, displayed in the works on the subject first referred above. Let us quote Terence Tao for a synthesis of the recent short history of the subject: *A rigorous proof of the circular law was then established by Bai, assuming additional moment and boundedness conditions on the individual entries. These additional conditions were then slowly removed in a sequence of papers by Gotze–Tikhimirov, Girko, Pan–Zhou, and Tao–Vu .*

We now refer to recent developments in the study of random matrices having some structure, the main topic that is dealt with in the present work, in particular results on the spacing distribution, on invertibility, and appearance of large structures and on the spectral analysis of these random matrices. These works may give an idea of the amount of exploratory work needed in the subject of random matrices with structure.

In [26], the authors consider four specific sparse patterned random matrices, namely the Symmetric Circulant, Reverse Circulant, Toeplitz, and the Hankel matrices. The entries are assumed to be Bernoulli with success probability linearly decreasing to zero. The moment approach is used to show that the expected empirical spectral distribution converges weakly for all these sparse matrices. The work in [27] is a complementary reference where the author investigates the existence and properties of the limiting spectral distribution of different patterned random matrices as the dimension grows. The method of moments and normal approximation with some combinatorics is used to deal with the Wigner matrix, the sample covariance matrix, the Toeplitz matrix, the Hankel matrix, the sample auto-covariance matrix, and the k-Circulant matrices.

In [28], a bound on the growth of the smallest singular value is found for random matrices with independent uniformly anti-concentrated entries with no restrictions on the null mean or identical distribution of the entries. The result obtained covers inhomogeneous matrices with different variances of the entries as long as the sum of second moments has sub-quadratic growth with the order of the matrix. Following this work, the reference [29] extends the results of Tao and Vu and Krishnapur on the universality of empirical spectral distributions to a class of inhomogeneous complex random matrices where the entries are linear images of standardised independent random variables satisfying a lower bound and Pastur's condition. The proof uses an anti-concentration for sums of non-identically distributed independent complex random variables.

In [30], the semicircle law is established for a sequence of random symmetric matrices that may be considered as adjacency matrices of random graphs; the random matrices have independent entries given by the product of independent standardised random variables, the weight of the edges, with Bernoulli random variables that gives the probability of the edge. The empirical distribution of the eigenvalues of the normalised random matrix converges in the Kolmogorov distance to the distribution function of the semicircle law under boundedness and average conditions.

The work [31] deals with random ray pattern matrices that is matrices for which each of its nonzero entries has modulus one. A ray pattern matrix corresponds to a weighted digraph. A random model of ray pattern matrices with order n is introduced, where a uniformly random ray pattern matrix is defined to be the adjacency matrix of a simple random digraph whose arcs are weighted with i.i.d. random variables uniformly distributed over the unit circle in the complex plane. In this paper, it is shown that the threshold function for a random ray pattern matrix to be ray nonsingular is $1/n$. This function is also a threshold function for the property that giant strong components appear in the simple random digraph.

The work [32] deals with patterned random matrices which are real symmetric with substantially less independent entries than in real symmetric matrices. The main results are the calculation of spacing distribution for order three matrices deriving the distributions analytically. As expected, spacing distribution displays a range of behaviours based on the structural constraints imposed on the matrices.

In this work, we propose and study an algorithm to build sequences of random matrices, with independent entries, that have a built in structure. Furthermore, we explore some aspects of this kind of random matrices related to identification, spectral analysis, and an idea for applications. An overview of the content of this work is now detailed.

- In Section 2, we present a first example of the algorithm, used to build structured matrices, given by the iterative application of matrix valued substitutions; the second example uses powers of the Kronecker product of a given matrix and is a particular case of the generic algorithm of matrix substitutions. A general procedure of construction of the sequence of structured matrices by substitutions is detailed in Section 3.1.
- In Section 3, we present the results on fixed points of matrix substitutions.
- The randomisation of structured matrices defined by matrix substitutions is studied in Section 4. Preliminary results on the spectral analysis of these random matrices are presented in Section 4.3. An application to modelling is detailed in Section 4.4 with an algorithm to associate a random field to an infinite random matrix of the kind studied in this work.

2. Structured Matrices Built by Substitutions

We start by presenting two examples of an algorithm to build sequences of arbitrary large matrices with entries in a finite set. For technical reasons we suppose that the entries of the structured matrices take values in some finite field, for instance:

$$\mathbb{Z}_p = \mathbb{Z}/p\mathbb{Z} = \{0, 1, 2, \ldots, p-1\},$$

p being a prime number. The identification of the entries of the matrix as elements of $\mathbb{Z}_p$ matters, essentially for the matrix substitution procedure used to build these structured matrices. Further ahead we will also consider that the entries of the matrix represent integer real numbers.

We will proceed to show, in Section 3, that in a certain class of matrix substitution maps we define, namely the affine matrix substitution maps, every such map admits either a fixed point or a periodic point.

2.1. A Matrix Sequence Built by Iterated Application of a Matrix Substitution

In the following examples, we suppose that the matrices entries take values in the field $\mathbb{Z}_3 = \{0, 1, 2\}$. We now consider an example of a sequence of matrices with a structure defined by substitutions. The main idea of the construction of this sequence of matrices is the following. We start with some initial matrix M_0. The second matrix in the sequence, the matrix M_1, is obtained by replacing each term of the M_0 matrix by the matrices given by $\sigma_0, \sigma_1, \sigma_2$ according to the entry of M_0 we are replacing is, respectively, 0, 1, 2.

$$M_0 = \begin{pmatrix} 2 & 0 & 1 \\ 1 & 2 & 1 \\ 1 & 0 & 2 \end{pmatrix} \quad \sigma_0 = \begin{pmatrix} 0 & 1 & 2 \\ 1 & 1 & 2 \\ 2 & 0 & 1 \end{pmatrix} \quad \sigma_1 = \begin{pmatrix} 1 & 0 & 0 \\ 0 & 2 & 0 \\ 1 & 0 & 1 \end{pmatrix} \quad \sigma_2 = \begin{pmatrix} 1 & 2 & 2 \\ 0 & 1 & 2 \\ 0 & 0 & 1 \end{pmatrix}. \quad (1)$$

In Section 3 we present a formal description of this procedure in a more general case. With this algorithm we have that,

$$M_1 = \begin{pmatrix} 1 & 2 & 2 & 0 & 1 & 2 & 1 & 0 & 0 \\ 0 & 1 & 2 & 1 & 1 & 2 & 0 & 2 & 0 \\ 0 & 0 & 1 & 2 & 0 & 1 & 1 & 0 & 1 \\ 1 & 0 & 0 & 1 & 2 & 2 & 1 & 0 & 0 \\ 0 & 2 & 0 & 0 & 1 & 2 & 0 & 2 & 0 \\ 1 & 0 & 1 & 0 & 0 & 1 & 1 & 0 & 1 \\ 1 & 0 & 0 & 0 & 1 & 2 & 1 & 2 & 2 \\ 0 & 2 & 0 & 1 & 1 & 2 & 0 & 1 & 2 \\ 1 & 0 & 1 & 2 & 0 & 1 & 0 & 0 & 1 \end{pmatrix} \quad (2)$$

and also,

$$M_2 = \begin{pmatrix} \text{(27} \times \text{27 matrix)} \end{pmatrix}$$

2.2. A Matrix Sequence Built by Kronecker Power Iterations

An apparently different way of building substitution structured matrices is by means of Kronecker powers of an initially given matrix that we now illustrate. The initial matrix is given by:

$$R_0 = \begin{pmatrix} 2 & 1 & 0 \\ 0 & 1 & 1 \\ 1 & 0 & 2 \end{pmatrix}$$

The sequence of the matrices taking values in $\mathbb{Z}_3 = \{0, 1, 2\}$ is defined by induction for $n + 1$ by taking the Kronecker product of the matrix for index n with R_0 modulo 3 to keep the entries of the matrix in $\mathbb{Z}_3$, that is,

$$R_{n+1} := [R_n \otimes R_0] \pmod{3}.$$

So, the second matrix of the sequence is,

$$R_1 = \begin{pmatrix} 1 & 2 & 0 & 2 & 1 & 0 & 0 & 0 & 0 \\ 0 & 2 & 2 & 0 & 1 & 1 & 0 & 0 & 0 \\ 2 & 0 & 1 & 1 & 0 & 2 & 0 & 0 & 0 \\ 0 & 0 & 0 & 2 & 1 & 0 & 2 & 1 & 0 \\ 0 & 0 & 0 & 0 & 1 & 1 & 0 & 1 & 1 \\ 0 & 0 & 0 & 1 & 0 & 2 & 1 & 0 & 2 \\ 2 & 1 & 0 & 0 & 0 & 0 & 1 & 2 & 0 \\ 0 & 1 & 1 & 0 & 0 & 0 & 0 & 2 & 2 \\ 1 & 0 & 2 & 0 & 0 & 0 & 2 & 0 & 1 \end{pmatrix},$$

and the third matrix of the sequence is:

$$R_2 = \begin{pmatrix} \cdots \end{pmatrix}.$$

Remark 1 (Kronecker power matrices are matrix substitutions). *We observe that the above example of a Kronecker power matrix sequence corresponds to a special kind of substitution, the linear matrix substitution (see Definition 3 ahead). In fact, the algorithm for building a Kronecker power series of matrices is given by the substitutions in the sense of Section 2.1 with the matrices σ_0, σ_1 and σ_2 defined by:*

$$\sigma_0 = \begin{pmatrix} 0 & 0 & 0 \\ 0 & 0 & 0 \\ 0 & 0 & 0 \end{pmatrix} \quad \sigma_1 = R_0 = \begin{pmatrix} 2 & 1 & 0 \\ 0 & 1 & 1 \\ 1 & 0 & 2 \end{pmatrix} \quad \sigma_2 = \begin{pmatrix} 1 & 2 & 0 \\ 0 & 2 & 2 \\ 2 & 0 & 1 \end{pmatrix}.$$

This is a consequence of the fact that computing a Kronecker power sequence starting with the matrix R_0 is equivalent to computing a matrix substitution given by:

$$\sigma_0 = (0 \cdot R_0 \bmod 3) = \mathbf{0}_{3 \times 3}, \quad \sigma_1 = (1 \cdot R_0 \bmod 3) = R_0, \quad \sigma_2 = (2 \cdot R_0 \bmod 3).$$

We observe that the two kinds of substitutions give rise to different structured matrices. For instance, the distribution of the absolute values of the eigenvalues—in $\mathbb{C}$, that is, supposing that the entries are complex—of the seventh iteration of substitutions for these two types of matrix substitutions are different and is shown, as histograms in Figure 1.

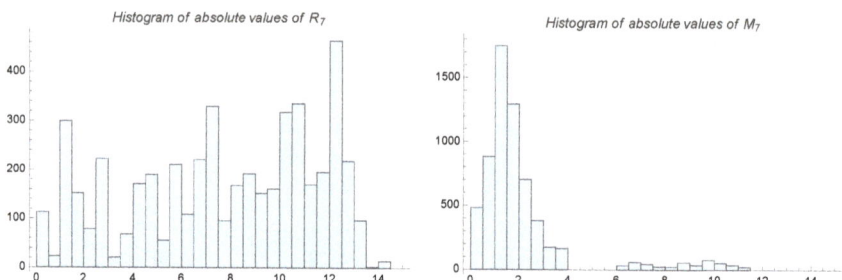

Figure 1. Histogram of absolute values of the eigenvalues of the structured matrices R_7 and M_7.

Another significant difference between the two constructions is noticeable in the form of the dispersion, in the plane, of the eigenvalues that can be seen in Figure 2.

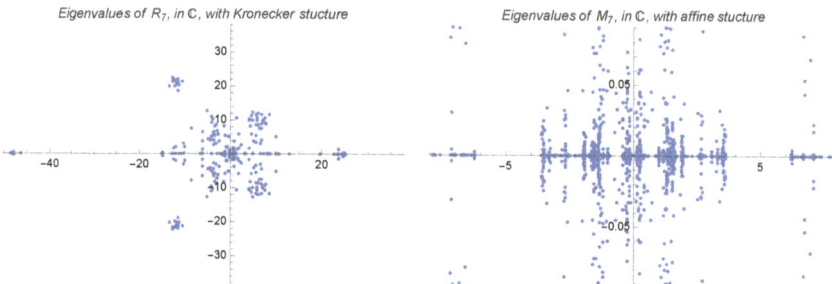

Figure 2. Dispersion or real and imaginary parts of eigenvalues of R_7 and M_7.

Remark 2. *The dispersion of eigenvalues observed in Figure 2 is to be compared to the dispersion of samples of randomised matrices of both kinds, Kronecker and simple, presented in Figure 3 ahead. It is as if the general structure of this dispersion remains despite the randomisation, at least whenever the variance of the random variables is small. This leads to conjecture that it may be important to determine the spectral distribution of the substitution matrices in order to infer for the spectral distribution of the randomised matrices.*

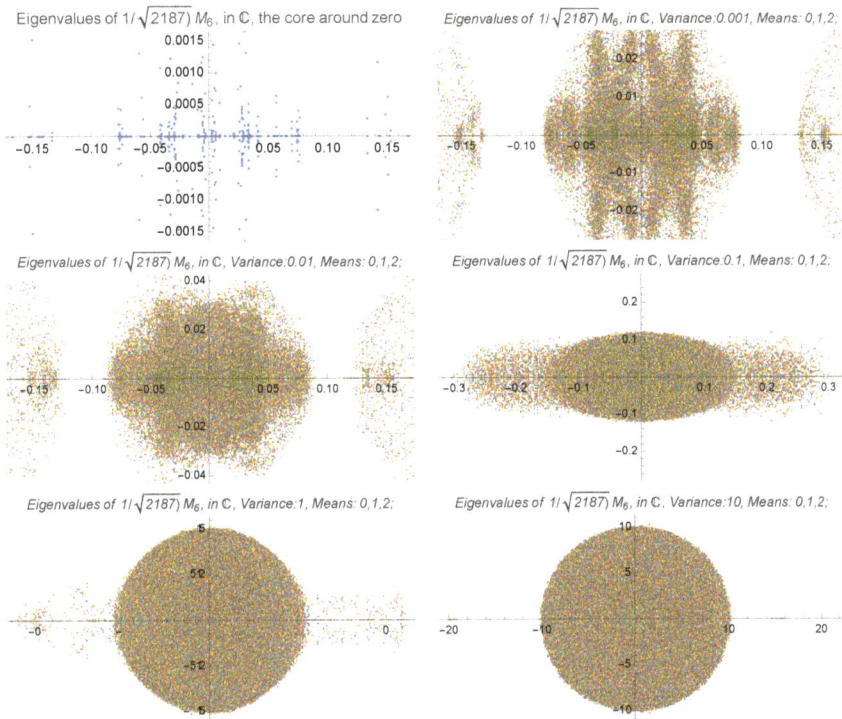

Figure 3. Eigenvalues distribution in $\mathbb{C}$ of a sample of 40 matrices with affine substitution induced structure and increasing variance

3. On the Fixed Points of Affine Matrix Substitutions

In this Section we present fixed point theorems for *affine matrix substitutions*. The work here presented rests upon a procedure to build sequences of structured matrices, by means of matrix substitutions. In order for such matrices to be a usable model, subject to observation, some stable resulting structure should result from the procedure. Our view is that this stable structure should be either a fixed point or at least a periodic point of a map on some space of matrices. We opt to consider spaces of infinite matrices. A general and historic approach to the subject of infinite matrices is given in [33]. A more recent account of important results on this subject is given in [34]. Furthermore, a flavour of a specific kind of problems can be read in [35]. The perspective of considering an infinite matrix as a linear operator on some Banach space of power summable sequences is exploited in the reference book [36] in which the concept of band-dominated operators, corresponding to operators that are limits of operators defined by infinite matrices with a finite number of non-null lines and columns, plays an important role. A particular case of this concept is of crucial importance in our work to prove the existence of a particular kind of observable fixed point.

To begin with we define some spaces of finite and infinite matrices with entries in $\mathbb{Z}_p$.

3.1. Some Spaces of Matrices

Let us briefly describe the setting. For simplicity, let p be a prime number and let $\mathbb{Z}_p = \{0, 1, \ldots, p-1\}$ be the finite field with $\#\mathbb{Z}_p = p$. The set $\mathbb{Z}_p$ may be though as the alphabet when the perspective of finite automata is adopted or, in the context of Big Data the set that codifies the possible answers. We next define the space of infinite matrices with entries in the field $\mathbb{Z}_p$.

$$\mathcal{M}_{+\infty} := \left\{ M = [a_{ij}]_{i,j \geq 1} : a_{ij} \in \mathbb{Z}_p \right\} = \mathbb{Z}_p^{(\mathbb{N}\setminus\{0\}\times\mathbb{N}\setminus\{0\})}. \tag{3}$$

We have that $\mathcal{M}_{+\infty}$ is a vectorial space over the field $\mathbb{Z}_p$. Let $\mathcal{M}_0$ be a particular subspace of $\mathcal{M}_{+\infty}$ which may be identified to a set of finite square matrices if all infinite parts of rows and infinite parts of columns having as entries only $0 \in \mathbb{Z}_p$ are discarded, that is:

$$\mathcal{M}_0 := \left\{ M = [a_{ij}]_{i,j \geq 1} \in \mathcal{M}_{+\infty} : \exists n \geq 1 \ \forall i,j \geq n \ a_{ij} = 0 \right\}.$$

We have that $\mathcal{M}_0$ is a vectorial subspace of $\mathcal{M}_{+\infty}$ and we observe that $M \in \mathcal{M}_0$ can have null lines and columns. We now decompose $\mathcal{M}_0$ by observing that for each $M \in \mathcal{M}_0$ there always exists n_M, the first integer $n \geq 1$ such that for all $i,j > n_M$ we have that $a_{ij} = 0$. Using this property, let us define $\mathcal{M}_{n \times n}^{\#} = \mathcal{M}_{n \times n}^{\#}(\mathbb{Z}_p) \subset \mathcal{M}_0$ as:

$$\mathcal{M}_{n \times n}^{\#} := \left\{ M = [a_{ij}]_{i,j \geq 1} : \exists n \geq 1, (\exists i, a_{in} \neq 0 \lor \exists j, a_{nj} \neq 0) \land (\forall i,j > n, a_{ij} = 0) \right\}.$$

that is, $\mathcal{M}_{n \times n}^{\#}$ is a subset of $\mathcal{M}_0$ of infinite square matrices having a leading principal matrix of exact order n such that neither the column or the line of order n have all its entries equal to zero and such that all columns or rows of order greater or equal to $n+1$ have only zero entries. $\mathcal{M}_{n \times n}^{\#}$ is not a subspace as the sum of two matrices in $\mathcal{M}_{n \times n}^{\#}$ may be an element of $\mathcal{M}_{n-1 \times n-1}^{\#}$ by the fact that the entries belong to $\mathbb{Z}_p$ and the sum is to be computed modulus p. We then may define:

$$\mathcal{M}_{n \times n}(\mathbb{Z}_p) = \mathcal{M}_{n \times n} := \bigcup_{1 \leq k \leq n} \mathcal{M}_{k \times k}^{\#}, \tag{4}$$

which is a vectorial space of infinite matrices over $\mathbb{Z}_p$, a subset of $\mathcal{M}_0$, defined in such a way such that the decomposition is of partition type, and that we have,

$$\mathcal{M}_0 = \bigcup_{n \geq 1} \mathcal{M}_{n \times n}(\mathbb{Z}_p). \tag{5}$$

We now introduce a sequence of infinite matrices associated with a given matrix substitution map. This sequence will be obtained by operating substitutions either on the finite matrix corresponding to the leading principal matrix of the infinite matrix or, directly, on the infinite matrix.

Definition 1 (Matrix substitution map). *The matrix substitution map associated with matrix substitution rules is defined in the following sequence of steps.*

1. *Let us consider the initial state as $M_0 \in \mathcal{M}_{n \times n}(\mathbb{Z}_p)$ for some $n \geq 1$.*
2. *We associate to M_0 its **leading principal matrix** of order n, denoted by $M_0^{<\infty}$ which, we stress, is a finite matrix of order n. Let $\mathcal{M}_{n \times n}^{<\infty}(\mathbb{Z}_p)$ denote the set of the leading principal matrices of order n associated with the elements of $\mathcal{M}_{n \times n}(\mathbb{Z}_p)$, $\mathcal{M}_0$ or $\mathcal{M}_{+\infty}$.*
3. *For technical reasons we will restrain our study by considering that we chose $d \geq 1$ such that for all $k \in \mathbb{Z}_p$ we have σ_k a finite matrix of order d that is, such that $\sigma_k \in \mathcal{M}_{d \times d}^{<\infty}(\mathbb{Z}_p)$. In the applications we may have $d = n$. Let us define the **global substitution rule** $\sigma : \mathbb{Z}_p \mapsto \mathcal{M}_{d \times d}^{<\infty}(\mathbb{Z}_p)$, associated with $\{\sigma_0, \sigma_1, \ldots, \sigma_{p-1}\}$ by:*

$$\forall j \in \mathbb{Z}_p \ \ \sigma(j) = \sum_{k=0}^{p-1} \sigma_k \mathbb{1}_{\{k=j\}}(j), \tag{6}$$

We now have an associated ***finite matrix substitution map*** denoted by $\Phi_\sigma^{<\infty}$ defined by:

$$\forall A = [a_{i,j}]_{1\leq i,j\leq r} \in \mathcal{M}_{n\times n}^{<\infty} \quad \Phi_\sigma^{<\infty}(A) = [\sigma(a_{i,j})]_{1\leq i,j\leq r} \in \mathcal{M}_{d\cdot n\times d\cdot n}^{<\infty}. \quad (7)$$

4. We define ***matrix substitution map*** denoted by Φ_σ by adding to the finite matrix $\Phi_\sigma^{<\infty}(A) \in \mathcal{M}_{d\cdot n\times d\cdot n}^{<\infty}$ infinite rows and columns of entries of $0 \in \mathbb{Z}_p$ in such a way that $\Phi_\sigma(A)$ is an infinite matrix such that we have $\Phi_\sigma(A) \in \mathcal{M}_{n\times n}(\mathbb{Z}_p)$ and such that the leading principal matrix of order n of $\Phi_\sigma(A)$ is precisely $\Phi_\sigma^{<\infty}(A)$.

5. We now define the extension of the notion of a matrix substitution map for matrices in $\mathcal{M}_{n\times n}$, to the space of infinite matrices $\mathcal{M}_{+\infty}$. Given that we supposed that global substitution $\sigma: \mathbb{Z}_p \mapsto \mathcal{M}_{d\times d}^{<\infty}(\mathbb{Z}_p)$ take values in a space of finite matrices of order d, we may define $\Phi_\sigma(M)$ for $M \in \mathcal{M}_{+\infty}$, with $M = [a_{ij}]_{i,j\geq 1}$ as the matrix $[\sigma(a_{ij})]_{i,j\geq 1}$, that is, an infinite matrix having entries matrices $[\sigma_k(a_{ij})]$, for $a_{ij} = k$ with $k \in \mathbb{Z}_p$.

6. The ***matrix substitutions sequence*** denoted by $\mathbf{M}_\sigma \equiv (M_m)_{m\geq 0}$ is defined by induction, for $M_0 = M$ with $M \in \mathcal{M}_{d\cdot n\times d\cdot n}^{<\infty}$ or $M \in \mathcal{M}_{+\infty}$, by:

$$\forall n \geq 0 \quad M_{m+1} = \Phi_\sigma^{<\infty}(M_m), M \in \mathcal{M}_{d\cdot n\times d\cdot n}^{<\infty}; \; M_{m+1} = \Phi_\sigma(M_m), M \in \mathcal{M}_{+\infty}. \quad (8)$$

Remark 3 (A substantiation for operating on finite order matrices). *The procedure of applying matrix substitutions to the leading principal matrix of the infinite matrices is designed to overcome the restriction of having σ_0 always equal to the null matrix with only $0 \in \mathbb{Z}_p$ entries.*

Remark 4 (Generalisations and open problems). *It is possible to generalize this procedure in several ways. For instance, we could have two different matrix substitution maps applied successively. There are several interesting problems under the perspective of this setting.*

(I) Given a sequence of matrices $(A_n)_{n\geq 0}$, satisfying some compatibility conditions, is it possible to determine conditions under which there exists an initial state M_0 and a matrix substitution map Φ_σ such that $(A_n)_{n\geq 0} = \mathbf{M}_\sigma$?

(II) A related and very important problem is to determine the properties of the eigenvalues of the matrices of the sequence $\mathbf{M}_\sigma$ that may be derived from the properties of Φ_σ.

3.2. On the Existence of Fixed Points for Matrix Substitution Maps

In this Section we consider the existence of fixed points of matrix substitution maps both for matrices in $\mathcal{M}_{+\infty}$ and in $\mathcal{M}_0$.

3.2.1. Fixed Points for Matrix Substitution Maps over Infinite Matrices

Let us first deal with fixed points in $\mathcal{M}_{+\infty}$ (see the definition in Formula (3)) of a linear matrix substitution map Φ_σ. We consider the definition of a matrix substitution map given in Definition 1 for matrices in the space of infinite matrices $\mathcal{M}_{+\infty}$. For infinite matrices we will show that a matrix substitution map defined on $\mathcal{M}_{+\infty}$ may be seen as a usual substitution of constant length on a finite set in the sense of ([3], p. 87).

Theorem 2 (On the existence of fixed points for infinite matrices). *Let $\sigma: \mathbb{Z}_p \mapsto \mathcal{M}_{d\times d}^{<\infty}(\mathbb{Z}_p)$ be a global substitution taking values in a space of finite matrices, of order d, with entries in $\mathbb{Z}_p$, and let Φ_σ be the associated matrix substitution map defined on $\mathcal{M}_{+\infty}$. Then, there exists an integer ρ and $M \in \mathcal{M}_{+\infty}$ such that,*

$$M = \Phi_\sigma^\rho(M) := \underbrace{\Phi_\sigma \circ \Phi_\sigma \circ \cdots \circ \Phi_\sigma}_{\rho \text{ times}}(M),$$

that is, M is a fixed point for the matrix substitution map $\Phi_\sigma^\rho(M)$ defined for $M \in \mathcal{M}_{+\infty}$.

Proof. We will show that to each matrix substitution map there corresponds a univocal substitution map in the usual sense and then, we will apply a well known result that guarantees the existence of fixed points for usual substitution maps (see [3], pp. 87–88). We first observe that given $s = [s_{ij}]_{1 \leq i,j \leq d}$ a $d \times d$ matrix with entries in $\mathbb{Z}_p$ we have an enumeration of these entries given by $(\widetilde{s}_k)_{k=1,\ldots,d^2}$ with:

$$s_{ij} = \widetilde{s}_{(i-1)d+j} = \widetilde{s}_k .$$

This type of enumeration of a finite matrix will be applied to to the matrices of the substitutions σ_k in order to convert the matrix σ_k in a *word* of length constituted by letters taken from $\mathbb{Z}_p$. The reversion of this enumeration works as follows. Given a finite word having d^2 letters we associate to it a $d \times d$ square matrix having as its first line the first d letters of the word, as its second line the letters of order $d+1$ to $2d^2$ and so on and so forth. It is clear that applying the enumeration and then the reversion gives the initial matrix.

Next, we have that given an infinite matrix, $M = [m_{ij}]_{i,j \geq 1}$ with entries in $\mathbb{Z}_p$ we have an enumeration of these entries given by $(\widetilde{m}_l)_{l \geq 1}$ with:

$$m_{ij} = \widetilde{m}_{\frac{(i+j-1)(i+j-2)}{2}+i} = \widetilde{m}_l .$$

This second type of enumeration will be applied to convert an infinite matrix with entries in $\mathbb{Z}_p$ in an infinite *word*. Again, let us detail how the reversion of this enumeration process works. Take an infinite word and consider the associated infinite matrix as follows: the first letter of the word is the first entry of the matrix; the second and the third letters of the word give the first diagonal, just below the first entry, in the direction up-down; the forth, fifth, and sixth letters of the word give the second diagonal, just below the first diagonal, in the direction up–down and so on and so forth. It is clear also that applying the second enumeration and then this reversion process gives the initial matrix. Now, take the global matrix substitution rule σ that replaces each $k \in \mathbb{Z}_p$ by the $d \times d$ matrix σ_k. Consider the associated words $\widetilde{\sigma}_k$ with letters in $\mathbb{Z}_p$ obtained by applying the first enumeration to the matrices σ_k. Take an infinite matrix M with entries in $\mathbb{Z}_p$ and apply the second enumeration rule to M to obtain an infinite word $\widetilde{M} = (\widetilde{m}_l)_{l \geq 1}$; we may define first an usual substitution rule $\widetilde{\sigma}$ on $\mathbb{Z}_p$ by $\widetilde{\sigma}(k) = \widetilde{\sigma}_k$ and also an usual word substitution map $\widetilde{\Phi}_\sigma$ on the set of infinite words built with letters in $\mathbb{Z}_p$ by:

$$\widetilde{\Phi}_\sigma(\widetilde{M}) = (\widetilde{\Phi}_\sigma(\widetilde{m}_l))_{l \geq 1} ,$$

which is an infinite word obtained from the infinite word $\widetilde{M}$ by replacing each one of its letters $k \in \mathbb{Z}_p$ by the correspondent word $\widetilde{\sigma}_k$. Recall Proposition V.1 in ([3], p. 88) that guarantees the existence of some infinite word $\widetilde{M}$ and some integer ρ such that:

$$\widetilde{\Phi}_\sigma^\rho(\widetilde{M}) = \underbrace{\widetilde{\Phi}_\sigma \circ \widetilde{\Phi}_\sigma \circ \cdots \circ \widetilde{\Phi}_\sigma}_{\rho \text{ times}}(M) = \widetilde{M} ,$$

and consider the infinite matrix M such that the second type of enumeration applied to it returns $\widetilde{M}$. It is clear that if we apply the second enumeration process to $\Phi_\sigma^\rho(M)$ we obtain $\widetilde{\Phi}_\sigma^\rho(\widetilde{M})$ which is equal to $\widetilde{M}$ and by reverting the enumeration process on $\widetilde{M}$ we finally obtain M, that is:

$$\Phi_\sigma^\rho(M) = M ,$$

as stated above. □

3.2.2. Fixed Points for Matrix Affine Substitutions Maps Defined over Finite Matrices

We can obtain finite dimensional fixed points of matrix substitution maps by applying Theorem 2.

Definition 2 (Generalised fixed points for a finite matrix substitution map)**.** *Let us consider a given integer $n \geq 1$. The matrix $M \in \mathcal{M}_{n \times n}^{<\infty}(\mathbb{Z}_p)$ (see Definition 1) is a finite matrix fixed point*

of the matrix substitution map $(\Phi_\sigma^{<\infty})$ if and only if there exists an integer $\rho \geq 1$ such that the leading principal part of order n of $(\Phi_\sigma^{<\infty})^\rho(M)$ is equal to M.

Proposition 1. *For any integer $n \geq 2$ and a given matrix substitution map $(\Phi_\sigma^{<\infty})$ there exists fixed points in the sense of Definition 2.*

Proof. We only have to apply Theorem 2 in order to obtain a fixed point of order ρ of $M \in \mathcal{M}_{+\infty}$ for the matrix substitution map Φ_σ and then to consider the leading principal matrix of order n of M. We obtain that $(\Phi_\sigma^{<\infty})^\rho(M) \in \mathcal{M}_{nd\rho \times nd\rho}^{<\infty}(\mathbb{Z}_p)$ and since we have that the leading principal part of $\Phi_\sigma^\rho(M)$ of order $nd\rho$ is equal to the finite matrix $(\Phi_\sigma^{<\infty})^\rho(M)$ we will have that the leading principal part of order n of $(\Phi_\sigma^{<\infty})^\rho(M)$ is equal to M. □

We will pursue next the goal of obtaining fixed points of matrix substitution maps in an algorithmic way, that is, by dealing with finite matrices. Let us now introduce topological structures over the spaces of matrices defined in Section 3. In order to define semi-norms over $\mathcal{M}_{n\times n}$, a space we may identify to the space of finite matrices of order n over the field $\mathbb{Z}_p = \mathbb{Z}/p\mathbb{Z}$, we will consider the trivial absolute value $|\cdot|_p$ (see [37], pp. 197–198), given by:

$$\forall k \in \mathbb{Z}_p \quad |k|_p = \begin{cases} 0 & \text{if } k = 0 \\ 1 & \text{if } k \neq 0 \end{cases}.$$

If $\mathbb{Z}_p$ is considered as a vectorial space over itself then, due to the properties of an absolute value over a field, we have that $|\cdot|_p$ may be considered as a norm over the vectorial space $\mathbb{Z}_p$. For $M \in \mathcal{M}_{n\times n}(\mathbb{Z}_p)$ let the modified sum semi-norm be given, for $m > 1$, by:

$$\|M\|_m := \frac{1}{m^2} \sum_{1 \leq i,j \leq m} |a_{ij}|_p \leq 1. \tag{9}$$

Essentially, $\|M\|_m$ counts the proportion of nonzero elements in the leading principal matrix of order m of M. We observe that—with m the order of the semi-norm and n the order of the matrix—as $m > n$ grows, $\|M\|_m$ will tend to zero. $\|\cdot\|_m$ is a semi-norm as the proportion of nonzero entries of the sum of two matrices—with entries in the field $\mathbb{Z}_p$—can only decrease with respect with the sum of the proportions of each matrix. As a consequence of the decomposition of $\mathcal{M}_{n\times n}(\mathbb{Z}_p)$ in Formula (4), we have that:

$$\|M\|_{[n]} = \|M\|_{\mathcal{M}_{n\times n}(\mathbb{Z}_p)} := \frac{1}{n^2} \sum_{1 \leq i,j \leq n} |a_{ij}|_p \leq 1, \tag{10}$$

is a norm over $\mathcal{M}_{n\times n}(\mathbb{Z}_p)$ and, with the norm $\|M\|_{\mathcal{M}_{n\times n}(\mathbb{Z}_p)}$ the space of matrices $\mathcal{M}_{n\times n}(\mathbb{Z}_p)$ is, obviously, a Fréchet space. Now, let $j : \mathcal{M}_{n\times n} \mapsto \mathcal{M}_{(n+1)\times(n+1)}$ be the natural injection which is well defined taking into account Formula (4). Since we have that, for $M \in \mathcal{M}_{n\times n} \setminus \mathcal{M}_{n+1\times n+1}$ that for $i = n+1$ or $j = n+1$, $|a_{ij}|_p = 0$, we then have,

$$\begin{aligned}\|j(M)\|_{[n+1]} &= \frac{1}{(n+1)^2} \sum_{1 \leq i,j \leq n+1} |a_{ij}|_p \\ &\leq \frac{1}{(n+1)^2} \sum_{1 \leq i,j \leq n} |a_{ij}|_p + \frac{1}{(n+1)^2} \sum_{i=n+1 \vee j=n+1} |a_{ij}|_p \\ &\leq \frac{1}{n^2} \sum_{1 \leq i,j \leq n} |a_{ij}|_p = \|M\|_{[n]}.\end{aligned} \tag{11}$$

As a consequence j maps continuously $(\mathcal{M}_{n\times n}, \|\cdot\|_n)$ into $(\mathcal{M}_{n+1\times n+1}, \|\cdot\|_{n+1})$. Furthermore, as a consequence, we may consider over $\mathcal{M}_0$ the inductive topology generated by the family of Fréchet spaces $(\mathcal{M}_{n\times n}, \|\cdot\|_n)_{n\geq 1}$ (see ([38], pp. 53–65) or ([39], pp. 57–60), or ([40], pp. 222–225)).

Remark 5 (On the topology of the space $\mathcal{M}_0$). *Let τ be this topology over $\mathcal{M}_0$. As a consequence of the well known results in the theory of LF spaces, we have that:*

1. *The restriction of τ to $\mathcal{M}_{n\times n}$ coincides with the norm topology $\|\cdot\|_n$.*
2. *$(\mathcal{M}_0, \tau)$ is a Hausdorf space.*
3. *We have the Dieudonné–Schwartz lemma, that is, if a set B is bounded in $(\mathcal{M}_0, \tau)$ then there exists some $n_b \geq 1$ such that $B \subset \mathcal{M}_{n_b \times n_b}$.*
4. *A sequence $(M_n)_{n\geq 1}$ converges in $(\mathcal{M}_0, \tau)$ if and and only if there exists some $n_c \geq 1$ such that $\{M_n : n \geq 1\} \subset \mathcal{M}_{n_c \times n_c}$ and the sequence $(M_n)_{n\geq 1}$ converges in $\left(\mathcal{M}_{n_c \times n_c}, \|\cdot\|_{n_c}\right)$.*
5. *We have Köthe's theorem, that is, $(\mathcal{M}_0, \tau)$ is a complete space.*

Remark 6 (A comparable topology). *If we consider over $\mathcal{M}_{+\infty}$ the family of semi-norms $(s_m)_{m\geq 1}$, given by:*

$$s_m\left([a_{ij}]_{i,j\geq 1}\right) := \sup_{n \leq m} \frac{1}{n^2} \sum_{1 \leq i,j \leq n} |a_{ij}|_p, \tag{12}$$

we have that (see [38], p. 64 for a proof of this result) $\mathcal{M}_{+\infty}$ is a Fréchet space, we have that $(\mathcal{M}_0, \tau)$ embeds continuously in $\mathcal{M}_{+\infty}$ and that the closure of $(\mathcal{M}_0, \tau)$ is $\mathcal{M}_{+\infty}$.

Now, let us consider $M_\sigma \equiv (M_n)_{n\geq 0}$ with $M_{n+1} = \Phi_\sigma(M_n)$ Our first goal is to study the contraction properties of Φ_σ over $\mathcal{M}_0$. The second goal is to extend Φ_σ to $\mathcal{M}_{+\infty}$, also as a contraction. This allows us to identify an invariant set. For that purpose we have to identify conditions under which Φ_σ is linear, or affine over $\mathcal{M}_0$.

Definition 3 (Linear matrix substitutions). *The matrix substitution map Φ_σ (see Formulas (6)–(8)) is defined to be a **linear matrix substitution map** over $\mathcal{M}_0$ iff for all $k, k' \in \mathbb{Z}_p$ we have that:*

$$\sigma_k + \sigma_{k'} = \sigma_{(k+k' \bmod p)} \quad \text{and} \quad k' \cdot \sigma_k = \sigma_{(k' \cdot k \bmod p)}. \tag{13}$$

Remark 7 (A substantiation of Definition 3). *With $k + k' \in \mathbb{Z}_p$ and $k \cdot k' \in \mathbb{Z}_p$ we will obviously have that,*

$$\begin{aligned}\Phi_\sigma(M + N) &= [\sigma(a_{ij} + b_{ij})]_{1\leq i,j \leq n} = [\sigma(a_{ij})]_{1\leq i,j\leq n} + [\sigma(b_{ij})]_{1\leq i,j\leq n} \\ &= \Phi_\sigma(M) + \Phi_\sigma(N).\end{aligned}$$

In fact, for the sum property—as for the product property the justification is similar—we have by definition,

$$[\sigma(a_{ij}) = \sigma_k \text{ iff } a_{ij} = k] \quad \text{and} \quad [\sigma(b_{ij}) = \sigma_{k'} \text{ iff } b_{ij} = k'],$$

and so,

$$\sigma(a_{ij}) + \sigma(b_{ij}) = \sigma_k + \sigma_{k'} = \sigma_{(k+k' \bmod p)} = \sigma(a_{ij} + b_{ij}) \text{ iff } a_{ij} + b_{ij} = (k + k' \bmod p).$$

Remark 8 (A consequence of Definition 3). *Condition (13) for having a matrix substitution linear implies that $\sigma_0 = 0 \in \mathbb{Z}_p$ because we should have for all $k \in \{0, 1, 2, \ldots p-1\}$ that $\sigma_0 + \sigma_k = \sigma_k$.*

Remark 9 (Examples of linear matrix global substitution rules). *A first example of a linear matrix substitution in $\mathbb{Z}_3$ is given by:*

$$\sigma_0 = \begin{pmatrix} 0 & 0 \\ 0 & 0 \end{pmatrix} \quad \sigma_1 = \begin{pmatrix} 0 & 2 \\ 1 & 1 \end{pmatrix} \quad \sigma_2 = \begin{pmatrix} 0 & 1 \\ 2 & 2 \end{pmatrix}.$$

Let us return to the example of Section 2.2. We observe that:

$$\sigma_2 + \sigma_1 (\bmod 3) = \sigma_{(2+1 \bmod 3)} = \sigma_0 = 0_{3\times 3},$$

thus showing that the substitution is a linear matrix substitution. A linear matrix substitution is essentially defined by its σ_1 substitution and so, every linear matrix substitution is derived from a Kronecker power matrix equal to σ_1 as defined in Section 2.2. We stress that not all matrix substitutions are linear as the first example in Section 2.1 shows. In fact, with the notations and definitions of this first example, we have that:

$$(\sigma_1 + \sigma_1)_{(\bmod 3)} = \begin{pmatrix} 2 & 0 & 0 \\ 0 & 1 & 0 \\ 2 & 0 & 2 \end{pmatrix} \quad (\sigma_2 - \sigma_0)_{(\bmod 3)} = \begin{pmatrix} 1 & 1 & 0 \\ 2 & 0 & 0 \\ 1 & 0 & 0 \end{pmatrix},$$

and $(\sigma_2 - \sigma_0 \bmod 3) \neq (\sigma_1 + \sigma_1 \bmod 3)$ thus showing that the substitution is not linear.

Remark 10 (On the contraction character of a matrix substitution map). *Let us suppose that we have some matrix with constant entries, for instance:*

$$M = [a_{ij}]_{i,j \geq 1} \in \mathcal{M}_{n \times n} \text{ with } a_{ij} \equiv p - 1.$$

Then, with the usual absolute value over $\mathbb{Z}_p$,

$$\|M\|_{[n]} = \frac{1}{n^2} \sum_{1 \leq i,j \leq n} |a_{ij}|_p = \frac{1}{n^2} \sum_{1 \leq i,j \leq n} 1 = 1.$$

Now suppose, in the worst case scenario, that $\sigma_{p-1} \in \mathcal{M}_{d \times d}^{<\infty}$ is a matrix with all its entries, except one, equal to $p - 1$ and the exception is 0. We now have as a consequence that all the entries of leading principal matrix of order $n + 1$ of $M_{n+1} = \Phi_\sigma(M_n)$ will be equal to $p - 1$ with n^2 entries that will be equal to 0. It then follows that,

$$\|M_{n+1}\|_{[d \cdot n]} = \|\Phi_\sigma(M_n)\|_{[d \cdot n]} = \frac{1}{(d \cdot n)^2} \sum_{1 \leq i,j \leq d \cdot n} |a_{ij}|_p$$

$$= \frac{1}{(d \cdot n)^2} \left[(d \cdot n)^2 - n^2 \right] = 1 - \frac{1}{d^2} = \left(1 - \frac{1}{d^2}\right) \|M\|_{[n]},$$

since $\|M\|_n = 1$. This example shows that the contraction properties of Φ_σ depend on the proportion of zeros vis-a-vis the nonzero entries of the substitutions.

Proposition 2 (Linear matrix substitutions that are contractions). *Let Φ_σ be a linear matrix substitution map associated with a global substitution rule σ such that the maximum number of zeros in each σ_k, for $k \in \{1, \ldots, k-1\}$, is r with $1 \leq r < d^2$. We recall that σ_0 is the square matrix with d^2 entries all equal to $0 \in \mathbb{Z}_p$. Then, the map Φ_σ is a contraction from $\mathcal{M}_{n \times n}$ into $\mathcal{M}_{n \cdot d \times n \cdot d}$ for every $n \geq 1$.*

Proof. Take a matrix $A \in \mathcal{M}_{n \times n}$ such that the number of zero entries in the leading principal matrix of order n of A is s with $0 \leq s < n^2$. The case where A is a null matrix is irrelevant because, in this case, $\Phi_\sigma(A)$ is the null matrix. Then in the leading principal matrix of order nd of $\Phi_\sigma(A)$ there will be at least sd^2 zero entries due to the substitution of each zero in A by d^2 zeros of the matrix σ_0 which is a matrix of order d. Now, there are $n^2 - s$ entries on A which are different of zero and for each of these non-null entries there correspond a maximum of r zero entries in $\Phi_\sigma(A)$. As a consequence the total number of zero entries in $\Phi_\sigma(A)$ is bounded by $sd^2 + (n^2 - s)r$. As such, we have that the proportion of nonzero elements in $\Phi_\sigma(A)$ has the following upper bound:

$$\|\Phi_\sigma(A)\|_{[d \cdot n]} \leq 1 - \frac{sd^2 + (n^2-s)r}{n^2 d^2} = \left(1 - \frac{s}{n^2}\right)\left(1 - \frac{r}{d^2}\right) = \left(1 - \frac{r}{d^2}\right)\|M\|_{[n]}, \quad (14)$$

and so, Φ_σ is a contraction with constant $1 - r/d^2 < 1$. □

Remark 11 (On the fixed points of linear matrix substitutions maps). *We have first to observe that if Φ_σ is a linear matrix substitution map associated with any global substitution rule σ then any null matrix $M = [a_{ij}]_{i,j \geq 1} \in \mathcal{M}_{n \times n}$, that is, such that $a_{ij} \equiv 0 \in \mathbb{Z}_p$, is a fixed point of Φ_σ. In fact, since h $a_{ij} \equiv 0 \in \mathbb{Z}_p$ and $\sigma_0 = 0$ we have,*

$$\Phi_\sigma(M) = M = 0.$$

Let us describe now the non-null other fixed points of Φ_σ, a linear matrix substitution map belonging to $\mathcal{M}_0$ (see Formula (5)). Consider a non-null matrix $M = [a_{ij}]_{i,j \geq 1} \in \mathcal{M}_{n \times n}$ such that $\Phi_\sigma(M) = M$. By recalling that $\Phi_\sigma(M) \in \mathcal{M}_{nd \times nd}$ and reverting to the leading principal matrices of both M—a finite matrix of order n—and $\Phi_\sigma(M)$—which in turn is a finite matrix of order nd—we may conclude that, with $0 \neq a_{11}$, if $a_{11} = k$ for $k \in \{1,2,\ldots,p-1\} \subset \mathbb{Z}_p$, then $\sigma(a_{11}) = \sigma_k(a_{11}) = M \neq 0$. Moreover, we should also have, due to $\Phi_\sigma(M) = M$, that:

$$\forall (i,j) \neq (1,1), a_{ij} \neq a_{11} \text{ and } \forall l \in \{1,2,\ldots,p-1\}, l \neq k \Rightarrow \sigma_l = 0.$$

We may conclude that if we are given a linear matrix substitution map then either the the correspondent global substitution rule has the particular structure described above or there exists no other fixed points in $\mathcal{M}_0$ besides the null matrix.

In order to overcome the limitation of the fixed points for linear matrix substitutions maps we may consider other matrix substitution maps such as the ones defined next.

Definition 4 (Affine matrix substitutions). *A matrix substitution map Φ is an **affine matrix substitution map** if there exists a **linear** global substitution rule σ and a **constant** global substitution rule ν_c such that,*

$$\Phi = \Phi_\sigma +_{(\text{mod } p)} \Phi_{\nu_c} = \Phi_{\sigma +_{(\text{mod } p)} \nu_c}, \quad (15)$$

with Φ_σ the linear matrix substitution map associated with σ and Φ_{ν_c} the constant matrix substitution map associated with ν_c.

Remark 12. *The important equality in the right-hand side of Formula (15) can be verified by resorting to the definition of a matrix substitution map associated with a global substitution rule.*

We will now consider Definition 2 of the generalised fixed points for finite matrix substitution maps. Recall that according to the definition in Formula (7) for we have that $\Phi_\sigma^{<\infty}(M) \in \mathcal{M}_{d \cdot n \times d \cdot n}^{<\infty}$ and introduce the following notation,

$$\Phi_{\sigma + \nu_c}^{<\infty}(M)\big|_n, \quad (16)$$

to denote the leading principal part of order n of $\Phi_{\sigma + \nu_c}^{<\infty}(M)$ for $M \in \mathcal{M}_{n \times n}$.

Theorem 3 (Fixed points of affine matrix substitutions). *Consider an affine matrix substitution $\Phi_{\sigma + \nu_c} = \Phi_\sigma + \Phi_{\nu_c}$ such that for the linear part global substitution rule σ, the maximum number of zeros in each σ_k, for $k \in \{1, \ldots, k-1\}$, is r with $1 \leq r < d^2$. Then we have that:*

1. *$\Phi_{\sigma + \nu_c}$ is a contraction from $\mathcal{M}_{n \times n}$ into $\mathcal{M}_{n \cdot d \times n \cdot d}$ for every $n \geq 1$.*
2. *$\Phi_{\sigma + \nu_c}$ is a contraction from $\mathcal{M}_0$ into $\mathcal{M}_0$.*

3. There exists $s \geq 1$ and $L = [a_{ij}]_{i,j \geq 1} \in \mathcal{M}_{s \times s}$ a fixed point of $\Phi_{\sigma+v_c}$, that is, such that
$$\Phi_{\sigma+v_c}^{<\infty}(L)|_s = L.$$

Proof. The first statement follows from Formula (14) of Proposition 2. Recall that, by Formula (10) we have that $\|M\|_{[n]} = \|M\|_n$ for $M \in \mathcal{M}_{n \times n}$ where for m integer $\|M\|_m$ is the semi-norm defined in Formula (9). For $M, N \in \mathcal{M}_{n \times n}$ we have that:

$$\|\Phi_{\sigma+v_c}(M) - \Phi_{\sigma+v_c}(N)\|_{[d \cdot n]} = \|\Phi_\sigma(M-N)\|_{[d \cdot n]} \leq \left(1 - \frac{r}{d^2}\right) \|M-N\|_{[n]}, \quad (17)$$

thus showing that the second statement is a consequence of the definition of the inductive topology of $\mathcal{M}_0$ and of a natural definition of a contraction in an *LF* topological vector space. The last statement follows from a usual Banach fixed point theorem type argument, suitably modified. We first show the Cauchy sequence contraction inequality. Let $M \in \mathcal{M}_{n \times n}$ be given and, consider the matrix substitutions sequence $M_{\sigma+v_c} \equiv (M_n)_{n \geq 0}$ that is defined, by induction, by:

$$\forall n \geq 0 \quad M_{n+1} = \Phi_{\sigma+v_c}(M_n) = \Phi_{\sigma+v_c}^{(n+1)}(M_0),$$

with $M_0 = M$ and, the iterated application map given, for instance for the second order iteration by $\Phi_{\sigma+v_c}^{(2)} = \Phi_{\sigma+v_c} \circ \Phi_{\sigma+v_c}$. We now show that $M_{\sigma+v_c}$ is a Cauchy sequence in $\mathcal{M}_0$. For that, see ([38], p. 30), we have to show that for every U, a neighbourhood of zero in $\mathcal{M}_0$ there exists some integer $m_0 \geq 1$ such that for all $p \geq 1$ and $m \geq m_0$ we have $M_{m+p} - M_m \in U$. We start by using Formula (17) to establish a contraction Cauchy sequence type inequality.

$$\begin{aligned}
\|M_{m+p} - M_m\|_{[d^{m+p} \cdot n]} &\leq \sum_{k=1}^{p} \|M_{m+k} - M_{m+k-1}\|_{[d^{m+k} \cdot n]} \\
&\leq \sum_{k=1}^{p} \left\|\Phi_{\sigma+v_c}^{(m+k)}(M_0) - \Phi_{\sigma+v_c}^{(m+k-1)}(M_0)\right\|_{[d^{m+k} \cdot n]} \\
&\leq \left(\sum_{k=1}^{p} \left(1 - \frac{r}{d^2}\right)^{m+k-1}\right) \|\Phi_{\sigma+v_c}(M_0) - M_0\|_{[d \cdot n]} \\
&= \left(\frac{d^2}{r}\right)\left(1 - \frac{r}{d^2}\right)^m \|\Phi_{\sigma+v_c}(M_0) - M_0\|_{[d \cdot n]}.
\end{aligned} \quad (18)$$

Since by Köthe's Theorem $\mathcal{M}_0$ is a complete space the conclusion now follows by the following argument. Let us rewrite the inequality (18) in the form:

$$M_{m+p} - M_m \in B_{[d^{m+p} \cdot n]}(0, c\lambda^m), \quad (19)$$

with $B_{[d^{m+p} \cdot n]}(0, c\lambda^m)$ the ball centred on zero with radius $c\lambda^m$ in $\mathcal{M}_{d^{m+p} \cdot n \times d^{m+p} \cdot n}$ with,

$$c := \frac{d^2}{r} \|\Phi_{\sigma+v_c}(M_0) - M_0\|_{[d \cdot n]} \text{ and } \lambda := \left(1 - \frac{r}{d^2}\right).$$

Now, let U be a convex neighbourhood of zero in $\mathcal{M}_0$. Then, see ([38], p. 57), for all $n \geq 1$ we have that $U \cap \mathcal{M}_{n \times n}$ is a neighbourhood of zero in $\mathcal{M}_{n \times n}$ and so,

$$\exists \epsilon > 0 \; B_{\mathcal{M}_{n \times n}}(0, \epsilon) \subseteq U \cap \mathcal{M}_{n \times n}(\subset U).$$

Let m_0 be an integer such that for all $m \geq m_0$ we have that $c\lambda^m < \epsilon$, which is possible as $\lambda < 1$. Now, due to the decreasing properties of the norms of the spaces $\mathcal{M}_{n \times n}$ we have that

$$\forall p \geq 1, M \geq m_0 \; B_{[d^{m+p} \cdot n]}(0, c\lambda^m) \subset B_{\mathcal{M}_{n \times n}}(0, \epsilon) \subset U,$$

thus showing that $M_{\sigma+v_c}$ is a Cauchy sequence in $\mathcal{M}_0$. Finally, as a consequence of the properties of the topology of the space $\mathcal{M}_0$, we have that the sequence $M_{\sigma+v_c}$ converges in $\mathcal{M}_0$ and so, for some $s \geq 1$ we have that $M_{\sigma+v_c}$ converges in $\mathcal{M}_{s\times s}$. As a consequence, there exists $L \in \mathcal{M}_{s\times s}$ such that:

$$\lim_{n\to+\infty} \left\| L - \Phi_{\sigma+v_c}^{(n)}(M)) \right\|_{[s]} = 0 \qquad (20)$$

We now observe that:

$$\| L - \Phi_{\sigma+v_c}(L) \|_{[s+1]} \leq \left\| \Phi_{\sigma+v_c}(L) - \Phi_{\sigma+v_c}^{(n+1)}(M)) \right\|_{[s+1]}$$
$$+ \left\| \Phi_{\sigma+v_c}^{(n)}(M) - \Phi_{\sigma+v_c}^{(n+1)}(M)) \right\|_{[s+1]}$$
$$+ \left\| L - \Phi_{\sigma+v_c}^{(n)}(M)) \right\|_{[s+1]}.$$

Now by the contraction property of $\Phi_{\sigma+v_c}$ shown in Formula (17) by the canonical injection of $\mathcal{M}_{s+1\times s+1}$ in $\mathcal{M}_{s\times s}$ shown in Formula (11) we have that:

$$\left\| \Phi_{\sigma+v_c}(L) - \Phi_{\sigma+v_c}^{(n+1)}(M)) \right\|_{[s+1]} \leq \left\| L - \Phi_{\sigma+v_c}^{(n)}(M)) \right\|_{[s+1]} \leq \left\| L - \Phi_{\sigma+v_c}^{(n)}(M)) \right\|_{[s]},$$

and so, by Formulas (18) and (20) we have that $\| L - \Phi_{\sigma+v_c}(L) \|_{[s+1]} = 0$ and this implies that $\Phi_{\sigma+v_c}^{<\infty}(L)\big|_s = L$, that is, L is a generalised fixed point for the finite matrix substitution map $\Phi_{\sigma+v_c}$. □

Remark 13 (Comparing Theorem 3 and Proposition 2). *Theorem 3 is an improvement of Proposition 2 in two directions. It is a constructive result since it gives an algorithm to obtain a fixed point and while in Proposition 2 the fixed point was a fixed point of some number of iterations of the matrix substitution map in Theorem 3 the fixed point obtained is a fixed point of only one iteration of the matrix substitution map.*

4. Random Matrices Associated to Structured Matrices

In this Section we consider structured random matrices derived from the structured matrices considered in Section 2. Our approach to the spectral analysis of random matrices derived from matrices built with a matrix substitution procedure relies on the general theory of random linear operators as exposed in [41]. Other more recent approaches to this subject are given in [42–44]. Take a structured matrix built by substitutions—that we will denominate the **skeleton** of the random matrix—and consider the associated random matrix having as entries random variables such that to the occurrence of each field element $i \in \mathbb{Z}_p$ in the skeleton structured matrix there corresponds a random variable with at least the same expected value as the expected value of a given random variable X_i, the same for a given $i \in \mathbb{Z}_p$. We will also consider the more stringent assumption that the entries in the random matrix corresponding to same field element $i \in \mathbb{Z}_p$ are equi-distributed with a given random variable X_i. The random matrix can have independent entries or not. As usual the study of the independent case is easier and we will assume independence. For instance, take the matrix M_1 in Formula (2), that is:

$$M_1 = \left[m_{i,j}^1\right]_{i,j} = \begin{pmatrix} 1 & 2 & 2 & 0 & 1 & 2 & 1 & 0 & 0 \\ 0 & 1 & 2 & 1 & 1 & 2 & 0 & 2 & 0 \\ 0 & 0 & 1 & 2 & 0 & 1 & 1 & 0 & 1 \\ 1 & 0 & 0 & 1 & 2 & 2 & 1 & 0 & 0 \\ 0 & 2 & 0 & 0 & 1 & 2 & 0 & 2 & 0 \\ 1 & 0 & 1 & 0 & 0 & 1 & 1 & 0 & 1 \\ 1 & 0 & 0 & 0 & 1 & 2 & 1 & 2 & 2 \\ 0 & 2 & 0 & 1 & 1 & 2 & 0 & 1 & 2 \\ 1 & 0 & 1 & 2 & 0 & 1 & 0 & 0 & 1 \end{pmatrix}$$

This matrix is the skeleton of the following random matrix:

$$M_1(X_\#) = \begin{pmatrix} X_{\#1} & X_{\#2} & X_{\#2} & X_{\#0} & X_{\#1} & X_{\#2} & X_{\#1} & X_{\#0} & X_{\#0} \\ X_{\#0} & X_{\#1} & X_{\#2} & X_{\#1} & X_{\#1} & X_{\#2} & X_{\#0} & X_{\#2} & X_{\#0} \\ X_{\#0} & X_{\#0} & X_{\#1} & X_{\#2} & X_{\#0} & X_{\#1} & X_{\#1} & X_{\#0} & X_{\#1} \\ X_{\#1} & X_{\#0} & X_{\#0} & X_{\#1} & X_{\#2} & X_{\#2} & X_{\#1} & X_{\#0} & X_{\#0} \\ X_{\#0} & X_{\#2} & X_{\#0} & X_{\#0} & X_{\#1} & X_{\#2} & X_{\#0} & X_{\#2} & X_{\#0} \\ X_{\#1} & X_{\#0} & X_{\#1} & X_{\#0} & X_{\#0} & X_{\#1} & X_{\#1} & X_{\#0} & X_{\#1} \\ X_{\#1} & X_{\#0} & X_{\#0} & X_{\#0} & X_{\#1} & X_{\#2} & X_{\#1} & X_{\#2} & X_{\#2} \\ X_{\#0} & X_{\#2} & X_{\#0} & X_{\#1} & X_{\#1} & X_{\#2} & X_{\#0} & X_{\#1} & X_{\#2} \\ X_{\#1} & X_{\#0} & X_{\#1} & X_{\#2} & X_{\#0} & X_{\#1} & X_{\#0} & X_{\#0} & X_{\#1} \end{pmatrix},$$

built with the rules detailed above and so it is a structured random matrix $M_1(X_\#) = \left[X_\#(m_{i,j}^1)\right]_{i,j}$ with skeleton $M_1 = \left[m_{i,j}^1\right]_{i,j}$ such that the entries are independent and verify, at least, $\mathbb{E}\left[X_\#(m_{i,j}^1)\right] = m_{i,j}^1$.

We will address, in Sections 4.1, 4.2 and 4.4 several questions regarding these structured random matrices, to wit:

1. Identification of a random matrix model (Section 4.1);
2. Convergence in law of random matrices built on skeletons matrices derived from substitution maps having a fixed point (Section 4.2);
3. Spectral analysis of some random structured matrices (Section 4.3);
4. Random surfaces associated with random matrices built on skeletons matrices derived from substitution maps having a fixed point (Section 4.4).

4.1. Testing for a Given Matrix Structure in a Realisation of a Stochastic Matrix

In this Section we will address the problem of testing if a given observed matrix can be considered as a realisation of a random matrix associated with a structured matrix built by a substitution map; this will be performed in a simple case. Let us suppose that we are given a realisation $M = [x_{ij}]_{1 \leq i,j \leq N}$ of a random matrix $\mathbb{M} = [X_{ij}]_{1 \leq i,j \leq N}$ having a structure derived from a matrix substitution map. We will admit the following assumptions.

(A) The matrix $\mathbb{M}$ has its skeleton—that is, a matrix $M = [m_{i,j}]_{i,j}$ with entries in $\mathbb{Z}_p$—which is a fixed point of the matrix substitution map. This assumption is justified on the grounds of the process that originated the skeleton being over its transient phase.

(B) The random variables which are entries of the random matrix $\mathbb{M}$ form a set of independent random variables.

Consider now, for each $i \in \mathbb{Z}_p$ the sequence $\mathbb{X}_{N_i}^i = (X_n^i)_{1 \leq n \leq N_p}$ formed by the random variables of the random matrix $\mathbb{M}$ that correspond to the entries in the skeleton with value i; we observe that $\sum_{i \in \mathbb{Z}_p} N_i = N^2$. We assume furthermore that:

(C) For each $i \in \mathbb{Z}_p$ we have that $X_i \frown \mathcal{G}_i(\theta)$, that is, the correspondent random variable X_i has a probability law $\mathcal{G}_i(\theta)$ with $\theta \in \Theta_i \subset \mathbb{R}^q$ a parameter.

Due to hypothesis **(B)** and **(C)**, the sequence $\mathbb{X}_{N_i}^p$ is a sample of the given random variable X_i. Furthermore, so a test procedure such as, a likelihood ratio test can be applied to determine if the matrix realisation M comes from a prescribed model of a random matrix with entries distributions verifying assumption **(C)** and with the skeleton given by a fixed point of the substitution map according to assumption **(A)**.

Remark 14 (On the detection of a structured random matrix). *Let us suppose that we have an observed large matrix which we suppose to be a realisation of a random matrix with independent centred entries. If the random variables are identically distributed then by force of the circular law, as quoted in Theorem 1 the spectral distribution of the normalised random matrix should be approximately the uniform distribution in the unit circle; a rejection of such a null hypothesis can be thought to be a strong indication of the existence of some particular structure in the matrix, namely that the entries are not identically distributed. For a formulation of such a statistical test, see [45] and also [46–48] and other references therein. Let us observe that it may be impossible to discern between possible existing structure or not; in fact, we have examples that show that if the coefficient of variation is large the distribution of eigenvalues of a structured matrix may have a similar pattern to the distribution of eigenvalues of a unstructured matrix.*

4.2. Convergence in Law of Random Structured Matrices Built by Arbitrary Substitutions

In this section, we show that if we consider a matrix fixed point of a matrix substitution map then the sequence of random matrices having as skeletons the sequence of iterates, by the matrix substitution map, of a given matrix converges in law to the random matrix that has as skeleton the fixed point of the matrix substitution map. We suppose that we are in the following context and notations.

- A global substitution given by : $\sigma : \mathbb{Z}_p \mapsto \mathcal{M}_{d \times d}^{<\infty}(\mathbb{Z}_p)$;
- The associated matrix substitution map Φ_σ defined on $\mathcal{M}_{+\infty}$;
- A fixed point M_∞ of the substitution map Φ_σ.
- The entries in the random matrix corresponding to same field element $p \in \mathbb{Z}_p$ are equi-distributed with a given random variable X_p.

We recall that if $M_0 \in \mathcal{M}_{+\infty}$ and $M_n = \Phi_\sigma(M_{n-1})$ for $n \geq 1$ then $M_\infty =_{\mathcal{M}_\infty} \lim_{n \to +\infty} M_n$ the convergence taking place in the topology of $\mathcal{M}_\infty$ defined by the increasing sequence of semi-norms given in Formula (12) (see Remark 6).

Theorem 4 (Convergence in law of random structured matrices). *Suppose that for each $i \in \mathbb{Z}_p$ the characteristic function of the random variable X_i is continuous at zero. If for $n \geq 1$, $M_n(X_\#)$ and $M_\infty(X_\#)$ are the random structured matrices with skeletons M_n and M_∞, , respectively, and as defined above then:*

$$Law(M_n(X_\#)) \xrightarrow[n \to +\infty]{} Law(M_\infty(X_\#)) . \tag{21}$$

Proof. Before applying Levy's continuity theorem we clarify the convergence in $\mathcal{M}_\infty$. The increasing family of semi-norms $(s_m)_{m \geq 1}$ defined by:

$$s_m(M) = s_m\left([a_{ij}]_{i,j \geq 1}\right) := \sup_{n \leq m} \frac{1}{n^2} \sum_{1 \leq i,j \leq n} |a_{ij}|_p ,$$

gives the maximum proportion of non-null terms in the leading principal parts of dimension less or equal to m of the matrix $M = [a_{ij}]_{i,j \geq 1}$. Taking $M_0 \in \mathcal{M}_{+\infty}$ and $M_n = \Phi_\sigma(M_{n-1})$ for $n \geq 1$, we have that $M_\infty =_{\mathcal{M}_\infty} \lim_{n \to +\infty} M_n$ if and only if:

$$\forall m \geq 1 , \lim_{n \to +\infty} s_m(M_n - M_\infty) = 0 .$$

If this is the case, taking now $\epsilon < 1/m$, for a given $m \geq 1$, and if $s_m(M_n - M_\infty) \leq \epsilon$ we have necessarily the leading principal parts of order m of M_n and M_∞ are equal. This implies that all the entries of the leading principal parts of order m of $M_n(X_\#)$ and $M_\infty(X_\#)$ have that same laws. Now given an infinite random matrix $M(X_\#)) = [a_{ij}(X_\#)]_{i,j\geq 1}$ with skeleton $M = [a_{ij}]_{i,j\geq 1}$ we may consider its characteristic function $\varphi_{M(X_\#)}$, for each $t \in \mathbb{R}$, by:

$$\forall t \in \mathbb{R}, \; \varphi_{M(X_\#)}(t) = \left[\varphi_{a_{ij}(X_\#)}(t)\right]_{i,j\geq 1} = \left[\mathbb{E}\left[e^{ita_{ij}(X_\#)}\right]\right]_{i,j\geq 1}.$$

For each $t \in \mathbb{R}$, we have that $\varphi_{M_n(X_\#)}(t)$ and $\varphi_{M_\infty(X_\#)}(t)$ are infinite matrices with coefficients in $\mathbb{C}$. We consider on the space $\mathcal{M}_\infty(\mathbb{C})$ of infinite matrices $[z_{ij}]_{i,j\geq 1}$ with coefficients in $z_{ij} \in \mathbb{C}$ the topology defined by the increasing family of semi-norms:

$$\rho_m\left([z_{ij}]_{i,j\geq 1}\right) = \sup_{n\leq m} \sum_{1\leq i,j\leq n} |z_{ij}|,$$

and we now show that:

$$\lim_{n\to+\infty} \varphi_{M_n(X_\#)}(t) =_{\mathcal{M}_\infty(\mathbb{C})} \varphi_{M_\infty(X_\#)}(t)$$
$$\Leftrightarrow \forall m \geq 1 \; \lim_{n\to+\infty} \rho_m\left(\varphi_{M_n(X_\#)}(t) - \varphi_{M_\infty(X_\#)}(t)\right) = 0,$$

for every fixed $t \in \mathbb{R}$. It is enough to consider $\epsilon < 1/m$ for any fixed $m \geq 1$. As seen above if $n \geq 1$ is such that $s_m(M_n - M_\infty) \leq \epsilon$ we have necessarily the leading principal parts of order m of $M_n(X_\#)$ and $M_\infty(X_\#)$ have that same laws and so their the characteristic functions of the entries of the respective leading principal parts of order m also coincide and so $\rho_m\left(\varphi_{M_n(X_\#)}(t) - \varphi_{M_\infty(X_\#)}(t)\right) = 0$. As a consequence of Levy's continuity theorem (see ([49], p. 389) or ([50], p. 144)), we have the thesis of the theorem in Formula (21). □

4.3. Spectral Analysis of Some Structured Random Matrices

In this Section we will provide results shedding light on the spectral analysis of some random structured matrices. The first result shows that under some mild assumptions a random structured matrix defines, almost surely for each one of its realisations, a Hilbert–Schmidt operator on $l^2(\mathbb{N})$, the Hilbert space of square summable sequences. The two main references needed in this Section are [51,52] for the results on Hilbert–Schmidt operators and [41] for random linear operators.

Theorem 5 (Random structured matrices with vanishing second moments). *Consider a random structured matrix $M(X(\#)) = \left[X_{ij}^{m_{ij}}\right]_{i,j}$ with skeleton $M = [m_{ij}]_{i,j}$ only verifying $\mathbb{E}[X_{ij}^{m_{ij}}] = m_{ij}$ besides the independence of the entries. Let $(e_i)_{i\geq 1}$ be the canonical orthonormal basis of $l^2(\mathbb{N})$, that is, $e_i = (e_i^1, e_i^2, \ldots e_i^n, \ldots)$ with $e_i^n = \delta_i^n$ the Kronecker's delta. We assume that the second moments $\mathbb{E}\left[\left|X_{ij}^{m_{ij}}\right|^2\right]$ of the random matrix entries go to zero, sufficiently fast as i,j grow indefinitely, more precisely:*

$$\sum_{i,j} \mathbb{E}\left[\left|X_{ij}^{m_{ij}}\right|^2\right] = C < +\infty. \tag{22}$$

Then we have that:

$$\mathbb{P}\left[\sum_{i,j} |\langle M(X(\#))e_i, e_j\rangle|^2 < +\infty\right] = 1. \tag{23}$$

Moreover, for $\omega \in \Omega$ almost surely, $M(X(\#))(\omega)$ defines a bounded operator in $l^2(\mathbb{N})$ which is also a Hilbert–Schmidt operator in $l^2(\mathbb{N})$.

Proof. The proof essentially relies on a Skorohod's sufficient condition for random linear operators in Hilbert space. We observe that:

$$\sum_{i,j}|\langle M(X(\#))e_i, e_j\rangle|^2 = \sum_{i,j}\left|X_{ij}^{m_{ij}}\right|^2.$$

Condition in Formula (22) implies, by Lebesgue's monotone convergence theorem that:

$$\mathbb{E}\left[\sum_{i,j}\left|X_{ij}^{m_{ij}}\right|^2\right] = \sum_{i,j}\mathbb{E}\left[\left|X_{ij}^{m_{ij}}\right|^2\right] = C < +\infty$$

Furthermore, so, by a standard argument we have the conclusion announced in Formula (23),

$$\mathbb{P}\left[\sum_{i,j}|\langle M(X(\#))e_i, e_j\rangle|^2 < +\infty\right] = \mathbb{P}\left[\sum_{i,j}\left|X_{ij}^{m_{ij}}\right|^2 < +\infty\right] = 1.$$

We first have for $\omega \in \Omega$ almost surely, that the operator $M(\omega) := M(X(\#)(\omega))$ is bounded, since, for all $s \in l^2(\mathbb{N})$, that is such that $s = (s_i)_{i\geq 1}$ with $\sum_{i\geq 1}|s_i|^2 < +\infty$, we have, by Parseval's equality and by Cauchy–Schwartz's inequality:

$$\|M(\omega)(s)\|^2 = \sum_{j\geq 1}|\langle M(\omega)(s), e_j\rangle|^2 = \sum_{j\geq 1}\left|\sum_{i\geq 1}\langle M(\omega)(e_i), e_j\rangle\langle s, e_i\rangle\right|^2$$

$$\leq \sum_{j\geq 1}\left[\left(\sum_{i\geq 1}|\langle M(\omega)(e_i), e_j\rangle|^2\right)\left(\sum_{i\geq 1}|\langle s, e_i\rangle|^2\right)\right] \quad (24)$$

$$= \left(\sum_{i,j\geq 1}|\langle M(\omega)(e_i), e_j\rangle|^2\right)\|s\|^2,$$

and thus, by Formula (23), the operator $M(\omega)$ is bounded. The final conclusion results from Remark 2 in Skorohod's treaty ([41], p. 8) stating that the condition expressed in Formula (23), is suffices for the matrix operator defined by the random matrix $M(X(\#))$ to be a Hilbert–Schmidt operator, almost surely. In fact, by Theorem 2 in ([51], p. 34) we have that a sufficient condition for the operator $M(\omega)$ to be an Hilbert–Schmidt operator is that:

$$\sum_{i\geq 1}\|M(\omega)(e_i)\|^2 = \sum_{j\geq 1}\sum_{i\geq 1}|\langle M(\omega)(e_i), e_i\rangle|^2 < +\infty,$$

and so the last result announced follows. □

As a consequence of Theorem 5 and of the spectral theorem we obtain the spectral representation of the kind of structured random matrices we studied in this Section.

Remark 15 (On the definition of eigenvalues of random structured matrices). *Since every Hilbert–Schmidt operator is compact and the random matrix entries are real the spectral theorem for compact self adjoint operators (see [52], p. 113) shows that, for $\omega \in \Omega$ almost surely, there is an orthonormal system $(\phi_i(\omega))_{i\geq 1}$ of eigenvectors of $M(\omega)$ and the corresponding eigenvalues $(\lambda_i(\omega))_{i\geq 1}$ such that for all $s \in l^2(\mathbb{N})$ we have that:*

$$M(\omega)(s) = \sum_{i\geq 1}\lambda_i(\omega)\langle s, (\phi_i(\omega))\rangle\phi_i(\omega),$$

and since the operator $M(\omega)$ is Hilbert–Schmidt we have that:

$$\sum_{j\geq 1}\|M(\omega)(\phi_j(\omega))\|^2 = \sum_{j\geq 1}\left\|\sum_{i\geq 1}\lambda_i(\omega)\langle\phi_j(\omega),(\phi_i(\omega)\rangle\phi_i(\omega)\right\|^2 = \sum_{j\geq 1}\|\lambda_j(\omega)\phi_j(\omega)\|^2$$
$$= \sum_{j\geq 1}|\lambda_j(\omega)|^2 < +\infty.$$

So, the random structured matrices studied in this Section have, almost surely, square integrable eigenvalues sequences.

The next result shows that the image of a nonrandom vector by some of the structured random matrices in this Section is, asymptotically, a Gaussian vector.

Theorem 6 (Gaussian character of images of nonrandom vectors by some structured random matrices). *Consider a random structured matrix $M(X(\#)) = \left[X_{ij}^{m_{ij}}\right]_{i,j}$ with skeleton $M = [m_{ij}]_{i,j}$ only verifying $\mathbb{E}[X_{ij}^{m_{ij}}] = m_{ij}$ and that and $\mathbb{V}\left[X_{ij}^{m_{ij}}\right]$ is bounded, besides the independence of the entries. Suppose that $x \in l^2(\mathbb{N}) \cap l^1(\mathbb{N})$. Suppose additionally that:*

$$\delta_L := \max_{j\leq L} \frac{\mathbb{E}\left[\left|\langle x,e_j\rangle X_{ij}^{m_{ij}}\right|^3\right]}{\mathbb{E}\left[\left|\langle x,e_j\rangle X_{ij}^{m_{ij}}\right|^2\right]} \xrightarrow[L\to+\infty]{} 0. \qquad (25)$$

Then $M(X(\#))(x)$ is a vector which has components that are asymptotically Gaussian, a property that we summarise in the form:

$$\sum_{j\geq 1}\langle x,e_j\rangle X_{ij}^{m_{ij}} \underset{a(j)}{\frown} \mathcal{N}(D,C^2) = \mathcal{N}\left(\sum_{j\geq 1}\langle x,e_j\rangle m_{ij}, \sum_{j\geq 1}|\langle x,e_j\rangle|^2 \mathbb{V}\left[X_{ij}^{m_{ij}}\right]\right),$$

for each component of $M(X(\#))(x)$.

Proof. The proof is an application of Lyapunov's central limit theorem for independent but not identically distributed random variables (see [53], p. 362). We consider the operator $M(X(\#)) : l^2(\mathbb{N}) \mapsto l^2(\mathbb{N})$ and for notational purposes that $(e_i)_{i\geq 1}$ is the canonical orthonormal basis of $l^2(\mathbb{N})$ and that $(e_i^\star)_{i\geq 1}$ is its the dual basis. With the notation $M(\omega) := M(X(\#))(\omega)$ we have that $M(\omega)(x) = \sum_{i\geq 1}\langle M(\omega)(x), e_i^\star\rangle e_i^\star$ and if we take a nonrandom vector $x = \sum_{i\geq 1}\langle x, e_i\rangle e_i$ we have that $M(\omega)(x) = \sum_{i\geq 1}\langle x, e_i\rangle M(\omega)(e_i)$, an expression that may be developed into:

$$M(\omega)(x) = \sum_{i\geq 1}\left\langle\sum_{j\geq 1}\langle x,e_j\rangle M(\omega)(e_j), e_i^\star\right\rangle e_i^\star = \sum_{i\geq 1}\sum_{j\geq 1}\langle x,e_j\rangle\langle M(\omega)(e_j), e_i^\star\rangle e_i^\star$$
$$= \sum_{i\geq 1}\left(\sum_{j\geq 1}\langle x,e_j\rangle X_{ij}^{m_{ij}}\right)e_i^\star,$$

using the fact that $M(\omega) = \left[X_{ij}^{m_{ij}}\right]_{i,j}$. We observe that using previous notations we have that:

$$\mathbb{E}\left[\langle x,e_j\rangle X_{ij}^{m_{ij}}\right] = \langle x,e_j\rangle m_{ij} \text{ and } \mathbb{V}\left[\langle x,e_j\rangle X_{ij}^{m_{ij}}\right] = |\langle x,e_j\rangle|^2 \mathbb{V}\left[X_{ij}^{m_{ij}}\right].$$

Now due to Lyapunov central limit theorem, the assumption made in Formula (25) and Berry estimate for the rate of convergence, we may write, for a variable $A = A(L) = \mathcal{O}(L)$:

$$\mathbb{P}\left[\sum_{j \leq L} \frac{\langle x, e_j \rangle X_{ij}^{m_{ij}} - \mathbb{E}\left[\langle x, e_j \rangle X_{ij}^{m_{ij}}\right]}{\sqrt{\sum_{j \leq L} |\langle x, e_j \rangle|^2 \mathbb{V}\left[X_{ij}^{m_{ij}}\right]}} \leq x\right] = \frac{1}{\sqrt{2\pi}} \int_{-\infty}^{x} e^{-\frac{t^2}{2}} dt + A\delta_L \,.$$

The above expression may be written as:

$$\mathbb{P}\left[\sum_{j \leq L} \langle x, e_j \rangle X_{ij}^{m_{ij}} \leq x \sqrt{\sum_{j \leq L} |\langle x, e_j \rangle|^2 \mathbb{V}\left[X_{ij}^{m_{ij}}\right]} + \sum_{j \leq L} \langle x, e_j \rangle m_{ij}\right]$$
$$= \frac{1}{\sqrt{2\pi}} \int_{-\infty}^{x} e^{-\frac{t^2}{2}} dt + A\delta_L \,. \qquad (26)$$

Since $x \in l^2(\mathbb{N})$ and $\mathbb{V}\left[X_{ij}^{m_{ij}}\right]$, the variances of the entries of the matrix $M(\omega)$, are bounded we have that:

$$\sum_{j \geq 1} |\langle x, e_j \rangle|^2 \mathbb{V}\left[X_{ij}^{m_{ij}}\right] = C^2 < +\infty \,.$$

Since $x \in l^1(\mathbb{N}) \cap l^2(\mathbb{N})$ and $m_{ij} \in \mathbb{Z}_p$ we have that $\sum_{j \geq 1} |\langle x, e_j \rangle| m_{ij} < +\infty$. As a consequence let:

$$\sum_{j \geq 1} \langle x, e_j \rangle m_{ij} = D \in \mathbb{R} \,.$$

Consider the partial sums $\sum_{j \leq L} \langle x, e_j \rangle m_{ij} = D_L$ and $\sqrt{\sum_{j \leq L} |\langle x, e_j \rangle|^2 \mathbb{V}\left[X_{ij}^{m_{ij}}\right]} := C_L$. We may write Formula (26) in the form:

$$\mathbb{P}\left[\sum_{j \leq L} \langle x, e_j \rangle X_{ij}^{m_{ij}} \leq xC_L + D_L\right] = \frac{1}{\sqrt{2\pi}} \int_{-\infty}^{x} e^{-\frac{t^2}{2}} dt + A\delta_L \,,$$

which, by a change of variable, amounts to:

$$\mathbb{P}\left[\sum_{j \leq L} \langle x, e_j \rangle X_{ij}^{m_{ij}} \leq y\right] = \frac{1}{\sqrt{2\pi C^2}} \int_{-\infty}^{y} e^{-\frac{(u-D)^2}{2C^2}} du + A\delta_L \,. \qquad (27)$$

Since we have that:

$$\frac{1}{\sqrt{2\pi C^2}} \int_{-\infty}^{y} e^{-\frac{(u-D)^2}{2C^2}} du = \frac{1}{\sqrt{2\pi}} \int_{-\infty}^{xC+D} e^{-\frac{t^2}{2}} dt = \lim_{L \to +\infty} \frac{1}{\sqrt{2\pi}} \int_{-\infty}^{xC_L+D_L} e^{-\frac{t^2}{2}} dt$$
$$= \lim_{L \to +\infty} \frac{1}{\sqrt{2\pi C_L^2}} \int_{-\infty}^{y} e^{-\frac{(u-D_L)^2}{2C_L^2}} du \,,$$

and from Formula (27), we have immediately:

$$\lim_{L \to +\infty} \mathbb{P}\left[\sum_{j \leq L} \langle x, e_j \rangle X_{ij}^{m_{ij}} \leq y\right] = \frac{1}{\sqrt{2\pi C^2}} \int_{-\infty}^{y} e^{-\frac{(u-D)^2}{2C^2}} du \,.$$

We may conclude that, on account of the independence of the entries of the random matrix, we have that $M(X(\#))(x)$, for all nonrandom x, is a random vector which has components $\sum_{j \geq 1} \langle x, e_j \rangle X_{ij}^{m_{ij}}$ that are asymptotically Gaussian. □

Remark 16. *The spectral analysis discussed in Remark 15 ensures a spectral decomposition of the random structured matrix operator $M(X(\#)(\omega))$ to exist for ω almost surely and so not only the eigenvalues but also the eigenvectors are random variables. Theorem 6 shows that if there exist an almost surely constant eigenvector of the operator $M(X(\#)(\omega))$ then the correspondent eigenvalue is Gaussian.*

Whenever the distributions for the three symbols are identical the effect of having a structured matrix naturally disappears as a consequence of Theorem 1. With different distributions the effects of having structured matrices appear.

For an illustration example in Figure 3 we have chosen,

$$X_0 \frown \mathcal{N}(0,\sigma^2) \text{ and } X_1 \frown \mathcal{N}(1,\sigma^2) \text{ and } X_2 \frown \mathcal{N}(2,\sigma^2)$$

and we took successively larger values for the variance.

Remark 17 (Identifying a random structured model by spectral analysis). *There are two conclusions that we may obtain from a first analysis of Figure 3. The first is that, as expected, for smaller variances there is a similarity between the distribution of the eigenvalues in the plane of the structure matrix, the skeleton of the random matrix with entries considered in the complex field, and of the associated random matrix; a second observation, stressing well known facts, is that for sufficiently large variance the distribution of the eigenvalues of the random matrix is similar to the distribution of eigenvalues of a random matrix with independent and identically distributed entries as in Theorem 1.*

4.4. Modelling: Random Surfaces Associated to Random Matrices

In this Section we show that to each structured infinite matrix, under some hypothesis, we can associate in a canonical way a random field, for instance, defining a random surface over the unit square in the plane. The procedure is akin to the ones used to define the multiplicative chaos of Mandelbrot, Kahane, and Peyrière (see [54]) with the difference that we use products of real valued random variables instead of non-negative ones.

Prior to that we first provide a technical observation. The general theory of infinite products of random variables of arbitrary sign is quite elaborated when compared with the theory of infinite sums of random variables (see, for instance, [55–57]). Nevertheless, in the case that the sequence of products is a (sub or super) martingale there are immediately convergence results that can be taken to be used. Consider an infinite matrix M which is a fixed point of some matrix substitution map. This assumption is motivated by the idea that an observed matrix structure must have some permanence in time in order to be observed. We will define an infinite random structured matrix with given skeleton M as a matrix $[X_{i,j}]_{i,j\geq 1}$ having as entries independent random variables, such that $\mathbb{E}\left[X_{i,j}^{m_{i,j}}\right] = m_{i,j}$.

We now associate to the columns of the random matrix $[X_{i,j}]_{i,j\geq 1}$ the following sequence of random variables $(L_j)_{j\geq 1}$.

$$L_j = L_j(\alpha,\gamma) := \gamma \frac{1}{x_j^\alpha} \sum_{i=1}^{+\infty} \frac{X_{i,j}^{m_{i,j}}}{p^i} \text{ with } x_j := \sum_{i=1}^{+\infty} \frac{m_{i,j}}{p^i}$$

with $\alpha \geq 1$ and $0 < \gamma \leq 1$. We will also suppose that there are no columns with only zeros in any of the substitution matrices, which implies that there exists $\epsilon > 0$ such that $x_j > \epsilon$. The parameters α and γ will be chosen to satisfy certain conditions ahead. In order to define the random surface we take a partition of $]0,1[^2$ by a sequence of dyadic cells. A representation of a decreasing sequence of dyadic cells in $]0,1[^2$ is given in Figure 4.

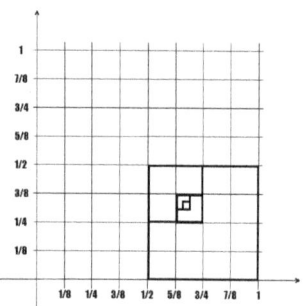

Figure 4. A decreasing sequence of dyadic cells.

In order to link the column random variables of the sequence $(L_j)_{j\geq 1}$ to the dyadic cells we consider for each decreasing sequence of dyadic cells such as:

$$C = (c(i_1, i_1 i_2, i_1 i_2 i_3, \ldots, i_1 i_2 i_3 \ldots i_N))_{N \geq 1}$$

which is uniquely identified by the indexes identifying the decreasing sequence of dyadic cells $i_1, i_1 i_2, i_1 i_2 i_3, \ldots, i_1 i_2 i_3 \ldots i_N, \ldots, i_1, i_2, i_3, \ldots, i_N, \cdots \in \{1, 2, 3, 4\}$. We have the following algorithm to rename the column random variables of the sequence $(L_j)_{j\geq 1} \equiv (L_j(\alpha))_{j\geq 1}$:

$$\begin{array}{llll}
W_1 = L_1 & W_2 = L_2 & W_3 = L_3 & W_4 = L_4 \\
W_{1,1} = L_5 & W_{1,2} = L_6 & W_{1,3} = L_7 & W_{1,4} = L_8 \\
W_{2,1} = L_9 & W_{2,2} = L_{10} & W_{2,3} = L_{11} & W_{2,4} = L_{12} \\
W_{3,1} = L_{13} & W_{3,2} = L_{14} & W_{3,3} = L_{15} & W_{3,4} = L_{16} \\
W_{4,1} = L_{17} & W_{4,2} = L_{18} & W_{4,3} = L_{19} & W_{4,4} = L_{20} \ldots
\end{array}$$

The linking algorithm of the column random variables to the dyadic cells of $[0,1]^2$ in its first step and second steps is as indicated in Figure 5.

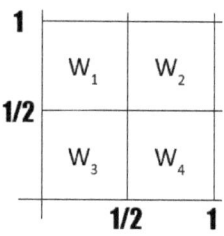
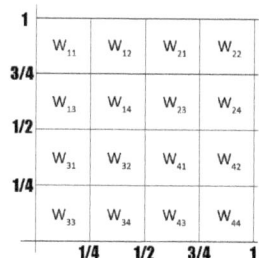

Figure 5. The placement of the first four random variables: first step (**left**); The placement of the next 16 random variables: second step (**right**).

We now detail the sequence of random variables that give the height of the random surface. For that purpose we define a sequence of random variables $(M_N)_{n\geq 1}$ uniquely associated with a decreasing sequence of dyadic cells in the following way:

$$M_N = M_N(c(i_1, i_1 i_2, \ldots, i_1 i_2 \ldots i_N)) := W_{i_1} \cdot W_{i_1 i_2} \cdot W_{i_1 i_2 i_3} \ldots W_{i_1 i_2 i_3 \ldots i_N} = \prod_{k=1}^{N} W_{i_1 i_2 i_3 \ldots i_k}, \quad (28)$$

observing that $M_N = M_N(c(i_1, i_1 i_2, \ldots, i_1 i_2 \ldots i_N))$ with $c(i_1, i_1 i_2, \ldots, i_1 i_2 \ldots i_N)$ the finite sequence of dyadic cells that goes until the Nth step. We further observe that for every

$(s,t) \in]0,1[\times]0,1[$ there exists an unique sequence $C(s,t) = (c(i_1, i_1i_2, \ldots, i_1i_2 \ldots i_N))_{N \geq 1}$ of decreasing dyadic cells such that:

$$\{(s,t)\} = \bigcap_{N \geq 1} c(i_1, i_1i_2, i_1i_2i_3, \ldots, i_1i_2i_3 \ldots i_N)$$

This decreasing sequence of dyadic cells of a given point allows, with an additional hypothesis, the definition of the random surface via the sequence $(M_N)_{N \geq 1} = (M_N(C(s,t)))_{N \geq 1}$. Consider the left (negative) tail average for the distribution of $X_{i,j}^{m_{i,j}}$ given by:

$$a_{i,j} := -\int_{-\infty}^{0} x dF_{X_{i,j}^{m_{i,j}}}(x).$$

We have the following result.

Theorem 7 (Existence of a nontrivial random field associated with a structured random matrix). *Suppose that the following assumptions are verified:*
(a) *The left tail averages verify:*

$$\sum_{i=1}^{\infty} \frac{a_{i,j}}{p^i} \leq m < +\infty,$$

for some constant m.
(b) *The variances of the random variables $X_{i,j}^{m_{i,j}}$ verify $\mathbb{V}\left[X_{i,j}^{m_{i,j}}\right] = x_j^{2\alpha_0} \cdot v_i$, for a certain $\alpha_0 = \alpha_0(m)$ to be determined later and with v_i such that:*

$$1 < V := \sum_{i=1}^{\infty} \frac{v_i}{p^{2i}} < +\infty.$$

Then, there is a combination of the parameters α, γ such that, for each $(s,t) \in]0,1[\times]0,1[$ the sequence $(M_N)_{N \geq 1} = (M_N(C(s,t)))_{N \geq 1}$ is a supermartingale that converges almost surely to a random variable $X_{(s,t)}$ defining the random field $(X_{(s,t)})_{(s,t) \in]0,1[^2}$, that is:

$$X_{(s,t)} := \lim_{N \to +\infty} M_N(c(i_1, i_1i_2, \ldots, i_1i_2 \ldots i_N)) \text{ a. s. },\quad (29)$$

and $\mathbb{E}\left[\left|X_{(s,t)}\right|\right] < +\infty$. Moreover, $\mathbb{V}\left[X_{(s,t)}\right] \geq 1$, that is, the random variable $X_{(s,t)}$ is not constant.

Proof. We first observe that since $x_j \geq \epsilon$ we have:

$$\mathbb{E}[|L_j(\alpha, \gamma)|] \leq \frac{\gamma}{x_j^\alpha} \left(\sum_{i=1}^{+\infty} \frac{\mathbb{E}\left[|X_{i,j}^{m_{i,j}}|\right]}{p^i}\right) = \frac{\gamma}{x_j^\alpha} \left(\sum_{i=1}^{+\infty} \frac{m_{i,j} + a_{i,j}}{p^i}\right) \leq \gamma \frac{1+m}{\epsilon^\alpha}.$$

We now choose $\alpha = \alpha_0$ such that $(1+m)/\epsilon^\alpha \leq 1$. Due to the independence of the of the random variables $X_{i,j}^{m_{i,j}}$, we have that:

$$\mathbb{V}[L_j] = \frac{\gamma^2}{x_j^{2\alpha_0}} \sum_{i=1}^{+\infty} \frac{\mathbb{V}\left[X_{i,j}^{m_{i,j}}\right]}{p^{2i}} = \frac{\gamma^2}{x_j^{2\alpha_0}} \sum_{i=1}^{+\infty} \frac{x_j^{2\alpha_0} \cdot v_i}{p^{2i}} = \gamma^2 V.$$

We now choose $\gamma = \gamma_0 \leq 1$ such that $\gamma_0^2 V = 1$. The random variables of the sequence $(W_{i_1}, W_{i_1i_2}, W_{i_1i_2i_3}, \ldots W_{i_1i_2i_3\ldots i_N})_{N \geq 1}$ are, in fact, distinct random variables of the sequence $(L_j(\alpha_0, \gamma_0))_{j \geq 1}$ and so, are independent. It is well known that, since

$$0 \leq \mathbb{E}[L_j(\alpha_0, \gamma_0)] = |\mathbb{E}[L_j(\alpha_0, \gamma_0)]| \leq \mathbb{E}[|L_j(\alpha_0, \gamma_0)|] \leq 1,$$

a sequence such as the one defined by Formula (28) is a supermartingale with respect to its natural filtration (see, for instance, ([58], p. 475)). Due to the independence we have that:

$$\mathbb{E}[|M_N|] = \mathbb{E}[|W_{i_1}|] \cdot \mathbb{E}[|W_{i_1 i_2}|] \cdot \mathbb{E}[|W_{i_1 i_2 i_3}|] \ldots \mathbb{E}[|W_{i_1 i_2 i_3 \ldots i_N}|]$$
$$= \prod_{k=1}^{N} \mathbb{E}[|W_{i_1 i_2 i_3 \ldots i_k}|] \leq 1,$$

that is, $\sup_{N \geq 1} \mathbb{E}[|M_N|] \leq 1$, and so, due to a well known theorem of Doob (see, for instance, ([58], p. 508)) the first conclusion follows. Using the facts that $\mathbb{V}[L_j(\alpha_0, \gamma_0)] = 1$ and that the random variables $W_{i_1 i_2 i_3 \ldots i_k}$ are distinct elements of the sequence $(L_j(\alpha_0, \gamma_0))_{j \geq 1}$, observing that for $k \neq l$ we have that,

$$\mathbb{V}[L_k \cdot L_l] = \mathbb{V}[L_k] \cdot \mathbb{V}[L_l] + \mathbb{V}[L_k] \cdot \mathbb{E}[L_l]^2 \mathbb{V}[L_l] \cdot \mathbb{E}[L_k]^2$$
$$= 1 + \mathbb{E}[L_l]^2 + \mathbb{E}[L_k]^2 \geq 1,$$

by induction, we now can state that:

$$\mathbb{V}[M_N] = \mathbb{V}\left[\prod_{k=1}^{N} W_{i_1 i_2 i_3 \ldots i_k}\right] \geq 1,$$

and so the second conclusion also follows. □

Let us give an idea of a random field built under the hypothesis of Theorem 7. In Figure 6, we present a low order approximation of the random surface associated with the example introduced by Formula (1) in Section 2.1. The skeleton for this approximation is the matrix M_7 a square matrix having around 43 million entries.

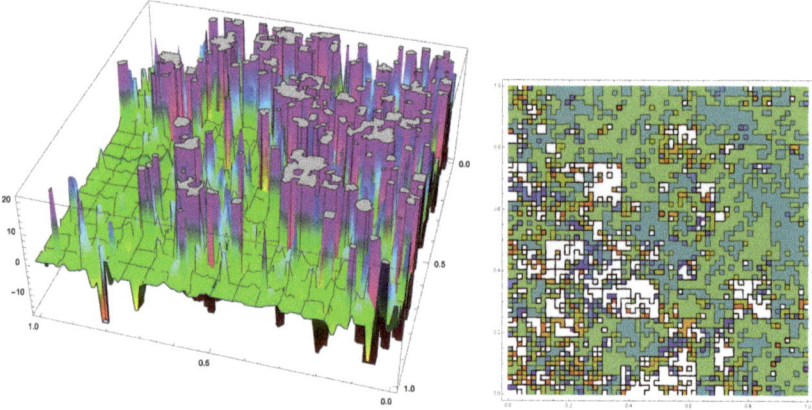

Figure 6. An approximation of low order of the random surface, built upon the skeleton M_7: surface plot (**left**); Contour plot: (**right**).

Remark 18 (On the covariance of the random field $(X_{(s,t)})_{(s,t) \in]0,1[^2}$). *Due to the general procedure considered in the construction of the random field it is possible to determine some interesting results on the covariance. In fact let, for two distinct points $(s,t), (s',t') \in]0,1[^2$, be the correspondent martingale sequences with elements $M_N(C(s,t))$ and $M_{N+P}(C(s',t'))$ with*

$N, P \geq 1$. Let us suppose that the integer $0 \leq N_0 < N$ is the largest integer such that the points $(s, t), (s', t')$ both belong to the same dyadic cell. It is then clear then that:

$$\text{Cov}[M_N(C(s,t)), M_{N+P}(C(s',t'))]$$
$$= \mathbb{E}\left[M_{N_0}(C(s,t))^2\right] \mathbb{E}\left[\prod_{k=N_0+1}^{N} W_{i_1 i_2 i_3 \ldots i_k}(C(s,t))\right] \mathbb{E}\left[\prod_{k=N_0+1}^{N+P} W_{i_1 i_2 i_3 \ldots i_k}(C(s',t'))\right]$$
$$- \mathbb{E}[M_N(C(s,t))] \mathbb{E}[M_{N+P}(C(s',t'))] .$$

If all the random variables of the sequence $(L_j)_{j \geq 1}$ have mean equal to 1 and then, forcefully, the absolute moment of second order is strictly larger than 1, for instance, equal to 2, then, again by Lebesgue convergence theorem we have that:

$$\text{Cov}\left[X_{(s,t)}, X_{(s',t')}\right] = 2^{N_0} - 1 ,$$

where, as already said, $N_0 \geq 0$ is the largest integer such that the points $(s,t), (s',t')$ both belong to the same dyadic cell. If the points do not belong to any common dyadic cell (see Figure 5), that is if $N_0 = 0$, the covariance is null. The closer the points are, the larger the integer N_0 is, and so, the larger the covariance.

5. Conclusions and Future Work

In this work, we introduced structured random matrices having a skeleton built from the a matrix substitution process with entries in a finite field. We showed that the iterated application of a particular kind of matrix substitution generates a sequence of matrices that admit a periodic point—that may be a fixed point—or a fixed point for the sequence of matrix principal parts of a given order. The random matrices, with independent entries, having as skeletons matrices derived from this matrix substitution process have remarkable properties whenever the random variables satisfy some uniform properties. It is showed, under adequate hypothesis, that:

- The existence of a particular type of structure of matrix substitution type is identifiable by simple statistical procedures;
- The convergence in law of a sequence of random matrices having as skeletons a sequence of matrices with entries in a finite field that, of matrix substitution type, converges to a fixed point;
- There is a generic result on the spectral analysis for the random matrices derived from a matrix substitution procedure;
- There is a canonical manner to associate a nontrivial random field with interesting properties to a random matrix having as a skeleton a matrix with entries in a finite field of matrix substitution type.

A more detailed analysis of the spectral properties of the random matrices here introduced is, for us, open to future work. Furthermore, matrices with a high percentage of zeros can be generated by considering special global matrix substitutions maps; the detailed properties of these matrices will be object of future work. Finally, a reciprocal problem to the one considered in this work is to determine if a large matrix is a fixed point of some global matrix substitution map. A reasonable conjecture is that for every large matrix there exists a global matrix substitution map admitting a fixed point that is close, in some sense, to the given matrix.

Author Contributions: Conceptualization, M.L.E.; methodology M.L.E.; software M.L.E.; validation M.L.E. and N.P.K.; formal analysis, M.L.E. and N.P.K.; investigation M.L.E. and N.P.K.; resources M.L.E. and N.P.K.; writing—original draft preparation M.L.E. and N.P.K.; writing—review and editing, M.L.E. and N.P.K.; visualization, M.L.E. and N.P.K.; supervision M.L.E.; project administration M.L.E.; funding acquisition M.L.E. All authors have read and agreed to the published version of the manuscript.

Funding: For the first author this work was partially supported through the project of the Centro de Matemática e Aplicações, UID/MAT/00297/2020 financed by the Fundação para a Ciência e a Tecnologia (Portuguese Foundation for Science and Technology). The APC was by supported by Fidelidade-Companhia de Seguros, S.A. to which the authors express their warmest acknowledgment.

Data Availability Statement: Not applicable.

Acknowledgments: This work was published with financial support from by the New University of Lisbon. The authors express gratitude to the comments, corrections, and questions of the referees that led to a revised and better version of this work.

Conflicts of Interest: The authors declare no conflict of interest.

References

1. Liu, S.; McGree, J.; Ge, Z.; Xie, Y. *Computational and Statistical Methods for Analysing Big Data with Applications*; Elsevier: Amsterdam, The Netherlands; Academic Press: Cambridge, MA, USA, 2016; pp. 11 + 194.
2. Pytheas Fogg, N.; Berthé, V.; Ferenczi, S.; Mauduit, C.; Siegel, A. (Eds.) *Substitutions in Dynamics, Arithmetics and Combinatorics*; Springer: Berlin/Heidelberg, Germany, 2002; Volume 1794, pp. 15 + 402. [CrossRef]
3. Queffélec, M. *Substitution Dynamical Systems. Spectral Analysis*, 2nd ed.; Springer: Dordrecht, The Netherlands, 2010; Volume 1294, pp. 15 + 351. [CrossRef]
4. von Haeseler, F. *Automatic Sequences*; Walter de Gruyter: Berlin/Heidelberg, Germany, 2003; pp. 6 + 191.
5. Allouche, J.P.; Shallit, J. *Automatic Sequences*; Theory, Applications, Generalizations; Cambridge University Press: Cambridge, UK, 2003; pp. 16 + 571. [CrossRef]
6. Frank, N.P. Multidimensional constant-length substitution sequences. *Topol. Its Appl.* **2005**, *152*, 44–69. [CrossRef]
7. Bartlett, A. Spectral theory of $\mathbb{Z}^d$ substitutions. *Ergod. Theory Dyn. Syst.* **2018**, *38*, 1289–1341. [CrossRef]
8. Jolivet, T.; Kari, J. Consistency of multidimensional combinatorial substitutions. *Theor. Comput. Sci.* **2012**, *454*, 178–188. [CrossRef]
9. Fogg, N.P.; Berthé, V.; Ferenczi, S.; Mauduit, C.; Siegel, A. (Eds.) Polynomial dynamical systems associated with substitutions. In *Substitutions in Dynamics, Arithmetics and Combinatorics*; Springer: Berlin/Heidelberg, Germany, 2002; pp. 321–342.
10. Ginibre, J. Statistical ensembles of complex, quaternion, and real matrices. *J. Math. Phys.* **1965**, *6*, 440–449. [CrossRef]
11. Girko, V. *Theory of Random Determinants*; Translated from the Russian; Kluwer Academic Publishers: Dordrecht, The Netherlands, 1988; pp. 25 + 677.
12. Girko, V. *Statistical Analysis of Observations of Increasing Dimension*; Translated from the Russian; Kluwer Academic Publishers: Dordrecht, The Netherlands, 1995; pp. 21 + 286.
13. Bai, Z.D. Methodologies in Spectral Analysis of Large Dimensional Random Matrices, a review. *Stat. Sin.* **1999**, *9*, 611–662.
14. Götze, F.; Tikhomirov, A. The circular law for random matrices. *Ann. Probab.* **2010**, *38*, 1444–1491. [CrossRef]
15. Alexeev, N.; Götze, F.; Tikhomirov, A. Asymptotic distribution of singular values of powers of random matrices. *Lith. Math. J.* **2010**, *50*, 121–132. [CrossRef]
16. Götze, F.; Naumov, A.; Tikhomirov, A. Distribution of linear statistics of singular values of the product of random matrices. *Bernoulli* **2017**, *23*, 3067–3113. [CrossRef]
17. Götze, F.; Naumov, A.; Tikhomirov, A.; Timushev, D. On the local semicircular law for Wigner ensembles. *Bernoulli* **2018**, *24*, 2358–2400. [CrossRef]
18. Götze, F.; Tikhomirov, A. Rate of convergence in probability to the Marchenko-Pastur law. *Bernoulli* **2004**, *10*, 503–548. [CrossRef]
19. Mehta, M.L. *Random Matrices*, 3rd ed.; Pure and Applied Mathematics (Amsterdam); Elsevier: Amsterdam, The Netherlands; Academic Press: Cambridge, MA, USA, 2004; Volume 142, pp. 18 + 688.
20. Anderson, G.W.; Guionnet, A.; Zeitouni, O. *An Introduction to Random Matrices*; Cambridge Studies in Advanced Mathematics; Cambridge University Press: Cambridge, UK, 2010; Volume 118, pp. 14 + 492.
21. Guionnet, A. Grandes matrices aléatoires et théorèmes d'universalité (d'après Erdős, Schlein, Tao, Vu et Yau). *Astérisque* **2011**, *1*, 203–237.
22. Tao, T. *Topics in Random Matrix Theory*; Graduate Studies in Mathematics; American Mathematical Society: Providence, RI, USA, 2012; Volume 132, pp. 10 + 282. [CrossRef]
23. Vu, V.H. (Ed.) Modern aspects of random matrix theory. In Proceedings of the Symposia in Applied Mathematics, San Diego, CA, 6–7 January 2013; Papers from the AMS Short Course on Random Matrices; American Mathematical Society: Providence, RI, USA, 2014; Volume 72, pp. 8 + 174. [CrossRef]
24. Akemann, G.; Baik, J.; Di Francesco, P. (Eds.) *The Oxford Handbook of Random Matrix Theory*; Paperback edition of the 2011 original [MR2920518]; Oxford University Press: Oxford, UK, 2015; pp. 31 + 919.
25. Erdős, L.; Yau, H.T. *A Dynamical Approach to Random Matrix Theory*; Courant Lecture Notes in Mathematics; Courant Institute of Mathematical Sciences: New York, NY, USA; American Mathematical Society: Providence, RI, USA, 2017; Volume 28, pp. 9 + 226.
26. Banerjee, D.; Bose, A. Patterned sparse random matrices: A moment approach. *Random Matrices Theory Appl.* **2017**, *6*, 1750011. [CrossRef]
27. Bose, A. *Patterned Random Matrices*; CRC Press: Boca Raton, FL, USA, 2018; pp. 21 + 267. [CrossRef]

28. Livshyts, G.V.; Tikhomirov, K.; Vershynin, R. The smallest singular value of inhomogeneous square random matrices. *Ann. Probab.* **2021**, *49*, 1286–1309. [CrossRef]
29. Jain, V.; Silwal, S. A note on the universality of ESDs of inhomogeneous random matrices. *ALEA Lat. Am. J. Probab. Math. Stat.* **2021**, *18*, 1047–1059. [CrossRef]
30. Tikhomirov, A.N. On the Wigner law for generalizided random graphs. *Sib. Adv. Math.* **2021**, *31*, 301–308. [CrossRef]
31. Liu, Y.; Chen, A.; Lin, F. Threshold function of ray nonsingularity for uniformly random ray pattern matrices. *Linear Multilinear Algebra* **2022**, *70*, 5708–5715. [CrossRef]
32. Ali, M.S.; Srivastava, S.C.L. Patterned random matrices: deviations from universality. *J. Phys. A* **2022**, *55*, 495201. [CrossRef]
33. Bernkopf, M. A history of infinite matrices. A study of denumerably infinite linear systems as the first step in the history of operators defined on function spaces. *Arch. History Exact Sci.* **1968**, *4*, 308–358. [CrossRef]
34. Shivakumar, P.N.; Sivakumar, K.C. A review of infinite matrices and their applications. *Linear Algebra Appl.* **2009**, *430*, 976–998. [CrossRef]
35. Williams, J.J.; Ye, Q. Infinite matrices bounded on weighted ℓ^1 spaces. *Linear Algebra Appl.* **2013**, *438*, 4689–4700. [CrossRef]
36. Lindner, M. *Infinite Matrices and Their Finite Sections*; Frontiers in Mathematics; An introduction to the limit operator method; Birkhäuser Verlag: Basel, Switzerland, 2006; pp. 15 + 191.
37. Warusfel, A. *Structures Algébriques Finies. Groupes, Anneaux, Corps*; Collection Hachette Université, Librairie Hachette: Paris, France, 1971; p. 271.
38. Koan, V.K. *Distributions, Analyse de Fourier, Opérateurs aux Dérivées Partielles*; Number tome 1 in Cours et exercices résolus maîtrise de mathématiques: Certficat C2; Vuibert: Paris, France, 1972.
39. Schaefer, H.H. *Topological Vector Spaces*; Springer: New York, NY, USA, 1971; Volume 3.
40. Köthe, G. *Topological Vector Spaces. I*; Die Grundlehren der mathematischen Wissenschaften in Einzeldarstellungen. 159; Garling, D.J.H., Translator; Springer: Berlin/Heidelberg, Germany; New York, NY, USA, 1969; pp. 15, 456.
41. Skorohod, A.V. *Random Linear Operators*; Mathematics and its Applications (Soviet Series); Translated from the Russian; D. Reidel Publishing Co.: Dordrecht, The Netherlands, 1984; pp. 16 + 199. [CrossRef]
42. Guo, T.X. Extension theorems of continuous random linear operators on random domains. *J. Math. Anal. Appl.* **1995**, *193*, 15–27. [CrossRef]
43. Thang, D.H.; Thinh, N. Generalized random linear operators on a Hilbert space. *Stochastics* **2013**, *85*, 1040–1059. [CrossRef]
44. Quy, T.X.; Thang, D.H.; Thinh, N. Abstract random linear operators on probabilistic unitary spaces. *J. Korean Math. Soc.* **2016**, *53*, 347–362. [CrossRef]
45. Chiu, S.N.; Liu, K.I. Generalized Cramér-von Mises goodness-of-fit tests for multivariate distributions. *Comput. Stat. Data Anal.* **2009**, *53*, 3817–3834. [CrossRef]
46. Thas, O. *Comparing Distributions*; Springer: New York, NY, USA, 2010; pp. 18 + 353.
47. McAssey, M.P. An empirical goodness-of-fit test for multivariate distributions. *J. Appl. Stat.* **2013**, *40*, 1120–1131. [CrossRef]
48. Fan, Y. Goodness-of-Fit Tests for a Multivariate Distribution by the Empirical Characteristic Function. *J. Multivar. Anal.* **1997**, *62*, 36–63. [CrossRef]
49. Shiryaev, A.N. *Probability. 1*, 3rd ed.; Boas, R.P., Chibisov, D.M., Eds.; Graduate Texts in Mathematics; Translated from the fourth (2007) Russian; Springer: New York, NY, USA, 2016; Volume 95, pp. 17 + 486.
50. Kallenberg, O. *Foundations of Modern Probability*; Probability Theory and Stochastic Modelling; Third edition [of 1464694]; Springer: Cham, Switzerland, 2021; Volume 99, pp. 12 + 946. [CrossRef]
51. Gel'fand, I.M.; Vilenkin, N.Y. *Generalized Functions. Vol. 4: Applications of Harmonic Analysis*; Translated by Amiel Feinstein; Academic Press: New York, NY, USA; London, UK, 1964; pp. 14 + 384.
52. Gohberg, I.; Goldberg, S. *Basic Operator Theory*; Birkhäuser: Boston, MA, USA, 1980; pp. 13 + 285.
53. Billingsley, P. *Probability and Measure*, 3rd ed.; Wiley Series in Probability and Mathematical Statistics; A Wiley-Interscience Publication; John Wiley & Sons, Inc.: New York, NY, USA, 1995; pp. 14 + 593.
54. Kahane, J.P.; Peyrière, J. Sur certaines martingales de Benoit Mandelbrot. *Adv. Math.* **1976**, *22*, 131–145. [CrossRef]
55. Lévy, P. Esquisse d'une théorie de la multiplication des variables aléatoires. *Ann. Sci. École Norm. Sup.* **1959**, *76*, 59–82. [CrossRef]
56. Zolotarev, V.M. General theory of the multiplication of random variables. *Dokl. Akad. Nauk SSSR* **1962**, *142*, 788–791.
57. Simonelli, I. Convergence and symmetry of infinite products of independent random variables. *Statist. Probab. Lett.* **2001**, *55*, 45–52. . Erratum in *Statist. Probab. Lett.* **2003**, *62*, 323. [CrossRef]
58. Shiryaev, A.N. *Probability*, 2nd ed.; Graduate Texts in Mathematics; Translated from the first (1980) Russian edition by R. P. Boas; Springer: New York, NY, USA, 1996; Volume 95, pp. 16 + 623. [CrossRef]

Disclaimer/Publisher's Note: The statements, opinions and data contained in all publications are solely those of the individual author(s) and contributor(s) and not of MDPI and/or the editor(s). MDPI and/or the editor(s) disclaim responsibility for any injury to people or property resulting from any ideas, methods, instructions or products referred to in the content.

MDPI
St. Alban-Anlage 66
4052 Basel
Switzerland
www.mdpi.com

Mathematics Editorial Office
E-mail: mathematics@mdpi.com
www.mdpi.com/journal/mathematics

Disclaimer/Publisher's Note: The statements, opinions and data contained in all publications are solely those of the individual author(s) and contributor(s) and not of MDPI and/or the editor(s). MDPI and/or the editor(s) disclaim responsibility for any injury to people or property resulting from any ideas, methods, instructions or products referred to in the content.

www.ingramcontent.com/pod-product-compliance
Lightning Source LLC
LaVergne TN
LVHW070209100526
838202LV00015B/2024